American Mosaic

pg.
568 - 616

American Mosaic

MULTICULTURAL READINGS IN CONTEXT

Barbara Roche Rico
Loyola Marymount University

Sandra Mano
University of California, Los Angeles

Houghton Mifflin Company   **BOSTON**

Dallas   **Geneva, Illinois**   **Palo Alto**   **Princeton, New Jersey**

For Our Students

Library of Congress Catalogue Card Number: 90-83046

ISBN: 0-395-53690-1

CDEFGHIJ-B-954321

ACKNOWLEDGMENTS

From THE SACRED HOOP by Paula Gunn Allen. Copyright © 1986 by Paula Gunn Allen. Reprinted by permission of Beacon Press.

Excerpt from "LimIts of the Border" by Houston A. Baker, Jr. Reprinted by permission of the author.

"Brown v. The Board of Education of Topeka (1954)" reprinted from A MORE PERFECT UNION: DOCUMENTS IN U.S. HISTORY, 2/e, by Paul F. Boller, Jr. and Ronald Story. Reprinted by permission of Houghton Mifflin Company.

(Acknowledgments continue on page 713.)

◆ CONTENTS ◆

3   AFRICAN AMERICANS
The Migration North and the Harlem Renaissance
163

4   PUERTO RICANS
The View from the Mainland
243

5   JAPANESE AMERICANS
The Internment Experience
323

6 AFRICAN AMERICANS
The Struggle for Civil Rights
399

7 CHICANOS
Negotiating Economic and Cultural Boundaries
475

8 NATIVE AMERICANS
Pride and Cultural Heritage
567

9 CONTEMPORARY VOICES
Diversity and Renewal
637

◆ PREFACE ◆

Using a chronological framework, *American Mosaic: Multicultural Readings in Context* celebrates diversity by presenting the writings of many ethnic groups at a particularly generative period in their histories. We believe that all students will be enriched by hearing these voices and by understanding the period in which the authors were writing. Moreover, students will come to appreciate the contributions these writers have made to American culture.

Each chapter reflects what we consider to be an important period in the development of a particular ethnic group, by using readings that are representative of the attitudes and concerns of that time. Our intention is to let the authors speak for themselves about issues important to them. Our desire is not to provide a comprehensive coverage of American ethnic literature and history, but instead to suggest the richness of the American experience. *American Mosaic* is designed to allow students to develop historical awareness and critical thinking skills while they study the development of literary, political, and cultural voices within our country.

We have begun our historical examination during the late nineteenth century. Clearly one can find earlier examples of immigrant writings, Puritan celebrations of the land and its possibilities, narratives and poems of Native American peoples, and the writings of the "forced immigrants," Africans brought here as slaves. However, the late 1800s witnessed three important developments: the large influx of immigrants primarily from Europe and Asia who came for religious and economic reasons; the altering of the parameters of American society through nativist groups, exclusionary laws, and the establishment of reservations; and the change in the national character brought about by the growth of cities and the migration north of African Americans. Throughout the text we have tried to reflect not only the changes experienced by the ethnic groups, but also the interaction of given ethnic groups with the majority culture. As importantly, the readings selected illustrate how the quality of American life was altered and enriched by the contributions of each group.

To help students perceive the mosaic, we have presented in each chapter a combination of literary and historical material. The excerpt from the legal document included in each section suggests ways in which the dominant culture responded to each ethnic group. (These documents are, however, only a sampling; we urge students to explore further the legal context that can only be outlined in the chapter.) The readings themselves illustrate the emergence of multicultural voices. In addition to essays, we have included first person narratives, journalistic pieces, oratory, fiction, and poetic works, because we believe that expository essays alone do not reflect the richness of the literature that was produced. By concluding each chapter with an essay by an academic who has extensively studied the culture of the group, we hope to illustrate how issues of culture can be explored across the disciplines.

The text's apparatus is designed to inform students and to encourage them to respond to and to challenge what they read. Every chapter includes an introductory essay intended to be a starting point for discussion. The headnotes provide further background information and suggest connections among the readings. Pre-reading and post-reading questions foster critical thinking skills and allow students to respond creatively to the texts. Suggestions for class discussions, group projects, and library research, as well as lists of supplemental materials, give students an opportunity to explore issues further.

From these encounters, students will, we hope, strengthen their abilities to think critically and to respond to what they read. They will come to see American culture not as a single monologic entity, but as an ongoing conversation involving many ethnic groups. And we trust they will find in the interplay of historical, literary, and cultural concerns an opportunity to assert their own voices.

ACKNOWLEDGMENTS

We would like to thank the Research Program in Ethnic Studies administered by UCLA's Institute for American Cultures, Norris Hundley, Chair, and the Chicano Studies Research Center Faculty Advisory Committee, David Hayes-Bautista, Chair, for the two-year grant that enabled us to pursue our research. We would also like to thank the Loyola Marymount University Department of English, Mel Bertolozzi, Chair, and the College of Liberal Arts, Rev. Anthony B. Brzoska, S.J., Dean, for their support of this project.

In the preparation of this text, we have received the help and encouragement of many people who have shared their ideas with us and who have responded with frankness and enthusiasm to ours. Mike Rose has acted from the outset as a mentor, commenting on and encouraging us in our work. We also appreciate the support of Linda Bannister, Héctor Calderón, Sandra Cisneros, Maria Cuevas, Robert Cullen, Michael Fried, Lucy Garza, Lee Leeson, Russell Leong, Kenneth Lincoln, Bonnie Lisle, Sharon Locy, Cathy Machado, Regina Mandanici, Bernice Mirenda, Steven Osborn, Louise Phelps, John Reilly, Manuel Rezende, Henrietta Rico, Alice Roy, Rose Shalom,

Santiago Sia, Ted Simpson, Robin Strayhorn, Betty Takahashi, Tracey Thompson, Carol Turner, Lucy Wilson, W. Ross Winterowd, and Gail Wronsky.

In addition, we would like to thank the professors of history and English who reviewed the manuscript and helped us to make it an accurate, fair, useful, and stimulating text exploring American multiculturalism: Poonam Arora, University of Michigan, Dearborn; Betty Bamberg, University of Southern California; John Bodnar, Indiana University, Bloomington; Ron Estes, St. Louis Community College at Forest Park; Donald Fixico, Western Michigan University; Eugene Howard, Bucks County Community College, PA; Jacquelyn Jackson, Middle Tennessee State University; Yolette Jones, Volunteer State Community College, TN; Malcolm Kiniry, Rutgers University, Newark, NJ; Rhonda Levine, University of California, Santa Barbara; Shirley Lim, University of California, Santa Barbara; Lois Marchino, University of Texas, El Paso; Beverly Moss, Ohio State University; Dottie Perry, Norfolk State University, VA; Georgia Rhoades, University of Louisville; Vicki Ruiz, University of California, Davis; Melita Schaum, University of Michigan, Dearborn; Lacreta Scott, Cerritos College; Joseph Skerrett, University of Massachusetts, Amherst; Bruce Southerd, East Carolina University, Greenville; Antonio Stevens-Arroyo, Brooklyn College, City University of New York; Franklin O. Sutton, Community College of Allegheny County, PA; Michael Vivion, University of Missouri, Kansas City; Linda Woodson, University of Texas, San Antonio; and Maria Elena Yepes, East Los Angeles College.

We owe special thanks to the editorial and production team at Houghton Mifflin whose encouragement and gentle prodding have made this a better book.

Finally, we would like to add a special note of thanks to our husbands, Morris Mano and Richard Rico, who have contributed so much to this book.

B.R.R.
S.M.

American Mosaic

Sweatshop in a Division Street tenement, New York City. Photographed by Jacob Riis. (Jacob A. Riis Collection/Museum of the City of New York)

Orchard Street, New York, 1898. The Lower East Side was the destination for many newly arrived Eastern European Jews. (Museum of the City of New York)

Chapter **1**

EARLY IMMIGRANTS
Living in America

Homesteaders in East Custer County, Nebraska, 1887.
(Soloman D. Butcher Collection/Nebraska State Historical Society)

Ellis Island, about 1910. Newly arrived immigrants
wait to be processed in the Great Hall, before being
permitted entry into the U.S. (United States History,
Local History and Genealogy Division, The New York
Public Library/Astor, Lenox and Tilden Foundations)

◆ Setting the Historical Context ◆

IN HER FAMOUS POEM "The New Colossus," first published in 1883, Emma Lazarus expressed for many the symbolism of the Statue of Liberty:

> Not like the brazen giant of Greek fame,
> With conquering limbs astride from land to land;
> Here at our sea-washed, sunset gates shall stand
> A mighty woman with a torch, whose flame
> Is the imprisoned lightning, and her name
> Mother of Exiles. From her beacon-hand
> Glows world-wide welcome; her mild eyes command
> The air-bridged harbor that twin cities frame.
> "Keep, ancient lands, your storied pomp!" cries she
> With silent lips. "Give me your tired, your poor,
> Your huddled masses yearning to breathe free,
> The wretched refuse of your teeming shore.
> Send these, the homeless, tempest-tost to me,
> I lift my lamp beside the golden door!"

In the rather florid language of the time, Lazarus depicted the United States as a refuge for the poor and the oppressed, a land of freedom and opportunity with a "golden door" open to all. Published at the height of the second great wave of immigration from Europe, the poem seemed so expressive of the American ideal that civic leaders had it engraved on the pedestal of the Statue of Liberty. Yet this gesture was not without a certain irony, for the dedication of the Statue of Liberty coincided with the initiation of legal restrictions on immigration and with the eruption of prejudice and economic discrimination that interfered with immigrants' pursuit of the American Dream.

Except for the Native Americans, all Americans, from colonial days onward, were immigrants or descendants of immigrants searching for political or religious freedom, or economic opportunity. The nineteenth century, however, saw two particularly intensive periods of European immigration. From 1820 to 1860, social and economic conditions in Europe—overcrowded cities, poverty, depression, or a series of bad harvests—encouraged thousands

to sail to America. Most of these immigrants, Protestants and Catholics from northern and western Europe, settled in cities on the northeastern coast. Most stayed permanently, but others, called "sojourners" or "birds of passage," planned to return to their homelands.

Between 1880 and 1902, migration swelled again, predominantly with Jewish and Catholic immigrants from southern and eastern Europe. In addition to social and economic motivations, religious persecution drove thousands to emigrate from their homes. Many Jews, particularly those from Russia, emigrated to escape the violent anti-Semitic attacks known as pogroms, and many Armenians fled religious persecution and torture inflicted by the Turks.

Urged by the glowing accounts of America found in advertisements, newspaper stories, and letters from friends and family members, immigrants came to the United States with great expectations. They anticipated finding vast, unsettled farmland, theirs for the taking, and cities that would welcome both skilled and unskilled workers. These expectations were often violated first by the immigration process itself, an experience that has become a part of the nation's collective memory and identity. Detained upon landing, immigrant families were subjected to a series of dehumanizing examinations. In recording a family's name, careless or ignorant immigration officials sometimes shortened it, changed its spelling, or reversed first and last names, using them interchangeably. Each family member underwent a series of medical examinations, and those who failed were detained indefinitely or deported, separating families for long periods. Although over three quarters of the people arriving at immigration centers were admitted to the country, the other twenty to twenty five percent were sent back to their homelands.

The enforced detention and helplessness of the immigrants made them vulnerable to exploitation. An investigation of Ellis Island during Theodore Roosevelt's administration exposed the corrupt practices of some immigration officials and of commercial enterprises that cheated immigrants by using unfair currency exchange rates. As a result of this investigation, the Federal Bureau of Immigration was established to oversee the practices of government officials. Although the immigration system was more closely monitored as a result of these actions, some of the abuses proved difficult to eliminate.

Newly arrived immigrants were sometimes exploited by earlier immigrants from their own ethnic groups. Unprincipled attorneys would claim to have immigrants' best interests at heart, only to charge them exorbitant fees for minor tasks. As Constantine Panunzio relates, *padroni* or other middlemen would take advantage of the immigrants' naiveté to promise wonderful employment opportunities that turned out to be only "pick and shovel" work. But at other times earlier immigrants offered encouragement and support. Panunzio reports that one such immigrant gave him food and shelter upon his arrival, and Gregory Orfalea traces the ways in which the Syrian Ladies' Aid Society and other organizations founded by immigrants worked to protect new immigrants' rights and to welcome them into the community.

Even after they had settled, immigrants found life more difficult than they had expected. Some immigrants to the Northeast and Midwest settled in rural areas, taking advantage of the Homestead Act of 1846, which guaranteed property ownership to those who lived on a parcel of land for five years. As the selection from Ole Rolvaag's novel reflects, however, the quality of life often contrasted sharply with what many of these people had expected. Life on the plains demanded a continual battle with the elements and with isolation. Homesteaders struggled both to provide their families with the essentials of life and to establish a sense of community, even among distant neighbors.

The contrast between expectation and reality can be perceived most dramatically in the descriptions of life within the cities. Anzia Yezierska's story contrasts the prosperity enjoyed by a few (in what one of her characters calls the "land flowing with milk and honey") with the poverty and hunger encountered by many others. Yezierska's image of neighbors talking to each other across a narrow airshaft helps us envision the dwellings where early immigrants were forced to live—crowded apartments in tenement buildings where sanitation, heat, and even light were at a premium. Often the landlords, who lived at a safe distance from these structures, could remain comfortably oblivious to the conditions inside them. It took photographers and writers such as Jacob Riis in New York and John Spago in Chicago to make the public more aware of these abuses.

Working conditions were also substandard. Many immigrants were forced to work in overcrowded sweatshops without adequate sanitation facilities. Men were often required to work sixteen-hour shifts, and women and children also worked long hours for low pay. By the mid-nineteenth century laws prohibited women from working shifts longer than ten hours. But it was not until the first decades of the twentieth century that laws were passed protecting the rights of children and making the education of minors compulsory.

In Myra Kelly's story, the main character tries to improve his fortunes by obtaining a union card. The benefits conferred by the card raise questions about the problematic relationship between labor unions and immigrants. Because immigrants were sometimes brought in as contract laborers and used, often unwittingly, to break up strikes, the unions initially refused to help them achieve equitable pay and decent working conditions. After a time, however, some of the unions began to recognize the immigrant workers' potential to strengthen their position. The American Federation of Labor (under the direction of immigrant Samuel Gompers) began to represent workers. In some urban areas competing unions took opposing stances, with some, such as the American Federation of Labor, admitting immigrants, and others, such as the Knights of Labor, excluding them—a situation that persisted throughout the nineteenth century.

The struggle for acceptance by the unions, and thus for a secure place in the economy, mirrors the immigrants' struggle for assimilation and thus for a secure place in society. Many natives and other immigrants believed that the key to success in the United States was to become "Americanized," and writers such as the philosopher John Dewey and the journalist Abraham Cahan supported this view. The title of Israel Zangwill's play, *The Melting Pot*, became the accepted term for this process, and was used throughout the period and long after. Writings and cartoons of the period mocked the "greenhorn," the person who, naively or not, clings to the ways and trappings of the Old Country. As Yezierska's story suggests, however, assimilation was not accomplished without loss and pain. In adopting the American way, immigrants often sacrificed the security, sense of identity, and comfort of their traditional way of life.

Even during this early period some social critics opposed assimilation as the immigrants' ultimate goal. Some who saw *The Melting Pot*, for example, objected to its depiction of the intermarriage of a Jew and a Gentile, which they contended violated Jewish law. And while some reformers, such as Jacob Riis, advocated assimilation, others suggested different forms of acculturation. Jane Addams, a reformer who founded the Hull House settlement in Chicago and who wrote extensively on issues relating to immigrants, proposed, for example, a two-way process of acculturation: as the immigrant learned the ways of the adopted country, the adopted country would learn and be enriched by the cultural contributions of the immigrant.

Although many Americans celebrated the arrival of the immigrants, many did not. During the 1880s, as the Statue of Liberty grew in importance as a symbol of invitation, the nation's attention was increasingly given to nativist doctrines and exclusionist legislation. The rejection of immigrants took several forms. Some members of the labor force resented the newcomers as a source of competition for jobs. Others, even some government officials, entertained stereotyped notions about immigrants, believing that some groups included numerous dangerous radicals. Some nativists subscribed to a theory of eugenics, using arguments based on genetics to assert the native superiority of their own and related ethnic groups. Still others claimed that the national identity might be diluted if the country were allowed to become a melting pot.

As a result of pressure from such groups, Congress passed exclusionist legislation, establishing immigration quotas that favored Protestant immigrants from northern or western Europe over those with other religious beliefs and from other areas. Congress also instituted a so-called head tax, a one-time charge that each immigrant paid upon entering the country; each subsequent exclusionist act was accompanied by an increase in this tax.

Despite these obstacles, immigrants continued to come. They formed civic organizations, built synagogues and churches, and dreamed of providing their children with easier, more rewarding lives. As time passed they began to exercise some power, if not in Congress, at least at the municipal level. In a very real way, the "huddled masses" of which Lazarus wrote made the "American Dream" more than simply an expression.

EXPLORING THE LITERARY AND
◆ CULTURAL CONTEXT ◆

The experiences of the early immigrants have become a part of the nation's collective memory. The selections that follow recount characteristic elements of that experience: the immigrants' expectations, their struggles for social and economic security and success, their problems and disappointments, and their attempts to institute reforms. These readings sometimes confirm commonly accepted interpretations of the immigrant experience and sometimes challenge them. Each writer, however, enlarges our view of these crucial experiences, leading us to reflect on the "American Dream" and on the conflicting values that phrase can encompass.

Constantine Panunzio uses the literal and figurative image of a storm to describe and analyze his first impressions of America. Contrary to having the optimism usually attributed to the hopeful immigrant, Panunzio describes his reluctance to live in America and his desire to return to Italy. The passage also reflects the immigrants' vulnerability to exploitation by unscrupulous and indifferent people.

In city or country, many immigrants struggled to survive, as several of the chapter's readings graphically describe. Panunzio, after being allowed to stay one night in another immigrant's home, is forced to sleep the next on a park bench. In Anzia Yezierska's story, "The Fat of the Land," the main character's hungry children fight over a potato. In the excerpt from Ole Edvart Rolvaag's *Giants in the Earth*, the family tries to make a dinner out of unwholesome badger meat. As several of the readings suggest, the struggle for survival is often connected to a struggle to keep the family together. In Yezierska's story, keeping the family together takes a literal form as the mother searches the crowded streets of her urban neighborhood for her lost child. In Rolvaag's novel, by contrast, the isolated mother attempts to exercise control over her children and herself in a vast, empty landscape where her sense of identity and her self-discipline are continually put to the test.

What some saw as a struggle for survival, others regarded as an opportunity for profit. The excerpt from Jacob Riis's *How the Other Half Lives*, which outlines the development of the tenement, provides one example of this exploitation, as it describes how dwellings were often expanded without regard to the health or safety of potential residents. Panunzio also describes exploitation, in his case spurred by the competition within or among immigrant groups for good jobs at good wages.

A large part of the immigrant experience was the struggle with linguistic and cultural differences. Orfalea tells how his grandparents' inability to speak English made them feel powerless when they faced immigration officials. Even after long residence in this country, immigrants without good English skills might feel at a social or economic disadvantage, as the main character in Yezierska's story demonstrates.

Throughout the readings, characters work to resolve conflicts and changes in their value systems. Sometimes cultural differences are acted out within a family. In Yezierska's story, for example, the main character feels that her children are attempting to separate her from the traditions that she values, while her children regard her speech and mannerisms as constant reminders of a grim past and a source of shame. In other readings, the larger social structures reflect tensions. Myra Kelly's story, "A Soul Above Buttons," examines conflicting attitudes toward education, acculturation, and success. In the story, the teacher views education as a means to achieve acculturation, but the small boy expects his education to provide him with more immediate keys to success. Their clash of wills provides a humorous, thoughtful examination of the educational process and its relation to the proverbial "American Dream."

The last two pieces make use of historical and critical distance to reexamine elements of the immigrant experience. Returning to Ellis Island, the Isle of Tears through which his grandparents immigrated to this country from Syria, Gregory Orfalea reflects on the significance of the place in the

national consciousness. David M. Fine, writing from the historian's perspective, reexamines the ideals and roles of assimilation and acculturation as
they were presented in the literature written by early immigrants. The
article also explains the way in which the expression "melting pot" has often
been misunderstood.

Taken together, the readings in this chapter present a complex picture
of some of the immigrants who have enriched the meaning of being an
American.

BEGINNING: PRE-READING/WRITING

◆ *Working in a group, use the knowledge you have gained from reading the introduction
to this chapter or your own experience to list the possible reasons that immigrants flocked
to America during the period between 1880 and 1920. Share your list with the class.
How do you think these reasons compare with those motivating immigrants today?*

---

*T*he *Bill of Rights comprises the first ten amendments to the Constitution of the United States. They resulted from an agreement between those who wanted a strong federal government and those who sought to restrict the power of that government. These amendments, added in 1791, were designed to prevent the federal government from making laws that violated such basic rights as freedom of speech, press, assembly, expression of religious faith, and trial by jury. The Supreme Court later extended the power of the Bill of Rights by applying the document to state governments as well.*

The Bill of Rights clearly articulates the rights guaranteed to each individual. As such it has assumed a special importance for many immigrants who have fled from repressive regimes or religious persecution in their homelands.

◆ THE BILL OF RIGHTS ◆

Articles in addition to, and Amendment of the Constitution of the United States of America, proposed by Congress, and ratified by the Legislatures of the several States, pursuant to the fifth Article of the original Constitution.

ART. I

Congress shall make no law respecting an establishment of religion, or prohibiting the free exercise thereof; or abridging the freedom of speech, or of the press; or the right of the people peaceably to assemble, and to petition the government for a redress of grievances.

ART. II

A well regulated Militia, being necessary to the security of a free State, the right of the people to keep and bear Arms, shall not be infringed.

ART. III

No Soldier shall, in time of peace be quartered in any house, without the consent of the Owner, nor in time of war, but in a manner to be prescribed by law.

ART. IV

The right of the people to be secure in their persons, houses, papers, and effects, against unreasonable searches and seizures, shall not be violated, and no Warrants shall issue, but upon probable cause, supported by Oath or affirmation, and particularly describing the place to be searched, and the persons or things to be seized.

ART. V

No person shall be held to answer for a capital, or otherwise infamous crime, unless on a presentment or indictment of a Grand Jury, except in cases arising in the land or naval forces, or in the Militia, when in actual service in time of War or public danger; nor shall any person be subject for the same offence to be twice put in jeopardy of life or limb; nor shall be compelled in any criminal case to be a witness against himself, nor be deprived of life, liberty, or property, without due process of law; nor shall private property be taken for public use, without just compensation.

ART. VI

In all criminal prosecutions, the accused shall enjoy the right to a speedy and public trial, by an impartial jury of the State and district wherein the crime shall have been committed, which district shall have been previously ascertained by law, and to be informed of the nature and cause of the accusation; to be confronted with the witnesses against him; to have compulsory process for obtaining witnesses in his favor, and to have the Assistance of Counsel for his defence.

ART. VII

In Suits at common law, where the value in controversy shall exceed twenty dollars, the right of trial by jury shall be preserved, and no fact tried by a jury, shall be otherwise re-examined in any Court of the United States, than according to the rules of the common law.

ART. VIII

Excessive bail shall not be required, nor excessive fines imposed, nor cruel and unusual punishments inflicted.

ART. IX

The enumeration in the Constitution, of certain rights, shall not be construed to deny or disparage others retained by the people.

ART. X

The powers not delegated to the United States by the Constitution, nor prohibited by it to the States, are reserved to the States respectively, or to the people. ◆

◆ Responding

1. Explain in your own words what one of the provisions in the Bill of Rights guarantees or implies.

2. Choose one of the rights guaranteed in the Bill of Rights. Then, using information in the introduction to the chapter and your own knowledge, explain why that right was particularly important to early immigrants.

CONSTANTINE PANUNZIO

Constantine Panunzio, who was born in Bari, Italy, in 1884, arrived in the United States on July 3, 1902. After completing studies in theology at Wesleyan University, Boston University, and New York University, he earned a doctorate from the Brookings Institution in 1925. During the period between 1915 and 1920, Panunzio was active in the immigrant community, working at settlement houses and at the YMCA; in 1919 he became the superintendent of immigrant labor for the Interchurch World Movement. After 1920 he devoted most of his time to teaching, serving on the sociology faculty of several universities, including the State University of New York and the University of California, Los Angeles. Many of Panunzio's published works treated the issues of immigration and deportation. He died in 1964, at the age of seventy-nine.

Panunzio's book The Soul of an Immigrant *(1922) recounts the author's own experiences and celebrates his assimilation into his new culture. Despite the text's general optimism, the excerpt that follows tells of his struggles to find housing and work just after arriving in America. We can sense the vulnerability of the immigrant and his need to rely on others. We see not only exploitation and rivalry, but also the capacity for friendship. In the midst of difficulty and deception, there emerges a strong sense of self-reliance and a will to endure.*

◆ IN THE AMERICAN STORM ◆

> *Not that they starve, but starve so dreamlessly,*
> *Not that they sow, but that they seldom reap,*
> *Not that they serve, but have no gods to serve,*
> *Not that they die, but that they die like sheep.*
>
> VACHEL LINDSAY

The *Francesco* put out to sea from Trapani, Sicily, on May 3, 1902, and a week or so later passed the Pillars of Hercules. Then she plunged into the wake of the trade winds and for about three weeks she sailed majestically before them like a gull, stirring not a sail all the while. Then followed a period of varying weather, which in turn was succeeded by a few days when the ocean was breathless and motionless. Frequently we could see whole schools of dolphins as they came to the surface, or monster whales spurting pillars of water into the air, a sight especially beautiful on calm moonlit nights. 1

The little brig had reached a distance of about three hundred miles from 2 the coast of North America, when one day the very weight of heaven seemed to be pressing down upon her. The clouds were yellow, sullen and angry-looking; the air was breathless with pent-up power. As the day advanced the barometer went lower and lower, and with the approach of evening this invisible, uncontrollable power seemed to be seizing the little ship as if with mighty claws. The sea rumbled beneath her, the thick masses of clouds pressed closer upon her, the waters became deep-dyed black. At five-thirty we heard the call: "All hands on deck," and a few moments later: "All sails in but lower-topsail and jib." Climbing like monkeys after coconuts, we made short work of the task. We knew, however, that something more strenuous was coming. At six, just as the four bells were striking, the very bowels of sea and sky opened upon us with amazing suddenness and force. The seasoned Tuscan sailor, whose every word was wont to be an oath, struck with sudden fear, fell upon his knees by the bulwark and began to say his prayers. Some one kicked him as you would a dog. The moment the terrific gale struck the ship it tore the heavy lower-topsail and flapped it madly in the air as if it were a piece of tissue paper. The brave little ship beat pitifully beneath the gale; its mainroyalmast was broken like a reed; its cargo was shifted to one side like a handful of pebbles, and its hull sprung a leak. The blast was over in an hour or so, but all hands worked steadily for three days and nights to shift the cargo back in place, while four men were kept at the hand-pump night and day until we reached shore a week or more later.

Some years afterward an American friend, reflecting upon this incident as I had described it to him remarked, "That storm was indeed prophetic of your early experiences in America, was it not?" It may be that it was, and perhaps we shall soon discover the analogy as it appeared in my friend's mind. 3

On July 3rd, 1902, after a voyage of sixty-one days, the *Francesco* anchored in Boston Harbor. As the next day was the "Fourth," the city was already decked in festal array. The captain hastened to register his arrival. A boat was lowered, and I was ordered to take him ashore; thus it was my good fortune to be the first to touch land. "America!" I whispered to myself as I did so. 4

In a day or two the ship was towed to a pier in Charlestown, where it lay until its cargo of salt was unloaded and a cargo of lumber consigned to Montevideo was put on board of her. 5

In the meantime a desire had arisen within me to return home. There were several reasons for this. In the first place, it was becoming increasingly unpleasant for me to remain in the midst of that crew. It chanced that I was the only person on board hailing from southern Italy; the rest of the men were mostly Genoese, with one or two Tuscans. Now, the feeling of sectional provincialism between north and south Italy is still so strong, and the North always assumes such airs of superiority, that I had become the butt of every joke and the scapegoat of every occasion. This was becoming more and more unbearable, and as time went on I decided that my self-respect could not and would not stand it. To this was added the fact that the captain was one of those creatures 6 who seem to be more brute than man, especially in dealing with youth. During that voyage he had more than once beaten me in a way that would have made the hardest punishments of my father blush. He was so cruel and unreasonable that before he left Boston several of the crew, including the first mate, left him.

In the face of these circumstances I began to think that if the captain would only let me go, I would return home. Accordingly, one day I went to him and very respectfully told him of my intention to return to Italy immediately if he would permit me, and would pay me the money which was due me. The stern, sea-hardened sailor brushed me aside without even an answer. A day or so later I again went to him; this time he drove me from his presence with a sharp kick. Whatever manhood there ever was in my being rose up and stood erect within me; with a determination as quick and as sharp as his kick had been, I decided I would now go at any cost. 7

I began to look about for ways and means to carry out my determination. On the pier was an elderly watchman, an Italian by birth, who had been in America for several years. To him I confided my difficulties. He was a sane and conservative man, cautious in giving advice. My desire was to find a ship which was returning to some European port. He did not know of any, but one evening he suggested that if worse came to worst, I could do some kind of work for a few days and thereby earn enough money to buy a third-class passage back to Naples, which at that time cost only fifty or sixty dollars. This gave me a new idea. I decided to take my destiny in my own hands and in some way find my way back to Italy. Two months had already passed since our arrival in Boston, and almost any day now the vessel would take to sea. If I were to act it must be now or never. I had been ashore twice and had become acquainted with a barber near the pier. To him I also confided my troubles, and he offered to keep my few belongings for me, should I finally decide to leave the ship. 8

Late in the evening of September 8, 1902, when the turmoil of the street traffic was subsiding, and the silence of the night was slowly creeping over the city, I took my sea chest, my sailor bag and all I had and set foot on American soil. I was in America. Of immigration laws I had not even a knowledge of their existence; of the English language I knew not a word; of friends I had none in Boston or elsewhere in America to whom I might turn for counsel or help. I had exactly fifty cents remaining out of a dollar which the captain had finally seen fit to give me. But as I was soon to earn money and return to Molfetta, I felt no concern. 9

My Charlestown barber friend took me in that first night with the distinct understanding that I could stay only one night. So the next morning bright and early, leaving all my belongings with the barber, I started out in search of a job. I roamed about the streets, not knowing where or to whom to turn. That day and the next four days I had one loaf of bread each day for food and at night, not having money with which to purchase shelter, I stayed on the rec- 10 reation pier on Commercial Street. One night, very weary and lonely, I lay upon a bench and soon dozed off into a light sleep. The next thing I knew I cried out in bitter pain and fright. A policeman had stolen up to me very quietly and with his club had dealt me a heavy blow upon the soles of my feet. He drove me away, and I think I cried; I cried my first American cry. What became of me that night I cannot say. And the next day and the next. . . . I just roamed aimlessly about the streets, between the Public Garden with its flowers and the water-side, where I watched the children at play, even as I had played at the water's brink in old Molfetta.

Those first five days in America have left an impression upon my mind   11
which can never be erased with the years, and which gives me a most profound sense of sympathy for immigrants as they arrive. On the fifth day, by mere chance, I ran across a French sailor on the recreation pier. We immediately became friends. His name was Louis. Just to look at Louis would make you laugh. He was over six feet tall, lank, queer-shaped, freckle-faced, with small eyes and a crooked nose. I have sometimes thought that perhaps he was the "missing link" for which the scientist has been looking. Louis could not speak Italian; he had a smattering of what he called "italien," but I could not see it his way. On the other hand, I kept imposing upon his good nature by giving a nasal twang to Italian words and insisting on calling it "francese." We had much merriment. Two facts, however, made possible a mutual understanding. Both had been sailors and had traveled over very much the same world; this made a bond between us. Then too, we had an instinctive knowledge of "esperanto," a strange capacity for gesticulation and facial contortion, which was always our last "hope" in making each other understand.

Not far from the recreation pier on which we met is located the Italian   12
colony of "North End," Boston. To this Louis and I made our way, and to an Italian boarding house. How we happened to find it and to get in I do not now recall. It was a "three-room apartment" and the landlady informed us that she was already "full," but since we had no place to go, she would take us in. Added to the host that was already gathered there, our coming made fourteen people. At night the floor of the kitchen and the dining table were turned into beds. Louis and I were put to sleep in one of the beds with two other men, two facing north and two south. As I had slept all my life in a bed or bunk by myself this quadrupling did not appeal to me especially. But we could not complain. We had been taken in on trust, and the filth, the smells and the crowding together were a part of the trust.

We began to make inquiries about jobs and were promptly informed that   13
there was plenty of work at "pick and shovel." We were also given to understand by our fellow-boarders that "pick and shovel" was practically the only work available to Italians. Now these were the first two English words I had heard and they possessed great charm. Moreover, if I were to earn money to return home and this was the only work available for Italians, they were very weighty

words for me, and I must master them as soon and as well as possible and then set out to find their hidden meaning. I practised for a day or two until I could say "peek" and "shuvle" to perfection. Then I asked a fellow-boarder to take me to see what the work was like. He did. He led me to Washington Street, not far from the colony, where some excavation work was going on, and there I did see, with my own eyes, what the "peek" and "shuvle" were about. My heart sank within me, for I had thought it some form of office work; but I was game and since this was the only work available for Italians, and since I must have money to return home, I would take it up. After all, it was only a means to an end, and would last but a few days.

It may be in place here to say a word relative to the reason why this idea   14 was prevalent among Italians at the time, and why so many Italians on coming to America find their way to what I had called "peek and shuvle." It is a matter of common knowledge, at least among students of immigration, that a very large percentage of Italian immigrants were "contadini" or farm laborers in Italy. American people often ask the question, "Why do they not go to the farms in this country?" This query is based upon the idea that the "contadini" were farmers in the sense in which we apply that word to the American farmer. The facts in the case are that the "contadini" were not farmers in that sense at all, but simply farm-laborers, more nearly serfs, working on landed estates and seldom owning their own land. Moreover, they are not in any way acquainted with the implements of modern American farming. Their farming tools consisted generally of a "zappa," a sort of wide mattock; an ax and the wooden plow of biblical times. When they come to America, the work which comes nearest to that which they did in Italy is not farming, or even farm labor, but excavation work. This fact, together with the isolation which inevitably would be theirs on an American farm, explains, in a large measure, why so few Italians go to the farm and why so many go into excavation work. There is another factor to be considered, and that is that the "padrone" perhaps makes a greater per capita percentage in connection with securing and managing workers for construction purposes than in any other line, and therefore he becomes a walking delegate about the streets of Italian colonies spreading the word that only "peek and shuvle" is available.

Now, though Louis and I had never done such work, because we were   15 Italians we must needs adapt ourselves to it and go to work with "peek and shuvle." (I should have stated that Louis, desiring to be like the Romans while living with them, for the time being passed for an Italian.)

So we went out to hunt our first job in America. For several mornings   16 Louis and I went to North Square, where there were generally a large number of men loitering in groups discussing all kinds of subjects, particularly the labor market. One morning we were standing in front of one of those infernal institutions which in America are permitted to bear the name of "immigrant banks," when we saw a fat man coming toward us. "Buon giorno, padrone," said one of the men. "Padrone?" said I to myself. Now the word "padrone" in Italy is applied to a proprietor, generally a respectable man, at least one whose dress and appearance distinguish him as a man of means. This man not only showed no signs of good breeding in his face, but he was unshaven and dirty and his clothes were shabby. I could not quite understand how he could be called "padrone." However, I said nothing, first because I wanted to get back home, and second because I wanted to be polite when I was in *American* society!

The "padrone" came up to our group and began to wax eloquent and to   17 gesticulate (both in Sicilian dialect) about the advantages of a certain job. I remember very clearly the points which he emphasized: "It is not very far, only twelve miles from Boston. For a few cents you can come back any time you wish, to see 'i parenti e gli amici,' your relatives and friends. The company has a 'shantee' in which you can sleep, and a 'storo' where you can buy your 'grosserie' all very cheap. 'Buona paga,' " he continued, "(Good pay), $1.25 per day, and you only have to pay me fifty cents a week for having gotten you this 'gooda jobba.' I only do it to help you and because you are my countrymen. If you come back here at six o'clock to-night with your bundles, I myself will take you out."

The magnanimity of this man impressed Louis and me very profoundly;   18 we looked at each other and said, "Wonderful!" We decided we would go; so at the appointed hour we returned to the very spot. About twenty men finally gathered there and we were led to North Station. There we took a train to some suburban place, the name of which I have never been able to learn. On reaching our destination we were taken to the "shantee" where we were introduced to two long open bunks filled with straw. These were to be our beds. The "storo" of which we had been told was at one end of the shanty. The next morning we were taken out to work. It was a sultry autumn day. The "peek" seemed to grow heavier at every stroke and the "shuvle" wider and larger in its capacity to hold the gravel. The second day was no better than the first, and the third was worse than the second. The work was heavy and monotonous to Louis and myself especially, who had never been "contadini" like the rest. The "padrone" whose magnanimity had so stirred us was little better than a brute. We began to do some simple figuring and discovered that when we had paid for our groceries at the "storo," for the privilege of sleeping in the shanty, and the fifty cents to the "padrone" for having been so condescending as to employ us, we would have nothing left but sore arms and backs. So on the afternoon of the third day Louis and I held a solemn conclave and decided to part company with "peek and shuvle,"—for ever. We left, without receiving a cent of pay, of course.

Going across country on foot we came to a small manufacturing village.   19 We decided to try our luck at the factory, which proved to be a woolen mill, and found employment. Our work was sorting old rags and carrying them in wheelbarrows into a hot oven, in which the air was almost suffocating. Every time a person went in it he was obliged to run out as quickly as possible, for the heat was unbearable. Unfortunately for us, the crew was composed almost entirely of Russians, who hated us from the first day, and called us "dagoes." I had never heard the word before; I asked Louis if he knew its meaning, but he did not. In going in and out of the oven the Russians would crowd against us and make it hard for us to pass. One morning as I was coming out, four of the men hedged me in. I thought I would suffocate. I finally succeeded in pushing out, my hand having been cut in the rush of the wheelbarrows.

The superintendent of the factory had observed the whole incident. He was a very kindly man. From his light complexion I think he was a Swede. He came to my rescue, reprimanded the Russians, and led me to his office, where he bandaged my hand. Then he called Louis and explained the situation to us. The Russians looked upon us as intruders and were determined not to work side by side with "the foreigners," but to drive them out of the factory. Therefore, much as he regretted it, the superintendent was obliged to ask us to leave, since there were only two of us, as against the large number of Russians who made up his unskilled crew. 20

So we left. My bandaged hand hurt me, but my heart hurt more. This kind of work was hard and humiliating enough, but what went deeper than all else was the first realization that because of race I was being put on the road. And often since that day have I felt the cutting thrusts of race prejudice. They have been dealt by older immigrants, who are known as "Americans," as well as by more recent comers. All have been equally heart-rending and head-bending. I hold no grudge against any one; I realize that it is one of the attendant circumstances of our present nationalistic attitude the world over, and yet it is none the less saddening to the human heart. I have seen prejudice, like an evil shadow, everywhere. It lurks at every corner, on every street and in every mart. I have seen it in the tram and on the train; I have felt its dreaded power in school and college, in clubs and churches. It is an ever-present evil spirit, felt though unseen, wounding hearts, cutting souls. It passes on its poison like a serpent from generation to generation, and he who would see the fusion of the various elements into a truly American type must ever take into cognizance its presence in the hearts of some human beings. ◆ 21

◆ Responding

1. Using examples from Panunzio's autobiography, illustrate how the storm he encountered on his journey was "indeed prophetic of [his] early experiences in America."

2. What working conditions made life particularly unbearable for Panunzio? What would you have found most intolerable?

3. Panunzio arrived in Boston in 1902, almost one hundred years ago. How have employment opportunities and working conditions for immigrants changed since then?

4. Compare Panunzio's experiences in a new situation and country with the experiences your family had when they first came to the United States or when they moved to another part of the country, or with your own experiences in a new environment.

JACOB RIIS

Jacob Riis, who was born in Denmark in 1849, immigrated to the United States in 1870. After working at various jobs in New York City, he became a police reporter for the New York Tribune *in 1877; later he worked for the* Sun. *Riis was a strong believer in personal initiative. In the public lectures he held during the 1880s, he encouraged immigrants to learn the language of their adopted country and adapt themselves to its customs. Jacob Riis died in 1914.*

How the Other Half Lives *is the most famous of the ten books Riis wrote. The text and its accompanying photographs, both by Riis, were first published as a series in* Scribner's Magazine. *The work was praised by Theodore Roosevelt, who then served as police commissioner of New York City. Riis's publications are credited with helping to effect reform in the poorest sections of the city.*

The selection that follows describes the development of tenements, from once ornate single-family homes of the well-to-do to the overcrowded dwellings of the very poor. The excerpt presents the squalor of these buildings in strongly visual terms and raises questions about the public's responsibility for those who find themselves destitute.

◆ GENESIS OF THE TENEMENT ◆

The first tenement New York knew bore the mark of Cain from its birth, though a generation passed before the writing was deciphered. It was the "rear house," infamous ever after in our city's history. There had been tenant-houses before, but they were not built for the purpose. Nothing would probably have shocked their original owners more than the idea of their harboring a promiscuous crowd; for they were the decorous homes of the old Knickerbockers, the proud aristocracy of Manhattan in the early days.

It was the stir and bustle of trade, together with the tremendous immigration that followed upon the war of 1812 that dislodged them. In thirty-five years the city of less than a hundred thousand came to harbor half a million souls, for whom homes had to be found. Within the memory of men not yet in their prime, Washington had moved from his house on Cherry Hill as too far out of town to be easily reached. Now the old residents followed his example; but they moved in a different direction and for a different reason. Their comfortable dwellings in the once fashionable streets along the East River front fell into the hands of real-estate agents and boarding-house keepers; and here, says the report to the Legislature of 1857, when the evils engendered had excited just alarm, "in its beginning, the tenant-house became a real blessing to that class of industrious poor whose small earnings limited their expenses, and whose employment in workshops, stores, or about the warehouses and thoroughfares, render a near residence of much importance." Not for long, however. As business increased, and the city grew with rapid strides, the necessities of the poor became the opportunity of their wealthier neighbors, and the stamp was set upon the old houses, suddenly become valuable, which the best thought and effort of a later age has vainly struggled to efface. Their "*large* rooms were partitioned into *several smaller ones*, without regard to light or ventilation, the rate of rent being lower in proportion to space or height from the street; and they soon became filled from cellar to garret with a class of tenantry living from hand to mouth, loose in morals, improvident in habits, degraded, and squalid as beggary itself." It was thus the dark bedroom, prolific of untold depravities, came into the world. It was destined to survive the old houses. In their new rôle, says the old report, eloquent in its indignant denunciation of "evils more destructive than wars," "they were not intended to last. Rents were fixed high enough to cover damage and abuse from this class, from whom nothing was expected, and the most was made of them while they lasted. Neatness, order, cleanliness, were never dreamed of in connection with the tenant-house system, as it spread its localities from year to year; while reckless slovenliness, discontent, privation, and ignorance were left to work out their invariable results, until the entire premises reached the level of tenant-house dilapidation, containing, but sheltering not, the miserable hordes that crowded beneath smouldering, water-rotted roofs or burrowed among the rats of clammy cellars." Yet so illogical is human greed that, at a later day, when called to account, "the proprietors frequently urged the filthy habits of the tenants as an excuse for the condition of their property, utterly losing sight of the fact that it was the tolerance of those habits which was the real evil, and that for this they themselves were alone responsible."

Still the pressure of the crowds did not abate, and in the old garden where 3 the stolid Dutch burgher grew his tulips or early cabbages a rear house was built, generally of wood, two stories high at first. Presently it was carried up another story, and another. Where two families had lived ten moved in. The front house followed suit, if the brick walls were strong enough. The question was not always asked, judging from complaints made by a contemporary witness, that the old buildings were "often carried up to a great height without regard to the strength of the foundation walls." It was rent the owner was after; nothing was said in the contract about either the safety or the comfort of the tenants. The garden gate no longer swung on its rusty hinges. The shell-paved walk had become an alley; what the rear house had left of the garden, a "court." Plenty such are yet to be found in the Fourth Ward, with here and there one of the original rear tenements.

Worse was to follow. It was "soon perceived by estate owners and agents 4 of property that a greater percentage of profits could be realized by the conversion of houses and blocks into barracks, and dividing their space into smaller proportions capable of containing human life within four walls. . . . Blocks were rented of real estate owners, or 'purchased on time,' or taken in charge at a percentage, and held for under-letting." With the appearance of the middleman, wholly irresponsible, and utterly reckless and unrestrained, began the era of tenement building which turned out such blocks as Gotham Court, where, in one cholera epidemic that scarcely touched the clean wards, the tenants died at the rate of one hundred and ninety-five to the thousand of population; which forced the general mortality of the city up from 1 in 41.83 in 1815, to 1 in 27.33 in 1855, a year of unusual freedom from epidemic disease, and which wrung from the early organizers of the Health Department this wail: "There are numerous examples of tenement-houses in which are lodged several hundred people that have a *pro rata* allotment of ground area scarcely equal to two square yards upon the city lot, court-yards and all included." The tenement-house population had swelled to half a million souls by that time, and on the East Side, in what is still the most densely populated district in all the world, China not excluded, it was packed at the rate of 290,000 to the square mile, a state of affairs wholly unexampled. The utmost cupidity of other lands and other days had never contrived to herd much more than half that number within the same space. The greatest crowding of Old London was at the rate of 175,816. Swine roamed the streets and gutters as their principal scavengers.[1] The death of a child in a tenement was registered at the Bureau of Vital Statistics as "plainly due to suffocation in the foul air of an unventilated apartment," and the Senators, who had come down from Albany to find out what was the matter with New York, reported that "there are annually cut off from the population by disease and death enough human beings to people a city, and enough human labor to sustain it." And yet experts had testified that, as compared with uptown, rents were from twenty-five to thirty per cent. higher in the worst slums of the lower wards, with such accommodations as were enjoyed, for instance, by a "family with boarders" in Cedar Street, who fed hogs in the cellar that contained eight or ten loads of manure; or "one room 12 × 12 with five families living in it, comprising twenty persons of both sexes and all ages, with only two beds, without partition, screen, chair, or table." The rate of rent has been successfully maintained to the present day, though the hog at least has been eliminated.

Lest anybody flatter himself with the notion that these were evils of a day that is happily past and may safely be forgotten, let me mention here three very recent instances of tenement-house life that came under my notice. One was the burning of a rear house in Mott Street, from appearances one of the original tenant-houses that made their owners rich. The fire made homeless ten families, who had paid an average of $5 a month for their mean little cubby-holes. The owner himself told me that it was *fully* insured for $800, though it brought him in $600 a year

5

---

[1]It was not until the winter of 1867 that owners of swine were prohibited by ordinance from letting them run at large in the built-up portions of the city. [Author's note]

rent. He evidently considered himself especially entitled to be pitied for losing such valuable property. Another was the case of a hard-working family of man and wife, young people from the old country, who took poison together in a Crosby Street tenement because they were "tired." There was no other explanation, and none was needed when I stood in the room in which they had lived. It was in the attic with sloping ceiling and a single window so far out on the roof that it seemed not to belong to the place at all. With scarcely room enough to turn around in they had been compelled to pay five dollars and a half a month in advance. There were four such rooms in that attic, and together they brought in as much as many a handsome little cottage in a pleasant part of Brooklyn. The third instance was that of a colored family of husband, wife, and baby in a wretched rear rookery in West Third Street. Their rent was eight dollars and a half for a single room on the top-story, so small that I was unable to get a photograph of it even by placing the camera outside the open door. Three short steps across either way would have measured its full extent.

There was just one excuse for the early tenement-house builders, and 6 their successors may plead it with nearly as good right for what it is worth. "Such," says an official report, "is the lack of house-room in the city that any kind of tenement can be immediately crowded with lodgers, if there is space offered." Thousands were living in cellars. There were three hundred underground lodging-houses in the city when the Health Department was organized. Some fifteen years before that the old Baptist Church in Mulberry Street, just off Chatham Street, had been sold, and the rear half of the frame structure had been converted into tenements that with their swarming population became the scandal even of that reckless age. The wretched pile harbored no less than forty families, and the annual rate of deaths to the population was officially stated to be 75 in 1,000. These tenements were an extreme type of very many, for the big barracks had by this time spread east and west and far up the island into the sparsely settled wards. Whether or not the title was clear to the land upon which they were built was of less account than that the rents were collected. If there were damages to pay, the tenant had to foot them. Cases were "very frequent when property was in litigation, and two or three different parties were collecting rents." Of course under such circumstances "no repairs were ever made."

The climax had been reached. The situation was summed up by the 7 Society for the Improvement of the Condition of the Poor in these words: "Crazy old buildings, crowded rear tenements in filthy yards, dark, damp basements, leaking garrets, shops, outhouses, and stables[2] converted into dwellings, though scarcely fit to shelter brutes, are habitations of thousands of our

---

[2]"A lot 50 × 60, contained twenty stables, rented for dwellings at $15 a year each; cost of the whole $600." [Author's note]

fellow-beings in this wealthy, Christian city." "The city," says its historian, Mrs. Martha Lamb, commenting on the era of aqueduct building between 1835 and 1845, "was a general asylum for vagrants." Young vagabonds, the natural offspring of such "home" conditions, overran the streets. Juvenile crime increased fearfully year by year. The Children's Aid Society and kindred philanthropic organizations were yet unborn, but in the city directory was to be found the address of the "American Society for the Promotion of Education in Africa." ◆

◆ Responding

1. Compare Riis's description of the New York tenements of the 1880s to any part of your own or a nearby city today.

2. Working individually or in a group, list the rights and responsibilities of landlords and tenants. Whose rights have primary importance if there is a conflict? Share your lists in class.

3. Consider the statement that "experts had testified that, as compared with uptown, rents were from twenty-five to thirty per cent higher in the worst slums of the lower wards." How do you account for that difference? Compare that situation to conditions in a city you know. Are rents, goods, and services more expensive in poor neighborhoods than in middle-class or rich neighborhoods?

4. Riis quotes a report on slum conditions that says, "The proprietors frequently urged the filthy habits of the tenants as an excuse for the condition of their property, utterly losing sight of the fact that it was the tolerance of those habits which was the real evil, and that for this they themselves were alone responsible." Do you agree or disagree?

OLE EDVART ROLVAAG

*Ole Edvart Rolvaag was born in Norway in 1876. After immigrating in
1896, he spent his early years in this country working on his uncle's farm
in South Dakota. He later earned undergraduate and advanced degrees from
Augustana College (in South Dakota), St. Olaf College (in Minnesota), and
the University of Oslo. From 1906 to 1931 Rolvaag served as professor of
Norwegian letters and literature at St. Olaf College. His publications include*
Giants in the Earth: A Saga of the Prairie *(1924–25, Norwegian;
1927, English);* Peder Victorious *(1929),* Their Father's God *(1931),
and* Boat of Longings *(1933), published after his death in 1931.*

*Giants in the Earth has been praised for its psychological realism and
for the intensity with which it depicts a pioneer family's struggles with the
isolation of their environment. The excerpt that follows explores the tensions
experienced by the woman of the family, who is in many ways a reluctant
pioneer. It depicts her struggle to maintain a sense of routine amid the pressures
her family faces in the remote landscape.*

◆ FACING THE GREAT DESOLATION ◆

VI

The days were long for the boys during their father's absence. Ole soon tired
of standing at the chopping block without the company of his brother; he idled
aimlessly about, and made frequent errands into the house to see whether he
couldn't hatch up something to break the monotony. Store-Hans wasn't much
better off; the secret which his father had entrusted to him was certainly interesting; but it wasn't quite fascinating enough to hold its own with the vision
of the ducks out there in the swamps. The father would surely bring something
home from town to solve this problem; he and his brother ought to be over
west reconnoitering every spare minute of the time. And now the Irish had all
gone away, too; their sod huts were standing empty; there would be many
curious things to look at and pry into! . . . Besides, their mother said so little
these days; it was no fun to be with her any longer. Often when he spoke to
her she was not there; she neither saw nor heard him, said only yes and no,
which seemed to come from far away. . . . Probably she was brooding over
the strange thing about to happen, Store-Hans told himself; he often looked
wonderingly at her, thinking many thoughts beyond his years. . . . He remembered his father's words, and never left her for long, although it was very
lonesome for him in the house.

A couple of days after the men's departure, she sent the boy over to Kjersti to borrow a darning needle; she had hidden her own away so carefully that she could not find it. Such things occurred commonly now; she would put something away, she could not remember where, and would potter around looking for it without really searching; at last, she would forget altogether what she was about, and would sit down with a peculiarly vacant look on her face; at such times she seemed like a stranger. . . . Ole was sitting in the house that morning, finishing a sling-shot which he had just made.

Suddenly Store-Hans came darting back with the needle; he had run until he was all out of breath. He burst out with the strangest news, of Tönseten's having killed a big animal; it was awfully big—almost like a bear! . . . Tönseten said it *was* a bear, so it must be true! Tönseten and Kjersti were skinning him right now; Kjersti had told him that if he would bring a pail, they could have fresh meat for supper. Both boys immediately began pleading for permission to go and see the animal; their mother scarcely answered; she gave them a pail and asked them not to stay long. 3

The boys came running down the hill just as Kjersti was cutting up the carcass; Tönseten was struggling with the hide, trying to stretch it on the barn door; his mouth bristled with nails, his hands were bloody—he was a frightful spectacle! 4

"What's that you've got?" asked Ole. 5

"Bear, my boy—bear!" . . . Tönseten wagged his head, took the nails out of his mouth, and spat a gob of tobacco juice. 6

"Bear!" snorted Ole, scornfully. 7

"That's no bear!" put in Store-Hans, though less doubtingly. 8

"By George! boys, to-day he had to bite the dust!" . . . 9

"But there aren't any bears out here, I tell you!" Ole protested. 10

"Is that so—huh? . . . There isn't an animal living that you can't find out here!" Tönseten spoke with such certainty that it was difficult for the boys to gainsay him. 11

"Where did you get him?" Store-Hans asked. 12

"Out west of the Irish a little way. . . . There were two of 'em; they had gone into the ground for the winter; this is the young one, you see—the old mammy got away from me!" 13

"But you didn't have any gun!" was Ole's next objection. 14

"Better than that, my boy! . . . I went for him with the crowbar!" Tönseten spat fiercely and looked at the boys. . . . "I smashed in his skull! . . . With that old bar I'd tackle either a tiger or a rhinoceros!" 15

"What became of the old she-bear?" Ole asked, falling under the spell of Tönseten's enthusiasm. 16

"She went north across the prairie, lickety-split! . . . Come here, now— take some of these chunks of meat home with you. . . . This will make delicious stew, let me tell you!" 17

"Is it fit to eat?" asked Store-Hans, still doubting. 18

"Fit to eat? No finer meat to be found than bear meat—don't you know   19
that?"

The boys followed him over to where Kjersti was still cutting up the   20
animal; it must have been a large carcass, for the cut meat made a sizable heap.

"Is it . . . is it really bear?" asked Ole, in a more humble tone.   21

"He's meaty enough for it! . . . Here, give me the pail; Beret needs some   22
good, strengthening food. . . . Maybe you'll take a little to Sörrina, too; you
can stop in with it on the way. . . . Careful—don't spill it, now!"

The boys loitered along on the way home; from time to time they had to   23
put down the pail, in order to discuss this extraordinary event. . . . So there
actually were bears slinking about this country! . . . If bears, there must be
lions and tigers and other such wild beasts; this was worth while! . . . Suppose
they were to go home and get Old Maria, hunt up the she-bear herself, and
put a big bullet clear through her head? They thrilled with excitement. . . . "Do
you dare to shoot her off?" Store-Hans demanded of his brother; Ole scowled
ominously and clenched his fists. . . . "*I!* . . . I'd aim straight for her temple,
and she'd drop deader than a herring!" . . . "Yes, aim at her *temple!*" Store-
Hans advised, soberly. "And if it's close range, you must draw the bead very
fine!" . . . "Fine as a hair!" said Ole, excitedly.

They picked up the pail at last, and finally succeeded in reaching Sörine's,   24
where there was another long delay; a detailed account had to be given of the
marvellous feat which Tönseten had performed.

When they were about to leave Sofie came out and wanted to know if   25
they weren't frightened; maybe the old mother bear was slinking about the
prairie right now looking for her cub! The boys lingered to talk with her; they
drew a glowing picture for the girl of how they were going home this minute
to get Old Maria, and then go hunting for the she-bear herself . . . just watch
them bring home a real roast pretty soon! . . . But weren't they scared? she
asked. . . . "Scared?" exclaimed Store-Hans. . . . "Oh, fiddle-sticks!" cried Ole.
"Only girls and old women get scared!"

Sofie only laughed; at which they affected a swaggering gruffness and   26
tried to spit like Tönseten—but theirs wouldn't come brown. . . .

They were gone such a long time that their mother grew anxious; when   27
they came over from Sörine's at last she stood outside the door watching for
them. She had dressed And-Ongen, and was almost on the point of starting
out to search; the boys were too preoccupied to notice this; Store-Hans spoke
first:

"Just think, there's a big she-bear over there to the westward!" . . .   28

"We're going to take the gun and shoot her!" exclaimed Ole, gleefully.   29

"We'll aim straight for her temple!" Store-Hans assured his mother.   30

"Now we'll have plenty of bear meat!" continued Ole in the next breath,   31
with absolute confidence.

The boys were all raging excitement; their mood frightened Beret still   32 more; she grasped them frantically, one hand on the shoulder of each, and gave them a hard shake. . . . They were to go inside this very minute, and take their books! They weren't going out of this house to-day! . . . "Go in, don't you hear me! . . . Go in!" . . .

. . . But this wasn't fair! Ole began reasoning with his mother; he used   33
strong words, his eyes flaming. . . . Didn't she realize that there was a real bear over to the westward—a real full-grown *grizzly* bear! . . . Mother . . . please . . . *please!* . . . Dad wasn't home, but the gun was all loaded and ready; they could easily manage the rest of it! In an hour's time they would have that bear's hide! Store-Hans even thought that he could go straight to the lair. . . . *Right through the temple* they would put the bullet! . . . The boys carried on like a raging hurricane.

The mother had to use force to get them indoors. . . . "Go in, I say, and   34
take your books! Can't you hear what I'm saying?" . . .

This was hard on them; they burst into the house like two mad bull calves;   35
she had to repeat the order several times more before they finally submitted and began to hunt for their books. At last Ole snatched up the "Epitome," his brother the "Bible History." They sat down to read by the table in front of the window, in a state of mutinous rebellion.

Trouble soon arose. Each wanted the seat immediately in front of the   36
window, where the most light fell; and neither would give up the position. A terrible battle broke out; Ole was the stronger, but his brother the quicker. On account of his age and size Ole considered himself the legitimate master of the house in the absence of his father, and therefore had the right to do anything; he now burst out with words which he had heard in the mouths of the men when something went wrong with their work. As soon as Store-Hans heard this he too began to use vile language; if Ole dared, he certainly did; he knew those words, and plenty more! . . . The boys kept up their scrimmage until they almost upset the table; their books suffered bad treatment and lay scattered about on the floor. And-Ongen watched them open-mouthed until she suddenly grew frightened and set up a howl.

Over by the stove the mother was washing the meat, putting it into a   37
kettle which she had placed on the fire. . . . Although she heard every word, she kept on working in silence; but her face turned ashen grey.

When she had finished the task she went out hurriedly; in a moment she   38
came back with a willow switch in her hand. Going straight over to the table, she began to lay about her with the switch; she seemed beside herself, struck out blindly, hit whatever she happened to aim at, and kept it up without saying a word. The switch whizzed and struck; shrieks of pain arose. The boys at once stopped fighting and gazed horror-stricken at their mother; they could not remember that she had ever laid a hand on them before. . . . And now there was such a strange, unnatural look in her eyes! . . .

They flew out on the floor to gather up their books, while the blows   39 continued to rain down upon them; And-Ongen stood in the middle of the floor, screaming with terror. . . .

Not until the mother struck amiss, breaking the switch against the edge of the table, did she stop. . . . Suddenly she seemed to come to her senses; she left the child screaming in the middle of the floor, went out of the house, and was gone a long time. When she came back, she carried an armful of wood; she went over to the stove and fed the fire; then she picked up And-Ongen, and lay down on the bed with her. . . . The boys sat quietly at the table reading; neither of them had the courage to look up. . . . 40

The house seemed strangely still after the passage of the storm. Ole put his fingers into his ears to shut out the terrible silence; his brother began to read aloud. It was bad enough for Ole, but worse for Store-Hans; he now recalled clearly what his father had confided in him; he thought of his own solemn promise; here he had been away from the house nearly the whole day! He felt burning hot all over his body. . . . He had opened the book where it told about the choosing of the twelve disciples, and now he tried to read; but *that* wasn't the stuff for him just now! . . . He turned the pages forward to the story of Samson, and read it diligently; then to David and Goliath; then to the story about Joseph and his brethren. The last eased his heart somewhat. . . . Joseph was just the sort of boy that he longed to be! 41

Ole had felt ashamed at the sight of his mother bringing in the wood, though that was not his task; his brother was to be the hired girl! . . . Suddenly anger seized him; this time it certainly was the fault of Store-Hans—he should have given him the place! . . . He dragged himself through the *Third Article*, which he knew perfectly well already; when the tumult within him had somewhat subsided he sat there thinking of how shamefully Tönseten must have deceived them. . . . *He* kill a bear! It was nothing but a measly old badger! And now this nasty stuff was cooking on the stove—they were going to have it for supper! And mother was so angry that one would never dare to explain it to her! . . . There sat his younger brother, snuffling and reading his brains out; plain to be seen that he would never amount to anything! . . . Ole closed his book with a bang, got up, and went outdoors to chop more wood; but he did not dare to look at the bed as he passed. . . . 42

Store-Hans sat over his book until it grew so dark that he could no longer distinguish the letters. . . . From time to time he looked up; his mother lay on the bed perfectly still; he could not see her face; And-Ongen was fast asleep with her head high on the pillow. The boy rose quietly, looked around—then took an empty pail and went out for water. He left the pailful of water outside the door; then he brought Rosie and Injun and the two oxen into the stable, and tied them up for the night. He spoke loudly and gruffly to the animals; mother should hear that he was tending to business! . . . When he finally brought in the water his mother was up again; he could see nothing unusual about her. 43

. . . No, she hadn't been crying this time! The thought made Store-Hans 44 so happy that he went straight to his brother, who was toiling over the chopping block as if possessed, and made friends with him again. The boys stayed outside until it was pitch dark; they talked fast and nervously, about a multitude of things; but that which weighed most heavily on their hearts— the way their mother's face had looked when she whipped them—they could not mention.

Inside the house the lamp had been lit. And-Ongen toddled about the floor, busy over her own little affairs; the boys came in quietly and sat down to their books again; but very little reading was done now. . . . At last the kettle of meat that had been boiling on the stove was ready; the mother put the food on the table; the boys drew up, Ole somewhat reluctantly. . . . "You get that troll stuff down!" he whispered to his brother, making a wry face. To this command Store-Hans made no answer; he had stuck his spoon into a crack between the boards of the table; they were large, those cracks—he could see a broad section of floor when he laid his eye down close. The earthen floor had such a rich brown colour in the dim sheen of the lamp; the cracks in the table made stripes across the shadow down there; it looked pretty, too—and just then it had occurred to Store-Hans how nice it would be if they could only have the floor looking like that by daylight. *45*

The mother filled the big bowl from the kettle and put it on the table; she had made a thick stew, with potatoes, carrots, and pieces of the meat; it looked appetizing enough but somehow the boys felt in no hurry to start. The mother came and sat down, bringing And-Ongen with her; the child was so delighted over the holiday fare they had to-night that she hurried to say grace. *46*

She and the mother immediately began to eat; the boys no longer had an excuse to sit watching. Store-Hans dipped up a spoonful of stew, blew on it, closed his eyes, and gulped it down. Ole did the same, but coughed as if he had swallowed the wrong way; then he leaned under the table and spat it out. . . . *47*

The mother asked quietly how they liked the supper. . . . At that, Ole could no longer restrain himself; he looked at his mother imploringly, and said in a tear-choked voice as he laid his spoon aside: *48*

"It tastes like dog to me!" *49*

To Store-Hans it seemed a shameful thing for Ole to speak that way of food which their mother had prepared for them; he swallowed spoonful after spoonful, while sweat poured from him. *50*

"I have heard it said many times," the mother went on, quietly, "that bear meat is all right. . . . The stew has a tangy taste, I notice, but not so bad that it can't be eaten. . . . You'd better leave the meat if you don't like it." *51*

"It isn't bear at all!" Ole blurted out. *52*

"What?" cried the mother in alarm, lowering her spoon. *53*

"It's only a lousy old badger! . . . I've heard dad say often that they aren't fit to eat!" . . . *54*

"It's true, every word of it!" cried Store-Hans, suddenly feeling frightened *55* and jamming his spoon farther down into the crack. . . . "I could tell it by his tail—Syvert had forgotten to cut it off! . . . Oh, I'm going to be sick—I can feel it coming!"

Beret got up, trembling in every limb; she took the bowl and carried it out into the darkness; a long way from the house she emptied it on the ground; And-Ongen cried and toddled after her. . . . The boys sat on at the table glaring reproachfully at each other; in the eyes of both blazed the same accusation: 56

"A nice mess you've made of things! Why didn't you keep your mouth shut?" 57

The mother came in again; she set the empty kettle on the stove and scoured it out carefully. . . . Then she cooked porridge for them, but when it was ready she could eat nothing herself. . . . 58

. . . That night she hung still more clothes over the window than she had the evening before. She sat up very late; it seemed as if she was unable to go to bed. 59

VII

She had been lying awake a long time; sleep would not come. Her thoughts drifted. . . . 60

. . . So it had come to this; they were no longer ashamed to eat troll food; they even sent it from house to house, as lordly fare! 61

All night long as she tossed in bed, bitter revolt raged within her. *They should not stay here through the winter!* . . . As soon as Per Hansa came home they must start on the journey back east; he, too, ought to be able to see by this time that they would all become wild beasts if they remained here much longer. Everything human in them would gradually be blotted out. . . . They saw nothing, learned nothing. . . . It would be even worse for their children— and what of their children's children? . . . Couldn't he understand that if the Lord God had intended these infinities to be peopled, He would not have left them desolate down through all the ages . . . until now, when the end was nearing? . . . 62

After a while the bitterness of her revolt began to subside; her thoughts became clear and shrewd, she tried to reason out the best way of getting back to civilization. That night she did not sleep at all. 63

The next morning she got up earlier than usual, kindled the fire, got the breakfast and waked the children. The food was soon prepared; first she poured some water into the pot, put in a spoonful or two of molasses, and added a few pieces of cinnamon; then she cut into bits the cold porridge from last night, and put them into the big bowl; when the sweetened water was hot she poured it over the porridge. . . . This was all they had—and no one asked for more. 64

While she ate she looked repeatedly at the big chest, trying to recall how everything had been packed when they came out last summer. Where did she 65 keep all the things now? She had better get the packing done at once—then that job would be out of the way when he came home. . . .

The greatest difficulty would be to obtain wagons. . . . Alas! those old wagons! The smaller one he had taken apart and used in making the very table around which they were now seated; as for the larger wagon, she knew only too well that it would never hang together through the long journey back; only the other day she had heard Per Hansa mention that he intended to break it up, and see if he couldn't make something or other out of it. . . . Well—how to get the wagons would be his business! They certainly couldn't perish out here for want of a wagon or two! Was there not One who once upon a time had had mercy on a great city full of wicked people, only because one just human being interceded? 66

. . . One just human being. . . . Alas! . . . Beret sighed heavily and put her hand up under her breast. 67

When there was no more porridge left in the bowl she rose, washed the dish, and put it away on the shelf. Ole had nothing to do in the house that morning; he walked toward the door, motioning to his brother to follow; but Store-Hans shook his head. Then Ole went out; the other boy sat there looking at his mother, not knowing what to do, unhappy and heavy-hearted; he felt a sudden impulse to throw himself down on the floor and weep aloud. 68

The mother was pottering about at some trifles, her thoughts constantly occupied with the idea of returning to civilization. Into her serious, grey-pale face, still soft and beautiful, had crept an expression of firmness and defiance; soon this aspect grew so marked that her face appeared to simulate anger, like that of one playing at being ferocious with a child. 69

As soon as she had finished her housework she went over to the big chest, opened the lid, sank down on her knees beside it, and began to rearrange the contents. The task was quickly done; then she took the clothes from the last washing, folded them up, and laid them carefully in the chest; there weren't many clothes left now! He ought to realize that they would soon be naked if they stayed here much longer! And where were they to get money for everything they needed out here? . . . Beret stood up and looked around the room, trying to decide what to pack first. On the shelf above the window lay an old Bible, a gift to her from her grandfather; it was so old that it was hard to read now, because of the many changes the language had undergone since then; but it was the only one they had. This book had been in her family many generations; her great-grandfather had owned it before her grandfather; from her it should pass on to Store-Hans; thus she had always determined when she thought of the matter. On top of the Bible lay the hymn book, in which she had read a little every Sunday since their arrival here. . . . 70

She put both books in the chest. 71

Again Beret rose and glanced around the room. Perhaps she had better take the school books, too; the boys were none too eager to use them; they 72 might as well be excused for the rest of the day; either that day or the next the father would surely come. . . . She asked Store-Hans to bring the books to her so that she could pack them.

Not until then did the boy fully take in what his mother was doing; it startled him so that for a moment he could not get up. 73

"Mother, what are you doing?" . . . 74

"We must begin to get ready!" . . . She sighed, and pressed her hands tightly under her burden; it was painful to her, stooping over so long at a time. 75

"Get ready? Are . . . are we going *away?*" . . . Store-Hans's throat contracted; his eyes stared big and terror-stricken at his mother. 76

"Why, yes, Hansy-boy—we had better be going back where people live before the winter is upon us," she told him, sadly. 77

The boy had risen, and now stood at the end of the table; he wanted to go to his mother but fear chained him to the spot; he stared at her with his mouth wide open. At last he got out: 78

"What will dad say?" . . . The words came accusingly but there were tears in them. 79

She looked at him like one in a dream; again she looked, but could not utter a word. . . . The sheer impossibility of what she was about to do was written as if in fire on the face and whole body of the boy—as if in rays that struck her, lighted everything up with an awful radiance, and revealed the utter futility of it all. . . . She turned slowly toward the chest, let down the lid, and sank on it in untold weariness. . . . Again the child stirred within her, kicking and twisting, so that she had to press her hand hard against it. 80

. . . O God! . . . now *he* was protesting, too! Was it only by ruthless sacrifice of life that this endless desolation could ever be peopled? 81

. . . "Thou canst not be so cruel!" she moaned. . . . "Demand not this awful sacrifice of a frail human being!" . . . 82

She rose slowly from the chest; as she walked across the floor and opened the door she felt as if she were dragging leaden weights. . . . Her gaze flitted fearfully toward the sky line—reached it, but dared not travel upward. . . . 83

Store-Hans remained at the end of the table, staring after her; he wanted to scream, but could not utter a sound. Then he ran to her, put his arms around her, and whispered hoarsely between sobs: 84

"Mother, are you . . . are you . . . getting sick now?" 85

Beret stroked the head that was pressed so hard against her side; it had such a vigorous, healthy warmth, the hair was soft and pleasant to the touch; she had to run her fingers through it repeatedly. . . . Then she stooped over and put her arm around the boy; his response to her embrace was so violent that it almost choked her. . . . O God! how sorely she needed some one to be kind to her now! . . . She was weeping; Store-Hans, too, was struggling with wild, tearing sobs. Little And-Ongen, who could not imagine what the two were doing over there by the door, came toddling to them and gazed up into 86 their faces; then she opened her mouth wide, brought her hand up to it, and shrieked aloud. . . . At that moment Ole came running down the hill, his feet flying against the sky, and shouted out to them:

"They are coming! . . . Get the coffee on!"   87

. . . Gone was the boy like a gust of wind; he threw himself on the pony   88
and galloped away to meet the returning caravan.

Beret and Store-Hans had both sprung to their feet and stood looking   89
across the prairie. . . . Yes, there they were, away off to the southeast! . . . And now Store-Hans, also, forgot himself; he glanced imploringly into his mother's face, his eyes eagerly questioning:

"Would it be safe to leave you while I run to meet dad?"   90

She smiled down into the eager face—a benign, spreading smile.   91

"Don't worry about me. . . . Just run along." . . .   92

VIII

The father sat at the table eating, with And-Ongen on his knee; the boys stood   93
opposite him, listening enthusiastically to the story of his adventures along the way; the mother went to and fro between the stove and the table. There was an enchanting joyousness about Per Hansa to-day which coloured all he said; no matter how much he told, it always sounded as if he were keeping back the best till later on. This had a positively intoxicating effect on the boys; it made them impatient and eager for more, and caused a steady flood of fresh questions.

Even Beret was smiling, though her hand trembled.   94

At last the boys had to give an account of how they had managed affairs   95
at home. When, after much teasing and banter, Per Hansa had finally heard the whole absurd story—it came little by little, in disjointed outbursts—of Tönseten and the bear, and their ill-starred badger stew of the night before, he laughed until the tears came and he had to stop eating. His mirth was so free and hearty that the boys, too, began to see the real fun of the incident, and joined in boisterously. Beret stood over by the stove, listening to it all; their infectious merriment carried her away, but at the same time she had to wipe her eyes. . . . She was glad that she had remembered to take out of the chest the things that she had begun to pack awhile before!

"Come here, Store-Hans," said the father, still laughing. "What's that   96
across the back of your neck?"

The question caught the boy unawares; he ran over and stood beside his   97
father.

"Why, it's a big red welt! . . . Have you been trying to hang yourself,   98
boy?"

Store-Hans turned crimson; he suddenly remembered the fearful blows   99
of last night.

Ole glanced quickly at his mother. . . . "Oh, pshaw!" he said with a manly   100
air. . . . "That was only Hans and me fighting!"

"Ah-ha!" exclaimed the father, with another laugh. "So that's the way 101
you two have been acting while I was away? Mother couldn't manage you,
eh? . . . Well, now you'll soon be dancing to a different tune; we've got so
much work on our hands that there won't be any peace here day or
night. . . . Thanks for good food, Beret-girl!"

He got up, took the boys with him, and began to carry things in from 102
the wagon. Most of the load they stored away in the house; some extra things,
however, had to find a temporary place in the stable.

At length Per Hansa brought in a small armful of bottles and set them 103
on the table.

"Come here, Beret-girl of mine! You have earned a good drink, and a 104
good drink you shall have!" . . . He went over to the water pail with the coffee
cup from which he had just been drinking, rinsed it out with a little water, and
emptied it on the floor; then he poured out a good half cupful of whisky and
offered it to her. She put out her hand as if to push him away. . . . Yes, indeed,
she would have to take it, he told her, putting his arm around her waist and
lifting the cup to her lips. She took the cup and emptied it in one draught. . . .
"There, that's a good little wife! . . . You're going to have just another little
drop!" He went to the table again and poured out a second drink, but not so
much this time. "Two legs, and one for each! Just drink it down! . . . And
now you take care of the bottles!"

That was a busy day in the humble dwelling of Per Hansa. First of all, 105
he had promised a load of potatoes to the Hallings, who waited back east
somewhere under a bleak sky, without even a potato peeling to put in their pot;
he must carry food to them. When Beret heard how poorly things were in that
hut—about the woman with the drawn cheeks and the starved look in her
eyes—she straightway began to hurry him up; he must go while he had the
horses and wagon here. Couldn't he get started to-day?

"Not so hasty there, my girl, not so hasty!" laughed Per Hansa, his face 106
beaming. . . . "I'm not going to sleep with any *Halling woman* to-night—that I
can tell you!"

Now he was his old irresistible self again. How strong, how precious to 107
her, he seemed! . . . She felt a loving impulse to grasp his hair and shake
him. . . .

Ole was immediately put to work knitting the net. The father had already 108
knitted four fathoms of it, by the light of the camp fire the night before; he
had sat up working over the net long after the others had turned in. . . . The
boys grew wild with enthusiasm at the sight of the net; were they going fishing
in the Sioux River? Both of them immediately began begging to be taken
along. . . . "Just keep your fingers moving, Olamand—hurry them up, I tell
you!" . . . The father made a great mystery of it, and refused to give any further
explanation.

As for himself and Store-Hans, they busied themselves over the lime; it 109
was all carried inside and placed in a corner where no moisture could reach it.

The preparations for the mixing required a good deal of work; the first thing was to make a wooden box sufficiently tight to hold water. Well, there was plenty of lumber now, at any rate! Per Hansa built the box and carried it down to the creek; there he placed it under water, hoping that it would swell enough to be tight by the time he needed it.

Evening fell all too soon on a wonderfully busy and joyful day. The boys were at last in bed, fast asleep. 110

But Per Hansa had no time for rest; to-night that net simply had to be finished. He finally made Beret go to bed, but she wasn't a bit sleepy; she lay there talking to him and filling the shuttles whenever they were empty. He explained fully to her how he intended to use the net; first he would set it in the Sioux River as he passed by there to-morrow; he knew of just the place; he would leave it there until he came back from the Hallings'. Unless the cards were stacked against him he would bring back a nice mess of fish. . . . That, however, wasn't his great plan with the net, he told her; but she mustn't say a word about this to the boys. It was to be a big surprise for them; they were such brave fellows! The fact of the matter was, he planned to catch *ducks* with that net; that had been the real reason for his buying the twine; there would be other fare than badger stew in this hut, he would just let her know, if the weather only held a few days more! 111

All at once it occurred to Beret that she had forgotten to cover up the windows to-night; she smiled to herself at the discovery. . . . What was the need of it, anyway? Cover the windows . . . what nonsense! . . . She smiled again, feeling a languorous drowsiness creep over her. 112

Per Hansa knit away on the net, chatting happily with her as he worked; a confident ring of joy sounded in all he said. He had fastened the net to the bedpost, just as her father always had done. She listened peacefully to his warm, cheerful voice, which after a while began to sound more distant, like the indolent swish and gurgle of lapping ocean waves on a fair summer's night. Gradually she was borne away on this sound, and slept the whole night through without stirring. 113

When she awoke next morning Per Hansa, still fully dressed, lay beside her, over against the wall; he evidently had thrown himself down to rest only a little while before. Light was creeping into the room; directly in front of the bed lay a big white heap of something. . . . Those careless boys—had they thrown their clothes on the floor again? . . . She stooped over to pick the clothes up and put them on the bench; she grasped hold of the heap—and it was a new net, sheeted and fully rigged, as a new net ought to be! 114

. . . Poor man!—he must have sat up all night! . . . She spread the quilt carefully over him. 115

That morning Beret took some of the precious white flour and made a batch of pancakes. He deserved to have one good meal before he went away again! 116

He left right after breakfast. Beret worked industriously throughout the day, while many thoughts came and went. . . . It must be her destiny, this! There was One who governed all things. . . . He knew what was best, and against His will it was useless to struggle! . . . 117

   . . . Often that day she went to the window to look eastward. Every time she looked, it seemed to be growing darker over there. . . . 118

   . . . That evening she again covered the window. . . . ◆

◆ Responding

1. Although still young, Ole and Store-Hans have already internalized traditional roles and attitudes about gender. Using the evidence in the reading, list the behaviors and duties they expect from males and females.

2. Analyze Beret's responses to the boys' fight. What pressures produced her reaction? What was she thinking and feeling when she "left the child screaming in the middle of the floor, went out of the house, and was gone a long time"? Pretend you are Beret and write an entry in your diary about the event.

3. Compare Beret's and Per Hansa's attitudes to life in the wilderness. How do you account for the differences? Some factors to consider are personal temperament, gender, upbringing, activities, responsibilities, ambitions, and expectations for the future.

4. Beret has great difficulty dealing with life on the prairie. Using your own knowledge, describe the pioneer heroine often portrayed in stories and films. Compare her character and behavior with Beret's.

MYRA KELLY

Myra Kelly was born in Dublin, Ireland, in 1875 and immigrated with her parents while she was still a child. She was educated at Horace Mann High School and at Columbia Teacher's College in New York City. After college she taught in the Bowery and then worked as a teaching mentor at Columbia Teacher's College.

Kelly's short stories, based on her teaching experiences, first appeared in magazines; they were later collected in book form as Little Citizens *(1904),* Wards of Liberty *(1907),* Isle of Dreams *(1907),* Rosnah *(1908), and* Little Aliens *(1910). Kelly also examined the effect of the public school on immigrant populations in an article entitled "The American Public School as a Factor in International Conciliation." She died of tuberculosis in 1910, at the age of thirty-five.*

The short story that follows explores the role of education in the immigrant's life by contrasting the main character's expectations with those of the teacher. The story's climax, in which the other students are asked to choose between their leader's values and those of the teacher, raises questions about the relationship between education and success. It also leads us to consider the ways in which institutions traditionally respond to demonstrations of assertiveness and personal initiative.

◆ A SOUL ABOVE BUTTONS ◆

The Boss staggered down the cellar steps and dropped the pile of coats from his small shoulder to the floor. The "boarders," for a breath's space, ceased from sewing buttons upon other coats and turned expectant eyes toward their employer, their landlord, their gaoler,[1] and their only source of news.   1

But he brought no tidings of the outer world on this particular afternoon. He had been through crowded blocks where the very air was full of war and murder and his only report was the banality: 2

"The day is upon me wherein I must go to school."   3

No one was interested. Even the mother of the Boss, frying fish in one corner of the cellar, was busy with her own gloomy preoccupations and reached her son's communication only after a long delay. Then she asked dully: 4

"Why?"   5

"For learn the reading and the writing of the English. A man at the factory where I waited for my turn told me of how he had learned these things and he showed me the card he had won by his learning. 'It is from the Union,' he told   6

---

[1]jailor

me, and behold! when he stood before the manager he received gents' vests for the finishing. The pay is good for that work. So when my turn came I, too, asked for finishing to do. But the manager laughed. 'Are you of the Union?' he demanded, 'show me then your card!' And I, having no card, received only buttons. For such a card I shall go to school."

On the next morning he waited upon the Principal of the nearest Public School and proved a grievous trial to that long-suffering official. The Boss's alert and well formulated knowledge of the world of the streets was only exceeded by his blandly abysmal ignorance of the world of books. And it was after careful deliberation and with grave misgiving that the Principal sent for the roll-book of the First Reader Class and consigned the newcomer to Miss Bailey's dominion. 7

Teacher welcomed him with careful patience but his advent created something akin to a riot in Room 18. There was hardly a child within its walls who was not familiar with his history and awed by his proximity. They all knew how his father had finished gents' garments and his own tired life in a cellar under Henry Street, and how the son, having learned the details of the business by acting as his father's messenger, was now the successful manager of that dead father's business. They knew how he had induced his mother to work for him, though she had at first preferred—sensibly enough—to die. How he had then impressed a half-witted sister into service, had acquired an uncanny dexterity with his own needle, and had lately enlarged his establishment to include three broken-spirited exiles who paid for their board and lodging by their ceaseless labor. 8

And now he had come to their school! Was in the First Reader Class! No wonder that Eva Gonorowsky tingled with excitement and preened the butterfly bow which threatened her right eye. No wonder that Sarah Schodsky, Monitor of Fashionable Intelligence, broke through all restrictions, and the belt of her apron, in her eagerness to impart these biographical details to Miss Bailey. No wonder that Patrick Brennan pondered how far a Leader of the Line might safely boss a professional Boss. No wonder that Morris Mogilewsky, Monitor of Goldfish and of Manners, was obliged to call Teacher's attention to the extent to which the "childrens longed out their necks und rubbered." 9

The Boss cared little for the commotion of which he was the cause. His red-lidded eyes were everywhere, saw everything, but found no trace of the "Cards off of Unions" of which he was in search. Nothing else interested him, and he grew uneasy as the class fell into its morning routine. An interval of Swedish Exercises prompted him to remonstrate. 10

"Say, missus, ain't you goin' to learn us to read? I ain't got no time to fool with me legs an' arms." 11

"We shall have reading in a few moments," Teacher assured him. "Are you so fond of it?" 12

"Don't know nothings about it," the Boss answered. "When are ye goin' to quit your foolin' an' learn us some?" 13

Teacher turned to survey her newest charge. Stripped of his authority [14] and removed from his cellar, the Boss was only a little more stunted of stature and crafty of eye than his nine years of life on the lower East Side of New York entitled him to be. And yet his criticism impressed itself through Constance Bailey's armor of pedagogic self-righteousness and left her rather at a loss.

"We shall have reading in a few moments," she repeated. "But first we [15] must try a little arithmetic. Wouldn't you like that?" And out of an ignorance as great as his ambition he answered tentatively:

"I'll try it. But I *comes* for learn readin' an' writin'." [16]

He didn't like arithmetic at all. It struck him as being a shade more inane [17] than Swedish Exercises, and almost as bad as singing and praying. The Boss who could calculate, entirely without written figures, the number of boarders necessary to make his business a paying one and the number of hours and dollars he could allow his mother to devote to domesticity, the Boss who had already estimated the depressing sum which the vagaries of the official Course of Study had thus far cost him, listened in contemptuous amazement to the problems proposed to his consideration by this Teacher's words and the Boss's thoughts followed one another in some such sequence as:

"I had ten dollars and I spent six dollars for a dress—" [18]

"Gee, ain't she easy!" [19]

"Two dollars for a waist—" [20]

"For her size! It was stealin'." [21]

"Fifty cents for a belt and fifty cents for three handkerchiefs. Who can [22] tell me how much I had left?"

"I kin," said the Boss, "but that's no way to do. You'd ought to count [23] your change. An' I kin tell you, too, you was skinned when you paid six dollars fer that dress. I ain't seen the coat but I kin tell by the skirt. An' that waist ain't worth no two dollars. I could show you a place where you'd get your money's worth. The man what owns half of it is a friend of mine."

But before he had arranged details he was swept into silence by the First [24] Reader Class's divergent estimates of Teacher's present financial standing.

"You've got nineteen dollars left," cried the optimistic Eva Gonorowsky, [25] while Ignatius Aloysius Diamantstein, with a pecuniary pessimism contracted from his Irish stepmother, shrieked the evil tidings:

"You're dead broke. You ain't got nothin' at all." [26]

Finally the unashamed Miss Bailey set her extravagances in neat figures [27] upon the blackboard and the Boss's spirits rose. This was the sort of thing he had come for. This was like business. And he marveled much that so idiotic a shopper could be "smart" enough to write with so easy a grace.

After further waiting and other wilful waste of time the readers were at [28] last distributed, and the mouse-colored head of the Boss, which might have been sleeker if the latest "boarder" had had greater skill or a sharper pair of scissors, was buried between the pages of a book. A half hour of the most desperate mental exertion left him spent, hot-eyed, gasping, but master of the fact that certain black marks upon a white surface proclaimed to those desiring tickets off of Unions that:

"Baby's eyes are blue. Baby's cheeks are pink. Baby has a ball. See the pretty ball." 29

Followed days of ceaseless effort and nights of sleepy toil. Followed headaches, hunger, weariness. But followed, too, a dim understanding of a relationship between letters and sounds. This Teacher called reading. 30

Writing he found even more difficult, but here Miss Bailey was able to manage some of that "correlation with the environment" which educators preach. While more frivolous First Readers wrote of flowers and birds and babies, the Boss stuck tongue in pallid cheek and traced: "Buttons are round," "Pants have pockets," and other legends calculated to make straight the way to Cards and Unions. 31

During his first week at school he managed to reimburse himself for some of his wasted hours. On the afternoon of his second day he spared time from his cellar to ask: 32

"Say, Mrs. Bailey, did you spend that other dollar yit?" 33

"What dollar?" asked that improvident young woman. 34

"The dollar you had left over when you bought that waist an' suit." 35

"No, I'm keeping that," Miss Bailey informed him, "to buy a house on Fifth Avenue." 36

"Where do you live now?" the Boss inquired, and Teacher told him a combination of numbers which conveyed nothing to his mind. 37

"Alone?" 38

"No, with my family." 39

"An' they let you fool round down here all the time? Don't they need you home?" 40

"Not very much. They don't mind." 41

"I guess not," the Boss acquiesced. "I guess you don't help much. Your hands don't look like you did. Say, do you get pay fer teachin'?" 42

"Very good pay," she answered meekly, though she did not always think so. 43

"Then you'd better go right on livin' at home. You don't want to buy no real estate. You stay with the old folks an' buy a hat with that dollar. You'd ought to have a stylish hat to wear with that new suit." 44

"But a dollar seems so much for just one hat," Miss Bailey objected. "A whole dollar!" 45

"I might be able to fix you so you could git it fer less," the Boss encouraged her; "I know a lady what sells hats, an' she might let you have something cheap if I saw her about it." 46

"Oh, would you really!" cried the guileless young person, "that is very good of you," and thereupon fell into consideration of a suitable color scheme. 47

"You leave me 'tend to it," the Boss advised. "I'll fix you up all right, all right." 48

On his way to the cellar he stopped to visit an old crony of his mother's who kept a millinery establishment neatly combined with a candy counter and a barrel of sauerkraut. With tales of the approaching birthday of the weak-minded sister he induced this lady to part—at the reduced rate of thirty-four cents—with a combination of purple and parrot-green velveteen and diamond sunbursts. Departing with this grandeur he made the provident stipulation that unless the mind of the weak-minded sister were reached and pleasured the whole transaction might be rescinded. 49

And before school had formally opened on the next morning, Miss Bailey cheerfully paid ninety cents for the head-gear and for a lesson in the sharpest bargaining of which she had ever dreamed. 50

Teacher was as new and puzzling a type to the Boss as he was to her. He had seen ladies like her in fashion-plates, but he had never imagined that the road to Cards and Unions was adorned by such sentinels. He had not expected that a very soft hand would guide his own work-roughened one in the formation of strange letters: that a very gentle accent would guide his own street-toughened one in the pronunciation of strange words. But least of all had he expected to enjoy these things and to work as much for the lady's commendation as for Cards and Unions, to be interested in her impossible stories, to admire her clothes, to entrap her into ill-advised purchases, and to be heavy of heart when his early doubts grew into sad certainties and he knew that Constance Bailey, so gay, so gullible, so friendly, so good to look upon, was woefully weak in mentality. 51

And yet what other explanation could there be of her wastefulness of time and effort and material. Why spend hours in the painting of a flower or the learning of a string of words which—when they meant anything at all—meant lies. Why close her ears to truth? Why reject his answer, founded upon fact and observation, to her question: "Where did you come from, Baby dear?" in favor of Isidore Belchatosky's inane doggerel: "Out of the everywhere into the here." 52

Then there was her Board of Monitors. The sons and daughters of great men were entrusted to her care and she allowed them to languish in officeless obscurity while Morris Mogilewsky, Yetta Aaronsohn, Eva Gonorowsky, Nathan Spiderwitz and Patrick Brennan basked in favor and high places. Was not Isaac Borrachsohn, the son of an Assemblyman and the grandson of a Rabbi, better fitted to "make good" than the daughter of a man who peddled notions "on the country," or a boy whose father even then was looking for a job? 53

But the saddest proof of her mental condition was her passion for washing. She was always at it. She had established a basin and a heap of towels in one corner of Room 18 and there she would wash a First Reader for no reason at all, or because of a mere obscurity of feature which might have been easily cleared away by the application of a slightly moistened coat cuff or the dampened 54 hem of an apron. In a paroxysm of cleanliness she washed the Boss, though his morning canvass of his person had shown him to be, with careful usage, good for at least a week. She washed paint brushes, desk covers, glasses, even pencils. All was fish that came to her net and she put it all in water.

There was one phase of her conversation which refused to classify itself either as fact or fiction. In the Course of Study it was described as "Moral Training," and Constance Bailey devoted a daily half hour to this part of her duty. She combined ethics with biography, and showed that virtue not only was its own cold reward but that the virtuous always held preferred stock in the business of life, and might realize at a moment's notice. There was Jack the Giant Killer and Abey Lincoln; King Alfred the Great and the Light Brigade; King Arthur and the David who slew Goliath; and—but this was the Boss's contribution to the galaxy of heroism—there was his own countryman Schonsky who had licked Paddy, The Terrible and many others. All these bright stars of history, all these examples of the good and true, had reaped great renown and profit from their purity and prowess; had triumphed over wrong; had demonstrated beyond the shadow of a doubt that "honesty is the best policy" and that "fortune favors the brave." 55

So things progressed in Room 18 until the Friday afternoon of the Boss's second week in the high halls of learning. On the preceding Friday he had been detained in the cellar by the sudden collapse of a boarder. But during the second week he had been constant in his attendance and Teacher handed him a blue ticket which announced to whom it might concern—and who could read it— that the punctuality, the application, and the deportment of the Boss had been all that could have been desired. She smiled approvingly when she gave it to him; she even laid an appreciative hand for an appreciable moment on the mouse-colored head and added a word of encouragement. 56

"You have done beautifully this week," she vouchsafed him. "I am very proud of my new little boy." 57

The new little boy retreated silently to his place and watched. He noted the joy and eagerness of such children as received tickets, the dejection of those who got none. He did not quite understand the details of the system but its general principles were familiar to him, so he waited until he and Miss Bailey were alone and she had given him such private instruction as their scanty leisure allowed. Then he drew out his certificate of merit and asked: 58

"Where do I git it cashed?" 59

"You don't get it cashed," said Teacher. "You take it home to show that you were a good little boy." 60

"Then where do I git me pay?" 61

"Your pay for being good!" Miss Bailey reproved him. 62

"Naw," said the Boss, "me pay fer sewin'. Didn't I make ye a book-mark an' mat, an' a horse reins fer a kid?" 63

"But not for pay," Teacher remonstrated. "You did it for—" 64

"Fer me health?" queried the Boss. "Well I guess nit. I done the work an' 65

I done it good, an' I want me pay. If you don't fix me up I'll report you and have your whole — shop raided."

In view of this awful threat and of the bursting indignation of the Boss, Teacher temporized with the hopeful-sounding but most doubting suggestion: 66

"Wouldn't you like to take the things home with you now? You will get all your sewing at promotion time, but if you would like to have those three pieces to-day I might let you take them." 67

"No you don't," said the good little boy grimly. "You don't work me with none of your con games. I done the work an' I want me pay." 68

Gently, but firmly, Miss Bailey explained the by-laws of the Board of Education to him. Stubbornly he refused to accept the explanation. 69

"You git *your* pay all right, all right," he unchivalrously reminded her. "You git your pay an' now you're tryin' to welsh on them poor little kids. Why, I wouldn't treat the greenest Greenie in my cellar like you treat them kids what you're paid to treat right." 70

Miss Bailey appealed to his common sense, to his thirst for learning, to the integrity of all her former dealings with her good little boy. In vain, again in vain. The commercialism of the Boss was rampant and vigilant. At the first pause in her justification he broke in with: 71

"An' I folded papers fer you, too. Don't I git no pay fer that? I don't know the rates on that kind of a job but a young lady friend of mine works to a paper-boxes factory an' she gets good money. What are you goin' to do about the house I folded for you? A house an' a barn, an' a darn fool bird. (I won't charge you nothin' on that bird 'cause it didn't look like nothin'.) But I want me pay on them other things, an' you'll be sorry if you don't fix me up now. I'll queer yer good and plenty if you don't. I—" and here the contempt and the maturity of the Boss were wonderful to see—"I don't want the crazy truck. I don't want no book-mark—I ain't got no book. Nor I don't want no paper house an' barn. An' do I look like I wanted a horse reins with bells on it? Bells on *me!*" cried the Boss who had his own reasons for going softly all his days. "Well I guess nit!" 72

Of course compromise, after attempted intimidation, was impossible, and Miss Bailey went home that afternoon in a most uncomfortable frame of mind. For the Boss had interested her. She had enjoyed working for and gaining his slow regard, was attracted by his independence. And she was sorry for the little chap with his tiny body and his great responsibilities. While he was pitying her for the omission of mind from her constitution she was grieving over him as a child defrauded of his childhood. But in this matter of paying children for the work they did at school, there was nothing she could say to make him understand her position. 73

On Monday morning the lowering expression of the Boss's visage and the truculent carriage of the corduroy head had become epidemic in Room 18. All the dark eyes, which for nearly a whole term had regarded Miss Bailey as a judicious combination of angel, Fairy-tale, and Benevolent Society, were now darker still with disillusionment and suspicion. Sulkily, the First Reader Class 74 obeyed the voice of authority. Slowly, the First Reader Class cast off the spell which had held them. Stealthily, the First Reader Class watched the mouse-colored crest of its new commander and waited for his signal to revolt. It came with the sewing hour in the late morning. Fat needles and gay worsted were distributed and the working-drawing of a most artistic iron-holder was traced upon the blackboard. The work was ready, but the workers were militantly not so. Teacher turned to Morris Mogilewsky:

"Is this a Jewish holiday?" she asked him, out of her disheartening experience of the enforced idleness of those frequent festivals. 75

"No, ma'am, this ain't no holiday," Morris answered. "On'y we dassent to sew fer you fer nothings, the while we likes we shall make mit you a hit." 76

"That is slang, dear," Teacher warned him. "But you could make much more of a hit with me by doing your sewing like good children." 77

"We dassent. The new boy he makes we shall make a swear over it. It's a fierce swear." 78

"Come here," Teacher commanded, and the Boss, abandoning a lurking desire to use his desk as a barricade and to entrench himself behind it, rose upon unsteady legs and obeyed. Teacher looked less harmless than he had expected as she demanded: 79

"What kind of a hit is this supposed to be?" 80

"It ain't no hit. It's a strike. I told the kids what their work is worth an' they feel like I do about doin' it fer nothin'. I guess you'll be sorry you turned me down, Friday," and for a baffled moment Teacher wished that the turning might be across her knee and accompanied with vigorous infringement of the by-laws. Here was a model class of the school, her pride, her enthusiasm, almost her creation, given over to mutiny and sedition. For a moment she thought of using coercion and then determined upon a *coup d'état*. Very gravely she stood beside her desk and made an address of farewell. 81

She touched upon the little joys and sorrows which had visited Room 18. She made artful allusions to flowers, canaries, goldfish, and rabbits. She cast one regretful eye back to the Christmas tree and she cast the other forwards to the proposed 'scursion to Central Park. She concluded, as well as she could through the satisfactory veil of tears which had enveloped the Class: 82

"But since you feel that I have treated you badly, since you feel that you should have been paid for learning those things which will help to make you useful when you are big and to keep you happy while you are little, I must ask you to take your hats and coats and everything which belongs to you and to leave your desks for the little boys and girls—there are plenty of them—who will be glad to come to school in Room 18 and who won't have to be paid for coming." 83

A long and wavering wail from the monitor of pencil points ended Miss Bailey's valedictory and was echoed by the monitors of goldfish and of buttons. 84

"I don't want I shall be promoted," snuffled Ignatius Aloysius Diamantstein with a damp cuff against a damper nose. "I have a fraid over Miss Blake und I likes it here all right." 85

"You won't be promoted," Miss Bailey comforted him. "You will stay at home or play on the street. You won't have to go to school at all." 86

"I don't likes it, I don't likes it!" wailed Morris Mogilewsky. "I don't need I shall be no rowdy what plays by blocks. I likes I shall stay by your side und make what is healthy mit them from-gold fishes." 87

"Very well, you may stay if you care to," Miss Bailey remarked with a coldness hitherto unknown in her dealings with this, the most devoted of her charges. "But the others must take their things and go at once." 88

But no one wanted to go. Teacher was buried under a landslide of moistly compunctious First Readers which launched itself upon her defenseless person with tearful pledges of fealty. When it was at last differentiated and driven back to the desks Miss Bailey delivered her ultimatum: 89

"The children who will stay at school only if they are paid for their work here may—Stand!" 90

Only the Boss arose. Fear, or love, or gratitude, or public opinion held the others in their seats and the Boss surveyed them with hot scorn. He had not reached that stage of Moral Training which would have taught him that the way of the reformer is as hard as that of the transgressor, and that the wages of the man who tries to awaken his fellow is generally derision and often death. 91

So he shared the lot of many leaders and stood without followers when the time for action had come. 92

"You're a bunch of sissies," he informed the neat and serried ranks of the First Readers. "You're a bunch of softies. You're a bunch of scabs." 93

"You really mustn't say such words," Teacher reproved him. "You just wait in the hall for a moment while I give the children something to do; I want to talk to you." 94

Some compromise between the Boss, Miss Bailey, and the By-laws might have been effected, but when Teacher had supplied her reclaimed and repentant charges with occupation, when she had placed Patrick Brennan in command and had uncoiled sundry penitent embraces which had again fastened upon her, she followed the Boss and found the hall empty. 95

Scouts were despatched and returned baffled. The truant officer was no more successful. Miss Bailey visited the cellar and retired discomfited, for she could neither breathe the air, believe the disclaimers, nor speak the speech which she encountered there. Other First Readers from time to time reported fleeting glimpses of the always fleeing Boss. But what could the inexperienced eyes of Constance Bailey, the hurried inspection of the truant officer, the innocent regard of the First Readers avail against his trained and constant watchfulness? More than ever now did he go softly all his days and many of his nights. 96

For he had presented himself before his friend, the manager of the shop, as one desiring examination in the elements of English Literature and Composition and had discovered that his two weeks had furthered him not at all upon the way to Cards off of Unions and that buttons were still to be his portion. 97

"Ain't this writin'?" he demanded and offered for his friend's inspection   98
some mystic marks of whose meaning—in the absence of a copy—he was a
little unsure.

"No, it ain't. It's foolin'," said the candid friend.   99

"She learned me that," the Boss maintained. "An' she learned me too,   100
'Honesty is the best Policy.' What's that?"

"That's a lie," the candid one informed him.   101

"An' she learned us about Jack the Giant Killer an' King Arthur. Who   102
was they?"

"Fakes," was the verdict of candor. "She worked you for all you was   103
worth."

"She fooled me all right, all right," the rueful Boss admitted. "But say,   104
you'd ought to see her. She sure looks like the real thing."

"Sure she does," acquiesced the friend, who combined worldly wisdom   105
with his frankness. "The slickest always does."

And so the Boss avoided the high halls of learning and all associated   106
therewith. For had he not bent thirstily over the Pierian Spring expecting to
quaff inspiration to Cards and to Unions, and had he not found that it flowed
forth misinformation, Swedish Exercise, unpaid labor, and that it bubbled
disgustingly with soap and water? ◆

◆ Responding

1. Working with a partner, write a dialogue in which one of you, pretending
   to be the Boss, complains that the curriculum is not relevant, and the other,
   pretending to be Miss Bailey, tries to convince the Boss to remain in school.
   Read the dialogue aloud to the class.

2. Define "street smart" and "book smart." Use characters and examples from
   the story and from your own experience to illustrate your definitions.

3. Part of the humor in this story comes from the different assumptions and
   expectations of the Boss and Miss Bailey. Read aloud or act out some of the
   scenes between the two characters. Analyze the class's spontaneous response.
   Compare these situations with other "fish-out-of-water" stories, such as the
   films *Crocodile Dundee I* and *II* and Mark Twain's *A Connecticut Yankee in King
   Arthur's Court*.

4. Miss Bailey defines the goal of education as teaching "those things which
   will help to make you useful when you are big and to keep you happy while
   you are little." Compare her goals with your personal educational goals.

ANZIA YEZIERSKA

Anzia Yezierska was born in Poland in 1885, the daughter of a Talmudic scholar. Her family immigrated to the United States during the 1890s. After attending night school, she graduated from the Teacher's College of Columbia University in 1904. Her publications include The Free Vacation House *(1915),* "The Fat of the Land" *(1919),* Salome of the Tenements *(1922),* Children of Loneliness *(1923),* The Bread Givers *(1925),* The Arrogant Beggar *(1927),* All I Could Never Be *(1932), and* The Red Ribbon on a White Horse *(1950).* "The Fat of the Land" *was awarded the O. Henry Prize for the best story of 1919; Yezierska's other literary prizes included the 1929–30 Zora Gale Fellowship at the University of Wisconsin and two awards from the National Institute of Arts and Letters (1962 and 1965).*

In the early part of Yezierska's career, her work enjoyed great popularity. She was friendly with many of the leading intellectuals of the day, including the philosopher John Dewey. In 1918 she was invited to Hollywood by film producer Sam Goldwyn to adapt one of her stories for the screen. Later in her life Yezierska had more difficulty getting her work published. She died in 1970.

Many of Yezierska's works explore elements of the immigrant experience. The selection that follows depicts the life of an immigrant from two perspectives—during the period just after she settles in this country and twenty-five years later—and invites us to compare the quality of her life and her assessment of her place in the world from those perspectives. It also asks us to consider the ways in which the character's altered status affects her relationship with her friends. Finally the story raises interesting questions about the expectations placed on immigrant parents by their children.

◆ THE FAT OF THE LAND ◆

In an air-shaft so narrow that you could touch the next wall with your bare hands, Hanneh Breineh leaned out and knocked on her neighbor's window.   1

"Can you loan me your wash-boiler for the clothes?" she called.   2

Mrs. Pelz threw up the sash.   3

"The boiler? What's the matter with yours again? Didn't you tell me you had it fixed already last week?"   4

"A black year on him, the robber, the way he fixed it! If you have no luck in this world, then it's better not to live. There I spent out fifteen cents to stop up one hole, and it runs out another. How I ate out my gall bargaining with him he should let it down to fifteen cents! He wanted yet a quarter, the swindler. Gottuniu! My bitter heart on him for every penny he took from me for nothing!"   5

"You got to watch all those swindlers, or they'll steal the whites out of your eyes," admonished Mrs. Pelz. "You should have tried out your boiler before you paid him. Wait a minute till I empty out my dirty clothes in a pillow-case; then I'll hand it to you." 6

Mrs. Pelz returned with the boiler and tried to hand it across to Hanneh Breineh, but the soap-box refrigerator on the window-sill was in the way. 7

"You got to come in for the boiler yourself," said Mrs. Pelz. 8

"Wait only till I tie my Sammy on to the high-chair he shouldn't fall on me again. He's so wild that ropes won't hold him." 9

Hanneh Breineh tied the child in the chair, stuck a pacifier in his mouth, and went in to her neighbor. As she took the boiler Mrs. Pelz said: 10

"Do you know Mrs. Melker ordered fifty pounds of chicken for her daughter's wedding? And such grand chickens! Shining like gold! My heart melted in me just looking at the flowing fatness of those chickens." 11

Hanneh Breineh smacked her thin, dry lips, a hungry gleam in her sunken eyes. 12

"Fifty pounds!" she gasped. "It ain't possible. How do you know?" 13

"I heard her with my own ears. I saw them with my own eyes. And she said she will chop up the chicken livers with onions and eggs for an appetizer, and then she will buy twenty-five pounds of fish, and cook it sweet and sour with raisins, and she said she will bake all her shtrudels on pure chicken fat." 14

"Some people work themselves up in the world," sighed Hanneh Breineh. "For them is America flowing with milk and honey. In Savel Mrs. Melker used to get shriveled up from hunger. She and her children used to live on potato-peelings and crusts of dry bread picked out from the barrels; and in America she lives to eat chicken, and apple shtrudels soaking in fat." 15

"The world is a wheel always turning," philosophized Mrs. Pelz. "Those who were high go down low, and those who've been low go up higher. Who will believe me here in America that in Poland I was a cook in a banker's house? I handled ducks and geese every day. I used to bake coffee-cake with cream so thick you could cut it with a knife." 16

"And do you think I was a nobody in Poland?" broke in Hanneh Breineh, tears welling in her eyes as the memories of her past rushed over her. "But what's the use of talking? In America money is everything. Who cares who my father or grandfather was in Poland? Without money I'm a living dead one. My head dries out worrying how to get for the children the eating a penny cheaper." 17

Mrs. Pelz wagged her head, a gnawing envy contracting her features. 18

"Mrs. Melker had it good from the day she came," she said, begrudgingly. "Right away she sent all her children to the factory, and she began to cook meat for dinner every day. She and her children have eggs and buttered rolls for breakfast each morning like millionaires." 19

A sudden fall and a baby's scream, and the boiler dropped from Hanneh Breineh's hands as she rushed into her kitchen, Mrs. Pelz after her. They found the high-chair turned on top of the baby. 20

"Gewalt! Save me! Run for a doctor!" cried Hanneh Breineh, as she 21
dragged the child from under the high-chair. "He's killed! He's killed! My only
child! My precious lamb!" she shrieked as she ran back and forth with the
screaming infant.

Mrs. Pelz snatched little Sammy from the mother's hands. 22

"Meshugneh! What are you running around like a crazy, frightening the 23
child? Let me see. Let me tend to him. He ain't killed yet." She hastened to
the sink to wash the child's face, and discovered a swelling lump on his forehead.
"Have you a quarter in your house?" she asked.

"Yes, I got one," replied Hanneh Breineh, climbing on a chair. "I got to 24
keep it on a high shelf where the children can't get it."

Mrs. Pelz seized the quarter Hanneh Breineh handed down to her. 25

"Now pull your left eyelid three times while I'm pressing the quarter, 26
and you'll see the swelling go down."

Hanneh Breineh took the child again in her arms, shaking and cooing over 27
it and caressing it.

"Ah-ah-ah, Sammy! Ah-ah-ah-ah, little lamb! Ah-ah-ah, little bird! Ah- 28
ah-ah-ah, precious heart! Oh, you saved my life; I thought he was killed,"
gasped Hanneh Breineh, turning to Mrs. Pelz. "Oi-i!" she sighed, "a mother's
heart! Always in fear over her children. The minute anything happens to them
all life goes out of me. I lose my head and I don't know where I am any more."

"No wonder the child fell," admonished Mrs. Pelz. "You should have a 29
red ribbon or red beads on his neck to keep away the evil eye. Wait. I got
something in my machine-drawer."

Mrs. Pelz returned, bringing the boiler and a red string, which she tied 30
about the child's neck while the mother proceeded to fill the boiler.

A little later Hanneh Breineh again came into Mrs. Pelz's kitchen, holding 31
Sammy in one arm and in the other an apronful of potatoes. Putting the child
down on the floor, she seated herself on the unmade kitchen-bed and began to
peel the potatoes in her apron.

"Woe to me!" sobbed Hanneh Breineh. "To my bitter luck there ain't no 32
end. With all my other troubles, the stove got broke. I lighted the fire to boil
the clothes, and it's to get choked with smoke. I paid rent only a week ago,
and the agent don't want to fix it. A thunder should strike him! He only comes
for the rent, and if anything has to be fixed, then he don't want to hear nothing.

"Why comes it to me so hard?" went on Hanneh Breineh, the tears 33
streaming down her cheeks. "I can't stand it no more. I came into you for a
minute to run away from my troubles. It's only when I sit myself down to peel
potatoes or nurse the baby that I take time to draw a breath, and beg only for
death."

Mrs. Pelz, accustomed to Hanneh Breineh's bitter outbursts, continued 34
her scrubbing.

"Ut!" exclaimed Hanneh Breineh, irritated at her neighbor's silence, "what 35
are you tearing up the world with your cleaning? What's the use to clean up
when everything only gets dirty again?"

"I got to shine up my house for the holidays."   36

"You've got it so good nothing lays on your mind but to clean your house.   37
Look on this little blood-sucker," said Hanneh Breineh, pointing to the wizened
child, made prematurely solemn from starvation and neglect. "Could anybody
keep that brat clean? I wash him one minute, and he is dirty the minute after."
Little Sammy grew frightened and began to cry. "Shut up!" ordered the mother,
picking up the child to nurse it again. "Can't you see me take a rest for a
minute?"

The hungry child began to cry at the top of its weakened lungs.   38

"Na, na, you glutton." Hanneh Breineh took out a dirty pacifier from her   39
pocket and stuffed it into the baby's mouth. The grave, pasty-faced infant shrank
into a panic of fear, and chewed the nipple nervously, clinging to it with both
his thin little hands.

"For what did I need yet the sixth one?" groaned Hanneh Breineh, turning   40
to Mrs. Pelz. "Wasn't it enough five mouths to feed? If I didn't have this child
on my neck, I could turn myself around and earn a few cents." She wrung her
hands in a passion of despair. "Gottuniu! The earth should only take it before
it grows up!"

"Shah! Shah!" reproved Mrs. Pelz. "Pity yourself on the child. Let it   41
grow up already so long as it is here. See how frightened it looks on you." Mrs.
Pelz took the child in her arms and petted it. "The poor little lamb! What did
it done you should hate it so?"

Hanneh Breineh pushed Mrs. Pelz away from her.   42

"To whom can I open the wounds of my heart?" she moaned. "Nobody   43
has pity on me. You don't believe me, nobody believes me until I'll fall down
like a horse in the middle of the street. Oi weh! Mine life is so black for my
eyes! Some mothers got luck. A child gets run over by a car, some fall from a
window, some burn themselves up with a match, some get choked with diph-
theria; but no death takes mine away."

"God from the world, stop cursing!" admonished Mrs. Pelz. "What do   44
you want from the poor children? Is it their fault that their father makes small
wages? Why do you let it all out on them?" Mrs. Pelz sat down beside Hanneh
Breineh. "Wait only till your children get old enough to go to the shop and
earn money," she consoled. "Push only through those few years while they are
yet small; your sun will begin to shine; you will live on the fat of the land,
when they begin to bring you in the wages each week."

Hanneh Breineh refused to be comforted.   45

"Till they are old enough to go to the shop and earn money they'll eat   46
the head off my bones," she wailed. "If you only knew the fights I got by each
meal. Maybe I gave Abe a bigger piece of bread than Fanny. Maybe Fanny
got a little more soup in her plate than Jake. Eating is dearer than diamonds.
Potatoes went up a cent on a pound, and milk is only for millionaires. And
once a week, when I buy a little meat for the Sabbath, the butcher weighs it
for me like gold, with all the bones in it. When I come to lay the meat out on
a plate and divide it up, there ain't nothing to it but bones. Before, he used to

throw me in a piece of fat extra or a piece of lung, but now you got to pay for everything, even for a bone to the soup."

"Never mind; you'll yet come out from all your troubles. Just as soon as   47
your children get old enough to get their working papers the more children you got, the more money you'll have."

"Why should I fool myself with the false shine of hope? Don't I know   48
it's already my black luck not to have it good in this world? Do you think American children will right away give everything they earn to their mother?"

"I know what is with you the matter," said Mrs. Pelz. "You didn't eat   49
yet to-day. When it is empty in the stomach, the whole world looks black. Come, only let me give you something good to taste in the mouth; that will freshen you up." Mrs. Pelz went to the cupboard and brought out the saucepan of gefülte fish that she had cooked for dinner and placed it on the table in front of Hanneh Breineh. "Give a taste my fish," she said, taking one slice on a spoon, and handing it to Hanneh Breineh with a piece of bread. "I wouldn't give it to you on a plate because I just cleaned up my house, and I don't want to dirty up more dishes."

"What, am I a stranger you should have to serve me on a plate yet!" cried   50
Hanneh Breineh, snatching the fish in her trembling fingers.

"Oi weh! How it melts through all the bones!" she exclaimed, brightening   51
as she ate. "May it be for good luck to us all!" she exulted, waving aloft the last precious bite.

Mrs. Pelz was so flattered that she even ladled up a spoonful of gravy.   52

"There is a bit of onion and carrot in it," she said, as she handed it to   53
her neighbor.

Hanneh Breineh sipped the gravy drop by drop, like a connoisseur sipping   54
wine.

"Ah-h-h! A taste of that gravy lifts me up to heaven!" As she disposed   55
leisurely of the slice of onion and carrot she relaxed and expanded and even grew jovial. "Let us wish all our troubles on the Russian Czar! Let him burst with our worries for rent! Let him get shriveled with our hunger for bread! Let his eyes dry out of his head looking for work!

"Shah! I'm forgetting from everything," she exclaimed, jumping up. "It   56
must be eleven or soon twelve, and my children will be right away out of school and fall on me like a pack of wild wolves. I better quick run to the market and see what cheaper I can get for a quarter."

Because of the lateness of her coming, the stale bread at the nearest   57
bakeshop was sold out, and Hanneh Breineh had to trudge from shop to shop in search of the usual bargain, and spent nearly an hour to save two cents.

In the meantime the children returned from school, and, finding the door   58
locked, climbed through the fire-escape, and entered the house through the window. Seeing nothing on the table, they rushed to the stove. Abe pulled a steaming potato out of the boiling pot, and so scalded his fingers that the potato fell to the floor; whereupon the three others pounced on it.

"It was my potato," cried Abe, blowing his burned fingers, while with the other hand and his foot he cuffed and kicked the three who were struggling on the floor. A wild fight ensued, and the potato was smashed under Abe's foot amid shouts and screams. Hanneh Breineh, on the stairs, heard the noise of her famished brood, and topped their cries with curses and invectives. [59]

"They are here already, the savages! They are here already to shorten my life! They heard you all over the hall, in all the houses around!" [60]

The children, disregarding her words, pounced on her market-basket, shouting ravenously: "Mamma, I'm hungry! What more do you got to eat?" [61]

They tore the bread and herring out of Hanneh Breineh's basket and devoured it in starved savagery, clamoring for more. [62]

"Murderers!" screamed Hanneh Breineh, goaded beyond endurance. "What are you tearing from me my flesh? From where should I steal to give you more? Here I had already a pot of potatoes and a whole loaf of bread and two herrings, and you swallowed it down in the wink of an eye. I have to have Rockefeller's millions to fill your stomachs." [63]

All at once Hanneh Breineh became aware that Benny was missing. "Oi weh!" she burst out, wringing her hands in a new wave of woe, "where is Benny? Didn't he come home yet from school?" [64]

She ran out into the hall, opened the grime-coated window, and looked up and down the street; but Benny was nowhere in sight. [65]

"Abe, Jake, Fanny, quick, find Benny!" entreated Hanneh Breineh, as she rushed back into the kitchen. But the children, anxious to snatch a few minutes' play before the school-call, dodged past her and hurried out. [66]

With the baby on her arm, Hanneh Breineh hastened to the kindergarten. [67]

"Why are you keeping Benny here so long?" she shouted at the teacher as she flung open the door. "If you had my bitter heart, you would send him home long ago and not wait till I got to come for him." [68]

The teacher turned calmly and consulted her record-cards. [69]

"Benny Safron? He wasn't present this morning." [70]

"Not here?" shrieked Hanneh Breineh. "I pushed him out myself he should go. The children didn't want to take him, and I had no time. Woe is me! Where is my child?" She began pulling her hair and beating her breast as she ran into the street. [71]

Mrs. Pelz was busy at a pushcart, picking over some spotted apples, when she heard the clamor of an approaching crowd. A block off she recognized Hanneh Breineh, her hair disheveled, her clothes awry, running toward her with her yelling baby in her arms, the crowd following. [72]

"Friend mine," cried Hanneh Breineh, falling on Mrs. Pelz's neck, "I lost my Benny, the best child of all my children." Tears streamed down her red, swollen eyes as she sobbed. "Benny! mine heart, mine life! Oi-i-i!" [73]

Mrs. Pelz took the frightened baby out of the mother's arms. [74]

"Still yourself a little! See how you're frightening your child." [75]

"Woe to me! Where is my Benny? Maybe he's killed already by a car. [76]

Maybe he fainted away from hunger. He didn't eat nothing all day long. Got-tuniu! Pity yourself on me!"

She lifted her hands full of tragic entreaty. 77

"People, my child! Get me my child! I'll go crazy out of my head! Get me my child, or I'll take poison before your eyes!" 78

"Still yourself a little!" pleaded Mrs. Pelz. 79

"Talk not to me!" cried Hanneh Breineh, wringing her hands. "You're having all your children. I lost mine. Every good luck comes to other people. But I didn't live yet to see a good day in my life. Mine only joy, mine Benny, is lost away from me." 80

The crowd followed Hanneh Breineh as she wailed through the streets, leaning on Mrs. Pelz. By the time she returned to her house the children were back from school; but seeing that Benny was not there, she chased them out in the street, crying: 81

"Out of here, you robbers, gluttons! Go find Benny!" Hanneh Breineh crumpled into a chair in utter prostration. "Oi weh! he's lost! Mine life; my little bird; mine only joy! How many nights I spent nursing him when he had the measles! And all that I suffered for weeks and months when he had the whooping-cough! How the eyes went out of my head till I learned him how to walk, till I learned him how to talk! And such a smart child! If I lost all the others, it wouldn't tear me so by the heart." 82

She worked herself up into such a hysteria, crying, and tearing her hair, and hitting her head with her knuckles, that at last she fell into a faint. It took some time before Mrs. Pelz, with the aid of neighbors, revived her. 83

"Benny, mine angel!" she moaned as she opened her eyes. 84

Just then a policeman came in with the lost Benny. 85

"Na, na, here you got him already!" said Mrs. Pelz. "Why did you carry on so for nothing? Why did you tear up the world like a crazy?" 86

The child's face was streaked with tears as he cowered, frightened and forlorn. Hanneh Breineh sprang toward him, slapping his cheeks, boxing his ears, before the neighbors could rescue him from her. 87

"Woe on your head!" cried the mother. "Where did you lost yourself? Ain't I got enough worries on my head than to go around looking for you? I didn't have yet a minute's peace from that child since he was born!" 88

"See a crazy mother!" remonstrated Mrs. Pelz, rescuing Benny from another beating. "Such a mouth! With one breath she blesses him when he is lost, and with the other breath she curses him when he is found." 89

Hanneh Breineh took from the window-sill a piece of herring covered with swarming flies, and putting it on a slice of dry bread, she filled a cup of tea that had been stewing all day, and dragged Benny over to the table to eat. 90

But the child, choking with tears, was unable to touch the food. 91

"Go eat!" commanded Hanneh Breineh. "Eat and choke yourself eating!" 92

"Maybe she won't remember me no more. Maybe the servant won't let me in," thought Mrs. Pelz, as she walked by the brownstone house on Eighty-Fourth 93

Street where she had been told Hanneh Breineh now lived. At last she summoned up enough courage to climb the steps. She was all out of breath as she rang the bell with trembling fingers. "Oi weh! even the outside smells riches and plenty! Such curtains! And shades on all windows like by millionaires! Twenty years ago she used to eat from the pot to the hand, and now she lives in such a palace."

A whiff of steam-heated warmth swept over Mrs. Pelz as the door opened, and she saw her old friend of the tenements dressed in silk and diamonds like a being from another world. 94

"Mrs. Pelz, is it you!" cried Hanneh Breineh, overjoyed at the sight of her former neighbor. "Come right in. Since when are you back in New York?" 95

"We came last week," mumbled Mrs. Pelz, as she was led into a richly carpeted reception-room. 96

"Make yourself comfortable. Take off your shawl," urged Hanneh Breineh. 97

But Mrs. Pelz only drew her shawl more tightly around her, a keen sense of her poverty gripping her as she gazed, abashed by the luxurious wealth that shone from every corner. 98

"This shawl covers up my rags," she said, trying to hide her shabby sweater. 99

"I'll tell you what; come right into the kitchen," suggested Hanneh Breineh. "The servant is away for this afternoon, and we can feel more comfortable there. I can breathe like a free person in my kitchen when the girl has her day out." 100

Mrs. Pelz glanced about her in an excited daze. Never in her life had she seen anything so wonderful as a white-tiled kitchen, with its glistening porcelain sink and the aluminum pots and pans that shone like silver. 101

"Where are you staying now?" asked Hanneh Breineh, as she pinned an apron over her silk dress. 102

"I moved back to Delancey Street, where we used to live," replied Mrs. Pelz, as she seated herself cautiously in a white enameled chair. 103

"Oi weh! What grand times we had in that old house when we were neighbors!" sighed Hanneh Breineh, looking at her old friend with misty eyes. 104

"You still think on Delancey Street? Haven't you more high-class neighbors uptown here?" 105

"A good neighbor is not to be found every day," deplored Hanneh Breineh. "Uptown here, where each lives in his own house, nobody cares if the person next door is dying or going crazy from loneliness. It ain't anything like we used to have it in Delancey Street, when we could walk into one another's rooms without knocking, and borrow a pinch of salt or a pot to cook in." 106

Hanneh Breineh went over to the pantry-shelf. 107

"We are going to have a bite right here on the kitchen-table like on Delancey Street. So long there's no servant to watch us we can eat what we please." 108

"Oi! How it waters my mouth with appetite, the smell of the herring and onion!" chuckled Mrs. Pelz, sniffing the welcome odors with greedy pleasure. 109

Hanneh Breineh pulled a dish-towel from the rack and threw one end of 110 it to Mrs. Pelz.

"So long as there's no servant around, we can use it together for a napkin. 111 It's dirty, anyhow. How it freshens up my heart to see you!" she rejoiced as she poured out her tea into a saucer. "If you would only know how I used to beg my daughter to write for me a letter to you; but these American children, what is to them a mother's feelings?"

"What are you talking!" cried Mrs. Pelz. "The whole world rings with 112 you and your children. Everybody is envying you. Tell me how began your luck?"

"You heard how my husband died with consumption," replied Hanneh 113 Breineh. "The five hundred dollars lodge money gave me the first lift in life, and I opened a little grocery store. Then my son Abe married himself to a girl with a thousand dollars. That started him in business, and now he has the biggest shirt-waist factory on West Twenty-Ninth Street."

"Yes, I heard your son had a factory." Mrs. Pelz hesitated and stammered; 114 "I'll tell you the truth. What I came to ask you—I thought maybe you would beg your son Abe if he would give my husband a job."

"Why not?" said Hanneh Breineh. "He keeps more than five hundred 115 hands. I'll ask him if he should take in Mr. Pelz."

"Long years on you, Hanneh Breineh! You'll save my life if you could 116 only help my husband get work."

"Of course my son will help him. All my children like to do good. My 117 daughter Fanny is a milliner on Fifth Avenue, and she takes in the poorest girls in her shop and even pays them sometimes while they learn the trade." Hanneh Breineh's face lit up, and her chest filled with pride as she enumerated the successes of her children. "And my son Benny he wrote a play on Broadway and he gave away more than a hundred free tickets for the first night."

"Benny? The one who used to get lost from home all the time? You always 118 did love that child more than all the rest. And what is Sammy your baby doing?"

"He ain't a baby no longer. He goes to college and quarterbacks the football 119 team. They can't get along without him.

"And my son Jake, I nearly forgot him. He began collecting rent in 120 Delancey Street, and now he is boss of renting the swellest apartment-houses on Riverside Drive."

"What did I tell you? In America children are like money in the bank," 121 purred Mrs. Pelz, as she pinched and patted Hanneh Breineh's silk sleeve. "Oi weh! How it shines from you! You ought to kiss the air and dance for joy and happiness. It is such a bitter frost outside; a pail of coal is so dear, and you got it so warm with steam heat. I had to pawn my feather bed to have enough for the rent, and you are rolling in money."

"Yes, I got it good in some ways, but money ain't everything," sighed 122 Hanneh Breineh.

"You ain't yet satisfied?" 123

"But here I got no friends," complained Hanneh Breineh. 124

"Friends?" queried Mrs. Pelz. "What greater friend is there on earth than 125
the dollar?"

"Oi! Mrs. Pelz; if you could only look into my heart! I'm so choked up! 126
You know they say a cow has a long tongue, but can't talk." Hanneh Breineh
shook her head wistfully, and her eyes filmed with inward brooding. "My
children give me everything from the best. When I was sick, they got me a
nurse by day and one by night. They bought me the best wine. If I asked for
dove's milk, they would buy it for me; but—but—I can't talk myself out in
their language. They want to make me over for an American lady, and I'm
different." Tears cut their way under her eyelids with a pricking pain as she
went on: "When I was poor, I was free, and could holler and do what I like in
my own house. Here I got to lie still like a mouse under a broom. Between
living up to my Fifth-Avenue daughter and keeping up with the servants, I am
like a sinner in the next world that is thrown from one hell to another." The
doorbell rang, and Hanneh Breineh jumped up with a start.

"Oi weh! It must be the servant back already!" she exclaimed, as she tore 127
off her apron. "Oi weh! Let's quickly put the dishes together in a dish-pan. If
she sees I eat on the kitchen table, she will look on me like the dirt under her
feet."

Mrs. Pelz seized her shawl in haste. 128

"I better run home quick in my rags before your servant sees me." 129

"I'll speak to Abe about the job," said Hanneh Breineh, as she pushed a 130
bill into the hand of Mrs. Pelz, who edged out as the servant entered.

"I'm having fried potato lotkes special for you, Benny," said Hanneh Breineh, 131
as the children gathered about the table for the family dinner given in honor
of Benny's success with his new play. "Do you remember how you used to lick
the fingers from them?"

"Oh, mother!" reproved Fanny. "Anyone hearing you would think we 132
were still in the pushcart district."

"Stop your nagging, sis, and let ma alone," commanded Benny, patting 133
his mother's arm affectionately. "I'm home only once a month. Let her feed
me what she pleases. My stomach is bomb-proof."

"Do I hear that the President is coming to your play?" said Abe, as he 134
stuffed a napkin over his diamond-studded shirt-front.

"Why shouldn't he come?" returned Benny. "The critics say it's the great- 135
est antidote for the race hatred created by the war. If you want to know, he is
coming to-night; and what's more, our box is next to the President's."

"Nu, mammeh," sallied Jake, "did you ever dream in Delancey Street 136
that we should rub sleeves with the President?"

"I always said that Benny had more head than the rest of you," replied 137
the mother.

As the laughter died away, Jake went on: 138

"Honor you are getting plenty; but how much mezummen does this play 139
bring you? Can I invest any of it in real estate for you?"

"I'm getting ten per cent royalties of the gross receipts," replied the youth- 140
ful playwright.

"How much is that?" queried Hanneh Breineh. 141

"Enough to buy up all your fish-markets in Delancey Street," laughed 142
Abe in good-natured raillery at his mother.

Her son's jest cut like a knife-thrust in her heart. She felt her heart ache 143
with the pain that she was shut out from their successes. Each added triumph
only widened the gulf. And when she tried to bridge this gulf by asking questions, they only thrust her back upon herself.

"Your fame has even helped me get my hat trade solid with the Four 144
Hundred," put in Fanny. "You bet I let Mrs. Van Suyden know that our box
is next to the President's. She said she would drop in to meet you. Of course
she let on to me that she hadn't seen the play yet, though my designer said she
saw her there on the opening night."

"Oh, Gosh, the toadies!" sneered Benny. "Nothing so sickens you with 145
success as the way people who once shoved you off the sidewalk come crawling
to you on their stomachs begging you to dine with them."

"Say, that leading man of yours he's some class!" cried Fanny. "That's 146
the man I'm looking for. Will you invite him to supper after the theater?"

The playwright turned to his mother. 147

"Say, ma," he said, laughingly, "how would you like a real actor for a 148
son-in-law?"

"She should worry," mocked Sam. "She'll be discussing with him the 149
future of the Greek drama. Too bad it doesn't happen to be Warfield, or mother
could give him tips on the 'Auctioneer.' "

Jake turned to his mother with a covert grin. 150

"I guess you'd have no objection if Fanny got next to Benny's leading 151
man. He makes at least fifteen hundred a week. That wouldn't be such a bad
addition to the family, would it?"

Again the bantering tone stabbed Hanneh Breineh. Everything in her 152
began to tremble and break loose.

"Why do you ask me?" she cried, throwing her napkin into her plate. "Do 153
I count for a person in this house? If I'll say something, will you even listen to
me? What is to me the grandest man that my daughter could pick out? Another
enemy in my house! Another person to shame himself from me!" She swept
in her children in one glance of despairing anguish as she rose from the table.
"What worth is an old mother to American children? The President is coming
to-night to the theater, and none of you asked me to go." Unable to check the
rising tears, she fled toward the kitchen and banged the door.

They all looked at one another guiltily. 154

"Say, sis," Benny called out sharply, "what sort of frame-up is this? 155
Haven't you told mother that she was to go with us to-night?"

"Yes—I—" Fanny bit her lips as she fumbled evasively for words. "I asked 156
her if she wouldn't mind my taking her some other time."

"Now you have made a mess of it!" fumed Benny. "Mother'll be too hurt 157
to go now."

"Well, I don't care," snapped Fanny. "I can't appear with mother in a 158
box at the theater. Can I introduce her to Mrs. Van Suyden? And suppose
your leading man should ask to meet me?"

"Take your time, sis. He hasn't asked yet," scoffed Benny. 159

"The more reason I shouldn't spoil my chances. You know mother. She'll 160
spill the beans that we come from Delancey Street the minute we introduce
her anywhere. Must I always have the black shadow of my past trailing after
me?"

"But have you no feelings for mother?" admonished Abe. 161

"I've tried harder than all of you to do my duty. I've *lived* with her." She 162
turned angrily upon them. "I've borne the shame of mother while you bought
her off with a present and a treat here and there. God knows how hard I tried
to civilize her so as not to have to blush with shame when I take her anywhere.
I dressed her in the most stylish Paris models, but Delancey Street sticks out
from every inch of her. Whenever she opens her mouth, I'm done for. You
fellows had your chance to rise in the world because a man is free to go up as
high as he can reach up to; but I, with all my style and pep, can't get a man
my equal because a girl is always judged by her mother."

They were silenced by her vehemence, and unconsciously turned to Benny. 163

"I guess we all tried to do our best for mother," said Benny, thoughtfully. 164
"But wherever there is growth, there is pain and heartbreak. The trouble with
us is that the ghetto of the Middle Ages and the children of the twentieth
century have to live under one roof, and—"

A sound of crashing dishes came from the kitchen, and the voice of Hanneh 165
Breineh resounded through the dining-room as she wreaked her pent-up fury
on the helpless servant.

"Oh, my nerves! I can't stand it any more! There will be no girl again 166
for another week!" cried Fanny.

"Oh, let up on the old lady," protested Abe. "Since she can't take it out 167
on us any more, what harm is it if she cusses the servants?"

"If you fellows had to chase around employment agencies, you wouldn't 168
see anything funny about it. Why can't we move into a hotel that will do away
with the need of servants altogether?"

"I got it better," said Jake, consulting a notebook from his pocket. "I have 169
on my list an apartment on Riverside Drive where there's only a small kitchenette; but we can do away with the cooking, for there is a dining service in
the building."

The new Riverside apartment to which Hanneh Breineh was removed by her   170
socially ambitious children was for the habitually active mother an empty desert
of enforced idleness. Deprived of her kitchen, Hanneh Breineh felt robbed of
the last reason for her existence. Cooking and marketing and puttering busily
with pots and pans gave her an excuse for living and struggling and bearing up
with her children. The lonely idleness of Riverside Drive stunned all her senses
and arrested all her thoughts. It gave her that choked sense of being cut off
from air, from life, from everything warm and human. The cold indifference,
the each-for-himself look in the eyes of the people about her were like stinging
slaps in the face. Even the children had nothing real or human in them. They
were starched and stiff miniatures of their elders.

But the most unendurable part of the stifling life on Riverside Drive was   171
being forced to eat in the public dining-room. No matter how hard she tried
to learn polite table manners, she always found people staring at her, and her
daughter rebuking her for eating with the wrong fork or guzzling the soup or
staining the cloth.

In a fit of rebellion Hanneh Breineh resolved never to go down to the   172
public dining-room again, but to make use of the gas-stove in the kitchenette
to cook her own meals. That very day she rode down to Delancey Street and
purchased a new market-basket. For some time she walked among the haggling
pushcart venders, relaxing and swimming in the warm waves of her old familiar
past.

A fish-peddler held up a large carp in his black, hairy hand and waved it   173
dramatically:

"Women! Women! Fourteen cents a pound!"   174

He ceased his raucous shouting as he saw Hanneh Breineh in her rich   175
attire approach his cart.

"How much?" she asked, pointing to the fattest carp.   176

"Fifteen cents, lady," said the peddler, smirking as he raised his price.   177

"Swindler! Didn't I hear you call fourteen cents?" shrieked Hanneh Brei-   178
neh, exultingly, the spirit of the penny chase surging in her blood. Diplomatically, Hanneh Breineh turned as if to go, and the fisherman seized her basket
in frantic fear.

"I should live; I'm losing money on the fish, lady," whined the peddler.   179
"I'll let it down to thirteen cents for you only."

"Two pounds for a quarter, and not a penny more," said Hanneh Breineh,   180
thrilling again with the rare sport of bargaining, which had been her chief joy
in the good old days of poverty.

"Nu, I want to make the first sale for good luck." The peddler threw the   181
fish on the scale.

As he wrapped up the fish, Hanneh Breineh saw the driven look of worry   182
in his haggard eyes, and when he counted out the change from her dollar, she
waved it aside. "Keep it for your luck," she said, and hurried off to strike a
new bargain at a pushcart of onions.

Hanneh Breineh returned triumphantly with her purchases. The basket 183
under her arm gave forth the old, homelike odors of herring and garlic, while
the scaly tail of a four-pound carp protruded from its newspaper wrapping. A
gilded placard on the door of the apartment-house proclaimed that all mer-
chandise must be delivered through the trade entrance in the rear; but Hanneh
Breineh with her basket strode proudly through the marble-paneled hall and
rang nonchalantly for the elevator.

The uniformed hall-man, erect, expressionless, frigid with dignity, stepped 184
forward:

"Just a minute, madam. I'll call a boy to take up your basket for you." 185

Hanneh Breineh, glaring at him, jerked the basket savagely from his hands. 186
"Mind your own business!" she retorted. "I'll take it up myself. Do you think
you're a Russian policeman to boss me in my own house?"

Angry lines appeared on the countenance of the representative of social 187
decorum.

"It is against the rules, madam," he said, stiffly. 188

"You should sink into the earth with all your rules and brass buttons. 189
Ain't this America? Ain't this a free country? Can't I take up in my own house
what I buy with my own money?" cried Hanneh Breineh, reveling in the
opportunity to shower forth the volley of invectives that had been suppressed
in her for the weeks of deadly dignity of Riverside Drive.

In the midst of this uproar Fanny came in with Mrs. Van Suyden. Hanneh 190
Breineh rushed over to her, crying:

"This bossy policeman won't let me take up my basket in the elevator." 191

The daughter, unnerved with shame and confusion, took the basket in 192
her white-gloved hand and ordered the hall-boy to take it around to the regular
delivery entrance.

Hanneh Breineh was so hurt by her daughter's apparent defense of the 193
hall-man's rules that she utterly ignored Mrs. Van Suyden's greeting and walked
up the seven flights of stairs out of sheer spite.

"You see the tragedy of my life?" broke out Fanny, turning to Mrs. Van 194
Suyden.

"You poor child! You go right up to your dear, old lady mother, and I'll 195
come some other time."

Instantly Fanny regretted her words. Mrs. Van Suyden's pity only roused 196
her wrath the more against her mother.

Breathless from climbing the stairs, Hanneh Breineh entered the apart- 197
ment just as Fanny tore the faultless millinery creation from her head and threw
it on the floor in a rage.

"Mother, you are the ruination of my life! You have driven away Mrs. 198
Van Suyden, as you have driven away all my best friends. What do you
think we got this apartment for but to get rid of your fish smells and your
brawls with the servants? And here you come with a basket on your arm
as if you had just landed from steerage! And this afternoon, of all times,

when Benny is bringing his leading man to tea. When will you ever stop disgracing us?"

"When I'm dead," said Hanneh Breineh, grimly. "When the earth will 199 cover me up, then you'll be free to go your American way. I'm not going to make myself over for a lady on Riverside Drive. I hate you and all your swell friends. I'll not let myself be choked up here by you or by that hall-boss policeman that is higher in your eyes than your own mother."

"So that's your thanks for all we've done for you?" cried the daughter. 200

"All you've done for me!" shouted Hanneh Breineh. "What have you done 201 for me? You hold me like a dog on a chain! It stands in the Talmud; some children give their mothers dry bread and water and go to heaven for it, and some give their mother roast duck and go to Gehenna because it's not given with love."

"You want me to love you yet?" raged the daughter. "You knocked every 202 bit of love out of me when I was yet a kid. All the memories of childhood I have is your everlasting cursing and yelling that we were gluttons."

The bell rang sharply, and Hanneh Breineh flung open the door. 203

"Your groceries, ma'am," said the boy. 204

Hanneh Breineh seized the basket from him, and with a vicious fling sent 205 it rolling across the room, strewing its contents over the Persian rugs and inlaid floor. Then seizing her hat and coat, she stormed out of the apartment and down the stairs.

Mr. and Mrs. Pelz sat crouched and shivering over their meager supper 206 when the door opened, and Hanneh Breineh in fur coat and plumed hat charged into the room.

"I come to cry out to you my bitter heart," she sobbed. "Woe is me! It 207 is so black for my eyes!"

"What is the matter with you, Hanneh Breineh?" cried Mrs. Pelz in 208 bewildered alarm.

"I am turned out of my own house by the brass-buttoned policeman that 209 bosses the elevator. Oi-i-i-i! Weh-h-h-h! What have I from my life? The whole world rings with my son's play. Even the President came to see it, and I, his mother, have not seen it yet. My heart is dying in me like in a prison," she went on wailing. "I am starved out for a piece of real eating. In that swell restaurant is nothing but napkins and forks and lettuce-leaves. There are a dozen plates to every bite of food. And it looks so fancy on the plate, but it's nothing but straw in the mouth. I'm starving, but I can't swallow down their American eating."

"Hanneh Breineh," said Mrs. Pelz, "you are sinning before God. Look 210 on your fur coat; it alone would feed a whole family for a year. I never had yet a piece of fur trimming on a coat, and you are in fur from the neck to the feet. I never had yet a piece of feather on a hat, and your hat is all feathers."

"What are you envying me?" protested Hanneh Breineh. "What have I 211 from all my fine furs and feathers when my children are strangers to me? All the fur coats in the world can't warm up the loneliness inside my heart. All the grandest feathers can't hide the bitter shame in my face that my children shame themselves from me."

Hanneh Breineh suddenly loomed over them like some ancient, heroic 212 figure of the Bible condemning unrighteousness.

"Why should my children shame themselves from me? From where did 213 they get the stuff to work themselves up in the world? Did they get it from the air? How did they get all their smartness to rise over the people around them? Why don't the children of born American mothers write my Benny's plays? It is I, who never had a chance to be a person, who gave him the fire in his head. If I would have had a chance to go to school and learn the language, what couldn't I have been? It is I and my mother and my mother's mother and my father and father's father who had such a black life in Poland; it is our choked thoughts and feelings that are flaming up in my children and making them great in America. And yet they shame themselves from me!"

For a moment Mr. and Mrs. Pelz were hypnotized by the sweep of her 214 words. Then Hanneh Breineh sank into a chair in utter exhaustion. She began to weep bitterly, her body shaking with sobs.

"Woe is me! For what did I suffer and hope on my children? A bitter old 215 age—my end. I'm so lonely!"

All the dramatic fire seemed to have left her. The spell was broken. They 216 saw the Hanneh Breineh of old, ever discontented, ever complaining even in the midst of riches and plenty.

"Hanneh Breineh," said Mrs. Pelz, "the only trouble with you is that you 217 got it too good. People will tear the eyes out of your head because you're complaining yet. If I only had your fur coat! If I only had your diamonds! I have nothing. You have everything. You are living on the fat of the land. You go right back home and thank God that you don't have any bitter lot."

"You got to let me stay here with you," insisted Hanneh Breineh. "I'll 218 not go back to my children except when they bury me. When they will see my dead face, they will understand how they killed me."

Mrs. Pelz glanced nervously at her husband. They barely had enough 219 covering for their one bed; how could they possibly lodge a visitor?

"I don't want to take up your bed," said Hanneh Breineh. "I don't care 220 if I have to sleep on the floor or on the chairs, but I'll stay here for the night."

Seeing that she was bent on staying, Mr. Pelz prepared to sleep by putting 221 a few chairs next to the trunk, and Hanneh Breineh was invited to share the rickety bed with Mrs. Pelz.

The mattress was full of lumps and hollows. Hanneh Breineh lay cramped 222 and miserable, unable to stretch out her limbs. For years she had been accustomed to hair mattresses and ample woolen blankets, so that though she covered herself with her fur coat, she was too cold to sleep. But worse than the cold were the creeping things on the wall. And as the lights were turned low, the mice came through the broken plaster and raced across the floor. The foul odors of the kitchen-sink added to the night of horrors.

"Are you going back home?" asked Mrs. Pelz, as Hanneh Breineh put on   223 her hat and coat the next morning.

"I don't know where I'm going," she replied, as she put a bill into Mrs.   224 Pelz's hand.

For hours Hanneh Breineh walked through the crowded ghetto streets.   225 She realized that she no longer could endure the sordid ugliness of her past, and yet she could not go home to her children. She only felt that she must go on and on.

In the afternoon a cold, drizzling rain set in. She was worn out from the   226 sleepless night and hours of tramping. With a piercing pain in her heart she at last turned back and boarded the subway for Riverside Drive. She had fled from the marble sepulcher of the Riverside apartment to her old home in the ghetto; but now she knew that she could not live there again. She had outgrown her past by the habits of years of physical comforts, and these material comforts that she could no longer do without choked and crushed the life within her.

A cold shudder went through Hanneh Breineh as she approached the   227 apartment-house. Peering through the plate glass of the door she saw the face of the uniformed hall-man. For a hesitating moment she remained standing in the drizzling rain, unable to enter, and yet knowing full well that she would have to enter.

Then suddenly Hanneh Breineh began to laugh. She realized that it was   228 the first time she had laughed since her children had become rich. But it was the hard laugh of bitter sorrow. Tears streamed down her furrowed cheeks as she walked slowly up the granite steps.

"The fat of the land!" muttered Hanneh Breineh, with a choking sob as   229 the hall-man with immobile face deferentially swung open the door—"the fat of the land!" ◆

◆ Responding

1. Compare Hanneh Breineh's life before and after her husband's death. Consider both her physcial and emotional circumstances.

2. We see Hanneh Breineh from the author's sympathetic point of view, but the other characters in the story view her differently. Imagine that you are one of her children and write a letter to a friend explaining your mother's behavior. Or write a journal entry about a time when you were torn between loyalty to a parent, sibling, or friend and embarrassment about that person's behavior in front of someone you wanted to impress.

3. Hanneh Breineh learns something in this story. "She had fled from the marble sepulcher of the Riverside apartment to her old home in the ghetto; but now she knew that she could not live there again. She had outgrown her past by the habits of years of physical comforts, and these material comforts that she could no longer do without choked and crushed the life within her." Working individually or in a group, write a moral to this story, then share it with the class.

4. Hanneh Breineh's friend and old neighbor Mrs. Pelz says that in America money is everything: "What greater friend is there on earth than the dollar?" She believes that the only trouble with Hanneh Breineh is that she "got it too good." Do you agree or disagree? Support your argument with evidence from the story as well as from your own experience.

GREGORY ORFALEA

Gregory Orfalea, whose grandparents immigrated to this country from Syria in 1878, was born in Los Angeles in 1949. He studied at Georgetown University, where he earned a bachelor's degree in 1971, and at the University of Alaska, where he earned a master of fine arts degree in 1977. Since then he has worked in journalism and in government (for the Small Business Administration); he has also taught college English. In addition to writing two volumes of poetry and monographs on United States-Arab relations, Orfalea has published the book-length study, Before the Flames: A Quest for the History of Arab Americans *(1988).*

The following excerpt from Before the Flames *uses a visit to Ellis Island to contrast the way in which the island was described by the author's grandparents and the way it appears today. As the passage describes some of the hardships endured by those who spent time on Ellis Island, it also explores the significance of the place for past and present generations.*

◆ WHO AM I?
THE SYRIANS DOCK IN AMERICA ◆

Assad Roum stood on Ellis Island in 1939, nineteen years after he had first   1
come ashore at the famous immigration processing center in America. He was
now a citizen, recently married in Syria, and had established an embroidery
and Corday handbag manufacturing business in Brooklyn. He waited in the
mist that day for his new bride to arrive. But when Nora Roum docked from
her month-long voyage across the sea, pregnant, Assad barely had a chance to
embrace her near the traditional "Kissing Pole" in the island. Immigration
authorities detained her for several months in the hospital ward there; for Nora
had trachoma, the dreaded eye disease that sent so many immigrants—Syrians
included—back to the homeland with no chance of becoming American. Nora
gave birth to the Roums' first child on Ellis Island. When she was approved as
an immigrant and could go to the mainland of New York to join her husband,
she was so ecstatic that she convinced Assad to name their infant daughter
Elsie, after Ellis Island itself. Today Elsie Roum is a physical education teacher
in California.

More than half the current U.S. population can trace its heritage through   2
Ellis Island; more than half have relatives who staggered through the doors of
the great emporium with its chandeliers, topped by magnificent steeples across
the water from the Statue of Liberty. In the period 1880–1924, 16 million
of the world's destitute (or 60 percent of the 27 million immigrants to America
at this time) were processed at the little islet made from the landfill of the New

York subway. Among them was the vast majority of 150,000 Syrians, including Assad Roum.

Today, Ellis Island is in ruins. Shut down by the Immigration Service in 1952, by which time airplane had replaced boat as primary conduit to freedom, Ellis Island became a hangout for daring teenagers, who would motorboat over from Jersey or Battery Park. It fell prey to mice, vandals, and, in 1976, the National Park Service, which today takes tourists through a mist of ghosts and huge empty halls with walls of peeling paint, rusty pipes, cobwebs. Old files and medical equipment are still there. One old wheelchair in the tent of a spider web has wooden footrests. It will take $300 million to restore this once majestic first home of so many whose hearts quickened at the sight of America and who, in fact, laid the foundation of the America we have today. As of this writing, some government officials want to turn Ellis Island into a hotel resort, against the hopes of the Statue of Liberty restoration committee, who want to preserve it as a historic site.

A Park Service tour guide at Ellis Island in 1983 started his hour-long discourse about immigrants with an anecdote of Golda Meir's father, who escaped a pogrom in Russia. The moving story was followed by a less interesting one about an immigrant from Barbados; three stirring references to Jewish immigrants were sandwiched in with mention of German, Irish, Italian, Greek, African, Chinese, Polish, Japanese, even Cambodian immigrants. But when told that by 1924 at least 150,000 Syrians had immigrated to America, the guide drew a blank. For me, it was a disconsolate note, as I listened to the ghosts of the Syrians, nauseous as so many were from the seas, try to spell out their names in English, or be turned away because of trachoma, or wander wide-eyed into the cacophonous corridors filled daily with up to 15,000 ragged but hopeful immigrants from around the world. They seemed as unknown in 1983 as they were a century back, when they were miscalled "Turks" and listed as such until 1899, a humiliating reference given the fact that most were Christian and had sacrificed so much to get away from Ottoman Turkish rule. Perhaps it was at Ellis Island that their identity crisis in America would begin, where Yaccoub quickly became Jacobs, and first names became last.

Perhaps it was due, too, to the fact that they were among the last in line of an immigrant surge that crested at the turn of the century and was shut down by law in 1924. Though by 1913 nearly 10,000 Syrians were leaving ships at American ports a year, they were but a drop in the bucket and a late drop at that. The largest single ethnic group in America—the Germans—had begun to immigrate as far back as 1710, and by 1900 German Americans numbered 5 million, accounting for a quarter of the population of America's largest fourteen cities. By the time of the first Syrian immigrant family to America in 1878, there were already 200,000 German Jews in the country. Nine thousand American Jews fought in the American Civil War at a time when "Hi Jolly" and Antonios Bishallany were just about the only Syrians in the United States. Syrian immigration at its peak between 1900 and 1914 was only 7 percent as large as Jewish immigration at the time. In the first decade of the twentieth century, the Syrians ranked 25 of 39 immigrant nationalities. Yet the Syrians came to America at such pace that they alarmed the Ottomans and other authorities who felt the very schools the Americans had set up for them would be emptied. By 1924, many of them were.

The Syrians at the end of the nineteenth century moved by donkeyback   6
or a three-day foot trip to the harbors—Beirut, Tripoli, Haifa, and Jaffa. Then they encountered eager steamship merchants, as well as a whole class of hucksters ("sharpers," poet Amin Rihani called them), who would do everything from bribing Ottoman officials for passports (*tadhkarahs*) to securing $30–$50 tickets for the short dinghy voyage to the steamer as well as the long overseas journey. All this was done for a price, of course, and middlemen made quite a profit. But the Syrians paid for their blankets and ferries, ready to take what would be the longest sea voyage anyone took east-to-west to America. Three bribes were not uncommon to receive the necessary endorsements to get on the ship in Beirut—a half *madjidy* (or Turkish dollar) to passport officials, another 50 cents to an inspector of the rowboat between wharf and steamer, and yet another 50 cents to the final inspector at the steamship's gangplank. As the Reverend Abraham Rihbany said after running this gauntlet at the end of a tiring trek, "We left our mother country with nothing but curses for her Government on our lips."

The ship ride across the old sea was "unfriendly," and Rihbany tried to   7
sleep on crates filled with quacking ducks: "Other human beings joined us in that locality, and we all lay piled on top of that heap of freight across one another's bodies much like the neglected wounded in a great battle." An argument broke out between a Syrian in the "duck apartment" and an Egyptian woman: "*Lawajh Allāh* (for the face of God), said the kind-hearted Damascene, and squeezed himself a few inches to one side. In an instant, the wrathful Egyptian wedged herself in, squirmed round until she secured the proper leverage, and then kicked mightily with both feet, pushed the beneficent Damascene clear out of the wave-washed deck."

In Marseilles, Rihbany saw electric lights for the first time in his twenty-   8
four years, as well as his first train. Marseilles unveiled the last Sirens for the Syrian peasant before he braved the Sea of Darkness to America. The port seethed with hawkers of everything from Western clothes to sex. Some Syrians ran hostelries and guided the weary Levantines, giving them directions and lodging for the nights they must wait. Rihbany bought a Western bowler hat, flinging his Oriental fez hat aside; it gave "a distinctly Occidental sensation . . . stiff and ill-fitting." Another immigrant through Marseilles from Zahle remembered meeting a merchant marine uncle who threw his newly purchased British safari hat into the sea, saying no one in America wore them.

Amin Rihani, the poet who came to the United States in 1888 from   9
Freiyka, Lebanon, compared the cramped lodgings in steerage to Lebanon's

sericulture: "I peeped into a little room, a dingy smelling box, which had in it six berths placed across and above each other like the shelves of the reed manchons we build for our silkworms at home." In his sardonic novel of the Syrian immigrant experience, *The Book of Khalid* (1911)—the only of its kind—Rihani called the pathway of the immigrant a virtual "Via Dolorosa" with the Stations of the Cross Beirut, Marseilles, and Ellis Island.

Salom Rizk remembered a cabin mate who "would dangle a rosary from the porthole when the seas were rough," and how, when he once left the porthole open after quieting a storm with a medallion of St. Christopher, a huge wave washed in and flooded the cabin. Two angry stewards mopped up the mess and threw the medallion into the sea. Steerage for most immigrants was time spent in the belly of the whale, with little hope for regurgitation, save that of their own sick stomachs. 10

Syrians and other immigrants went through the "boiling down" effect of steerage, and got their first taste—though a foul one—of life in a democracy, where accidents of race, class, privilege, and religion in the Old Country were steamed into a common "new man," linked by little more than the desire of a whiff of clear air, a foot on terra firma. Arab refugees from Jerusalem bartered crosses of olive wood for an extra cup of clear water. *Tarbushes* of the proud were tossed around like so many insignificant footballs, battered, lost at sea. How bizarre it must have been to be suddenly a minority as a Muslim, now amongst a horde of Christians and Jews. One Christian immigrant—who translated poetry by Kahlil Gibran—recalled being helped with food and comforting words by a Muslim on his journey across the sea. The enmities of sectarianism drained off in the sea and the agony of adjusting to a new country. At least they had Arabic—treasured tongue—in common. 11

Some avoided danger more threatening than the sharpers of Marseilles. Said Hanna, a Syrian immigrant from Damascus, told a story of initial frustration when he had arrived in Marseilles too late to catch his ship, which was to link up in Southampton, England, with a huge new oceanliner bound for New York. But when the *Titanic* sank at sea, he counted himself a lucky man and never again worried about being late. 12

The "Island of Tears" awaited them in New York as they entered the misty harbor, passing the great statue holding a flame surrounded by wire. "Tears" because, of the sixteen million immigrants who arrived in this period at Ellis Island, two million never got out of its examination rooms, except to be sent home because of disease, mostly trachoma. Actually, those who arrived before 1893 were processed at Castle Garden, attached to Battery Park by landfill. It was there that in 1877 seven Algerians who had escaped prison in French Guiana had been "exiled" by the mayor of Wilmington, Delaware, where they had been arrested as vagrants: "The men are quiet and very attentive to their religious duties. They go to the northeast side of the building four times a day and quietly perform their devotions, at the same time 'looking toward Mecca.' They are all somewhat proficient in the French language." 13

But Ellis Island was the site of entry for most Syrians (some came through 14 Pawtucket in Rhode Island, Philadelphia, or New Orleans). Woozy, disoriented by raucous shouts in five different languages to go "Forward! Quickly!," they found themselves herded into the throng in the huge emporiumlike structure, probably the largest building any of them had ever entered. They had to traverse three stations of doctors, the first of whom pulled out an average of one in six immigrants marked for further checking by crayon or chalk: *H* for heart, *K* for hernia, *Sc* for scalp, and *X* if the immigrants were suspected of being insane or mentally retarded. At Station Two, the immigrants had to walk up a long flight of stairs; if they hobbled, they were chalked. Surviving that, they were checked for communicable disease. Leprosy? A scalp disease called favus? Syphilis? (The latter had entered Lebanon for the first time when the French came into the country in 1861, bringing with them the "Franji sore.") The final, most dreaded stage of this gauntlet was the trachoma check. It was here that Brooklynite Sadie Stonbely from Aleppo, Syria, was poked so badly in the eye during the examination that she had bad vision in her left eye for the rest of her life. In spite of these pitfalls, according to one Syrian immigrant, Ellis Island was fondly called *bayt al-hurryah* (the house of freedom).

An American senator aided an early Syrian constituent from Worcester, 15 Massachusetts, whose two boys were being held at Ellis Island because they had trachoma. He telegraphed President Theodore Roosevelt to "prevent an outrage which will dishonor the country and create a foul blot on the American flag." Roosevelt responded quickly, and soon the boys were allowed to join their mother. Years later, Roosevelt visited Worcester himself and discovered that the boys' eyes had been damaged by the glare of sea water, not trachoma.

Arriving indigent, or penniless, could keep an immigrant mired on Ellis 16 Island. One man who escaped a Turkish pogrom against Armenians in Tripoli, Lebanon, at the turn of the century by disguising himself (with the help of Muslim friends) in Muslin clothes ("He had to step over dead people, the ground wasn't showing") had sons already in America when he arrived at Ellis Island. They worried that he had no money to show immigration officials. And they hatched a scheme:

> The story—it's a secret but I'll tell you now. It's too late; everybody's dead. My brother went and bought a box of candy and lined the bottom of it with gold pieces, and he put the candy on top. And he went to the boat dock, down in the pier. Downstairs they sell fish, they sell, you know, nibbles, things like that. My brother bought a lot of things there and put them in a basket (with the candy and gold). My father was standing up on the boat. And he told my father in Armenian, "Take the box of candy and leave everything else to anybody who wants it. Just take the candy and go to your room. You'll find out why I sent it up there." When he went he found, sure enough, I don't know how many pieces of gold. Because when he comes at Ellis Island they've got to show a certain amount of gold to come in here, that you were well enough to take care of yourself.

By 1907, the Syrian Ladies' Aid Society was in full force helping Syrians   17
acclimate themselves to New York once they got through the Ellis Island checks.
Many emigrants spoke with warmth and appreciation about Dr. Nageeb Arbeely, who was chief Arabic examiner in the early years on the Island, as well
as his brother, Dr. Ibrahim Arbeely, who published an English-Arabic grammar
for the immigrants in 1896. Relatives gathered at the famous "Kissing Pole" to
greet the newly processed arrival with anxiety and ecstasy before the new would-
be American from Syria crossed the lapping waters of the Narrows and caught
a first sight of that huge zither—the Brooklyn Bridge. ◆

◆ Responding

1. Explain the basis of Orfalea's observation that the Syrians who arrived at
   Ellis Island in 1883 seemed as unknown in 1983 as they were a century back.

2. Using specific examples from the reading, explain why poet Amin Rishani
   called "the pathway of the immigrant a virtual 'Via Dolorosa' with the Stations of the Cross Beirut, Marseilles, and Ellis Island."

3. For some immigrants, Ellis Island was an "Island of Tears"; for others, "the
   house of freedom." Explain the significance of the two names, and discuss
   the selection process that took place at Ellis Island. Was the American government too harsh in its treatment of arriving immigrants? What rationale
   might there have been for the selection process?

4. Working in a group, share family stories of immigration to the United States.
   List all of the different places you know of where people entered the country.
   Share your list with the class.

REFLECTING A CRITICAL CONTEXT

DAVID M. FINE

David M. Fine is a professor of history at California State University at Long Beach. He has studied the history and literature of American immigrant groups for many years. His publications include The City, the Immigrant, and American Fiction, 1820–1920 *(1977), as well as articles in* American Studies, American Jewish Historical Quarterly, *and* American Literary Realism.

The essay that follows explores the way in which early immigrant writers viewed assimilation. It discusses the controversies, both within and outside the immigrant community, about the interpretation of the term "melting pot" and the degree to which newcomers should be expected to assimilate.

◆ ATTITUDES TOWARD ACCULTURATION IN THE ENGLISH FICTION OF THE JEWISH IMMIGRANT, 1900–1917 ◆

When the Jewish immigrant began to write novels in the language of his adopted land, it was both natural and inevitable that his subject should have been his own adjustment to America. Having the leisure to write fiction meant having achieved some measure of success in America, and, as might be expected, the process the immigrant novelist characteristically described was one of assimilation and accommodation with the dominant culture. We are given most often an account of his own interpretation of "Americanization," a concept which could mean either the shedding of Old World customs and the absorption of native habits or the broader melting pot fusion of Old and New World culture. Rarely did cultural pluralism, or "cosmopolitanism"—the idea advanced by Horace Kallen that America existed as a confederation of culturally-distinct national and ethnic groups—play a part in the fiction written by the first generation immigrant, except as an idea to be rejected: the writer's own experience had moved in an opposite direction.

Like so many of the immigrant autobiographies which appeared during the period, the novels written by immigrant Jews had a hopeful message to preach. In a period characterized by the mounting distrust of foreigners and the suspicion that the newer arrivals from eastern Europe were unassimilable, these novels were optimistic affirmations of immigrant assimilability. There were exceptions, of course—among them Abraham Cahan's *The Rise of David*

Levinsky and Sidney Nyburg's *The Chosen People*. We would like to contrast these two novels with others written by Jewish writers, particularly Elias Tobenkin, Ezra Brudno, and Edward Steiner, at the same time placing the immigrant novel within the larger cultural context of assimilation attitudes which prevailed in these years.

Although they were not the largest of the "new immigrant" groups, the Jews produced most of the period's immigrant fiction.[1] Like other large groups from southern and eastern Europe the Jews were motivated to emigrate for a variety of reasons, but to a greater extent than with the other groups, repression provided the spur. As a result, they brought a sizeable number of educated men with them and thus were able to achieve culturally in the first generation what other groups had to wait until the second and third generations to achieve. Moreover, since many were fleeing Czarist oppression, there were relatively few "birds of passage." In far greater proportion than other immigrants they planned to remain in America, so that the whole question of acculturation was a crucial one.

To some Jews acculturation meant sloughing off of Old World habits and embracing Christian American values. No better testament to this assimilation ideal exists than the autobiography of Mary Antin, *The Promised Land*, which created something of a literary sensation when it appeared in 1912. Her story tells of the girl who emigrated in 1894 at the age of thirteen from Polotsk, Russia, to Boston. In Russia she had been a stranger in her own land, a victim of Christian maliciousness and persecution. In America she is made to feel at home, and, encouraged to adopt the ways of her new land, she is reborn as an entirely new person: "I was born, I have lived, and I have been made over. . . . I am absolutely other than the person whose story I have to tell. . . . My life I still have to live; her life ended when mine began.[2]

To Danish-born journalist Jacob Riis, whose autobiography, *The Making of an American*, was written in much the same spirit as Miss Antin's, the clannishness of the recent immigrants stood as one of the chief stumbling blocks to acculturation. While he recognized that the tenement building and the sweat shop system were major factors which fostered the immigrant's cultural isolation, he pointed out to readers of *How the Other Half Lives* (1890) that some immigrant groups had risen from the ghettos rapidly, while others had stubbornly resisted Americanization. As the immigrant who made it in America, he had little patience with foreigners who were slow to adopt native ways. His sympathies diminished in proportion to the immigrants' obstinacy in clinging to Old World manners and traditions. The Russian Jews were to him among

[1]Between 1881 and 1917 some four million Italians came to America as compared to two million East European Jews. Moses Rischin, *The Promised City: New York's Jews, 1900–1911* (Cambridge, Massachusetts: 1962), p. 20; Harvey Wish, *Society and Thought in Modern America: A Social and Intellectual History of the American People from 1865* (New York: 1962), pp. 242, 248. [Author's note]
[2]Mary Antin, *The Promised Land* (Boston: 1912), p. xi. [Author's note]

the most recalcitrant of the new immigrants, standing "where the new day that dawned on Calvary left them, stubbornly refusing to see the light."[3]

The immigrant novelist whose works came closest to advocating the kind   6 of assimilation Mary Antin and Jacob Riis were recommending was Russian-born Elias Tobenkin. In *Witte Arrives* (1916), he describes the Americanization of Emile Witte (born Wittowski), who emigrates as a youth from Russia and after attending a Western university becomes a commercial and artistic success as a journalist, while his father remains a peddler in America, too rooted in Old World habits to become Americanized. So thoroughly has Witte been made over that his articles on domestic issues, we are told, have an "Emersonian flavor" and that most readers "would have placed the writer of such articles as none other than a scion of one of the oldest American families."[4]

Witte seals his "arrival" at the end of the novel by marrying a Gentile girl   7 of wealthy, old New England stock, after his Jewish wife dies. His transformation from bewildered alien to successful citizen seems much too facile but for the fact that, like Tobenkin, Witte arrived in America as a young boy and grew up in the rural West and not in the urban ghetto. He became Americanized not as Mary Antin had, by erasing the stigmata of the past but as Jacob Riis had, by channeling his talents into the mainstream of the middle-class American reform movement, by putting his journalistic skills to the service of broad, native, democratic ideals.

The reviewers praised *Witte Arrives*, some likening it to *The Promised Land*,   8 others reading it—or misreading it—as an affirmation of the melting pot, ignoring the implications of fusing contained in the metaphor. Typical of the latter view was the comment of H. W. Boynton, who wrote in *Bookman* that "the main picture of the ardent young alien becoming in a brief score of years a loyal thoroughgoing American is of a sort to stiffen our faith in the melting pot." A reviewer for *Nation*, commenting a year and a half later on Tobenkin's next novel, *The House of Conrad*, reminded readers of *Witte Arrives*: "It was the story of the melting pot, of a young Russian who came to this country in boyhood and made himself at least as American as the Americans."[5]

Such remarks illustrate the looseness with which the term "melting pot"   9 was used during the period. As Philip Gleason has indicated in his essay on the melting pot in the *American Quarterly*, the term was employed in these years

---

[3]Jacob Riis, *How the Other Half Lives: Studies Among the Tenements of New York* (New York: 1892), p. 112. [Author's note]

[4]Elias Tobenkin, *Witte Arrives* (New York: 1916), p. 293. [Author's note]

[5]H. W. Boynton, "Witte Arrives," *Bookman*, XLIV (October, 1916), 183; "Dreams and the Main Chance," *Nation*, CVI (March 14, 1918), 295–296. For other reviews of *Witte Arrives* see *New York Times Book Review*, August 1916, 334; Edward Hale, "Recent Fiction," *Dial*, LXI (September 21, 1916), 194; and "Witte Arrives," *Nation*, CIII (September 28, 1916), 304–305. [Author's note]

to denote almost any view toward assimilation favored by those using it.[6] During the war years, with the fear of divided loyalties and the suspicion of all but "100 percent Americans," the traditional optimistic view that the melting pot was working to produce a stronger America by blending the best elements of Old and New World cultures lost ground to the view that the function of the pot was to purge the "foreign dross" and "impurities" from the immigrant. In the popular mind the melting pot was identified more and more closely with indoctrination. As a result of this shift in the meaning of the term, those liberal critics who rejected narrow Americanization as a cultural ideal tended also to reject the melting pot, with its connotations of conformity and standardization. One of these critics was Randolph Bourne. Following the lead of Horace Kallen, Bourne rejected fusion altogether as either a realistic possibility or a desirable goal and called for an ethnically diverse, "Trans-National" America.[7] Writing in the *Dial* in 1918, Bourne sarcastically denounced what he called the "insistant smugness" of Tobenkin's *The House of Conrad*, which again emphasized the theme of assimilation and identified success with the absorption of native ideals.[8]

Acculturation in the novels of Elias Tobenkin and in the immigrant autobiography of Mary Antin presumes movement in one direction only: the immigrant sheds his past and adjusts to his adopted land. Missing from such statements is the traditional attitude that cultural blending is a two-way process, that Old World culture is needed to enrich the nation. This attitude found expression at the turn of the century in the settlement ideals of Jane Addams and in the journalistic sketches of Hutchins Hapgood. In her work at Chicago's Hull House and in her writing, Miss Addams, daughter of a prominent Midwestern family, concentrated on what the native American can gain from the "gifts" of the newcomers, and instead of premising her urban reform program on the rapid Americanization of the immigrants, as Riis was doing, she urged them to retain the rich folk traditions of their former lives and share them with Americans.[9] Hapgood, product of one of America's oldest families (his ancestors arrived at Massachusetts Bay in the 1640's), looked to the new immigrants to supply cultural and spiritual values to a nation caught up in getting and spending. Like his brother Norman, who became an authority on New York's Yiddish

10

[6]Philip Gleason, "The Melting Pot: Symbol of Fusion or Confusion?" *American Quarterly*, XVI (Spring, 1964), 20–46. [Author's note]

[7]Randolph Bourne, "Trans-National America," *Atlantic Monthly*, CXVIII (July 1916), 86–97. For Horace Kallen's position, see "Democracy Versus the Melting Pot," *Nation*, C (1915), 217–220. A more recent statement by Kallen is contained in *Culture Pluralism and the American Idea: An Essay in Social Philosophy* (Philadelphia: 1956). [Author's note]

[8]Randolph Bourne, "Clipped Wings," *Dial*, LXIV (April 11, 1918), 358–359. [Author's note]

[9]See, for instance, her address, "The Objective Value of a Social Settlement," in *Philanthropy and Social Progress: Seven Essays* (New York: 1893), pp. 27–40, and her *Twenty Years at Hull House* (New York: 1910), especially p. 246. [Author's note]

theater before taking over the editorship of *Collier's Weekly*, "Hutch" was infatuated with the Lower East Side ghetto which he came to know as a New York reporter, working alongside Abraham Cahan on Lincoln Steffens' *Commercial Advertiser*. *The Spirit of the Ghetto* (1902), a collection of Hapgood's journalistic pieces, remains a moving if sentimental tribute to the cultural richness of New York's Lower East Side. In contrast to Jacob Riis, whose concern for slum reform and Americanization led him to sketch the ghetto's derelicts, paupers, and street arabs, Hapgood sketched its artists, poets, and scholars. Riis examined its crowded tenements, saloons, and stale beer dives; Hapgood its theaters, schools, and coffee houses.

By addressing themselves not merely to what the immigrants could gain   11 by becoming Americans but to what America could gain by keeping its immigrant ports open, Jane Addams and Hutchins Hapgood brought forward into the urban-industrial age the traditional belief that the New World is a place of new men, and that the national character would continue to be modified by those who chose to come here.

The term "melting pot," used to describe the fusing of Old and New   12 World cultures on American soil, was given currency by the English novelist-playwright Israel Zangwill, who used it as the title of his successful 1908 play about immigrant life in New York. The play concerns a young musician who has fled from Kishinev to his uncle's flat in New York following the pogrom in which his parents had been massacred before his eyes. Dedicated to the ideal of the melting pot, he composes an "American Symphony" which will passionately proclaim his faith in his new life. He is never allowed to forget the past, however; he carries as a reminder a Russian bullet in his shoulder and is given to hysterical paranoiac outbursts. The play's conflict arises when, incredulously, he learns that his fiancée, a non-Jewish Russian immigrant, is the daughter of the Czarist officer who led the Kishinev massacre. By the end of the play, though, his love for Vera and his ecstatic vision of America as a land where ancient hatreds can be put aside, prove stronger than the anguish of the past. At the opposite extreme from David's almost neurotic obsession with the melting pot is the cultural pluralism of the boy's uncle, Mendel Quixano, who rigorously opposes his nephew's marriage to a Christian girl even before he learns of Vera's past. The Jews, he argues, have survived in captivity and in the Diaspora only because they have sustained a separate identity and have refused to merge with the dominant culture. Assimilation would spell the death of the Jewish people.

Mendel's position had considerable support among America's immigrant   13 Jews. Those who had fled the pogroms of Russia came to America not to be fused into a different culture but in order to be free to retain old beliefs, customs, and cultural identity. Opposition to melting pot blending came not only from Orthodox Jews and Zionists, but from many of those immigrants who had reached maturity in eastern Europe during the eighties and who retained the vivid memory of Czarist persecution. Such elders of the immigrant community were unwilling to give up their loyalty to Old World traditions which satisfied social and emotional as well as religious needs.[10] *The American Hebrew*, an important organ of the older, more assimilated German Jews, voiced the feelings of at least part of the ghetto when it said of Zangwill:

> Certain it is that no man who has felt so distinctly the heart-beats of the great Jewish masses can be expected to be taken seriously if he proposes Assimilation as the solution of the Jewish problem. Not for this did prophets sing and martyrs die.[11]

Opinion among "arrived" Jews was divided. Louis Marshall, president of the American Jewish Committee and one of the most influential Jews in American life, wrote that "the melting pot, as advanced by Zangwill, produces mongrelization . . . our struggles should be not to create a hybrid civilization, but preserve the best elements that constitute the civilization we are still seeking, the civilization of universal brotherhood."[12] On the other hand, President Roosevelt's Secretary of Labor and Commerce, Oscar Straus, the highest ranking Jew in government, reportedly shared with the President an enthusiasm for the play's optimistic message of fusion.[13]

In the years just prior to the premiere of Zangwill's play two novels written by immigrants, Ezra Brudno's *The Fugitive* (1904) and Edward Steiner's *The Mediator* (1907), affirmed the melting pot credo in a manner quite similar to Zangwill's. The novels are remarkably alike and can conveniently be described together. Both tell of Russian-Jewish youths, victims of Old World persecution who come to America with apocalyptic visions of the reunification of Jew and Christian. The faith in the healing power of the New World both authors wrote into their novels had its roots in their own successful public careers in America. Brudno, born in Lithuania in 1879, attended Yale University and went on to a prominent legal career. Steiner, a convert to Christianity, was born in Vienna in 1866, taught theology and sociology at Grinnell College in Iowa, and authored several books on immigration.

The early chapters of both novels are devoted to the Old World childhood of the protagonists. Both young men are raised in Christian environments. Brudno's hero, Israel Rusakoff, the son of an Orthodox Jew falsely convicted of the ritual slaughter of a Christian girl, is adopted by a Russian landowner who it later turns out—in one of the ironic coincidences which plague this fiction—is the repentant betrayer of the boy's father. Steiner's hero, Samuel Cohen, has been raised by a Catholic nurse following the death of his mother.

---

[10]Solomon Liptzin, *Generation of Decision* (New York: 1958), pp. 175–176. [Author's note]

[11]Quoted in "Mr. Zangwill's New Dramatic Gospel," *Current Literature*, XLV (December, 1908), 672. [Author's note]

[12]Charles Reznikoff, ed., *Louis Marshall: Champion of Liberty* (New York: 1957) p. 809. [Author's note]

[13]*Current Literature, loc. cit.*, p. 671. [Author's note]

So awed is he by the beauty and pomp of Catholicism he enters a monastery to study for the priesthood, only to abandon his vocation when he witnesses a brutal pogrom perpetrated in the name of Christianity. Both youths conclude that Christianity is a false sanctuary, that they cannot escape their pasts, that their destinies have been shaped by their heritage. Yet to return to the Orthodoxy of their fathers is as impossible as to reject their birthright completely. Old World Judaism—particularly in Brudno's novel—is rendered in its most medieval, oriental, and reactionary aspects.

In both works the flight to America is a flight from forms of oppression   17 imposed by both Jew and Christian, but in the ghetto of New York's Lower East Side, they find further oppression. To indicate the debasement of the European Jew in the New World ghetto, both Brudno and Steiner employ the device, so common to the immigrant novel, of allowing figures from the protagonists' Old World past to reappear: prominent Russian Jews, forced to flee following the 1881 assassination of the Czar, turn up as sweatshop workers; former Talmudic scholars become Yankee "dandies" or "allrightniks." The usual metamorphosis places the Jew behind a sewing machine, tyrannized by the German-Jewish "sweater." Conventionally, the Americanized "uptown" German Jew is the villain in the fiction of the ghetto, both in these novels produced by immigrants and in the popular native-drawn sketches of immigrant life which were then appearing in the magazines. Between the poles of rigid Old World piety and traditionalism and New World secularism and materialism, the heroes of Brudno and Steiner seek to define their American and Jewish identities. To reconcile Old World and New, Russian and German, Jew and Gentile, becomes their mission.

Steiner's "mediator" assumes a more active role in bringing about the   18 rapprochement of the two worlds. Having been raised in a monastery and having fled with the traumatic recognition of the gulf between Christian teaching and Christian practice, he became an evangelist on the East Side, proclaiming the true spirit of Christ to Jew and Gentile. He is aided by the patrician philanthropist Mr. Bruce, but the mission he sets for himself is a broader one than the simple conversion advocated by Bruce. The conflict between the two men, which dominates the later chapters of the novel, centers on the distinction between the rival interpretations of Americanization, that is, one-sided assimilation with the dominant population group as against the more liberal melting pot ideal. Bruce seeks to Americanize the Jewish immigrant by converting him to Christianity; Samuel Cohen seeks to fuse the two faiths, preserving the highest ideals of both.

The protagonists in both novels confirm their roles as cultural mediators   19 by marrying Gentile women. Brudno's hero, like Zangwill's, marries the daughter of his Old World enemy. Thus the marriage which has been forbidden in the Old World is sanctioned in the New. Steiner's hero weds the daughter of the missionary with whom he has joined forces. As in *Witte Arrives*, *The Melting Pot*, and *The Fugitive*, the union of the Jewish male with the Gentile woman—

either a native-born aristocrat or the daughter of the Jew's Old World betrayer—provides the symbolism for the reconciliation of Old and New World. Marriage to a Christian American is both the badge signifying the immigrant's successful "arrival" and the broader symbol of the possibilities for cultural fusion in America.

The most interesting comment on the solution Steiner's mediator presents comes from another novel about a self-styled mediator written ten years later. In *The Chosen People* (1917) Sydney Nyburg, a Baltimore lawyer and grandson of a Dutch Jewish immigrant, tells the story of Philip Graetz, rabbi of an affluent urban synagogue who conceives his divinely-appointed mission to be the mediator between the Americanized, "uptown" German Jews of his own congregation and the recently-arrived "downtown" Russian Jews of the city's ghetto. Steiner's mediator sought to bring together Jew and Gentile; Nyburg's wants to join the two worlds of Jews in America. In both novels the clash is between the values of the Old World and those of the New; in both the protagonist is a self-appointed "prophet of peace," who, upheld by a visionary melting pot credo, directs his rhetoric to the fusion of two diverse worlds. The difference is that not only is Graetz singularly unfit for his chosen task, but the task itself is shown to be beyond the possibility of attainment by any single man. What the world needs, Graetz learns, is not the prophet with his abstract plea for justice, but the pragmatic bargainer—the tough-minded realist, who, if he cannot make the uptown Jew love his downtown brothers, can, at least, keep him from exploiting their labor. [20]

Graetz's teacher and foil in the novel is a cynical, Russian-born labor attorney, David Gordon. In the strike which serves in the novel as a focus for the struggle between uptown and downtown, the workers of the ghetto are able to achieve better working conditions not because Graetz has convinced the industrialists of his congregation of their selfishness, but because Gordon has marshalled an army of workers willing to challenge the Jewish plutocracy. To Gordon, the two worlds of Jews cannot be kept from fighting as long as they occupy opposite poles in a capitalistic, individualistic society. His own solution is Zionism, which he feels will bind all Jews together in the building of their own society. Like the cultural pluralists, he believes that the Jews can stay alive only by defining their identity outside the value system of America. At the other extreme are the German Jews of Graetz's congregation, who embrace their Americanization ardently and are embarrassed by the persistence of Old World habits in the Russian Jews. They live in fear that the vast presence of the newcomers will undermine their own hard-won position in Christian America, and yet because they rely on the cheap labor force supplied by the recent immigrant, they have a vested interest in perpetuating his ignorance. [21]

The Chosen People was a needed antidote to the facile affirmations of assimilation and the melting pot offered by such immigrant writers as Tobenkin, Brudno, and Steiner. Labor warfare between uptown German and downtown Russian Jews in Baltimore served Nyburg well as a vehicle for examining the [22] broader question of the cultural gulf between older and newer Americans in the early years of the twentieth century. Abraham Cahan's major novel, *The Rise of David Levinsky*, appeared within a few months of *The Chosen People* and a few reviewers, pairing the two in their columns, noted the thematic parallels.

Levinsky's "rise" in America is an ironic one, for it is achieved at the expense of what is deepest and truest in him. He has realized the American dream of material success, but the victory is hollow. His life has been a dismal failure, he recognizes from his millionaire's perspective, because his outer achievements fail to satisfy his inner hunger.

The Rise of David Levinsky restates the theme which occupied Cahan in his earlier, shorter fiction. Throughout his tales of Jewish immigrant life in New York City, the Diaspora, a central and definitive historical fact in the Jewish experience, dominates the consciousness of the immigrant protagonists. His heroes are painfully aware of their exile, and whatever outer success they achieve in America, they are never permitted to forget what they have lost. This is Cahan's reply to the novels of acculturation with their glib, optimistic generalizations about cultural reconciliation and fusion. Under the pressure of New World experience, Old World values totter but never collapse entirely, for his protagonists are both unable and unwilling to extricate themselves from the grip of the past. Yearning for the past becomes one of the inescapable conditions—and, indeed, positive forces—in their lives. "The gloomiest past is dearer than the brightest present," Levinsky confesses.[14] And even Jake Podkovnik, Cahan's "Yekl," the flashy "allrightnik" and the most vulgar of his Americanizers, sees his Old World past as "a charming tale, which he was neither willing to banish from his memory nor reconcile with the actualities of his American present."[15] As Cahan's heroes outwardly assimilate into American life, they become increasingly alienated from themselves. The outer self comes into conflict with the inner self, which cannot and will not be stilled.

The result is loneliness, ennui, and guilt. In the no-man's land in which Cahan's heroes reside, there are no enduring loves or happy marriages. There are no unions with native-born aristocratic Gentile women to symbolize the melting pot blending of Old and New World. Nor are marriages or friendships from the Old World permitted to continue in the New. Yekl divorces his Russian wife for the perfumed, gaudy Mamie Fein. Levinsky, despite his great wealth, is rejected by three women. The widowed Asriel Stroom in "The Imported Bridegroom" (1898) is denied the old-age dream of seeing his Americanized daughter married to a pious Talmudic scholar. In Cahan's many other stories which deal with love and marriage in the ghetto, only one, "A Ghetto Wedding,"

---

[14]Abraham Cahan, *The Rise of David Levinsky* (New York: 1917), p. 526. [Author's note]

[15]Abraham Cahan, *Yekl, A Tale of the New York Ghetto* (New York: 1896), p. 54. [Author's note]

seems to offer the prospect of a permanent, fulfilling liaison. Contacts with the past are always unnerving. Yekl sends to Russia for his family but is embarrassed by his wife's appearance at Ellis Island and forces her to remove the traditional wig which identifies her as a "greenhorn." Levinsky is always uncomfortable in the presence of Old World figures. In one scene he is unable—or unwilling—to leave a street car to offer aid to a destitute man he sees and recognizes as a fellow student from his boyhood in Russia. In a mood of nostalgia near the end of the novel he arranges a reunion with a "ship brother" twenty-five years after he and the other man, a tailor, arrived from Europe, but the affair is spoiled by mutual distrust and embarrassment, and Levinsky is made to feel guilty for his success. Throughout the book when faces from the past reappear, he is unable to contend with his mixed feelings of hostility and compassion. The faces remind him of all that he has striven to eliminate from his mind—his near starvation, the brutal death of his mother, the bitter Czarist oppression—and yet he cannot help identifying with these people, and he yearns for their company.

The conditions of Levinsky's present life have made it impossible for him to bridge the gulf to the past he yearns for, yet, paradoxically, he is never far removed from the past. Loneliness, hunger, and alienation have been so firmly stamped on his character since his boyhood, they seem the most authentic parts of him. And while he cries on the one hand for an end to his sorrows, the sorrows seem to have their own kind of value. Through his meteoric rise his inner identity has remained essentially unchanged. Neither the thorough Americanization prescribed by Mary Antin, Jacob Riis, and Elias Tobenkin, nor the cultural fusion urged by Jane Addams, Ezra Brudno, and Edward Steiner are, in the end, realizable states in Cahan's fictional world. With *The Rise of David Levinsky* the novel of immigrant acculturation is no longer the story of easy faith. David Levinsky, immigrant and entrepreneur, finds emptiness at the end of the American dream.[16]

It seems appropriately ironic that 1917, the year America entered the war and passed its first major immigration restriction law, should mark the publication of the two most probing novels of immigration acculturation. At the height of the xenophobia engendered by the foreign crisis, Sidney Nyburg and

[16]Our discussion of *The Rise of David Levinsky* follows the general lines of Isaac Rosenfeld's essay, "America, the Land of the Sad Millionaire," *Commentary*, XIV (August, 1952), 131–135. For a different approach see David Singer, "David Levinsky's Fall: A Note on the Liebman Thesis," *American Quarterly*, XIX (Winter, 1967), 696–697. Beginning with the thesis of Professor Charles Liebman that East European Jewish immigrants to America were not, in the main, Orthodox Jews as is commonly assumed, Singer attempts to demonstrate that Levinsky had rejected his Old World piety long before emigrating and that such gestures as cutting his earlocks in America are not to be interpreted as signs of his loss of faith but of his desire for cultural assimilation and social acceptance. For a recent account of Cahan's career and a discussion of his fiction, including the earlier magazine version of Levinsky, see Ronald Sanders, *The Downtown Jews: Portraits of an Immigrant Generation* (New York: 1969). [Author's note]

Abraham Cahan, the one a third-generation and the other a first-generation American, wrote the period's most compelling fictional accounts of the Jewish immigrant in urban America. *The Chosen People* and *The Rise of David Levinsky* stand apart from and above the other novels of immigrant acculturation in having resisted ideological formulas and doctrinaire solutions and in having succeeded in portraying realistically the ironies, complexities, and dilemmas of cultural assimilation. The setting for the conflict between Old and New World in both works is the urban industrial arena because it was here that older and newer Americans so often clashed. The industrial conflict served as a metaphor for the broader, more fundamental cultural conflict. Rabbi Philip Graetz, ideologically linked with the affluent industrialists of his congregation, discovered a deeper identity with the exploited proletariat of the ghetto. David Levinsky, whose outer identity shifted with his changing fortunes, discovered that his inner identity was inescapable.

One of the conclusions to be drawn from a study of the immigrant novel 28 is that it is dangerous to assume that the foreign-born writer, because he lived through the process of adjustment, would necessarily produce the most trenchant accounts of the process. Some immigrant writers seemed more to reflect what they had read than what they had experienced. Conventions which they absorbed from the popular ghetto melodramas appearing in the journals—stock figures like the malevolent German Jewish sweater and the fiery young ghetto idealist, for instance—and the ideological doctrines of the reformers and the social theorists proved irresistible. In the novels of Elias Tobenkin, Ezra Brudno, and Edward Steiner, the psychological complexities of acculturation are evaded in favor of overly-enthusiastic affirmations of Americanization. As immigrants who succeeded in America, they used the novel, as Mary Antin used autobiography, to chant the praises of their adopted land. While all the immigrant novelists of the period described the disparity between the expectations and the actualities of America, between the "imagined" and the "real" America, only Cahan among them pursued the psychological implications of that disparity, its permanent cost to the psyche. Only Cahan, among the pre-World War I, first-generation Jewish American novelists, refused to turn his immigrant heroes into propagandists or preachers, refused to blink his eyes as he faced the chasm which lay between Old World values and New World experience. ◆

◆ Responding

1. An important issue that is still controversial is whether immigrants should strive for assimilation or maintain cultural pluralism. Working individually or in a group, define the two concepts. Write an essay discussing the implications of each for the individual immigrant. Support your points with examples from the readings or from your own knowledge and experience.

2. Using information from Fine's article, define and trace the history of the term "melting pot." How might critics object to the image of America as a melting pot? What other image might replace it?

3. How does the melting-pot image, which many Americans have advocated for years, fit into a society that wants to encourage cultural diversity? Write an essay arguing that America should or should not try to be a melting pot.

4. Fine introduces Sidney Nyburg's *The Chosen People* as "a vehicle for examining the broader question of the cultural gulf between older and newer Americans in the early years of the twentieth century." Describe this gulf. Does a similar gulf exist between established Americans and new immigrants today?

◆

C O N N E C T I N G

Critical Thinking and Writing

1. Write an essay discussing the difficulties and misunderstandings that can occur between foreign-born parents and children raised in America. Support your points with examples from at least two readings in the text as well as from your own knowledge and experience. Some readings that particularly focus on this theme are "The Fat of the Land," *Facing the Great Desolation, No-no Boy,* "Father Cures a Presidential Fever," and "Ropes of Passage."

2. Discuss the problems that European immigrants faced at the turn of the century, such as poor working and living conditions, difficulty learning English, lack of government support, and prejudice against new immigrants. Compare these hardships with those of other immigrant groups, such as Japanese, Chinese, Puerto Ricans, or Latinos.

3. Evidence of folk beliefs and practices occurs in some of the readings when the characters prepare love potions, wear charms to ward off evil, or behave in certain ways to avoid bad luck. Compare folk beliefs that appear in stories such as "The Fat of the Land" and "Love Medicine," with those in your own culture. Argue that such beliefs and practices are or are not an important part of all or most cultures.

4. Explore the difficulties of adjusting to life in a new country. You can use examples from the readings as well as from your own experience.

5. Myra Kelly makes a serious point about a trivial issue in "A Soul Above Buttons." When the Boss tries to organize the children to strike and is outwitted by the teacher, the narrator comments, "He had not reached that stage of Moral Training which would have taught him that the way of the reformer is as hard as that of the transgressor, and that the wages of the man who tries to awaken his fellow is generally derision and often death." Using other examples from the text, such as the experiences of César Chávez, James Farmer, or Malcolm X, discuss the validity of this statement.

6. Compare characters from two stories in this section to show the variety of ways in which early immigrants reacted to the challenges of living in a new country. Analyze the circumstances and the personal qualities of the characters to explain their methods of coping.

7. An American clergyman, Canon Barnett, stated that "the things which make men alike are finer and better than the things that keep them apart, and that these basic likenesses, if they are properly accentuated, easily transcend the less essential differences of race, language, creed and tradition." Agree or disagree with this statement, using evidence from the readings in this section as well as from your own experience.

8. Research your family history and write the story of your family's journey to the United States and your relatives' experiences when they arrived in this country. If you are a Native American or are unable to find out anything about your family's immigration, record the circumstances in which your family moved to the place where they currently live.

9. First- and second-generation Americans often criticize new immigrants for failing to learn English and to adopt our way of doing things, citing their own parents or grandparents as examples of immigrants who easily became assimilated. Write an essay supporting or refuting the idea that early immigrant groups were absorbed into the national culture more easily than recent ones. Use examples from your own knowledge and experience as well as evidence from the readings in this chapter.

10. Design your own essay topic that analyzes or compares some aspect of two or more of these readings.

For Further Research

1. Review current immigration laws and compare them to laws at the turn of the century. Some issues to consider are the ways in which attitudes have changed as the country has become more populated, who currently makes up

the largest group of immigrants, whether certain groups are more welcome than others, and what policies we should have in the future.

2. Research social legislation in the United States at the turn of the century to protect children and adults. Some questions to consider include: (a) What were the child labor laws? (b) Was there compulsory education? (c) Were unemployment benefits available? (d) Were working conditions regulated? (e) Was there a minimum wage? Expand this topic by comparing the working person's rights at the turn of the century with those rights today. What laws have been enacted to guarantee such rights?

◆

REFERENCES AND ADDITIONAL SOURCES

Addams, Jane. *Twenty Years at Hull House*. New York: Macmillan, 1910.

————. *Forty Years at Hull House*. New York: Macmillan, 1935.

Cahan, Abraham. *The Education of Abraham Cahan*. Trans. Leo Stein et al. Philadelphia: Jewish Publication Society of America, 1969.

Dunne, Finley Peter. *Observations by Mr. Dooley*. New York: Harper, 1906.

Fine, David M. *The City, the Immigrant and American Fiction, 1880–1920*. Metuchen, N.J.: Scarecrow, 1977.

Handlin, Oscar. *Race and Nationality in American Life*. Garden City, N.Y.: Doubleday, 1957.

————. *Uprooted: The Epic Story of the Great Migrations that Made the American People*. Boston: Little Brown, 1951.

Jones, Maldwyn Allen. *American Immigration*. Chicago: University of Chicago Press, 1961.

Kraut, Alan M. *The Huddled Masses: The Immigrant in American Society, 1880–1921*. Arlington Heights, Ill.: Harlan Davidson, 1982.

Mindel, Charles H., and Robert W. Haberstein, eds. *Ethnic Families in America: Patterns and Variations*. New York: Elsevier, 1976.

Taylor, Philip. *The Distant Magnet: European Emigration to the U.S.A.* New York: Harper & Row, 1971.

Tifft, Wilton, and Thomas Dunne. *Ellis Island*. New York: Norton, 1971.

Chinatown, San Francisco, 1889.
(Courtesy, The Bancroft Library)

Northern Pacific tracks along the Clark Fork River,
Montana, 1890. (Haynes Foundation Collection/Mon-
tana Historical Society)

Chapter 2

CHINESE IMMIGRANTS
The Lure of the Gold Mountain

Gold miners' camp, 1850.
(Courtesy, The Bancroft Library)

Chinese store in San Francisco, 1904.
(Courtesy, The Bancroft Library)

◆ SETTING THE HISTORICAL CONTEXT ◆

IN A POEM WRITTEN BY A CHINESE IMMIGRANT, we hear a warning to the people still at home:

> My friends, remember by all means:
> Don't let yourselves be stranded in a foreign country
> Brows besieged by sorrow from frequent worries of home;
> Thousands of miles of clouds and mountains further
>   impede a gloomy stay.
> Separation brings out misery.
> A journey to America is only a search for wealth.
> Return to the old country quickly, to avoid going astray.

The language of this poem reflects the feelings expressed in many other works of the period. There is a clear contrast between the promise of the Gold Mountain and its actual cost in human terms. "Gold Mountain" was the term the Chinese applied to California, or more generally to America itself—a land of opportunity offering an escape from the poverty at home in China. But the promise of success contained in the Gold Mountain legend was too often shattered by prejudice and resentment. Despite these pressures, Chinese immigrants, relying on their strong traditions of family, community, and hard work, have contributed greatly to the cultural development of the United States. In order to understand these pressures and the Chinese immigrant community's response to them, we need to examine briefly the circumstances the immigrants encountered upon their arrival in America.

Although there were a few Chinese immigrants earlier, the Chinese first arrived in the United States in great numbers between 1849 and 1870. Most came from the area of Kwangtung, a province on China's south coast that is noted as a commercial rather than an agricultural region. Because Kwangtung was a port city, its residents were informed about distant events through contacts from around the world. After hearing about the gold rush in California, many citizens decided to leave China to seek new opportunities for success in America. A large percentage of those who emigrated were young males, who left their families behind but hoped to return to them within a few years with newly acquired prosperity.

Emigration often involved hardship. Until 1860 the act of emigration itself violated both Chinese custom and the emperor's laws; those apprehended were subject to capital punishment. Moreover, life aboard ship was often a test of endurance—quarters were cramped, and food supplies were often inadequate. For many immigrants, the hardships did not end even after they had arrived in California, for there they usually had to undergo a series of medical tests and interrogation sessions at immigration headquarters.

During the first twenty years of Chinese immigration, many new arrivals moved quickly from the coast to jobs inland, often serving as contract workers to repay managers for the costs of their passage. Although a small number of Chinese found employment in New England or in the South, most remained in the West, journeying inland to the gold mines of the Sierra Nevada. Many worked in the mines; others provided laundry and cooking services in the mining camps.

Although there were profits to be made, the Chinese in the mining camps also experienced many problems. Relations between the Chinese and whites sometimes became violent. Discriminatory taxes, later ruled unconstitutional by the Supreme Court, were levied by the State of California upon the income of the Chinese workers. Despite these obstacles, however, many Chinese were able to contribute significantly to the growth of the American West. They earned the praise of business and governmental leaders for their ability to perform difficult labor, including dangerous work handling explosives. In 1871, for example, a United States commission designated to report on the mining industry praised the efficiency and courage of Chinese immigrant workers.

After the gold rush had ended, some Chinese immigrants found work in other kinds of mines, but a much larger number was employed in building the transcontinental railroad. Railroad executives were so impressed by their efficiency and the quality of their work that they sent emissaries to Kwangtung to recruit additional workers. During the last years of the construction

(1865–1869), the great majority of railroad construction workers were Chinese immigrants. When the final piece of track connecting the eastern with the western railroads had been put into place, the Chinese workers were acknowledged to have made an important contribution to the growth of the nation.

When the railroad construction project was over, Chinese immigrants turned to other enterprises. Some moved to the San Joaquin Valley, where they applied their skills to a large land reclamation project. Others worked in agriculture, helping to cultivate California's citrus crops and to develop new strains of fruit. Other immigrants settled on the coast, where they worked to establish fisheries. By the 1870s, however, the large majority of Chinese immigrants had settled in urban areas.

The most important of these urban areas during the nineteenth century was San Francisco's Chinatown. This section underwent dramatic growth during the period after the completion of the Union Pacific Railroad. Chinatown offered a place to live when immigrants were able to find work in the larger society and a place of refuge during times of persecution. When immigrants were forced out of other areas of employment, Chinatown provided them with a place where they could establish their own small businesses and enterprises.

But Chinatown was more than a refuge; it was a social, political, and cultural center. By the mid-1850s it had its own theater and by the 1890s it had, in addition to many bookstores and locally published periodicals, the nation's first bilingual daily newspaper. In addition to fraternal and social organizations, literary societies and political organizations sprang up. Other Chinatowns developed in other urban centers as settlers moved down the California coast and took the railroad east to New York and Boston.

Chinatown, like many other communities settled right after the gold rush, had its share of social problems, including the nationwide problems of prostitution and gambling and the local problem of the opium trade. The difficulties of the immigrants' life sometimes exacerbated common problems. For example, the immigrants' resort to prostitutes can be attributed to state and federal laws barring Chinese men from having their wives join them or from marrying non-Asians.

Thus Chinatown, although providing Chinese immigrants with a community based on shared language and tradition, was not impervious to the forces affecting the larger society. It could provide little protection from the increasingly virulent anti-Chinese sentiments of the last decades of the nineteenth century, which were partially the result of an economic depression. With the mines exhausted and railroad construction completed, there was less work for the pool of available laborers. The railroad the Chinese immigrants had helped to build added to their problems by bringing to the West Coast many people unable to find work in the East. As in other periods, the unemployed often blamed their situation not on prevalent economic conditions but on their competition for jobs—in this case the Chinese immigrants, who, they claimed, would work for a cheaper wage. As a result of this misperception and the widely held racial prejudices of the time, Chinese immigrants became scapegoats for economic problems over which they had no control.

The prevalent atmosphere allowed nativist and protectionist organizations to be formed throughout the West. These groups exerted pressure on governmental officials at all levels to bar Chinese immigrants who were already settled from employment and to prevent new immigrants from entering the country. Ironically, some of the leaders in this call for sanctions were themselves immigrants to this country, the most notable example being Denis Kearney, an Irish immigrant and founder of the Workingmen's Party. The goal of this San Francisco-based organization was the exclusion of Asian workers from American commerce.

The media intensified exclusionary sentiments. Historians have been able to find anti-immigrant news stories as early as Civil War times; *The New York Times*, for example, ran a series of purported news stories in the 1860s warning against the influx of immigrants. By the 1890s, western papers, such as the *San Francisco Chronicle*, began to sensationalize the issue further by advertising and covering in depth the rallies and other media events organized by nativist and protectionist factions such as the Workingmen's Party.

The pressure exerted by media and special-interest groups was felt by many of the prominent politicians of the period, some of whom ran on nativist exclusionary platforms and others of whom became more exclusionary with time. Leland Stanford, who had praised Chinese workers when he was the head of the Pacific Railroad, became more exclusionary when he served as California governor and United States senator.

Exclusionary legislation was passed on the local, state, and federal levels. In San Francisco, for example, schools were ordered racially segregated. In addition to making the Chinese subject to discriminatory taxes, the State of California passed laws prohibiting Asians from obtaining business licenses and owning real estate. On the federal level, the Scott Act prohibited Chinese laborers from entering the country, and it prevented those immigrants who had returned to China from being readmitted to the United States.

The most serious discriminatory legislation passed during this period, however, was the federal Exclusion Act of 1882, which prohibited Chinese nationals from entering the United States. President Taft vetoed the act, but his veto was overridden. After its passage, some immigrants were able to enter the country from Mexico or Canada and a small number of others entered by claiming to be from those categories of immigrants exempted by the Exclusion Act. Generally, however, immigration from China to the United States was virtually halted until 1943.

The passage of the Exclusion Act was particularly deplorable given the way in which the Chinese government had welcomed American nationals as early as the 1840s. Indeed, in 1841 the Chinese had granted rather extensive rights to American citizens coming to China. These rights were granted unilaterally; the Americans were not required to reciprocate. By the time the first treaty was due to expire, however, the negotiators representing the Chinese government insisted that their subjects be guaranteed certain basic rights. The Burlingame Treaty, negotiated in the 1860s, had granted Chinese nationals in the United States the immigration and employment rights accorded to persons from "a most favored nation." The Exclusion Act was a clear violation of this treaty.

After the passage of the Exclusion Act, those Chinese nationals who attempted to enter the United States legally were routinely detained for questioning; after 1910 they were held at Angel Island in San Francisco Bay.

FOR JUSTICE—
For Chinese,
American Friendship
WRITE, WIRE
Your CONGRESSMAN Today
Asking Him To Support The
REPEAL of the CHINESE
EXCLUSION ACT!
Congress Convenes September 13th

Poster urging repeal of restrictive immigration laws that barred Chinese entry or settlement in the U.S.

During their detention at the facility, they were examined and questioned about their status. Those who were able to convince the examiners of their right to be in the United States were admitted; those who were not were deported. The examination process often took months, during which time detainees lived in squalid quarters and ate substandard food. Family members were separated by gender for the duration of the stay, and detainees were allowed no visitors. Even though the facility was declared "uninhabitable" as early as 1920, it remained in operation until the 1940s. Inmates protested their living conditions in poems written on the barrack walls, and these works provide a record of the suffering endured by many Chinese nationals at the hands of immigration officials. In many of these poems the promise of America is directly contrasted with the intolerant atmosphere that immigrants were forced to confront.

The Exclusion Act, renewed in the 1890s, remained in effect until 1943. Not until then did the American government's treatment of immigrants from China begin to change, and even then the change was due less to a change of heart than a change in strategic priorities. As the United States entered into the Second World War, American military strategists sought allies in Asia. Improved relations with China thus became extremely important, and repeal of the Exclusion Act followed, as part of the nation's attempt to improve its international strategic position.

During the first years after the repeal, however, only a token number of Chinese—approximately one hundred—were allowed to immigrate annually. In 1945 immigration laws were relaxed to allow the foreign spouses of American soldiers to immigrate. Another law, passed in 1947, allowed approximately one thousand Chinese nationals entry into the country. During the next forty years the number of Chinese immigrants to the United States increased with the easing of American immigration restrictions and the change of government in China. Some Chinese fled the country after the Communist victory in 1949; others left during the Cultural Revolution of the 1970s. More recently, young Chinese who had come to the United States to study sought and were granted political asylum after the massacre at Tiananmen Square in 1989. Like the immigrants who preceded them, the Chinese immigrants of the past forty years have enriched the quality of American life.

EXPLORING THE LITERARY AND
♦ CULTURAL CONTEXT ♦

Each of the selections that follow responds to the circumstances that Chinese immigrants found in America. Some, such as the Gold Mountain Poems, are immediate responses; others, such as Maxine Hong Kingston's "The Grandfather of the Sierra Nevada Mountains" are more reflective. But whether immediate or reflective, the works contrast the lure of the Gold Mountain with its cost in human terms. Against the resentment and injustice faced by the Chinese in the larger society, the authors create vivid images of the individual vitality and collective resolve that helped the early Chinese immigrants to endure and to prosper.

Several of the readings mention or allude in more general terms to the Gold Mountain legend. The expression suggested more than financial success. Ambitious young men in China found themselves bound by the strictures of law, tradition, and social expectation. A sojourn in the United States—from which they might return wealthy, experienced in the ways of the world, and adept at speaking English and other skills uncommon at home—offered the possibility of an improved social position for themselves and their families. In "The Pioneer Chinese," Betty Lee Sung describes one such émigré. Impressed with "exaggerated tales" of the land "somewhere beyond the oceans," he seeks passage to the United States, hoping to find there the means to alleviate his poverty without loss of face.

Often, however, these hopes were unfulfilled, because the pursuit itself threatened to rob people of their dignity. In the Gold Mountain Poems, detainees protest because, far from reaping riches from the Gold Mountain, they have instead been treated as criminals. In Maxine Hong Kingston's work, a gold nugget represents the lure of the Gold Mountain; but when the mountain is approached, it threatens to devour self and spirit. The dehumanizing work demanded of the Chinese workers, who were lowered down cliffs in baskets to plant explosives or sent into the mines to bite "like a rat through that mountain," reflects the proprietors' assumptions about the expendable nature of this labor force.

Yet the Chinese remained willing, hard, and resourceful workers, seeing the connection between effort and the ability to determine one's own destiny. The émigré in the selection by Sung follows the work wherever it leads, in pursuit of his goal. In the selection from *Father and Glorious Descendant*, Pardee Lowe looks for employment in the classified advertisements. His fate is ultimately determined less by his own ambition than by the prejudice of others, proof that despite an individual's efforts toward self-determination, success or failure often depends on other people's acts. We can see this in the Gold Mountain Poems—exclamations to an audience that may or may not be listening. The parents in Siu Sin Far's story, "In the

Land of the Free," endure the bitter experience of helplessness before the law, greed, and bureaucratic indifference.

Mutual incomprehension emerges in the readings as the result of cultural boundaries, which tend to encourage both sides to make damaging and alienating comparative generalizations. Many American protectionist pamphlets attempted to present Asian immigrants as moral and racial out-siders, but the corresponding pamphlets for Chinese immigrants warned them against American ways. The Chinese caution toward, even suspicion of, Americans emerges in the selection by Maxine Hong Kingston when the grandfather refers to the Americans who control his destiny as "demons."

These readings illuminate the role taken by Chinese immigrants in shaping American history. "The Grandfather of the Sierra Nevada Mountains" challenges the traditional assumptions about the nation's west-ward expansion. Using the motto "My grandfather built the railroad," she explores the conflicts between agency and ownership, self-sacrifice and reward. Through Kingston's writing and that of the other Chinese Americans represented in this chapter, we are led to reflect on the dis-tinctions between what can be found and what must be built, and the sacrifices that must be made for each.

BEGINNING: PRE-READING/WRITING

◆ *Working in a group, use the knowledge of early Chinese immigrants you have gained from the introduction to this chapter, other books or media, and personal experience to try to construct profiles of some of the first Chinese immigrants in California. Consider sex, age, marital status, economic status, skills or profession, and reasons for immigrating. Share your profile with the class. What kind of person do you think would have made the journey from China to a foreign land in the mid-1800s?*

---

*T*he Exclusion Act barred Chinese nationals, with very few exceptions, from entering the United States. For the first time in American history, immigrants were excluded because of their country of origin. Congress passed the Act after much lobbying by nativist and protectionist groups such as Denis Kearney's Workingmen's Party. The Exclusion Act was later renewed and remained in effect until 1943.

◆ *From* **THE CHINESE EXCLUSION ACT** ◆

May 6, 1882. CHAP. 126.—*An act to execute certain treaty stipulations relating to Chinese.*

Whereas, in the opinion of the Government of the United States the coming 1
of Chinese laborers to this country endangers the good order of certain localities within the territory thereof: Therefore,

Be it enacted by the Senate and House of Representatives of the United States of 2
America in Congress assembled, That from and after the expiration of ninety days next after the passage of this act, and until the expiration of ten years next after the passage of this act, the coming of Chinese laborers to the United States be, and the same is hereby, suspended; and during such suspension it shall not be lawful for any Chinese laborer to come, or, having so come after the expiration of said ninety days, to remain within the United States.

SEC. 2. That the master of any vessel who shall knowingly bring within 3
the United States on such vessel, and land or permit to be landed, any Chinese laborer, from any foreign port or place, shall be deemed guilty of a misdemeanor, and on conviction thereof shall be punished by a fine of not more than five hundred dollars for each and every such Chinese laborer so brought, and may also be imprisoned for a term not exceeding one year.

SEC. 3. That the two foregoing sections shall not apply to Chinese laborers 4
who were in the United States on the seventeenth day of November, eighteen hundred and eighty, or who shall have come into the same before the expiration of ninety days next after the passage of this act, and who shall produce to such master before going on board such vessel, and shall produce to the collector of the port in the United States at which such vessel shall arrive, the evidence hereinafter in this act required of his being one of the laborers in this section mentioned; nor shall the two foregoing sections apply to the case of any master whose vessel, being bound to a port not within the United States, shall come within the jurisdiction of the United States by reason of being in distress or in stress of weather, or touching at any port of the United States on its voyage to any foreign port or place: *Provided*, That all Chinese laborers brought on such vessel shall depart with the vessel on leaving port.

April 29, 1902.   CHAP. 641.—An act to prohibit the coming into and to regulate the residence within the United States, its Territories, and all territory under its jurisdiction, and the District of Columbia, of Chinese and persons of Chinese descent.

Be it enacted by the Senate and House of Representatives of the United States of America in Congress assembled, That all laws now in force prohibiting and regulating the coming of Chinese persons, and persons of Chinese descent, into the United States, and the residence of such persons therein, including sections five, six, seven, eight, nine, ten, eleven, thirteen, and fourteen of the Act entitled "An Act to prohibit the coming of Chinese laborers into the United States" approved September thirteenth, eighteen hundred and eighty-eight, be, and the same are hereby, re-enacted, extended, and continued so far as the same are not inconsistent with treaty obligations, until otherwise provided by law, and said laws shall also apply to the island territory under the jurisdiction of the United States, and prohibit the immigration of Chinese laborers, not citizens of the United States, from such island territory to the mainland territory of the United States, whether in such island territory at the time of cession or not, and from one portion of the island territory of the United States to another portion of said island territory: *Provided, however,* That said laws shall not apply to the transit of Chinese laborers from one island to another island of the same group; and any islands within the jurisdiction of any State or the District of Alaska shall be considered a part of the mainland under this section.

SEC. 2. That the Secretary of the Treasury is hereby authorized and empowered to make and prescribe, and from time to time to change, such rules and regulations not inconsistent with the laws of the land as he may deem necessary and proper to execute the provisions of this Act and of the Acts hereby extended and continued and of the treaty of December eighth, eighteen hundred and ninety-four, between the United States and China, and with the approval of the President to appoint such agents as he may deem necessary for the efficient execution of said treaty and said Acts.

SEC. 3. That nothing in the provisions of this Act or any other Act shall be construed to prevent, hinder, or restrict any foreign exhibitor, representative, or citizen of any foreign nation, or the holder, who is a citizen of any foreign nation, of any concession or privilege from any fair or exposition authorized by Act of Congress from bringing into the United States, under contract, such mechanics, artisans, agents, or other employees, natives of their respective foreign countries, as they or any of them may deem necessary for the purpose of making preparation for installing or conducting their exhibits or of preparing for installing or conducting any business authorized or permitted under or by virtue of or pertaining to any concession or privilege which may have been or may be granted by any said fair or exposition in connection with such exposition, under such rules and regulations as the Secretary of the Treasury may prescribe, both as to the admission and return of such person or persons.

SEC. 4. That it shall be the duty of every Chinese laborer, other than a citizen, rightfully in, and entitled to remain in any of the insular territory of the United States (Hawaii excepted) at the time of the passage of this Act, to obtain within one year thereafter a certificate of residence in the insular territory wherein he resides, which certificate shall entitle him to residence therein, and upon failure to obtain such certificate as herein provided he shall be deported from such insular territory; and the Philippine Commission is authorized and required to make all regulations and provisions necessary for the enforcement of this section in the Philippine Islands, including the form and substance of the certificate of residence so that the same shall clearly and sufficiently identify the holder thereof and enable officials to prevent fraud in the transfer of the same: *Provided, however,* That if said Philippine Commission shall find that it is impossible to complete the registration herein provided for within one year from the passage of this Act, said Commission is hereby authorized and empowered to extend the time for such registration for a further period not exceeding one year.

Approved, April 29, 1902. ◆

◆ Responding

1. Using material from the introduction to the chapter, your own knowledge, or sources in your school library, gather information to answer the following questions.
   a. Why were the Chinese invited to the United States in the 1800s?
   b. How many laborers were imported from China?
   c. What projects did they primarily work on?

2. Working individually or in a group, use the information gained from your research into the importation of laborers to speculate about the reactions of other groups already in the West.

3. Discuss the ways in which the Exclusion Act of 1882 tried to curtail Chinese immigration. What effect did the passage of this act have on the image of America as a land of opportunity?

BETTY LEE SUNG

Betty Lee Sung was born in Baltimore. She studied at the University of Illinois, Queens College, and the City College of New York, where she earned undergraduate and graduate degrees. In addition to doing editorial work and translation, Sung worked for the United States Army Map Service during World War II and The Voice of America just after the war. More recently, she has been on the faculty of the Asian studies department at the City University of New York, and she has written extensively on immigration and related subjects.

"The Pioneer Chinese," a chapter from Sung's book Mountain of Gold: The Story of the Chinese in America *(1967), describes some of the experiences of early sojourners from China. By discussing some of their goals and motivations, as well as the reactions of family members remaining in China, the essay illustrates the interplay of social and economic factors that contributed to the decision to immigrate.*

◆ THE PIONEER CHINESE ◆

Surprisingly, the very first Chinese to set foot on United States soil were not adventurers or laborers in search of gold but students in search of knowledge. In 1847, a year before the glitter of that metallic substance caught the eye of John Marshall on the south bank of the American River, an American missionary, the Reverend S. R. Brown, had brought with him three Chinese boys to the United States to study at the Monson Academy in Massachusetts. One of them was Yung Wing, who later graduated from Yale and who attained high office in the Chinese government. He was successful in persuading the Emperor to send other students to the United States for specialized training and education, almost all of whom eventually rendered distinguished service to their country, then emerging from her self-isolation. 1

Historian J. O'Meara said the first Chinese to arrive on the West Coast were merchants with beautiful silks, tea, and *objets d'art*.[1] The first Chinese immigrants, according to H. H. Bancroft, were two men and a woman who arrived aboard the *Bard Eagle* in 1848. The two men went directly to the mines and the woman went to work in the home of a missionary named Charles Gillespie, who had also come on the same boat from Hong Kong.[2] 2

Under ordinary circumstances, the number of Chinese who would venture 3

---

[1]J. O'Meara, "The Chinese in Early Days," *Overland Monthly*, n.s.v. 3 (1884). [Author's note]
[2]H. H. Bancroft, *History of California* (San Francisco: The San Francisco History Co., 1884–1890), Vol. III, p. 336. [Author's note]

beyond their native shores across 7,000 miles of ocean would have been inconsequential. The deterrents were too many. But when merchant ships put in to Canton with exaggerated tales of the gold discovery in California, mountains crumbled, oceans dried up, distances shrank, and dangers were shrugged off for men of ambition quick to take advantage of a situation that promised fortunes in nothing less than gold. By 1851, in a matter of three years, there were 25,000 Chinese in California.

Fatt Hing was one of these 25,000. His story is typical of the pioneer 4 Chinese, many who came with him and many who came after him.

As a lad of nineteen, Fatt Hing had already seen and heard and learned 5 more about the world than most of the men in his village, who had seldom set foot beyond the nearest town square. For Fatt Hing was a fish peddler who went frequently from Toishan to Kwanghai on the coast to buy his fish to sell at the market.

Down by the wharves, where the fishing boats came in, Fatt Hing had 6 often seen foreign ships with their sails fluttering in the wind. He had seen hairy white men on the decks, and he had often wondered and dreamed about the lands they came from. Fatt Hing had been fortunate in that he had been to school, although this schooling lasted no more than two years. In this short period of time, he had gained an awareness that China was not the center of the universe and that foreign white devils with guns and boats had been pushing China around.

One morning there was a great deal of commotion and excitement on the 7 wharves. Elbowing his way to the center of the crowd, Fatt Hing caught snatches of the cause of the commotion amidst the shouting and the pushing. By putting together a word here and a word there, he surmised that there were mountains of gold for the picking, somewhere beyond the oceans.

In the gray dawn of early mornings following, Fatt Hing's ears strained 8 to catch every word pertaining to the Mountain of Gold on the wharves. His mind was already made up. How to get there was the question he sought to answer.

Fatt Hing was cautious. He confided in no one, for he did not wish to 9 alarm his parents. True, they were not solely dependent upon him for support. He had two older brothers, but his parents would forbid him to go and he did not want to upset them. By the time Fatt Hing had gathered enough information to learn that he could buy passage on one of the huge foreign ships, he was shocked into a cold sweat to discover that the magistrate's soldiers had arrested many of the less discreet who had tried to board a ship. Belatedly, they had learned that it was a crime punishable by capital punishment for a subject of the Emperor to emigrate from his homeland.

Many more months of cautious probing rewarded Fatt Hing with the 10 knowledge that the garrison leader could be bribed. It took longer to persuade his parents to let him go. By that time, reports were filtering back that the Mountain of Gold was no myth and that the gold was free to any who would come and mine it. Then there was no holding Fatt Hing back. His father sold the water buffalo and Fatt Hing's mother pawned her earrings for his passage. Together they bade their son a tearful farewell, and he was smuggled on board a Spanish ship bound for California.

After he was secreted on board, Fatt Hing discovered to his surprise that the entire hold was filled with young men like himself. They slept, sat, ate, and waited on straw mats on the floor. The air in the hold was stifling and foul, putrid from the vomiting of those who had yet to acquire their sea legs. Most of the time, the wind-swept decks were much too cold for the thin cotton or flax garments which Fatt Hing and his fellow passengers wore. Besides, most of the deck was roped off, absolutely forbidden grounds to the human cargo. Fatt Hing spent many days and nights with this nose pressed against a crack in the board covering the hold. Those days and nights were given to a lot of thinking with misgivings about the step that he had taken. 11

The uncertainties of what they were headed for and the rigors of the trip drew the men together. None actually knew anything beyond what he had learned through hearsay gathered surreptitiously from the grapevine. Yet they had committed themselves totally to embarkation for lands unknown. None had expected the trip to take more than three months. Ten days—twenty days— a month on ship, some had anticipated. Each day after that added to their apprehensions and fear. 12

Fatt Hing recognized no familiar face when he came aboard. As his surname was Chin, he quickly sought out others with the same name, for presumably a Chin was related to another Chin regardless of how many generations back they may have shared a common ancestor. Those without name relations sought out others from the same vicinity or district. It was imperative to their sense of security to know that they belonged to a group. Had they remained in China and been thrown together under different circumstances, their relationship most likely would have been characterized by surface formality demanded by social conventions. Here in the stifling hold of a Spanish ship, an invisible bond welded the men together so that Fatt Hing felt closer to these men than he had ever felt toward his own brothers. 13

The fears of some that they had been hoodwinked and were being transported to a foreign land to be sold as slaves proved unfounded. Toward dusk on the ninety-fifth day, the hills of San Francisco rose over the horizon. The captain ordered the holds opened and the men swarmed out onto the decks. None slept that night as they watched the ship inch in toward the harbor. 14

When the ship docked the next day, a delegation of Chinese was on hand to greet the new arrivals. "Come with us," said the spokesman for the group, "and we will take you to the Chinese Street." 15

After the new arrivals were fed and refreshed with cups of strong hot tea, the leader spoke again. 16

"I am Wong Wing Dock, chairman of the Six Companies," he said. "We came as you came on board one of those ships, and we came for the same 17 purpose—to seek gold. When we set foot on these shores, however, there were no Chinese faces to greet us, for we were among the first to arrive. Weak and wearied from our long journey, we were bewildered and lost. We did not know where to turn for shelter or food. Fortunately, there were enough of us so that some set to putting up these houses while others looked for food. We followed the white men into the hills and found out how they sifted the sands for gold and we did the same.

"One valuable lesson we have learned and which you will soon appreciate is that we must stick together and help one another, even though we are not kin. That is why we have formed this organization called the Six Companies representing the six districts which most of us come from. Our compatriots have honored me by choosing me chairman. [18]

"You will always find food and shelter here among us. Any needed supplies can be purchased from the shops on this street. No doubt you will want to send a letter home to let your families know of your safe arrival. Elder brother Leong is a learned man, and he will help you write your letters. [19]

"When you have earned money from your diggings or from your wages, you will pay dues into the company fund. This fund helps us to maintain the company headquarters and helps us set up an orderly system to take care of our own. [20]

"We are Chinese in a land of foreigners. Their ways are different from our ways. Their language is different from our language. Most of them are loud and rough. We are accustomed to an orderly society, but it seems as if they are not bound by any rules of conduct. It is best, if possible, to avoid any contact with them. [21]

"Try not to provoke the foreigners. But you will find that they like to provoke us. We are comfortable in our loose cotton jackets and trousers and we are used to going barefooted. They like to wear rough coarse clothing with high-laced boots. They cut their hair short and let the hair grow on their faces. We wear our hair long and braided and we shave the hair from our faces. Since we all want to return to our homeland, we cannot cut off our queues.[3] [22]

"Be patient and maintain your dignity. If you are lucky you may not have to stay here long. Some of us and many white men have made rich finds. They need workers to help them. As new arrivals you may want to work for these men, or you may choose to prospect on your own. [23]

"You will need a pick, a shovel and a few supplies," continued Chairman Wong. "You may take what you need from our headquarters now, and the sum will be entered in the company books against your name." [24]

---

[3]The queue was a symbol of subjugation forced upon the Chinese by the ruling Manchus. The Chinese hated the queue but were compelled to wear it. In 1911, with the overthrow of the Manchus, the Chinese were liberated from this loathsome reminder of subjugation and immediately cut off their queues. [Author's note]

As soon as Chairman Wong had finished speaking, some of the men hastily   25
asked where they should go for their pick and shovel. Though the strangeness
of their environment was disconcerting, and though they were weak from their
confinement in the ship's hold, they were impatient to be off into the hills.

Fatt Hing held back. As one of the younger men, he did not want to push   26
ahead of his elders, but he also wanted time to think. "What do I know about
mining?" he pondered. "Where should I start looking? Perhaps it would be
better if I hired myself out until I get to know more about this new land."

The thoughts of Fatt Hing's shipmates ran in the same vein. Chairman   27
Wong had received many requests for Chinese workers and he knew exactly
where to send them. The terms were generous. Each worker was to receive
half of the gold he mined.

Early next morning, the men set out on foot for the hills. When they   28
arrived at their destination, Fatt Hing saw that hundreds of his fellow countrymen who had come previously had set up camp. It was comforting for him
to know that he would be among his own people—people who spoke his own
language and observed his own customs—though he was thousands of miles
away from home.

Dig and sift, dig and sift. Fatt Hing and his fellow workers pecked at the   29
mountainsides, in the ravines and gulches, working loose the earth and washing
out the fine gold particles which sank to the bottom of the pan. It seemed as if
other miners had worked the claim before, taking out the larger pieces while
scorning the fine gold particles which required more laborious work. To Fatt
Hing, however, the glitter of the gold dust in the loose earth drove him to work
with unrelenting fury. "Truly, these are mountains of gold," he cried. "I must
write my brothers and my cousins and tell them to come."

Thus each boatload brought more Chinese and more. Brothers sent for   30
brothers and even distant kin so that Chinese immigration snowballed. No
sooner had a ship disgorged its passengers than they were off to the mines.
Although Canton, China, was 7,000 miles and a three months' journey away,
it was a less hazardous and quicker trip than the overland route across the
American continent or the boat trip around Cape Horn. From Canton also came
lumber for the houses, cottons and silks, and even bundles of clean laundry
which had been sent clear across the Pacific for washing.

In 1850, the new state legislature, casting about for a source of revenue,   31
passed a Foreign Miners' License Law imposing $20.00 per month on all
foreign miners. Instead of bringing into the state treasury the expected revenue, the law had the effect of depopulating the miners' camps. By the time
the legislators realized that the tax was a mistake and repealed it a year later,
many Chinese miners had quit the hills and swarmed into San Francisco.
Quick to grasp at the excellent opportunities for making money in the city,
the Chinese took to carpentering, washing and ironing, and operating restaurants and hotels. Everywhere, the Chinese were considered indispensable

and were praised for their industry and efficiency. Noting these virtues, Mary Coolidge wrote:

> The editor of the Pacific News remarked upon their industry, quietness, cheerfulness and cleanliness of their personal habits. Whatever the white man scorned to do, the Chinaman took up; whatever the white men did, the Chinese could learn to do; he was a gapfiller, doing what no one else would do, or what remained undone, adapting himself to the white man's tastes and slipping away unprotestingly to other tasks when the white man wanted his job.[4]

When California was admitted as the thirty-first state to the Union, the Chinese took a prominent part in the ceremonies and the parade. The *Alta California*, a San Francisco newspaper, said: "The China Boys will yet vote at the same polls, study at the same schools, and bow at the same altar as our countrymen." 32

Governor McDougal recommended in 1852 a system of land grants to induce the further immigration and settlement of the Chinese, whom he called "one of the most worthy of our newly adopted citizens."[5] 33

Renewed agitation by late-arriving Americans who complained that foreigners were carrying off millions in American wealth resulted in the repassage of a foreign miners' tax, set this time at $4.00 per month. Although the levy was intended against all foreigners, it amounted to a tax almost exclusively against the Chinese. Though Irish outnumbered the Chinese and the Germans were a close third, the Chinese *looked* more foreign. Besides, the Chinese always paid up, and it was easier for the tax collector to collect from a willing payer. It was estimated that the Chinese paid 85 percent of the revenue from the miners' tax, an amount approximating five million dollars during the time the law was in force. This tax was later declared unconstitutional, but none of it was refunded.[6] 34

Nearly two years went by for Fatt Hing, and his little hoard of gold had increased steadily. He had continued to work for others, hiring himself out when he heard of a particularly rich find. He had gone into San Francisco on a few occasions to write a letter and send some money home, or to meet his brothers when they arrived. Otherwise, he had worked unremittingly. But the claim he now worked was yielding less each day, and he found himself thinking more and more about his parents and home. Finally he decided that he would take his gold and return to China. 35

Before he set sail, he cleared his account with the Six Companies and was 36

---

[4]Mary Coolidge, *Chinese Immigration* (New York: Henry Holt & Co., 1909), pp. 34–37. [Author's note]
[5]*Ibid.* [Author's note]
[6]*Ibid.*, p. 80. [Author's note]

delegated by Chairman Wong to see that the bones of several of his compatriots who had met death in this foreign land were returned to their ancestral homes for proper burial. This time, he made sure there was a bunk for him on ship and that his trip home would be more pleasant than his trip over, for now he could afford better accommodations.

To while away the time on board, Fatt Hing and his fellow travelers fell 37 into the habit of playing *pai-gow*. Before the journey's end, each man's hoard of gold had exchanged owners several times. When the ship docked at Canton, Fatt Hing was lucky enough to have retained half of what he started out with.

This was enough to enable Fatt Hing to take a bride, build a house, and 38 buy four *mous* of land. His parents and relatives could not believe their eyes when he unwrapped his packets of gold, and Fatt Hing had moments of regrets about his gambling losses on board the ship. He could have stayed home, farmed his land, and lived unpretentiously, but within a year Fatt Hing became restless. He missed the excitement of California, and he was eager to get back to the mines. But his parents would not allow him to depart until he had presented them with a grandson. Nevertheless, as soon as Fatt Hing knew that his wife was pregnant, he bought passage back to California. This time there was no need to slip aboard surreptitiously. California gold had enriched the country, and the magistrate was happy to see the men come and go.

A lot of changes took place in San Francisco during Fatt Hing's year or 39 so of absence. It was certainly not like the same San Francisco that Fatt Hing saw when he landed the first time. Houses were strung out like beads on a string. Ships of every nation were anchored in the bay. Goods were piled high on the piers. There were so many Chinese faces in the crowd, he almost felt as if he were standing on a wharf in Canton.

Gold mining was another story. The furious pace of activity had died 40 down. The surface gold was pretty much worked over. That below the ground was more difficult to get at, and a day's labor yielded less. More and more, the Chinese were moving into the city. Fatt Hing was uncertain. He knew the hills and he had been unusually lucky before. He wanted to try again. He finally decided to prospect for his own gold and work his own claim if he found one. One of his brothers was persuaded to join him.

Month after weary month, the two trudged up and down the river banks 41 and mountain ravines. First they followed the Sacramento north and then they swung south to follow the San Joaquin. Throughout the vast expanse, they found that other miners held prior claim to the choice areas while abandoned claims yielded little. To keep themselves in food and supplies, Fatt Hing and his brother gathered firewood, worked in the sawmills, watered other men's horses, or cooked for other miners.

"We are opening a restaurant on Jackson Street," said his cousin. "Tong- 42 Ling charges a dollar a meal and his place is overflowing with foreigners through- out the day. What did he know about cooking before he came to *Gum Shan*? If the foreign devils will eat his food, they will eat ours. Why don't you two brothers join us?" By then, the two needed little persuasion. Fatt Hing, who had picked up a smattering of English, worked in the dining room. When business was slow, he stood outside the door banging on his gong, entreating customers to come in. No matter what the request, Fatt Hing always answered his customers with repeated nods of the head, a broad smile, and several yeses.

For Fatt Hing, this life was more comfortable than mining or prospecting. Business picked up steadily, and the money came in regularly. "Let others go after the gold in the hills," he said. "I'll wait for the gold to come to the city."   43

In 1864 the chairman of the Six Companies received a call for workers from an entirely new line of work—railroad construction. After thirty years of bickering and wrangling, mistrust and contention, the Federal government finally decided to build a transcontinental railroad linking the West with the East. The Act of 1862 called for the construction of a railroad and telegraph line from the Missouri River to the Pacific coast.   44

The Union Pacific and Central Pacific were commissioned to build the railroad. The Union Pacific was to start at the Missouri River and build westward while the Central Pacific was to begin from the west coast building eastward, both rails to link up and form one continuous line after completion. The railroad companies were paid by the miles of rails laid. Thus the stage was set for a furious race between the Union Pacific and Central Pacific to see which could lay more miles of track.   45

An immediate cry went up for men, for boys, for any pair of hands that could do the work. Labor was made more scarce by men diverted to battle in the Civil War. Charles Crocker, one of the Big Four partners of the Central Pacific in charge of construction, was faced immediately with the acute shortage of labor. Of the thousands sent into the hills during 1863 to 1864, only two in five reported for work, and of these all but a few quit as soon as they had earned enough to pay stage fare to Virginia City, where new discoveries in mineral wealth excited the adventurers' hopes for a windfall fortune. For a while, there was talk about importing peons from Mexico; at another time, Crocker thought of hiring prisoners or asking the government to send out rebels captured during the Civil War.   46

The situation was desperate; there was little likelihood that the railroad could be completed within the fourteen years called for, or be completed at all, as long as labor continued to be such a thorny problem. Charles Crocker, an ingenious and resourceful man, thought of the Chinese. His superintendent, J. H. Strobridge, was skeptical. "They are physically incapable of the heavy manual labor," he argued. But at no one time could Crocker recruit more than 800 whites. He issued circulars, posted ads in the post office, and gave work to any person who applied. After pay day, the force would dwindle to 600 and gradually increase to 800 but no more.   47

When no other recourse appeared in sight, Strobridge dubiously decided to try the experiment and fifty Chinese were hired. They were hauled to the end of the track. They disembarked, glanced without curiosity at the surrounding forest, then tranquilly established camp, cooked a meal of rice and dried cuttlefish and went to sleep. By sunrise, they were at work with picks, shovels and wheelbarrows. At the end of their first twelve hours of plodding industry, Crocker and his engineers viewed the results with gratified astonishment. Those who through the day had been momentarily expecting the weaklings to fall in their tracks from exhaustion permanently revised their opinion of the Chinaman's endurance.[7]

Crocker came to rely on and place his trust completely in the Chinese   48
laborer, so much so that they were labeled "Crocker's pets." At first the Chinese worked as graders, leveling the ground with their picks and shovels for the railbed. A shortage of masons temporarily halted the work. Strobridge reported to Crocker, who boomed, "Put your Chinamen to work."

With all his faith in the Chinaman as a grader, Strobridge protested, "Make   49
masons out of Chinamen?"

"Sure," replied Crocker, "didn't they build the Chinese wall, the biggest   50
piece of masonry in the world?"[8]

At one time, over 10,000 Chinese were employed on the Central Pacific.   51
Their heroism in making the Central Pacific a reality is described vividly in a book by Oscar Lewis entitled *The Big Four*.[9]

Almost immediately after work began on the western terminal of the   52
Central Pacific, the builders were up against the sheer granite walls of the Sierra Nevadas. Work had to be continued, for the Union Pacific was racing across the western plains, and every mile of rail laid by the Union Pacific meant more money in their pockets and less for the Central Pacific coffers. Yet the blinding snowstorms, the extreme cold, and the roaring avalanches defied man to pitch himself against the elements. This is Mr. Lewis' description of the heroism of Crocker's men:

> The winter of 1865–1866 was severe as any on record. Snow fell in quantity as early as October, and the next five months saw an almost continuous succession of storms. As ground froze and the tracks and construction lines were blanketed under an icy mass fifteen feet thick, the work slowed down to a walk.[10]

Nearly half of the work force of 9,000 men had to be put to work clearing   53
the snow. Five locomotives strained futilely to drive a snowplow through thirty-foot drifts. Before half the winter was up, they had to admit defeat except in tunnels or in the deep cuts. Mr. Lewis continues:

> Tunnels were dug beneath forty-foot drifts, and for months, three thousand work-men lived curious mole-like lives, passing from work to living quarters in dim

---

[7]Oscar Lewis, *The Big Four* (New York: Alfred Knopf, 1938), P. 71. [Author's note]
[8]Edwin L. Sabin, *Building the Pacific Railway* (Philadelphia: J.B. Lippincott Co., 1919). [Author's note]
[9]The Big Four were Leland Stanford, Collis P. Huntington, Mark Hopkins, and Charles Crocker, the four partners who organized and directed the work of the Central Pacific. [Author's note]
[10]Lewis, *op. cit.*, pp. 72–73. [Author's note]

passages far beneath the snow's surface. This eerie existence was complicated by constant danger, for as snows accumulated on the upper ridges, avalanches grew frequent, their approach heralded only by a brief thunderous roar. A second later, a work crew, a bunkhouse, sometimes an entire camp, would go hurtling at a dizzy speed down miles of frozen canyons. Not until months later were the bodies recovered; sometimes groups were found with shovels or picks still clutched in their frozen hands.[11]

Oswald Garrison Villard, in his testimony to a House committee on Chinese exclusion, paid tribute to the heroism of the Chinese who worked for him under the same conditions on the Northwest Pacific line. He said: 54

> I want to remind you of the things that Chinese labor did for us in opening up the western portion of this country. I am a son of the man who drove the first transcontinental railroad across the American Northwest, the first rail link from Minnesota to Oregon and the waters of the Puget Sound. I was near him when he drove the last spike and paid an eloquent tribute to the men who had built that railroad by their manual labor, for there were no road-making machines in those days.
>
> He never forgot and never failed to praise the Chinese among them, of whom nearly 10,000 stormed the forest fastnesses, endured cold and heat and the risk of death at the hands of the hostile Indians to aid in the opening up of our great northwestern empire.
>
> I have a dispatch from the chief engineer of the Northwestern Pacific, telling how the Chinese laborers went out into eight feet of snow with the temperature far below zero to carry on the work when no American dared face the conditions.[12]

Winter had its hazards, but summer had its share too. Again, to quote from Oscar Lewis: 55

> Throughout the summer of 1866, "Crocker's pets," six thousand strong, swarmed over the upper canyon, pecking methodically at the broken rock of the cuts, trooping in long lines beneath their basket hats to pour wheelbarrow-loads of debris down the canyon-side, threading precarious paths with seventy pound kegs of black powder suspended from both ends of bamboo poles, refreshing themselves at intervals with sips of tea kept near at hand in whisky kegs emptied and abandoned by their white confreres. The Chinese were presently found to be adept at the backbreaking work of drilling and placing blasts, by then a major part of the work, for the upper ridges were scraped clear of soil by the winter deposits of ice.
>
> Track-layers followed close behind the graders, and locomotives pushed strings of flatcars loaded with construction iron, lumber, explosives, food, drink and more men to the rail head. Cape Horn, a sheer granite buttress, proved the most formidable obstacle of the year; its lower sides dropped away in a thousand-foot vertical cliff that offered no vestige of a foothold. The indomitable Chinese were lowered from above on ropes, and there suspended between sky and earth, chipped

---

[11]*Ibid.* [Author's note]
[12]Villard, O.G. "Justice for the Chinese," *Christian Century* Vol. 60 (May 26, 1943), pp. 633–634. [Author's note]

way with hammer and chisel to form the first precarious ledge which was then laboriously deepened to a shelf wide enough to permit the passage of cars. Three years later, when overland trains crept cautiously along this ledge, passengers gazed straight down from their windows into thin air.[13]

John Galloway, famous transportation engineer, in his book, *The First Transcontinental Railroad, Central Pacific and Union Pacific*, called the construction of the transcontinental railroad—1,800 miles across grassy plains and sagebrush desert, through the passes of the Rockies and High Sierras—without doubt the greatest engineering feat of the nineteenth century.   56

The majority of the workmen on the Central Pacific were Chinese, while on the Union Pacific the Irish predominated. So, in addition to the fierce race to add trackage to their own lines, there was an undercurrent spirit of competition between the Irish and the Chinese.   57

Some of this competition resulted in outright animosity, but it was a spur in their flanks, each side driving the other to outperform themselves.   58

One day, the Union Pacific men laid down six miles of track and boasted to the Central Pacific of their accomplishment. The Central Pacific answered with seven.   59

"No Chinaman is going to beat us," replied the Irish. Thus goaded, they laid down seven and a half miles of track and said they would lay eight if Crocker didn't call it quits.   60

Crocker pulled up his haughty frame and promised the Union Pacific ten miles. Durant, president of the Union Pacific, immediately put up $10,000 in wager that Crocker couldn't do it.   61

"Wait and see," smiled Crocker.   62

Crocker was a sly devil. He waited until the day before the last sixteen miles were to be laid. Then he assembled his men and his supplies and laid down the ten miles of track with 1,800 feet added for good measure. It was an achievement that has never been equaled nor approached even by modern methods in the United States.   63

Of the two portions of the railroad, there was no doubt that the Central Pacific portion was the more difficult. The Central was obliged to overcome 7,000 feet of mountain rise in 100 miles, whereas the Union Pacific had 500 miles in which to overcome a gradual rise of 5,000 feet and fifty miles more of a leeway in which to attain the summit of the Black Hills, 2,000 feet higher. This appeared slight compared with the rise of 2,000 feet in twenty miles accomplished by the Central Pacific. Editor Bowles of the *Springfield Republican* proclaimed that the building of the Union Pacific from Omaha to the Rocky Mountains was mere baby work in comparison.   64

---

[13]Lewis, *op. cit.*, pp. 74–75. [Author's note]

Chinese labor also built the Northwest Pacific Railroad, extending the 65
benefits of the transcontinental to the Northwest Territory. They were also
the main labor force of the Southern Pacific, which began pushing its tributaries
southward and westward.

When work on the railroads slackened, some Chinese turned to manu- 66
facturing, as goods imported from the East were expensive. One day, a farmer
sent into town for some temporary farm hands to pick his tomato crop. Much
of the crop was already overripe, but in farming as with the railroads, labor
was scarce and temperamental. When workers could be found, they were rough-
necks who bruised the fruit and caused heavy losses.

When told that he should try the Chinese, the farmer asked for a group 67
of workers who were told to report in the morning. Even before the sun came
up, the Chinese were at the farm ready for work. Diligently and quietly, they
plucked the ripe tomatoes from the stalks, laying them gently in the baskets.
At sundown, the baskets were arranged and piled neatly in rows and the workers
faded away. Before dawn the next day, the workers were back in the fields.

By word of mouth the news spread, and the Chinese were in great demand 68
as agricultural workers. According to Carey McWilliams, Chinese made up one-
tenth of the farm labor supply in 1870. In 1880, they constituted one-third. By
1884, half of the farm workers in California were Chinese.[14]

Much of the city of San Francisco today stands on man-made land. When 69
the first white settlers saw her, she was a half-submerged peninsula of marsh-
land, swamps, lagoons, and rocky hills covered with sagebrush. Five million
acres of lush garden and farm land at the mouths of the Sacramento and San
Joaquin rivers were reclaimed by hardy Chinese laborers who performed their
tasks without benefit of drainage machinery, cranes, bulldozers, or trucks when
malaria took a heavy toll of white laborers.[15]

Early historians of California are unanimous in their opinions about the 70
contributions rendered by the pioneer Chinese. Theirs were the muscles that
opened up the bowels of the earth and wrested from her the riches of gold to
add to the wealth of the nation. They tilled the land and harvested the fruit so
that the vast hordes pouring into the West to populate and tame the wilderness
would not hunger. They added dignity and stability, order and tranquility to
a frontier land where laws were yet to be made. They were a colorful part of
the scenery, their dress and their ways so different from what the Occident
was accustomed to seeing. Their patronage and their lion's share of the taxes
kept many a county from bankruptcy. Their feats and heroism in the construc-

---

[14]Carey McWilliams, *California, the Great Exception* (New York: Current Books, Inc., 1949), p. 152.
[Author's note]
[15]Testimony of George D. Roberts, President of the Tideland Reclamation Co., 1877 Report, p.
436. [Author's note]

tion of the transcontinental railroads and tributaries are recorded in history. Their industry and physical stamina salvaged for the West millions of acres of the richest farm lands and urban real estate.

They could not have given more! ◆   71

◆ Responding

1. Discuss the lure that attracted early Chinese immigrants to America. Why were so many anxious to come to San Francisco in spite of the dangers involved in leaving China?

2. Fatt Hing's experience is presented as typical of that of many Chinese immigrants. Outline the main events that characterized his life as an immigrant.

3. Chairman Wong says, "One valuable lesson we have learned and which you will soon appreciate is that we must stick together and help one another, even though we are not kin." Write an essay explaining the ways in which early Chinese immigrants helped later immigrants.

4. According to the reading, what aspects of Chinese culture and character helped the immigrants become successful in America? After isolating those characteristics, list the values that seemed to be important in Chinese culture. Compare these values to your own. Are these values important to you? To contemporary American society?

FROM THE GOLD MOUNTAIN POEMS

The Gold Mountain poems are anonymous works written by some of the earliest Chinese immigrants to the United States. It was not until several generations later that the poems were edited by Marlon K. Hom and published by the University of California Press.

These three poems express the discontentment the immigrants felt with their homeland as well as the disillusionment and bitter reality they faced when arriving in America.

◆ IMMIGRATION BLUES ◆

In search of a pin-head gain,
I was idle in an impoverished village.
I've risked a perilous journey to come to the Flowery
    Flag Nation.
Immigration officers interrogated me:
And, just for a slight lapse of memory,
I am deported, and imprisoned in this barren
    mountain.
A brave man cannot use his might here,
And he can't take one step beyond the confines. ◆

At home I was in poverty,
    constantly worried about firewood and rice.
I borrowed money
    to come to Gold Mountain.
Immigration officers cross-examined me;
    no way could I get through.
Deported to this island,
    like a convicted criminal.
Here—
Mournful sighs fill the gloomy room.
A nation weak; her people often humiliated
Like animals, tortured and destroyed at others'
    whim. ◆

So, liberty is your national principle;
Why do you practice autocracy?
You don't uphold justice, you Americans,
You detain me in prison, guard me closely.
Your officials are wolves and tigers,
All ruthless, all wanting to bite me.
An innocent man implicated, such an injustice!
When can I get out of this prison and free
    my mind? ◆

◆ Responding

1. Describe the attitude of the speaker in any of the poems. How does he feel
   about the United States government?

2. We don't know why the speaker in these poems is imprisoned. Write your
   own story about the circumstances that might have caused him to be "deported to this island, like a convicted criminal."

3. Write a letter from a government official to a San Francisco newspaper
   justifying the speaker's imprisonment. Alternatively, write an editorial for a
   San Francisco newspaper condemning the treatment of prisoners held on
   Angel Island.

4. Unlike most of the poetry in this book, these poems were not written by
   professional poets who wanted to publish their work, but by immigrants
   who used poetry as a way of understanding their experiences and expressing
   their feelings. Write a poem about some experience that affected you strongly,
   or write a journal entry discussing the benefits of writing as an emotional
   outlet.

SUI SIN FAR

*Sui Sin Far is a pseudonym assumed by the writer Edith Maude Eaton.
Born in 1867, Edith Eaton was the eldest of fourteen children of a Chinese
mother and an English father. Her earliest jobs included work in stenography
and in the advertising department of a railroad company. Most of her stories
were published in such magazines as* The Overland Monthly, Century,
and Good Housekeeping. *She died in 1909.*

*The stories of Sui Sin Far are among the first works published by an
Asian-American author. "In the Land of the Free," which explores the
consequences of the immigration process for one family, also depicts the family's
vulnerability to exploitation by unscrupulous people.*

◆ IN THE LAND OF THE FREE ◆

I

"See, Little One—the hills in the morning sun. There is thy home for years   1
to come. It is very beautiful and thou wilt be very happy there."

The Little One looked up into his mother's face in perfect faith. He was   2
engaged in the pleasant occupation of sucking a sweetmeat; but that did not
prevent him from gurgling responsively.

"Yes, my olive bud; there is where thy father is making a fortune for thee.   3
Thy father! Oh, wilt thou not be glad to behold his dear face. 'Twas for thee
I left him."

The Little One ducked his chin sympathetically against his mother's knee.   4
She lifted him on to her lap. He was two years old, a round, dimple-cheeked
boy with bright brown eyes and a sturdy little frame.

"Ah! Ah! Ah! Ooh! Ooh! Ooh!" puffed he, mocking a tugboat steaming   5
by.

San Francisco's waterfront was lined with ships and steamers, while other   6
craft, large and small, including a couple of white transports from the Philippines, lay at anchor here and there off shore. It was some time before the *Eastern
Queen* could get docked, and even after that was accomplished, a lone Chinaman
who had been waiting on the wharf for an hour was detained that much longer
by men with the initials U.S.C. on their caps, before he could board the steamer
and welcome his wife and child.

"This is thy son," announced the happy Lae Choo.   7

Hom Hing lifted the child, felt of his little body and limbs, gazed into   8
his face with proud and joyous eyes; then turned inquiringly to a customs officer
at his elbow.

"That's a fine boy you have there," said the man. "Where was he born?" 9

"In China," answered Hom Hing, swinging the Little One on his right 10
shoulder, preparatory to leading his wife off the steamer.

"Ever been to America before?" 11

"No, not he," answered the father with a happy laugh. 12

The customs officer beckoned to another. 13

"This little fellow," said he, "is visiting America for the first time." 14

The other customs officer stroked his chin reflectively. 15

"Good day," said Hom Hing. 16

"Wait!" commanded one of the officers. "You cannot go just yet." 17

"What more now?" asked Hom Hing. 18

"I'm afraid," said the customs officer, "that we cannot allow the boy to 19
go ashore. There is nothing in the papers that you have shown us—your wife's
papers and your own—having any bearing upon the child."

"There was no child when the papers were made out," returned Hom 20
Hing. He spoke calmly; but there was apprehension in his eyes and in his
tightening grip on his son.

"What is it? What is it?" quavered Lae Choo, who understood a little 21
English.

The second customs officer regarded her pityingly. 22

"I don't like this part of the business," he muttered. 23

The first officer turned to Hom Hing and in an official tone of voice, said: 24

"Seeing that the boy has no certificate entitling him to admission to this 25
country you will have to leave him with us."

"Leave my boy!" exclaimed Hom Hing. 26

"Yes; he will be well taken care of, and just as soon as we can hear from 27
Washington he will be handed over to you."

"But," protested Hom Hing, "he is my son." 28

"We have no proof," answered the man with a shrug of his shoulders; 29
"and even if so we cannot let him pass without orders from the Government."

"He is my son," reiterated Hom Hing, slowly and solemnly. "I am a 30
Chinese merchant and have been in business in San Francisco for many years.
When my wife told to me one morning that she dreamed of a green tree with
spreading branches and one beautiful red flower growing thereon, I answered
her that I wished my son to be born in our country, and for her to prepare to
go to China. My wife complied with my wish. After my son was born my
mother fell sick and my wife nursed and cared for her; then my father, too,
fell sick, and my wife also nursed and cared for him. For twenty moons my
wife care for and nurse the old people, and when they did they bless her and
my son, and I send for her to return to me. I had no fear of trouble. I was a
Chinese merchant and my son was my son."

"Very good, Hom Hing," replied the first officer. "Nevertheless, we take 31
your son."

"No, you not take him; he my son too." 32

It was Lae Choo. Snatching the child from his father's arms she held and 33
covered him with her own.

The officers conferred together for a few moments; then one drew Hom 34
Hing aside and spoke in his ear.

Resignedly Hom Hing bowed his head, then approached his wife. " 'Tis 35
the law," said he, speaking in Chinese, "and 'twill be but for a little while—
until tomorrow's sun arises."

"You, too," reproached Lae Choo in a voice eloquent with pain. But 36
accustomed to obedience she yielded the boy to her husband, who in turn
delivered him to the first officer. The Little One protested lustily against the
transfer; but his mother covered her face with her sleeve and his father silently
led her away. Thus was the law of the land complied with.

II

Day was breaking. Lae Choo, who had been awake all night, dressed herself, 37
then awoke her husband.

" 'Tis the morn," she cried. "Go, bring our son." 38

The man rubbed his eyes and arose upon his elbow so that he could see 39
out of the window. A pale star was visible in the sky. The petals of a lily in a
bowl on the windowsill were unfurled.

" 'Tis not yet time," said he, laying his head down again. 40

"Not yet time. Ah, all the time that I lived before yesterday is not so 41
much as the time that has been since my Little One was taken from me."

The mother threw herself down beside the bed and covered her face. 42

Hom Hing turned on the light, and touching his wife's bowed head with 43
a sympathetic hand inquired if she had slept.

"Slept!" she echoed, weepingly. "Ah, how could I close my eyes with 44
my arms empty of the little body that has filled them every night for more than
twenty moons! You do not know—man—what it is to miss the feel of the little
fingers and the little toes and the soft round limbs of your little one. Even in
the darkness his darling eyes used to shine up to mine, and often have I fallen
into slumber with his pretty babble at my ear. And now, I see him not; I touch
him not; I hear him not. My baby, my little fat one!"

"Now! Now! Now!" consoled Hom Hing, patting his wife's shoulder 45
reassuringly; "there is no need to grieve so; he will soon gladden you again.
There cannot be any law that would keep a child from its mother!"

Lae Choo dried her tears. 46

"You are right, my husband," she meekly murmured. She arose and 47
stepped about the apartment, setting things to rights. The box of presents
she had brought for her California friends had been opened the evening before;
and silks, embroideries, carved ivories, ornamental laccquer-ware, brasses,
camphorwood boxes, fans, and chinaware were scattered around in confused heaps. In the midst of unpacking the thought of her child in the hands

of strangers had overpowered her, and she had left everything to crawl into bed and weep.

Having arranged her gifts in order she stepped out on to the deep balcony. 48

The star had faded from view and there were bright streaks in the western 49 sky. Lae Choo looked down the street and around. Beneath the flat occupied by her and her husband were quarters for a number of bachelor Chinamen, and she could hear them from where she stood, taking their early morning breakfast. Below their dining-room was her husband's grocery store. Across the way was a large restaurant. Last night it had been resplendent with gay colored lanterns and the sound of music. The rejoicings over "the completion of the moon," by Quong Sum's firstborn, had been long and loud, and had caused her to tie a handkerchief over her ears. She, a bereaved mother, had it not in her heart to rejoice with other parents. This morning the place was more in accord with her mood. It was still and quiet. The revellers had dispersed or were asleep.

A roly-poly woman in black sateen, with long pendant earrings in her 50 ears, looked up from the street below and waved her a smiling greeting. It was her old neighbor, Kuie Hoe, the wife of the gold embosser, Mark Sing. With her was a little boy in yellow jacket and lavender pantaloons. Lae Choo remembered him as a baby. She used to like to play with him in those days when she had no child of her own. What a long time ago that seemed! She caught her breath in a sigh, and laughed instead.

"Why are you so merry?" called her husband from within. 51

"Because my Little One is coming home," answered Lae Choo. "I am a 52 happy mother—a happy mother."

She pattered into the room with a smile on her face. 53

The noon hour had arrived. The rice was steaming in the bowls and a fragrant 54 dish of chicken and bamboo shoots was awaiting Hom Hing. Not for one moment had Lae Choo paused to rest during the morning hours; her activity had been ceaseless. Every now and again, however, she had raised her eyes to the gilded clock on the curiously carved mantelpiece. Once, she had exclaimed:

"Why so long, oh! why so long?" Then, apostrophizing herself: "Lae 55 Choo, be happy. The Little One is coming! The Little One is coming!" Several times she burst into tears, and several times she laughed aloud.

Hom Hing entered the room; his arms hung down by his side. 56

"The Little One!" shrieked Lae Choo. 57

"They bid me call tomorrow." 58

With a moan the mother sank to the floor. 59

The noon hour passed. The dinner remained on the table. 60

III

The winter rains were over: the spring had come to California, flushing the 61 hills with green and causing an ever-changing pageant of flowers to pass over them. But there was no spring in Lae Choo's heart, for the Little One remained away from her arms. He was being kept in a mission. White women were caring for him, and though for one full moon he had pined for his mother and refused to be comforted he was now apparently happy and contented. Five moons or five months had gone by since the day he had passed with Lae Choo through the Golden Gate; but the great Government at Washington still delayed sending the answer which would return him to his parents.

Hom Hing was disconsolately rolling up and down the balls in his abacus box when a keen-faced young man stepped into his store. 62

"What news?" asked the Chinese merchant. 63

"This!" The young man brought forth a typewritten letter. Hom Hing read the words: 64

"Re Chinese child, alleged to be the son of Hom Hing, Chinese merchant, doing business at 425 Clay street, San Francisco. 65

"Same will have attention as soon as possible." 66

Hom Hing returned the letter, and without a word continued his manipulation of the counting machine. 67

"Have you anything to say?" asked the young man. 68

"Nothing. They have sent the same letter fifteen times before. Have you not yourself showed it to me?" 69

"True!" The young man eyed the Chinese merchant furtively. He had a proposition to make and was pondering whether or not the time was opportune. 70

"How is your wife?" he inquired solicitously—and diplomatically. 71

Hom Hing shook his head mournfully. 72

"She seems less every day," he replied. "Her food she takes only when I bid her and her tears fall continually. She finds no pleasure in dress or flowers and cares not to see her friends. Her eyes stare all night. I think before another moon she will pass into the land of spirits." 73

"No!" exclaimed the young man, genuinely startled. 74

"If the boy not come home I lose my wife sure," continued Hom Hing with bitter sadness. 75

"It's not right," cried the young man indignantly. Then he made his proposition. 76

The Chinese father's eyes brightened exceedingly. 77

"Will I like you to go to Washington and make them give you the paper to restore my son?" cried he. "How can you ask when you know my heart's desire?" 78

"Then," said the young fellow, "I will start next week. I am anxious to see this thing through if only for the sake of your wife's peace of mind." 79

"I will call her. To hear what you think to do will make her glad," said Hom Hing. 80

He called a message to Lae Choo upstairs through a tube in the wall. 81

In a few moments she appeared, listless, wan, and hollow-eyed; but when 82 her husband told her the young lawyer's suggestion she became electrified; her form straightened, her eyes glistened; the color flushed to her cheeks.

"Oh," she cried, turning to James Clancy. "You are a hundred man good!" 83

The young man felt somewhat embarrassed; his eyes shifted a little under 84
the intense gaze of the Chinese mother.

"Well, we must get your boy for you," he responded. "Of course"— 85
turning to Hom Hing—"it will cost a little money. You can't get fellows to hurry the Government for you without gold in your pocket."

Hom Hing stared blankly for a moment. Then: "How much do you want, 86
Mr. Clancy?" he asked quietly.

"Well, I will need at least five hundred to start with." 87

Hom Hing cleared his throat. 88

"I think I told to you the time I last paid you for writing letters for me 89
and seeing the Custom boss here that nearly all I had was gone!"

"Oh, well then we won't talk about it, old fellow. It won't harm the boy 90
to stay where he is, and your wife may get over it all right."

"What that you say?" quavered Lae Choo. 91

James Clancy looked out of the window. 92

"He says," explained Hom Hing in English, "that to get our boy we have 93
to have much money."

"Money! Oh, yes." 94

Lae Choo nodded her head. 95

"I have not got the money to give him." 96

For a moment Lae Choo gazed wonderingly from one face to the other; 97
then, comprehension dawning upon her, with swift anger, pointing to the lawyer, she cried: "You not one hundred man good; you just common white man."

"Yes, ma'am," returned James Clancy, bowing and smiling ironically. 98

Hom Hing pushed his wife behind him and addressed the lawyer again: 99
"I might try," said he, "to raise something; but five hundred—it is not possible."

"What about four?" 100

"I tell you I have next to nothing left and my friends are not rich." 101

"Very well!" 102

The lawyer moved leisurely toward the door, pausing on its threshold to 103
light a cigarette.

"Stop, white man; white man, stop!" 104

Lae Choo, panting and terrified, had started forward and now stood beside 105
him, clutching his sleeve excitedly.

"You say you can go to get paper to bring my Little One to me if Hom 106
Hing give you five hundred dollars?"

The lawyer nodded carelessly; his eyes were intent upon the cigarette 107
which would not take the fire from the match.

"Then you go get paper. If Hom Hing not can give you five hundred 108
dollars—I give you perhaps what more that much."

She slipped a heavy gold bracelet from her wrist and held it out to the 109
man. Mechanically he took it.

"I go get more!" 110

She scurried away, disappearing behind the door through which she had 111
come.

"Oh, look here, I can't accept this," said James Clancy, walking back to 112
Hom Hing and laying down the bracelet before him.

"It's all right," said Hom Hing, seriously, "pure China gold. My wife's 113
parent give it to her when we married."

"But I can't take it anyway," protested the young man. 114

"It is all same as money. And you want money to go to Washington," 115
replied Hom Hing in a matter-of-fact manner.

"See, my jade earrings—my gold buttons—my hairpins—my comb of 116
pearl and my rings—one, two, three, four, five rings; very good—very good—
all same much money. I give them all to you. You take and bring me paper for
my Little One."

Lae Choo piled up her jewels before the lawyer. 117

Hom Hing laid a restraining hand upon her shoulder. "Not all, my wife," 118
he said in Chinese. He selected a ring—his gift to Lae Choo when she dreamed
of the tree with the red flower. The rest of the jewels he pushed toward the
white man.

"Take them and sell them," said he. "They will pay your fare to Wash- 119
ington and bring you back with the paper."

For one moment James Clancy hesitated. He was not a sentimental man; 120
but something within him arose against accepting such payment for his services.

"They are good, good," pleadingly asserted Lae Choo, seeing his hesi- 121
tation.

Whereupon he seized the jewels, thrust them into his coat pocket, and 122
walked rapidly away from the store.

IV

Lae Choo followed after the missionary woman through the mission nursery 123
school. Her heart was beating so high with happiness that she could scarcely
breathe. The paper had come at last—the precious paper which gave Hom Hing
and his wife the right to the possession of their own child. It was ten months
now since he had been taken from them—ten months since the sun had ceased
to shine for Lae Choo.

The room was filled with children—most of them wee tots, but none so 124
wee as her own. The mission woman talked as she walked. She told Lae Choo
that little Kim, as he had been named by the school, was the pet of the place,
and that his little tricks and ways amused and delighted every one. He had
been rather difficult to manage at first and had cried much for his mother; "but

children so soon forget, and after a month he seemed quite at home and played around as bright and happy as a bird."

"Yes," responded Lae Choo. "Oh, yes, yes!"   125

But she did not hear what was said to her. She was walking in a maze of   126 anticipatory joy.

"Wait here, please, " said the mission woman, placing Lae Choo in a chair.   127 "The very youngest ones are having their breakfast."

She withdrew for a moment—it seemed like an hour to the mother—then   128 she reappeared leading by the hand a little boy dressed in blue cotton overalls and white-soled shoes. The little boy's face was round and dimpled and his eyes were very bright.

"Little One, ah, my Little One!" cried Lae Choo.   129

She fell on her knees and stretched her hungry arms toward her son.   130

But the Little One shrunk from her and tried to hide himself in the folds   131 of the white woman's skirt.

"Go 'way, go 'way!" he bade his mother.◆

◆ Responding

1. Explain the irony of the title.

2. Analyze the motivation and behavior of James Clancy. Do you think he is sincerely trying to help Hom Hing? He hesitates before taking the jewels in payment for his services. What do you think is going through his mind at that moment? Why does he accept them as payment? What do you think he should have done?

3. In what ways might the story represent the fears of loss of culture and identity that plague many new immigrants to the United States?

4. Although the language and writing style of this story are dated, the theme of being caught in the trap of official bureaucracy is current. Rewrite the story with a contemporary setting. Alternatively, write about a time when you or someone you know had to fight what seemed to be endless red tape.

PARDEE LOWE

Pardee Lowe was born in California in 1905 to parents who had emigrated from south China. (They named their son Pardee after the governor of California, George Pardee.) He earned his bachelor's degree from Stanford University and his master's in business from Harvard University. During the 1930s he served as the international secretariat of the Institute for Pacific Relations, a cultural and civic organization. He later assisted in the Chinese War Relief Organization, which supplied food and medicine to Chinese war refugees. He began publishing articles on these efforts in The Yale Review *and other journals during the 1940s.*

In his book Father and Glorious Descendant, *Pardee Lowe uses his father's biography as the focal point from which to examine his own family's and other immigrants' experiences in the United States. The book recounts the early days in San Francisco's Chinatown, the effects of the Great Earthquake of 1906, and the family's resettlement in the Stockton area. Throughout the text Lowe expresses both a faith in the potential for success in the new country and a respect for the ritual and customs that comprise the family's cultural heritage.*

The selection that follows, a chapter from Father and Glorious Descendant, *shows the ways in which the American dream, held out to many immigrants, was often shattered by prejudice.*

◆ FATHER CURES A PRESIDENTIAL FEVER ◆

How I came to be infected with Presidentitis even now I find somewhat difficult to explain. That it was not congenital was amply demonstrated by Father's matter-of-fact superiority over such divine foolishness. And Mother, bless her realistic Chinese soul, never affected awareness of such mundane matters until the political clubs of our neighborhood (we lived in the toughest one in East Belleville) celebrated under her very nose with torchlight parades, drunken sprees, black eyes and cracked skulls the glorious victories of their Men of the People. Whenever this happened she would exclaim, "My, my, what queer people the Americans are!"

The first time Father discovered how long the first-born man child of his household had been exposed to the ravages of this dread disease, he was horrified. "Unbelievable!" he stormed. But Mother, who had a strong will of her own, flew right back at him. And when she cried aloud, with Heaven as her witness, that she did not know how I caught it or how she could have prevented it, Father recognized the justice of her remarks. She couldn't. Kwong Chong, our own neighborhood dry-goods store, household duties, and two new babies kept Mother so harassed that she had no time to chase us about the streets or down the back alleys. Later, to still her flow of tears, Father even grudgingly admitted his full responsibility. By moving our family to an American neighborhood, according to Mother, he had needlessly exposed us all to the malady.

That this was the source of the trouble, probably no one knew better than 3
Father. When the 1906 San Francisco earthquake and fire consumed all his worldly goods and forced him to flee Chinatown with his wife, two babies in arms, and a motley feudal retinue of kinsmen, relatives, and garment-sewing employees, he merely considered it more or less a blessing in disguise. From the ashes of this catastrophe, which represented for Mother the end of her Chinatownian world, Father's thoughts and plans for the future soared like a phoenix.

At long last the visions and dreams for his offspring, present and potential, 4
would be realized. His family would rub shoulders with Americans. They would become good American citizens albeit remaining Chinese. They would inhabit a hyphenated world. By some formula, which he never was able to explain, they would select only the finest attributes of each contributory culture. They would reflect everlasting credit on him and on the name of Lowe.

(Even then, Father's faith passed all human understanding. He expected 5
us somehow to muddle through. We did—but in a manner totally unexpected.)

From Father's point of view, we children were to be raised at home 6
according to the old and strict Chinese ideal. But in that ever-widening circle of American neighborhood life beyond the narrow confines of our home, Father had no control. A daily commuter to his shop in San Francisco's Chinatown, an hour's ride away by steam train and ferry, he was never fully apprised of our actions until too late.

He was ignorant, for instance, of what transpired in the large wooden 7
public school situated some three short blocks from our home. He was confident we were in good hands. If he had only known what was awaiting his son there, he might not have been so eager to have me acquire an American schooling.

When at the age of five I entered the portals of this mid-Victorian archi- 8
tectural firetrap, surrounded by its iron-spiked fence and tall trees, for the first time, I recognized it as an international institution in which I was free to indulge my own most un-Chinese inclinations—and, unintentionally to be sure, to undermine Father's high hopes.

I can still vividly remember the strange excitement of the first morning 9
roll call, which was to be repeated daily for many years to come. Clumsily, the teacher pronounced our names. As we rose, she checked our nationality.

"Louisa Fleishhacker—*Austrian*." She underlined the word *Austrian*. "Elsie 10
Forsythe—*English*. Penelope Lincoln—*American Negro*. Yuri Matsuyama—*Japanese*. Nancy Mullins—*Irish*. Maria Pucinelli—*Italian*. Stella Saceanu—*Rumanian*. Anna Zorich—*Serbian*." Finishing with the girls, she turned the page. "Michael Castro—*Portuguese*. Heinz Creyer—*German*. Thorvald Ericson—*Swedish*. Philippe Etienne—*French*. Nicholas Katanov—*Russian*. Pardee Lowe—*Chinese*. Robert MacPherson—*Scotch*. And Francisco Trujillo—*Mexican*."

There we stood. In the company of fifteen other beginners, no two in the 11 entire group of the same nationality, I was embarking upon a new and glorious adventure, the educational melting pot, which was to make every one of us, beyond peradventure, an American.

It pleased Father no end to know that I liked to go to American school. 12 He informed Mother proudly that it denoted a scholarly spirit well-becoming a Chinese. If he had only glimpsed what lay back of my mind as I saw him gaily off on the morning seven-forty commuters' train he might have derived much less satisfaction.

No sooner was Father's back turned than I would dash madly to the 13 streetcar line. On my way I would stop and pick a bunch of posies from our neighbors' back yards, praying fervently that I would be the only pupil waiting for Miss McIntyre, our teacher. Disappointment invariably awaited me, for I was not alone. Anna, Nancy, Penelope, and Robert, sharing exactly the same sentiments, always managed to get there ahead of me.

As soon as we spotted Miss McIntyre's tall figure alighting from the car, 14 we sprang forward. With a warm smile of affection which enfolded us all, she allowed us to grab her hands, snatch her books from her arms and literally drag her from the rear step of the car to the front steps of the school, happily protesting every step of the way: "Now, children! . . . Now *children!*"

Coming mainly from immigrant homes where parents were too preoc- 15 cupied with earning a living to devote much time to their children, we transferred our youthful affections to this one person who had both the time and the disposition to mother us. We showered upon our white-haired teacher the blind, wholehearted loyalty of the young. Our studies we readily absorbed, not because we particularly liked them so much as because it was "she" who taught us. Thus, with the three R's, games, stories, a weekly bath which she personally administered in the school's bathroom—two pupils at a time—and her love, she whom we staunchly enshrined in our hearts laid the rudimentary but firm foundation of our personal brand of American culture.

Then, one day it happened. Miss McIntyre, herself the daughter of an 16 Irish immigrant who had come to California during the Gold Rush, read to us with deep emotion the life of George Washington. The virtues displayed by the Father of Our Country, particularly when confessing his act of chopping down the cherry tree, were, she led us to believe, the very ones which would, if faithfully practiced, win us equal fame. Concluding the narrative, she looked in turn at Anna, Penelope, and Robert. She was challenging us to higher things. As her eyes caught mine, she added with conviction, "And every single one of you can be President of the United States someday!"

I shall never forget that occasion. To be President in our minds was like 17 being God, with the difference that everybody knew what the President[1] looked like. His pictures were in every newspaper. Even in the funny sheets, I some-

---

[1]President Theodore Roosevelt

times saw him. Big as life, with his grinning mouthful of teeth, eyeglasses gleaming, and his mustache bristling in the breeze of the political opposition— he looked the spitting image of Father. The only difference I could detect was that Father preferred the bamboo duster to the "Big Stick," and "*Jun Ho Ah!*" was as near as he ever came to "Bully!"

Everything I did from this moment on served only to strengthen the grandiose dream whose chief interlocking threads included myself, Father, and the Presidency. Much to the disgust of my more active playmates and the envy of my bookworm friends, I became a walking encyclopedia of American history. I could repeat the full names and dates of every President of these United States. And I knew the vivid, gory details, authentic and apocryphal, of every important military engagement in which Americans took part—and always victoriously. 18

I hounded the settlement librarian for books, and more books. Like one famished, I devoured all of James Fenimore Cooper's novels. Lodge and Roosevelt's *Hero Tales from American History* fascinated me. As I read Abbot's *The Story of Our Navy* and Johnston's *Famous Scouts, Including Trappers, Pioneers and Soldiers of the Frontier*, my sense of patriotism quickened. So stirred was I by Tomlinson's narrative that in my childish imagination I followed George Washington as a young scout, or marched resolutely forward to engage the Iroquois and Red Coats. Of all the books, however, Coffin's *Boys of '76* was my favorite. And many were the evenings in which I descended from the New Hampshire hills with sixteen-year-old Elijah Favor to fight at Lexington and Concord and finally to share the fruits of Revolutionary victory at Yorktown. 19

However, by the time I could recite with relish and gusto Scott's lines:— 20

> "Breathes there the man, with soul so dead,
> Who never to himself hath said,
> This is my own, my native land! . . ."

the President's picture had changed. In the course of the years, he had become huge, the size of a bear, but he still wore a mustache. He was less like Father now. And while I found it difficult to imagine myself becoming as stout, I felt that even flabby avoirdupois, if associated with the Presidency, had its compensations. No matter what his shape, I told myself, everybody still loved and worshiped the President of the United States.

Of this deadly and insidious fever that racked my chubby frame, Father was totally ignorant. Nor would he have ever divined my secret if it had not been for our journey to the Mother Lode country. 21

It was our first long overnight trip away from home together. The train ride, needless to say, was nothing short of glorious. For two whole days I had all to myself a father whom I seldom saw, but to whom I was thoroughly devoted. Besides, a city boy, I had never seen mountains so tall or sights so strange and fleeting. But the most enjoyable part of all was to bounce on the red-plush train seats and stop the vendor whenever he passed by with his hamper filled with peanuts, candies, and soda pop. 22

After a full day's ride, we arrived at our destination, a small silver-mining 23 town in the Sierra Nevada. At the station platform, Father and I were met by a roly-poly Westerner dressed in baggy clothes, riding boots, and a huge sombrero and mouthing ominously an equally formidable black cigar. After "How-de-doing" us, the stranger offered Father a cigar. A "cheroot" I think he called it. Then followed a ritual that filled me with amazement.

While Mr. Brown sized up Father skeptically, Father planted himself 24 firmly on both feet, rolled the unlighted cigar in his hands, stroked it gently, and drew it slowly beneath his nose. With a deep sign of satisfaction, he inhaled deeply.

"Havana Perfecto?" inquired Father, more as a statement of fact than a 25 question.

"Splendid!" assented Mr. Brown with a vigorous nod. Smiling broadly 26 for the first time, he slapped Father approvingly on the back and swept me up into his arms. As we drove majestically down the dusty street in his creaky cart, our now genial host vouchsafed that Father was one of the few "damned furriners" and certainly the first "Chinaman" to pass this unusual inspection.

By the way that Father puffed at his cigar and blew magnificent smoke 27 rings, I could see that he was pleased with Mr. Brown's compliment. But never a word did he mention about his being the proprietor of Sun Loy, the largest tobacco shop in Chinatown. Since he didn't, neither did I.

Arriving at a large two-story hotel, resembling in size, shape, and color 28 an old Southern mansion, Mr. Brown, whom we now knew to be the proprietor, roared from his sagging wagon seat: "Hi there, folks! I've picked up my Chinamen!"

Out trooped the few American residents of the hotel, glad to witness 29 anything that would break the monotony of a long hot summer's day, followed by six white-clad Chinese domestics who greeted us with an explosion of the Fragrant Mountain dialect. *"Ah Kung Ah!"* (Respected Great-Uncle!) "We hope all is well with you!"

It gave me a great thrill to see everybody, even the Americans, so def- 30 erential to Father. There was something about him that commanded universal respect. Chinese in Western clothes, especially of the latest cut, were a decided rarity in those days. And Father in his first suit of tailor-mades from a nobby American clothier looked simply grand. Tall, well-built, and sporting a bushy mustache, he looked every inch a distinguished personage. I could well understand why his American business associates persisted in nicknaming him "The Duke."

Mr. Brown, having already been informed of the purpose of our visit, 31 drew quietly aside. So did the Americans, no longer interested in a group of jabbering, gesticulating Orientals. This gave a few of my kinsmen an opportunity to converse with me in our dialect, which I understood, but, much to their chagrin, could not speak. Shocked that a Chinese boy should be ignorant of his own dialect, the eldest exclaimed, *"Chow Mah!"* (Positively disgraceful!) The way he said it made me more than a little ashamed of myself.

However, Father cut short my uncomfortable moment by introducing me 32 to the object of our visit. "This—" indicating a short, slender chap who appeared exceedingly glum—"is your Fourth Paternal Uncle, Precious Fortune."

Fourth Uncle, despite his title, was only a distant kinsman and, from his 33 point of view, had every reason for sulkiness. Just as he had conveniently forgotten about his grieving mother and childless wife in China for the pleasures of Chinatown's gambling tables, Father appeared—and Fourth Uncle didn't like it one bit. Father was the personification of outraged Chinese family conscience on the warpath. To him, in place of his own father, Fourth Uncle had to account for his glaring lapses in filial piety. He had to explain, for example, why he had not written them in three years; why he never sent them money; and, worst of all, why he persisted in leaving his aging mother grandchildless.

As the Clan's Senior Elder Uncle, Father took his Greater Family re- 34 sponsibilities very seriously. All through dinner, he informed Mr. Brown spiritedly that Fourth Uncle would have to leave. At first, Mr. Brown replied that he hated to part with an excellent cook, but when we came to dessert he finally agreed that in view of Fourth Uncle's wicked profligacy, it appeared the wisest course.

Having disposed of the fried chicken, apple pie, and Fourth Uncle so 35 satisfactorily, Mr. Brown next turned to me. "Son," he inquired, "what are you studying to become? Would you like to stay with me and be my cook, taking your uncle's place?"

The last question passed me by completely; I answered the first one. "I 36 want to be President," I said.

A sharp silence smote the mellow dining room. Now the secret was out. 37 I was amazed at my own stupidity. Happily absorbed with my second helping of apple pie and fresh rich country milk, I had recklessly given vent to my Presidential aspirations. Now what would Father say?

Father, uncertain of the exact nature of the enchantment that had suddenly 38 ensnared his son, looked at me queerly as though he doubted his ears. Mr. Brown laughed long and loud with a strange catch in his voice. "Sure, son, that's right," he added. "Study hard and you'll be President someday."

I wondered then why Mr. Brown's laughter sounded so odd, but I never 39 associated this with pity until much, much later. By then, however, I had been thoroughly cured by Father.

Homeward bound Father said precious little. Not even to Fourth Uncle, 40 still glum, whom we brought home with us to start life anew. Father's silence was disturbing and he attempted to cloak it, and his thoughts, with liberal benefactions. When we reached Belleville Junction I had no further use for the newspaper vendor and his basket of allurements—and Father no use for silence. In his own mind he had worked out a series of special therapeutic treatments to counteract my desperate malady, Presidentitis.

A few days after our return from the Sierra Nevada, Father said gently, "Glo- 41 rious Descendant, how would you like to go to a private boarding school in China?"

I shuddered at the full significance of his suggestion. To be separated 42
from America and from my family? And never to see them again for years and
years? "No! No!" I wailed. "I don't want to go!" Rejecting the idea with all
the vehemence at my command, I added, "I want to stay in America!"

Father dwelt patiently on all the advantages of such a schooling but to no 43
avail. Nothing he said moved me. What about my future, inquired Father,
didn't I care? Of course, I replied, but I didn't want to be a mandarin or a
Chinese merchant prince at such a terrific sacrifice. Father's questions became
more penetrating; they stripped the future of everything but realities. Could I,
as a Chinese, ever hope to find a good job in American society? At this, I
laughed. Miss McIntyre, I told him, had plainly said that I could even be
President.

In these sessions, I revealed to Father the seriousness of my infection. I 44
opened the gates to that part of my youthful life he had never known. I told
him in no uncertain terms that I loved America, particularly East Belleville,
which I considered to be the grandest place in all the world. Besides, I continued,
why would I wish to go to China? All the things I had heard from our kinsfolk
about the old country were bad, with no redeeming features. After all, I added
as my clinching argument, if this were not so, why should our kinsmen wish
to come to the United States?

Our cousins and uncles, Father tried desperately to explain, really wanted 45
to stay at home with their wives and children, but because times seemed so
difficult in China they were compelled, by economic necessity, to come and
work in the Golden Mountains. "Don't think you're the only one who loves
his family and hates to leave it," concluded Father somewhat angrily.

The argument became endless. The more Father pleaded, the more de- 46
termined I became. America, I swore, was God's own country. It abounded
in free public schools, libraries, newspapers, bathtubs, toilets, vaudeville theaters, and railroad trains. On the other hand, I reminded him, China was a place
where anything might happen: One might be kidnaped, caught in a revolution,
die from the heat, perish from the cold, or even pick up ringworm diseases
which left huge bald patches on one's scalp.

Finally Father was convinced. Since I did not personally regard his idea 47
with favor, trying to send me to China was hopeless. This by no means ex-
hausted Father's remedial efforts on my behalf. Plan number one having failed,
Father put number two into operation. He decided that if I wouldn't go to
China I was to spend an extra hour each day on my Chinese studies for Tutor
Chun.

Now I knew leisure no longer. My American playmates, and endless 48
trips to the settlement library, were given up—but not forgotten. And I discovered to my painful sorrow that I had only substituted one necessary evil for
another. Every evening from five to eight I despondently memorized, recited,
and copied endless columns of queer-shaped characters which bore not
the slightest resemblance to English. As I went to this school on Saturday
mornings and studied my lessons on Sunday, I envied Penelope, Heinz, and

Francisco, my poorest foreign playmates, their luxurious freedom. They did not have to learn Chinese.

Unlike my American education, my Chinese one was not crowned with success. It was not that I was entirely unwilling to learn, but simply that my brain was not ambidextrous. Whenever I stood with my back to the teacher, my lips attempted to recite correctly in poetical prose Chinese history, geography, or ethics, while my inner spirit was wrestling victoriously with the details of the Battle of Bunker Hill, Custer's Last Stand, or the tussle between the *Monitor* and *Merrimac.*

When it became apparent to Tutor Chun that, in spite of my extra hour a day, I was unable to balance cultural waters on both shoulders, he mercifully desisted flailing me with the bamboo duster. No amount of chastising, he informed me bitterly, would ever unravel the cultural chop suey I was making of my studies. But, in the long run, even the gentle soul of the Chinese teacher could not tolerate my muddle-headedness. One day after a particularly heart-rending recitation on my part, he telephoned Mother in despair. "Madame," he exclaimed in mortal anguish, "never have I had a pupil the equal of your son. I strain all my efforts but, alas, I profoundly regret that I am unable to teach him anything!"

Father was appalled at this news, but since he was not the kind of man who gave up easily, his determination waxed all the stronger. Subtler methods, bribery, were tried. Perhaps, he reasoned, I might develop a taste for Chinese as well as English literature if it were only made financially worth my while. Each Sunday a shining quarter would be mine, he said, if I would present him with a daily ten-minute verbal Chinese translation of the latest newspaper reports on European war developments.[1]

Lured by this largess, I made my translations. They were, to be sure, crude and swiftly drawn. But then, ten minutes was all too brief a period in which to circumnavigate the globe and report on its current events. I endowed the military movements of von Kluck's, Foch's, and Haig's armies with the élan of Sheridan's sweep down the Shenandoah, unencumbered with the intricate mechanized paraphernalia of modern warfare. And long before Wilson, Clemenceau, and Lloyd George assembled at Versailles, I had made and remade the map of Europe a dozen times.

Father's clever scheme not only worked, but it proved mutually beneficial. During the four years of the war, we kept it up. Thanks to the revolutionary *Young China*, and the *Christian Chinese Western Daily*, he was never entirely in the dark as to which armies won which campaign and who finally won the war. Naturally, Father learned a great deal about history that wasn't so, but he did not particularly mind. I was improving my Chinese.

49

50

51

52

53

---

[1] World War I

During this period my youthful cup of patriotism was filled to overflowing. 54
In the first place our Americanism had finally reached the ears of the White
House. The christening of my twin brothers brought two important letters of
congratulation from Washington, which Father proudly framed and hung con-
spicuously in his private office. As might be imagined, they exerted a profound
influence on all our lives.

When I felt particularly in need of encouragement, I would go to the back 55
wall of Father's office and read aloud Vice President Marshall's letter to Father.
It was a human one, glowing with warmth and inspiration. There was one
sentence which stood out: "To be a good American citizen, in my judgment,
is about the best thing on earth, and while I cannot endow your children with
any worldly goods, I can bless them with the hope that they may grow up to
be an honor to their parents and a credit to the commonwealth."

I recall this Vice-Presidential blessing so vividly because it was the crux 56
of our family problem. It summed up our difficulties as well as our goal. For
me, at least, it was difficult to be a filial Chinese son and a good American
citizen at one and the same time. For many years I used to wonder why this
was so, but I appreciate now it was because I was the eldest son in what was
essentially a pioneering family. Father was pioneering with Americanism—and
so was I. And more often than not, we blazed entirely different trails.

When America finally entered the War, even Father's sturdy common 57
sense softened somewhat under the heat waves of patriotism that constantly
beat down upon us. I was in paradise. My youthful fancies appreciated that
only strife and turmoil made heroes. When I recalled that practically every
great President—Washington, Jackson, Lincoln, Grant, and Roosevelt—had
once been a soldier, I bitterly lamented the fact that I was not old enough. I'd
show those "Huns" (by this time I had already imbibed freely at the fount of
propaganda) a thing or two, I informed Father. But Father only snorted something about waiting until I could shoulder a gun, and studying Chinese.

The next summer, my thirteenth, I decided to go to work during vacation. 58
I needed spending money badly for my first term in high school. Father applauded this show of independence until I informed him that I intended, if
possible, to become an office boy in an American business firm. Then he was
seized with profound misgivings. "Would they hire you?" Father inquired.

Why shouldn't they, I replied, with overweening self-confidence. "See!" 59
I pointed to the Sunday editions of the *San Francisco Chronicle*. "I can hold any
of these jobs."

Father looked at the classified advertisements I had checked. Whether he 60
knew what all the abbreviations meant, I wasn't certain. I didn't, but that was
totally immaterial. The world was new, I was young, and for $40 a month I
was willing to learn the ins. or exp. bus., work for good opps., be ready to
asst. on files, and, for good measure, do gen. off. wk. for perm. adv.

Father remarked that he wasn't so certain that the millennium had arrived, 61
but he was open to conviction. He agreed to let me proceed on one condition:

If I failed to find a job I was to return to Tutor Chun and study my Chinese lessons faithfully.

Blithely one sunny July morning I went forth job hunting, well-scrubbed, wearing my Sunday suit and totally unaware of the difficulties that confronted me. In my pocket were ten clipped newspaper advertisements, each one, I thought, with a job purposely made for me.   62

I took out the most promising one. It was for seven enterp. boys, between the ages of 12 and 16; and they were wanted at once for a bond house which offered good opps. as well as $50 per month. The address was on California Street.   63

Stopping in front of an imposing marble palace of San Francisco finance, I compared the address with the clipping. It checked. How simply grand it would be to work for such a firm, I thought, as the elevator majestically pulled us up to the ninth floor. I trembled with eager anticipation as I pushed open the glass door of Richards and Mathison, for it seemed as though a new world were swimming into view.   64

"Wad-a-ya-wunt?" barked the sharp voice of a young lady. I looked in her direction. There she sat behind a shiny, thin brass cage, just like a bank teller—or a monkey, for above her head hung a sign. It read INFORMATION.   65

"Please, ma'am," I asked, "can you tell me where I can find Mr. Royal?"   66

"Humph!" she snorted, as she looked me up and down as if to say I didn't have a chance. "He's busy, you'll have to wait."   67

After what seemed hours, the girl threw open the office gate and motioned me to enter. I followed her down a long aisle of desks, every one as large as a kitchen table. At each desk sat a man or a girl shuffling large cards or scribbling on long sheets of paper. As we passed, they stopped their work and looked at me queerly. I noticed several boys of my own age putting their heads together. I knew they were talking about me. And when they snickered, I wanted to punch their noses.   68

Opening a door marked PRIVATE, the girl announced: "Mr. Royal, here is another boy." He raised his head.   69

There it was. On Mr. Royal's lean, smooth-shaven face was the same look of incredulity that I had once noticed on Mr. Brown's. But only for a moment. For he suddenly reached for a cigarette, lit it, and looked at me quizzically, while I hopped on one foot and then on the other.   70

"Young man," he said, "I understand you would like to work for us? Well then, you'd better tell us something of yourself."   71

"Why, of course," I said, "of course." And impulsively I told everything: all about my graduation from grammar school, my boy-scout training, and my desire to earn my own keep during the summer.   72

Mr. Royal seemed visibly impressed. When a faint smile replaced his frown, I stopped fidgeting. I fully expected him to ask me to come to work in the morning. Therefore, I was appalled when he told me that he was sorry,   73 but all the jobs were taken. It never occurred to me that our interview would end like this.

My face fell. I hadn't expected such an answer. To soften the blow, Mr. Royal added that if I filled out an application he would call me if there were any openings.   74

I filled out the application under the unsympathetic eyes of the information girl, and stumbled miserably out of the office, vaguely sensible of the fact that there would never be any opening.   75

The feeling was intensified as I made the round of the other nine firms. Everywhere I was greeted with perturbation, amusement, pity, or irritation— and always with identically the same answer. "Sorry," they invariably said, "the position has just been filled." My jaunty self-confidence soon wilted. I sensed that something was radically, fundamentally wrong. It just didn't seem possible that overnight all of the positions could have been occupied, particularly not when everybody spoke of a labor shortage. Suspicion began to dawn. What had Father said? "American firms do not customarily employ Chinese." To verify his statement, I looked again in the newspaper the next morning and for the week after and, sure enough, just as I expected, the same ten ads were still in the newspaper.   76

For another week, I tried my luck. By now I was thoroughly shellshocked. What had begun as a glorious adventure had turned into a hideous, long-drawn nightmare.   77

Father during this trying period wisely said nothing. Then, one morning, he dusted off my dog-eared paper-bound Chinese textbooks. When I came to breakfast I found them on my desk, mute but eloquent reminders of my promise. I looked at them disconsolately. A bargain was a bargain.   78

When our clock struck nine, I picked up my bundle of books. Fortunately for me, Father had already commuted to work. Only Mother saw me off. Patting me sympathetically on the shoulder, she regarded me reflectively. It was an invitation for me to unburden my heart. But not even for her would I confess my full recovery from a nearly fatal disease. That moment was reserved for my long walk to language school.   79

I marched out of the house insouciant. When I wasn't whistling I was muttering to myself a Jewish slang phrase I had just picked up. It was "Ish-kabibble" and it meant that I didn't care. And I didn't until I reached the park where all my most vivid daydreaming periods were spent. There, I broke down and wept. For the first time I admitted to myself the cruel truth— I didn't have a "Chinaman's chance" of becoming President of the United States. In this crash of the lofty hopes which Miss McIntyre had raised, it did not occur to me to reflect that the chances of Francisco Trujillo, Yuri Matsuyama, or Penelope Lincoln were actually no better than mine. But after a good cry I felt better—anyway, I could go to an American school again in the fall. ◆   80

♦ **Responding**

1. Explain what happens to Pardee Lowe to change his original optimism about equal opportunity in America to an understanding that in post–World War I San Francisco there would never be an opening for him with an American company and that, as he says in the story, he didn't have "a 'Chinaman's chance' of becoming President of the United States." What opportunities would be open to Pardee Lowe today? Could he be elected President of the United States?

2. Discuss the problems Pardee Lowe has in being a "filial Chinese son and good American citizen at one and the same time." Do you agree that it is difficult to be a part of two cultures? In writing your essay, use the reading as well as the experiences of you and your friends to support your argument.

3. Lowe's father holds certain hopes and aspirations for his son. Compare those with the aspirations he holds for himself.

4. Working individually or in a group, list the roles and responsibilities of the members of the extended Lowe family. Share your list with the class. Write an esssay comparing this family with other families presented in this book, or with your own family.

REFLECTING A CRITICAL CONTEXT

MAXINE HONG KINGSTON

Maxine Hong Kingston was born in Stockton, California, in 1940, the daughter of Chinese immigrants. Kingston attended the University of California at Berkeley, earning her bachelor's degree in 1962, and later a teaching certificate. After college she taught high school English in California and Hawaii, then college English in Hawaii.

Kingston's first book, Woman Warrior: Memoirs of a Girlhood among Ghosts, *was published in 1976. Combining realism and fantasy,* Woman Warrior *tells Kingston's mother's story, describing her life as a medical student in China and then as an immigrant to the United States. It was awarded the National Book Critics Circle Award in 1976.*

Kingston considers China Men *the companion volume to* Woman Warrior. China Men *relates some of the experiences of the male family members, who often immigrated first to make a home for their families in the new land. This volume received the American Book Award in 1981.*

The following selection, a chapter from China Men, *describes Kingston's grandfather's experiences while working in the mines and building the railroads. In fictional and nonfictional episodes, the chapter dramatizes the immigrants' struggles for success. In describing the sacrifice and determination required of these men, it also reflects on the legacy they left for their descendents.*

◆ THE GRANDFATHER OF THE SIERRA NEVADA MOUNTAINS ◆

The trains used to cross the sky. The house jumped and dust shook down from the attic. Sometimes two trains ran parallel going in opposite directions; the railroad men walked on top of the leaning cars, stepped off one train onto the back of the other, and traveled the opposite way. They headed for the caboose while the train moved against their walk, or they walked toward the engine while the train moved out from under their feet. Hoboes ran alongside, caught the ladders, and swung aboard. I would have to learn to ride like that, choose my boxcar, grab a ladder at a run, and fling myself up and sideways into an open door. Elsewhere I would step smoothly off. Bad runaway boys lost their legs trying for such rides. The train crunched past—pistons stroking like elbows and knees, the coal cars dropping coal, cows looking out between the slats of the cattlecars, the boxcars almost stringing together sentences—Hydro-Cushion, Georgia Flyer, Route of the Eagle—and suddenly sunlight filled the windows again, the slough wide again and waving with tules, for which the city was once named; red-winged blackbirds and squirrels settled. We children ran to the tracks and found the nails we'd placed on them; the wheels had flattened them into knives that sparked.

Once in a while an adult said, "Your grandfather built the railroad." (Or 2 "Your grandfathers built the railroad." Plural and singular are by context.) We children believed that it was that very railroad, those trains, those tracks running past our house; our own giant grandfather had set those very logs into the ground, poured the iron for those very spikes with the big heads and pounded them until the heads spread like that, mere nails to him. He had built the railroad so that trains would thunder over us, on a street that inclined toward us. We lived on a special spot of the earth, Stockton, the only city on the Pacific coast with three railroads—the Santa Fe, Southern Pacific, and Western Pacific. The three railroads intersecting accounted for the flocks of hoboes. The few times that the train stopped, the cows moaned all night, their hooves stumbling crowdedly and banging against the wood.

Grandfather left a railroad for his message: We had to go somewhere 3 difficult. Ride a train. Go somewhere important. In case of danger, the train was to be ready for us.

The railroad men disconnected the rails and took the steel away. They 4 did not come back. Our family dug up the square logs and rolled them downhill home. We collected the spikes too. We used the logs for benches, edged the yard with them, made bases for fences, embedded them in the ground for walkways. The spikes came in handy too, good for paperweights, levers, wedges, chisels. I am glad to know exactly the weight of ties and the size of nails.

Grandfather's picture hangs in the dining room next to an equally large 5 one of Grandmother, and another one of Guan Goong, God of War and Literature. My grandparents' similarity is in the set of their mouths; they seem to have hauled with their mouths. My mouth also feels the tug and strain of weights in its corners. In the family album, Grandfather wears a greatcoat and Western shoes, but his ankles show. He hasn't shaved either. Maybe he became sloppy after the Japanese soldier bayoneted his head for not giving directions. Or he was born slow and without a sense of direction.

The photographer came to the village regularly and set up a spinet, potted 6 trees, an ornate table stacked with hardbound books of matching size, and a backdrop with a picture of paths curving through gardens into panoramas; he lent his subjects dressy ancient mandarin clothes, Western suits, and hats. An aunt tied the fingers of the lame cousin to a book, the string leading down his sleeve; he looks like he's carrying it. The family hurried from clothes chests to mirrors without explaining to Grandfather, hiding Grandfather. In the family album are group pictures with Grandmother in the middle, the family arranged on either side of her and behind her, second wives at the ends, no Grandfather. Grandmother's earrings, bracelets, and rings are tinted jade green, everything and everybody else black and white, her little feet together neatly, two knobs at the bottom of her gown. My mother, indignant that nobody had readied

Grandfather, threw his greatcoat over his nightclothes, shouted, "Wait! Wait!" and encouraged him into the sunlight. "Hurry," she said, and he ran, coat flapping, to be in the picture. She would have slipped him into the group and had the camera catch him like a peeping ghost, but Grandmother chased him away. "What a waste of film," she said. Grandfather always appears alone with white stubble on his chin. He was a thin man with big eyes that looked straight ahead. When we children talked about overcoat men, exhibitionists, we meant Grandfather, Ah Goong, who must have yanked open that greatcoat—no pants.

MaMa was the only person to listen to him, and so he followed her everywhere, and talked and talked. What he liked telling was his journeys to the Gold Mountain. He wasn't smart, yet he traveled there three times. Left to himself, he would have stayed in China to play with babies or stayed in the United States once he got there, but Grandmother forced him to leave both places. "Make money," she said. "Don't stay here eating." "Come home," she said. 7

Ah Goong sat outside her open door when MaMa worked. (In those days a man did not visit a good woman alone unless married to her.) He saw her at her loom and came running with his chair. He told her that he had found a wondrous country, really gold, and he himself had gotten two bags of it, one of which he had had made into a ring. His wife had given that ring to their son for his wedding ring. "That ring on your finger," he told Mother, "proves that the Gold Mountain exists and that I went there." 8

Another of his peculiarities was that he heard the crackles, bangs, gunshots that go off when the world lurches; the gears on its axis snap. Listening to a faraway New Year, he had followed the noise and come upon the blasting in the Sierras. (There is a Buddhist instruction that that which is most elusive must, of course, be the very thing to be pursued; listen to the farthest sound.) The Central Pacific hired him on sight; chinamen had a natural talent for explosions. Also there were not enough workingmen to do all the labor of building a new country. Some of the banging came from the war to decide whether or not black people would continue to work for nothing. 9

Slow as usual, Ah Goong arrived in the spring; the work had begun in January 1863. The demon that hired him pointed up and up, east above the hills of poppies. His first job was to fell a redwood, which was thick enough to divide into three or four beams. His tree's many branches spread out, each limb like a little tree. He circled the tree. How to attack it? No side looked like the side made to be cut, nor did any ground seem the place for it to fall. He axed for almost a day the side he'd decided would hit the ground. Halfway through, imitating the other lumberjacks, he struck the other side of the tree, above the cut, until he had to run away. The tree swayed and slowly dived to earth, creaking and screeching like a green animal. He was so awed, he forgot he was supposed to yell. Hardly any branches broke; the tree sprang, bounced, pushed at the ground with its arms. The limbs did not wilt and fold; they were a small forest, which he chopped. The trunk lay like a long red torso; sap ran 10 from its cuts like crying blind eyes. At last it stopped fighting. He set the log across sawhorses to be cured over smoke and in the sun.

He joined a team of men who did not ax one another as they took alternate 11 hits. They blew up the stumps with gunpowder. "It was like uprooting a tooth," Ah Goong said. They also packed gunpowder at the roots of a whole tree. Not at the same time as the bang but before that, the tree rose from the ground. It stood, then plunged with a tearing of veins and muscles. It was big enough to carve a house into. The men measured themselves against the upturned white roots, which looked like claws, a sun with claws. A hundred men stood or sat on the trunk. They lifted a wagon on it and took a photograph. The demons also had their photograph taken.

Because these mountains were made out of gold, Ah Goong rushed over 12 to the root hole to look for gold veins and ore. He selected the shiniest rocks to be assayed later in San Francisco. When he drank from the streams and saw a flash, he dived in like a duck; only sometimes did it turn out to be the sun or the water. The very dirt winked with specks.

He made a dollar a day salary. The lucky men gambled, but he was not 13 good at remembering game rules. The work so far was endurable. "I could take it," he said.

The days were sunny and blue, the wind exhilarating, the heights godlike. 14 At night the stars were diamonds, crystals, silver, snow, ice. He had never seen diamonds. He had never seen snow and ice. As spring turned into summer, and he lay under that sky, he saw the order in the stars. He recognized constellations from China. There—not a cloud but the Silver River, and there, on either side of it—Altair and Vega, the Spinning Girl and the Cowboy, far, far apart. He felt his heart breaking of loneliness at so much blue-black space between star and star. The railroad he was building would not lead him to his family. He jumped out of his bedroll. "Look! Look!" Other China Men jumped awake. An accident? An avalanche? Injun demons? "The stars," he said. "The stars are here." "Another China Man gone out of his mind," men grumbled. "A sleepwalker." "Go to sleep, sleepwalker." "There. And there," said Ah Goong, two hands pointing. "The Spinning Girl and the Cowboy. Don't you see them?" "Homesick China Man," said the China Men and pulled their blankets over their heads. "Didn't you know they were here? I could have told you they were here. Same as in China. Same moon. Why not same stars?" "Nah. Those are American stars."

Pretending that a little girl was listening, he told himself the story about 15 the Spinning Girl and the Cowboy: A long time ago they had visited earth, where they met, fell in love, and married. Instead of growing used to each other, they remained enchanted their entire lifetimes and beyond. They were too happy. They wanted to be doves or two branches of the same tree. When they returned to live in the sky, they were so engrossed in each other that they neglected their work. The Queen of the Sky scratched a river between them with one stroke of her silver hairpin—the river a galaxy in width. The lovers suffered, but she did devote her time to spinning now, and he herded his cow. The King of the Sky took pity on them and ordered that once each year, they be allowed to meet. On the seventh day of the seventh month (which is not the same as July 7), magpies form a bridge for them to cross to each other. The lovers are together for one night of the year. On their parting, the Spinner cries the heavy summer rains.

Ah Goong's discovery of the two stars gave him something to look forward to besides meals and tea breaks. Every night he located Altair and Vega and gauged how much closer they had come since the night before. During the day he watched the magpies, big black and white birds with round bodies like balls with wings; they were a welcome sight, a promise of meetings. He had found two familiars in the wilderness: magpies and stars. On the meeting day, he did not see any magpies nor hear their chattering jaybird cries. Some black and white birds flew overhead, but they may have been American crows or late magpies on their way. Some men laughed at him, but he was not the only China Man to collect water in pots, bottles, and canteens that day. The water would stay fresh forever and cure anything. In ancient days the tutelary gods of the mountains sprinkled corpses with this water and brought them to life. That night, no women to light candles, burn incense, cook special food, Grandfather watched for the convergence and bowed. He saw the two little stars next to Vega—the couple's children. And bridging the Silver River, surely those were black flapping wings of magpies and translucent-winged angels and faeries. Toward morning, he was awakened by rain, and pulled his blankets into his tent. 16

The next day, the fantailed orange-beaked magpies returned. Altair and Vega were beginning their journeys apart, another year of spinning and herding. Ah Goong had to find something else to look forward to. The Spinning Girl and the Cowboy met and parted six times before the railroad was finished. 17

When cliffs, sheer drops under impossible overhangs, ended the road, the workers filled the ravines or built bridges over them. They climbed above the site for tunnel or bridge and lowered one another down in wicker baskets made stronger by the lucky words they had painted on four sides. Ah Goong got to be a basketman because he was thin and light. Some basketmen were fifteen-year-old boys. He rode the basket barefoot, so his boots, the kind to stomp snakes with, would not break through the bottom. The basket swung and twirled, and he saw the world sweep underneath him; it was fun in a way, a cold new feeling of doing what had never been done before. Suspended in the quiet sky, he thought all kinds of crazy thoughts, that if a man didn't want to live any more, he could just cut the ropes or, easier, tilt the basket, dip, and never have to worry again. He could spread his arms and the air would momentarily hold him before he fell past the buzzards, hawks, and eagles, and landed impaled on the tip of a sequoia. This high and he didn't see any gods, no Cowboy, no Spinner. He knelt in the basket though he was not bumping his head against the sky. Through the wickerwork, slivers of depths darted like 18 needles, nothing between him and air but thin rattan. Gusts of wind spun the light basket. "Aiya," said Ah Goong. Winds came up under the basket, bouncing it. Neighboring baskets swung together and parted. He and the man next to him looked at each other's faces. They laughed. They might as well have gone to Malaysia to collect bird nests. Those who had done high work there said it had been worse; the birds screamed and scratched at them. Swinging near the cliff, Ah Goong stood up and grabbed it by a twig. He dug holes, then inserted gunpowder and fuses. He worked neither too fast nor too slow, keeping even with the others. The basketmen signaled one another to light the fuses. He struck match after match and dropped the burnt matches over the sides. At last his fuse caught; he waved, and the men above pulled hand over hand hauling him up, pulleys creaking. The scaffolds stood like a row of gibbets. Gallows trees along a ridge. "Hurry, hurry," he said. Some impatient men clambered up their ropes. Ah Goong ran up the ledge road they'd cleared and watched the explosions, which banged almost synchronously, echoes booming like war. He moved his scaffold to the next section of cliff and went down in the basket again, with bags of dirt, and set the next charge.

This time two men were blown up. One knocked out or killed by the 19
explosion fell silently, the other screaming, his arms and legs struggling. A desire shot out of Ah Goong for an arm long enough to reach down and catch them. Much time passed as they fell like plummets. The shreds of baskets and a cowboy hat skimmed and tacked. The winds that pushed birds off course and against mountains did not carry men. Ah Goong also wished that the conscious man would fall faster and get it over with. He hands gripped the ropes, and it was difficult to let go and get on with the work. "It can't happen twice in a row," the basketmen said the next trip down. "Our chances are very good. The trip after an accident is probably the safest one." They raced to their favorite basket, checked and double-checked the four ropes, yanked the strands, tested the pulleys, oiled them, reminded the pulleymen about the signals, and entered the sky again.

Another time, Ah Goong had been lowered to the bottom of a ravine, 20
which had to be cleared for the base of a trestle, when a man fell, and he saw his face. He had not died of shock before hitting bottom. His hands were grabbing at air. His stomach and groin must have felt the fall all the way down. At night Ah Goong woke up falling, though he slept on the ground, and heard other men call out in their sleep. No warm women tweaked their ears and hugged them. "It was only a falling dream," he reassured himself.

Across a valley, a chain of men working on the next mountain, men like 21
ants changing the face of the world, fell, but it was very far away. Godlike, he watched men whose faces he could not see and whose screams he did not hear roll and bounce and slide like a handful of sprinkled gravel.

After a fall, the buzzards circled the spot and reminded the workers for 22
days that a man was dead down there. The men threw piles of rocks and branches to cover bodies from sight.

The mountainface reshaped, they drove supports for a bridge. Since hammering was less dangerous than the blowing up, the men played a little; they rode the baskets swooping in wide arcs; they twisted the ropes and let them unwind like tops. "Look at me," said Ah Goong, pulled open his pants, and pissed overboard, the wind scattering the drops. "I'm a waterfall," he said. He had sent a part of himself hurtling. On rare windless days he watched his piss fall in a continuous stream from himself almost to the bottom of the valley.

One beautiful day, dangling in the sun above a new valley, not the desire to urinate but sexual desire clutched him so hard he bent over in the basket. He curled up, overcome by beauty and fear, which shot to his penis. He tried to rub himself calm. Suddenly he stood up tall and squirted out into space. "I am fucking the world," he said. The world's vagina was big, big as the sky, big as a valley. He grew a habit: whenever he was lowered in the basket, his blood rushed to his penis, and he fucked the world.

Then it was autumn, and the wind blew so fiercely, the men had to postpone the basketwork. Clouds moved in several directions at once. Men pointed at dust devils, which turned their mouths crooked. There was ceaseless motion; clothes kept moving; hair moved; sleeves puffed out. Nothing stayed still long enough for Ah Goong to figure it out. The wind sucked the breath out of his mouth and blew thoughts from his brains. The food convoys from San Francisco brought tents to replace the ones that whipped away. The baskets from China, which the men saved for high work, carried cowboy jackets, long underwear, Levi pants, boots, earmuffs, leather gloves, flannel shirts, coats. They sewed rabbit fur and deerskin into the linings. They tied the wide brims of their cowboy hats over their ears with mufflers. And still the wind made confusing howls into ears, and it was hard to think.

The days became nights when the crews tunneled inside the mountain, which sheltered them from the wind, but also hid the light and sky. Ah Goong pickaxed the mountain, the dirt filling his nostrils through a cowboy bandanna. He shoveled the dirt into a cart and pushed it to a place that was tall enough for the mule, which hauled it the rest of the way out. He looked forward to cart duty to edge closer to the entrance. Eyes darkened, nose plugged, his windy cough worse, he was to mole a thousand feet and meet others digging from the other side. How much he'd pay now to go swinging in a basket. He might as well have gone to work in a tin mine. Coming out of the tunnel at the end of a shift, he forgot whether it was supposed to be day or night. He blew his nose fifteen times before the mucus cleared again.

The dirt was the easiest part of tunneling. Beneath the soil, they hit granite. Ah Goong struck it with his pickax, and it jarred his bones, chattered his teeth. He swung his sledgehammer against it, and the impact rang in the dome of his skull. The mountain that was millions of years old was locked against them and was not to be broken into. The men teased him, "Let's see you fuck the world now." "Let's see you fuck the Gold Mountain now." But he no longer felt like it. "A man ought to be made of tougher material than flesh," he said. "Skin is too soft. Our bones ought to be filled with iron." He lifted the hammer high, careful that it not pull him backward, and let it fall forward of its own weight against the rock. Nothing happened to that gray wall; he had to slam with strength and will. He hit at the same spot over and over again, the same rock. Some chips and flakes broke off. The granite looked everywhere the same. It had no softer or weaker spots anywhere, the same hard gray. He learned to slide his hand up the handle, lift, slide and swing, a circular motion, hammering, hammering, hammering. He would bite like a rat through that mountain. His eyes couldn't see; his nose couldn't smell; and now his ears were filled with the noise of hammering. This rock is what is real, he thought. This rock is what real is, not clouds or mist, which make mysterious promises, and when you go through them are nothing. When the foreman measured at the end of twenty-four hours of pounding, the rock had given a foot. The hammering went on day and night. The men worked eight hours on and eight hours off. They worked on all eighteen tunnels at once. While Ah Goong slept, he could hear the sledgehammers of other men working in the earth. The steady banging reminded him of holidays and harvests; falling asleep, he heard the women chopping mincemeat and the millstones striking.

The demons in boss suits came into the tunnel occasionally, measured   28 with a yardstick and shook their heads. "Faster," they said. "Faster. Chinamen too slow. Too slow." "Tell us we're slow," the China Men grumbled. The ones in top tiers of scaffolding let rocks drop, a hammer drop. Ropes tangled around the demons' heads and feet. The cave China Men muttered and flexed, glared out of the corners of their eyes. But usually there was no diversion—one day the same as the next, one hour no different from another—the beating against the same granite.

After tunneling into granite for about three years, Ah Goong understood   29 the immovability of the earth. Men change, men die, weather changes, but a mountain is the same as permanence and time. This mountain would have taken no new shape for centuries, ten thousand centuries, the world a still, still place, time unmoving. He worked in the tunnel so long, he learned to see many colors in black. When he stumbled out, he tried to talk about time. "I felt time," he said. "I saw time. I saw world." He tried again, "I saw what's real. I saw time, and it doesn't move. If we break through the mountain, hollow it, time won't have moved anyway. You translators ought to tell the foreigners that."

Summer came again, but after the first summer, he felt less nostalgia at   30 the meeting of the Spinning Girl and the Cowboy. He now knew men who had been in this country for twenty years and thirty years, and the Cowboy's one year away from his lady was no time at all. His own patience was longer. The stars were meeting and would meet again next year, but he would not have seen his family. He joined the others celebrating Souls' Day, the holiday a week later, the fourteenth day of the seventh month. The supply wagons from San Francisco and Sacramento brought watermelon, meat, fish, crab, pressed duck.

"There, ghosts, there you are. Come and get it." They displayed the feast complete for a moment before falling to, eating on the dead's behalf.

In the third year of pounding granite by hand, a demon invented dynamite. The railroad workers were to test it. They had stopped using gunpowder in the tunnels after avalanches, but the demons said that dynamite was more precise. They watched a scientist demon mix nitrate, sulphate, and glycerine, then flick the yellow oil, which exploded off his fingertips. Sitting in a meadow to watch the dynamite detonated in the open, Ah Goong saw the men in front of him leap impossibly high into the air; then he felt a shove as if from a giant's unseen hand—he fell backward. The boom broke the mountain silence like fear breaking inside stomach and chest and groin. No one had gotten hurt; they stood up laughing and amazed, looking around at how they had fallen, the pattern of the explosion. Dynamite was much more powerful than gunpowder. Ah Goong had felt a nudge, as if something kind were moving him out of harm's way. "All of a sudden I was sitting next to you." "Aiya. If we had been nearer, it would have killed us." "If we were stiff, it would have gone through us." "A fist." "A hand." "We leapt like acrobats." Next time Ah Goong flattened himself on the ground, and the explosion rolled over him.

He never got used to the blasting; a blast always surprised him. Even when he himself set the fuse and watched it burn, anticipated the explosion, the bang—*bahng* in Chinese—when it came, always startled. It cleaned the crazy words, the crackling, and bingbangs out of his brain. It was like New Year's, when every problem and thought was knocked clean out of him by firecrackers, and he could begin fresh. He couldn't worry during an explosion, which jerked every head to attention. Hills flew up in rocks and dirt. Boulders turned over and over. Sparks, fires, debris, rocks, smoke burst up, not at the same time as the boom (*bum*) but before that—the sound a separate occurrence, not useful as a signal.

The terrain changed immediately. Streams were diverted, rockscapes exposed. Ah Goong found it difficult to remember what land had looked like before an explosion. It was a good thing the dynamite was invented after the Civil War to the east was over.

The dynamite added more accidents and ways of dying, but if it were not used, the railroad would take fifty more years to finish. Nitroglycerine exploded when it was jounced on a horse or dropped. A man who fell with it in his pocket blew himself up into red pieces. Sometimes it combusted merely standing. Human bodies skipped through the air like puppets and made Ah Goong laugh crazily as if the arms and legs would come together again. The smell of burned flesh remained in rocks.

In the tunnels, the men bored holes fifteen to eighteen inches deep with a power drill, stuffed them with hay and dynamite, and imbedded the fuse in sand. Once, for extra pay, Ah Goong ran back in to see why some dynamite had not gone off and hurried back out again; it was just a slow fuse. When the explosion settled, he helped carry two-hundred-, three-hundred-, five-hundred-pound boulders out of the tunnel.

As a boy he had visited a Taoist monastery where there were nine rooms, 36 each a replica of one of the nine hells. Lifesize sculptures of men and women were spitted on turning wheels. Eerie candles under the suffering faces emphasized eyes poked out, tongues pulled, red mouths and eyes, and real hair, eyelashes, and eyebrows. Women were split apart and men dismembered. He could have reached out and touched the sufferers and the implements. He had dug and dynamited his way into one of these hells. "Only here there are eighteen tunnels, not nine, plus all the tracks between them," he said.

One day he came out of the tunnel to find the mountains white, the 37 evergreens and bare trees decorated, white tree sculptures and lace bushes everywhere. The men from snow country called the icicles "ice chopsticks." He sat in his basket and slid down the slopes. The snow covered the gouged land, the broken trees, the tracks, the mud, the campfire ashes, the unburied dead. Streams were stilled in mid-run, the water petrified. That winter he thought it was the task of the human race to quicken the world, blast the freeze, fire it, redden it with blood. He had to change the stupid slowness of one sunrise and one sunset per day. He had to enliven the silent world with sound. "The rock," he tried to tell the others. "The ice." "Time."

The dynamiting loosed blizzards on the men. Ears and toes fell off. Fingers 38 stuck to the cold silver rails. Snowblind men stumbled about with bandannas over their eyes. Ah Goong helped build wood tunnels roofing the track route. Falling ice scrabbled on the roofs. The men stayed under the snow for weeks at a time. Snowslides covered the entrances to the tunnels, which they had to dig out to enter and exit, white tunnels and black tunnels. Ah Goong looked at his gang and thought, If there is an avalanche, these are the people I'll be trapped with, and wondered which ones would share food. A party of snow-bound barbarians had eaten the dead. Cannibals, thought Ah Goong, and looked around. Food was not scarce; the tea man brought whiskey barrels of hot tea, and he warmed his hands and feet, held the teacup to his nose and ears. Someday, he planned, he would buy a chair with metal doors for putting hot coal inside it. The magpies did not abandon him but stayed all winter and searched the snow for food.

The men who died slowly enough to say last words said, "Don't leave 39 me frozen under the snow. Send my body home. Burn it and put the ashes in a tin can. Take the bone jar when you come down the mountain." "When you ride the fire car back to China, tell my descendants to come for me." "Shut up," scolded the hearty men. "We don't want to hear about bone jars and dying." "You're lucky to have a body to bury, not blown to smithereens." "Stupid man to hurt yourself," they bawled out the sick and wounded. How their wives would scold if they brought back deadmen's bones. "Aiya. To be buried here, nowhere." "But this is somewhere," Ah Goong promised. "This is the Gold Mountain. We're marking the land now. The track sections are numbered, and your family will know where we leave you." But he was a crazy man, and they didn't listen to him.

Spring did come, and when the snow melted, it revealed the past year, 40 what had happened, what they had done, where they had worked, the lost tools, the thawing bodies, some standing with tools in hand, the bright rails. "Remember Uncle Long Winded Leong?" "Remember Strong Back Wong?" "Remember Lee Brother?" "And Fong Uncle?" They lost count of the number dead; there is no record of how many died building the railroad. Or maybe it was demons doing the counting and chinamen not worth counting. Whether it was good luck or bad luck, the dead were buried or cairned next to the last section of track they had worked on. "May his ghost not have to toil," they said over graves. (In China a woodcutter ghost chops eternally; people have heard chopping in the snow and in the heat.) "Maybe his ghost will ride the train home." The scientific demons said the transcontinental railroad would connect the West to Cathay. "What if he rides back and forth from Sacramento to New York forever?" "That wouldn't be so bad. I hear the cars will be like houses on wheels." The funerals were short. "No time. No time," said both China Men and demons. The railroad was as straight as they could build it, but no ghosts sat on the tracks; no strange presences haunted the tunnels. The blasts scared ghosts away.

When the Big Dipper pointed east and the China Men detonated nitro- 41 glycerine and shot off guns for the New Year, which comes with the spring, these special bangs were not as loud as the daily bangs, not as numerous as the bangs all year. Shouldn't the New Year be the loudest day of all to obliterate the noises of the old year? But to make a bang of that magnitude, they would have to blow up at least a year's supply of dynamite in one blast. They arranged strings of chain reactions in circles and long lines, banging faster and louder to culminate in a big bang. And most importantly, there were random explosions— surprise. Surprise. SURPRISE. They had no dragon, the railroad their dragon.

The demons invented games for working faster, gold coins for miles of 42 track laid, for the heaviest rock, a grand prize for the first team to break through a tunnel. Day shifts raced against night shifts, China Men against Welshmen, China Men against Irishmen, China Men against Injuns and black demons. The fastest races were China Men against China Men, who bet on their own teams. China Men always won because of good teamwork, smart thinking, and the need for the money. Also, they had the most workers to choose teams from. Whenever his team won anything, Ah Goong added to his gold stash. The Central Pacific or Union Pacific won the land on either side of the tracks it built.

One summer day, demon officials and China Man translators went from 43 group to group and announced, "We're raising the pay—thirty-five dollars a month. Because of your excellent work, the Central Pacific Railroad is giving you a four-dollar raise per month." The workers who didn't know better cheered. "What's the catch?" said the smarter men. "You'll have the opportunity to put in more time," said the railroad demons. "Two more hours per shift." Ten-hour shifts inside the tunnels. "It's not ten hours straight," said the demons. "You have time off for tea and meals. Now that you have dynamite, the work isn't so hard." They had been working for three and a half years already, and the track through the Donner Summit was still not done.

The workers discussed the ten-hour shift, swearing their China Man ob- 44 scenities. "Two extra hours a day—sixty hours a month for four dollars." "Pig catcher demons." "Snakes." "Turtles." "Dead demons." "A human body can't work like that." "The demons don't believe this is a human body. This is a chinaman's body." To bargain, they sent a delegation of English speakers, who were summarily noted as troublemakers, turned away, docked.

The China Men, then, decided to go on strike and demand forty-five 45 dollars a month and the eight-hour shift. They risked going to jail and the Central Pacific keeping the pay it was banking for them. Ah Goong memorized the English, "Forty-five dollars a month—eight-hour shift." He practiced the strike slogan: "Eight hours a day good for white man, all the same good for China Man."

The men wrapped barley and beans in ti leaves, which came from Hawai'i 46 via San Francisco, for celebrating the fifth day of the fifth month (not May but mid-June, the summer solstice). Usually the way the red string is wound and knotted tells what flavors are inside—the salty barley with pickled egg, or beans and pork, or the gelatin pudding. Ah Goong folded ti leaves into a cup and packed it with food. One of the literate men slipped in a piece of paper with the strike plan, and Ah Goong tied the bundle with a special pattern of red string. The time and place for the revolution against Kublai Khan had been hidden inside autumn mooncakes. Ah Goong looked from one face to another in admiration. Of course, of course. No China Men, no railroad. They were indispensable labor. Throughout these mountains were brothers and uncles with a common idea, free men, not coolies, calling for fair working conditions. The demons were not suspicious as the China Men went gandying up and down the tracks delivering the bundles tied together like lines of fish. They had exchanged these gifts every year. When the summer solstice cakes came from other camps, the recipients cut them into neat slices by drawing the string through them. The orange jellies, which had a red dye stick inside soaked in lye, fell into a series of sunrises and sunsets. The aged yolks and the barley also looked like suns. The notes gave a Yes strike vote. The yellow flags to ward off the five evils—centipedes, scorpions, snakes, poisonous lizards, and toads—now flew as banners.

The strike began on Tuesday morning, June 25, 1867. The men who 47 were working at that hour walked out of the tunnels and away from the tracks. The ones who were sleeping slept on and rose as late as they pleased. They bathed in streams and shaved their moustaches and wild beards. Some went fishing and hunting. The violinists tuned and played their instruments. The drummers beat theirs at the punchlines of jokes. The gamblers shuffled and played their cards and tiles. The smokers passed their pipes, and the drinkers bet for drinks by making figures with their hands. The cooks made party food. The opera singers' falsettos almost perforated the mountains. The men sang new songs about the railroad. They made up verses and shouted Ho at the good ones, and laughed at the rhymes. Oh, they were madly singing in the mountains. The storytellers told about the rise of new kings. The opium smokers when they roused themselves told their florid images. Ah Goong sifted for gold. All the while the English-speaking China Men, who were being advised by the shrewdest bargainers, were at the demons' headquarters repeating the demand: "Eight hours a day good for white man, all the same good for China Man." They had probably negotiated the demons down to nine-hour shifts by now.

The sounds of hammering continued along the tracks and occasionally there were blasts from the tunnels. The scabby white demons had refused to join the strike. "Eight hours a day good for white man, all the same good for China Man," the China Men explained to them. "Cheap John Chinaman," said the demons, many of whom had red hair. The China Men scowled out of the corners of their eyes. — 48

On the second day, artist demons climbed the mountains to draw the China Men for the newspapers. The men posed bare-chested, their fists clenched, showing off their arms and backs. The artists sketched them as perfect young gods reclining against rocks, wise expressions on their handsome noble-nosed faces, long torsos with lean stomachs, a strong arm extended over a bent knee, long fingers holding a pipe, a rope of hair over a wide shoulder. Other artists drew faeries with antennae for eyebrows and brownies with elvish pigtails; they danced in white socks and black slippers among mushroom rings by moonlight. — 49

Ah Goong acquired another idea that added to his reputation for craziness: The pale, thin Chinese scholars and the rich men fat like Buddhas were less beautiful, less manly than these brown muscular railroad men, of whom he was one. One of ten thousand heroes. — 50

On the third day, in a woods—he would be looking at a deer or a rabbit or an Injun watching him before he knew what he was seeing—a demon dressed in a white suit and tall hat beckoned him. They talked privately in the wilderness. The demon said, "I Citizenship Judge invite you to be U.S. citizen. Only one bag gold." Ah Goong was thrilled. What an honor. He would accept this invitation. Also what advantages, he calculated shrewdly; if he were going to be jailed for this strike, an American would have a trial. The Citizenship Judge unfurled a parchment sealed with gold and ribbon. Ah Goong bought it with one bag of gold. "You vote," said the Citizenship Judge. "You talk in court, buy land, no more chinaman tax." Ah Goong hid the paper on his person so that it would protect him from arrest and lynching. He was already a part of this new country, but now he had it in writing. — 51

The fourth day, the strikers heard that the U.S. Cavalry was riding single file up the tracks to shoot them. They argued whether to engage the Army with dynamite. But the troops did not come. Instead the cowardly demons blockaded — 52 the food wagons. No food. Ah Goong listened to the optimistic China Men, who said, "Don't panic. We'll hold out forever. We can hunt. We can last fifty days on water." The complainers said, "Aiya. Only saints can do that. Only magic men and monks who've practiced." The China Men refused to declare a last day for the strike.

The foresighted China Men had cured jerky, fermented wine, dried and strung orange and grapefruit peels, pickled and preserved leftovers. Ah Goong, one of the best hoarders, had set aside extra helpings from each meal. This same quandary, whether to give away food or to appear selfish, had occurred during each of the six famines he had lived through. The foodless men identified themselves. Sure enough, they were the shiftless, piggy, arrogant type who didn't worry enough. The donors scolded them and shamed them the whole while they were handing them food: "So you lived like a grasshopper at our expense." "Fleaman." "You'll be the cause of our not holding out long enough." "Rich man's kid. Too good to hoard." Ah Goong contributed some rice crusts from the bottoms of pans. He kept how much more food he owned a secret, as he kept the secret of his gold. In apology for not contributing richer food, he repeated a Mohist saying that had guided him in China: " 'The superior man does not push humaneness to the point of stupidity.' " He could hear his wife scolding him for feeding strangers. The opium men offered shit and said that it calmed the appetite.

On the fifth and sixth days, Ah Goong organized his possessions and patched his clothes and tent. He forebore repairing carts, picks, ropes, baskets. His work-habituated hands arranged rocks and twigs in designs. He asked a reader to read again his family's letters. His wife sounded like herself except for the polite phrases added professionally at the beginnings and the ends. "Idiot," she said, "why are you taking so long? Are you wasting the money? Are you spending it on girls and gambling and whiskey? Here's my advice to you: Be a little more frugal. Remember how it felt to go hungry. Work hard." He had been an idle man for almost a week. "I need a new dress to wear to weddings. I refuse to go to another banquet in the same old dress. If you weren't such a spendthrift, we could be building the new courtyard where we'll drink wine among the flowers and sit about in silk gowns all day. We'll hire peasants to till the fields. Or lease them to tenants, and buy all our food at market. We'll have clean fingernails and toenails." Other relatives said, "I need a gold watch. Send me the money. Your wife gambles it away and throws parties and doesn't disburse it fairly among us. You might as well come home." It was after one of these letters that he had made a bonus checking on some dud dynamite.

Ah Goong did not spend his money on women. The strikers passed the word that a woman was traveling up the railroad and would be at his camp on the seventh and eighth day of the strike. Some said she was a demoness and some that she was a Chinese and her master a China Man. He pictured a nurse coming to bandage wounds and touch foreheads or a princess surveying her subjects; or perhaps she was a merciful Jesus demoness. But she was a pitiful woman, led on a leash around her waist, not entirely alive. Her owner sold lottery tickets for the use of her. Ah Goong did not buy one. He took out his penis under his blanket or bared it in the woods and thought about nurses and princesses. He also just looked at it, wondering what it was that it was for, what a man was for, what he had to have a penis for.

There was a rumor also of an Injun woman called Woman Chief, who 56 led a nomadic fighting tribe from the eastern plains as far as these mountains. She was so powerful that she had four wives and many horses. He never saw her though.

The strike ended on the ninth day. The Central Pacific announced that 57 in its benevolence it was giving the workers a four-dollar raise, not the fourteen dollars they had asked for. And that the shifts in the tunnels would remain eight hours long. "We were planning to give you the four-dollar raise all along," the demons said to diminish the victory. So they got thirty-five dollars a month and the eight-hour shift. They would have won forty-five dollars if the thousand demon workers had joined the strike. Demons would have listened to demons. The China Men went back to work quietly. No use singing and shouting over a compromise and losing nine days' work.

There were two days that Ah Goong did cheer and throw his hat in the 58 air, jumping up and down and screaming Yippee like a cowboy. One: the day his team broke through the tunnel at last. Toward the end they did not dynamite but again used picks and sledgehammers. Through the granite, they heard answering poundings, and answers to their shouts. It was not a mountain before them any more but only a wall with people breaking through from the other side. They worked faster. Forward. Into day. They stuck their arms through the holes and shook hands with men on the other side. Ah Goong saw dirty faces as wondrous as if he were seeing Nu Wo, the creator goddess who repairs cracks in the sky with stone slabs; sometimes she peeks through and human beings see her face. The wall broke. Each team gave the other a gift of half a tunnel, dug. They stepped back and forth where the wall had been. Ah Goong ran and ran, his boots thudding to the very end of the tunnel, looked at the other side of the mountain, and ran back, clear through the entire tunnel. All the way through.

He spent the rest of his time on the railroad laying and bending and 59 hammering the ties and rails. The second day the China Men cheered was when the engine from the West and the one from the East rolled toward one another and touched. The transcontinental railroad was finished. They Yippee'd like madmen. The white demon officials gave speeches. "The Greatest Feat of the Nineteenth Century," they said. "The Greatest Feat in the History of Mankind," they said. "Only Americans could have done it," they said, which is true. Even if Ah Goong had not spent half his gold on Citizenship Papers, he was an American for having built the railroad. A white demon in top hat tap-tapped on the gold spike, and pulled it back out. Then one China Man held the real spike, the steel one, and another hammered it in.

While the demons posed for photographs, the China Men dispersed. It 60 was dangerous to stay. The Driving Out had begun. Ah Goong does not appear in railroad photographs. Scattering, some China Men followed the north star in the constellation Tortoise the Black Warrior to Canada, or they kept the constellation Phoenix ahead of them to South America or the White Tiger west or the Wolf east. Seventy lucky men rode the Union Pacific to Massachusetts for jobs at a shoe factory. Fifteen hundred went to Fou Loy Company in New Orleans and San Francisco, several hundred to plantations in Mississippi, Georgia, and Arkansas, and sugarcane plantations in Louisiana and Cuba. (From the South, they sent word that it was a custom to step off the sidewalk along with the black demons when a white demon walked by.) Seventy went to New Orleans to grade a route for a railroad, then to Pennsylvania to work in a knife factory. The Colorado State Legislature passed a resolution welcoming the railroad China Men to come build the new state. They built railroads in every part of the country—the Alabama and Chattanooga Railroad, the Houston and Texas Railroad, the Southern Pacific, the railroads in Louisiana and Boston, the Pacific Northwest, and Alaska. After the Civil War, China Men banded the nation North and South, East and West, with crisscrossing steel. They were the binding and building ancestors of this place.

Ah Goong would have liked a leisurely walk along the tracks to review 61 his finished handiwork, or to walk east to see the rest of his new country. But instead, Driven Out, he slid down mountains, leapt across valleys and streams, crossed plains, hid sometimes with companions and often alone, and eluded bandits who would hold him up for his railroad pay and shoot him for practice as they shot Injuns and jackrabbits. Detouring and backtracking, his path wound back and forth to his railroad, a familiar silver road in the wilderness. When a train came, he hid against the shaking ground in case a demon with a shotgun was hunting from it. He picked over camps where he had once lived. He was careful to find hidden places to sleep. In China bandits did not normally kill people, the booty the main thing, but here the demons killed for fun and hate. They tied pigtails to horses and dragged chinamen. He decided that he had better head for San Francisco, where he would catch a ship to China.

Perched on hillsides, he watched many sunsets, the place it was setting, 62 the direction he was going. There were fields of grass that he tunneled through, hid in, rolled in, dived and swam in, suddenly jumped up laughing, suddenly stopped. He needed to find a town and human company. The spooky tumbleweeds caught in barbed wire were peering at him, waiting for him; he had to find a town. Towns grew along the tracks as they did along rivers. He sat looking at a town all day, then ducked into it by night.

At the familiar sight of a garden laid out in a Chinese scheme—vegetables 63 in beds, white cabbages, red plants, chives, and coriander for immortality, herbs boxed with boards—he knocked on the back door. The China Man who answered gave him food, the appropriate food for the nearest holiday, talked story, exclaimed at how close their ancestral villages were to each other. They exchanged information on how many others lived how near, which towns had Chinatowns, what size, two or three stores or a block, which towns to avoid. "Do you have a wife?" they asked one another. "Yes. She lives in China. I have been sending money for twenty years now." They exchanged vegetable seeds, slips, and cuttings, and Ah Goong carried letters to another town or China.

Some demons who had never seen the likes of him gave him things and touched him. He also came across lone China Men who were alarmed to have him appear, and, unwelcome, he left quickly; they must have wanted to be the only China Man of that area, the special China Man. **64**

He met miraculous China Men who had produced families out of no-where—a wife and children, both boys and girls. "Uncle," the children called him, and he wanted to stay to be the uncle of the family. The wife washed his clothes, and he went on his way when they were dry. **65**

On a farm road, he came across an imp child playing in the dirt. It looked at him, and he looked at it. He held out a piece of sugar; he cupped a grassblade between his thumbs and whistled. He sat on the ground with his legs crossed, and the child climbed into the hollow of his arms and legs. "I wish you were my baby," he told it. "My baby." He was very satisfied sitting there under the humming sun with the baby, who was satisfied too, no squirming. "My daughter," he said. "My son." He couldn't tell whether it was a boy or a girl. He touched the baby's fat arm and cheeks, its gold hair, and looked into its blue eyes. He made a wish that it not have to carry a sledgehammer and crawl into the dark. But he would not feel sorry for it; other people must not suffer any more than he did, and he could endure anything. Its mother came walking out into the road. She had her hands above her like a salute. She walked tentatively towards them, held out her hand, smiled, spoke. He did not understand what she said except "Bye-bye." The child waved and said, "Bye-bye," crawled over his legs, and toddled to her. Ah Goong continued on his way in a direction she could not point out to a posse looking for a kidnapper chinaman. **66**

Explosions followed him. He heard screams and went on, saw flames outlining black windows and doors, and went on. He ran in the opposite direction from gunshots and the yell—*eeha awha*—the cowboys made when they herded cattle and sang their savage songs. **67**

Good at hiding, disappearing—decades unaccounted for—he was not working in a mine when forty thousand chinamen were Driven Out of mining. He was not killed or kidnapped in the Los Angeles Massacre, though he gave money toward ransoming those whose toes and fingers, a digit per week, and ears grotesquely rotting or pickled, and scalped queues, were displayed in Chinatowns. Demons believed that the poorer a chinaman looked, the more gold he had buried somewhere, that chinamen stuck together and would always ransom one another. If he got kidnapped, Ah Goong planned, he would whip out his Citizenship Paper and show that he was an American. He was lucky not to be in Colorado with the Denver demons burned all chinamen homes and businesses, nor in Rock Springs, Wyoming, when the miner demons killed **68** twenty-eight or fifty chinamen. The Rock Springs Massacre began in a large coal mine owned by the Union Pacific; the outnumbered chinamen were shot in the back as they ran to Chinatown, which the demons burned. They forced chinamen out into the open and shot them; demon women and children threw the wounded back in the flames. (There was a rumor of a good white lady in Green Springs who hid China Men in the Pacific Hotel and shamed the demons away.) The hunt went on for a month before federal troops came. The count of the dead was inexact because bodies were mutilated and pieces scattered all over the Wyoming Territory. No white miners were indicted, but the government paid $150,000 in reparations to victims' families. There were many family men, then. There were settlers—abiding China Men. And China Women. Ah Goong was running elsewhere during the Drivings Out of Tacoma, Seattle, Oregon City, Albania, and Marysville. The demons of Tacoma packed all its chinamen into boxcars and sent them to Portland, where they were run out of town. China Men returned to Seattle, though, and refused to sell their land and stores but fought until the army came; the demon rioters were tried and acquitted. And when the Boston police imprisoned and beat 234 chinamen, it was 1902, and Ah Goong had already reached San Francisco or China, and perhaps San Francisco again.

In Second City (Sacramento), he spent some of his railroad money at the theater. The main actor's face was painted red with thick black eyebrows and long black beard, and when he strode onto the stage, Ah Goong recognized the hero, Guan Goong; his puppet horse had red nostrils and rolling eyes. Ah Goong's heart leapt to recognize hero and horse in the wilds of America. Guan Goong murdered his enemy—crash! bang! of cymbals and drum—and left his home village—sad, sad flute music. But to the glad clamor of cymbals entered his friends—Liu Pei (pronounced the same as Running Nose) and Chang Fei. In a joyful burst of pink flowers, the three men swore the Peach Garden Oath. Each friend sang an aria to friendship; together they would fight side by side and live and die one for all and all for one. Ah Goong felt as warm as if he were with friends at a party. Then Guan Goong's archenemy, the sly Ts'ao Ts'ao, captured him and two of Liu Pei's wives, the Lady Kan and the Lady Mi. Though Ah Goong knew they were boy actors, he basked in the presence of Chinese ladies. The prisoners traveled to the capital, the soldiers waving horsehair whisks, signifying horses, the ladies walking between horizontal banners, signifying palanquins. All the prisoners were put in one bedroom, but Guan Goong stood all night outside the door with a lighted candle in his hand, singing an aria about faithfulness. When the capital was attacked by a common enemy, Guan Goong fought the biggest man in one-to-one combat, a twirling, jumping sword dance that strengthened the China Men who watched it. From afar Guan Goong's two partners heard about the feats of the man with the red face and intelligent horse. The three friends were reunited and fought until they secured their rightful kingdom.

69

Ah Goong felt refreshed and inspired. He called out Bravo like the demons 70 in the audience, who had not seen theater before. Guan Goong, the God of War, also God of War and Literature, had come to America—Guan Goong, Grandfather Guan, our own ancestor of writers and fighters, of actors and gamblers, and avenging executioners who mete out justice. Our own kin. Not a distant ancestor but Grandfather.

In the Big City (San Francisco), a goldsmith convinced Ah Goong to have 71 his gold made into jewelry, which would organize it into one piece and also delight his wife. So he handed over a second bag of gold. He got it back as a small ring in a design he thought up himself, two hands clasping in a handshake. "So small?" he said, but the goldsmith said that only some of the ore had been true gold.

He got a ship out of San Francisco without being captured near the docks, 72 where there was a stockade full of jailed chinamen; the demonesses came down from Nob Hill and took them home to be servants, cooks, and baby-sitters.

Grandmother liked the gold ring very much. The gold was so pure, it 73 squished to fit her finger. She never washed dishes, so the gold did not wear away. She quickly spent the railroad money, and Ah Goong said he would go to America again. He had a Certificate of Return and his Citizenship Paper.

But this time, there was no railroad to sell his strength to. He lived in a 74 basement that was rumored to connect with tunnels beneath Chinatown. In an underground arsenal, he held a pistol and said, "I feel the death in it." "The holes for the bullets were like chambers in a beehive or wasp nest," he said. He was inside the earth when the San Francisco Earthquake and Fire began. Thunder rumbled from the ground. Some say he died falling into the cracking earth. It was a miraculous earthquake and fire. The Hall of Records burned completely. Citizenship Papers burned, Certificates of Return, Birth Certificates, Residency Certificates, passenger lists, Marriage Certificates—every paper a China Man wanted for citizenship and legality burned in that fire. An authentic citizen, then, had no more papers than an alien. Any paper a China Man could not produce had been "burned up in the Fire of 1906." Every China Man was reborn out of that fire a citizen.

Some say the family went into debt and sent for Ah Goong, who was 75 not making money; he was a homeless wanderer, a shiftless, dirty, jobless man with matted hair, ragged clothes, and fleas all over his body. He ate out of garbage cans. He was a louse eaten by lice. A fleaman. It cost two thousand dollars to bring him back to China, his oldest sons signing promissory notes for one thousand, his youngest to repay four hundred to one neighbor and six hundred to another. Maybe he hadn't died in San Francisco, it was just his papers that burned; it was just that his existence was outlawed by Chinese Exclusion Acts. The family called him Fleaman. They did not understand his accomplishments as an American ancestor, a holding, homing ancestor of this place. He'd gotten the legal or illegal papers burned in the San Francisco

Earthquake and Fire; he appeared in America in time to be a citizen and to father citizens. He had also been seen carrying a child out of the fire, a child of his own in spite of the laws against marrying. He had built a railroad out of sweat, why not have an American child out of longing? ◆

◆ Responding

1. Maxine Hong Kingston calls her grandfather "an American ancestor, a holding, homing ancestor of this place," even though he was never legally an American citizen. Explain his contribution to this country.

2. Working in a group, discuss the ways in which Kingston's grandfather's life was shaped by the place where he was living and the opportunities available to him. Write a journal entry or an essay about the ways in which you or any of your relatives have been directly affected by the period or place in which you happen to be born or live.

3. Imagine that you are a reporter for a San Francisco newspaper in the late 1800s. You have just returned from interviewing Chinese railroad workers. Write a feature story for your newspaper arguing that they are being exploited and mistreated by the "demon" bosses, or write a story from the bosses' point of view about working conditions on the railroad.

4. Choose one of the atrocities Kingston writes about and expand your knowledge of the circumstances by researching the incident in your school library. Write your own version and share it with the class.

◆

CONNECTING

Critical Thinking and Writing

1. Write an essay speculating about the possible social, psychological, and economic effects of the Exclusion Act on Chinese already in the United States when it was passed. Use examples from the readings to support your opinions.

2. Compare the working conditions of the Chinese on the railway to the working conditions of other groups described in readings by Kingston, Colón, Panunzio, and Chávez, among others. How was each group treated? You may compare the treatment of a group or the experiences of individuals.

3. Discuss the causes and effects of organized resistance among the Chinese railroad workers, as reported by Kingston, and compare them with Chávez's description of Chicano efforts to organize almost one hundred years later.

4. The issue of parents wishing to maintain a native culture while raising their children in an alien culture is a recurrent theme in these readings. Some parents find it easier than others to accept the assimilation of their children. Compare the reactions of any two families in this or other chapters when their children begin to become Americanized.

5. Trace the struggles for civil rights and acceptance that faced the immigrant Chinese in America. Using information from this chapter and the chapter about Japanese-American experiences during World War II, compare the problems facing the Chinese during the late 1800s with those of the Japanese during the 1940s.

6. Discuss the influence of the American school system on the children of immigrants. Is education a force that melds society? Is it also a force that separates parents and children?

7. Using information from these readings, describe the role of women in traditional Chinese culture. Compare the Chinese woman immigrant of the late 1800s to women from other immigrant groups of the same period, such as European immigrants.

8. Many Chinese came to the United States in the nineteenth century. Using evidence from the readings, write an essay comparing their reasons for immigrating with those of other groups.

9. Using the readings as a resource, compile a list of the customs and folklore that were a part of Chinese culture in the late 1800s. Write an essay discussing the folklore of your family or culture, or of another culture with which you are familiar.

10. Discuss the relationship between parents and children portrayed in this chapter. What duties did a Chinese child of late 1800s and early 1900s owe to parents and to the rest of the family?

For Further Research

1. Angel Island has been called the Ellis Island of the West Coast. Research and compare the situation at the two ports of entry to the United States.

2. Research the changes in family life that have taken place in Chinese families living in America over the past sixty years.

◆

REFERENCES AND ADDITIONAL SOURCES

Barth, Gunther. *Bitter Strength: A History of the Chinese in the United States, 1850–1870.* Cambridge, Mass.: Harvard University Press, 1964.

Chinn, Thomas, et al. *A History of the Chinese in California.* San Francisco: Chinese Historical Society of America, 1969.

Genthe, Arnold and John K. Tchen. *Genthe's Photographs of San Francisco's Old Chinatown.* New York: Dover, 1984.

Hom, Marlon K. *Songs of the Gold Mountain: Cantonese Rhymes from San Francisco Chinatown.* Berkeley and Los Angeles: University of California Press, 1987.

Kim, Elaine. *Asian American Literature.* Philadelphia: Temple University Press, 1982.

Kim, Hyung-Chan, ed. *Dictionary of Asian American History.* Westwood, CT: Greenwood, 1986.

Lai, Him Mark, et al. *Island: Poetry and History of Chinese Immigrants on Angel Island. 1910–1940.* San Francisco: HOC DOI Project, 1980.

Saxton, Alexander. *The Indispensible Enemy: Labor and the Anti-Chinese Movement in California.* Berkeley: University of California Press, 1971.

Solberg, S.E. "Sui, Storyteller: Sui Sin Far," in *Turning Shadows into Light: Art and Culture of the Northwest's Early Asian/Pacific Community*. Muyumi Tsutakawa and Alan Chong Lau, eds. Seattle: Young Pine Press, Asian Multi-Media Center, 1982.

_____. "Sui Sin Far/Edith Eaton: First Chinese American Fictionalist," in *Melus* 8:1 (1981), 27–39.

Takaki, Ronald. *Strangers from a Different Shore: A History of Asian Americans*. Boston: Little, Brown, 1989.

Tsai, Shih Shan Henry. *The Chinese Experience in America*. Bloomington: Indiana University Press, 1986.

Tung, William L. *The Chinese in America: Chronology and Fact Book*. Dobbs Ferry, N.Y.: Oceana, 1974.

Family moving into Harlem, 1905.
(© Brown Brothers)

Chapter 3

AFRICAN AMERICANS
The Migration North and the Harlem Renaissance

World War I veterans returning home, 1919.
(© Culver Pictures, Inc.)

Parade on Seventh Avenue in Harlem, 1920s.
(© James Van Der Zee Collection/photo
courtesy The Studio Museum)

◆ SETTING THE HISTORICAL CONTEXT ◆

IN HIS POEM "Afro American Fragment," Langston Hughes writes of the importance of recovering a sense of history, a past that was lost for too long:

> So long,
> So far away,
> Is Africa.
> Not even memories alive
> Save those that history books create,
> Save those that songs
> Beat back into the blood—
>
> . . . Subdued and time-lost
> Are the drums — and yet
> Through some vast mist of race
> There comes this song
> I do not understand
> This song of atavistic land . . .

Through images of awakening, recovery, and rebirth, the poem explores several themes important during the Harlem Renaissance, a period when African Americans used music, literature, painting, sculpture, and theater to assert their pride in their traditions and communities. Like other cultural renaissances, the Harlem Renaissance sought renewal through the recovery of history. Just as the poets and artists of the Italian Renaissance turned away from the Middle Ages and toward the classical ages of Greece and Rome, African American writers and artists during the 1920s turned away from the years of slavery by looking back to the traditions of Africa.

Yet the Harlem Renaissance was a movement with roots and repercussions in American society and politics. Occurring in the wake of the great African American migration north during the first two decades of the twentieth century, the Harlem Renaissance became, in the words of critic Alain Locke, a corresponding "migration of the spirit." This cultural and political coming of age was in part a consequence of the new urban concentration and some accumulation of capital among African Americans.

During this time the debate over the best way to achieve social justice grew more insistent and spread to include larger segments of society, both inside and outside the African American community.

The migration of large numbers of African Americans from southern farms to northern cities began in the 1880s. Years of poor weather and insect infestations had depressed the South's agricultural economy, so that African Americans—mostly sharecroppers—doubted that the area could offer them a secure future. The economic position of African Americans in the South—and sometimes their very lives—were further threatened by the social injustices of prejudice and segregation.

The Reconstruction Act of 1867 and the Fourteenth and Fifteenth Amendments to the U.S. Constitution (1868 and 1870, respectively) had been intended to guarantee blacks the full exercise of their rights as citizens. Through these acts and with the support of the U.S. government, African Americans began to vote, hold office, participate in the southern states' constitutional conventions, and establish schools. Although Reconstruction afforded them some help in overcoming the accumulated liabilities of years of slavery, serious problems remained. Without federal resettlement or land redistribution programs, African Americans remained economically sub-servient to landowning whites. Some whites, unwilling to accept them as political and social equals, established racist organizations such as the Ku Klux Klan, which practiced systematic terror and violence against African Americans.

Even the meager support of Reconstruction ended when, in 1877, political maneuvering in Washington resulted in the federal government's withdrawal from its role in upholding the basic rights of African Americans. The federal government's support continued to erode over the next decades, reaching a low point in the Supreme Court's 1896 decision in *Plessy* v. *Ferguson*, which established the "separate but equal" doctrine. Throughout this period, white southerners who were hostile to black political and social participation took advantage of the weakening federal role to segregate and disfranchise African Americans through legislation and intimidation.

During the 1880s, when civic leaders in the North were celebrating

the United States as a land of opportunity and a refuge for the world's oppressed peoples, southern legislators were drafting measures limiting African
Americans' access to such public facilities as streetcars, waiting rooms,
water fountains, and restrooms; segregation spread as well to vital institutions such as schools and hospitals. One southern state after another altered
its constitution to segregate and exclude African Americans; by 1907 all
southern states had adopted such measures.

These states were able to maintain segregation by disfranchising many
African Americans. Beginning in the late 1890s, they circumvented the
intention of the Fifteenth Amendment through legislative actions requiring
potential voters to pay poll taxes, pass literacy tests, or prove that they were
property owners. Some states, for example, instituted the requirement that
people intending to vote first had to read and interpret a section of the
state constitution selected by the examining official. When the legislators
discovered that some whites were also having difficulty passing these tests,
they found another way in which to give whites preferential treatment:
they instituted so-called grandfather clauses, exempting from testing and
property requirements any man whose father or grandfather had been eligible
to vote in the state on a given date, usually in the early 1860s. Because
African Americans had not been allowed to vote during the years of slavery,
their descendants were effectively prevented from voting through these
discriminatory clauses.

In addition to instituting segregation and disfranchisement, southern
states denied African Americans educational and employment opportunities.
Despite the state governments' assertion that black and white schools were
"separate but equal," the facilities for blacks were clearly inferior to those
for whites. Moreover, African Americans were routinely excluded from
membership in unions and other professional organizations.

During the late nineteenth and early twentieth centuries, African
Americans maintained ongoing protests against and resistance to segregation
and voting restrictions, using forums such as the *Chicago Defender*, a popular
and outspoken black newspaper, and strategies such as economic boycotts
that were put to good use again decades later by Martin Luther King, Jr.

Despite occasional successes, however, these injustices remained substantially unchanged until the Civil Rights Act of 1964 and the Voting Rights Act of 1965. Driven from the South by poverty, discrimination, brutality, and political oppression, and responding to the assurances of the media and of paid recruiters that their labor was in demand, African Americans thus migrated—in small numbers to the West and in large numbers to the industrial cities of the north. They established homes and communities in many northern cities, but their cultural center was in Harlem.

In his introduction to *The New Negro*, the influential anthology of Harlem Renaissance literature that he edited, Alain Locke celebrated the "great migration" as an opportunity for African Americans to be not only transplanted but also transformed. With a greater concentration of African Americans in urban centers, the opportunities for political dialogue increased, and the philosophy of the community began to change. The "New Negro movement" of the 1920s accelerated the general rejection of the conciliatory attitude toward racial advancement exemplified by educator Booker T. Washington. In the late nineteenth century, Washington advocated that African Americans pursue moral, educational, and occupational self-improvement as a means of achieving acceptance by and respect from whites. The historian and scholar W. E. B. DuBois challenged this position. DuBois, one of the founders of the National Association for the Advancement of Colored People (NAACP), served as editor of the NAACP publication *Crisis*, one of the most important periodicals of the Harlem Renaissance. Rejecting Washington's position that mastery of technical and mechanical skills would lead to better-paying jobs and a place in white society, DuBois maintained that blacks would advance only by developing their own society and culture as they pressed for their full rights as citizens.

Many voices contributed to the lively debate in the African American community over how best to achieve social justice and to assert racial pride. A. Philip Randolph, a socialist, civil rights activist, and labor leader, organized the Brotherhood of Sleeping Car Porters and cofounded a weekly, *The Messenger*, critical of the positions of both Washington and DuBois. Marcus Garvey, born in Jamaica, founded the Universal Negro Improvement

Association (UNIA) in 1911, before emigrating to the United States in 1916. The UNIA sought equality for blacks through their total independence—social, political, and economic—from whites. In the United States, Garvey established a movement that advocated separatism and called on African Americans to unite to promote liberation and development in the African homeland. He received support from both blacks and whites before being imprisoned for mail fraud and later deported. Garvey's idea that blacks needed an independent power base continues to influence African American leaders, although it has been redefined in political rather than geographical terms.

Emerging from this historical context, the Harlem Renaissance was marked by voices of protest and voices of rebirth. Locke characterizes these voices as attempting to address "the discrepancy between the American social creed and American social practice." The conflicts within the African American community had become apparent in the debate over what its attitude toward and role in World War I should be. Although they were at first hesitant, many community leaders, DuBois among them, encouraged African Americans to support the war effort as a means of improving their status at home. Despite their distinguished service, however, African American soldiers returning from the war found themselves with little more than their military decorations. Even before the end of the war, the Wilson administration, in an effort to appease southerners, had begun to segregate facilities in all public buildings within the District of Columbia. African Americans in cities continued to be plagued by discrimination in housing and employment. In addition to the unfulfilled promise of equal opportunity, there was also a dramatic increase in racially motivated violence: eighty people were killed during the East St. Louis, Illinois, riots of 1917, and twenty five cities and towns had violent confrontations over race during the "red summer" riots of 1919.

Anger over violence and injustice found expression in some of the earliest Harlem Renaissance poetry. Claude McKay's "If We Must Die," now an American classic, was written to protest the dehumanization and fear of this period:

If we must die, let it not be like hogs
Hunted and penned in an inglorious spot,
While round us bark the mad and hungry dogs,
Making their mock at our accursed lot.
If we must die, O let us nobly die,
So that our precious blood may not be shed
In vain; then even the monsters we defy
Shall be constrained to honor us though dead!
O kinsmen! we must meet the common foe!
Though far outnumbered let us show brave,
And for their thousand blows deal one deathblow!
What though before us lies the open grave?
Like men we'll face the murderous, cowardly pack,
Pressed to the wall, dying, but fighting back!

But concurrently with publishing announcements and evidence of the new artistic renaissance, the periodicals *Crisis* and *Opportunity* printed monthly reports of the numbers of African Americans who had been lynched.

Art was used not only to reflect current social realities but also to transcend them. In "Invocation," McKay took inspiration from the African states obtaining their independence in the years following World War I. He advises American blacks to do as he did, to "turn east" for hope:

O my brothers and my sisters, wake! arise:
For the new birth rends the old earth and the very dead are
    waking.
Ghosts are turned flesh, throwing off the grave's disguise,
And the foolish, even children, are made wise;
For the big earth groans in travail for the strong, new world
    in the making
O my brother, dreaming for centuries,
Wake from sleeping; to the East turn, turn your eyes.

McKay here celebrates his readers' potential both to witness and to participate in social and cultural transformation. In its essays, poetry, and art, the Harlem Renaissance proclaimed the emergence of African Americans who were no longer willing to accept secondary status in the society: in the vernacular of the time, it proclaimed a "New Negro."

Invitation to awards dinner for first literary contest, May 1, 1925. "Opportunity, Journal of Negro Life" was published by the National Urban League. (Moorland-Spingarn Research Center, Mary O'H. Williamson Collection/Howard University)

The Harlem Renaissance ended abruptly with the stock market crash of 1929 and the Great Depression that followed. Writers such as Claude McKay, who found their audiences eroding, emigrated to Europe; in fact, so many African American writers moved to Europe that it is often said that the Harlem Renaissance was transferred to Paris. Others, such as Zora Neale

Hurston and Arna Bontemps, returned to the South and fell into obscurity. Although short-lived as an artistic movement, the Harlem Renaissance created among black writers a firm belief in the strength of their voices and created among both black and white readers an enduring expectation of fresh, penetrating, expressive black writing and art.

EXPLORING THE LITERARY AND
◆ CULTURAL CONTEXT ◆

In *Black Manhattan*, James Weldon Johnson explains how blacks established an autonomous culture and society in Harlem. Despite depictions of its residents as wild, unrestrained, and immoral—in the works of outsiders such as Carl van Vechten, for example—Johnson shows that in fact, Harlem represented stability, as exemplified by its churches and civic groups. If there were nightclubs and burlesques, there were also theaters and fraternal and cultural organizations. Harlem also supported its own newspaper and several nationally important journals, including *Crisis, Opportunity*, and *The Messenger*.

New York City attracted artists and writers from all over the country, and the African Americans gravitated toward Harlem. Indeed, few of the Harlem writers were actually from the Northeast. Although Countée Cullen was born in Harlem, Jean Toomer, Jessie Fauset, and Zora Neale Hurston were from the South, Langston Hughes was from the Midwest, and Claude McKay was from the Caribbean.

In fiction, poetry, essays, and drama, African American writers proclaimed the emergence of the "New Negro," who not only rejected accommodation with white culture but asserted the validity and power of the African American heritage and traditions. In his classic essay "The New Negro," the philosopher and critic Alain Locke announced the beginning of a new time for the African American—a time of cultural growth and freer self-expression. This theme was found in many of the poems of the period, among them Claude McKay's "America," in which the speaker, although admitting the difficulty of his task, asserts a willingness to fight for what is his.

Although Harlem became the center of intellectual exploration and artistic production, much of the art produced there had its inspiration and themes in other, often rural, settings. In some works, such as Hughes's "The Negro Speaks of Rivers," landscape reflects collective memory. Explorations of the African American heritage used elements and settings derived both from Africa and from the rural American South. Hurston's "Sweat," for example, reveals the persistence and importance of church and community conventions and of folk traditions. Works such as "Theater," from Jean Toomer's *Cane*, are written in a style that captures the energy and experimentation of jazz, thus filtering personal experience through cultural expression.

In "America," McKay calls the United States "the cultured hell that tests my youth." The body of writing emerging from the Harlem Renaissance reflects this tension. "The New Negro" conveys optimism about the ability of African Americans to confront and surmount circumstances, but other works are less sanguine about the individual's fate in a society that condones racial prejudice. The excerpt from Jessie Redmon Fauset's novel, for instance, introduces some of the ironies faced by African Americans fighting World War I for a freedom in Europe that they did not enjoy at home; indeed, as the passage continues, Fauset illustrates how racial prejudice can erupt and spread where it never before existed. Prejudice emerges in the selection from Wallace Thurman's novel *The Blacker the Berry*, in which African Americans are shown as perpetrators and victims of colorism (judging fellow African Americans by the relative lightness or darkness of their skin). In the chapter's last essay, Darwin Turner evaluates these and other attitudes expressed in works of the Harlem Renaissance from a historical perspective.

The Harlem Renaissance was an artistic movement characterized by contradictions. While asserting artistic "otherness"—their reliance not on an American but on an African aesthetic—many artists relied for financial and critical support of their ideas on the white avant-garde of Greenwich Village. While black writers proclaimed Harlem's rebirth as a cultural center, evidence of that rebirth was too often missing from the daily lives of residents, who continued to endure discrimination in housing and employment. Although founded in political activism, the Harlem Renaissance moved more and more toward personal experience and expression. But there is no controversy about the achievements of the Harlem Renaissance, a period when African Americans created a culture that the world was compelled to notice.

BEGINNING: PRE-READING/WRITING

◆ *What's in a name? A great deal, especially if it's the name of a group you belong to. Discuss why the name of an ethnic group is a particularly sensitive issue for people within that group. Consider the ways in which ethnic group names are chosen. Who does the naming, and who uses the name? Why do groups sometimes decide that they prefer to be called by a new name? For example, why was the name Negro rejected by the African American community? What are the psychological effects of names with positive or negative connotations? Why are some names appropriate when used by group members but not when used by outsiders?*

---

*T*he Constitution of South Carolina (1895) illustrates a trend that began in southern states in the 1880s and 1890s. In a process known as disfranchisement, the state legislature set limits on voting rights, based on such criteria as the applicant's ownership of property, payment of a poll tax, and ability to pass a literacy test. Such laws effectively excluded most African Americans from the voting process. It was not until the 1960s that these laws were repealed. Disfranchisement is considered one of the primary causes of the great migration of African Americans from the south.

◆ *From* THE CONSTITUTION OF SOUTH CAROLINA ◆

Article II: Right of Suffrage

SECTION 1. All elections by the people shall be by ballot, and elections shall never be held or the ballots counted in secret.   1

SEC. 2. Every qualified elector shall be eligible to any office to be voted for, unless disqualified by age, as prescribed in this Constitution. But no person shall hold two offices of honor or profit at the same time: *Provided*, That any person holding another office may at the same time be an officer in the militia or a Notary Public.   2

SEC. 3. Every male citizen of this State and of the United States twenty-one years of age and upwards, not laboring under the disabilities named in this Constitution and possessing the qualifications required by it, shall be an elector.   3

SEC. 4. The qualifications for suffrage shall be as follows: 4

(*a*) Residence in the State for two years, in the County one year, in the polling precinct in which the elector offers to vote four months, and the payment six months before any election of any poll tax then due and payable: *Provided*, That ministers in charge of an organized church and teachers of public schools shall be entitled to vote after six months' residence in the State, otherwise qualified.   5

(*b*) Registration, which shall provide for the enrollment of every elector once in ten years, and also an enrollment during each and every year of every elector not previously registered under the provisions of this Article.   6

(*c*) Up to January 1st 1898, all male persons of voting age applying for registration who can read any Section in this Constitution submitted to them by the registration officer, or understand and explain it when read to them by the registration officer, shall be entitled to register and become electors. A separate record of all persons registered before January 1st, 1898, sworn to by the registration officer, shall be filed, one copy with the Clerk of Court and one in the office of the Secretary of State, on or before February 1st, 1898, and such persons shall remain during life qualified electors unless disqualified by   7 the other provisions of this Article. The certificate of the Clerk of Court or Secretary of State shall be sufficient evidence to establish the right of said citizens to any subsequent registration and the franchise under the limitations herein imposed.

(*d*) Any person who shall apply for registration after January 1st, 1898, if otherwise qualified, shall be registered: *Provided*, That he can both read and write any Section of this Constitution submitted to him by the registration officer or can show that he owns, and has paid all taxes collectible during the previous year on property in this State assessed at three hundred dollars ($300) or more.

(*e*) Managers of election shall require of every elector offering to vote at any election, before allowing him to vote, proof of the payment of all taxes, including poll tax, assessed against him and collectible during the previous year. The production of a certificate or of the receipt of the officer authorized to collect such taxes shall be conclusive proof of the payment thereof.

(*f*) The General Assembly shall provide for issuing to each duly registered elector a certificate of registration, and shall provide for the renewal of such certificate when lost, mutilated or destroyed, if the applicant is still a qualified elector under the provisions of this Constitution, or if he has been registered as provided in subsection (*c*). ◆

◆ Responding

1. Find the provisions in this section of the constitution of South Carolina that could be used to keep someone from voting. Who has the discretion to grant someone the right to vote?

2. Working in a group, discuss the ways in which the power structure in a society can work to disfranchise certain citizens.

3. Are you surprised that such laws were not challenged in the courts? Compare these provisions with the guarantees in the Bill of Rights. Do they violate the rights guaranteed in the United States Constitution?

ALAIN LOCKE

Alain Locke was born in Philadelphia in 1886. After earning a bachelor's degree and a doctorate in philosophy from Harvard University, he later became the first African American Rhodes Scholar. He taught philosophy at Howard University and several other colleges, wrote more than half a dozen books, and served as literary editor of Opportunity *and* Phylon, *two important journals of the Harlem Renaissance. Throughout his life he also served as a patron and mentor for many writers and artists within the African American community.*

Credited with being the intellectual leader of the Harlem Renaissance, Locke oversaw the editing of The New Negro *anthology (1925). His classic essay, "The New Negro," which introduces the anthology, announces the goals of the movement and celebrates the talents of those given voice in the collection.*

◆ THE NEW NEGRO ◆

In the last decade something beyond the watch and guard of statistics has happened in the life of the American Negro and the three norns who have traditionally presided over the Negro problem have a changeling in their laps. The Sociologist, the Philanthropist, the Race-leader are not unaware of the New Negro, but they are at a loss to account for him. He simply cannot be swathed in their formulæ. For the younger generation is vibrant with a new psychology; the new spirit is awake in the masses, and under the very eyes of the professional observers is transforming what has been a perennial problem into the progressive phases of contemporary Negro life. 1

Could such a metamorphosis have taken place as suddenly as it has appeared to? The answer is no; not because the New Negro is not here, but because the Old Negro had long become more of a myth than a man. The Old Negro, we must remember, was a creature of moral debate and historical controversy. His has been a stock figure perpetuated as an historical fiction partly in innocent sentimentalism, partly in deliberate reactionism. The Negro himself has contributed his share to this through a sort of protective social mimicry forced upon him by the adverse circumstances of dependence. So for generations in the mind of America, the Negro has been more of a formula than a human being—a something to be argued about, condemned or defended, to be "kept down," or "in his place," or "helped up," to be worried with or worried over, harassed or patronized, a social bogey or a social burden. The thinking Negro even has been induced to share this same general attitude, to focus his attention on controversial issues, to see himself in the distorted perspective of a social problem. His shadow, so to speak, has been more real to him than his person- 2

ality. Through having had to appeal from the unjust stereotypes of his op-
pressors and traducers to those of his liberators, friends and benefactors he has
had to subscribe to the traditional positions from which his case has been viewed.
Little true social or self-understanding has or could come from such a situation.

But while the minds of most of us, black and white, have thus burrowed   3
in the trenches of the Civil War and Reconstruction, the actual march of development has simply flanked these positions, necessitating a sudden reorien-
tation of view. We have not been watching in the right direction; set North
and South on a sectional axis, we have not noticed the East till the sun has us
blinking.

Recall how suddenly the Negro spirituals revealed themselves; suppressed   4
for generations under the stereotypes of Wesleyan hymn harmony, secretive,
half-ashamed, until the courage of being natural brought them out—and behold,
there was folk-music. Similarly the mind of the Negro seems suddenly to have
slipped from under the tyranny of social intimidation and to be shaking off the
psychology of imitation and implied inferiority. By shedding the old chrysalis
of the Negro problem we are achieving something like a spiritual emancipation.
Until recently, lacking self-understanding, we have been almost as much of a
problem to ourselves as we still are to others. But the decade that found us
with a problem has left us with only a task. The multitude perhaps feels as yet
only a strange relief and a new vague urge, but the thinking few know that in
the reaction the vital inner grip of prejudice has been broken.

With this renewed self-respect and self-dependence, the life of the Negro   5
community is bound to enter a new dynamic phase, the buoyancy from within
compensating for whatever pressure there may be of conditions from without.
The migrant masses, shifting from countryside to city, hurdle several generations of experience at a leap, but more important, the same thing happens
spiritually in the life-attitudes and self-expression of the Young Negro, in his
poetry, his art, his education and his new outlook, with the additional advantage,
of course, of the poise and greater certainty of knowing what it is all about.
From this comes the promise and warrant of a new leadership. As one of them
has discerningly put it:

> We have tomorrow
> Bright before us
> Like a flame.
>
> Yesterday, a night-gone thing
> A sun-down name.
>
> And dawn today
> Broach arch above the road we came.
> We march!

This is what, even more than any "most creditable record of fifty years   6
of freedom," requires that the Negro of to-day be seen through other than the
dusty spectacles of past controversy. The day of "aunties," "uncles" and "mam-
mies" is equally gone. Uncle Tom and Sambo have passed on, and even the
"Colonel" and "George" play barnstorm rôles from which they escape with
relief when the public spotlight is off. The popular melodrama has about played
itself out, and it is time to scrap the fictions, garret the bogeys and settle down
to a realistic facing of facts.

First we must observe some of the changes which since the traditional   7
lines of opinion were drawn have rendered these quite obsolete. A main change
has been, of course, that shifting of the Negro population which has made the
Negro problem no longer exclusively or even predominantly Southern. Why
should our minds remain sectionalized, when the problem itself no longer is?
Then the trend of migration has not only been toward the North and the Central
Midwest, but city-ward and to the great centers of industry—the problems of
adjustment are new, practical, local and not peculiarly racial. Rather they are
an integral part of the large industrial and social problems of our present-day
democracy. And finally, with the Negro rapidly in process of class differentia-
tion, if it ever was warrantable to regard and treat the Negro *en masse* it is
becoming with every day less possible, more unjust and more ridiculous.

In the very process of being transplanted, the Negro is becoming trans-   8
formed.

The tide of Negro migration, northward and city-ward, is not to be fully   9
explained as a blind flood started by the demands of war industry coupled with
the shutting off of foreign migration, or by the pressure of poor crops coupled
with increased social terrorism in certain sections of the South and Southwest.
Neither labor demand, the boll-weevil nor the Ku Klux Klan is a basic factor,
however contributory any or all of them may have been. The wash and rush
of this human tide on the beach line of the northern city centers is to be explained
primarily in terms of a new vision of opportunity, of social and economic
freedom, of a spirit to seize, even in the face of an extortionate and heavy toll,
a chance for the improvement of conditions. With each successive wave of it,
the movement of the Negro becomes more and more a mass movement toward
the larger and the more democratic chance—in the Negro's case a deliberate
flight not only from countryside to city, but from medieval America to modern.

Take Harlem as an instance of this. Here in Manhattan is not merely the   10
largest Negro community in the world, but the first concentration in history
of so many diverse elements of Negro life. It has attracted the African, the
West Indian, the Negro American; has brought together the Negro of the North
and the Negro of the South; the man from the city and the man from the town
and village; the peasant, the student, the business man, the professional man,
artist, poet, musician, adventurer and worker, preacher and criminal, exploiter
and social outcast. Each group has come with its own separate motives and for

its own special ends, but their greatest experience has been the finding of one another. Proscription and prejudice have thrown these dissimilar elements into a common area of contact and interaction. Within this area, race sympathy and unity have determined a further fusing of sentiment and experience. So what began in terms of segregation becomes more and more, as its elements mix and react, the laboratory of a great race-welding. Hitherto, it must be admitted that American Negroes have been a race more in name than in fact, or to be exact, more in sentiment than in experience. The chief bond between them has been that of a common condition rather than a common consciousness; a problem in common rather than a life in common. In Harlem, Negro life is seizing upon its first chances for group expression and self-determination. It is—or promises at least to be—a race capital. That is why our comparison is taken with those nascent centers of folk-expression and self-determination which are playing a creative part in the world to-day. Without pretense to their political significance, Harlem has the same rôle to play for the New Negro as Dublin has had for the New Ireland or Prague for the New Czechoslovakia.

Harlem, I grant you, isn't typical—but it is significant, it is prophetic. 11 No sane observer, however sympathetic to the new trend, would contend that the great masses are articulate as yet, but they stir, they move, they are more than physically restless. The challenge of the new intellectuals among them is clear enough—the "race radicals" and realists who have broken with the old epoch of philanthropic guidance, sentimental appeal and protest. But are we after all only reading into the stirrings of a sleeping giant the dreams of an agitator? The answer is in the migrating peasant. It is the "man farthest down" who is most active in getting up. One of the most characteristic symptoms of this is the professional man, himself migrating to recapture his constituency after a vain effort to maintain in some Southern corner what for years back seemed an established living and clientele. The clergyman following his errant flock, the physician or lawyer trailing his clients, supply the true clues. In a real sense it is the rank and file who are leading, and the leaders who are following. A transformed and transforming psychology permeates the masses.

When the racial leaders of twenty years ago spoke of developing race- 12 pride and stimulating race-consciousness, and of the desirability of race soli- darity, they could not in any accurate degree have anticipated the abrupt feeling that has surged up and now pervades the awakened centers. Some of the rec- ognized Negro leaders and a powerful section of white opinion identified with "race work" of the older order have indeed attempted to discount this feeling as a "passing phase," an attack of "race nerves" so to speak, an "aftermath of the war," and the like. It has not abated, however, if we are to gauge by the present tone and temper of the Negro press, or by the shift in popular support from the officially recognized and orthodox spokesmen to those of the inde- pendent, popular, and often radical type who are unmistakable symptoms of a new order. It is a social disservice to blunt the fact that the Negro of the Northern centers has reached a stage where tutelage, even of the most interested and well-intentioned sort, must give place to new relationships, where positive self-direction must be reckoned with in ever increasing measure. The American mind must reckon with a fundamentally changed Negro.

The Negro too, for his part, has idols of the tribe to smash. If on the one hand the white man has erred in making the Negro appear to be that which would excuse or extenuate his treatment of him, the Negro, in turn, has too often unnecessarily excused himself because of the way he has been treated. The intelligent Negro of to-day is resolved not to make discrimination an extenuation for his shortcomings in performance, individual or collective; he is trying to hold himself at par, neither inflated by sentimental allowances nor depreciated by current social discounts. For this he must know himself and be known for precisely what he is, and for that reason he welcomes the new scientific rather than the old sentimental interest. Sentimental interest in the Negro has ebbed. We used to lament this as the falling off of our friends; now we rejoice and pray to be delivered both from self-pity and condescension. The mind of each racial group has had a bitter weaning, apathy or hatred on one side matching disillusionment or resentment on the other; but they face each other to-day with the possibility at least of entirely new mutual attitudes. 13

It does not follow that if the Negro were better known, he would be better liked or better treated. But mutual understanding is basic for any subsequent coöperation and adjustment. The effort toward this will at least have the effect of remedying in large part what has been the most unsatisfactory feature of our present stage of race relationships in America, namely the fact that the more intelligent and representative elements of the two race groups have at so many points got quite out of vital touch with one another. 14

The fiction is that the life of the races is separate, and increasingly so. The fact is that they have touched too closely at the unfavorable and too lightly at the favorable levels. 15

While inter-racial councils have sprung up in the South, drawing on forward elements of both races, in the Northern cities manual laborers may brush elbows in their everyday work, but the community and business leaders have experienced no such interplay or far too little of it. These segments must achieve contact or the race situation in America becomes desperate. Fortunately this is happening. There is a growing realization that in social effort the coöperative basis must supplant long-distance philanthropy, and that the only safeguard for mass relations in the future must be provided in the carefully maintained contacts of the enlightened minorities of both race groups. In the intellectual realm a renewed and keen curiosity is replacing the recent apathy; the Negro is being carefully studied, not just talked about and discussed. In art and letters, instead of being wholly caricatured, he is being seriously portrayed and painted. 16

To all of this the New Negro is keenly responsive as an augury of a new democracy in American culture. He is contributing his share to the new social understanding. But the desire to be understood would never in itself have been 17 sufficient to have opened so completely the protectively closed portals of the thinking Negro's mind. There is still too much possibility of being snubbed or patronized for that. It was rather the necessity for fuller, truer self-expression, the realization of the unwisdom of allowing social discrimination to segregate him mentally, and a counter-attitude to cramp and fetter his own living—and so the "spite-wall" that the intellectuals built over the "color-line" has happily been taken down. Much of this reopening of intellectual contacts has centered in New York and has been richly fruitful not merely in the enlarging of personal experience, but in the definite enrichment of American art and letters and in the clarifying of our common vision of the social tasks ahead.

The particular significance in the re-establishment of contact between the more advanced and representative classes is that it promises to offset some of the unfavorable reactions of the past, or at least to re-surface race contacts somewhat for the future. Subtly the conditions that are molding a New Negro are molding a new American attitude. 18

However, this new phase of things is delicate; it will call for less charity but more justice; less help, but infinitely closer understanding. This is indeed a critical stage of race relationships because of the likelihood, if the new temper is not understood, of engendering sharp group antagonism and a second crop of more calculated prejudice. In some quarters, it has already done so. Having weaned the Negro, public opinion cannot continue to paternalize. The Negro to-day is inevitably moving forward under the control largely of his own objectives. What are these objectives? Those of his outer life are happily already well and finally formulated, for they are none other than the ideals of American institutions and democracy. Those of his inner life are yet in process of formation, for the new psychology at present is more of a consensus of feeling than of opinion, of attitude rather than of program. Still some points seem to have crystallized. 19

Up to the present one may adequately describe the Negro's "inner objectives" as an attempt to repair a damaged group psychology and reshape a warped social perspective. Their realization has required a new mentality for the American Negro. And as it matures we begin to see its effects; at first, negative, iconoclastic, and then positive and constructive. In this new group psychology we note the lapse of sentimental appeal, then the development of a more positive self-respect and self-reliance; the repudiation of social dependence, and then the gradual recovery from hyper-sensitiveness and "touchy" nerves, the repudiation of the double standard of judgment with its special philanthropic allowances and then the sturdier desire for objective and scientific appraisal, and finally the rise from social disillusionment to race pride, from the sense of social debt to the responsibilities of social contribution, and offsetting the necessary working and commonsense acceptance of restricted conditions, the belief in ultimate esteem and recognition. Therefore the Negro to-day wishes to be known for what he is, even in his faults and shortcomings, 20 and scorns a craven and precarious survival at the price of seeming to be what he is not. He resents being spoken of as a social ward or minor, even by his own, and to being regarded a chronic patient for the sociological clinic, the sick man of American Democracy. For the same reasons, he himself is through with those social nostrums and panaceas, the so-called "solutions" of his "problem," with which he and the country have been so liberally dosed in the past. Religion, freedom, education, money—in turn, he has ardently hoped for and peculiarly trusted these things; he still believes in them, but not in blind trust that they alone will solve his life-problem.

Each generation, however, will have its creed, and that of the present is the belief in the efficacy of collective effort, in race co-operation. This deep feeling of race is at present the mainspring of Negro life. It seems to be the outcome of the reaction to proscription and prejudice; an attempt, fairly successful on the whole, to convert a defensive into an offensive position, a handicap into an incentive. It is radical in tone, but not in purpose and only the most stupid forms of opposition, misunderstanding or persecution could make it otherwise. Of course, the thinking Negro has shifted a little toward the left with the world-trend, and there is an increasing group who affiliate with radical and liberal movements. But fundamentally for the present the Negro is radical on race matters, conservative on others, in other words, a "forced radical," a social protestant rather than a genuine radical. Yet under further pressure and injustice iconoclastic thought and motives will inevitably increase. Harlem's quixotic radicalisms call for their ounce of democracy to-day lest to-morrow they be beyond cure.

The Negro mind reaches out as yet to nothing but American wants, American ideas. But this forced attempt to build his Americanism on race values is a unique social experiment, and its ultimate success is impossible except through the fullest sharing of American culture and institutions. There should be no delusion about this. American nerves in sections unstrung with race hysteria are often fed the opiate that the trend of Negro advance is wholly separatist, and that the effect of its operation will be to encyst the Negro as a benign foreign body in the body politic. This cannot be—even if it were desirable. The racialism of the Negro is no limitation or reservation with respect to American life; it is only a constructive effort to build the obstructions in the stream of his progress into an efficient dam of social energy and power. Democracy itself is obstructed and stagnated to the extent that any of its channels are closed. Indeed they cannot be selectively closed. So the choice is not between one way for the Negro and another way for the rest, but between American institutions frustrated on the one hand and American ideals progressively fulfilled and realized on the other.

There is, of course, a warrantably comfortable feeling in being on the right side of the country's professed ideals. We realize that we cannot be undone without America's undoing. It is within the gamut of this attitude that the thinking Negro faces America, but with variations of mood that are if anything more significant than the attitude itself. Sometimes we have it taken with the defiant ironic challenge of McKay:[1]

> Mine is the future grinding down to-day
> Like a great landslip moving to the sea,
> Bearing its freight of débris far away
> Where the green hungry waters restlessly
> Heave mammoth pyramids, and break and roar
> Their eerie challenge to the crumbling shore.

Sometimes, perhaps more frequently as yet, it is taken in the fervent and almost filial appeal and counsel of Weldon Johnson's:[2]

> O Southland, dear Southland!
> Then why do you still cling
> To an idle age and a musty page,
> To a dead and useless thing?

But between defiance and appeal, midway almost between cynicism and hope, the prevailing mind stands in the mood of the same author's *To America*, an attitude of sober query and stoical challenge:

> How would you have us, as we are?
>   Or sinking 'neath the load we bear,
> Our eyes fixed forward on a star,
>   Or gazing empty at despair?
>
> Rising or falling? Men or things?
>   With dragging pace or footsteps fleet?
> Strong, willing sinews in your wings,
>   Or tightening chains about your feet?

More and more, however, an intelligent realization of the great discrepancy 24 between the American social creed and the American social practice forces upon the Negro the taking of the moral advantage that is his. Only the steadying and sobering effect of a truly characteristic gentleness of spirit prevents the

---

[1]Claude McKay (1889–1948) Jamaican-born poet and novelist who figured prominently in the Harlem Renaissance.

[2]James Weldon Johnson (1871–1938), social reformer, educator, poet, essayist, song writer, and lawyer.

rapid rise of a definite cynicism and counter-hate and a defiant superiority feeling. Human as this reaction would be, the majority still deprecate its advent, and would gladly see it forestalled by the speedy amelioration of its causes. We wish our race pride to be a healthier, more positive achievement than a feeling based upon a realization of the shortcomings of others. But all paths toward the attainment of a sound social attitude have been difficult; only a relatively few, enlightened minds have been able as the phrase puts it "to rise above" prejudice. The ordinary man has had until recently only a hard choice between the alternatives of supine and humiliating submission and stimulating but hurtful counter-prejudice. Fortunately from some inner, desperate resourcefulness has recently sprung up the simple expedient of fighting prejudice by mental passive resistance, in other words by trying to ignore it. For the few, this manna may perhaps be effective, but the masses cannot thrive upon it.

Fortunately there are constructive channels opening out into which the balked social feelings of the American Negro can flow freely. 25

Without them there would be much more pressure and danger than there is. These compensating interests are racial but in a new and enlarged way. One is the consciousness of acting as the advance-guard of the African peoples in their contact with Twentieth Century civilization; the other, the sense of a mission of rehabilitating the race in world esteem from that loss of prestige for which the fate and conditions of slavery have so largely been responsible. Harlem, as we shall see, is the center of both these movements; she is the home of the Negro's "Zionism." The pulse of the Negro world has begun to beat in Harlem. A Negro newspaper carrying news material in English, French and Spanish, gathered from all quarters of America, the West Indies and Africa has maintained itself in Harlem for over five years. Two important magazines, both edited from New York, maintain their news and circulation consistently on a cosmopolitan scale. Under American auspices and backing, three pan-African congresses have been held abroad for the discussion of common interests, colonial questions and the future co-operative development of Africa. In terms of the race question as a world problem, the Negro mind has leapt, so to speak, upon the parapets of prejudice and extended its cramped horizons. In so doing it has linked up with the growing group consciousness of the dark-peoples and is gradually learning their common interests. As one of our writers has recently put it: "It is imperative that we understand the white world in its relations to the non-white world." As with the Jew, persecution is making the Negro international. 26

As a world phenomenon this wider race consciousness is a different thing from the much asserted rising tide of color. Its inevitable causes are not of our making. The consequences are not necessarily damaging to the best interests of civilization. Whether it actually brings into being new Armadas of conflict or argosies of cultural exchange and enlightenment can only be decided by the attitude of the dominant races in an era of critical change. With the American 27

Negro, his new internationalism is primarily an effort to recapture contact with the scattered peoples of African derivation. Garveyism[3] may be a transient, if spectacular, phenomenon, but the possible role of the American Negro in the future development of Africa is one of the most constructive and universally helpful missions that any modern people can lay claim to.

Constructive participation in such causes cannot help giving the Negro   28 valuable group incentives, as well as increased prestige at home and abroad. Our greatest rehabilitation may possibly come through such channels, but for the present, more immediate hope rests in the revaluation by white and black alike of the Negro in terms of his artistic endowments and cultural contributions, past and prospective. It must be increasingly recognized that the Negro has already made very substantial contributions, not only in his folk-art, music especially, which has always found appreciation, but in larger, though humbler and less acknowledged ways. For generations the Negro has been the peasant matrix of that section of America which has most undervalued him, and here he has contributed not only materially in labor and in social patience, but spiritually as well. The South has unconsciously absorbed the gift of his folk-temperament. In less than half a generation it will be easier to recognize this, but the fact remains that a leaven of humor, sentiment, imagination and tropic nonchalance has gone into the making of the South from a humble, unacknowl-edged source. A second crop of the Negro's gifts promises still more largely. He now becomes a conscious contributor and lays aside the status of a beneficiary and ward for that of a collaborator and participant in American civilization. The great social gain in this is the releasing of our talented group from the arid fields of controversy and debate to the productive fields of creative expression. The especially cultural recognition they win should in turn prove the key to that revaluation of the Negro which must precede or accompany any consid-erable further betterment of race relationships. But whatever the general effect, the present generation will have added the motives of self-expression and spir-itual development to the old and still unfinished task of making material headway and progress. No one who understandingly faces the situation with its sub-stantial accomplishment or views the new scene with its still more abundant promise can be entirely without hope. And certainly, if in our lifetime the Negro should not be able to celebrate its full initiation into American democracy, he can at least, on the warrant of these things, celebrate the attainment of a significant and satisfying new phase of group development, and with it a spiritual Coming of Age. ◆

---

[3]Movement named after Black Nationalist leader Marcus Garvey (1887–1940) which promoted separatism and encouraged liberation and development for the African homeland.

◆ Responding

1. Locke explains the movement of blacks from the South to the North "primarily in terms of a new vision of opportunity, of social and economic freedom, of a spirit to seize, even in the face of an extortionate and heavy toll, a chance for the improvement of conditions." Using information from the reading and from your own knowledge, write an essay agreeing or disagreeing with the argument that movement to the North improved conditions for southern blacks in the 1920s.

2. Define what Locke means by the old and new images of the Negro. What diverse elements made up the "largest Negro community in the world" in Harlem in the 1920s?

3. State the purpose of this essay in your own words. Who was Locke's audience? Do you think he was writing primarily for a white or a black audience?

4. Working individually or in a group, list the changes Locke describes as taking place in race relations during the 1920s. Are some of these changes now outdated by other changes in society? Describe the "contact and cooperation" today between diverse groups of people in your community.

ZORA NEALE HURSTON

Zora Neale Hurston, born in Eatonsville, Florida, in 1903, studied an-
thropology at Howard University and Barnard College. During the Harlem
Renaissance, Hurston worked with Langston Hughes and Wallace Thurman
on editorial projects such as the publication of the literary journal Fire!!!
Although she wrote some short stories during this period, much of Hurston's
work was not published until after the Harlem Renaissance. Her major
writings include Moses, Man of the Mountain *(1939),* Jonah, Gourd
Vine *(1934),* Their Eyes Were Watching God *(1937),* Seraph on the
Sewanee *(1948), and her autobiography,* Dust Tracks on the Road
(1941). In her later years she had less success publishing her works. She died
in poverty in 1960. Recently, through the efforts of Alice Walker and other
African American writers, Hurston's work has found a wider audience.

The short story that follows, like many others from the Harlem Renais-
sance, is set in the South. Using a rural setting and folk themes, it explores
the relationships between social and familial structures.

◆ SWEAT ◆

It was eleven o'clock of a Spring night in Florida. It was Sunday. Any other   1
night, Delia Jones would have been in bed for two hours by this time. But she
was a washwoman, and Monday morning meant a great deal to her. So she
collected the soiled clothes on Saturday when she returned the clean things.
Sunday night after church, she sorted and put the white things to soak. It saved
her almost a half-day's start. A great hamper in the bedroom held the clothes
that she brought home. It was so much neater than a number of bundles lying
around.

She squatted on the kitchen floor beside the great pile of clothes, sorting   2
them into small heaps according to color, and humming a song in a mournful
key, but wondering through it all where Sykes, her husband, had gone with
her horse and buckboard.

Just then something long, round, limp and black fell upon her shoulders   3
and slithered to the floor beside her. A great terror took hold of her. It softened
her knees and dried her mouth so that it was a full minute before she could cry
out or move. Then she saw that it was the big bull whip her husband liked to
carry when he drove.

She lifted her eyes to the door and saw him standing there bent over with   4
laughter at her fright. She screamed at him.

"Sykes, what you throw dat whip on me like dat? You know it would   5
skeer me—looks just like a snake, an' you knows how skeered Ah is of snakes."

"Course Ah knowed it! That's how come Ah done it." He slapped his leg 6
with his hand and almost rolled on the ground in his mirth. "If you such a big
fool dat you got to have a fit over a earth worm or a string, Ah don't keer how
bad Ah skeer you."

"You ain't got no business doing it. Gawd knows it's a sin. Some day 7
Ah'm gointuh drop dead from some of yo' foolishness. 'Nother thing, where
you been wid mah rig? Ah feeds dat pony. He ain't fuh you to be drivin' wid
no bull whip."

"You sho' is one aggravatin' nigger woman!" he declared and stepped into 8
the room. She resumed her work and did not answer him at once. "Ah done
tole you time and again to keep them white folks' clothes outa dis house."

He picked up the whip and glared at her. Delia went on with her work. 9
She went out into the yard and returned with a galvanized tub and set it on
the washbench. She saw that Sykes had kicked all of the clothes together again,
and now stood in her way truculently, his whole manner hoping, *praying*, for
an argument. But she walked calmly around him and commenced to re-sort the
things.

"Next time, Ah'm gointer kick 'em outdoors," he threatened as he struck 10
a match along the leg of his corduroy breeches.

Delia never looked up from her work, and her thin, stooped shoulders 11
sagged further.

"Ah ain't for no fuss t'night Sykes. Ah just come from taking sacrament 12
at the church house."

He snorted scornfully. "Yeah, you just come from de church house on a 13
Sunday night, but heah you is gone to work on them clothes. You ain't nothing
but a hypocrite. One of them amen-corner Christians—sing, whoop,and shout,
then come home and wash white folks' clothes on the Sabbath."

He stepped roughly upon the whitest pile of things, kicking them helter- 14
skelter as he crossed the room. His wife gave a little scream of dismay, and
quickly gathered them together again.

"Sykes, you quit grindin' dirt into these clothes! How can Ah git through 15
by Sat'day if Ah don't start on Sunday?"

"Ah don't keer if you never git through. Anyhow, Ah done promised 16
Gawd and a couple of other men, Ah ain't gointer have it in mah house. Don't
gimme no lip neither, else Ah'll throw 'em out and put mah fist up side yo'
head to boot."

Delia's habitual meekness seemed to slip from her shoulders like a blown 17
scarf. She was on her feet; her poor little body, her bare knuckly hands bravely
defying the strapping hulk before her.

"Looka heah, Sykes, you done gone too fur. Ah been married to you fur 18
fifteen years, and Ah been takin' in washin' fur fifteen years. Sweat, sweat,
sweat! Work and sweat, cry and sweat, pray and sweat!"

"What's that got to do with me?" he asked brutally. 19

"What's it got to do with you, Sykes? Mah tub of suds is filled yo' belly 20 with vittles more times than yo' hands is filled it. Mah sweat is done paid for this house and Ah reckon Ah kin keep on sweatin' in it."

She seized the iron skillet from the stove and struck a defensive pose, 21 which act surprised him greatly, coming from her. It cowed him and he did not strike her as he usually did.

"Naw you won't," she panted, "that ole snaggle-toothed black woman 22 you runnin' with ain't comin' heah to pile up on *mah* sweat and blood. You ain't paid for nothin' on this place, and Ah'm gointer stay right heah till Ah'm toted out foot foremost."

"Well, you better quit gittin' me riled up, else they'll be totin' you out 23 sooner than you expect. Ah'm so tired of you Ah don't know whut to do. Gawd! How Ah hates skinny wimmen!"

A little awed by this new Delia, he sidled out of the door and slammed 24 the back gate after him. He did not say where he had gone, but she knew too well. She knew very well that he would not return until nearly daybreak also. Her work over, she went on to bed but not to sleep at once. Things had come to a pretty pass!

She lay awake, gazing upon the debris that cluttered their matrimonial 25 trail. Not an image left standing along the way. Anything like flowers had long ago been drowned in the salty stream that had been pressed from her heart. Her tears, her sweat, her blood. She had brought love to the union and he had brought a longing after the flesh. Two months after the wedding, he had given her the first brutal beating. She had the memory of his numerous trips to Orlando with all of his wages when he had returned to her penniless, even before the first year had passed. She was young and soft then, but now she thought of her knotty, muscled limbs, her harsh knuckly hands, and drew herself up into an unhappy little ball in the middle of the big feather bed. Too late now to hope for love, even if it were not Bertha it would be someone else. This case differed from the others only in that she was bolder than the others. Too late for everything except her little home. She had built it for her old days, and planted one by one the trees and flowers there. It was lovely to her, lovely.

Somehow, before sleep came, she found herself saying aloud: "Oh well, 26 whatever goes over the Devil's back, is got to come under his belly. Sometime or ruther, Sykes, like everybody else, is gointer reap his sowing." After that she was able to build a spiritual earthworks against her husband. His shells could no longer reach her. AMEN. She went to sleep and slept until he announced his presence in bed by kicking her feet and rudely snatching the covers away.

"Gimme some kivah heah, an' git yo' damn foots over on yo' own side! 27 Ah oughter mash you in yo' mouf fuh drawing dat skillet on me."

Delia went clear to the rail without answering him. A triumphant indif- 28 ference to all that he was or did.

II

The week was as full of work for Delia as all other weeks, and Saturday found 29
her behind her little pony, collecting and delivering clothes.

It was a hot, hot day near the end of July. The village men on Joe Clarke's 30
porch even chewed cane listlessly. They did not hurl the cane-knots as usual.
They let them dribble over the edge of the porch. Even conversation had
collapsed under the heat.

"Heah come Delia Jones," Jim Merchant said, as the shaggy pony came 31
'round the bend of the road toward them. The rusty buckboard was heaped
with baskets of crisp, clean laundry.

"Yep," Joe Lindsay agreed. "Hot or col', rain or shine, jes'ez reg'lar ez 32
de weeks roll roun' Delia carries 'em an' fetches 'em on Sat'day."

"She better if she wanter eat," said Moss. "Syke Jones ain't wuth de shot 33
an' powder hit would tek tuh kill 'em. Not to *huh* he ain't."

"He sho' ain't," Walter Thomas chimed in. "It's too bad, too, cause she 34
wuz a right pretty li'l trick when he got huh. Ah'd uh mah'ied huh mahself if
he hadnter beat me to it."

Delia nodded briefly at the men as she drove past. 35

"Too much knockin' will ruin *any* 'oman. He done beat huh 'nough tuh 36
kill three women, let 'lone change they looks," said Elijah Moseley. "How Syke
kin stommuck dat big black greasy Mogul he's layin' roun' wid, gits me. Ah
swear dat eight-rock couldn't kiss a sardine can Ah done thowed out de back
do' 'way las' yeah."

"Aw, she's fat, thass how come. He's allus been crazy 'bout fat women," 37
put in Merchant. "He'd a' been tied up wid one long time ago if he could a'
found one tuh have him. Did Ah tell yuh 'bout him come sidlin' roun' *mah*
wife—bringin' her a basket uh peecans outa his yard fuh a present? Yessir, mah
wife! She tol' him tuh take 'em right straight back home, 'cause Delia works
so hard ovah dat washtub she reckon everything on de place taste lak sweat an'
soapsuds. Ah jus' wisht Ah'd a' caught 'im 'roun dere! Ah'd a' made his hips
ketch on fiah down dat shell road."

"Ah know he done it, too. Ah sees 'im grinnin' at every 'oman dat passes," 38
Walter Thomas said. "But even so, he useter eat some mighty big hunks uh
humble pie tuh git dat li'l 'oman he got. She wuz ez pritty ez a speckled pup!
Dat wuz fifteen years ago. He useter be so skeered uh losin' huh, she could
make him do some parts of a husband's duty. Dey never wuz de same in de
mind."

"There oughter be a law about him," said Lindsay. "He ain't fit tuh carry 39
guts tuh a bear."

Clarke spoke for the first time. "Tain't no law on earth dat kin make a 40
man be decent if it ain't in 'im. There's plenty men dat takes a wife lak dey do
a joint uh sugar-cane. It's round, juicy an' sweet when dey gits it. But dey

squeeze an' grind, squeeze an' grind an' wring tell dey wring every drop uh pleasure dat's in 'em out. When dey's satisfied dat dey is wrung dry, dey treats 'em jes' lak dey do a cane-chew. Dey thows 'em away. Dey knows whut dey is doin' while dey is at it, an' hates theirselves fuh it but they keeps on hangin' after huh tell she's empty. Den dey hates huh fuh bein' a cane-chew an' in de way."

"We oughter take Syke an' dat stray 'oman uh his'n down in Lake Howell swamp an' lay on de rawhide till they cain't say Lawd a' mussy. He allus wuz uh ovahbearin niggah, but since dat white 'oman from up north done teached 'im how to run a automobile, he done got too beggety to live—an' we oughter kill 'im," Old Man Anderson advised.   41

A grunt of approval went around the porch. But the heat was melting their civic virtue and Elijah Moseley began to bait Joe Clarke.   42

"Come on, Joe, git a melon outa dere an' slice it up for yo' customers. We'se all sufferin' wid de heat. De bear's done got *me!*"   43

"Thass right, Joe, a watermelon is jes' whut Ah needs tuh cure de ep-pizudicks," Walter Thomas joined forces with Moseley. "Come on dere, Joe. We all is steady customers an' you ain't set us up in a long time. Ah chooses dat long, bowlegged Floridy favorite."   44

"A god, an' be dough. You all gimme twenty cents and slice away," Clarke retorted. "Ah needs a col' slice m'self. Heah, everybody chip in. Ah'll lend y'all mah meat knife."   45

The money was all quickly subscribed and the huge melon brought forth. At that moment, Sykes and Bertha arrived. A determined silence fell on the porch and the melon was put away again.   46

Merchant snapped down the blade of his jackknife and moved toward the store door.   47

"Come on in, Joe, an' gimme a slab uh sow belly an' uh pound uh coffee—almost fuhgot 'twas Sat'day. Got to git on home." Most of the men left also.   48

Just then Delia drove past on her way home, as Sykes was ordering magnificently for Bertha. It pleased him for Delia to see.   49

"Git whutsoever yo' heart desires, Honey. Wait a minute, Joe. Give huh two bottles uh strawberry soda-water, uh quart parched ground-peas, an' a block uh chewin' gum."   50

With all this they left the store, with Sykes reminding Bertha that this was his town and she could have it if she wanted it.   51

The men returned soon after they left, and held their watermelon feast. 52

"Where did Syke Jones git da 'oman from nohow?" Lindsay asked.   53

"Ovah Apopka. Guess dey musta been cleanin' out de town when she lef'. She don't look lak a thing but a hunk uh liver wid hair on it."   54

"Well, she sho' kin squall," Dave Carter contributed. "When she gits ready tuh laff, she jes' opens huh mouf an' latches it back tuh de las' notch. No ole granpa alligator down in Lake Bell ain't got nothin' on huh."   55

III

Bertha had been in town three months now. Sykes was still paying her room- 56
rent at Della Lewis'—the only house in town that would have taken her in.
Sykes took her frequently to Winter Park to 'stomps'. He still assured her that
he was the swellest man in the state.

"Sho' you kin have dat li'l ole house soon's Ah git dat 'oman outa dere. 57
Everything b'longs tuh me an' you sho' kin have it. Ah sho' 'bominates uh
skinny 'oman. Lawdy, you sho' is got one portly shape on you! You kin git
anything you wants. Dis is *mah* town an' you sho' kin have it."

Delia's work-worn knees crawled over the earth in Gethsemane and up 58
the rocks of Calvary many, many times during these months. She avoided the
villagers and meeting places in her efforts to be blind and deaf. But Bertha
nullified this to a degree, by coming to Delia's house to call Sykes out to her
at the gate.

Delia and Sykes fought all the time now with no peaceful interludes. They 59
slept and ate in silence. Two or three times Delia had attempted a timid friend-
liness, but she was repulsed each time. It was plain that the breaches must
remain agape.

The sun had burned July to August. The heat streamed down like a 60
million hot arrows, smiting all things living upon the earth. Grass withered,
leaves browned, snakes went blind in shedding and men and dogs went mad.
Dog days!

Delia came home one day and found Sykes there before her. She won- 61
dered, but started to go on into the house without speaking, even though he
was standing in the kitchen door and she must either stoop under his arm or
ask him to move. He made no room for her. She noticed a soap box beside the
steps, but paid no particular attention to it, knowing that he must have brought
it there. As she was stooping to pass under his outstretched arm, he suddenly
pushed her backward, laughingly.

"Look in de box dere Delia, Ah done brung yuh somethin'!" 62

She nearly fell upon the box in her stumbling, and when she saw what 63
it held, she all but fainted outright.

"Syke! Syke, mah Gawd! You take dat rattlesnake 'way from heah! You 64
gottuh. Oh, Jesus, have mussy!"

"Ah ain't got tuh do nuthin' uh de kin'—fact is Ah ain't got tuh do nothin' 65
but die. Tain't no use uh you puttin' on airs makin' out lak you skeered uh dat
snake—he's gointer stay right heah tell he die. He wouldn't bite me cause Ah
knows how tuh handle 'im. Nohow he wouldn't risk breakin' out his fangs 'gin
yo skinny laigs."

"Naw, now Syke, don't keep dat thing 'round tryin' tuh skeer me tuh 66
death. You knows Ah'm even feared uh earth worms. Thass de biggest snake
Ah evah did see. Kill 'im Syke, please."

"Doan ast me tuh do nothin' fuh yuh. Goin' 'round tryin' tuh be so damn asterperious.[1] Naw, Ah ain't gonna kill it. Ah think uh damn sight mo' uh him dan you! Dat's a nice snake, an' anybody doan lak 'im kin jes' hit de grit." 67

The village soon heard that Sykes had the snake, and came to see and ask questions. 68

"How de hen-fire did you ketch dat six-foot rattler, Syke?" Thomas asked. 69

"He's full uh frogs so he cain't hardly move, thass how Ah eased up on 'm. But Ah'm a snake charmer an' knows how tuh handle 'em. Shux, dat ain't nothin'. Ah could ketch one eve'y day if Ah so wanted tuh." 70

"Whut he needs is a heavy hick'ry club leaned real heavy on his head. Dat's de bes' way tuh charm a rattlesnake." 71

"Naw, Walt, y'all jes' don't understand dese diamon' backs lak Ah do," said Sykes in a superior tone of voice. 72

The village agreed with Walter, but the snake stayed on. His box remained by the kitchen door with its screen wire covering. Two or three days later it had digested its meal of frogs and literally came to life. It rattled at every movement in the kitchen or the yard. One day as Delia came down the kitchen steps she saw his chalky-white fangs curved like scimitars hung in the wire meshes. This time she did not run away with averted eyes as usual. She stood for a long time in the doorway in a red fury that grew bloodier for every second that she regarded the creature that was her torment. 73

That night she broached the subject as soon as Sykes sat down to the table. 74

"Syke, Ah wants you tuh take dat snake 'way fum heah. You done starved me an' Ah put up widcher, you done beat me an Ah took dat, but you done kilt all mah insides bringin' dat varmint heah." 75

Sykes poured out a saucer full of coffee and drank it deliberately before he answered her. 76

"A whole lot Ah keer 'bout how you feels inside uh out. Dat snake ain't goin' no damn wheah till Ah gits ready fuh 'im tuh go. So fur as beatin' is concerned, yuh ain't took near all dat you gointer take ef yuh stay 'round *me*." 77

Delia pushed back her plate and got up from the table. "Ah hates you, Sykes," she said calmly. "Ah hates you tuh de same degree dat Ah useter love yuh. Ah done took an' took till mah belly is full up tuh mah neck. Dat's de reason Ah got mah letter fum de church an' moved mah membership tuh Woodbridge—so Ah don't haftuh take no sacrament wid yuh. Ah don't want-uh see yuh 'round me atall. Lay 'round wid dat 'oman all yuh wants tuh, but gwan 'way fum me an' mah house. Ah hates yuh lak uh suck-egg dog." 78

Sykes almost let the huge wad of corn bread and collard greens he was chewing fall out of his mouth in amazement. He had a hard time whipping himself up to the proper fury to try to answer Delia. 79

------

[1]haughty

"Well, Ah'm glad you does hate me. Ah'm sho' tiahed uh you hangin' on tuh me. Ah don't want yuh. Look at yuh stringey ole neck! Yo' rawbony laigs an' arms is enough tuh cut uh man tuh death. You looks jes' lak de devvul's doll-baby tuh *me*. You cain't hate me no worse dan Ah hates you. Ah been hatin' *you* fuh years."

"Yo' ole black hide don't look lak nothin' tuh me, but uh passle uh wrinkled up rubber, wid yo' big ole yeahs flappin' on each side lak uh paih uh buzzard wings. Don't think Ah'm gointuh be run 'way fum mah house neither. Ah'm goin' tuh de white folks 'bout *you*, mah young man, de very nex' time you lay yo' han's on me. Mah cup is done run ovah." Delia said this with no signs of fear and Sykes departed from the house, threatening her, but made not the slightest move to carry out any of them.

That night he did not return at all, and the next day being Sunday, Delia was glad she did not have to quarrel before she hitched up her pony and drove the four miles to Woodbridge.

She stayed to the night service—'love feast'—which was very warm and full of spirit. In the emotional winds her domestic trials were borne far and wide so that she sang as she drove homeward,

> Jurden water, black an' col
> Chills de body, not de soul
> An' Ah wantah cross Jurden in uh calm time.

She came from the barn to the kitchen door and stopped.

"Whut's de mattah, ol' Satan, you ain't kickin' up yo' racket?" She addressed the snake's box. Complete silence. She went on into the house with a new hope in its birth struggles. Perhaps her threat to go to the white folks had frightened Sykes! Perhaps he was sorry! Fifteen years of misery and suppression had brought Delia to the place where she would hope *anything* that looked towards a way over or through her wall of inhibitions.

She felt in the match-safe behind the stove at once for a match. There was only one there.

"Dat niggah wouldn't fetch nothin' heah tuh save his rotten neck, but he kin run thew whut Ah brings quick enough. Now he done toted off nigh on tuh haff uh box uh matches. He done had dat 'oman heah in mah house, too."

Nobody but a woman could tell how she knew this even before she struck the match. But she did and it put her into a new fury.

Presently she brought in the tubs to put the white things to soak. This time she decided she need not bring the hamper out of the bedroom; she would go in there and do the sorting. She picked up the pot-bellied lamp and went in. The room was small and the hamper stood hard by the foot of the white iron bed. She could sit and reach through the bedposts—resting as she worked.

"*Ah wantah cross Jurden in uh calm time.*" She was singing again. The mood of the 'love feast' had returned. She threw back the lid of the basket almost gaily. Then, moved by both horror and terror, she sprang back toward the door. *There lay the snake in the basket!* He moved sluggishly at first, but even as she turned round and round, jumped up and down in an insanity of fear, he began to stir vigorously. She saw him pouring his awful beauty from the basket upon the bed, then she seized the lamp and ran as fast as she could to the kitchen. The wind from the open door blew out the light and the darkness added to her terror. She sped to the darkness of the yard, slamming the door after her before she thought to set down the lamp. She did not feel safe even on the ground, so she climbed up in the hay barn.

There for an hour or more she lay sprawled upon the hay a gibbering wreck. 90

Finally she grew quiet, and after that came coherent thought. With this stalked through her a cold, bloody rage. Hours of this. A period of introspection, a space of retrospection, then a mixture of both. Out of this an awful calm. 91

"Well, Ah done de bes' Ah could. If things ain't right, Gawd knows tain't mah fault." 92

She went to sleep—a twitch sleep—and woke up to a faint gray sky. There was a loud hollow sound below. She peered out. Sykes was at the wood-pile, demolishing a wire-covered box. 93

He hurried to the kitchen door, but hung outside there some minutes before he entered, and stood some minutes more inside before he closed it after him. 94

The gray in the sky was spreading. Delia descended without fear now, and crouched beneath the low bedroom window. The drawn shade shut out the dawn, shut in the night. But the thin walls held back no sound. 95

"Dat ol' scratch is woke up now!" She mused at the tremendous whirr inside, which every woodsman knows, is one of the sound illusions. The rattler is a ventriloquist. His whirr sounds to the right, to the left, straight ahead, behind, close under foot—everywhere but where it is. Woe to him who guesses wrong unless he is prepared to hold up his end of the argument! Sometimes he strikes without rattling at all. 96

Inside, Sykes heard nothing until he knocked a pot lid off the stove while trying to reach the match-safe in the dark. He had emptied his pockets at Bertha's. 97

The snake seemed to wake up under the stove and Sykes made a quick leap into the bedroom. In spite of the gin he had had, his head was clearing now. 98

"Mah Gawd!" he chattered, "ef Ah could on'y strack uh light!" 99

The rattling ceased for a moment as he stood paralyzed. He waited. It seemed that the snake waited also. 100

"Oh, fuh de light! Ah thought he'd be too sick"—Sykes was muttering to himself when the whirr began again, closer, right underfoot this time. Long before this, Sykes' ability to think had been flattened down to primitive instinct and he leaped—onto the bed. 101

Outside Delia heard a cry that might have come from a maddened chimpanzee, a stricken gorilla. All the terror, all the horror, all the rage that man possibly could express, without a recognizable human sound. 102

A tremendous stir inside there, another series of animal screams, the intermittent whirr of the reptile. The shade torn violently down from the window, letting in the red dawn, a huge brown hand seizing the window stick, great dull blows upon the wooden floor punctuating the gibberish of sound long after the rattle of the snake had abruptly subsided. All this Delia could see and hear from her place beneath the window, and it made her ill. She crept over to the four-o'clocks and stretched herself on the cool earth to recover. 103

She lay there. "Delia, Delia!" She could hear Sykes calling in a most despairing tone as one who expected no answer. The sun crept on up, and he called. Delia could not move—her legs had gone flabby. She never moved, he called, and the sun kept rising. 104

"Mah Gawd!" She heard him moan, "Mah Gawd fum Heben!" She heard him stumbling about and got up from her flower-bed. The sun was growing warm. As she approached the door she heard him call out hopefully, "Delia, is dat you Ah heah?" 105

She saw him on his hands and knees as soon as she reached the door. He crept an inch or two toward her—all that he was able, and she saw his horribly swollen neck and his one open eye shining with hope. A surge of pity too strong to support bore her away from that eye that must, could not, fail to see the tubs. He would see the lamp. Orlando with its doctors was too far. She could scarcely reach the chinaberry tree, where she waited in the growing heat while inside she knew the cold river was creeping up and up to extinguish that eye which must know by now that she knew. ◆ 106

◆ Responding

1. Working in a group, discuss Delia's predicament and list possible solutions. What community resources might be available today to help her that were not available in the 1920s? Share your ideas with the class.

2. Delia says, "Oh well, whatever goes over the Devil's back, is got to come under his belly. Sometime or ruther, Sykes, like everybody else, is gointer reap his sowing." Summarize the events in the story that illustrate the truth of this proverb.

3. Delia has her revenge at the end of the story, but how will she, a very religious woman, feel the next day? Write a possible sequel to the story in which Delia writes a letter or talks to a trusted friend about her behavior.

Alternatively, write an essay discussing the psychological consequences and ethical implications of her actions.

4. Using the comments of the characters in the story, write a physical and psychological description of Sykes.

5. Since the men in the community are aware of Sykes's behavior, why don't they try to help Delia? Discuss whether individuals have a responsibility to try to intervene when they see one person abused by another. Explain Delia's threat to tell the "white folks" and not the black men about Sykes's abuse. What does that choice reveal about power relationships in her community?

LANGSTON HUGHES

Langston Hughes, who was born in Joplin, Missouri, in 1902, studied at Columbia University and Lincoln University. During a literary career of over forty years, he wrote poetry, fiction, drama, and a two-volume auto-biography, The Big Sea *(1940) and* I Wonder as I Wander *(1956). His work has been praised for its simplicity and its wit. During the 1920s, Hughes participated in many of the editorial activities and the lively debates of the Harlem Renaissance.*

The three poems that follow explore the issues of heritage, identity, and ambition. They invite us to consider the relationships between individuals and groups, and the power that each of us has to make others feel accepted or rejected.

◆ MOTHER TO SON ◆

Well, son, I'll tell you:
Life for me ain't been no crystal stair.
It's had tacks in it,
And splinters,
And boards torn up,
And places with no carpet on the floor—
Bare.
But all the time
I'se been a-climbin' on,
And reachin' landin's,
And turnin' corners,
And sometimes goin' in the dark
Where there ain't been no light.
So boy, don't you turn back.
Don't you set down on the steps
'Cause you finds it's kinder hard.
Don't you fall now—
For I'se still goin', honey,
I'se still climbin',
And life for me ain't been no crystal stair. ◆

◆ Responding

1. Write a letter or poem that the son might write in response to his mother.

2. We don't know many details about the speaker's life. Fill out her character by adding some of the specific facts that you imagine have made her life "no crystal stair."

3. Using your own knowledge and experience, describe some of the problems that the boy might encounter in growing up that would make him "set down on the steps."

4. Critics have called this a poem of racial affirmation. Explain why you agree or disagree.

◆ THE NEGRO SPEAKS OF RIVERS ◆

I've known rivers:
I've known rivers ancient as the world and older than the
    flow of human blood in human veins.

My soul has grown deep like the rivers.

I bathed in the Euphrates when dawns were young.
I built my hut near the Congo and it lulled me to sleep.
I looked upon the Nile and raised the pyramids above it.
I heard the singing of the Mississippi when Abe Lincoln
    went down to New Orleans, and I've seen its muddy
    bosom turn all golden in the sunset.

I've known rivers:
Ancient, dusky rivers.

My soul has grown deep like the rivers. ◆

◆ Responding

1. With the class, stage a choral reading of the poem for multiple voices. Select parts of the poem to be read by individuals and others to be read by the group. After the reading, discuss the effectiveness of your selections.

2. Discuss Hughes's use of stanza breaks and line lengths to achieve his effects.

3. Identify and discuss the "I" in the poem.

4. Using the campus library, look up all the rivers mentioned in the poem. Share your information with the class. What relation do the rivers have to people of African descent? Write a poem about a place or a part of nature that is particularly important to you.

◆ THEME FOR ENGLISH B ◆

The instructor said,

> *Go home and write*
> *a page tonight.*
> *And let that page come out of you—*
> *Then, it will be true.*

I wonder if it's that simple?

I am twenty-two, colored, born in Winston-Salem.
I went to school there, then Durham, then here
to this college on the hill above Harlem.
I am the only colored student in my class.
The steps from the hill lead down into Harlem,
through a park, then I cross St. Nicholas,
Eighth Avenue, Seventh, and I come to the Y,
the Harlem Branch Y, where I take the elevator
up to my room, sit down, and write this page:

It's not easy to know what is true for you or me
at twenty-two, my age. But I guess I'm what
I feel and see and hear. Harlem, I hear you:
hear you, hear me—we two—you, me, talk on this page.
(I hear New York, too.) Me—who?

Well, I like to eat, sleep, drink, and be in love.
I like to work, read, learn, and understand life.
I like a pipe for a Christmas present,
or records—Bessie, bop, or Bach.
I guess being colored doesn't make me *not* like
the same things other folks like who are other races.

So will my page be colored that I write?
Being me, it will not be white.
But it will be
a part of you, instructor.
You are white—
yet a part of me, as I am a part of you.
That's American.
Sometimes perhaps you don't want to be a part of me.
Nor do I often want to be a part of you.
But we are, that's true!
As I learn from you,
I guess you learn from me—
although you're older—and white—
and somewhat more free.

This is my page for English B. ◆

◆ Responding

1. Discuss the ways in which the speaker sees himself as similar to everyone else in his class, and the ways in which he sees himself as different.

2. Discuss what the speaker means when he says "you are . . . a part of me, as I am a part of you. That's American." After the discussion, write a prose version of these lines.

3. The speaker is the only "colored" student in his university class. How do you think he feels about that situation? Write about a time when you, a relative, or a friend were the only representative of a group—for example, the only woman or man, the only American, the only northerner—among a group of "others." How did you respond in that situation? How did the others treat you?

JEAN TOOMER

Jean Toomer was born in Washington, D.C., in 1894. He studied at several universities, including the University of Wisconsin, New York University, and the City University of New York, before deciding to become a writer. In the 1920s he settled in Harlem and became a part of the literary circle there. His first book, Cane *(1925) received great critical acclaim. In his later years he spent time in Europe, where he studied philosophy and served on the faculty of the George Gurdieff Institute in Fontainbleau, France. His later writing—including short stories, poetry, and a play—did not enjoy the critical success of* Cane. *Toomer died in poverty in 1967.*

Cane, from which this excerpt is taken, was celebrated during its time as one of the pre-eminent works of the Harlem Renaissance. Its combination of prose and verse as well as its use of dialect, drama, and narrative was considered especially innovative. "Theater" employs richly descriptive language to convey the tension between the two characters. The reader can sense the interplay between stage performers and audience that helps to give the piece its dramatic quality.

◆ THEATER ◆

Life of nigger alleys, of pool rooms and restaurants and near-beer saloons soaks into the walls of Howard Theater[1] and sets them throbbing jazz songs. Black-skinned, they dance and shout above the tick and trill of white-walled buildings. At night, they open doors to people who come in to stamp their feet and shout. At night, road-shows volley songs into the mass-heart of black people. Songs soak the walls and seep out to the nigger life of alleys and near-beer saloons, of the Poodle Dog and Black Bear cabarets. Afternoons, the house is dark, and the walls are sleeping singers until rehearsal begins. Or until John comes within them. Then they start throbbing to a subtle syncopation. And the space-dark air grows softly luminous.   1

John is the manager's brother. He is seated at the center of the theater, just before rehearsal. Light streaks down upon him from a window high above. One half his face is orange in it. One half his face is in shadow. The soft glow of the house rushes to, and compacts about, the shaft of light. John's mind coincides with the shaft of light. Thoughts rush to, and compact about it. Life of the house and of the slowly awakening stage swirls to the body of John, and thrills it. John's body is separate from the thoughts that pack his mind.   2

Stage-lights, soft, as if they shine through clear pink fingers. Beneath   3

---

[1]A theater in the Afro-American section of Washington, D.C.: the audiences and the performers were also Afro-American. [Author's note]

them, hid by the shadow of a set, Dorris. Other chorus girls drift in. John feels them in the mass. And as if his own body were the mass-heart of a black audience listening to them singing, he wants to stamp his feet and shout. His mind, contained above desires of his body, singles the girls out, and tries to trace origins and plot destinies.

A pianist slips into the pit and improvises jazz. The walls awake. Arms   4
of the girls, and their limbs, which . . . jazz, jazz . . . by lifting up their tight street skirts they set free, jab the air and clog the floor in rhythm to the music. (Lift your skirts, Baby, and talk t papa!) Crude, individualized, and yet . . . monotonous . . .

John: Soon the director will herd you, my full-lipped, distant beauties,   5
and tame you, and blunt your sharp thrusts in loosely suggestive movements, appropriate to Broadway. (O dance!) Soon the audience will paint your dusk faces white, and call you beautiful. (O dance!) Soon I . . . (O dance!) I'd like . . .

Girls laugh and shout. Sing discordant snatches of other jazz songs. Whirl   6
with loose passion into the arms of passing show-men.

John: Too thick. Too easy. Too monotonous. Her whom I'd love I'd leave   7
before she knew that I was with her. Her? Which? (O dance!) I'd like to . . .

Girls dance and sing. Men clap. The walls sing and press inward. They   8
press the men and girls, they press John towards a center of physical ecstasy. Go to it, Baby! Fan yourself, and feed your papa! Put . . . nobody lied . . . and take . . . when they said I cried over you. No lie! The glitter and color of stacked scenes, the gilt and brass and crimson of the house, converge towards a center of physical ecstasy. John's feet and torso and his blood press in. He wills thought to rid his mind of passion.

"All right, girls. Alaska. Miss Reynolds, please."   9

The director wants to get the rehearsal through with.   10

The girls line up. John sees the front row: dancing ponies. The rest are   11
in shadow. The leading lady fits loosely in the front. Lack-life, monotonous. "One, two, three—" Music starts. The song is somewhere where it will not strain the leading lady's throat. The dance is somewhere where it will not strain the girls. Above the staleness, one dancer throws herself into it. Dorris. John sees her. Her hair, crisp-curled, is bobbed. Bushy, black hair bobbing about her lemon-colored face. Her lips are curiously full, and very red. Her limbs in silk purple stockings are lovely. John feels them. Desires her. Holds off.

John: Stage-door johnny;[2] chorus-girl. No, that would be all right. Dictie,[3]   12
educated, stuck-up; show-girl. Yep. Her suspicion would be stronger than her passion. It wouldnt work. Keep her loveliness. Let her go.

---

[2]Slang term referring to men who dated actresses, singers, and dancers and who, after performances, waited for them at the stage door. [Author's note]

[3]Slang term referring to educated, middle-class Afro-Americans who behave as though they consider themselves socially superior to other Afro-Americans—similar to "stuck-up," "snobbish." [Author's note]

Dorris sees John and knows that he is looking at her. Her own glowing 13
is too rich a thing to let her feel the slimness of his diluted passion.

"Who's that?" she asks her dancing partner. 14

"Th manager's brother. Dictie. Nothin doin, hon." 15

Dorris tosses her head and dances for him until she feels she has him. 16
Then, withdrawing disdainfully, she flirts with the director.

Dorris: Nothin doin? How come? Aint I as good as him? Couldnt I have 17
got an education if I'd wanted one? Dont I know respectable folks, lots of em,
in Philadelphia and New York and Chicago? Aint I had men as good as him?
Better. Doctors an lawyers. Whats a manager's brother, anyhow?

Two steps back, and two steps front. 18

"Say, Mame, where do you get that stuff?" 19

"Whatshmean, Dorris?" 20

"If you two girls cant listen to what I'm telling you, I know where I can 21
get some who can. Now listen."

Mame: Go to hell, you black bastard. 22

Dorris: Whats eatin at him, anyway? 23

"Now follow me in this, you girls. Its three counts to the right, three 24
counts to the left, and then you shimmy—"

John: —and then you shimmy. I'll bet she can. Some good cabaret, with 25
rooms upstairs. And what in hell do you think you'd get from it? Youre going
wrong. Here's right: get her to herself—(Christ, but how she'd bore you after
the first five minutes)—not if you get her right she wouldnt. Touch her, I mean.
To herself—in some room perhaps. Some cheap, dingy bedroom. Hell no. Cant
be done. But the point is, brother John, it can be done. Get her to herself
somewhere, anywhere. Go down in yourself—and she'd be calling you all sorts
of asses while you were in the process of going down. Hold em, bud. Cant be
done. Let her go. (Dance and I'll love you!) And keep her loveliness.

"All right now, Chicken Chaser.[4] Dorris and girls. Where's Dorris? I told 26
you to stay on the stage, didnt I? Well? Now thats enough. All right. All right
there, Professor? All right. One, two, three—"

Dorris swings to the front. The line of girls, four deep, blurs within the 27
shadow of suspended scenes. Dorris wants to dance. The director feels that
and steps to one side. He smiles, and picks her for a leading lady, one of these
days. Odd ends of stage-men emerge from the wings, and stare and clap. A
crap game in the alley suddenly ends. Black faces crowd the rear stage doors.
The girls, catching joy from Dorris, whip up within the footlights' glow. They
forget set steps; they find their own. The director forgets to bawl them out.
Dorris dances.

John: Her head bobs to Broadway. Dance from yourself. Dance! O just 28
a little more.

---

[4]A dance

Dorris' eyes burn across the space of seats to him.   29

Dorris: I bet he can love. Hell, he cant love. He's too skinny. His lips   30
are too skinny. He wouldnt love me anyway, only for that. But I'd get a pair
of silk stockings out of it. Red silk. I got purple. Cut it, kid. You cant win him
to respect you that away. He wouldnt anyway. Maybe he would. Maybe he'd
love. I've heard em say that men who look like him (what does he look like?)
will marry if they love. O will you love me? And give me kids, and a home,
and everything? (I'd like to make your nest, and honest, hon, I wouldnt run
out on you.) You will if I make you. Just watch me.

Dorris dances. She forgets her tricks.[5] She dances.   31

Glorious songs are the muscles of her limbs.   32

And her singing is of canebrake loves and mangrove feastings.   33

The walls press in, singing. Flesh of a throbbing body, they press close   34
to John and Dorris. They close them in. John's heart beats tensely against her
dancing body. Walls press his mind within his heart. And then, the shaft of
light goes out the window high above him. John's mind sweeps up to follow
it. Mind pulls him upward into dream.   Dorris dances. . .
John dreams:

> Dorris is dressed in a loose black gown splashed with lemon ribbons. Her feet
> taper long and slim from trim ankles. She waits for him just inside the stage door.
> John, collar and tie colorful and flaring, walks towards the stage door. There are
> no trees in the alley. But his feet feel as though they step on autumn leaves whose
> rustle has been pressed out of them by the passing of a million satin slippers. The
> air is sweet with roasting chestnuts, sweet with bonfires of old leaves. John's
> melancholy is a deep thing that seals all senses but his eyes, and makes him whole.
>
> Dorris knows that he is coming. Just at the right moment she steps from the
> door, as if there were no door. Her face is tinted like the autumn alley. Of old
> flowers, or of a southern canefield, her perfume. "Glorious Dorris." So his eyes
> speak. And their sadness is too deep for sweet untruth. She barely touches his
> arm. They glide off with footfalls softened on the leaves, the old leaves powdered
> by a million satin slippers.
>
> They are in a room. John knows nothing of it. Only, that the flesh and blood
> of Dorris are its walls. Singing walls. Lights, soft, as if they shine through clear
> pink fingers. Soft lights, and warm.
>
> John reaches for a manuscript of his, and reads. Dorris, who has no eyes, has
> eyes to understand him. He comes to a dancing scene. The scene is Dorris. She
> dances. Dorris dances. Glorious Dorris. Dorris whirls, whirls, dances. . .

Dorris dances.

The pianist crashes a bumper chord. The whole stage claps. Dorris, flushed,
looks quick at John. His whole face is in shadow. She seeks for her dance in
it. She finds it a dead thing in the shadow which is his dream. She rushes from

---

[5]Her practiced or stylized dance routine. [Author's note]

the stage. Falls down the steps into her dressing-room. Pulls her hair. Her eyes, over a floor of tears, stare at the whitewashed ceiling. (Smell of dry paste, and paint, and soiled clothing.) Her pal comes in. Dorris flings herself into the old safe arms, and cries bitterly.

"I told you nothin doin," is what Mame says to comfort her. ◆   35

◆ Responding

1. Discuss Toomer's use of the word "nigger." In what ways does its use offend contemporary readers? Do you think it offended readers when the story was written?

2. Working in a group, list the arguments for and against John's approaching Dorris, or the arguments for and against Dorris's approaching John. Combine groups and compare lists.

3. Describe a situation in which you wanted to do something but your anxiety, shyness, or fear of embarrassment kept you from taking risks.

4. Write the scene that might occur if John decided to talk to Dorris. Or describe how John feels afterward about not talking to Dorris.

JESSIE REDMON FAUSET

Jessie Redmon Fauset is one of the more controversial writers of the Harlem Renaissance period. Born in 1882, she received her bachelor's degree at Cornell University, her master's at the University of Pennsylvania, and pursued further studies at the Sorbonne. During her college years, Fauset was involved in protests against discriminatory residence policies at neighboring colleges. From 1911 to 1926 she worked on the editorial staff of the NAACP pub-lication Crisis, *traveling throughout Europe and Africa and contributing articles relevant to the Pan-Africa movement and the African American community in general. Fauset wrote four novels:* There Is Confusion *(1924),* Plum Bun *(1929),* The Chinaberry Tree *(1931), and* Comedy American Style *(1933). Although her work had been praised during the Renaissance, it was later criticized as being melodramatic and too focused on the values of the middle class. More recently, scholars have returned to her work, noting Fauset's willingness to take risks and to challenge conventional assumptions.*

The excerpt that follows, from There is Confusion, *provides some of the emotional background for the Renaissance movement. It recounts, with clear irony, the situation of African American soldiers sent to Europe during World War I. Even as they fight for the rights of others, the soldiers witness their own rights being compromised.*

◆ *From* **THERE IS CONFUSION** ◆

The interminable voyage was over and Peter debarked to spend still more 1
interminable days at Brest. Dr. Meriwether Bye left immediately for La Courtine, where Peter later caught sight of him once more on his way to the front.
The somewhat exalted mood to which his long and intimate talks with Meriwether had raised him vanished completely under the strain of the dirt, the
racial and national clashes, and above all the persistent bad weather of Brest.

This town, the end of Brittany and the furthest western outpost of France, 2
always remained in Peter's memory as a horrible prelude to a most horrible
war. Brest up to the time that Europe had gone so completely and so suddenly
insane, had been the typical, stupid, monotonous French town with pictur-
esquely irregular pavements, narrow tortuous streets, dark, nestling little shops
and the inevitable public square. Around and about the city to all sides stretched
well ordered farms.

Then came the march of two million American soldiers across the town 3
and the surrounding country. Under their careless feet the farms became mud,
so that the name Brest recalls to the minds of thousands nothing if not a picture
of the deepest, slimiest, stickiest mud that the world has known. All about were
people, people, too many people, French and Americans. And finally the re-

lations between the two nations, allies though they were, developed from mis-understandings into hot irritations, from irritations into clashes. First white Americans and Frenchmen clashed; separate restaurants and accommodations had to be arranged. Then came the inevitable clash between white and colored Americans; petty jealousies and meannesses arose over the courtesies of French-women and the lack of discrimination in the French cafés. The Americans found a new and inexplicable irritation in the French colored colonials. Food was bad, prices were exorbitant; officers became tyrants. Everyone was at once in Brest and constantly about to leave it; real understanding and acquaintanceship were impossible.

Peter thought Dante might well have included this place in the description of his Inferno. Here were Disease and Death, Mutilation and Murder. Steve-dores and even soldiers became cattle and beasts of burden. Many black men were slaves. The thing from which France was to be defended could hardly be worse than this welter of human misunderstandings, the clashing of unknown tongues, the cynical investigations of the government, the immanence of war and the awful, persistent wretchedness of the weather. 4

The long wait turned into sudden activity and Peter's outfit was ordered to Lathus, thence to La Courtine, one of the large training centers. It was at this latter place that he caught sight of more of Meriwether Bye. He seemed unusually alert and cheerful, Peter thought, and when the two got a chance to speak to each other, this impression was confirmed. The young white physician had the look of a man who sees before him a speedy deliverance. 5

"He thinks he's going to die and chuck this whole infernal business," Peter said to himself. "Wish I could be as sure of getting out of it as he is." Somehow the brief encounter left him more dispirited than ever. "Come out of it, ole hoss," Harley Alexander used to say to him. "What'd your 'grand white' friend do to you?" 6

"Oh, you shut up!" Peter barked at him. 7

His real depression, however, dated back to the time immediately after his company had left Brest. The awful condition of things in the seaport town was general rather than specific, and for the first time since Peter had entered the war he was feeling comparatively calm. His long and intimate talks with Meriwether had produced their effect. He had not realized that any such man as the young Quaker physician had existed in the white world. He had too much sense and too many cruel experiences to believe that there were many of Meriwether's kind to be found in a lifetime's journey, but somehow his long bitterness of the years had been assuaged. Henceforth, he told himself, he would try to be more generous in his thoughts of white men—perhaps his attitude invited trouble which he was usually only too willing to meet halfway. 8

At Lathus, Harley Alexander met him in the little *place*.[1] "Seems to 9

---

[1] square

me you're got up regardless," Peter had commented. Alexander, one of the trimmest men in the regiment, was looking unusually shipshape, almost dapper.

The other struck him familiarly across the shoulder. "And that ain't all. 10 Say, fellow, there's a band concert to-night right here in this little old square. I'm goin' and I'm goin' to take a lady."

"Lady! Where'd you get her?" 11

"Right here. These girls are all right. Not afraid of a dark skin. 'How 12 should we have fear, m'soo,' one of them says to me, 'when you fight for our *patrie*[2] and when you are so *beau*?' '*Beau*' that's handsome, ain't it? Say this is some country to fight for; got some sense of appreciation. Better come along, old scout. There's a pile of loots getting ready to come, each with a French dame in tow."

"I'll be there," Peter told him, laughing. "But count me out with the 13 ladies. I can't get along with the domestic brand and I know I'll be out of luck with the foreign ones."

Some passing thought wiped the joy of anticipation from Harley's face. 14 "My experience is that these foreign ones are a damn sight less foolish than some domestic ones I've met. Well, me for the concert."

But that band concert never came off. At sunset a company of white 15 American Southerners marched into Lathus down the main street, past the little *place*. There was a sudden uproar.

"Look! Darkies and white women! Come on, fellows, kill the damned 16 niggers!"

There was a hasty onslaught in which the colored soldiers even taken by 17 surprise gave as good as they took. Between these two groups from the same soil there was grimmer, more determined fighting than was seen at Verdun. The French civil population stood on the church-steps opposite the square and watched with amazement.

"*Nom de dieu!* Are they crazy, then, these Americans, that they kill each 18 other!"

The next day saw Peter's company on its way to La Courtine, a training 19 center, where there were no women. Thence they moved presently to the front in the Metz Sector.

The injustice and indignity rendered the colored troups at Lathus, plus 20 the momentary glimpses which he caught of Meriwether and his exaltation, plunged Peter into a morass of melancholy and bitter self-communing which shut him off as effectually as a smoke-screen from any real appreciation of the dangers which surrounded him on the front.

In the midst of all that ineffable danger, that hellish noise, he was harassed 21 by the inextricable confusion, the untidiness of his own life. God, to get rid of

---

[2]country

it all! Once he spent forty-eight hours with nine other men on the ridge of a hill under fire. The other fellows told stories and swapped confidences. But he stayed unmoved through it all, impervious alike to the danger and the good man-talk going on about him.

When the call came for a reconnoitering party, he was one of the first to step forward. He went out that night into the blackness, the hellishness of No Man's Land. He saw a dark figure rise in front of him, heard a guttural sound and the next moment his left arm, drenched with blood, hung useless at his side. Raising himself he shot at the legs which showed a solid blackness against the thinner surrounding darkness. Wriggling on his belly, he pushed forward to where he thought he heard sounds, a struggle. "Something doing," he told himself, "might as well get in on that." 22

But when he drew near the darkness was so intense that he did not dare interfere. Two men, at least, were struggling terribly but he could not tell which was which. They were breathing in terrific grunts, so heavily that they had not noticed the approach of his smoothly sliding body. Suddenly what he had hoped for, happened. A rocket shot up in the air flared briefly and showed him the two men. One was Meriwether Bye, the other was a German, his hand in the act of throwing a hand grenade. 23

Peter lurched forward and at that ghastly short range shot the German through the stomach. But he was too late, the grenade had left the man's hand. The earth rocked about him, he could see Meriwether fall, a toppling darkness in the darkness. He started toward him but his foot caught in a depression and he himself fell sideways on his wounded arm. There was a moment of exquisite pain and then the darkness grew even more dark about him, the silent night more silent. 24

When he came to, it was still dark, though the day, he felt, rather than saw, was approaching. His arm hurt unmercifully. He had never known such pain. He raised himself on his one arm, and felt around with his foot. Yes, there was a body, he prayed it might not be the German. Crawling forward he plunged his hand into blood, a depthless pool of sticky blood. Sickened, he drew back and dried it, wiping it on his coat. More cautiously, then, he reached out again, searching for the face, yes, that was Meriwether's nose. Those canny finger-tips of his recognized the facial structure. His hand came back to Meriwether's chest. The heart was beating faintly and just above it was a hole, with the blood gushing, spurting, hot and thick. 25

He sat upright and wrenching open his tunic tore at his shirt. The stuff was hard to tear but it finally gave way under the onslaught of teeth and fingers. Faint with the pain of his left arm and the loss of his own blood, he set his lips hard, concentrating with all his strength on the determination not to lose consciousness again. Finally grunting, swearing, almost crying, he got Meriwether's head against his knee, then against his shoulder, and staunched the wound with the harsh, unyielding khaki. His canteen was full and he drenched the chilly, helpless face with its contents. All this time he was sitting with no support for his back and the strain was telling on him. 26

Against the surrounding gray of the coming morning, southward toward 27
his own lines, he caught sight of darker shapes, trees perhaps, perhaps men—
if he could only get to them! Placing Meriwether's face upwards he caught him
about his lean waist, buckling him to his side with an arm of steel, and rising
to his knees he crawled for what seemed a mile toward that persistent blackness.
Twice he fell, once he struck his left arm against a dead man's boot. The awful
throbbing in his shoulder increased. But at last he was there, at last in the
shelter of a clump of low, stunted trees. With a sob he braced himself against
them, letting Meriwether's head and shoulders rest against his knees. The blood
had begun to spurt again and Meriwether stirred. Peter whispered:

"Bye, for God's sake, speak to me. This is Peter, Peter, Bye, you re- 28
member?"

The young doctor repeated the name thickly. "Yes, Peter. I know. I'm 29
dying."

"Not yet. Man, it's almost day, they'll come to us. Pull yourself together. 30
We'll save you somehow."

Meriwether whispered, "I'm cold." 31

Could he get his coat off? How could he ever pull it off that shattered 32
arm? Still he achieved even this, wrapping it around the white man's shivering
form, raising that face, gray as the gray day above them, high on his chest,
cradling him like a baby.

The chill was the chill of death, a horrible death. Meriwether coughed 33
and choked; Peter could feel the life struggling within the poor torn body. Once
the cold lips said: "Peter, you're a good scout."

Just before a merciful unconsciousness enveloped him for the last time, 34
Meriwether sat upright in the awful agony of death. "Grandfather," he called
in a terrible voice, "this is the last of the Byes."

When the stretcher-bearers found them, Meriwether was lying across 35
Peter's knees, his face turned childwise toward Peter's breast. The colored man's
head had dropped low over the fair one and his black curly hair fell forward
straight and stringy, caked in the blood which lay in a well above Meriwether's
heart.

"Cripes!" said one of the rescue men, "I've seen many a sight in this war, 36
but none ever give me the turn I got seein' that smoke's hair dabblin' in the
other fellow's blood." ◆

◆ Responding

1. Using your school library, research the history of segregation within the
   armed forces. Discuss the practical effects of segregation on black soldiers
   during World War I.

2. Fauset writes "Peter thought Dante might well have included this place in the description of his Inferno." Explain why the battlefield was like an image of hell.

3. Discuss the irony of Americans fighting each other when they had been sent to France to fight the Germans. Why do you think the white soldiers were unable to put aside their attitudes toward blacks and concentrate on the war effort?

4. After Peter had numerous intimate talks with the young Quaker physician, "his long bitterness of the years had been assuaged. Henceforth, he told himself, he would try to be more generous in his thoughts of white men." Describe an experience you have had that changed your negative feelings or ideas. Alternatively, discuss whether it is realistic on the author's part to believe that a positive experience with one individual can change attitudes that have been building throughout a lifetime of negative contacts.

WALLACE THURMAN

Wallace Thurman was born in Salt Lake City in 1902. After studying at the University of Southern California, he settled in Harlem where he worked on several of the important periodicals of the Harlem Renaissance period, including The Messenger. *He collaborated with many of the foremost writers of the movement: with W. J. Rapp he wrote the play* Harlem, *and with Zora Neale Hurston and Langston Hughes he edited the literary publication* Fire!!!. *Thurman also wrote two novels,* The Blacker the Berry *(1929) and* Infants of the Spring *(1932). By caricaturing leading literary figures of the time, the second novel satirized some of the pretensions of the Harlem Renaissance itself. Thurman died of tuberculosis at the age of thirty-two.*

The following excerpt, from The Blacker the Berry, *examines the influence of unconscious prejudices on first impressions. Its ending provides an ironic commentary on the main character's reliance on such prejudices.*

◆ *From* **THE BLACKER THE BERRY** ◆

Summer vacation was nearly over and it had not yet been decided what to do with Emma Lou now that she had graduated from high school. She herself gave no help nor offered any suggestions. As it was, she really did not care what became of her. After all it didn't seem to matter. There was no place in the world for a girl as black as she anyway. Her grandmother had assured her that she would never find a husband worth a dime, and her mother had said again and again, "Oh, if you had only been a boy!" until Emma Lou had often wondered why it was that people were not able to effect a change of sex or at least a change of complexion.

It was her Uncle Joe who finally prevailed upon her mother to send her to the University of Southern California in Los Angeles. There, he reasoned, she would find a larger and more intelligent social circle. In a city the size of Los Angeles there were Negroes of every class, color, and social position. Let Emma Lou go there where she would not be as far away from home as if she were to go to some eastern college.

Jane and Maria, while not agreeing entirely with what Joe said, were nevertheless glad that at last something which seemed adequate and sensible could be done for Emma Lou. She was to take the four year college course, receive a bachelor degree in education, then go South to teach. That, they thought, was a promising future, and for once in the eighteen years of Emma Lou's life every one was satisfied in some measure. Even Emma Lou grew elated over the prospects of the trip. Her Uncle Joe's insistence upon the differences of social contacts in larger cities intrigued her. Perhaps he was right after all in continually reasserting to them that as long as one was a Negro, one's specific color had little to do with one's life. Salvation depended upon the individual. And he also told Emma Lou, during one of their usual private talks, that it was only in small cities one encountered stupid color prejudice such as she had encountered among the blue vein circle in her home town.

"People in large cities," he had said, "are broad. They do not have time   4
to think of petty things. The people in Boise are fifty years behind the times, but you will find that Los Angeles is one of the world's greatest and most modern cities, and you will be happy there."

On arriving in Los Angeles, Emma Lou was so busy observing the colored   5
inhabitants that she had little time to pay attention to other things. Palm trees and wild geraniums were pleasant to behold, and such strange phenomena as pepper trees and century plants had to be admired. They were very obvious and they were also strange and beautiful, but they impinged upon only a small corner of Emma Lou's consciousness. She was minutely aware of them, nec-essarily took them in while passing, viewing the totality without pondering over or lingering to praise their stylistic details. They were, in this instance, exquisite theatrical props, rendered insignificant by a more strange and a more beautiful human pageant. For Emma Lou, who, in all her life, had never seen over five hundred Negroes, the spectacle presented by a community containing over fifty thousand, was sufficient to make relatively commonplace many more important and charming things than the far famed natural scenery of Southern California.

She had arrived in Los Angeles a week before registration day at the   6
university, and had spent her time in being shown and seeing the city. But whenever these sightseeing excursions took her away from the sections where Negroes lived, she immediately lost all interest in what she was being shown. The Pacific Ocean in itself did not cause her heart beat to quicken, nor did the roaring of its waves find an emotional echo within her. But on coming upon Bruce's Beach for colored people near Redondo, or the little strip of sandied shore they had appropriated for themselves at Santa Monica, the Pacific Ocean became an intriguing something to contemplate as a background for their ac-tivities. Everything was interesting as it was patronized, reflected through, or acquired by Negroes.

Her Uncle Joe had been right. Here, in the colored social circles of Los   7
Angeles, Emma Lou was certain that she would find many suitable companions, intelligent, broad-minded people of all complexions, intermixing and being too occupied otherwise to worry about either their own skin color or the skin color of those around them. Her Uncle Joe had said that Negroes were Negroes whether they happened to be yellow, brown, or black, and a conscious effort to eliminate the darker elements would neither prove nor solve anything. There was nothing quite so silly as the creed of the blue veins: "Whiter and whiter, every generation. The nearer white you are the more white people will respect you. Therefore all light Negroes marry light Negroes. Continue to do so gen-

eration after generation, and eventually white people will accept this racially bastard aristocracy, thus enabling those Negroes who really matter to escape the social and economic inferiority of the American Negro."

Such had been the credo of her grandmother and of her mother and of their small circle of friends in Boise. But Boise was a provincial town, given to the molding of provincial people with provincial minds. Boise was a backward town out of the mainstream of modern thought and progress. Its people were cramped and narrow, their intellectual concepts stereotyped and static. Los Angeles was a happy contrast in all respects.

On registration day, Emma Lou rushed out to the campus of the University of Southern California one hour before the registrar's office was scheduled to open. She spent the time roaming around, familiarizing herself with the layout of the campus and learning the names of the various buildings, some old and vineclad, others new and shiny in the sun, and watching the crowds of laughing students, rushing to and fro, greeting one another and talking over their plans for the coming school year. But her main reason for such an early arrival on the campus had been to find some of her fellow Negro students. She had heard that there were to be quite a number enrolled, but in all her hour's stroll she saw not one, and finally somewhat disheartened she got into the line stretched out in front of the registrar's office, and, for the moment, became engrossed in becoming a college freshman.

All the while, though, she kept searching for a colored face, but it was not until she had been duly signed up as a student and sent in search of her advisor that she saw one. Then three colored girls had sauntered into the room where she was having a conference with her advisor, sauntered in, arms interlocked, greeted her advisor, then sauntered out again. Emma Lou had wanted to rush after them—to introduce herself, but of course it had been impossible under the circumstances. She had immediately taken a liking to all three, each of whom was what is known in the parlance of the black belt as high brown, with modishly-shingled bobbed hair and well formed bodies, fashionably attired in flashy sport garments. From then on Emma Lou paid little attention to the business of choosing subjects and class hours, so little attention in fact that the advisor thought her exceptionally tractable and somewhat dumb. But she liked students to come that way. It made the task of being advisor easy. One just made out the program to suit oneself, and had no tedious explanations to make as to why the student could not have such and such a subject at such and such an hour, and why such and such a professor's class was already full.

After her program had been made out, Emma Lou was directed to the bursar's office to pay her fees. While going down the stairs she almost bumped into two dark-brown-skinned boys, obviously brothers if not twins, arguing as to where they should go next. One insisted that they should go back to the registrar's office. The other was being equally insistent that they should go to the gymnasium and make an appointment for their required physical examination. Emma Lou boldly stopped when she saw them, hoping they would speak, but they merely glanced up at her and continued their argument, bringing cards and pamphlets out of their pockets for reference and guidance. Emma Lou wanted to introduce herself to them, but she was too bashful to do so. She wasn't yet used to going to school with other Negro students, and she wasn't exactly certain how one went about becoming acquainted. But she finally decided that she had better let the advances come from the others, especially if they were men. There was nothing forward about her, and since she was a stranger it was no more than right that the old-timers should make her welcome. Still, if these had been girls . . . , but they weren't, so she continued her way down the stairs.

In the bursar's office, she was somewhat overjoyed at first to find that she 12
had fallen into line behind another colored girl who had turned around immediately, and, after saying hello, announced in a loud, harsh voice:

"My feet are sure some tired!" 13

Emma Lou was so taken aback that she couldn't answer. People in college 14
didn't talk that way. But meanwhile the girl was continuing:

"Ain't this registration a mess?" 15

Two white girls who had fallen into line behind Emma Lou snickered. 16
Emma Lou answered by shaking her head. The girl continued:

"I've been standin' in line and climbin' stairs and talkin' and a-signin' till 17
I'm just 'bout done for."

"It is tiresome," Emma Lou returned softly, hoping the girl would take 18
a hint and lower her own strident voice. But she didn't.

"Tiresome ain't no name for it," she declared more loudly than ever before, 19
then, "Is you a new student?"

"I am," answered Emma Lou, putting much emphasis on the "I am." 20

She wanted the white people who were listening to know that she knew 21
her grammar if this other person didn't. "Is you," indeed! If this girl was a specimen of the Negro students with whom she was to associate, she most certainly did not want to meet another one. But it couldn't be possible that all of them—those three girls and those two boys for instance—were like this girl. Emma Lou was unable to imagine how such a person had ever gotten out of high school. Where on earth could she have gone to high school? Surely not in the North. Then she must be a southerner. That's what she was, a southerner— Emma Lou curled her lips a little—no wonder the colored people in Boise spoke as they did about southern Negroes and wished that they would stay South. Imagine anyone preparing to enter college saying "Is you," and, to make it worse, right before all these white people, these staring white people, so eager and ready to laugh. Emma Lou's face burned.

"Two mo', then I goes in my sock." 22

Emma Lou was almost at the place where she was ready to take even this 23
statement literally, and was on the verge of leaving the line. Supposing this creature did "go in her sock"! God forbid!

"Wonder where all the spades keep themselves? I ain't seen but two 'sides 24
you."

"I really do not know," Emma Lou returned precisely and chillily. She 25
had no intentions of becoming friendly with this sort of person. Why she would
be ashamed even to be seen on the street with her, dressed as she was in a red-
striped sport suit, a white hat, and white shoes and stockings. Didn't she know
that black people had to be careful about the colors they affected?

The girl had finally reached the bursar's window and was paying her fees, 26
and loudly differing with the cashier about the total amount due.

"I tell you it ain't that much," she shouted through the window bars. "I 27
figured it up myself before I left home."

The cashier obligingly turned to her adding machine and once more ob- 28
tained the same total. When shown this, the girl merely grinned, examined the
list closely, and said:

"I'm gonna' pay it, but I still think you're wrong." 29

Finally she moved away from the window, but not before she had turned 30
to Emma Lou and said,

"You're next," and then proceeded to wait until Emma Lou had finished. 31

Emma Lou vainly sought some way to escape, but was unable to do so, 32
and had no choice but to walk with the girl to the registrar's office where they
had their cards stamped in return for the bursar's receipt. This done, they went
onto the campus together. Hazel Mason was the girl's name. Emma Lou had
fully expected it to be either Hyacinth or Geranium. Hazel was from Texas,
Prairie Valley, Texas, and she told Emma Lou that her father, having become
quite wealthy when oil had been found on his farm lands, had been enabled to
realize two life ambitions—obtain a Packard touring car and send his only
daughter to a "fust-class" white school.

Emma Lou had planned to loiter around the campus. She was still eager 33
to become acquainted with the colored members of the student body, and this
encounter with the crass and vulgar Hazel Mason had only made her the more
eager. She resented being approached by any one so flagrantly inferior, any
one so noticeably a typical southern darky, who had no business obtruding into
the more refined scheme of things. Emma Lou planned to lose her unwelcome
companion somewhere on the campus so that she could continue unhindered
her quest for agreeable acquaintances.

But Hazel was as anxious to meet one as was Emma Lou, and having 34
found her was not going to let her get away without a struggle. She, too, was
new to this environment and in a way was more lonely and eager for the
companionship of her own kind than Emma Lou, for never before had she come
into such close contact with so many whites. Her life had been spent only
among Negroes. Her fellow pupils and teachers in school had always been
colored, and as she confessed to Emma Lou, she couldn't get used "to all these
white folks."

"Honey, I was just achin' to see a black face," she had said, and, though 35
Emma Lou was experiencing the same ache, she found herself unable to sym-
pathize with the other girl, for Emma Lou classified Hazel as a barbarian who

had most certainly not come from a family of best people. No doubt her mother had been a washerwoman. No doubt she had innumerable relatives and friends all as ignorant and as ugly as she. There was no sense in any one having a face as ugly as Hazel's, and Emma Lou thanked her stars that though she was black, her skin was not rough and pimply, nor was her hair kinky, nor were her nostrils completely flattened out until they seemed to spread all over her face. No wonder people were prejudiced against dark skin people when they were so ugly, so haphazard in their dress, and so boisterously mannered as was this present specimen. She herself was black, but nevertheless she had come from a good family, and she could easily take her place in a society of the right sort of people.

The two strolled along the lawn-bordered gravel path which led to a vine-covered building at the end of the campus. Hazel never ceased talking. She kept shouting at Emma Lou, shouting all sorts of personal intimacies as if she were desirous of the whole world hearing them. There was no necessity for her to talk so loudly, no necessity for her to afford every one on the crowded campus the chance to stare and laugh at them as they passed. Emma Lou had never before been so humiliated and so embarrassed. She felt that she must get away from her offensive companion. What did she care if she had to hurt her feelings to do so? The more insulting she could be now, the less friendly she would have to be in the future.

"Good-bye," she said abruptly, "I must go home." With which she turned away and walked rapidly in the opposite direction. She had only gone a few steps when she was aware of the fact that the girl was following her. She quickened per pace, but the girl caught up with her and grabbing hold of Emma Lou's arm, shouted,

"Whoa there, Sally."

It seemed to Emma Lou as if every one on the campus was viewing and enjoying this minstrel-like performance. Angrily she tried to jerk away, but the girl held fast.

"Gal, you sure walk fast. I'm going your way. Come on, let me drive you home in my buggy."

And still holding on to Emma Lou's arm, she led the way to the side street where the students parked their cars. Emma Lou was powerless to resist. The girl didn't give her a chance, for she held tight, then immediately resumed the monologue which Emma Lou's attempted leave-taking had interrupted. They reached the street, Hazel still talking loudly, and making elaborate gestures with her free hand.

"Here we are," she shouted, and releasing Emma Lou's arm, salaamed before a sport model Stutz roadster. "Oscar," she continued, "meet the new girl friend. Pleased to meetcha, says he. Climb aboard."

And Emma Lou had climbed aboard, perplexed, chagrined, thoroughly angry, and disgusted. What was this little black fool doing with a Stutz roadster? And of course, it would be painted red—Negroes always bedecked themselves and their belongings in ridiculously unbecoming colors and ornaments. It seemed to be a part of their primitive heritage which they did not seem to have sense enough to forget and deny. Black girl—white hat—red and white striped sport suit—white shoes and stockings—red roadster. The picture was complete. All Hazel needed to complete her circus-like appearance, thought Emma Lou, was to have some purple feathers stuck in her hat.

Still talking, the girl unlocked and proceeded to start the car. As she was   44
backing it out of the narrow parking space, Emma Lou heard a chorus of semi-suppressed giggles from a neighboring automobile. In her anger she had failed to notice that there were people in the car parked next to the Stutz. But as Hazel expertly swung her machine around, Emma Lou caught a glimpse of them. They were all colored and they were all staring at her and at Hazel. She thought she recognized one of the girls as being one of the group she had seen earlier that morning, and she did recognize the two brothers she had passed on the stairs. And as the roadster sped away, their laughter echoed in her ears, although she hadn't actually heard it. But she had seen the strain in their faces, and she knew that as soon as she and Hazel were out of sight, they would give free rein to their suppressed mirth.

Although Emma Lou had finished registering, she returned to the uni-   45
versity campus on the following morning in order to continue her quest for collegiate companions without the alarming and unwelcome presence of Hazel Mason. She didn't know whether to be sorry for that girl and try to help her or to be disgusted and avoid her. She didn't want to be intimately associated with any such vulgar person. It would damage her own position, cause her to be classified with some one who was in a class by herself, for Emma Lou was certain that there was not, and could not be, any one else in the university just like Hazel. But despite her vulgarity, the girl was not all bad. Her good nature was infectious, and Emma Lou had surmised from her monologue on the day before how utterly unselfish a person she could be and was. All of her store of the world's goods were at hand to be used and enjoyed by her friends. There was not, as she had said "a selfish bone in her body." But even that did not alter the disgusting fact that she was not one who would be welcome by the "right sort of people." Her flamboyant style of dress, her loud voice, her raucous laughter, and her flagrant disregard or ignorance of English grammar seemed inexcusable to Emma Lou, who was unable to understand how such a person could stray so far from the environment in which she rightfully belonged to enter a first-class university. Now Hazel, according to Emma Lou, was the type of Negro who should go to a Negro college. There were plenty of them in the South whose standard of scholarship was not beyond her ability. And, then, in one of those schools, her darky-like clownishness would not have to be paraded in front of white people, thereby causing discomfort and embarrassment to others of her race, more civilized and circumspect than she.

The problem irritated Emma Lou. She didn't see why it had to be. She   46
had looked forward so anxiously, and so happily to her introductory days on

the campus, and now her first experience with one of her fellow colored students had been an unpleasant one. But she didn't intend to let that make her unhappy. She was determined to return to the campus alone, seek out other companions, see whether they accepted or ignored the offending Hazel, and govern herself accordingly.

It was early and there were few people on the campus. The grass was still wet from a heavy overnight dew, and the sun had not yet dispelled the coolness of the early morning. Emma Lou's dress was of thin material and she shivered as she walked or stood in the shade. She had no school business to attend to; there was nothing for her to do but to walk aimlessly about the campus. 47

In another hour, Emma Lou was pleased to see that the campus walks were becoming crowded, and that the side streets surrounding the campus were now heavy with student traffic. Things were beginning to awaken. Emma Lou became jubilant and walked with jaunty step from path to path, from building to building. It then occurred to her that she had been told that there were more Negro students enrolled in the School of Pharmacy than in any other department of the university, so finding the Pharmacy building she began to wander through its crowded hallways. 48

Almost immediately, she saw a group of five Negro students, three boys and two girls, standing near a water fountain. She was both excited and perplexed, excited over the fact that she was so close to those she wished to find, and perplexed because she did not know how to approach them. Had there been only one person standing there, the matter would have been comparatively easy. She could have approached with a smile and said, "Good morning." The person would have returned her greeting, and it would then have been a simple matter to get acquainted. 49

But five people in one bunch all known to one another and all chatting intimately together!—it would seem too much like an intrusion to go bursting into their gathering—too forward and too vulgar. Then, there was nothing she could say after having said "good morning." One just didn't break into a group of five and say, "I'm Emma Lou Morgan, a new student, and I want to make friends with you." No, she couldn't do that. She would just smile as she passed, smile graciously and friendly. They would know that she was a stranger, and her smile would assure them that she was anxious to make friends, anxious to become a welcome addition to their group. 50

One of the group of five had sighted Emma Lou as soon as she had sighted them: 51

"Who's this?" queried Helen Wheaton, a senior in the College of Law. 52

"Some new 'pick,' I guess," answered Bob Armstrong, who was Helen's fiance and a senior in the School of Architecture. 53

"I bet she's going to take Pharmacy," whispered Amos Blaine. 54

"She's hottentot enough to take something," mumbled Tommy Brown. "Thank God, she won't be in any of our classes, eh Amos?" ◆ 55

◆ Responding

1. Emma Lou is a victim of prejudice within her family because she is dark-skinned and female. Yet when she goes to college, she is prejudiced against Hazel Mason because of her behavior. She is aware of her victimization but unaware of her victimizing. In contemporary terms, Emma Lou needs her consciousness raised. Write her a letter making her aware of what she is doing.

2. Working individually or in a group, list all of Hazel Mason's good and bad qualities according to Emma Lou's assessment. From Emma Lou's point of view consider whether she should befriend her. Do you think the two young women would become friends? Share your reasons with the class.

3. Emma Lou is rejected by the students whom she wishes to befriend. Explain their reasons for rejecting her. This selection illustrates the phenomenon of prejudice within a racial group. Whose criteria are the group members using as their model? Using examples from the selection, your own experience, or sources such as Spike Lee's film *School Daze*, explain the ways in which prejudice within a racial group can distort relationships and undermine the members of the group.

4. Thurman takes the title, *The Blacker the Berry*, from the folk saying "The blacker the berry, the sweeter the juice." Explain why he chose this title, and what it reveals about his attitudes toward racial characteristics. Speculate about what he will have Emma Lou come to realize by the end of the novel.

REFLECTING A CRITICAL CONTEXT

DARWIN TURNER

Darwin Turner was born in Cincinnati in 1931. He earned his bachelor's and master's degrees at the University of Cincinnati in 1947 and 1949, respectively, and his doctorate at the University of Chicago in 1949. He has taught English at several universities, including North Carolina Agricultural and Technical State, Indiana University, and the University of Michigan; since 1980 he has been on the faculty of the University of Iowa, where he is currently a professor of English and chair of the Afro-American Studies Department. Turner has written extensively on the African American literary experience. His publications include In a Minor Chord: Three African American Writers and Their Search for Identity *and* The Wayward and the Seeking: Selected Writings of Jean Toomer. *He has also edited the critical edition of Jean Toomer's* Cane.*

In the essay that follows, Turner evaluates the contribution of Harlem Renaissance writers from a contemporary perspective. In contrast to earlier critics, who stressed the elitism or excessiveness of the movement, he explores the Harlem Renaissance as a "serious way of examining the problems of living."

◆ THE HARLEM RENAISSANCE: ONE FACET OF AN UNTURNED KALEIDOSCOPE ◆

Geraldine's brash cry, "What you see is what you get," is appropriate comment on the tendency of many Americans to fix their attention on only a particular aspect of Black life in America—usually the most spectacular aspect. If they would twist the base of the kaleidoscope of Black life, the multicolored fragments would rearrange themselves into different patterns, some of them startlingly different. But few viewers choose to adjust the kaleidoscope.

As a result, out of the many patterns of Black life during the 1920's, the dominant image emblazoned on the vision of America is the Harlem Renaissance. By the same process, from the Harlem Renaissance itself, a Jazzed Abandon has become the most memorable spectacle. James Weldon Johnson's description of reactions to Harlem summarizes the legend of the Harlem Renaissance:

> It is known in Europe and the Orient, and it is talked about by natives in the interior of Africa. It is farthest known as being exotic, colourful [*sic*], and sensuous; a place of laughing, singing, and dancing; a place where life wakes up at night. This phase of Harlem's fame is most widely known because, in addition to being

spread by ordinary agencies, it has been proclaimed in story and song. And certainly this is Harlem's most striking and fascinating aspect. New Yorkers and people visiting New York from the world over go to the night-clubs of Harlem and dance to such jazz music as can be heard nowhere else; and they get an exhilaration impossible to duplicate. Some of these seekers after new sensations go beyond the gay night-clubs; they peep in under the more seamy side of things; they nose down into lower strata of life. A visit to Harlem at night—the principal streets never deserted, gay crowds skipping from one place of amusement to another, lines of taxicabs and limousines standing under the sparkling lights of the entrances to the famous night-clubs, the subway kiosks swallowing and disgorging crowds all night long—gives the impression that Harlem never sleeps and that the inhabitants thereof jazz through existence.[1]

Johnson continued, "But, of course, no one can seriously think that the two hundred thousand and more Negroes in Harlem spend their nights on any such pleasance."[2] So we too can say, "Surely, no one seriously thinks that this picture or even the entire 'Renaissance' constitutes the totality of the patterns housed in the kaleidoscope of Black life during the 1920's, the decade of the 'New Negro.' "   3

Even if one examines only the literary portraiture of the decade, one discerns more than a single image as the minute, tinted mirrors arrange and rearrange themselves into diverse patterns reflecting the actuality of Black life or reflecting the psyches of the Black and white artists who depicted that life. A knowledgeable individual twists the instrument to view the primitivism depicted by such white authors as Julia Peterkin, Eugene O'Neill, Sherwood Anderson, Dubose Heyward, Mary Wiborg, and William Faulkner, or the exotic abandon simulated by Carl Van Vechten. But a slight adjustment reshapes those images into the cultural elitism revealed by Van Vechten and cherished by W. E. B. DuBois. Another adjustment reveals the integrationist optimism of Langston Hughes, or the pan-Africanism of W. E. B. DuBois, or the Black nationalism of Marcus Garvey. Examine rural southern Blacks from the perspectives of Peterkin, Heyward, Faulkner, and Jean Toomer; or scrutinize the urban northerners of Toomer, Claude McKay, Rudolph Fisher, Langston Hughes, and Countée Cullen. Smile at the enthusiastic and naive Carl Van Vechtens, Mabel Dodges, and other white patrons as they prance about with their trophies collected on safaris into the Black jungles; then scowl at the lynchers painted by Claude McKay and photographed by Walter White. Admire the "patient endurance," with which William Faulkner colored his Dilsey; but do not overlook the militant impatience that inflames McKay's poetic voice. Consider the African nationalism vaguely sketched by Cullen, Hughes, and McKay; but compare it with Hughes' poetic demands for American integration   4

---

[1] James W. Johnson, *Black Manhattan* (New York, 1968; originally published, 1930), pp. 160–161. [Author's note]

[2] Ibid., p. 161. [Author's note]

and McKay's impressionistic sketches of the damnable siren, America, that fascinates, challenges, and captivates Blacks. Excite yourselves with sexual abandon garishly painted by Van Vechten, Anderson, McKay, and Toomer; but study also the conservative, often frustrated Blacks portrayed by Jessie Fauset and Toomer. Weep for the impotent failures depicted by O'Neill and Paul Green; but rejoice with the bold, determined aspirants of Fauset and Fisher.

Beyond the literary spectrum, the images are equally diverse. The decade of the 1920's was ushered in by the triumphant return in 1919 of the highly decorated Black 369th Infantry, which marched from the docks, down Broadway, and through Harlem, led every step of the way by James Europe's jazz band. But the decade was ushered in also by the "Red Summer" of 1919. In that year alone, according to historian John Hope Franklin, approximately twenty-five race riots throughout the nation spilled blood on the streets of the democratic land that, less than a year earlier, had won the war (so Americans said) that, President Wilson boasted, would end all wars and would safeguard democracy. Jazz was in vogue: such Black musicians as Duke Ellington and Fletcher Henderson attracted thousands of excited people to hear their bands, and Louis Armstrong gained new fans with each performance. But poverty was in vogue also: Black migrants who could not find jobs and older residents who had lost theirs to a new influx of whites gave rent parties, which remained joyous as long as no one remembered that the only reason for the party was the inability to pay the rent. Occupants of Harlem for less than a decade, Blacks were buying homes for residence and for profit on a scale rivaling the stock market speculations of their white contemporaries; but hard times had already established residence in the South, as Waring Cuney revealed in "Hard Times Blues":

> I went down home
> About a year ago
> Things looked so bad
> My heart was sore.
> People had nothing
> It was a sinning shame,
> Everybody said
> Hard times was to blame.
>
> Great-God-A-Mighty
> Folks feeling bad,
> Lost all they ever had.
>
> Sun was shining fourteen
> Days and no rain,
> Hoeing and planting
> Was all in vain.
> It was hard times, Lawd,
> All around,
> Meal barrels empty,
> Crops burnt to the ground.

Great-God-A-Mighty
Folks feeling bad,
Lost all they ever had.

Skinny looking children
Bellies poking out,
Old pellagra
Without a doubt,
Old folks hanging 'round
The cabin door
Aint seen things
This bad before.

Great-God-A-Mighty
Folks feeling bad,
Lost all they ever had.

Went to the Boss
At the Commissary Store,
Folks all hungry
Please don't close the door,
Want more food, little time to pay.
Boss man laughed
And walked away.

Great-God-A-Mighty
Folks feeling bad,
Lost all they ever had.

Landlord coming 'round
When the rent's due,
Aint got the money
Take your home from you.
Takes your mule and horse
Even take your cow,
Says get off this land
You no good no how.

Great-God-A-Mighty
Folks feeling bad,
Lost all they ever had.

For Black folks, and many rural whites, times were bad—at the very height 6
of the Jazz Age when Scott Fitzgerald's sheiks, flappers, and Gatsbys were stag-
ing their most lavish parties. Blacks were not naive about the times. With the assistance of Walter White, a Caucasian-looking Black, the N.A.A.C.P. launched its
three-decades-long campaign against lynching. The *Messenger*, a Black newspaper, advocated socialism as the only solution to the economic problems of Black
Americans; and *The Crusader*, another Black newspaper, denounced American

bigotry in tones that a subsequent generation would believe originated in the 1960's. Recognizing the inability of nonunionized workers to withstand the arbitrary practices of the bosses, Black workers struggled to enter or establish unions: in the Brotherhood of Sleeping Car Porters, A. Philip Randolph created the most enduring of them all. Scorning any hope for Black economic or political power in the United States, Marcus Garvey, a West Indian, enlisted thousands of new followers who wished to sail the Black Star Line back to Africa. Ironically, Garvey, an actual Black from an island, won more power and financial support in America than Eugene O'Neill ever envisaged for his Emperor Jones, a fictional Black American who seizes control of a Black island.

Such awareness of the multiplicity of patterns of Black life during the 1920's justifies a reexamination, necessarily brief and somewhat superficial, of the Harlem Renaissance, particularly the literary Renaissance—to determine the reasons for its image as Jazzed Abandon, to trace more closely the more serious themes of the literature, and to reassess the significance of the Renaissance. 7

If we of the 1970's picture Black life in the 1920's as a riotous night-club tour, we cannot blame the best-known white writers for our misconception. Ironically, although Blacks became so popular as a subject that almost every prominent American author of the decade featured them in at least one major work, most of these authors ignored the Harlem scene in their literature. Such obvious neglect prompts speculation about the reasons: Were the authors describing the Afro-Americans they knew best? Or were they deliberately creating Black characters who would contrast with, and perhaps obscure, the image of the proud Renaissance Blacks? 8

Of course, in 1920, when O'Neill's *Emperor Jones* appeared, the Harlem Renaissance was less than a flutter in the heart of Alain Locke, the Black philosopher and cultural historian who named that era. O'Neill cannot be accused of ignoring what he could not have been expected to see. Situating his Black on a Caribbean island, O'Neill showed how fear, stripping away civilized veneer, reduces a man—in this instance, a southern Black—to a primitive. 9

The contrast between the Renaissance and O'Neill's work, however, appears in *All God's Chillun Got Wings* (1924). This drama, necessarily set in the North, describes the pathetic relationship between a Black man, who aspires to be a lawyer, and the "fallen" white woman whom he marries. The woman, betrayed and deserted by a white lover, marries the Black but becomes insane— or more insane, according to your view. The Black fails to become a lawyer partly because his wife, not wanting him to succeed, interferes with his study. The more crucial reason for his failure, however, is that whenever he is examined by whites, he forgets whatever he knows. In 1924, the year the play appeared, Jessie Fauset and Walter White published the first Black novels of the decade: *There Is Confusion*, which centers on the lives of middle-class Blacks in Philadelphia, among them a Black graduate of a white medical school, and *The Fire in the Flint*, a protest against lynching. For three years, Black musicals had been 10 the rage of Broadway theater. BLACK was in, by 1924. The next year *Survey Graphic* would focus an entire issue on the "New Negro," James Weldon Johnson would hail Harlem as the capital of Black America, others would call it "Mecca." Despite these events, O'Neill provided New York theatergoers with a Black protagonist whose aspirations exceed his ability. Whatever O'Neill's reasons for the theme, the choice of an actor to portray the protagonist could not have been more ironic. The Black who panics when examined by whites was played by Paul Robeson, all-American football player (I believe that he was the first Black selected by Walter Camp as an All-American), a twelve-letter man in athletics, and a Phi Betta Kappa graduate, who earned one of the highest academic averages in the history of Rutgers University.

The spectacle of Black failure was continued by Paul Green, a North 11
Carolinian who wrote more plays about Blacks than any other white person during the decade. In 1926 Green won the Pulitzer Prize for *In Abraham's Bosom*, a drama in which Black Abe McCrannie, during Reconstruction, tries futilely to establish a school for Blacks. In the same year, 1926, W. E. B. DuBois, editor of *The Crisis*, the voice of the N.A.A.C.P., continuing a practice intended to encourage Black scholarship, published the pictures of the year's Black college graduates. Within a few years, DuBois would proudly announce that the large number of graduates prohibited his publishing the pictures of all.

Another memorable drama of the decade was Dubose Heyward's *Porgy*, 12
now an American "classic," a story of a Black and crippled junk dealer, who strives to win Bess, a fallen woman, from Crown, a bad, bad man. Perhaps the most appropriate evaluation of the drama comes from W. E. B. DuBois, who insisted that he did not object to the play. Then, sniffing delicately from the rarified atmosphere surrounding a New England Brahmin who was a Ph.D. graduate from Harvard and had been a graduate student at Heidelberg, DuBois explained that, although he did not doubt that Heyward's Blacks existed in Charleston, South Carolina, he regretted Heyward's failure to portray the educated Blacks DuBois associated with when he visited that city.

During the 1920's William Faulkner foreshadowed his future stature with 13
The Sound and the Fury, located primarily in Mississippi, with a glance at Cambridge, Massachusetts. Faulkner's major Black character in this novel is Dilsey, prototype of "the Black who endures." Like Green and O'Neill, Faulkner probably had not read Alain Locke's introduction to *The New Negro* (1925). Locke asserted: "Sentimental interest in the Negro has ebbed. We used to lament this as the falling off of our friends; now we rejoice and pray to be delivered both from self-pity and condescension. The mind of each racial group has had a better weaning, apathy or hatred on one side matching disillusionment or resentment on the other; but they face each other today with the possibility at least of entirely new mutual attitudes."[3]

---

[3]Locke, "The New Negro," *The New Negro* (New York, 1968), p. 8. [Author's note]

The decade ended with a production of the extraordinarily popular *Green* 14
Pastures (1930) by Marc Connelly. Based on Roark Bradford's *Ol' Man Adam*
and His Chillun, the drama seems to retell the Old Testament from the perspective of a Black child at a church fish-fry. The narrator is not a child, however;
he is an adult.

However distorted their vision of Blacks may have been, well-known white 15
American authors of the 1920's cannot be blamed for the exotic image of the
nightclub Black. That image comes from Blacks themselves and from a few
whites who identified themselves as promoters of Blacks or as sympathizers.

The image may have begun with *Shuffle Along* (1921), a brilliant and 16
popular musical, written and directed by four Blacks—Flournoy Miller, Eubie
Blake, Noble Sissel, and Aubrey Lyles. In the same year, *Shuffle Along* was
succeeded by *Put and Take*, another musical by a Black—Irving C. Miller, who
also produced *Liza* (1923), which was followed in the same year by *Runnin' Wild*
by Miller and Lyles. The beauty of Afro-American chorus girls such as Florence
Mills and Josephine Baker, the exotic foreign settings, the gaiety and the frenzy
of these musicals and their successors may have cultivated in Broadway audiences a taste for particular depictions of Black life. Furthermore, these musicals
may have created an image difficult to change.

Although it is located in the South, Sherwood Anderson's *Dark Laughter* 17
(1925) conjures up the image of a joyful, untroubled people who, themselves
freed from the need to read Freud, laugh gently at frustrated whites, who
repress their own sexual desires. The image of joy continues in Carl Van
Vechten's novel, *Nigger Heaven* (1926), set in Harlem. Although Van Vechten
later proclaimed his desire to familiarize white readers with a cultural Black
society which gives soirées and speaks French, he glamorized the Scarlet Cree-
per, a "sweetman" (gigolo), and he depicted Black night life with an excitement
certain to allure readers.

The exoticism and gaiety appear in the works of Black writers themselves. 18
Even Countée Cullen, known to subsequent generations as a somewhat prim
purveyor of high art, contrasted the warmth of Blacks with the coldness of
whites, wrote atavistically of the African rhythm inherent in the walk of a Black
waiter (in *Color*, 1925), and rhapsodized the wildness of the African heritage.

In his first collection, *The Weary Blues* (1926), Langston Hughes not only 19
created jazz/blues poems but also wrote with an exuberance tending to promote
the image of an uninhibited people:

Dream Variation

To fling my arms wide
In some place of the sun,
To whirl and to dance
Till the white day is done.
Then rest at cool evening

Beneath a tall tree
While night comes on gently,
    Dark like me,—
That is my dream!

To fling my arms wide
In the face of the sun,
Dance! whirl! whirl!
Till the quick day is done.
Rest at pale evening. . . .
A tall, slim tree. . . .
Night coming tenderly
    Black like me.[4]

Black novelists also contributed to the image of an uninhibited people whose lives are exotic whirls. In *Home to Harlem* (1928), Claude McKay, a Black West Indian, drowned social protest in a flood of night life—prostitutes, sweetmen, jazz, nightclub fights—as he told the story of a Black deserter from the armed services who searches through Harlem for the prostitute whom he loves. Succeeding novelists, such as Rudolph Fisher (*The Walls of Jericho*, 1928) and Wallace Thurman (*The Blacker the Berry*, 1929), seemed almost compelled to include irrelevant nightclub scenes as though they had become clichés of Black life.

It should not be wondered then that W. E. B. DuBois, editor of *The Crisis*, 20 reserved sections of several issues to question whether writers and publishers shared his fear that Black writers were being encouraged to create derogatory pictures of Blacks. Seriously concerned about respectable images of Blacks, DuBois, more than two decades earlier, had rationalized their enthusiasm as a primitivism promoted by the experience of slavery, a primitivism which would be modified when Black Americans matured into the sophistication of Euro-American society. Now that his "Talented Tenth" seemed to promote spectacles of frenzy, however, DuBois suspected that their desire to publish persuaded them to ignore the truth of Black life and to pander to whites by creating images designed to titillate.

Beneath the surfaces of gay abandon during the 1920's, however, are more 21 somber issues, more sober themes which should be examined more closely. The same writers who seem to rejoice in the enthusiasm of Black life also sounded what Langston Hughes described as "the sob of the jazz band"—the melancholy undertone of Black life, ever present but sometimes unheard by those who fail to listen carefully.

Claude McKay pictured a Harlem dancer who guards her soul from the 22 lascivious image suggested by her dance (*Harlem Shadows*, 1922), and Langston Hughes described the weariness of a jazz pianist (*The Weary Blues*, 1926). In

---

[4]Hughes, *The Weary Blues* (New York, 1926). [Author's note]

The Walls of Jericho (1928) Fisher overshadowed the scenes of night life with a quieter depiction of the romance of two working people of Harlem. Thurman tempered his scenes of night life and dances in *The Blacker the Berry* by revealing that some Blacks visited dance halls not to gorge themselves with gaiety but to discover companionship to ease their loneliness. In the same novel a white Chicagoan confirms his impression that the exotic savagery of Harlemites is grossly exaggerated by their white press agents. While his actress-sister revels in what she considers the barbaric splendor of the Black club they visit, the Chicagoan sees a generally decorous behavior which assures him that Harlemites are no wilder than the Blacks he has known in Chicago (and perhaps not as wild as the whites in either city). Countée Cullen asserted that he wrote *One Way to Heaven* (1932) to counter Carl Van Vechten's *Nigger Heaven* by showing the humanity of Black life in Harlem. In scene after scene, Cullen balances superficial exuberance with sober explanation: The enthusiasm of a religious revival does not obscure the fact that in attendance also are some morally respectable Blacks who are not swept away by the emotion. The heroine, a morally circumspect, hard-working woman, has attended several revivals to which she has been indifferent. A male's illicit love affair is ascribed partly to the nature of the wandering male and partly to a desire to find companionship because his wife, who has become a religious fanatic, is engaged in an affair with Jesus.

These more serious vestiges of Black life in America should not be ignored when one considers the literature of the Renaissance; for, far from being mere entertainers, many Black writers regarded literature as a means of seriously examining problems of living. Moreover, they did not restrict their examinations to problems of Blacks in an adversary relationship with white society. Almost from the first they were concerned with issues which might be considered universal if American critics were more willing to discover universality in the lives of Black people. [23]

The interest in human conditions appears in Jean Toomer's *Cane* (1923), the work of the Renaissance which is the best known and the most highly respected in academic circles. Toomer delineates many protagonists whose difficulties do not depend primarily upon their ancestry: Karintha has matured too soon sexually; Carma lives in a society which pretends that a woman should become sexless if her husband does not live with her; Esther cannot reconcile her sexual urges with the education by a society which has taught her that "good" girls do not feel such urges; John, in "Theater," cannot adapt his idealized romanticizing into a satisfactory relationship with an actual woman; Dorris, in "Theater," dreams of a companionship that will provide a real substitute for the artificiality of the theater; Muriel, in "Box Seat," fears to defy the little-minded, social regulators of the world; Avery finds it more pleasurable to be supported by men than to labor as a teacher in a normal school. The problems of these individuals may be complicated or intensified by their condition as Blacks in America, but the problems would exist regardless of their race. [24]

Jessie Fauset, the too little-known author of *There Is Confusion* (1924), *Plum*   25
Bun (1929), *The Chinaberry Tree* (1933), and *Comedy: American Style* (1933), contrived her novels to focus on the problems of Blacks whose lives are not continuously affected by their interrelationships with whites. Most often their
problems derive from their ambition or from a society excessively willing to
evaluate individuals according to false criteria. In *There Is Confusion*, for example,
an ambitious young Black protagonist disrupts and nearly destroys the people
around her because she tries to regulate their lives according to her delusions.
Because she believes that people should not marry outside their class, she
interferes with her brother's romance with a young woman whose family background is different. Doing "the right thing," by withdrawing from the relationship, the second young woman then rushes into an unfortunate marriage.
Because the protagonist believes that suitors must be trained into suitably devoted servants, she refuses to apologize to the man she loves even though she
is wrong. After he apologizes in order to effect a reconciliation, she delays a
response with the deliberate intention of causing him to learn that he cannot
win her too easily. She begins to realize her error only when he, jolted by her
rebuff, proposes to a woman who offers him affection without reservation.

In stories which she published during the 1920's, Zora Neale Hurston of   26
Florida explores such an "in-group" issue as the manner in which townspeople
affect individuals by forcing them to act out of character in order to maintain
the respect of the mob ("Spunk"). In addition, she vividly revealed the problems
which disturb male-female relationships: the alienation which develops when a
naive wife is seduced by a traveling salesman ("The Gilded Six-Bits"); the tragic
consequences when a self-centered husband who has exploited his wife tries to
replace her ("Sweat").

Black dramatists, such as Willis Richardson and Georgia D. Johnson,   27
prepared domestic dramas for the Black community: the tensions between a
man and his improvident brothers-in-law ("The Broken Banjo"); the pathos of
a situation in which a child is permitted to die because the mother favors the
healing power of faith above that of man's medicine.

In such ways as these, Black people of the Renaissance explored serious   28
issues involving Black people but not deriving primarily from the racial ancestry
or from their relationship with whites. This statement, however, should not
encourage a fallacious assumption that the Black writers evaded their racial
identity or ignored problems which do derive from interracial conflict. To the
contrary, Black Renaissance writers frequently expressed concerns which strik-
ingly anticipate major themes identified with the revolutionary Black Arts writers of the 1960's: a search for and affirmation of ancestral heritage, a feeling of
alienation from the white Euro-American world; a presentation of and protest
against oppression; and even militant defiance of oppression.

Just as Black Arts writers of today affirm their African heritage, so many   29
Renaissance writers sought identity through identification with an ancestral
past. Jean Toomer sought identity derived in part from the consciousness of
the slave South and Africa (*Cane*, 1923, and "Natalie Mann"). As I have pointed

out earlier, Countée Cullen proclaimed that the sober teachings of Christian
civilization could not curb the memories and the urges which linked him with
Africa ("Heritage"). Langston Hughes found pride in identification with a race
so old in human history that it had lived when rivers were young ("The Negro
Speaks of Rivers"). Although some of these ancestral searches may seem rhetorical rather than actual, although some of the thoughts of Africa are sufficiently
atavistic to promote a concept of exotic primitivism, the quests respond partly
at least to Alain Locke's urgings that Black artists search for subject and style
in an African tradition.

For the Black American writer of the 1920's, however, the search for   30
ancestry proved more difficult than for white Americans. Some Blacks, ashamed
of their ancestry as slaves and as descendants of Africans whom they judged
to have been savages, attempted to evolve more respectable ancestry from identification with former masters. In *There Is Confusion* (1924) Jessie Fauset suggested
the problems sometimes posed by the quest for European ancestry. Moreover,
Blacks who wished to affirm a Black heritage were forced to identify with a
continent rather than with a particular tribe or nation. Hence, the identification
sometimes became intellectual and abstract rather than personal. The problem
is suggested by Hughes:

Afro-American Fragment

So long,
So far away
Is Africa.
Not even memories alive
Save those that history books create,
Save those that songs
Beat back into the blood—
Beat out of blood with words sad-sung
In strange un-Negro tongue—
So long
So far away.

Subdued and time-lost
Are the drums—and yet
Through some vast mist of race
There comes this song
I do not understand,
This song of atavistic land,
Of bitter yearning lost
Without a place—
So long,
So far away
Is Africa's
Dark face.

Failure to establish psychological identity with the Black heritage and   31
corresponding awareness of exclusion from the European heritage sometimes
produced a sense of alienation comparable to that expressed by Black Arts
writers today. The feeling resounds vividly from McKay's "Outcast."

> For the dim regions whence my fathers came
> My spirit, bondaged by the body, longs.
> Words felt, but never heard, my lips would frame:
> My soul would sing forgotten jungle songs.
> I would go back to darkness and to peace,
> But the great western world holds me in fee,
> And I may never hope for full release,
> While to its alien gods I bend my knee.
> Something in me is lost, forever lost,
> Some vital thing has gone out of my heart,
> And I must walk the way of life a ghost
> Among the sons of earth, a thing apart;
> For I was born, far from my native clime,
> Under the white man's menace, out of time.

The serious themes that Renaissance writers explored most frequently,   32
as might be expected, are protests against oppression. The presence of such
themes has been obscured by three facts: (1) many readers remember the glamorous gaiety and forget the serious comments; (2) some protests appear as brief
asides rather than fully developed explanations; (3) some protests seem mild
because, rather than directly assaulting whites, they adumbrate the manner in
which external oppression causes Blacks to oppress themselves. The way that
serious protest can be ignored is evidenced by the customary reactions of casual
readers to McKay's *Home to Harlem* (1928), which appears, even in this paper,
as a prototype of a Black work that promotes exoticism. The vividly exotic
spectacles blind many readers to McKay's presentation of such facts as the
following: During World War I many Black soldiers who enlisted to fight for
democracy were restricted to service as laborers; during the 1920's some Harlem
clubs, whether owned by whites or Blacks, discriminated against Blacks by
refusing them admission—except as entertainers or waiters; in many occupations
Black workers surrendered their dignity to the caprice of white supervisors.

It is true that no *Native Son* burst from the Renaissance to denounce   33
American oppression. But Walter White's novel *The Fire in the Flint* (1924)
decries the brutality of lynchings, as does Claude McKay's "The Lynching."
Toomer's "Blood-Burning Moon" and "Kabnis" (*Cane*) reveal the powerlessness
of Blacks to protect themselves from white brutality: a successful self-defense
summons the lynch mob as quickly as a murder would.

Much more prevalent is the Renaissance writers' tendency to attack oppres-   34
sion indirectly by showing how it causes Blacks to turn against themselves.
Because color, as an evidence of African ancestry, was a shibboleth of whites

against Blacks, many Blacks used color as a criterion of intra-group evaluation. In *The Blacker the Berry* the protagonist, because of her dark skin, suffers within her family, in school and college, and in efforts to secure employment. Yet pathetically, as Thurman shows, the heroine cherishes the same criteria which have victimized her. She desires only men who are of lighter complexion and Caucasian appearance; and she undervalues herself, believing for a time at least that her Blackness is an ineradicable blot upon her record. In *Comedy: American Style* (1933), Fauset censured a Negro mother who values her children according to the degree of their approximation to Caucasian appearance. Walter White's *Flight* (1928) and Nella Larsen's *Passing* (1929) show the dilemmas of heroines who, repressed by the conditions of life as Blacks, attempt to improve their lot by passing for white.

In ironic repudiation of the images of Blacks as amoral beings, Jean Toomer repeatedly stressed the necessity for middle-class Negroes to liberate themselves from conscious imitation of the restrictive morality of Anglo-Saxons. "Esther," "Theater," and "Box-Seat" all reveal the frustrations of Black people who, desiring social approval, repress their emotions, their humanness. In "Kabnis" Carrie K., fearing censure by others, represses her instinctual attraction to Lewis. Paul ("Rona and Paul," *Cane*) loses a female companion because of his self-conscious desire to explain to a bystander that the relationship is not lustful. Toomer's most fully developed attack on middle-class morality appears in the unpublished drama "Natalie Mann." Mert, a school teacher, dies because she perceives too late that she must enjoy passion fully without concern for society's censure. Natalie, the protagonist, develops to this awareness only through the assistance of a Christ-like male who himself has experienced the rebukes of the middle class.

Toomer was not the only writer to question the excessive effort of Blacks to conform to the standards presumed to be those of whites. The protagonist in Walter White's *Flight* is forced to leave town and, temporarily, to deny her race because Blacks will not permit her to forget that she has had a child out of wedlock: her lover's proposal of abortion so diminished him in her esteem that she refused his subsequent efforts to marry her.

During the 1920's few writers reacted militantly to oppression with the kind of rhetoric for which Black revolutionary literature became notorious during the 1960's. There are several reasons. A generally optimistic faith that talented Blacks soon would emerge with the mainstream muted rhetorical violence and violent rhetoric. Furthermore, publishers during the 1920's did not permit the kind of language and the explicit description of violent action which became almost commonplace in later decades. Third, the publishing houses were controlled by whites. It should be remembered that much of the Black revolutionary literature of the 1960's issued from Black publishers of poetry and in Black community drama.

Under the circumstances it is not surprising that the militant reaction often was expressed as self-defense, as in Claude McKay's well-known "If We

Must Die" (*Harlem Shadows*). Less frequently came prayers for destruction, as in McKay's "Enslaved" (*Harlem Shadows*). Most often the militancy is a proud hostility toward whites. At the end of *Flight* the male protagonist learns why his father abhorred whites: they had deprived him of inheritance by refusing to recognize him as their offspring. In turn he refuses to permit an elderly white to ease his own conscience by making a monetary donation while continuing to ignore the blood relationship.

I cannot conclude without reassessing the significance of the literary Har- 39
lem Renaissance. If it is remembered for expression of gaiety rather than for the serious concerns of the Black authors; if it was a movement which involved only talented artists in one segment of the Black American population; if it reflects primarily the life of only one part of one city inhabited by Blacks; if it evidences little awareness of such a significant issue for Blacks as DuBois' dreams and promotions of Pan-Africanism and even less awareness of or respect for Marcus Garvey's Back-to-Africa movement—if the literary Renaissance is so limited, does it merit serious study? Was it, as Harold Cruse has suggested, an era to be examined only as a pathetic example of a time when Black artists might have established criteria for their art but failed to do so? Was it, as W. E. B. DuBois stated and as LeRoi Jones insisted more forcefully later, a movement that lost validity as it became a plaything of white culture? In fact, is the very attention given to it by historians of Black culture evidence of the willingness of Blacks and whites to glorify, or permit glorification of, inferior art by Blacks?

Each of these allegations has partial validity. But such objections based 40
on idealistic absolutes fail to consider the actual significances of the literary Renaissance. First, in no other decade had Black novelists been afforded such opportunity for publication. If fewer than twenty original, non-vanity-press novels appeared between 1924 and 1933, that figure nevertheless exceeded the number published by American commercial houses in all the years since the publication of the first Black American novel, Williams Wells Brown's *Clotel* (1853). Even the Depression and the closing of some outlets could not dispel the new awareness that possibilities existed for Blacks who wished to write novels. The field was open to many writers, not merely to the individual geniuses—the Paul Dunbar or the Charles Chesnutt of an earlier decade. This productivity, as well as the later success of Richard Wright, undoubtedly encouraged such novelists as Chester Hines, Ann Petry, Frank Yerby, and William G. Smith, who developed during the late 1930's and early 1940's.

The literary examples and inspirations were not limited to the novel. Only 41
a few serious Black dramas reached Broadway, but the enthusiastic establishment of Black community theaters during the 1920's furthered the creation of a Black audience for drama and promoted awareness of the need for writers to create material for that audience.

Perhaps the productivity in poetry had less significant influence because 42
Blacks previously had found outlets for poetry—the national reputation of Paul

Laurence Dunbar was known by Blacks. Moreover, poetry was still to be considered an avocation which one supported by revenue derived from a stable vocation. But there was hope that Black writers might be able to sustain themselves partly through grants, for Countée Cullen had established a precedent by winning a Guggenheim fellowship for his proposal of a poetry-writing project.

Of final benefit to future writers was the mere fact that entrées had been 43 established. A Langston Hughes or Wallace Thurman or Countée Cullen or, later, an Arna Bontemps knew publishers and knew other people who might be able to assist prospective authors. In all these senses, the Renaissance was not a rebirth but, in very significant ways, a first birth for Black Americans in literature.

A second significance of the literary Renaissance is its inspiration for 44 African and Caribbean poets such as Léopold Senghor, Aimé Césaire, and Léon Damas who, a generation later in the 1930's and 1940's, promoted Negritude, a literary-cultural movement which emphasized consciousness of African identity and pride in the Black heritage. More than a decade after the Negritude writers, newer Black American writers of the 1960's looked to African Negritude for inspiration. Thus, both directly and circuitously, the Renaissance promoted Black American literature and Black consciousness of future decades.

Finally, the Renaissance has importance as a symbol. In many respects, 45 the actuality of a culture is less important than the myth which envelops and extends from that culture. The memory that Black Americans had been recognized and respected for literary achievements, as well as other artistic achievements, established awareness that there could be a literary culture among Blacks. If the memory faded rapidly from the consciousness of white America, it did not fade from the minds of Blacks responsible for continuing the culture among their people. Marcus Garvey did not succeed in restoring Black Americans to Africa; consequently, he is remembered as a dream that faded. But the Renaissance, for Black Americans and others, has gained strength as the mythic memory of a time when Blacks first burst into national consciousness as a talented group that was young, rebellious, proud, and beautiful. ◆

◆ Responding

1. Explain why Turner wants us to twist the kaleidoscope of black life for a different view of the Harlem Renaissance.

2. Contrast the "spectacle" of black failure presented by many white writers of the 1920s with some of the successes Turner mentions. What reasons does he present to explain the distorted picture of blacks in the literature and theater of the time?

3. Working individually or in group illustrate the serious themes dealt with by African American writers during the Harlem Renaissance using examples from the selections in this chapter. Discuss the reasons Turner gives to explain why the importance of this work has been obscured.

4. Review Turner's comments about one of the selections in this chapter. Write an essay supporting his statements with fully developed examples from the reading.

5. Write an essay responding to the criticism by W. E. B. DuBois and Imamu Amiri Baraka (LeRoi Jones) that the Harlem Renaissance was "a movement that lost validity as it became a plaything of white culture."

◆

CONNECTING

Critical Thinking and Writing

1. Compare the situation for people of color in universities today with the situation for the speaker in "Theme for English B," for Emma Lou in *The Blacker the Berry,* or for Santos in "Ropes of Passage." In what ways has your university tried to welcome and encourage people of color? How successful have these attempts been?

2. Describe Delia's life as an example of the trials described in the poem "Mother and Son." Explain the ways in which she "kept climbing" in spite of hardships.

3. Discuss the differences in intention and effect when Toomer opens his story with "Life of nigger alleys . . ." and when the white soldiers in *There Is Confusion* say, "Kill the damned niggers!"

4. Locke says, "Each generation . . . will have its creed." Using evidence from the readings, identify the creed of the Harlem Renaissance. Write an essay explaining how this creed influenced the writing of the period.

5. Define *renaissance* as used by Locke and illustrated in this chapter. Compare this movement to other renaissances for people of color in this country. Discuss the similarities and differences between the impetus that sparked a rebirth and the artistic production that resulted.

6. Locke writes of "the racial leaders of twenty years ago [who] spoke of developing race-pride and stimulating race-consciousness, and of the desirability of race solidarity." These were also the goals of the Harlem Renaissance. Compare these goals to those of later movements, such as the civil rights movement, which is the subject of Chapter 6. What would various leaders of the movement such as Rev. Martin Luther King, Jr., and Malcolm X say about these goals?

7. Characters such as Emma Lou in *The Blacker the Berry* and Hanneh Breineh in "The Fat of the Land" are rejected by their own families. Compare their situations. Analyze what such a rejection reveals about the families themselves.

8. Both Delia in "Sweat" and Socorro in "Illegal Alien" have physically abusive husbands. Compare the response of each woman to the situation. Using your own knowledge and examples from books and other media, investigate the

cultural factors that might influence their methods of dealing with their husbands' abuse.

9. Both the Harlem Renaissance and the Native American Renaissance of the 1960s celebrated pride and cultural heritage. Compare a reading from this chapter with one from Chapter 8 to show the different ways in which each group uses cultural materials as the inspiration for new works of art.

For Further Research

1. In the 1920s, Harlem was a flourishing community for artists, writers, and entertainers. Research the rise and decline of that community, and compare the Harlem of the twenties with Harlem today.

2. Trace the development of African Americans' interest in African language and culture from the 1920s to the present.

3. Research Marcus Garvey and his Back-to-Africa movement. Discuss the history of the movement and its status today.

◆

REFERENCES AND ADDITIONAL SOURCES

Baker, Houston A., Jr. *Modernism and the Harlem Renaissance*. Chicago: University of Chicago Press, 1989.

Bell, Bernard W. *The Afro-American Novel and its Tradition*. Amherst: University of Massachusetts Press, 1987.

Berghahn, Marion. *Images of Africa in Black American Literature*. Totowa, New Jersey: Rowman and Littlefield, 1977.

Bontemps, Arna, ed. *The Harlem Renaissance Remembered: Essays Edited with a Commentary by Arna Bontemps*. New York: Dodd, 1984.

Brown, Sterling. *Negro Poetry and Drama*. New York: Arno, 1969.

Cruse, Harold. *The Crisis of the Negro Intellectual: A Historical Analysis of the Failure of Black Leadership*. New York: Morrow, 1984.

Davis, Arthur P., and Michael Peplow, eds. *The New Negro Renaissance: An Anthology*. New York: Holt, 1975.

Huggins, Nathan I. *Harlem Renaissance*. London: Oxford University Press, 1971.

Ikonné, Chidi. *From Du Bois to Van Vechten: The Early New Negro Literature, 1903–1926.* Westport, Conn.: Greenwood, 1981.

Johnson, James Weldon. *Black Manhattan.* New York: Athenaeum, 1969.

Locke, Alain. *The New Negro.* New York: Athenaeum, 1968.

Perry, Margaret. *Silence to the Drums.* New York: Garland Pub., 1982.

Wagner, Jean. *Black Poets of the United States: From Paul Laurence Dunbar to Langston Hughes.* Champagne-Urbana: University of Illinois Press, 1973.

Detail of background photo, sugarcane fields, Puerto Rico. (The Bettman Archive)

Puerto Rican immigrants arriving in the U.S., 1945. First immigrants to arrive by air to U.S. (Culver Pictures, Inc.)

Chapter 4

PUERTO RICANS
The View from the Mainland

(© Cliff Garboden/Stock Boston)

◆ SETTING THE HISTORICAL CONTEXT ◆

IN "PUERTO RICAN OBITUARY," Pedro Pietro describes the feelings of many persons from Puerto Rico who migrated to the U.S. mainland expecting a better life for their families:

> Juan
> Miguel
> Milagros
> Olga
> Manuel
> All died yesterday today
> And will die tomorrow . . .
> Waiting for the Garden of Eden
> To open up again,
> All died
> Dreaming about america.

In one sense the bitterness expressed here can be compared to the experiences of other immigrants. In another more important sense, however, the Puerto Rican experience is unique. Puerto Ricans, whether they live on the island or on the mainland, are American citizens.

The island is referred to as a "free state associated" with the United States. Drawn to the United States by promises of employment or pushed from the island by the pressures of a large population and high unemployment, Puerto Ricans have become a significant presence in U.S. cities, especially since World War II. (Forty percent of the population now lives on the mainland.) Despite their status as citizens, however, they have met barriers to economic success. Externally, they have had to contend with prejudice and discrimination over differences in race, culture, and language; internally, they remain ambivalent about assimilation, retaining roots in their home island and a stake in its centuries-old debate over cultural identity and political future.

In 1493, Columbus claimed the island, then inhabited by the peaceful Arawaks, for Spain. The island, exploited for its agricultural production and strategic importance, remained in Spanish hands until it was ceded to the

United States in 1898, following the Spanish-American War. Liberal forces had campaigned throughout the nineteenth century for reform of the colonial government, winning two major achievements: the abolition of slavery and the institution of an autonomous island government. But the second of these reforms was swept away when the United States established military control. Puerto Rico was now subject to the U.S. Congress, which shaped policy through a series of legislative acts.

The first of these, the Foraker Act (1900), replaced the interim military government with a civil administration under a presidentially appointed governor. The Jones Act (1917), passed in response to demands by the Puerto Rican people for self-government, made the island a U.S. territory and granted citizenship to its residents. The benefits of this act were limited, however. Puerto Ricans gained representation in Congress, but their representative could neither speak nor vote; the governor of the island continued to be appointed rather than elected; and, during the final months of World War I, eligible males became subject to the draft. Not until 1948 did Congress permit Puerto Ricans to elect their governor by popular vote, and not until 1952 did it permit them to adopt a constitution. Under this document, the island became fully self-governing as the Commonwealth of Puerto Rico, while remaining in voluntary association with the United States.

U.S. economic policies for the island have tended to consolidate land and the means of production of food and other commodities, changes usually spurred by and predominantly benefitting mainland investors. One important initiative was Operation Bootstrap, begun in the 1940s under Franklin Delano Roosevelt's New Deal, which gave investors tax benefits and helped them clear agricultural land and construct hotels, factories, and other businesses. The standard of living on the island improved, substandard housing was replaced, and roads were paved. Supporters of Operation Bootstrap point to increased literacy, decreased infant mortality, and other social benefits of industrialization and the importation of technology. Critics, however, have charged that such controlled economic programs interfere with rather than promote local development, and that in Puerto Rico they have led to the displacement of agricultural workers without creating enough new jobs for them. When the ownership of businesses and capital assets remain in American hands, the labor and resources of the island are drained to profit the mainland, and unemployed Puerto Ricans are forced to live on food stamps and welfare or to migrate.

Migration from Puerto Rico to the mainland began in the mid-nineteenth century. Although it has sometimes been politically motivated, as when Puerto Ricans involved in an unsuccessful rebellion against Spain in the 1870s sought refuge in New York, it has more often been economically motivated. Under the increased prosperity brought about by American investment, migration has reduced the population pressures resulting from a high birth rate and improved public health. In fact, it has been so important for the island's economic stability that the Puerto Rican government long maintained an office in New York City to facilitate it. By 1930, a large majority of Puerto Rican migrants had settled in East Harlem (now called Spanish Harlem) and in parts of Brooklyn and the Bronx, finding employment in the garment and tobacco industries. Despite discrimination, which limited their opportunities—their housing was often substandard, for example, with inadequate heat and sanitation—these immigrants formed supportive communities.

Migration has also served American commercial interests: in the 1950s, New York Mayor Robert Wagner visited Puerto Rico to recruit workers, and American corporations routinely sent recruiters there. In fact, the most significant period of Puerto Rican migration occurred soon after World War II, when the postwar economic boom created a high demand for labor. Reinforcing this demand was the introduction of cheap air fares, which brought the island and mainland closer together. Although some Puerto Ricans were recruited for agricultural work in the western states and Hawaii, the great majority settled in the industrial cities of the Northeast, especially New York.

At first, the social and cultural cohesiveness of their scattered communities helped Puerto Ricans endure a hostile climate and culture. While their social status was generally lower than it would have been in Puerto

Rico, they were compensated by health and educational opportunities, increased wages, and a higher standard of living. But increasing estrangement from Puerto Rican family, religious, and cultural values began to weaken these communities, and the eroding mainland economy of the 1970s further undermined Puerto Ricans' social and economic position. As the industries that used their semi-skilled labor began to close, automate, or leave the cities, many Puerto Ricans turned to lower-paying, lower-status jobs in the service economy, finding employment as maids, waiters, dishwashers, and busboys. Discrimination prevented even educated, professional people from finding more rewarding work, since their professional licenses were often not honored on the mainland.

Education, which has traditionally been a means for immigrant populations to improve their economic and social status, began to fail the Puerto Rican communities. Access to free university education and other social services shrank as the economy deteriorated, and the needs of Puerto Rican children in the elementary and high schools were neglected because of inadequate facilities and discrimination. The Report of the United States Civil Rights Commission (1976) condemned both substandard conditions in public schools and the lack of opportunities for higher education, and found that Puerto Rican children were often treated unfairly; because their first language was Spanish, they were misidentified as slow learners and kept back, which often discouraged them and prolonged their time in school. Students cited in the report complained of being pressured into taking vocational or basic courses instead of college-preparatory classes. Under these conditions, many Puerto Rican children did not finish school, which further diminished their prospects for finding good jobs.

In the early part of the century, Puerto Ricans attempted to address such socioeconomic problems by establishing and participating in political and labor organizations that worked for social change. Especially after gaining citizenship in 1917, Puerto Ricans became increasingly involved in party politics and local government. In the 1940s and 1950s social and cultural organizations were founded to help ease the tensions between those already settled on the mainland and the large numbers of new arrivals. In the

1960s, organizations such as the Puerto Rican Community Development Project were founded to unify old and new members of the community and to take advantage of federal programs and other opportunities for collective improvement and advancement.

In recent years, the increasing integration of Puerto Ricans into the political mainstream has been symbolized by the close race Herman Badillo ran for mayor of New York and by his influence as Bronx borough president. However, impatience with dependence on federal money and political alliances has given rise to militancy, especially among Puerto Rican college students. In New York and Chicago, respectively, the Young Lords' Party and the Young Lords' Organization have protested society's failure to meet the community's needs. Among other actions, they have seized churches and hospitals to dramatize the situation and have established breakfast programs, day-care centers, clinics, and other services.

The ongoing political debate in Puerto Rico between those who favor statehood and those who favor independence mirrors the two self-images of mainland Puerto Ricans, who see their communities as culturally autonomous or as economically and politically dependent. Exposed to and hampered by discrimination from the larger society, many mainland Puerto Ricans feel equally estranged from an island past and culture that they may never have experienced personally. Solutions to this marginalized, uncertain status are not easy to find, and thus achievement and pride continue to be mixed with distress and loss. Like the despairing figures in Pietro's poem, mainland Puerto Ricans wait to enter the seemingly unattainable Eden of opportunity.

EXPLORING THE LITERARY AND ◆ CULTURAL CONTEXT ◆

Arranged chronologically, the readings in this chapter reveal glimpses of the changing roles and concerns of Puerto Ricans in the United States from early in the century until the 1960s.

The selection from *The Memoirs of Bernardo Vega* describes the solidarity and sense of self-worth among workers in a cigar factory. Recognizing the need for social change, the men find the means to prepare themselves to take an informed role in political debate, even while they continue to earn their living.

Arriving in the United States at the same time as Vega, Jesús Colón encountered discrimination and unemployment. In the three short essays included here, he describes his hopes and expectations, his willingness and efforts to improve himself, and finally a moment of bitter despair.

The chapter from Piri Thomas's book *Down These Mean Streets* explores two strong weapons against such despair: family and cherished memories. Thomas gently raises questions about the effect on one's sense of identity of the unresolvable tension between nostalgia for the past and commitment to the present. Strength through tradition and family also underlie Nicholasa Mohr's "A Thanksgiving Celebration."

In "Ropes of Passage," a chapter from Edward Rivera's *Family Installments*, a young man's acceptance of his family's values, traditions, and expectations is weakened by exposure to the conflicting systems that prevail at his job and in his college classes. The selection from Judith Ortiz Cofer's *The Line of the Sun* shows the same struggle from two perspectives: that of a child, just beginning to recognize and grapple with these difficulties, and that of a grown man, already all but defeated by them.

Yet Juan Flores's essay "Puerto Rican Literature in the United States" creates a context of hope, even given Cofer's disturbing vision of the mainland Puerto Rican community. Flores helps us to see the relation between language and community.

BEGINNING: PRE-READING/WRITING

◆ *In a class discussion, speculate about the political, economic, and personal reasons why Puerto Ricans emigrate to the United States. Consider whether the political relationship between Puerto Rico and the United States creates circumstances for Puerto Ricans that are different from those of immigrants from other countries.*

The Foraker Act, which was passed in 1900, instituted a civil government for Puerto Rico, under the jurisdiction of an American military governor and an eleven-member executive council with an American majority. The act also designated English as the Island's official language. It remained in effect until 1917, when the Jones Act granted Island residents American citizenship. Puerto Ricans were not allowed to elect their own governor, however, until 1948; they could not write their own constitution until 1950.

◆ *From* **THE FORAKER ACT** ◆

The Governor

SEC. 17. That the official title of the chief executive officer shall be "The Governor of Porto Rico." He shall be appointed by the President, by and with the advice and consent of the Senate; he shall hold his office for a term of four years and until his successor is chosen and qualified unless sooner removed by the President; he shall reside in Porto Rico during his official incumbency, and shall maintain his office at the seat of government; he may grant pardons and reprieves, and remit fines and forfeitures for offenses against the laws of Porto Rico, and respites for offenses against the laws of the United States, until the decision of the President can be ascertained; he shall commission all officers that he may be authorized to appoint, and may veto any legislation enacted, as hereinafter provided; he shall be the commander in chief of the militia, and shall at all times faithfully execute the laws, and he shall in that behalf have all the powers of governors of the Territories of the United States that are not locally inapplicable; and he shall annually, and at such other times as he may be required, make official report of the transactions of the government in Porto Rico, through the Secretary of State, to the President of the United States: *Provided,* That the President may, in his discretion, delegate and assign to him such executive duties and functions as may in pursuance with law be so delegated and assigned.

The Executive Council

SEC. 18. That there shall be appointed by the President, by and with the advice and consent of the Senate, for the period of four years, unless sooner removed by the President, a secretary, an attorney-general, a treasurer, an auditor, a commissioner of the interior, and a commissioner of education, each of whom shall reside in Porto Rico during his official incumbency and have the powers and duties hereinafter provided for them, respectively, and who, together with five other persons of good repute, to be also appointed by the President for a like term of four years, by and with the advice and consent of the Senate, shall constitute an executive council, at least five of whom shall be native inhabitants of Porto Rico, and, in addition to the legislative duties hereinafter imposed upon them as a body, shall exercise such powers and perform such duties as are hereinafter provided for them, respectively, and who shall have power to employ all necessary deputies and assistants for the proper discharge of their duties as such officials and as such executive council. ◆

◆ Responding

1. Summarize these provisions of the Foraker Act in your own words. What duties and responsibilities are given to the governor?

2. Consider the way in which officials are chosen to govern Puerto Rico. Who makes these appointments? What role do Puerto Ricans themselves play?

3. How do you think local people reacted to these provisions at the time they were written? Do you think they would react the same way today? Explain any changes in attitude that might have taken place.

BERNARDO VEGA

Bernardo Vega was born in Farallon, Puerto Rico, in 1885. During his early years as a tabaquero, *or tobacco worker, Vega participated in the island's first labor union. After leaving Puerto Rico for New York in 1916, he worked for many years as a cigar maker, once again actively participating in the organized labor movement. His involvement in New York's political and social organizations also put him into contact with some of the leading members of the Latino intellectual community in exile, such as the Cuban poet Jose Martí. Vega spent his final years working for the pro-independence movement in Puerto Rico, where he died in 1965.*

Vega's Memoirs *provide a vivid account of the experiences of Puerto Rican workers who settled in New York during the early 1900s. Although he wrote them in the 1940s, the memoirs were not published until after his death. The manuscript version was edited by Cesar Andreu Iglesias, who altered the third-person account to the first person. Juan Flores translated the book into English.*

◆ THE CUSTOMS AND TRADITIONS OF THE TABAQUEROS AND WHAT IT WAS LIKE TO WORK IN A CIGAR FACTORY IN NEW YORK CITY ◆

Since the day we had our street clothes stolen and had to come home from work in rags, Pepe and I started thinking of quitting work at the munitions plant. But we had no other job in mind, or time to look for one. One day I found Pepe gloomier than a rooster after a cockfight. I tried to console him, but he just broke down, crying his heart out. The job was even more unbearable for him than it was for me. He got sick and gave up. 1

I kept up that fierce daily battle for another few weeks. But one morning I caught sight of a bunch of rags on fire alongside a powder keg and, had I not grabbed an extinguisher and put out the fire just in time, right there and then I might have taken leave of the world of the living. 2

For fear of losing my skin, time had come to give notice. Payday was every two weeks, and I had worked only half that. I decided to leave that day no matter what, though I wanted to be sure of collecting what was due me. The only way I would see was to pick a fight with someone and force them to fire me. I chose as my victim the first co-worker who showed up. The foreman pulled us apart and took us to the office to fire us both. Once I got my pay, I assured the foreman that it was I who had started the trouble and that the other guy was innocent. The foreman shouted, "You son of a bitch!" That was the first time, though certainly not the last, that I was called by that name in the United States. 3

One day a few weeks later I picked up the morning newspaper and felt my heart skip a beat—that same plant had been blown to bits in an explosion! 4

With what savings I had I bought myself some clothes for winter. Having no notion yet what that season would demand, I made the sinful mistake of buying two loud colored suits and an equally flashy overcoat. Friends who had already spent a few winters in New York made fun of my new purchases. So there I was, after all that hardship, in the same old straits—flat broke and without the clothes I needed for winter. 5

It took "El Salvaje," as Ramón Quiñones—another fellow townsman from Cayey and a first-rate *tabaquero*[1]—was called, to get me out of my predicament. Though gentle and good-hearted, he would resort to his fists at the slightest provocation, and was always quick to seize the limelight. He never carried firearms, but tried to solve all his problems with his bare hands. That's how he got the nickname "Wild Man." 6

One day my friend "El Salvaje" took me down to Fuentes & Co., a cigar factory located on Pearl Street, near Fulton Street, in lower Manhattan. I started work immediately, but within a week they had marked down the price of my make of cigar, and I quit.[2] When "El Salvaje" found out, he went down to the shop in person and, as was his custom, had it out with the foreman with his bare fists. He had to pay a fine to stop them from locking him up. 7

As for me, I was actually lucky to leave that job. A few days later I found work at another cigar factory, "El Morito" ("The Little Moor"), on 86th Street off Third Avenue, a few steps from where I was living. At that wonderful place I struck up friendships with a lot of Cubans, Spaniards, and some fellow countrymen, all of whom awakened in me an eagerness to study. Among them, two Cubans remain prominently in my mind. One of them, Juan Bonilla, had been a close friend of José Martí. He was a noted orator and one of the editors of *Patria*, the newspaper founded in New York by the Apostle of the Cuban Revolution himself. The other was T. de Castro Palomino, a man of vast erudition, who had also gained renown for his role in the liberation struggles of the Antilles. 8

Of the Spaniards I remember fondly Maximiliano Olay, still hardly more than a boy in those years, who had had to flee Spain to escape charges of complicity in an anarchist assassination of a leading political figure. He was a loyal friend of many Puerto Rican migrants; more than once I heard him claim 9

[1]Cigarmaker

[2]Cigar prices varied according to the "make" or *vitola*—the quality of the tobacco and the cigarmakers' reputation. The *vitola* was indicated by the cigar ring.

Cigar factories ranged in size from the *chinchal* (workshop), which might include no more than the master cigarmaker and two or three apprentices, to *fábricas* (factories), which employed from fifty to four hundred workers. Some *fábricas* engaged in all phases of cigar production; in others, called *despalillados*, most of the workers were women, who separated the tobacco leaves from the stems. [Author's note] that destiny had made him a brother of the Puerto Ricans, for one of them had once saved his life.

Maximiliano was born in Collota, a village in the Asturian mountains of Spain. Two of the Guardia Civil on duty in his town were from Puerto Rico. They were friends of his family, who had watched him grow up from early childhood. As a young man he got himself into serious trouble for political activities. He was arrested and the charges against him would have cost him his head. But one of the Guardia Civil hid him and arranged for his escape. He crossed the border into France and managed to get away to New York. "Now you see why all Puerto Ricans are my brothers," Maximiliano would say.

Another good Spaniard and dear friend of Puerto Ricans was Rufino Alonso, whom they used to call "Primo Bruto" ("Dumb Cousin"). Another of the Puerto Ricans I got to know there and still remember was Juan Hernández, the director of the workers' paper *El Internacional*. There was also the fine writer Enrique Rosario Ortiz, and J. Navas, Tomás Flores, Francisco Guevara, Ramón Rodríguez, Matías Nieves—known as "El Cojo Ravelo" ("Limping Ravelo")—all of whom were active in the cigarworkers' struggle and in the Hispanic community in general.

With workers of this caliber, "El Morito" seemed like a university. At the time the official "reader" was Fernando García. He would read to us for one hour in the morning and one in the afternoon. He dedicated the morning session to current news and events of the day, which he received from the latest wireless information bulletins. The afternoon sessions were devoted to more substantial readings of a political and literary nature. A Committee on Reading suggested the books to be read, and their recommendations were voted on by all the workers in the shop. The readings alternated between works of philosophical, political, or scientific interest, and novels, chosen from the writings of Zola, Dumas, Victor Hugo, Flaubert, Jules Verne, Pierre Loti, Vargas Vila, Pérez Galdós, Palacio Valdés, Dostoyevsky, Gogol, Gorky, or Tolstoy.[3] All these authors were well known to the cigarworkers at the time.

It used to be that a factory reader would choose the texts himself, and they were mostly light reading, like the novels of Pérez Escrich, Luis Val, and the like. But as they developed politically, the workers had more and more to say in the selection. Their preference for works of social theory won out. From then on the readings were most often from books by Gustave LeBon, Ludwig Buchner, Darwin, Marx, Engels, Bakunin.[4] . . . And let me tell you, I never knew a single *tabaquero* who fell asleep.

---

[3]Popular French, Spanish, and Russian novelists of the 19th century.

[4]Prominent scientists and theorists of the nineteenth century, several of whom—Marx, Engels, and Bakunin—were instrumental in the development of modern socialism.

The institution of factory readings made the *tabaqueros* into the most 14
enlightened sector of the working class. The practice began in the factories of
Viñas & Co., in Bejucal, Cuba, around 1864. Of course there were readings
before then, but they weren't daily. Emigrants to Key West and Tampa introduced the practice into the United States around 1869—at least, I was told that
in that year the shop owned by Martínez Ibor in Key West had an official
reader.

In Puerto Rico the practice spread with the development of cigar pro- 15
duction, and it was Cubans and Puerto Ricans who brought it to New York.
It is safe to say that there were no factories with Hispanic cigarworkers without
a reader. Things were different in English-speaking shops where, as far as I
know, no such readings took place.

During the readings at "El Morito" and other factories, silence reigned 16
supreme—it was almost like being in church. Whenever we got excited about
a certain passage we showed our appreciation by tapping our tobacco cutters
on the worktables. Our applause resounded from one end of the shop to the
other. Especially when it came to polemical matters no one wanted to miss a
word. Whenever someone on the other side of the room had trouble hearing,
he would let it be known and the reader would raise his voice and repeat the
whole passage in question.

At the end of each session there would be a discussion of what had been 17
read. Conversation went from one table to another without our interrupting
our work. Though nobody was formally leading the discussion, everyone took
turns speaking. When some controversy remained unresolved and each side
would stick to a point of view, one of the more educated workers would act as
arbiter. And should dates or questions of fact provoke discussion, there was
always someone who insisted on going to the *mataburros* or "donkey-slayers"—
that's what we called reference books.

It was not uncommon for one of the workers to have an encyclopedia right 18
there on his worktable. That's how it was at "El Morito," where Juan Hernández, Palomino, Bonilla, Rosario, and young Olay stood out as the arbiters
of discussion. And when a point of contention escaped even their knowledge,
the dogfight, as we used to call it, was laid to rest by appealing to the authority
of the *mataburro*.

I remember times when a *tabaquero* would get so worked up defending 19
his position that he didn't mind losing an hour's work—it was piecework—
trying to prove his point. He would quote from the books at hand, and if there
weren't any in the shop he'd come back the next day with books from home,
or from the public library. The main issues in these discussions centered around
different trends in the socialist and anarchist movements.

In those years of World War I, a central topic was imperialism and its 20
relation to pacifism. In "El Morito" we had just been reading Henri Barbusse's
Le feu (*Under Fire*). The hair-raising depiction of life in the trenches gave rise
to an endless discussion among the socialists, anarchists, and the handful of

Germanophiles in the factory. Earlier we had read *La Hyene enragée* (*The Trial of the Barbarians*) by Pierre Loti, one of the writers often read to pass the time. But this particular book did a great deal to disarm the pacifists. The forceful description of the ruins of Rheims and Arras, the destructive avalanche of the Kaiser's soldiers, so graphically depicted, stirred us to thoughts of revenge and gained our deepest sympathy for the Allies. Just like so many of our comrades in both France and Germany, we fell prey to the call to "defend the fatherland," losing sight of the proletarian internationalism on which socialism is founded. Needless to say, Lenin and Bolshevism were still totally unknown in New York at the time.

When the Catholic newspapers in France took up their campaign against Marx and Marxism, we read the rigorous defense made by the socialist Jean Longuet. His articles kindled lively debates among the *tabaqueros*. For a while the sentiment in defense of France, inspired by Barbusse and Loti, began to lose support. The most militant pacifists among us struck back by arguing: "The French and the Germans both represent imperialist capitalism. We workers should not favor either one of them!" But this revolutionary position was again undermined by the reading of the Manifesto of March 1916, signed by the leaders of pacifist internationalism—Jean Grave, Carlo Malato, Paul Reclus, and Peter Kropotkin. This declaration struck a mortal blow to the worldwide anti-imperialist movement. "To talk of peace," it read, "is to play into the hands of the German government. . . . Teutonic aggression is a threat not only to our hopes for social emancipation but to human progress in general. For that reason we, who are antimilitarists, archenemies of war, and ardent partisans of peace and brotherhood among all nations, stand alongside of those who resist."

"Those who resist," of course, were the French. As a result, a growing current of Francophilia spread among socialists. A great majority of *tabaqueros* saw France as the standardbearer of democracy and progress, if not of socialism.

The dominant trend among North American socialists, however, and perhaps among the people of the United States in general, was neutrality. The leading pacifist and anarchist among the Spanish-speaking workers in New York was Pedro Esteves, who put out the paper *Cultura Proletaria*. As I mentioned before, most of the *tabaqueros* believed that the Germans had to be defeated. Many of them enlisted in the French army. Outstanding among them were Juan Sanz and Mario César Miranda, two leaders of the workers' movement who left Puerto Rico and were killed in combat in the first battle of Verdun. Florencio Lumbano, a Puerto Rican cigarworker in New York, also fell on the battlefields of France. Another *tabaquero* to take up arms was Justo Baerga. Years later I was told that he had been seen, old and sickly, in Marseilles.

Many, in fact, are the Puerto Ricans who have fought in defense of other countries. Perhaps for that reason, they have found themselves so alone in their own land. It was right there in "El Morito" that I first heard of the role of the *tabaqueros* in the Cuban wars of independence. There, too, I began to learn of the distinguished contribution our countrymen made to the Cuban revolution.

I heard many true stories from the lips of Juan Bonilla and Castro Palomino, who had experienced them first hand. From then on, I was determined to write an account of the participation of Puerto Ricans in the Cuban independence struggle, which after all was a struggle for the independence of Puerto Rico as well.

But life among the *tabaqueros* was not all serious and sober. There was a   25
lot of fun, too, especially on the part of the Cuban comrades. Many were the times that, after a stormy discussion, someone would take his turn by telling a hilarious joke. Right away tempers would cool down and the whole shop would burst out laughing.

None of the factories was without its happy-go-lucky fellow who would   26
spend the whole time cracking jokes. In "El Morito" our man of good cheer was a Cuban named Angelito, who was known for how little work he did. He would get to the shop in the morning, take his place at his worktable, roll a cigar, light it, and then go change his clothes. When he returned to his table he would take the cigar from his mouth and tell his first joke. The co-workers nearest him would laugh, and after every cigar he'd tell another joke. He would announce when he had made enough cigars to cover that day's rent. Then he'd set out to roll enough to take care of his expenses. Once this goal was reached, he wouldn't make one more cigar, but would leave his workplace, wash up, get dressed, and head for the Broadway theaters.

A good-looking man, Angelito was tall and slender. He had a charming   27
face and was an elegant dresser. He had arrived in the United States with a single, fixed idea in mind, which he admitted openly to anyone who would listen: he wanted to hook up with a rich woman. Pursuing his prey, he would walk up and down the streets, looking, as he himself would say, for his lottery prize. And the truth is that it didn't take him long to find it. A few months after I started at "El Morito" he landed a rich girl, who was beautiful and a violinist to boot. He married her and lived—in his own words—like a prince. But he never forgot us: time and again he would show up at the shop to tell us of his exploits and bless us with the latest addition to his vast repertoire of jokes.

Around that time news reached us at "El Morito" of a major strike in the   28
sugar industry in Puerto Rico. A call went out for a rally in solidarity with the strikers. It took place on 85th Street near Lexington Avenue, and was attended by over a hundred *tabaqueros*, mostly Puerto Ricans. Santiago Rodríguez presided, and Juan Fonseca served as secretary. Many of those attending stood up to speak, including Ventura Mijón, Herminio Colón, Angel María Dieppa, Enrique Plaza, Pedro San Miguel, Miguel Rivera, Alfonso Dieppa, Rafael Correa, and Antonio Vega. The last mentioned immediately attracted my attention because of the way he spoke, and even more because of his appearance.

While I was listening to Antonio Vega I recalled how my father used to   29
talk all the time about his lost brother, who had never been seen or heard from since he was very young. I'm not sure if it was the memory that did it, but I

know I felt deeply moved by the man who bore my last name. He was a tall fellow, with a broad forehead, a full head of gray hair, a big handle-bar mustache, green eyes, and an oval-shaped face. . . . When I went up to him he jumped to his feet with the ease of an ex-soldier and responded very courteously when I congratulated him for his speech. We then struck up a conversation, at the end of which we hugged each other emotionally. He was none other than my father's long lost brother. ◆

◆ Responding

1. Think about the image of blue-collar workers that you have formed from your own experience and from the way they have been portrayed in books and in the media. Compare that image to Vega and his fellow *tabaqueros* at the turn of the century. Why did he call them "the most enlightened sector of the working class"? Why were education and political ideas so important to these particular people?

2. Compare the education Vega received in the factory to the formal education he would have received in a traditional school. What are the strengths and weaknesses of each?

3. Vega says, "I remember times when a *tabaquero* would get so worked up defending his position that he didn't mind losing an hour's work—it was piecework—trying to prove his point. He would quote from the books at hand, and if there weren't any in the shop he'd come back the next day with books from home, or from the public library." Why did the workers become so engaged in these issues? Explore the lessons we can learn from this example to promote literacy and improve our educational system.

4. Working individually or in a group, design your own curriculum for an adult literacy class at your local library. Choose readings and discussion topics. Compare your choices with those of the *tabaqueros*.

Jesús Colón

Jesús Colón, born in Puerto Rico, immigrated to the United States around 1916, as a stowaway aboard ship. He spent his early years working at odd jobs in order to support himself, and later drew on these experiences for a column for the Daily Worker. *His column became the source of many of the essays in* A Puerto Rican in New York.*

Throughout this collection, Colón explores the tension between what he expected to find in the United States and what he actually discovered. As a black Puerto Rican emigré, Colón had to confront American society's prejudices against his language and his race. In the third selection he describes his reaction to being judged not by the quality of his work but by the color of his skin.

◆ STOWAWAY ◆

I still remember the name of the boat—S.S. Carolina. An old ship painted in funeral black around the hull and in hospital white from the deck up. Everything was planned with one of the crew. I just walked up the narrow wooden ladder of thin timber rungs far apart. This ladder connected the dock with the ships.

I think I don't have to explain that I did not carry a valise or other bundles with me. Just myself.

The sailor at the top of the ladder must have thought that I was one of those kids always going up and down with messages to the passengers. I was sixteen years old. As soon as I was inside the S.S. Carolina the friend on the crew installed me uncomfortably inside one of the linen closets, banging the door practically right on my nose. Time passed. The minutes seemed like hours. The hours felt like days. At last I heard the clanking of chains as the anchor was hoisted. After a little while I listened to the metallic noise of the propellers as they started their enormous metal four leaf clovers circling in the waters of San Juan Bay.

The third shrill whistle of the ship gave me the sign that we were finally getting away from the dock. I imagined from my hiding place in the linen closet that the S.S. Carolina was now on its course pointing its prow toward the entrance under the watchful eye of Morro Castle. In my mind I could see that the Door of San Juan, centuries old with its gate surrounded by old granite blocks that had grown indefinite in color, would now be looking at the ship. This very door had also seen the wooden vessels of Ponce de Leon, one of Puerto Rico's first Governors, passing by and the powerful galleons of pirates like Drake, Morgan and Cumberland, about whom I so fondly read in my childhood. And now, after a few more brief moments, I would be able to see none of San Juan's walls and Puerto Rico's palm decorated shores even if I were on deck.

As it had to happen, somebody came for fresh new linen eventually. They   5
found me there together with the linen they came to get. I was brought to the
Captain. After a scene mixed with ire and sermonizing on his part, I was placed
in the "merciful" hands of the chef steward who passed me over to the chef in
charge of the kitchen.

There I was introduced to the tallest mountain of pots, pans and cauldrons   6
I had ever seen in my life. The general idea was that I was supposed to keep
them shiny as a new Lincoln copper penny all through the voyage. I was also
entrusted with the cleaning and washing of mounds of plates and cups of all
shapes and sizes made out of cheap heavy porcelain. In an argument you could
strike somebody with one of the heavy coffee cups and knock him cold. There
was no regard for extra fine cleaning and washing. No taking your time in the
precise and artistic handling of plates, saucers and other dishes. It seemed to
me as if they had assigned a quota on each porcelain item that they could break
during the voyage and they were very much afraid that they would not do
enough breaking to fulfill and surpass their stated quotas.

It was simply a question of quantity against quality in dish washing. You   7
just could not stop to see if the image of your sweaty, dirty face would truly
be reflected in the plate that you just cleaned, washed and shined, for the chef
might think that you were just stalling for time or perhaps just trying to get
one minute's rest. And that was unthinkable. And the water in which you
washed those dishes! We should not really call it water. We should rather call
it steam converted into water. When you dipped your hands and forearms into
it, you felt for a moment as if they were being melted into nothingness. It took
me a few days to get my skin accustomed to the pain produced by the steam
they called warm water, used on ships to wash dishes in those days.

Besides these kitchen chores, the other tasks of an average stowaway were   8
to mop the floors, shine brass,—and do anything that anybody aboard ship
thought he might place upon your shoulders to lighten his particular daily
responsibilities. And don't you dare protest!

Good thing that I had a little experience at serving on tables in Puerto   9
Rico! Little by little the steward of the second class dining room took notice of
the fact, and I graduated into the class of an overworked bus boy who ran from
table to table bringing back to the kitchen each time two armfuls of empty
china.

Thus passed the days and nights traveling under strict war regulations,   10
darkness during the night—for the United States was at war with Germany.
During the day, I was shining dishes and pans or collecting china from the
tables. During the night I went to bed too tired even to be able to dream about
them.

One day I heard a voice hollering: "Sandy Hook, Sandy Hook!" I asked,   11
"What is Sandy Hook?" "Sandy Hook is the name of one place in the land,"
somebody answered. None of Columbus' companions could have been happier
than I at hearing that word LAND!

The steward had been watching the way I worked in the kitchen and   12 dining room. One day he came to me. "How would you like to stay and work on this ship? Thirty dollars a month, room and board. One day off when we come to port." I did not answer him one way or the other. I just told him that I would think it over.

As the ship dropped anchor alongside a Brooklyn dock, and a plank 13 connecting dock and ship was securely fastened in its place, I went ashore as unobtrusively as I had come into the boat in San Juan Bay in Puerto Rico. I never came back to accept the steward's offer to remain on the ship.

Good thing that I didn't, for a few trips later the S.S. Carolina was sent 14 to the bottom of the Caribbean by a German submarine. ◆

◆ EASY JOB, GOOD WAGES ◆

This happened early in 1919. We were both out of work, my brother and I. 1 He got up earlier to look for a job. When I woke up, he was already gone. So I dressed, went out and bought a copy of the *New York World* and turned its pages until I got to the "Help Wanted Unskilled" section of the paper. After much reading and re-reading the same columns, my attention was held by a small advertisement. It read: "Easy job. Good wages. No experience necessary." This was followed by a number and street on the west side of lower Manhattan. It sounded like the job I was looking for. Easy job. Good wages. Those four words revolved in my brain as I was travelling toward the address indicated in the advertisement. Easy job. Good wages. Easy job. Good wages. Easy . . .

The place consisted of a small front office and a large loft on the floor of 2 which I noticed a series of large galvanized tubs half filled with water out of which I noticed protruding the necks of many bottles of various sizes and shapes. Around these tubs there were a number of workers, male and female, sitting on small wooden benches. All had their hands in the water of the tub, the left hand holding a bottle and with the thumb nail of the right hand scratching the labels.

The foreman found a vacant stool for me around one of the tubs of water. 3 I asked why a penknife or a small safety razor could not be used instead of the thumb nail to take off the old labels from the bottles. I was expertly informed that knives or razors would scratch the glass thus depreciating the value of the bottles when they were to be sold.

I sat down and started to use my thumb nail on one bottle. The water 4 had somewhat softened the transparent mucilage used to attach the label to the bottle. But the softening did not work out uniformly somehow. There were always pieces of label that for some obscure reason remained affixed to the bottles. It was on those pieces of labels tenaciously fastened to the bottles that my right hand thumb nail had to work overtime. As the minutes passed I noticed that the coldness of the water started to pass from my hand to my body giving me intermittent body shivers that I tried to conceal with the greatest of effort from those sitting beside me. My hands became deadly clean and tiny little wrinkles started to show, especially at the tip of my fingers. Sometimes I stopped a few seconds from scratching the bottles, to open and close my fists in rapid movements in order to bring blood to my hands. But almost as soon as I placed them in the water they became deathly pale again.

But these were minor details compared with what was happening to the 5 thumb of my right hand. From a delicate, boyish thumb, it was growing by the minute into a full blown tomato colored finger. It was the only part of my right hand remaining blood red. I started to look at the workers' thumbs. I noticed that these particular fingers on their right hands were unusually developed with a thick layer of corn-like surface at the top of their right thumb. The nails on their thumbs looked coarser and smaller than on the other fingers—thumb and nail having become one and the same thing—a primitive unnatural human instrument especially developed to detach hard pieces of labels from wet bottles immersed in galvanized tubs.

After a couple of hours I had a feeling that my thumb nail was going to 6 leave my finger and jump into the cold water in the tub. A numb pain imperceptibly began to be felt coming from my right thumb. Then I began to feel such pain as if coming from a finger bigger than all of my body.

After three hours of this I decided to quit fast. I told the foreman so, 7 showing him my swollen finger. He figured I had earned 69 cents at 23 cents an hour.

Early in the evening I met my brother in our furnished room. We started 8 to exchange experiences of our job hunting for the day. "You know what?" my brother started, "early in the morning I went to work where they take labels off old bottles—with your right hand thumb nail . . . Somewhere on the West Side of Lower Manhattan. I only stayed a couple of hours. 'Easy job . . . Good wages' . . . they said. The person who wrote that ad must have had a great sense of humor." And we both had a hearty laugh that evening when I told my brother that I also went to work at that same place later in the day.

Now when I see ads reading, "Easy job. Good wages," I just smile an 9 ancient, tired, knowing smile. ◆

◆ KIPLING AND I ◆

Sometimes I pass Debevoise Place at the corner of Willoughby Street. . . . I 1 look at the old wooden house, gray and ancient, the house where I used to live some forty years ago. . . .

My room was on the second floor at the corner. On hot summer nights 2 I would sit at the window reading by the electric light from the street lamp which was almost at a level with the window sill.

It was nice to come home late during the winter, look for some scrap of **3**
old newspaper, some bits of wood and a few chunks of coal and start a sparkling
fire in the chunky fourlegged coal stove. I would be rewarded with an intimate
warmth as little by little the pigmy stove became alive, puffing out its sides,
hot and red, like the crimson cheeks of a Santa Claus.

My few books were in a soap box nailed to the wall. But my most prized **4**
possession in those days was a poem I had bought in a five and ten cent store
on Fulton Street. (I wonder what has become of these poems, maxims and
sayings of wise men that they used to sell at the five and ten cent stores?) The
poem was printed on gold paper and mounted in a gilded frame ready to be
hung in a conspicuous place in the house. I bought one of those fancy silken
picture cords finishing in a rosette to match the color of the frame.

I was seventeen. This poem to me then seemed to summarize the wisdom **5**
of all the sages that ever lived in one poetical nutshell. It was what I was looking
for, something to guide myself by, a way of life, a compendium of the wise,
the true and the beautiful. All I had to do was to live according to the counsel
of the poem and follow its instructions and I would be a perfect man—the
useful, the good, the true human being. I was very happy that day, forty years
ago.

The poem had to have the most prominent place in the room. Where **6**
could I hang it? I decided that the best place for the poem was on the wall right
by the entrance to the room. No one coming in and out would miss it. Perhaps
someone would be interested enough to read it and drink the profound waters
of its message. . . .

Every morning as I prepared to leave, I stood in front of the poem and **7**
read it over and over again, sometimes half a dozen times. I let the sonorous
music of the verse carry me away. I brought with me a handwritten copy as I
stepped out every morning looking for work, repeating verses and stanzas from
memory until the whole poem came to be part of me. Other days my lips kept
repeating a single verse of the poem at intervals throughout the day.

In the subways I loved to compete with the shrill noises of the many **8**
wheels below by chanting the lines of the poem. People stared at me moving
my lips as though I were in a trance. I looked back with pity. They were not
so fortunate as I who had as a guide to direct my life a great poem to make me
wise, useful and happy.

And I chanted: **9**

> If you can keep your head when all about you
> Are losing theirs and blaming it on you . . .

> If you can wait and not be tired by waiting
> Or being hated don't give way to hating . . .

> If you can make one heap of all your winnings
> And risk it on a turn of pitch and toss . . .
> And lose and start again at your beginnings . . .

"If," by Kipling, was the poem. At seventeen, my evening prayer and 10 my first morning thought. I repeated it every day with the resolution to live up to the very last line of that poem.

I would visit the government employment office on Jay Street. The con- 11 versations among the Puerto Ricans on the large wooden benches in the employment office were always on the same subject. How to find a decent place to live. How they would not rent to Negroes or Puerto Ricans. How Negroes and Puerto Ricans were given the pink slips first at work.

From the employment office I would call door to door at the piers, factories 12 and storage houses in the streets under the Brooklyn and Manhattan bridges. "Sorry, nothing today." It seemed to me that "today" was a continuation and combination of all the yesterdays, todays and tomorrows.

From the factories I would go to the restaurants looking for a job as a 13 porter or dishwasher. At least I would eat and be warm in a kitchen.

"Sorry" . . . "Sorry" . . . 14

Sometimes I was hired at ten dollars a week, ten hours a day including 15 Sundays and holidays. One day off during the week. My work was that of three men: dishwasher, porter, busboy. And to clear the sidewalk of snow and slush "when you have nothing else to do." I was to be appropriately humble and grateful not only to the owner but to everybody else in the place.

If I rebelled at insults or at a pointed innuendo or just the inhuman amount 16 of work, I was unceremoniously thrown out and told to come "next week for your pay." "Next week" meant weeks of calling for the paltry dollars owed me. The owners relished this "next week."

I clung to my poem as to a faith. Like a potent amulet, my precious poem 17 was clenched in the fist of my right hand inside my second-hand overcoat. Again and again I declaimed aloud a few precious lines when discouragement and disillusionment threatened to overwhelm me.

> If you can force your heart and nerve and sinew 18
> To serve your turn long after you are gone . . .

The weeks of unemployment and hard knocks turned into months. I 19 continued to find two or three days of work here and there. And I continued to be thrown out when I rebelled at the ill treatment, overwork and insults. I kept pounding the streets looking for a place where they would treat me half decently, where my devotion to work and faith in Kipling's poem would be appreciated. I remember the worn out shoes I bought in a second-hand store on Myrtle Avenue at the corner of Adams Street. The round holes in the soles that I tried to cover with pieces of carton were no match for the frigid knives of the unrelenting snow.

One night I returned late after a long day of looking for work. I was hungry. My room was dark and cold. I wanted to warm my numb body. I lit a match and began looking for some scraps of wood and a piece of paper to start a fire. I searched all over the floor. No wood, no paper. As I stood up, the glimmering flicker of the dying match was reflected in the glass surface of the framed poem. I unhooked the poem from the wall. I reflected for a minute, a minute that felt like an eternity. I took the frame apart, placing the square glass upon the small table. I tore the gold paper on which the poem was printed, threw its pieces inside the stove and placing the small bits of wood from the frame on top of the paper I lit it, adding soft and hard coal as the fire began to gain strength and brightness.

I watched how the lines of the poem withered into ashes inside the small stove. ◆

◆ Responding

1. Colón had many problems earning a living in New York City. The cause may have been the economic conditions of the period, or Colón's own lack of training and experience. Consider the possibility that he couldn't get a good job because there were no opportunities for Puerto Ricans. Working individually or in a group and using evidence from these selections, list Colón's difficulties and discuss the reasons for them. Share your conclusions with the class.

2. After reading Colón's work, one could argue that he had to confront a system in which material things were more important than human suffering. Write an essay agreeing or disagreeing with this view of American society. You may consider Colón's experience and the historical period he wrote about or deal with the issue in relation to contemporary society.

3. Power relationships seem to play a central role in these three pieces. Those who had the ability to hire and fire could set the working conditions. Discuss Colón's main objections to the jobs he was able to find. Have you ever been in a similar unpleasant situation? Perhaps you were afraid or unable to say anything because the person (an employer, a teacher, or a friend) was in a position of power. Compare your handling of the situation to Colón's.

4. Imagine that you are the manager of a restaurant. You have just fired Colón and he has filed a complaint with the Labor Relations Board. Write a letter to the board justifying your action.

5. Why does Colón burn the poem at the end of the third selection? Write an essay explaining why a reader might feel that it is a symbolic act as well as an actual one.

PIRI THOMAS

Piri Thomas, born in Spanish Harlem in 1928, began writing while in prison for armed robbery. His books include Down These Mean Streets *(1967);* Savior, Savior Hold My Hand *(1972);* Seven Times Long *(1974); and* The View from El Barrio *(1978).*

    The excerpt that follows is from Down These Mean Streets. *The stories in this book, describing Thomas's involvement with street gangs and drug addiction, are often raw in their use of language, sexually explicit and violent. However, in this story Thomas uses a more nostalgic, more pensive tone to describe gatherings in the small New York apartment that his family shared.*

◆ PUERTO RICAN PARADISE ◆

Poppa didn't talk to me the next day. Soon he didn't talk much to anyone. He lost his night job—I forget why, and probably it was worth forgetting—and went back on home relief. It was 1941, and the Great Hunger called Depression was still down on Harlem.

    But there was still the good old WPA. If a man was poor enough, he could dig a ditch for the government. Now Poppa was poor enough again.

    The weather turned cold one more time, and so did our apartment. In the summer the cooped-up apartments in Harlem seem to catch all the heat and improve on it. It's the same in the winter. The cold, plastered walls embrace that cold from outside and make it a part of the apartment, till you don't know whether it's better to freeze out in the snow or by the stove, where four jets, wide open, spout futile, blue-yellow flames. It's hard on the rats, too.

    Snow was falling. "My *Cristo*," Momma said, "*qué frío*. Doesn't that landlord have any *corazón*?[1] Why don't he give more heat?" I wondered how Pops was making out working a pick and shovel in that falling snow.

    Momma picked up a hammer and began to beat the beat-up radiator that's copped a plea from so many beatings. Poor steam radiator, how could it give out heat when it was freezing itself? The hollow sounds Momma beat out of it brought echoes from other freezing people in the building. Everybody picked up the beat and it seemed a crazy, good idea. If everybody took turns beating on the radiators, everybody could keep warm from the exercise.

    We drank hot cocoa and talked about summertime. Momma talked about Puerto Rico and how great it was, and how she'd like to go back one day, and how it was warm all the time there and no matter how poor you were over

---
[1] heart

there, you could always live on green bananas, *bacalao*,[2] and rice and beans. "*Dios mío*," she said, "I don't think I'll ever see my island again."

"Sure you will, Mommie," said Miriam, my kid sister. She was eleven. 7
"Tell us, tell us all about Porto Rico."

"It's not Porto Rico, it's Puerto Rico," said Momma. 8

"Tell us, Moms," said nine-year-old James, "about Puerto Rico." 9

"Yeah, Mommie," said six-year-old José. 10

Even the baby, Paulie, smiled. 11

Moms copped that wet-eyed look and began to dream-talk about her *isla* 12
verde,[3] Moses' land of milk and honey.

"When I was a little girl," she said, "I remember the getting up in the 13
morning and getting the water from the river and getting the wood for the fire
and the quiet of the greenlands and the golden color of the morning sky, the
grass wet from the *lluvia*[4] . . . Ai, Dios, the *coquís*[5] and the *pajaritos*[6] making all
the *música* . . ."

"Mommie, were you poor?" asked Miriam. 14

"*Sí, muy pobre*, but very happy. I remember the hard work and the very 15
little bit we had, but it was a good little bit. It counted very much. Sometimes
when you have too much, the good gets lost within and you have to look very
hard. But when you have a little, then the good does not have to be looked for
so hard."

"Moms," I asked, "did everybody love each other—I mean, like if every- 16
body was worth something, not like if some weren't important because they
were poor—you know what I mean?"

"*Bueno hijo*, you have people everywhere who, because they have more, 17
don't remember those who have very little. But in Puerto Rico those around
you share *la pobreza*[7] with you and they love you, because only poor people can
understand poor people. I like *los Estados Unidos*, but it's sometimes a cold place
to live—not because of the winter and the landlord not giving heat but because
of the snow in the hearts of the people."

"Moms, didn't our people have any money or land?" I leaned forward, 18
hoping to hear that my ancestors were noble princes born in Spain.

"Your grandmother and grandfather had a lot of land, but they lost that." 19

"How come, Moms?" 20

"Well, in those days there was nothing of what you call *contratos*,[8] and 21
when you bought or sold something, it was on your word and a handshake,
and that's the way your *abuelos*[9] bought their land and then lost it."

"Is that why we ain't got nuttin' now?" James asked pointedly. 22

"Oh, it—" 23

---

[2]codfish
[3]green island
[4]rain
[5]small treetoads
[6]little birds
[7]poverty
[8]contracts
[9]grandparents

The door opened and put an end to the kitchen yak. It was Poppa coming 24
home from work. He came into the kitchen and brought all the cold with him.
Poor Poppa, he looked so lost in the clothes he had on. A jacket and coat,
sweaters on top of sweaters, two pairs of long johns, two pairs of pants, two
pairs of socks, and a woolen cap. And under all that he was cold. His eyes
were cold; his ears were red with pain. He took off his gloves and his fingers
were stiff with cold.

"*Cómo está?*"[10] said Momma. "I will make you coffee." 25

Poppa said nothing. His eyes were running hot frozen tears. He worked 26
his fingers and rubbed his ears, and the pain made him make faces. "Get me
some snow, Piri," he said finally.

I ran to the window, opened it, and scraped all the snow on the sill into 27
one big snowball and brought it to him. We all watched in frozen wonder as
Poppa took that snow and rubbed it on his ears and hands.

"Gee, Pops, don't it hurt?" I asked. 28

"*Sí*, but it's good for it. It hurts a little first, but it's good for the frozen 29
parts."

I wondered why. 30

"How was it today?" Momma asked. 31

"Cold. My God, ice cold." 32

Gee, I thought, *I'm sorry for you, Pops. You gotta suffer like this.* 33

"It was not always like this," my father said to the cold walls. "It's all the 34
fault of the damn depression."

"Don't say 'damn,' " Momma said. 35

"Lola, I say 'damn' because that's what it is—*damn*." 36

And Momma kept quiet. She knew it was "damn." 37

My father kept talking to the walls. Some of the words came out loud, 38
others stayed inside. I caught the inside ones—the damn WPA, the damn
depression, the damn home relief, the damn poorness, the damn cold, the damn
crummy apartments, the damn look on his damn kids, living so damn damned
and his not being able to do a damn thing about it.

And Momma looked at Poppa and at us and thought about her Puerto 39
Rico and maybe being there where you didn't have to wear a lot of extra clothes
and feel so full of damns, and how when she was a little girl all the green was
wet from the *lluvias*.

And Poppa looking at Momma and us, thinking how did he get trapped 40
and why did he love us so much that he dug in damn snow to give us a piece
of chance? And why couldn't he make it from home, maybe, and keep running?

And Miriam, James, José, Paulie, and me just looking and thinking about 41
snowballs and Puerto Rico and summertime in the street and whether we were
gonna live like this forever and not know enough to be sorry for ourselves.

The kitchen all of a sudden felt warmer to me, like being all together 42

---

[10]How are you?

made it like we wanted it to be. Poppa made it into the toilet and we could hear everything he did, and when he finished, the horsey gurgling of the flushed toilet told us he'd soon be out. I looked at the clock and it was time for "Jack Armstrong, the All-American Boy."

José, James, and I got some blankets and, like Indians, huddled around 43 the radio digging the All-American Jack and his adventures, while Poppa ate dinner quietly. Poppa was funny about eating—like when he ate, nobody better bother him. When Poppa finished, he came into the living room and stood there looking at us. We smiled at him, and he stood there looking at us.

All of a sudden he yelled, "How many wanna play 'Major Bowes' Amateur 44 Hour'?"

"Hoo-ray! Yeah, we wanna play," said José. 45

"Okay, first I'll make some taffy outta molasses, and the one who wins 46 first prize gets first choice at the biggest piece, okay?"

"Yeah, hoo-ray, *chevere.*" 47

Gee, Pops, you're great, I thought, *you're the swellest, the bestest Pops in the* 48 *whole world, even though you don't understand us too good.*

When the candy was all ready, everybody went into the living room. 49 Poppa came in with a broom and put an empty can over the stick. It became a microphone, just like on the radio.

"Pops, can I be Major Bowes?" I asked. 50

"Sure, Piri," and the floor was mine. 51

"Ladies and gentlemen," I announced, "tonight we present 'Major Bowes' 52 Amateur Hour,' and for our first number—"

"Wait a minute, son, let me get my ukelele," said Poppa. "We need music." 53

Everybody clapped their hands and Pops came back with his ukelele. 54

"The first con-tes-tant we got is Miss Miriam Thomas." 55

"Oh no, not me first, somebody else goes first," said Miriam, and she hid 56 behind Momma.

"Let me! Let me!" said José. 57

Everybody clapped. 58

"What are you gonna sing, sir?" I asked. 59

"Tell the people his name," said Poppa. 60

"Oh yeah. Presenting Mr. José Thomas. And what are you gonna sing, 61 sir?"

I handed José the broom with the can on top and sat back. He sang well 62 and everybody clapped.

Everyone took a turn, and we all agreed that two-year-old Paulie's "gurgle, 63 gurgle" was the best song, and Paulie got first choice at the candy. Everybody got candy and eats and thought how good it was to be together, and Moms thought that it was wonderful to have such a good time even if she wasn't in Puerto Rico where the grass was wet with *lluvia.* Poppa thought about how cold it was gonna be tomorrow, but then he remembered tomorrow was Sunday and he wouldn't have to work, and he said so and Momma said "*Sí,*" and the talk got around to Christmas and how maybe things would get better.

The next day the Japanese bombed Pearl Harbor. 64

"My God," said Poppa. "We're at war." 65

"*Dios mío*," said Momma. 66

I turned to James. "Can you beat that," I said. 67

"Yeah," he nodded. "What's it mean?" 68

"What's it mean?" I said. "You gotta ask, dopey? It means a rumble is 69
on, and a big one, too."

I wondered if the war was gonna make things worse than they were for 70
us. But it didn't. A few weeks later Poppa got a job in an airplane factory.
"How about that?" he said happily. "Things are looking up for us."

Things *were* looking up for us, but it had taken a damn war to do it. A 71
lousy rumble had to get called so we could start to live better. I thought, *How
do you figure this crap out?*

I couldn't figure it out, and after a while I stopped thinking about it. Life 72
in the streets didn't change much. The bitter cold was followed by the sticky
heat; I played stickball, marbles, and Johnny-on-the-Pony, copped girls' drawers
and blew pot. War or peace—what difference did it really make? ◆

◆ Responding

1. How realistic are Thomas's mother's memories of Puerto Rico? Has she
   idealized her childhood? What does Thomas think? He calls the chapter
   "Puerto Rican Paradise." Is that title descriptive or ironic? Using examples
   from the reading, describe his mother's life in Puerto Rico and contrast it
   with the situation in which she finds herself in Harlem.

2. Sometimes when we are unhappy with our present circumstances we like to
   think about a time when we were happier. Describe a time when you compared your situation in the present to a happier period in the past. Were
   your memories accurate, or did you idealize the past? Did your memories
   help you or hinder you in accepting conditions in the present? What role
   did such memories play in the Thomas family?

3. The Thomas family had few material comforts, but family members contributed to one another's happiness. Describe the family's activities. How
   did these compensate or fail to compensate for some of the difficulties of
   their living conditions? How does your family or the family of someone you
   know provide financial and emotional support for its members?

4. Mrs. Thomas says, ". . . only poor people can understand poor people."
   Does this mean that only by being a member of a group can you understand
   the experience of someone in that group? Argue for or against this position.

EDWARD RIVERA

Born in Puerto Rico in 1944, the author Edward Rivera grew up in New York City. After attending the city's public schools, he earned a bachelor's degree in English from the City College of New York and a master of fine arts from Columbia University. He currently teaches English at the City College of New York.

Edward Rivera's Family Installments *(1983) recounts some of the experiences of a Puerto Rican family in New York. The passage that follows describes the narrator's attempts to assert his identity in the workplace, in class, and at home. Here, the speaker's struggle for identity is contrasted with the atmosphere of mistrust he finds in the outside world. At the same time, the narrator finds his parents' complete faith in him an additional burden. As he tries to negotiate his way from both inside and outside his family structure, the narrator finds he must cope with an increasing sense of isolation from both worlds.*

◆ ROPES OF PASSAGE ◆

Christmas Eve, a Friday, on the subway home from work—my first full-time job—I got off on impulse at 116th Street, the Columbia-Barnard stop. There were some good bookstores in the area (none in my neighborhood, only drugstore and candy-store classics: the Reverend Doctors Norman Vincent Peale and Billy Graham; His Eminence Fulton J. Sheen; His Pre-Eminence Francis Cardinal Spellman, who had written a *nihil obstat* novel, *The Foundling*, which he'd had no trouble getting imprimatured; a lot of unreadable sex, crime, and cowboy; and Dale Carnegie's book on how to make people like you. I'd given that one a try and decided I didn't have it in me). I also wanted to walk home, which was only a mile away, though it was so different from this Columbia-Barnard area that it might as well have been another country.

At work, Vulcan Office Equipment, Inc., I sat all day in the shipping department typing address labels and form letters to Dear Sirs or Madams who wanted to know when the latest catalog on our "new line of products" was coming out, or how come that new swivel chair or filing cabinet they'd just bought was caving in. We had a form letter for every emergency, very polite letters; we didn't want to get into trouble with the Small Claims Court. The one time I defied form and wrote my own reply to an angry customer, I almost got fired for telling the truth, which the head of sales insisted wasn't the truth, "just your own wise-ass misconception of the truth, Malánguez." I didn't agree, but I needed the job (fifty a week), so from then on I stuck to form and kept the truth to myself. No more caveat emptors[1] from Malánguez. "Because he

---

[1] Latin phrase meaning "Buyer beware."

should not be ignorant of the property that he is buying." I had a paperback dictionary of foreign phrases back in my room.

And after work, four days a week from six to ten, I sat in night-college classrooms and took notes or daydreamed, or looked out the window at five-story buildings burning down in Harlem, one a night, sometimes two. 3

After my last class I sat and read in the subway down to 96th and Broadway; then I sat and read in another subway, a one-stop ride up to 110th and Lenox, which was only a short walk from home, and not a dangerous one for me, because by that time I was so tired and sorry-looking that I must have resembled a mugger or desperate rapist myself. At home, in the dining room, I sat and read through one of Mami's warmed-over dinners (except for juice in the morning, and coffee all day, I fasted to keep my weight down, and not to purify my soul, as the priests of Saint Misericordia's Church recommended to their parishioners); then I sat in my room, doing homework till two or three; then I slept on my back till eight, when a new round of sitting set in. I was turning stiff, soft, and more cynical than was good for me. I blamed it all on too much sitting and almost no exercise, and the walk I intended to take across 110th Street on this cold Christmas Eve, with a fat soft-cover novel in my coat pocket, would do me good. 4

There was another reason, though, a more important one: I hadn't been able to buy Papi and Mami a couple of presents, and I didn't feel in a hurry to get home and tell them they'd have to wait three days, when the banks would reopen and I could cash my payroll check, which included a ten-dollar Christmas bonus for a total of sixty dollars, the most I'd made in any one week. Not that they gave a damn about presents, though they always had something for each other, and for me, but I did, even if I had a good reason, or excuse, for going home empty-handed. 5

Vulcan's payroll office hadn't distributed the week's checks till after the banks closed. The computer, or something else, had broken down. Dozens of workers, office and factory, had threatened insurrection over the "tragic breakdown of that goddam gizmo," as one of them had put it. Some said they were going to turn in their resignations. 6

The payroll manager, the personnel manager, the sales manager, the advertising manager, and their right-hand men and women, the vice-presidents to one thing or another, the vice-president to the president, and the president himself (over the phone; he was on Christmas vacation already) had teamed up and told "labor," as they called the rest of us, to go right ahead and turn in our resignations if we thought we were so unexpendable. "The labor pool in this metropolis," the president's vice-president told us, "is a dime a dozen. Inexhaustible is another way of putting it. But it adds up to the same thing. Another way of putting it," he went on, "is that there's plenty more unemployed people where you folks came from, and they wouldn't hesitate to jump at the vacancies you'll leave, due to mechanical failure." 7

"If you ask me," the payroll manager had added, "this is a clear-cut case of ingrate insurrection, and in my considered judgement, it will abort. Your grievance has no cornerstone to stand on, my friends." He was addicted to elegant language and snobbish misspellings. He spelled labor "labour," check "cheque," catalog "catalogue," and judgment "judgement." "Because that's the way the British spell it," he explained. "And they should know what they're talking about. It's their goddarn language, after all." Pronouncements like that, issued in an affected British accent with a heavy trace of Coney Islandese, intimidated labour; and his prophecy that the insurrection would abort was accurate.

No one resigned—at least not on the spot. And if you weren't going to resign on the spot, you might as well stay on till you were sixty-five, for all the effect it was going to have on management.

So those of us (most of us) who were counting on those Christmas checks with the Christmas-bonus "riders" to buy presents for our dear ones and others, would just have to wait till Monday, when the banks would be mobbed. That was the only reason so many of us at Vulcan were opposed to having Christmas fall on a weekend. "It's the kind of inconvenience," a woman from billing had said, "that those people up in Washington can do something about. That's why we vote for the bastards, isn't it?" No one answered her. She went on to denounce politicians, and the grievance against management was forgotten until it was time to go home, when it was too late to insurrect.

So we had an abortion instead of an uprising. Some of us said they were going to hunt down a check-cashing place on the way home, one of those ever-present usury outfits that charged 10 percent or upward of your weekly take for the privilege. That's what we got for Christmas falling on an arbitrary weekend, and for payroll gizmos breaking down. Things weren't looking up this year. There wasn't even snow in sight. The fifteen dollars I had on me wasn't enough to buy a couple of decent presents.

So while waiting for the light to change on the Columbia-Barnard corner, I began thinking of not going home at all this Eve. I had enough on me, just about enough, to sleep in an SRO for the night. The area was full of them. A lot of older people and others lived in them. They sat, weather permitting, on the benches that divided Broadway into uptown and downtown for traffic. Some of them fed pigeons, others stared, few talked.

After the Columbia-Barnard traffic light turned green, I walked up to a paperback bookstore with a Latin-looking name: The Papyrodorsal. Its display window was transparent, dust-free. I couldn't see my own reflection in it, despite the soft fluorescence highlighting its latest acquisitions: a quality-cover reissue of Bernard Berenson's *The Italian Painters of the Renaissance* ($4.95; the City College Bookstore still had it for a buck and a quarter); Lionel Trilling's life of Matthew Arnold; Ortega y Gasset's *The Dehumanization of Art* and *The Revolt of the Masses*; the Penguin *Don Quixote* with the cover by Daumier (I had this one back in my room, along with a Spanish edition, both marked up; I had read them almost simultaneously for a Spanish translation course. The antique Spanish had almost destroyed me; Chaucer had been a breeze by comparison); the *Studs Lonigan* trilogy (longer than the Bible; I'd read every word on the IRT over a two-month period); Kierkegaard, *Purity of Heart Is to Will One Thing*; *On the Genealogy of Morals* and *Ecce Homo* (I'd read about this ecce homo in a parochial school Vulgate: Thou art the man who's about to get it); and a bunch of others, all nicely lit up behind that smudgeless, dustless window. There were plenty more inside.

I headed for the fiction shelves, the ones that took up most store space. 14 The entire section was labeled FICTION (hand-lettered in old script, white paint on brown Formica), and under that, in the same script, the legend: "We House the Classics in Accecsible Editions." Another misspelling. This was some language, English, "full of orthographic booby traps," as one of my Spanish teachers had put it. Just the same, a misspelled word in a bookstore that housed the classics had to be some kind of sin. I ignored it and began browsing through the fictions.

But not for as long as I'd planned. There were only three other customers 15 in the place, plus the floorwalker, a student type, husky enough to be on the Columbia Lions football team. He was wearing a herringbone jacket, a button-down shirt, blue jeans, and striped track shoes. And he was trying to pass himself off as another customer, an innocent browser among the Penguins. His eyes kept shifting from the shelf of Penguins to the customers, and when I walked in he began looking at me as well. I tried to ignore him but couldn't. There must have been a lot of stealing going on in this place if they had to hire somebody special to spy on people.

I decided to pick out something in a hurry and leave before it started 16 snowing. *Moby Dick* would do. "Must reading," one of my instructors had called it. We had read *Benito Cereno*, "Bartleby," *Billy Budd*, and "The Town-Ho's Story." I had written a term paper on that last one. The point of my paper had been that Steel-kilt, the "inflexible mutineer," as I had called him (borrowing the phrase from my instructor), was really a "metaphor for those who will not serve the devil," who in this case was "personified by the captain of the ship." And I tried to back up my point by referring to the other Melville stories, and by throwing in a couple of casual comments the instructor had made in class, when he didn't think anyone was taking notes. I didn't give him credit for those comments, and maybe that was why he gave me a D-plus on the paper.

On the last page of my Town-Ho disaster, he had written that I didn't 17 have the slightest idea what I was talking about, that my interpretation didn't have a lame leg to stand on, and that I must have plagiarized it from some "unlettered hack." So much for me and the Town-Ho's paper. In a P.S. he had suggested I read *Moby Dick* and find out what Melville was really all about. "And don't go see the movie," he had gone on, carried away. "Gregory Peck is no titanic Ahab for my money. Orson Welles's Father Mapple is not as disastrous as the wooden Peck, but Ishmael was dismally miscast, and on the whole the movie should have been left unmade. On the other hand . . ."

He had run out of paper there, and I'd been too humiliated by my grade 18 to ask him about that other hand. Maybe if I read *Moby Dick*, not one of those editions abridged for the so-called modern reader, but the whole thing, from "Call me Ishmael" to the "devious-cruising Rachel, . . . Finis," cut, I'd find out what that other hand was all about.

The cashier was talking intimately to a high-I.Q.-looking young man 19 across the counter. He was puffing on a pipe (I guessed it went well with his intelligence) while she told him something down low. Then they had to break it up when I arrived with Melville's *Redburn*. (They had no *Moby Dick*s in sight; every copy must have been picked up in the Christmas rush.) But instead of moving aside a second while I paid for it, he put his right elbow on the counter. Now he had both elbows on it, and I had no room to pay his friend. I asked him to excuse me, and he didn't seem to like that. Neither did she. I got an unkind look from both. I must have barged in at the wrong time. Then she gave him a signal with her eyes, and he moved aside a little, just enough for me to hand her the *Redburn*. He stared down at me—he was over six feet— with the pipe in his mouth, while I pulled out my wallet. I had a ten and a five in there, plus the uncashed paycheck with the Christmas-bonus rider. I handed the cashier the five, and while she was ringing up the register, she asked me if I wanted a bag with the book.

"If it doesn't cost extra," I said, meaning no offense. I was nervous. And 20 I didn't want to spend more money than I had to.

But she was offended. "It's *free*." 21

And her friend puffed a little pipe smoke down on me. It smelled of 22 apples.

"Okay, I'll take it," I told her. 23

"A Christmas present," her friend said. 24

Then he grabbed a book that had been lying on the counter—a C. Wright 25 Mills—and said to her, "See you later." She nodded. "Eight-thirty." And he left, puffing away.

She put the *Redburn* on top of a little green bag that looked too small for 26 it, and put seven cents change on the counter.

"I think I gave you a five," I said. 27

She threw her head back. "You think?" 28

"No, I know I did. I gave you five dollars, and this book doesn't come to 29 four ninety-three. It's under a dollar. You owe me four more."

"I don't remember any five," she said. 30

"I do. If you'll look in the register, you'll see." 31

The floorwalker had come up and was standing at my side, looking straight 32 at me. I pretended not to notice him.

"This cash register's full of fives," she said, and to prove it she rang up 33

No Sale. She pulled out a bunch of fives and held them up for me to see. Then she said, "Which one is yours?"

I was about to tell her, but the floorwalker got his word in first. "They all look the same to me, Sue. A. Lincoln. Of course, you never know when you're going to find a counterfeit in the batch." 34

I ignored him. I had to. I didn't want to get into something uglier than I was in already. Besides, it wasn't any of his business. "I gave you a five," I told the cashier. 35

She looked at the floorwalker; he looked at me as if I'd just handed her a stick-up note. He was shifting his weight from one leg to the other, like a deckhand on a rolling ship, or an experienced standee on a subway. 36

"I think," I told the cashier, "maybe you were distracted when I gave you the five, and you thought it was a one. Maybe you weren't looking. It happens." 37

"Maybe *you* weren't looking," the floorwalker said. He was out to get me. I wouldn't stand a chance. He had about four inches on me, at least fifteen pounds, he had the reach, the four-square shoulders of someone who did push-ups before breakfast, and he had the much-used striped track shoes. In my corner, I had stiff joints from all that sitting, and a pair of eyes that could use a pair of strong eyeglasses (I kept putting those off). And I wasn't in the mood to fight over four dollars. If it was also a case of cold feet, I wasn't in a mood to stick around and find out. So I picked up the *Redburn*, minus the little green bag and the seven-cents change, and started to walk out. 38

"You forgot your change," the cashier said when I grabbed the door handle. 39

"It's your tip," I said, "for courteous service," and kept going. The floor-walker didn't follow. 40

Out on Broadway, there were many last-minute shoppers. Trees of all sizes, their branches lashed compactly with string or wrapped in netting, were selling fast on the sidewalk outside all-night vegetable vendors', Greek greengrocers whose neat displays of fruit and vegetables brightened up the area. There weren't many students around. Most of them, I knew, were out-of-towners, and they must have gone home for the vacation. 41

The previous year, we'd had a heavy snowfall. I'd gone with Papi and Mami to the midnight Mass—the Mass of the Roosters, we called it—one of the few family customs we bothered keeping up anymore. Tego had always gone with us, before he got married and moved to the Bronx. 42

We three, and the others who had packed Saint Misericordia's Church that last Eve, had walked out into something like a blizzard. But no one had minded. The three priests and their altar boys, Maestro Padilla and his organ, and the choir of amateurs had put on a good spectacle and left everyone cheered up. Then the three of us had broken our Rooster-Mass fast (I hadn't received, but I fasted anyway, to keep up the custom), and celebrated with a big meal— 43 chicken, rice, spiced bean sauce, salad, caramel custard, and rum-spiked eggnog, which we had made ourselves with coconut cream and nutmeg. Then we had opened up the presents, thanked each other more than was necessary, and danced for a while before calling it a night. They were a good dancing couple, though they kept apologizing to each other for their clumsiness, when in fact I was the one who kept tripping all over himself and stepping on Mami's toes, while Papi played something fast on the guitar. We slept late Christmas Day. They went to Tío Mito's house with presents; I went to a movie with a hangover.

But this time around I wasn't in the mood for the Rooster Mass and for what followed. So, instead of making a left turn when I got to 110th and Broadway, then a right turn toward Fifth Avenue, then another left three blocks down, I walked into a delicatessen and bought a pastrami-with-mustard-on-rye to go, a piece of cheesecake, and a bottle of Rheingold. There was an opener on a string next to the door; I removed the bottle's cap, replaced it, and went to look for a cheap SRO. I might as well get used to these places. Papi and Mami dropped hints from time to time about going back home, and I got the impression (maybe a paranoid one) that they were just waiting for me to finish school so they could put those hints to practice.

"Maybe I'll open up a chicken farm," I heard him tell Mami.   45

"With what money?" she asked.   46

"Household Finance, what else?" And then he laughed, but it was a serious 47 laugh, almost grim, and left me confused. And I had begun thinking about those SROs off Broadway.

The one I picked out had a green-and-white awning. Elysian Arms SRO, it 48 was called, a fly-by-night resting place. Transients and Semi-Permanents. Reasonable Rates. The "Reasonable Rates" won me over; I was down to $6.50. The night clerk wanted seven; we haggled; he made me promise to pay him the fifty-cent balance first thing Monday. I showed him my paycheck as collateral.

"I can fix you up with a girlie, Malánguez. Up to you."   49

"A what?"   50

"Come on, you know what I'm talking about."   51

"I'm broke."   52

"What happened, the banks closed down early or something?"   53

"We had a computer breakdown at work."   54

"Yeah, these things happen. So come see me when you cash your collat- 55 eral."

I walked up to my room on the third floor. I hung up my coat on a nail 56 on the door and my scarf on the doorknob to cover the keyhole. The room had a washstand-sink, no stove, a tiny refrigerator with an empty ice tray, a shadeless lamp on a night table decorated with cigarette burns, a single bed with a flower-print bedspread and a huge sag in the middle: a valley, a fault, a crevasse, a pit, an eyesore. The window was hidden by a pair of curtains that matched the bedspread. On one of the pink walls, a framed print of a landscape with figures. English, it looked, nineteenth-century panoramic: a hay wagon, dogs taking up the rear, a stream, trees, cliffs in the distance, a green sky, greenish clouds, wagon driver with pipe in mouth, hay on wagon, a young couple on the hay, birds between them and the clouds, no sign of snow. This was either a Constable or a Gainsborough, an early Turner, or maybe only an all-purpose Woolworth's. It was unsigned. I was reminded of an art teacher I'd once had, a fellow Puerto Rican in his forties from 111th Street between Fifth and Lenox. Now he lived down in the East Twenties, with his wife, who was shy and generous, and his three small sons, whose first names began with the letter *K*; his wife told me she'd had nothing to do with that. "He's nuts about Paul Klee," she told me. Who was this Paul Clay? She told me.

"How come you spelled it with a double *e* and pronounced it like clay?"   57

"Don't ask me," she said. "That's how *he* pronounced it, and he should   58 know." There were Klee prints and posters, framed and unframed, all over their walls, as if this Klee had been a baseball star or movie hero.

Every Friday evening, after work, he gave me and a few other boys from   59 the neighborhood free drawing lessons for two or three hours. He always came in smelling of alcohol. He told me he and a couple of friends from the "studio" liked to get together after work for a couple of drinks in a place called the Oyster Bar inside Grand Central Terminal, to unwind after a hard day's work. He worked in a place called Cartographers Unlimited, which had nothing to do with maps anymore. He was an art director there, he told me. "And I made it to the top with nobody's help," except for the man who had given him his start: a half-Irish, half-German illustrator (whose first name had begun with a *K*: Kraus-something), a practicing Catholic who came to the community center once a week to give local boys art lessons. Tito Puente had been a student of K.'s, but somehow Tito couldn't stay away from the percussion instruments and had eventually strayed into music and turned into a big-band man. "Today he could have been a well-known illustrator, old boy. Our own Paul Clay." He had picked up that "old boy" expression at work. I didn't like it; I thought he was patronizing me whenever he used it. But it was only much later that I realized he hadn't meant anything by it. He said it automatically, casually, as if he had picked it up in grammar school or on the raunchy block where he grew up, and not on Madison Avenue.

But worse than that affectation, for me, was his horrible spelling. How,   60 I used to wonder, could a man whose important position and livelihood depended on "cleints" like Lipton's Tea ("The Great Pacific and Atlantic People, old boy") and White Owl Cigars (his illustrations for their panatelas appeared everywhere, he told me) misspell their names in the beautiful pastel sketches he did for his students—on a tiny table with matching tiny chairs (our studio was a kindergarten or day-care center between nine and three).

"Litpons Flow-True Tae Gabs" was how he sometimes spelled his client's   61 product in those pastel sketches. Maybe the Oyster Bar was responsible for those misspellings; maybe he was putting us on, and himself as well, and his "cleint." If that was it, I missed the joke. I was serious about spelling, a snob when it came to putting the right letter in the right place. It was my only distinction. I had once won first prize in a fourth-grade spelling bee at Saint Misericordia's School. The nuns had awarded me a framed five-by-seven print of the Sacred Heart, which I had seen on sale in Woolworth's. The remarks our principal had made during the presentation ceremony implied that I was one of those students who were destined to do our parish proud. "Any boy who can spell this well," she said, "is bound to leave his handwriting on the wall, as it were." And she was right in a way she hadn't intended (I think): I left my well-spelled graffiti on many a neighborhood wall and stoop. Correct spelling in public places became my signature, my "logo," as my art teacher might have said. "Post No Bills Malánguez," my friends called me, even after I had kicked the habit.

Then my art teacher, looking for a sidekick in what I suspected must have been misery, had tried to talk Papi and Mami into signing me out of school. "That school you go to, Santos," he told me, "is nothing but a dead end. Some of their best graduates go straight to the Tombs; then they work their way up the river. Most of them never work their way out of the house of detention. They hang themselves, or they get hanged by the guards or fellow prisoners. It's called suicide any way you look at it. And nobody gives a shit. What you want is a career, old boy. Post haste. Seize the time. How's that said in Latin?" 62

"*Dies irae*, I think." 63

"That's the idea. Let me talk to your father and mother." 64

"I'll get him a job where I work," he told them over coffee and cake. They were impressed and told him it was up to me. I went along with it, and almost didn't sleep that night, a hint. 65

The night before the signing of my doom, I chickened out and told Papi and Mami I wanted no part of this proposal. Fine, they said, whatever I wanted, but how come I'd changed my mind? This important artist (he had put on some airs for them) was willing to start me out in an important career, one of those rare opportunities, and I was turning him down. I could always get my high-school diploma at night from Washington Irving High. In fact, I'd have to get it; they wouldn't give me any choice as long as I was living in their house, which was also my house, of course, but still . . . 66

"Because in the first place," I said, "I haven't got that kind of talent. In fact, it's almost nothing. I can't even copy a Mickey Mouse straight. And I don't have the vocation, either. I don't want to spend the rest of my life drawing tea bags, or smiling little men smoking panatelas, and naming my three sons with the letter *K* or something. It doesn't sound right to me. Besides, he can't spell too good." 67

And what did spelling have to do with pictures? they asked. I didn't have a good answer to that one, so I said, "Self-respect or something." 68

And that was that. I stayed in school, playing hooky three afternoons a week, sometimes four, depending on the weather; and I stopped going to Friday-night art lessons. If my art teacher felt betrayed by my refusal, he never said; 69

he never came around to ask. Maybe he found a more suitable sidekick. I hoped he did.

I put the lamp on the floor and dragged the night table in front of the bed,   70
pulled the pastrami-to-go out of the bag, removed the cap from the Rheingold, and sat on the edge of the bed, away from the pit. I read while I ate, holding the book with my left hand and eating and drinking by turns with my right.

Chapter One: "Wellingborough, as you are going to sea, suppose you take   71
this shooting-jacket of mine along . . ." That was Redburn's older brother speaking, "out of the goodness and simplicity of his heart." In addition to the shooting-jacket, he throws in his fowling-piece, "and sell it in New York for what you can get." "Sad disappointments in several plans which I had sketched for my future life; the necessity of doing something for myself, united to a naturally roving disposition, and now conspired within me, to send me to sea as a sailor." I fell asleep toward the end of Chapter One.

Next morning, an old woman with all-white hair and an Irish brogue   72
woke me up with a scream—"Christ, I'm in the wrong room!"—and slammed the door shut. My back hurt; in my sleep, I'd fallen into the bed's pit. I got up, put on my coat, looped the scarf around my neck, shoved the *Redburn* back inside my coat pocket, and left in a hurry. I knew I'd be back sometime, but no need to rush it. "Underarms SRO," I told myself on the way out.

I walked back home. No snow had fallen; most streets were empty. And when   73
I stepped inside the apartment, Mami gave me a gloomy, worried look. She and Papi had panicked, it seemed, and come close to calling the cops. Why hadn't I called? she asked. Because, I said, I'd gone to a party at one of the bosses' homes up in Riverdale, near the home of the late-great Italian conductor, Toscanini. A classy mansion this boss had, I said. Servants, pedigreed dogs and cats to spare, a musical doorbell, and a wife and kids to match. I said I'd gotten drunk on some expensive-tasting whiskey and the boss had put me up for the night in a classy guest room. Well, why hadn't I called at least? she wanted to know. For the same reason, I said, that I hadn't been able to take the subway back: I'd been out of it, as if I'd swallowed a pint of ether. She didn't pursue the matter.

And when Papi came in with a container of milk and a pound of coffee,   74
I told him the same lie. He hadn't even asked me. He said something about everything being closed except the church, which I took as a hint. He nodded while I told him my story, and when I was finished he excused himself and went into the dining room to do some leather tooling. Somebody from work, he said, had commissioned a leather wallet from him. Five dollars. He had promised this man the wallet by Monday, so there was no time to waste. I went back inside my room.

They hadn't eaten the post-Rooster-Mass meal. They hadn't even touched   75
the eggnog. Not only had they lost their appetite, they explained at the dinner

table, but they had seen no point in eating and drinking, and the rest, by themselves.

"If you're trying to make me feel bad about it," I told them, "please don't   76
waste your time. These things happen to people all the time." They looked at
each other as if they didn't know what I was talking about.

"Maybe," Mami said, "you should go to the seven o'clock Mass tonight."   77

"What for?" I said.   78

"To make up for the Rooster one."   79

"It's not the same."   80

"A Mass is a Mass, Santos."   81

I looked at Papi. He was giving his plate a deadpan look.   82

"It's not the same for me," I said.   83

"Why not?"   84

"Because the Rooster's special."   85

"All roosters are special," Papi said, looking up from his meal. This was   86
followed by silence. We chewed and swallowed for a while. We took sips of
eggnog. They were waiting for me to say something. And I did, just to say
something.

"I don't like those priests too much."   87

"What's wrong with them?" he said.   88

"They're all Irish."   89

"So?"   90

"I don't know."   91

"A priest is a priest," she said. "No matter what the nationality."   92

"Maybe you're right, Mami. They're all the same."   93

She looked at Papi, who was dabbing at the yellow rice with his fork. "It   94
sounds as though our son is turning into a bigot," she said. He didn't answer.
Then she looked at me. "Is this something one learns in college?"

"Depends," I said, offended. "It so happens I learned it before I got to   95
high school."

"Not in this house," she said.   96

"And you've been keeping it a secret all these years?" Papi said. He hadn't   97
looked up.

I put down my fork and stood up. "It wasn't hard to." And I excused   98
myself. In my room, I read some more *Redburn* and went over notes for an
exam. Finals were coming up the following week. She was in their room doing
something in silence, probably reading *The Wonderland*, and he was in the dining
room, working on the wallet. At fifteen to seven, I put on my coat and scarf
and went to church, out of spite. I dozed through half of it. I don't think I was
the only one. The priest, half-asleep himself, droned his prayers. There weren't
many people in there. Only a handful went up to receive.

When I got back home, she was still in their bedroom, and he was still   99
working on the wallet. I sat down again to study for the finals.

From a small space between the window shade and sill in my room, I   100 could see the dining room's lighted window, its shade drawn all the way to frustrate the peeping Toms, who seemed to get a sexual kick out of anything they saw, as long as they didn't think they were being noticed. Apparently even the sight of a partly blind man working on a wallet in his dining room, with the aid of thick eyeglasses, turned them on. Maybe brick walls did too.

The shade in our dining room was so old and worn that chinks of light 101 showed through. Like tiny stars, I thought, turning sentimental for a minute. "Continuous as the stars that shine," I went on, "And twinkle on the milky way . . ." English Lit. I, a survey course I'd taken, was paying off in unexpected ways.

From time to time I could hear him strumming his guitar, taking short 102 breaks from his leather tooling to give his eyes and head a rest. He stayed in there some two hours, and at ten-thirty he turned out the light and went to the john for his bath. He must have soaked in the tub, relaxing (or trying to) for twenty minutes, a long time for him; he wasn't used to indulging himself in water. On his way to bed he stopped in front of my door, which was shut, for almost a minute. The floorboards creaked every time he shifted his weight. He couldn't seem to make up his mind whether to knock or to leave me alone with my books and notes and anger. Maybe he was hoping I'd make the first move, but I thought I'd already done that by going to church, spite or no spite. At one point I was tempted to come out of hiding ("And hermits are contented with their cells; / And students with their pensive citadels"), but I fought off the urge. My anger won out; I sat still until he gave up and went to bed.

Finally, when he was snoring away and Mami had stopped coughing, I 103 came out. I tiptoed to the john for a leak, a slow one, as if my tubes had been stopped up; then to the kitchen for coffee. A little late in the day for coffee, but I was planning to stay up half the night. There was half a pot in the refrigerator. She left it there for him every night, because he always left the house in a hurry five mornings a week; he didn't like to get to work late.

I read and drank his coffee till after three A.M. Every now and then I got 104 the feeling, a frightening one, that they were both standing outside my door, waiting for me to come out, so we could eat the post-Rooster-Mass dinner in earnest. But when I left the room to go wash up, there was no one there, just the living room, dark.

I had a nightmare, a recurring one. A "Beowulf[2] dream," I called it. It 105 was a pretentious nightmare, another by-product of the survey Lit. I course I'd taken the semester before. The fight between the hero and the monster, and later between the hero and the monster's mother in her underwater hideout, had stayed with me, whereas most of the other students in the class had found

---

[2]An eighth century Old English poem depicting the deeds of the hero, Beowulf. One of his great feats included killing the monster, Grendel, and later, Grendel's avenging mother.

it boring (those who'd bothered reading it) and not nearly as gripping as *Frankenstein* or *The Wolf Man* (the movies). One of them had read Bram Stoker's *Dracula* and called it "ten times better than this Bearwolf."

"It's not Bear," I had told this student. "It's b-e-o-w. I think you mispronounced it." 106

And he had accused me, playfully, or maybe not, of being a show-off. 107 "A pedant," he said. And all I could say to that was that one could do worse. "For example, what?" he'd asked.

"For example, being a show-off in reverse. Meaning ignorant." So much 108 for that friendship, which had just started to get going.

In the dream I got the monsters mixed up; I merged them into one monster: 109 Grendel with huge breasts, enormous steel claws, and stringy, seaweed hair ("a certain evil-doer, a fearful solitary, on dark nights commits deeds of unspeakable malice—damage and slaughter"). Whenever I had this dream, my bedroom door was closed. (I'd once installed a latch on it. "For privacy," I had explained to Papi and Mami. They said they didn't understand what I was getting at, but they said nothing more about it and eventually I stopped latching myself in. But some of the hurt I'd inflicted on them had persisted, as had some of the rotten feeling I'd felt for installing that apparatus.)

The monster, whose face I couldn't make out in the dark, would slam the 110 door open and stand at the entrance, staring at me, something like the movie Wolf Man, before it pounced on its hysterical, fright-frozen victims. I knew I was wide awake, but I was also paralyzed, helpless. Only my eyes moved, staring at this thing that was staring back before turning and disappearing into the living room, or stalking up to me ("a horrible light, like a lurid flame, flickered in his eyes,") and settling its weight, a ton of it, on me. The only thing to do was to let it lie there along the length of my body, and make its point, whatever that was: This monster didn't go in for explanations. Then it would get off me, growling, snarling, leaving only its bad breath and underarm odor behind, and disappear. Sometimes it went out the window. I don't know how it got down to the alley; I never looked. And in the morning my bedroom door would be open; so I came around to believing that this hadn't been a dream, or not completely a dream. Maybe I had taken Lit. I too seriously, and this was the payoff.

I spent the next day, Sunday, studying for finals and drinking coffee, and 111 in the evening went to a movie. Afterward I treated myself (on money I'd "borrowed" from Papi) to a piece of German pastry and more coffee, in a place near the movie house, and by the time I got back home they were sleeping again. We'd hardly spoken all day.

The day of my first final exam, sociology, I stayed home from work. I didn't 112 think I had a choice. I hadn't been able to keep up with the course work, had found it agonizingly hard to concentrate on the material: the boring lectures delivered by a man who was himself bored, the deadly class discussions (whenever he let the students open their mouths), the jargon in the text (which taught me, if not much else, the meaning of the word *obscene*), which had been written by the instructor himself, assisted by others (according to his page of acknowledgments), without whose help, et cetera. It was in its eighth edition, each edition containing "new material," meaning he'd brought the jargon up to date—and the price of the book as well.

So I stayed home to study. And at five P.M., my eyes bloodshot, my hands shaking, my head short on oxygen, I was tying my shoes when the phone went off. We'd had a phone for years but almost never used it. It was there mostly for emergencies. Tío Mito called a couple of times a week, Papi called him a couple of times back, Chuito and his wife rarely called, Mami and I never called anyone, partly because we had no one to call and partly because we were afraid of the phone. (This was a problem at work: One of my bosses called me "phone-shy" and had sometimes ordered me to pick it up when it rang on his desk; I retaliated by taking down wrong messages, and now he seemed to be waiting for an excuse to get rid of me.) 113

The day of my sociology final, it rang about six times, stopped, and rang again in about ten seconds. This went on for about five minutes. Mami and I were both waiting for the other to pick it up, but it wasn't working out. 114

"Maybe it's Papi," I said from my room. 115

She mumbled something. The ringing drowned her out. She finally gave in and picked it up, and within seconds she was pleading with the caller in a nervous voice. Finally she said to the pest, whom she had called "señora," that she had the wrong number, and hung up. 116

"Who was it?" I asked, coming out of my room. 117

She looked frightened. "It's a woman who says we owe her money for a set of furniture." 118

"So if it rings again, take it off the hook. I have to go." 119

"You know the noise the operator makes if we take it off the hook." 120

"I know, Mami. But it's either her or the furniture woman." 121

It rang again. I picked it up. 122

"Malánguez?" 123

"No, his son. He's out on something urgent. You have the wrong number." 124

"Your father owes to us for a set of furniture." 125

"No, he don't. Our furniture's all paid up. We didn't get it from your boss, anyway." 126

Convinced that I was lying, she threatened us with a court summons, with the City Marshal, whoever that might be, with a dispossess, and while she was going on with these threats, I pushed down the receiver, put the nightmare apparatus down on the floor, and wiped my hands on my pants. 127

"Please leave it there," I told Mami. "Don't hang it up." 128

"When Gerán comes home," she said. "I don't want that thing in this house." 129

"Maybe we should cut the cord," I said. 130

She nodded, and I went back inside my room to put on my coat. I was 131
late for the sociology final.

I took a cab up to school, but I was still late. On the way there, I reviewed 132
the "material" in my head: almost total confusion, a jumble of jargon, ordinary
things passed off as profundities with the aid of "abstractionitis." ("The home
then is the specific zone of functional potency that grows about a live parent-
hood . . . an active interfacial membrane or surface furthering exchange . . . a
mutualizing membrane between the family and the society in which it lives. . . .")

The classroom was packed for the first time since the opening day of 133
classes, and filled with smoke. Over forty students were bent over their examination booklets, most of them looking confused by the questions. The professor, puffing an immense pipe, was at his desk (manufactured by Vulcan),
reading Riesman on *The Lonely Crowd*, casually, as if it were a murder mystery
whose ending he had figured out back on page one. He didn't look pleased
when I stepped up to his desk: another pair of lungs in a roomful of carbon
dioxide and cigarette smoke.

"Yes?" 134

I asked him for a question sheet and an examination booklet. They were 135
on the desk, weighted down with the eighth edition of his anthology.

"Are you registered in this course?" he asked. 136

Yes, I was. He wanted to know my name. I told him. He looked me up 137
in his roll book. Had I been coming to class regularly? Every time. How come
I never spoke up in class? Because I sat in the back. It was hard to be heard
from back there. I might try sitting up front, he said. I said I would. He said
it was a little late for that. For a moment I'd forgotten what day this was. *Dies
irae*, according to my paperback dictionary of foreign phrases. Do-or-die day.

There were no empty chairs, so I walked to the back of the room and 138
squatted in a corner, keeping my coat and scarf on.

"Answer one from Part A, one from Part B, and one from Part C." I had 139
no trouble understanding that much. But my mind blanked out on the choices
in Parts A, B, and C. There was something about "group membership as the
source of individual morality and social health" (Durkheim? I couldn't remember). I must have slept through that lecture, and I couldn't remember any
mention of it in the eighth edition. Another one asked for something or other
on Weber's contention that "minorities in 19th-century Europe—the Poles in
Russia, the Huguenots in France, the Non-comformists in England, and the
Jews in all countries—had offset their socio-political exclusion by engaging in
economic activity, whereas the Catholics had not." This one had to be explained
in fifteen minutes. I got around it by drawing a blank.

The easiest choice in Part C asked for "a sociological autobiography, 140
demonstrating your command of certain relevant aspects in this course, as well
as the terminology of sociology."

"Terminology of sociology." That wasn't even a good rhyme. It was also 141 asking too much for fifteen minutes. It wasn't even enough time for my nerves to calm down. Too bad. I got up and left the room. No one noticed.

I went down to the student cafeteria for a cup of coffee, and while I drank 142 it, I read the opening chapter of Dr. A. Alonso's *El Gibaro*, a Puerto Rican classic which I'd brought with me to reread on the subway back home. "I am one of those," it went, "and this can't matter much to my readers, who are in the habit of not sleeping without first having read something"—another one, I thought, nineteenth-century version—"and this something must be of the sort that requires more than usual seclusion, order and meditation, since I think that at no time other than the night's silence can one withdraw from the real world, to elevate oneself into the imaginary; above all when the day has been spent without affliction, something that a young man achieves from time to time, before he becomes the head of a family, or while he does not have to govern, on his own, the vessel of his future."

In the examination blue book, which I hadn't bothered returning, I trans- 143 lated some of these long, rhythmic sentences as best I could (no dictionary on me, for one thing), just for practice, and then, when I'd finished a second cup of coffee, I shoved the Alonso and the blue book back inside my coat pocket and left for the subway.

When I got home the phone was back on the hook. Mami was waxing the 144 kitchen floor. "I'll be through in a minute," she said.

"No hurry, Mami. I'm not hungry yet. How come the phone's back on 145 the hook?"

"I think you better ask your father. He took care of it." 146

He was in the living room watching TV, the weekly wrestling matches. 147 Tío Mito had given him his secondhand Philco when he and Agripina decided to get themselves a new one with a bigger screen. Papi had insisted on paying him for it, in installments, but Mito had told him not to insult him with talk of money. The only "shows" he was interested in were boxing and wrestling.

Minutes earlier, he hadn't heard or seen me walk past him to go hang up 148 my coat; and I hadn't recovered sufficiently from the sociology disaster to strike up a conversation, so I had walked past him twice without saying a word. Now I was feeling contrite about my rudeness—and curious about the phone-back-on-the-hook.

We exchanged a kiss on the cheek. He was wearing his thick glasses, and 149 I couldn't help wondering, nervously, whether I'd be wearing a similar pair myself someday.

"What happened with the phone, Papi?" 150

"Nothing. I gave that crazy woman a lesson in good manners." His gaze 151 was taking turns between me and the TV. "When I got in from work," he went on, "it was on the floor, making a horrible noise. Like a dying animal."

"That's the operator. Playing games." 152

"I know. Five minutes after I hung it up, this furniture woman called 153 again to threaten us with a court summons and other things. And when I told her I was going to call the police, she said they were on her side. So was the City Marshal."

Then, seeing that reasoning with her would get him nowhere, and that 154 keeping the phone off the hook was no solution, he hung up and went out to look for the people this woman really wanted, the fraudulent Malánguezes. "They must have taken our name from the phone book," he said.

"Did you find them?" 155

"It took me a long time, but I did." 156

He went into every building on all of three blocks looking for the fake 157 Malánguezes. He squinted at names on mailbox doors, some nineteen names per building, until he found them. Not Malánguez, actually, but "Malanga," which was close enough. He walked up four flights of stairs, his eyes hurting from all that squinting, and demanded an explanation. They had a new set of furniture in their living room: evidence. "The first thing they told me was that they didn't know what I was talking about."

"That's what they always say." 158

They had mistaken him, apparently, for a con man of some kind, and it 159 had taken some talking on his part to convince them he was on the level. Over a cup of coffee, which they had wasted no time offering him (an admission of guilt, I thought), they admitted that they hadn't paid a single installment on their new set of furniture and attributed it to a misunderstanding.

"Misunderstanding, nothing, Papi. They were just trying to save face 160 when you caught them redburned."

"Redburned?" 161

"Red*handed*, I mean. With the goods, the evidence, the dope. The fur- 162 niture. You should have demanded an apology, those frauds. Hypocrites."

"How could I? They never admitted to stealing, Santos. If anything, they 163 were the ones who got robbed. You should have seen that furniture. I give it six months, maybe eight."

"Must be a rococo set. They put you and Mami through a hard time, a 164 nightmare. Your eyes are red from all that squinting."

"That's from the TV. Why don't you sit down and watch some of this 165 wrestling with me for a while?"

"I have more homework to do." 166

"How was the examination?" 167

"Easy. I finished early." 168

"Good. I thought you would. But don't overdo it, Santos. Your eyes." 169

"Don't worry. I'll see you later." 170

They were asleep—at least I thought they were—when I came out of my 171 room for a leak and a cup of coffee. I hadn't eaten. No appetite. A little unintended fasting wouldn't kill me.

Not long after I fell asleep, Grendel-and-his-mother-merged-into-one paid 172 me another visit. They wouldn't let up. This time, in the dream, I had fallen halfway off the bed, and It—They—grabbed me from behind in a powerful grip, a full nelson. I pretended not to notice, which wasn't easy, and tried to get all of myself back into bed, but It knew I knew. I wasn't fooling Them. They were trying to rape me, and as usual I couldn't scream or fight back. So I saved myself by waking up, sweating, almost out of breath. I stayed up reading for a couple of hours.

During that time I decided to move out. The Elysian Arms escapade 173 hadn't been just an impulse after all. But back in bed, nearly asleep, I knew I wasn't going anywhere just yet, maybe never. ◆

◆ Responding

1. Santos is a victim of an injustice when he receives the wrong change at the bookstore. Discuss his response. Why doesn't he fight harder for his rights? Why doesn't the floorwalker believe him? What would your reaction be in a similar situation?

2. Santos criticizes the payroll manager's addiction to elegant language and British spelling and his art teacher's use of "old boy." These characters are appropriating elements of a culture that is not their own in order to impress others. Could they argue that Santos, too, is appropriating an identity that is not his own? Examine Santos's reading material and dreams and argue for or against this point of view.

3. Santos is unable or unwilling to write his "sociological autobiography" for the test. Consider how he might answer the question and write the answer for him, choosing incidents from the reading to illustrate how society's beliefs and attitudes influence his life.

4. Santos says, "During that time I decided to move out. The Elysian Arms escapade hadn't been just an impulse after all. But back in bed, nearly asleep, I knew I wasn't going anywhere just yet, maybe never." Working in two groups, list the factors that keep Santos at home and the reasons why he wants to move out, or list the pros and cons of his staying at home and moving out. After comparing the lists, write an essay describing what you think Santos will be doing in ten years.

NICHOLASA MOHR

Nicholasa Mohr, who was born in New York in 1935, studied at the Brooklyn Museum Art School and the Pratt School. Between 1952 and 1967 she worked as a painter and printmaker and taught in the New York public schools. Since 1972 she has held lectureships and visiting appointments in creative writing, Puerto Rican studies, and art at several universities, including the State University of New York at Stony Brook, the University of Illinois, and the University of Wisconsin. Mohr's publications include Nilda *(1973),* El Bronx Remembered: A Novella and Stories *(1975),* In Nueva York *(1977), and* Rituals of Survival *(1985).*

"A Thanksgiving Celebration," a part of Mohr's collection Rituals of Survival, *explores the way in which one woman relies on her creativity and strength of will to gain a sense of control over her decaying environment.*

◆ A THANKSGIVING CELEBRATION (AMY) ◆

Amy sat on her bed thinking. Gary napped soundly in his crib, which was placed right next to her bed. The sucking sound he made as he chewed on his thumb interrupted her thoughts from time to time. Amy glanced at Gary and smiled. He was her constant companion now; he shared her bedroom and was with her during those frightening moments when, late into the night and early morning, she wondered if she could face another day just like the one she had safely survived. Amy looked at the small alarm clock on the bedside table. In another hour or so it would be time to wake Gary and give him his milk, then she had just enough time to shop and pick up the others, after school. 1

She heard the plopping sound of water dropping into a full pail. Amy hurried into the bathroom, emptied the pail into the toilet, then replaced it so that the floor remained dry. Last week she had forgotten, and the water had overflowed out of the pail and onto the floor, leaking down into Mrs. Wynn's bathroom. Now, Mrs. Wynn was threatening to take her to small claims court, if the landlord refused to fix the damage done to her bathroom ceiling and wallpaper. All right, Amy shrugged, she would try calling the landlord once more. She was tired of the countless phone calls to plead with them to come and fix the leak in the roof. 2

"Yes, Mrs. Guzman, we got your message and we'll send somebody over. Yes, just as soon as we can . . . we got other tenants with bigger problems, you know. We are doing our best, we'll get somebody over; you gotta be patient . . ." 3

Time and again they had promised, but no one had ever showed up. And it was now more than four mouths that she had been forced to live like this. Damn, Amy walked into her kitchen, they never refuse the rent for that, there's 4 somebody ready any time! Right now, this was the best she could do. The building was still under rent control and she had enough room. Where else could she go? No one in a better neighborhood would rent to her, not the way things were.

She stood by the window, leaning her side against the molding, and looked out. It was a crisp sunny autumn day, mild for the end of November. She remembered it was the eve of Thanksgiving and felt a tightness in her chest. Amy took a deep breath, deciding not to worry about that right now.

Rows and rows of endless streets scattered with abandoned buildings and small houses stretched out for miles. Some of the blocks were almost entirely leveled, except for clumps of partial structures charred and blackened by fire. From a distance they looked like organic masses pushing their way out of the earth. Garbage, debris, shattered glass, bricks and broken, discarded furniture covered the ground. Rusting carcasses of cars that had been stripped down to the shell shone and glistened a bright orange under the afternoon sun.

There were no people to be seen nor traffic, save for a group of children jumping on an old filthy mattress that had been ripped open. They were busy pulling the stuffing out of the mattress and tossing it about playfully. Nearby, several stray dogs searched the garbage for food. One of the boys picked up a brick, then threw it at the dogs, barely missing them. Reluctantly, the dogs moved on.

Amy signed and swallowed, it was all getting closer and closer. It seemed as if only last month, when she had looked out of this very window, all of that was much further away; in fact, she recalled feeling somewhat removed and safe. Now the decay was creeping up to this area. The fire engine sirens screeching and screaming in the night reminded her that the devastation was constant, never stopping even for a night's rest. Amy was fearful of living on the top floor. Going down four flights to safety with the kids in case of a fire was another source of worry for her. She remembered how she had argued with Charlie when they had first moved in.

"All them steps to climb with Michele and Carlito, plus carrying the carriage for Carlito, is too much."

"Come on baby," Charlie had insisted "it's only temporary. The rent's cheaper and we can save something towards buying our own place. Come on . . ."

That was seven years ago. There were two more children now, Lisabeth and Gary; and she was still here, without Charlie.

"Soon it'll come right to this street and to my doorstep. God Almighty!" Amy whispered. It was like a plague: a disease for which there seemed to be no cure, no prevention. Gangs of youngsters occupied empty store fronts and basements; derelicts, drunk or wasted on drugs, positioned themselves on street corners and in empty doorways. Every day she saw more abandoned and burned-out sections.

As Amy continued to look out, a feeling that she had been in this same situation before, a long time ago, startled her. The feeling of déjà vu, so real to her, reminded Amy quite vividly of the dream she had had last night. In that dream, she had been standing in the center of a circle of little girls. She herself was very young and they were all singing a rhyme. In a soft whisper, Amy sang the rhyme: "London Bridge is falling down, falling down, falling down, London Bridge is falling down, my fair lady. . . ." She stopped and saw herself once again in her dream, picking up her arms and chanting, "Wave your arms and fly away, fly away, fly away . . ."

She stood in the middle of the circle waving her arms, first gently, then   14
more forcefully, until she was flapping them. The other girls stared silently at her. Slowly, Amy had felt herself elevated above the circle, higher and higher until she could barely make out the human figures below. Waving her arms like the wings of a bird, she began to fly. A pleasant breeze pushed her gently, and she glided along, passing through soft white clouds into an intense silence. Then she saw it. Beneath her, huge areas were filled with crumbling buildings and large caverns; miles of destruction spread out in every direction. Amy had felt herself suspended in this silence for a moment and then she began to fall. She flapped her arms and legs furiously, trying to clutch at the air, hoping for a breeze, something to get her going again, but there was nothing. Quickly she fell, faster and faster, as the ground below her swirled and turned, coming closer and closer, revealing destroyed, burned buildings, rubble and a huge dark cavern. In a state of hysteria, Amy had fought against the loss of control and helplessness, as her body descended into the large black hole and had woken up with a start just before she hit bottom.

Amy stepped away from the window for a moment, almost out of breath   15
as she recollected the fear she had felt in her dream. She walked over to the sink and poured herself a glass of water.

"That's it, Europe and the war," she said aloud. "In the movies, just like   16
my dream."

Amy clearly remembered how she had sat as a very little girl in a local   17
movie theatre with her mother and watched horrified at the scenes on the screen. Newsreels showed entire cities almost totally devastated. Exactly as it had been in her dream, she recalled seeing all the destruction caused by warfare. Names like "Munich, Nuremburg, Berlin" and "the German people" identified the areas. Most of the streets were empty, except for the occasional small groups of people who rummaged about, searching among the ruins and huge piles of debris, sharing the spoils with packs of rats who scavenged at a safe distance. Some people pulled wagons and baby carriages loaded with bundles and household goods. Others carried what they owned on their backs.

Amy remembered turning to her mother, asking, "What was going on?   18
Mami, who did this? Why did they do it? Who are those people living there?"

"The enemy, that's who," her mother had whispered emphatically. "Bad   19
people who started the war against our country and did terrible things to other people and to us. That's where your papa was for so long, fighting in the army. Don't you remember, Amy?"

"What kinds of things, Mami? Who were the other people they did bad things to?" 20

"Don't worry about them things. These people got what they deserved. Besides, they are getting help from us, now that we won the war. There's a plan to help them, even though they don't deserve no help from us." 21

Amy had persisted. "Are there any little kids there? Do they go to school? Do they live in them holes?" 22

"Shh . . . let me hear the rest of the news . . ." her mother had responded, annoyed. Amy had sat during the remainder of the double feature, wondering where those people lived and all about the kids there. And she continued to wonder and worry for several days, until one day she forgot all about it. 23

Amy sipped from the glass she held, then emptied most of the water back into the sink. She sat and looked around at her small kitchen. The ceiling was peeling and flakes of paint had fallen on the kitchen table. The entire apartment was in urgent need of a thorough plastering and paint job. She blinked and shook her head, and now? Who are we now? What have I done? Who is the enemy? Is there a war? Are we at war? Amy suppressed a loud chuckle. 24

"Nobody answered my questions then, and nobody's gonna answer them now," she spoke out loud. 25

Amy still wondered and groped for answers about Charlie. No one could tell her what really happened . . . how he had felt and what he was thinking before he died. Almost two years had gone by, but she was still filled with an overwhelming sense of loneliness. That day was just like so many other days; they were together, planning about the kids, living from one crisis to the next, fighting, barely finding the time to make love without being exhausted; then late that night, it was all over. Charlie's late again, Amy had thought, and didn't even call me. She was angry when she heard the doorbell. He forgot the key again. Dammit, Charlie! You would forget your head if it weren't attached to you! 26

They had stood there before her; both had shown her their badges, but only one had spoken. 27

"Come in . . . sit down, won't you." 28

"You better sit down, miss." The stranger told her very calmly and soberly that Charlie was dead. 29

"On the Bruckner Boulevard Expressway . . . head on collision . . . dead on arrival . . . didn't suffer too long . . . nobody was with him, but we found his wallet." 30

Amy had protested and argued—No way! They were lying to her. But after a while she knew they brought the truth to her, and Charlie wasn't coming back. 31

Tomorrow would be the second Thanksgiving without him and one she could not celebrate. Celebrate with what? Amy stood and walked over and opened the refrigerator door. She had enough bread, a large pitcher of powdered 32 milk which she had flavored with Hershey's cocoa and powdered sugar. There was plenty of peanut butter and some graham crackers she had kept fresh by sealing them in a plastic bag. For tonight she had enough chopped meat and macaroni. But tomorrow? What could she buy for tomorrow?

Amy shut the refrigerator door and reached over to the money tin set way   33
back on one of the shelves. Carefully she took out the money and counted every cent. There was no way she could buy a turkey, even a small one. She still had to manage until the first; she needed every penny just to make it to the next check. Things were bad, worse than they had ever been. In the past, when things were rough, she had turned to Charlie and sharing had made it all easier. Now there was no one. She resealed the money tin and put it away.

Amy had thought of calling the lawyers once more. What good would   34
that do? What can they do for me? Right now . . . today!

"These cases take time before we get to trial. We don't want to take the   35
first settlement they offer. That wouldn't do you or the children any good. You have a good case, the other driver was at fault. He didn't have his license or the registration, and we have proof he was drinking. His father is a prominent judge who doesn't want that kind of publicity. I know . . . yes, things are rough, but just hold on a little longer. We don't want to accept a poor settlement and risk your future and the future of your children, do we?" Mr. Silverman of Silverman, Knapp and Ullman was handling the case personally. "By early Spring we should be making a date for trial . . . just hang in there a bit longer . . ." And so it went every time she called: the promise that in just a few more months she could hope for relief, some money, enough to live like people.

Survivor benefits had not been sufficient, and since they had not kept up   36
premium payments on Charlie's G.I. insurance policy, she had no other income. Amy was given a little more assistance from the Aid to Dependent Children agency. Somehow she had managed so far.

The two food stores that extended her credit were still waiting for Amy   37
to settle overdue accounts. In an emergency she could count on a few friends; they would lend her something, but not for this, not for Thanksgiving dinner.

She didn't want to go to Papo and Mary's again. She knew her brother   38
meant well, and that she always had an open invitation. They're good people, but we are five more mouths to feed, plus they've been taking care of Papa all these years, ever since Mami died. Enough is enough. Amy shut her eyes. I want my own dinner this year, just for my family, for me and the kids.

If I had the money, I'd make a dinner tomorrow and invite Papa and Lou   39
Ann from downstairs and her kids. She's been such a good friend to us. I'd get a gallon of cider and a bottle of wine . . . a large cake at the bakery by Alexander's, some dried fruits and nuts . . . even a holiday centerpiece for the table. Yes, it would be my dinner for us and my friends. I might even invite Jimmy. She hadn't seen Jimmy for a long time. Must be over six months . . . almost a year? He worked with Charlie at the plant. After Charlie's death, Jimmy had come by often, but Amy was not ready to see another man, not just then, so

she discouraged him. From time to time, she thought of Jimmy and hoped he would visit her again.

Amy opened her eyes and a sinking feeling flowed through her, as she [40] looked down at the chips of paint spread out on the kitchen table. Slowly, Amy brushed them with her hand, making a neat pile.

These past few months, she had seriously thought of going out to work. [41] Before she had Michele, she had worked as a clerk-typist for a large insurance company, but that was almost ten years ago. She would have to brush up on her typing and math. Besides, she didn't know if she could earn enough to pay for a sitter. She couldn't leave the kids alone; Gary wasn't even three and Michele had just turned nine. Amy had applied for part-time work as a teacher's aide, but when she learned that her check from Aid to Dependent Children could be discontinued, she withdrew her application. Better to go on like this until the case comes to trial.

Amy choked back the tears. I can't let myself get like this. I just can't! [42] Lately, she had begun to find comfort at the thought of never waking up again. What about my kids, then? I must do something. I have to. Tomorrow is going to be for us, just us, our day.

Her thoughts went back to her own childhood and the holiday dinners [43] with her family. They had been poor, but there was always food. We used to have such good times. Amy remembered the many stories her grandmother used to tell them. She spoke about her own childhood on a farm in a rural area of Puerto Rico. Her grandmother's stories were about the animals, whom she claimed to know personally and very well. Amy laughed, recalling that most of the stories her grandmother related were too impossible to be true, such as a talking goat who saved the town from a flood, and the handsome mouse and beautiful lady beetle who fell in love, got married and had the biggest and fanciest wedding her grandmother had ever attended. Her grandmother was very old and had died before Amy was ten. Amy had loved her best, more than her own parents, and she still remembered the old woman quite clearly.

"Abuelita, did them things really happen? How come them animals talked? [44] Animals don't talk. Everybody knows that."

"Oh, but they do talk! And yes, everything I tell you is absolutely the [45] truth. I believe it and you must believe it too." The old woman had been completely convincing. And for many years Amy had secretly believed that when her grandmother was a little girl, somewhere in a special place, animals talked, got married and were heroes.

"Abuelita," Amy whispered, "I wish you were here and could help me [46] now." And then she thought of it. Something special for tomorrow. Quickly, Amy took out the money tin, counting out just the right amount of money she needed. She hesitated for a moment. What if it won't work and I can't convince them? Amy took a deep breath. Never mind, I have to try, I must. She counted out a few more dollars. I'll work it all out somehow. Then she warmed up Gary's milk and got ready to leave.

Amy heard the voices of her children with delight. Shouts and squeals of laughter bounced into the kitchen as they played in the living room. Today they were all happy, anticipating their mother's promise of a celebration. Recently, her frequent moods of depression and short temper had frightened them. Privately, the children had blamed themselves for their mother's unhappiness, fighting with each other in helpless confusion. The children welcomed their mother's energy and good mood with relief. 47

Lately Amy had begun to realize that Michele and Carlito were constantly fighting. Carlito was always angry and would pick on Lisabeth. Poor Lisabeth, she's always so sad. I never have time for her and she's not really much older than Gary. This way of life has been affecting us all . . . but not today. Amy worked quickly. The apartment was filled with an air of festivity. She had set the table with a paper tablecloth, napkins and paper cups to match. These were decorated with turkeys, pilgrims, Indian corn and all the symbols of the Thanksgiving holiday. Amy had also bought a roll of orange paper streamers and decorated the kitchen chairs. Each setting had a name-card printed with bright magic markers. She had even managed to purchase a small holiday cake for dessert. 48

As she worked, Amy fought moments of anxiety and fear that threatened to weaken her sense of self-confidence. What if they laugh at me? Dear God in heaven, will my children think I'm a fool? But she had already spent the money, cooked and arranged everything; she had to go ahead. If I make it through this day, Amy nodded, I'll be all right. 49

She set the food platter in the center of the table and stepped back. A mound of bright yellow rice, flavored with a few spices and bits of fatback, was surrounded by a dozen hardboiled eggs that had been colored a bright orange. Smiling, Amy felt it was all truly beautiful; she was ready for the party. 50

"All right." Amy walked into the living room. "We're ready!" The children quickly followed her into the kitchen. 51

"Oooh, Mommy," Lisabeth shouted, "everything looks so pretty." 52

"Each place has got a card with your own name, so find the right seat." Amy took Gary and sat him down on his special chair next to her. 53

"Mommy," Michele spoke, "is this the whole surprise?" 54

"Yes," Amy answered, "just a minute, we also have some cider." Amy brought a small bottle of cider to the table. 55

"Easter eggs for Thanksgiving?" Carlito asked. 56

"Is that what you think they are, Carlito?" Amy asked. "Because they are not Easter eggs." 57

The children silently turned to one another, exchanging bewildered looks. 58

"What are they?" Lisabeth asked. 59

"Well," Amy said, "these are . . . turkey eggs, that's what. What's better than a turkey on Thanksgiving day? Her eggs, right?" Amy continued as all of them watched her. "You see, it's not easy to get these eggs. They're what you call a delicacy. But I found a special store that sells them, and they agreed to sell me a whole dozen for today." 60

"What store is that, Mommy?" Michele asked. "Is it around here?" 61

"No. They don't have stores like that here. It's special, way downtown." 62

"Did the turkey lay them eggs like that? That color?" Carlito asked. 63

"I want an egg," Gary said, pointing to the platter. 64

"No, no . . . I just colored them that way for today, so everything goes 65
together nicely, you know . . ." Amy began to serve the food. "All right, you
can start eating."

"Well then, what's so special about these eggs? What's the difference 66
between a turkey egg and an egg from a chicken?" Carlito asked.

"Ah, the taste, Carlito, just wait until you have some." Amy quickly 67
finished serving everyone. "You see, these eggs are hard to find because they
taste so fantastic." She chewed a mouthful of egg. "Ummm . . . fantastic, isn't
it?" She nodded at them.

"Wonderful, Mommy," said Lisabeth. "It tastes real different." 68

"Oh yeah," Carlito said, "you can taste it right away. Really good." 69

Everyone was busy eating and commenting on how special the eggs tasted. 70
As Amy watched her children, a sense of joy filled her, and she knew it had
been a very long time since they had been together like this, close and loving.

"Mommy, did you ever eat these kinds of eggs before?" asked Michele. 71

"Yes, when I was little," she answered. "My grandmother got them for 72
me. You know, I talked about my abuelita before. When I first ate them, I
couldn't get over how good they tasted, just like you." Amy spoke with assur-
ance, as they listened to every word she said. "Abuelita lived on a farm when
she was very little. That's how come she knew all about turkey eggs. She used
to tell me the most wonderful stories about her life there."

"Tell us!" 73

"Yeah, please Mommy, please tell us." 74

"All right, I'll tell you one about a hero who saved her whole village from 75
a big flood. He was . . . a billy goat."

"Mommy," Michele interrupted, "a billy goat?" 76

"That's right, and you have to believe what I'm going to tell you. All of 77
you have to believe me. Because everything I'm going to say is absolutely the
truth. Promise? All right, then, in the olden days, when my grandmother was
very little, far away in a small town in Puerto Rico . . ."

Amy continued, remembering stories that she had long since forgotten. 78
The children listened, intrigued by what their mother had to say. She felt a
calmness within. Yes, Amy told herself, today's for us, for me and the kids. ◆

◆ Responding

1. Amy says to herself, "If I make it through this day . . . I'll be all right."
   Explain why this Thanksgiving is so important to her.

2. Amy lies to her children about the eggs. What is the reason for the lie? If she had asked your advice, what would you have advised her to tell her children?

3. The family stories represent more than just pleasant memories. Discuss their importance to Amy. Why does she choose this time to tell them to her children? What is the role of stories in your family? Share a family story that is important to you.

4. At the beginning of the story we learn that Amy, a widow with four children, is living on welfare in a run-down apartment in a poor neighborhood. Given this situation, explain why you might have expected an optimistic or a pessimistic resolution. Mohr chooses an optimistic ending. What do you think she is saying about Amy? Write an alternate ending for the story, and compare it with Mohr's.

Judith Ortiz Cofer

Born in Puerto Rico in 1952, the writer Judith Ortiz Cofer immigrated to the United States with her family in 1956. After earning her bachelor's degree from Augusta College and her master's degree from Florida Atlantic University, she spent a year at Oxford University in 1977. Since then she has taught English and Spanish at several universities in the South, including the University of Miami and the University of Georgia. Cofer's publications include the autobiographical work The Line of the Sun *and four volumes of poetry.*

The following excerpt from The Line of the Sun *explores some of the contrasts between what the narrator calls life in "the tropical paradise" and life in the streets of Paterson, New Jersey. The narrator speculates about how her life would have been different if her family had remained in Puerto Rico. In so doing, the narrative suggests the importance of the imagination in fashioning one's view of both the present and the past.*

◆ *From* THE LINE OF THE SUN ◆

It was a bitter winter in Paterson. The snow fell white and dry as coconut shavings, but as soon as it touched the dirty pavement it turned into a muddy soup. Though we wore rubber boots, our feet stayed wet and cold all day. The bitter wind brought hot tears to our eyes, but it was so cold that we never felt them streaking our cheeks.

During Lent the nuns counted attendance at the seven o'clock mass and gave demerits if we did not take into our dry mouths Christ's warm body in the form of a wafer the priest held in his palm. The church was dark at that hour of the morning, and thick with the steaming garments of children dropped off by anxious mothers or, like us, numb from a seven-block walk.

In the hour of the mass, I thawed in the sweet unctuousness of the young Italian priest's voice chanting his prayers for the souls of these young children and their teachers, for their parents, for the dead and the living, for our deprived brothers and sisters, some of whom had not found comfort in Christ and were now in mortal danger of damning their souls to the raging fire of hell. He didn't really say hell, a word carefully avoided in our liturgy: it was all innuendo and Latin words that sounded like expletives. *Kyrie Eleison*, he would challenge; *Christe Eleison*, we would respond heartily, led by the strong voice of Sister Mary Beata, our beautiful homeroom teacher, whose slender body and perfect features were evident in spite of the layers of clothing she wore and the coif that surrounded her face. She was the envy of our freshman-class girls. In the classroom I sat in the back watching her graceful movements, admiring the translucent quality of her unblemished skin, wondering whether both her calm and her beauty were a gift from God, imagining myself in the medieval clothes of her nun's habit.

I sat in the last desk of the last row of the girl's side of the room, the 4
smallest, darkest member of a class full of the strapping offspring of Irish immigrants with a few upstart Italians recently added to the roll. The blazing red hair of Jackie O'Connell drew my eyes like a flame to the center of the room, and the pattern of freckles on her nose fascinated me. She was a popular girl with the sisters; her father was a big-shot lawyer with political ambitions. Donna Finney was well developed for her age, her woman's body restrained within the angular lines of the green-and-white plaid uniform we would wear until our junior year, when we would be allowed to dress like young ladies in a pleated green skirt and white blouse. Donna sat in the row closest to the boys' side of the room.

The boys were taller and heavier than my friends at El Building; they 5
wore their blue ties and opened doors for girls naturally, as if they did it at home too. At school we were segregated by sex: every classroom was divided into girlside and boyside, and even the playground had an imaginary line right down the middle, where the assigned nun of the day would stand guard at recess and lunchtime. There were some couples in the school, of course. Everyone knew Donna went with a junior boy, a basketball player named Mickey Salvatore, an Italian playing on our Fighting Irish team—and it was a known fact that they went out in his car. After school some girls met their boyfriends at Schulze's drugstore for a soda. I saw them go in on my way home. My mother, following Rafael's instructions, gave us thirty minutes to get home before she put on her coat and high heels and came looking for us. I had just enough time to round up my brother at the grammar-school building across the street and walk briskly the seven blocks home. No soda for me with friends at Schulze's.

Ramona had come looking for us one day when an afternoon assembly 6
had held me up, and that episode had taught me a lesson. Her long black hair loose and wild from the wind, she was wearing black spiked shoes and was wrapped in a red coat and black shawl when she showed up outside the school building. The kids stared at her as if she were a circus freak, and the nuns looked doubtful, thinking perhaps they should ask the gypsy to leave the school grounds. One boy said something about her that made a hot blush of shame creep up my neck and burn my cheeks. They didn't know—couldn't know— that she was my mother, since Rafael made all our school arrangements every year, explaining that his wife could not speak English and therefore would not be attending PTA meetings and so forth. My mother looked like no other mother at the school, and I was glad she did not participate in school activities. Even on Sunday she went to the Spanish mass while we attended our separate service for children. My gypsy mother embarrassed me with her wild beauty. I wanted her to cut and spray her hair into a sculptured hairdo like the other ladies; I wanted her to wear tailored skirts and jackets like Jackie Kennedy; I even

resented her youth, which made her look like my older sister. She was what I would have looked like if I hadn't worn my hair in a tight braid, if I had allowed myself to sway when I walked, and if I had worn loud colors and had spoken only Spanish.

I was beginning to understand why Rafael wanted to move us away from El Building. The older I got, the more embarrassed I felt about living in this crowded, noisy tenement, which the residents seemed intent on turning into a bizarre facsimile of an Island barrio. But for a while my fascination with Guzmán overpowered all other feelings, and when I came home from the organized, sanitized world of school, I felt drawn into his sickroom like an opium addict. I looked forward to the air thick with the smells of many cigarettes and of alcohol. More and more I took over the nursing duties which Ramona, with her impatient hands, relished little. She was used to fast-healing children and an absent husband. Guzmán's bleeding wound and his careful movements tried her patience.   7

And so it happened that my uncle and I began talking. Guzmán told me about his childhood on the Island in general terms, leaving out things he did not think I would understand, but his silences and omissions were fuel to my imagination and I filled in the details. I questioned him about his friend Rosa, whose name came up whenever he began to describe the Island. It was as if she were the embodiment of all that was beautiful, strange, and tempting about his homeland. He told me about her amazing knowledge of plants and herbs, how she knew what people needed just by talking to them. Once I asked him to describe her to me. His eyes had been closed as he spoke, seeing her, I suppose; but he opened them like one who slowly rises from a dream and looked at me, sitting by the side of his bed in my blue-and-white first Friday uniform, my hair pulled back in a tightly wound bun.   8

"Let your hair down," he said.   9

I reached back and pulled the long black pins out of my thick hair, letting it fall over my shoulders. It was quite long, and I never wore it loose.   10

"She had long black hair like yours," he said rising on his elbows to look intently into my face as if seeing me for the first time. I noticed his knuckles going white from the effort. "And she was light-complexioned like you." He fell back on the pillow, groaning a little. Ramona came in at that moment with fresh bandages and looked strangely at me sitting there with my hair undone, but did not say anything. Ordering Guzmán to shift to his side, she changed his bandage briskly.   11

"I need you to go to the bodega for me, Marisol," she said, not looking at me. I hated going into the gloomy little Spanish grocery store with its fishy smell and loiterers who always had something smart to say to women.   12

"Why can't you send Gabriel?" I asked petulantly, feeling once again that strain developing between my mother and me which kept getting more in the way of all our attempts at communication. She refused to acknowledge the fact that I was fast becoming too old to order around.   13

"He is doing his homework." Tucking the sheet around her brother as if   14
he were another child, she turned to me. "Just do what I tell you, niña, without
arguments or back talk. It looks like we are going to have a serious discussion
with your father when he comes home." She looked at me meaningfully.

When she left the room I braided my hair slowly. It was the new impasse   15
we had reached. I would obey her but I would take my time doing so, pushing
her to a steady burning anger which could no longer be relieved by the familiar
routine of spanking, tears, reconciliation. It was a contest of wills that I knew
no one could win, but Ramona was still hoping Rafael would know how to
mediate. He was the absent disciplinarian—Solomon, the wise judge, the threat
and the promise that hung over us day after day in her constant "when your
father comes home."

I couldn't understand how she continued to treat me like a child when   16
she had not been much older than I when she married Rafael. If I were on the
Island I would be respected as a young woman of marriageable age. I had heard
Ramona talking with her friends about a girl's fifteenth year, the *Quinceañera*,
when everything changes for her. She no longer plays with children; she dresses
like a woman and joins the women at coffee in the afternoon; she is no longer
required to attend school if there is more pressing need for her at home, or if
she is engaged. I was almost fifteen now—still in my silly uniform, bobby socks
and all; still not allowed to socialize with my friends, living in a state of limbo,
halfway between cultures. No one at school asked why I didn't participate in
the myriad parish activities. They all understood that Marisol was *different*.

Talking with my uncle, listening to stories about his life on the Island,   17
and hearing Ramona's constant rhapsodizing about that tropical paradise—all
conspired to make me feel deprived. I should have grown up there. I should
have been able to play in emerald-green pastures, to eat sweet bananas right
off the trees, to learn about life from the women who were strong and wise
like the fabled Mamá Cielo. How could she be Ramona's mother? Ramona,
who could not make a decision without invoking the name of our father, whose
judgment we awaited like the Second Coming.

As I reached for the door to leave Guzmán's room, he stirred.   18

"Rosa," he said, groggy from medication.   19

"Do you need anything?" I was trembling.   20

Alert now, he pointed to the dresser against the wall. "Take my wallet   21
from the top drawer and get me a carton of L&M's when you go to the bodega."
He closed his eyes again, whispering, "Thanks, niña."

I took his wallet, unwilling to make more noise by looking through it for   22
money. In the kitchen Ramona was washing dishes at the sink, her back to me,
but she was aware of my presence, and her anger showed in the set of her
shoulders. I suddenly remembered how much she used to laugh, and still did
when she was around her women friends.

"The list and the money are on the table, Marisol. Don't take long. I need   23
to start dinner soon."

I put my coat on and left the apartment. The smells of beans boiling in   24
a dozen kitchens assailed my nostrils. Rice and beans, the unimaginative staple
food of all these people who re-created every day the same routines they had
followed in their mamá's houses so long ago. Except that here in Paterson, in
the cold rooms stories about the frozen ground, the smells and sounds of a lost
way of life could only be a parody.

Instead of heading out the front door and to the street, an impulse carried   25
my feet down an extra flight of stairs to El Basement. It was usually deserted
at this hour when everyone was preparing to eat. I sat on the bottom step and
looked around me at the cavernous room. A yellow light hung over my head.
I took Guzmán's wallet from my coat pocket. Bringing it close to my face, I
smelled the old leather. Carefully I unfolded it flat on my lap. There were
several photos in the plastic. On top was a dark Indian-looking woman whose
features looked familiar. Her dark, almond-shaped eyes were just like Ramona's,
but her dark skin and high cheekbones were Guzmán's. I guessed this was an
early picture of my grandmother, Mamá Cielo. Behind that there was one of
two teenage boys, one dark, one blond. They were smiling broadly, arms on
each other's shoulders. There was a fake moon in the background like the ones
they use in carnival photo booths. Though the picture was bent, cutting the
boys at the neck, and of poor quality, I recognized them: it was Guzmán and
Rafael. I looked at it for a long time, especially at my father's face, almost
unrecognizable to me with its unfamiliar look of innocent joy. Perhaps they
had been drinking that night. I had often heard Ramona talking about the
festivals dedicated to Our Lady of Salud, the famous smiling Virgin. Maybe
they had the photo taken then. Was this the night that Guzmán had seen Rosa
dressed like a gypsy at the fair? I had heard that story told late at night in my
mother's kitchen, eavesdropping while I pretended to sleep. Did Rafael know
Ramona then—was he happy because he was in love with the beautiful fourteen-
year-old sister of his best friend?

In one of the plastic windows there was a newspaper clipping, yellow and   26
torn, of a Spanish actress, wild black hair falling like a violent storm around a
face made up to look glamorous, eyelashes thickened black, glossy lips parted
in an open invitation. She was beautiful. I had seen her face often in the
magazines my mother bought at the bodega, but why did Guzmán carry this
woman's picture around? Was this what Rosa had looked like, or was she just
his fantasy?

Deeply engrossed in my secret activity of going through my uncle's wallet,   27
I was startled to hear men's voices approaching the top of the landing. I sat
still waiting for them to go up the stairs, but they came down instead. There
were four or five whose faces I recognized in the dim light as the working men
of El Building, young husbands whose wives were Ramona's friends. I was not
afraid, but I hid the wallet in my coat pocket and quickly got to my feet. My
mind raced to come up with an excuse, though it was *their* presence in El

Basement that was odd. The laundry room was used legitimately by women and otherwise by kids. The only other users, as I very well knew from my encounter with José and the woman, were people who wanted to hide what they were doing.

The voice I heard most clearly was that of Santiago, the only man from   28
El Building ever to have been invited by Rafael into our apartment. After a severe winter week several years before, we had been left without heat until this man went down to city hall and got a judge to force the building super-intendent to do something about the frozen heater pipes. Rafael had been in Europe at the time, but he obviously respected Santiago.

Coming down the steps, Santiago's voice directed the others. One man   29
was to stand at the top and wait for the others, the rest were to follow him into the basement. He nearly stumbled over me in the dim light, not seeing me wrapped in my gray coat.

"Niña, *por Dios*, what are you doing here at this hour?" His voice was   30
gentle but I detected irritation.

"My mother lost something here earlier and sent me down to try to find   31
it." I explained rather rapidly in my awkward formal Spanish.

He took my elbow in a fatherly way: "Marisol, I don't believe your mother   32
would be so careless as to send you down here to this dark place at the dinner hour alone. But I won't mention that I saw you here, and you must do the same for me, for us. These men and I want to have a private conversation. Do you understand?

"Yes," I said quickly, wanting to be released from his firm grasp, "I won't   33
say anything." He let go of my arm and I ran up the stairs. Several other men had arrived and were talking in hushed tones at the top of the steps. I managed to catch a few sentences as I slipped by their surprised faces and into the streets. It was the factory they were discussing. Someone had said *huelga*, a strike. They were planning a strike.

Outside it was cold, but not bitter; a hint of spring in the breeze cooled   34
my cheeks without biting into my skin. For once I felt a sense of pride in my father, who had managed to escape the horrible trap of factory work, though he was paying a high price for it. Tonight I'd have something to talk about with Guzmán. He would be interested in the secret basement meeting and the strike. ◆

◆ Responding

1. Marisol describes herself as "halfway between cultures." Compare her life-style at fifteen in Paterson, New Jersey, with what her life would have been like if she had been born and raised in Puerto Rico.

2. Describe Puerto Rico as Marisol pictures it. In what ways do you think she idealizes the Island? Discuss the role of Puerto Rico in helping her deal with her everyday life. Is there a place or a person you think about when you want to escape from current problems?

3. Discuss Marisol's reaction to her mother's visit to her school. What image does she have in mind for her ideal mother? Describe a time when you or someone you know was in a situation where you felt out of place and wanted to fit in.

4. Working individually or in a group, discuss the conflict of wills between mother and daughter. List examples of their encounters and the reaction of each. How much of Marisol's behavior do you think is adolescent rebellion, and how much is a response to her mother's personality?

REFLECTING A CRITICAL CONTEXT

JUAN FLORES

Born in 1943, Juan Flores has studied the sociology and culture of Puerto Rico for many years. In addition to publishing essays in Daedalus, Latin American Perspectives, Journal of Ethnic Studies, *and other publications in the U.S. and Latin America, he also translated the* Memoirs of Bernardo Vega *into English. In 1980 he received the Casa de las Americas award for the best essay in Latin American studies. He currently teaches in the International Studies Department at the City College of New York, and is affiliated with the Center for Puerto Rican Studies at Hunter College.*

In the essay that follows, Juan Flores uses an historical perspective to examine Puerto Rican literature written on the Island, and that produced on the mainland.

◆ PUERTO RICAN LITERATURE IN THE UNITED STATES: STAGES AND PERSPECTIVES ◆

Can anyone name the great Puerto Rican novel? It's *La charca* by Manuel Zeno   1
Gandía, published in 1894 and first available to American readers in English translation in 1984. The lapse, of course, is symptomatic. After nearly a century of intense economic and political association, endless official pledges of cultural kinship, and the wholesale importation of nearly half the Puerto Rican people to the United States, Puerto Rican literature still draws a blank among American readers and students of literature. Major writers and authors are unknown and, with a handful of exceptions, untranslated; English-language and bilingual anthologies are few and unsystematic, and there is still not a single introduction to the literature's history available in English. Even the writing of Puerto Ricans living in the United States, mostly in English and all expressive of life in this country, has remained marginal to any literary canon, mainstream or otherwise: among the "ethnic" or "minority" literatures it has probably drawn the least critical interest and the fewest readers.

Yet, as a young Puerto Rican friend once put it, "Puerto Rico is this   2
country's 'jacket.' " In no other national history are twentieth-century American social values and priorities more visibly imprinted than in Puerto Rico's. Puerto Rico, in fact, or at least its treatment at the hands of the United States, is part of American history. Its occupation in 1898 after four centuries of Spanish

colonialism, the decades of imposition of English, the unilateral decreeing of American citizenship in 1917, economic and social crisis during the Depression years, externally controlled industrialization, unprecedented migration of the work force and sterilization of the women, ecological depletion and contamination, relentless cultural saturation—all these events pertain not only to Puerto Rican historical reality but to the recent American past as well. And in no foreign national literature is this seamy, repressed side of the "American century" captured at closer range than in the novels of Zeno Gandía and Enrique Laguerre, the stories of José Luis González and Pedro Juan Soto, the poetry of Luis Palés Matos and Julia de Burgos, or the plays of René Marqués and Jaime Carrero. Understandably, Puerto Rican literature in the twentieth century has been obsessed with the United States, whose presence not only lurks, allegorically, as the awesome colossus to the north but is manifest in every aspect of national life. Those intent on reworking literary curricula and boundaries would thus do well to heed this telling record of United States politics and culture as they bear on neighboring peoples and nationalities.

Closer still, of course, and more directly pertinent to a "new" American literary history, is the Puerto Rican literature produced in the United States. Not until the late 1960s, when distinctly Nuyorican voices emerged on the American literary landscape, did it occur to anyone to speak of a Puerto Rican literature emanating from life in this country. How, indeed, could such an uprooted and downtrodden community even be expected to produce a literature? Such relative newcomers, many lacking in basic literacy skills in either English or Spanish, were assumed to be still caught up in the immigrant syndrome, or worse, to be languishing in what Oscar Lewis termed the "culture of poverty." But in books like Piri Thomas's *Down These Mean Streets* and Pedro Pietri's *Puerto Rican Obituary*, there was suddenly a literature by Puerto Ricans, in English and decidedly in—and against—the American grain. 3

This initial impetus has since grown into a varied but coherent literary movement, and over the past decade the Nuyoricans have come to make up an identifiable current in North American literature. That this movement also retains its association to Puerto Rico's national literature and, by extension, to Latin American literary concerns is a crucial though more complex matter. In fact, it is Nuyorican literature's position straddling two national literatures and hemispheric perspectives that most significantly distinguishes it among the American minority literatures. In any case, those years of cultural and political awakening in the late 1960s generated an active literary practice among Puerto Ricans born and raised in the United States, who have managed to expound a distinctive problematic language with a bare minimum of institutional or infrastructural support. 4

Critical and historical interest in this new literature has also grown. Journal articles and introductions to books and anthologies, though scattered, have helped provide some context and approaches. Along with critics like Edna Acosta-Belén, Efraín Barradas, and John Miller, Wolfgang Binder, professor 5 of American studies at the University of Erlangen, deserves special mention. His substantial work on contemporary Puerto Rican literature is based on an ample knowledge of the material and close familiarity with many of the authors. Further study of this kind has ascertained with increasing clarity that Puerto Rican literature in the United States was not born, sui generis, in the late 1960s and that its scope, like that of other emerging literatures, cannot be properly accounted for if analysis is limited by the reigning norms of genre, fictionality, language, or national demarcation.

In 1982 there appeared the first, and still the only, book on Puerto Rican literature in the United States, Eugene Mohr's *The Nuyorican Experience*. Mohr, professor of English at the University of Puerto Rico, offers a helpful overview of many of the works and authors and suggests some lines of historical periodization. I will therefore refer to Mohr's book, and especially to some of its omissions, in reviewing briefly the contours of Puerto Rican literature in the United States. How far back does it go, and what were the major stages leading to the present Nuyorican style and sensibility? To what extent does its very existence challenge the notion of literary and cultural canons, and how does this literature relate to other noncanonical and anticanonical literatures in the United States?

The first Puerto Ricans to write about life in the United States were political exiles from the independence struggle against Spain, who came to New York in the late decades of the nineteenth century to escape the clutches of the colonial authorities. Some of Puerto Rico's most prominent intellectual and revolutionary leaders, such as Eugenio María de Hostos, Ramón Emeterio Betances, Lola Rodríguez de Tío, and Sotero Figueroa, spent more or less extended periods in New York, where along with fellow exiles from Cuba they charted further steps to free their countries from Spanish rule. The lofty ideals of "Antillean unity" found concrete expression in the establishment of the Cuban and Puerto Rican Revolutionary Party, under the leadership of the eminent Cuban patriot Jose Martí. This early community was largely composed of the radical patriotic elite, but there was already a solid base of artisans and laborers who lent support to the many organizational activities. It should also be mentioned that one of these first settlers from Puerto Rico was Arturo Alfonso Schomburg, a founder of the Club Dos Antillas and, in later years, a scholar of the African experience.

The writings that give testimonial accounts and impressions of those years in New York are scattered in diaries, correspondences, and the often short-lived revolutionary newspapers and still await compilation and perusal. Perhaps the most extended and revealing text to have been uncovered thus far is a personal article by the Puerto Rican poet and revolutionary martyr Francisco Gonzalo Marín. "Pachín" Marín, a typesetter by trade who died in combat in the mountains of Cuba, figures significantly in the history of Puerto Rican poetry because of his emphatic break with the stale, airy clichés of romantic verse and his introduction of an ironic, conversational tone and language. In

"Nueva York por dentro: Una faz de su vida bohemia," he offers a pointed critical reflection on New York City as experienced by the hopeful but destitute Puerto Rican immigrant.

In *The Nuyorican Experience* Eugene Mohr makes no mention of "Pachín" Marín or of these first, nineteenth-century samples of Puerto Rican writing in New York, though the Cuban critic Emilio Jorge Rodríguez has drawn proper attention to them. The sources are of course still scarce, and that period of political exile was clearly distinct in character from the later stages, which were conditioned by the labor immigration under direct colonial supervision. Nevertheless, writings like that of "Pachín" Marín and some of the diary entries and letters of Hostos and others carry immense prognostic power in view of subsequent historical and literary developments. In a history of Puerto Rican literature in the United States they provide an invaluable antecedent perspective, a prelude of foreboding, even before the fateful events of 1898. When read along with the essays and sketches of Jose Martí on New York and the United States, these materials offer the earliest "inside" view of American society by Caribbean writers and intellectuals. [9]

Mohr dates the origins of "the Nuyorican experience" from Bernardo Vega's arrival in New York in 1916, as recounted in the opening chapter of Vega's memoirs. While the *Memorias de Bernardo Vega* (*Memoirs of Bernardo Vega*) is a logical starting point, since it chronicles the Puerto Rican community from the earliest period, the book was actually written in the late 1940s and was not published until 1977. (An English translation appeared in 1984.) Despite the book's belated appearance, though, Bernardo Vega was definitely one of the "pioneers." He and his work belong to and stand for that period from the First through the Second World War (1917–45), which saw the growth and consolidation of the immigrant community following the Jones Act that decreed citizenship (1917) and preceding the mass migration after 1945. In contrast to the political exiles and other temporary or occasional sojourners to New York, Bernardo Vega was also, in Mohr's terms, a "proto-Nuyorican": though he eventually returned to Puerto Rico late in life (he lived there in the late 1950s and the 1960s), Vega was among the first Puerto Ricans to write about New York as one who was here to stay. [10]

Puerto Rican literature of this first stage showed many of the signs of an immigrant literature, just as the community itself, still relatively modest in size, resembled that of earlier immigrant groups in social status, hopes for advancement, and civic participation. The published writing was overwhelmingly of a journalistic and autobiographical kind: personal sketches and anecdotes, jokes and *relatos* printed in the scores of Spanish-language newspapers and magazines that cropped up and died out over the years. It is a first-person testimonial literature: the recent arrivals capturing, in the home language, the jarring changes and first adjustments as they undergo them. [11]

Yet the analogy to European immigrant experience was elusive even then, long before the momentous changes of midcentury made it clear that something [12] other than upward mobility and eventual assimilation awaited Puerto Ricans on the mainland. The most important difference, which has conditioned the entire migration and settlement, is the abiding colonial relationship between Puerto Rico and the United States. Puerto Ricans came here as foreign nationals, a fact that American citizenship and accommodationist ideology tend to obscure; but they also arrived as a subject people. The testimonial and journalistic literature of the early period illustrate that Puerto Ricans entering this country, even those most blinded by illusions of success and fortune, tended to be aware of this discrepant, disadvantageous status.

For that reason, concern for the home country and attachment to national cultural traditions remained highly active, as did the sense of particular social vulnerability in the United States. The discrimination met by the "newcomers" was compounded by racial and cultural prejudice, as the black Puerto Rican writer and political leader Jesús Colón portrays so poignantly in his book of autobiographical sketches set in those earlier decades, *A Puerto Rican in New York*. In both of these senses—the strong base in a distinct and maligned cultural heritage and the attentiveness and resistance to social inequality—Puerto Rican writing in the United States, even in this initial testimonial stage, needs to be read as a colonial literature. Its deeper problematic makes it more akin to the minority literatures of oppressed groups than to the literary practice and purposes of "ethnic" immigrants. 13

Another sign of this kinship, and of the direct colonial context, has to do with the boundaries of literary expression established by the norms of print culture. For in spite of the abundant periodical literature, with its wealth of narrative and poetic samples, in that period and in subsequent periods of Puerto Rican immigrant life surely the most widespread and influential form of verbal culture has been transmitted, not through publication, but through oral testimony and through the music. The work of oral historians in gathering the reminiscences of surviving "pioneers" will be indispensable in supplementing the study of printed texts. Also of foremost importance in this regard is the collection and analysis of the popular songs of the migration, the hundreds of boleros, plenas, and example of *jíbaro* or peasant music dealing with Puerto Rican life in the United States, which enjoyed immense popularity throughout the emigrant community. Starting in the 1920s, when many folk musicians joined the migration from the Island to New York, the popular song has played a central role in the cultural life of Puerto Ricans in this country. It needs to be recognized as an integral part of the people's "literary" production. Only in recent years, and mainly in reference to the "salsa" style of the present generation, have there been any attempts to cull these sources for broader cultural and theoretical meanings. But it was in those earlier decades, when favorites like Rafael Hernández, Pedro Flores, Ramito, Mon Rivera, Cortijo, and Tito Rodríguez were in New York composing and performing songs about Puerto Rican life here, that this tradition of the popular song began. 14

A turning point in Puerto Rican literature, before the advent of the Nuyoricans   15
in the late 1960s, came around 1950. This second stage covers the years 1945–65.
Those two decades after World War II saw the rapid industrialization of Puerto
Rico under Operation Bootstrap, and hundreds of thousands of Puerto Rican workers
migrated to New York and other United States cities. This avalanche of newly
arriving families, a significant part of the country's displaced agricultural proletariat, drastically changed the character of the Puerto Rican immigrant community, distancing it still further from the familiar immigrant experience. The "Puerto
Rican problem" became more urgent than ever for official and mainstream America, as did the infusion of drugs, criminality, and the forces of incrimination into
the crowded Puerto Rican neighborhoods. It should be remembered that *West Side
Story*, written and first performed in the mid-1950s, was intended to ease this ex-
plosive situation, though it actually has had the long-term effect of reinforcing
some of the very stereotypes, so rampant in the dominant culture, that it sought
to dispel. The same must be said of Oscar Lewis's book *La vida* and its infamous
notion of the "culture of poverty."

It was in this period and because of these conditions that the migration   16
and the emigrant community in the United States became major themes in
Puerto Rican national literature. In prior decades some authors from the Island
had of course shown an interest in their uprooted compatriots, setting their
works in New York and choosing immigrants as their protagonists: parts of *El
negocio* and *Los redentores*, the later novels of Manuel Zeno Gandía, take place in
the United States, and frequent bibliographical reference is made to still another
unpublished novel by Zeno Gandía entitled *Hubo un escándalo* (or *En Nueva
York*), though it has not yet been possible to study that manuscript. José de
Diego Padró, an interesting but neglected writer active between 1910 and 1930,
set much of his long bizarre novel *En Babia* in New York, as did the dramatist
Fernando Sierra Berdecía in his comedy *Esta noche juega el jóker*. But these are
random and rare exceptions and still do not indicate any inclusion of emigrant
experience in the thematic preoccupations of the national literature.

By midcentury, though, accompanying the more general shift in the lit-   17
erature from a rural to an urban focus, the attention of Island authors turned
decisively to the reality of mass migration and the emigrant barrio. Many
writers, such as René Marqués, Enrique Laguerre, José Luis González, and
Emilio Díaz Valcárcel, came here in those years to witness it directly, while a
writer like Pedro Juan Soto, later identified more with the Island literature,
actually lived through the emigration firsthand. The result was a flurry of
narrative and theatrical works, all appearing in the 1950s and early 1960s, some
of which still stand today as the most powerful fictional renditions of Puerto
Rican life in the United States. In contrast to the primarily testimonial writings
of the previous period, this was the first "literature," in the narrow sense, about
the community here, in which imaginative invention, dramatic structure, and
stylistic technique are used to heighten the impact of historical and autobiographical experience.

Despite the undeniable artistic merit of some of this work—I would single   18 out the stories of José Luis González, Soto's *Spiks*, and, for historical reasons, René Marqués's *La carreta*—it is also clearly a literature *about* Puerto Ricans in the United States rather than *of* that community. Mohr aptly entitles his second chapter "Views from an Island." That these are the "views" of visiting or temporary sojourners is evident in various ways but is not necessarily a detriment to their literary value. The tendency is to present the arrival and settlement experience in strict existential and instantaneous terms; instead of process and interaction there is above all culture shock and intense personal dislocation. What these glimpses and miniatures gain in emotional intensity they often lose in their reduction of a complex, collective, and unfolding reality to a snapshot of individual behavior. Another sign of the unfamiliarity and distance between the writer and the New York community is the language: though an occasional English or "Spanglish" usage appears for authenticating purposes, there is a general reliance on standard literary Spanish or, as in *La carreta*, a naturalistic transcription of Puerto Rican dialect. What is missing is any resonance of the community's own language practice, which even then, in the 1950s, was already tending toward the intricate mixing and code switching characteristic of Puerto Rican speech in the United States.

But despite such problems, these "views from an island" rightly remain   19
some of the best-known works of Puerto Rican literature in the United States, their literary impact generally strengthened by the critical, anticolonial standpoint of the authors. The pitiable condition of the authors' compatriots in United States cities is attributed and linked to the status of Puerto Rico as a direct colony. This perspective, and the constant focus on working-class characters, helps dispel the tone of naive optimism and accommodationism that had characterized the writings of such earlier petit bourgeois observers of the emigrant community as Juan B. Huyke and Pedro Juan Labarthe. The writings of Soto, González, and others, because of their quality and the authors' grounding in the national literature of the Island, form an important link to Latin American literature. A story like González's "La noche que volvimos a ser gente," for example, is clearly a work of contemporary Latin American fiction, even though it is set in New York and its attention focuses on the subways and streets of the urban United States. The same is true of Díaz Valcárcel's novel *Harlem todos los días* and many more of these works.

It should be emphasized that during the 1950s there was also a "view from   20
within" the Puerto Rican community, a far less known literature by Puerto Ricans who had been here all along and who, lovingly or not, considered the barrio home. Here again Bernardo Vega and Jesús Colón come to mind, for although the *Memorias* and *A Puerto Rican in New York* chronicle the arrival and settlement over the decades, they were not written until the late 1940s and 1950s. There were also a number of Puerto Rican poets who had been living in New York for decades and who by the 1950s began to see themselves as a distinctive voice within the national poetry; among them were Juan Avilés, Emilio Delgado, Clemente Soto Vélez, Pedro Carrasquillo, Jorge Brandon, and José Dávila Semprít. Back in the 1940s this group had included as well Puerto

Rico's foremost woman poet, Julia de Burgos. What little is available of this material shows it to be largely conventional Spanish-language verse making little reference to the migration or to life in New York, much less anticipating in any way the complex bilingual situation of the generation to come. But much more of interest may still be found with further study, and it is important to refer to Pedro Carrasquillo for his popular *décimas* about a *jíbaro* in New York, to Dávila Sempít for his forceful political poetry, and to Soto Vélez and Brandon for the examples they set for many of the younger poets.

Perhaps the best example of literature from within the community at midcentury is the novel *Trópico en Manhattan* by Guillermo Cotto-Thorner. The contrast with the Island authors' treatment of the emigrant experience is striking: the shock of arrival and first transitions is extended and lent historical depth; individual traumas and tribulations are woven into a more elaborate interpersonal and social context. Most interesting of all as a sign of the author's proximity to and involvement in the community is, once again, the language. The Spanish of *Trópico en Manhattan*, especially in certain dialogue passages, is at times interspersed with bilingual neologisms of various kinds. And at the end of the book there is a lengthy glossary of what Cotto-Thorner calls "Neorkismos." [21]

The contrast between the observers' and the participants' views in Puerto Rican literature of this period does not reflect so much the literary quality as the relation of the writers to the literature's historical development. A novel like *Trópico en Manhattan* may not surpass the stories of José Luis González and Pedro Juan Soto, but it does more extensively reveal the social contradictions internal to the community and give them a sense of epic duration and process. With regard to literary history, that relatively unknown and forgotten novel, with its early sensitivity to "Neorkismos," may more directly prefigure the voice and vantage point of the Nuyoricans than does *La carreta*, or even *Spiks*. [22]

Another such transitional author of the period 1945–65 is Jaime Carrero, who also works to clarify that the "outsider-insider" contrast refers not only to place of residence but to cultural perspective. Carrero, whose bilingual poetry volume *Jet neorriqueño: Neo-Rican Jet Liner* directly foreshadowed the onset of Nuyorican literature in New York, is from the Island, having been to New York for college and other visits. As Eugene Mohr points out, what distinguishes Carrero from those other Island-based writers is "the persistence of his interest in the *colonia* and his sympathy with the Nuyorican viewpoint." His attempts at bilingual verse and especially his plays, from *Pipo subway no sabe reir* to *El lucky seven*, give vivid literary expression to this internal, participants' perspective. Carrero has also written a novel (*Raquelo tiene un mensaje*) about the trauma of Nuyorican return migration to the Island, but Pedro Juan Soto's *Ardiente suelo fría estación* is as yet unequaled in its treatment of that experience. [23]

The third, Nuyorican stage in emigrant Puerto Rican literature arose with no direct reference to or evident knowledge of the writings of either earlier period. Yet despite this apparent disconnection, Nuyorican creative expression effectively draws together the firsthand testimonial stance of the "pioneer" stage and [24] the fictional, imaginative approach of writers of the 1950s and 1960s. This combining of autobiographical and imaginative modes of community portrayal is clearest perhaps in the prose fiction: *Down These Mean Streets*, Nicholasa Mohr's *Nilda* and Edward Rivera's *Family Installments* are all closer to the testimonial novel than to any of the narrative works of previous years.

This sense of culminating and synthesizing of the earlier phases indicates 25 that with the Nuyoricans the Puerto Rican community in the United States has arrived at a modality of literary expression corresponding to its position as a nonassimilating colonial minority. The most obvious mark of this new literature emanating from the community is the language; the switch from Spanish to English and bilingual writing. This language transfer should not be mistaken for assimilation in a wide cultural sense: as the content of the literature indicates, using English is a sign of being here, not necessarily of liking it here or of belonging.

By now, the Nuyorican period of United States-based Puerto Rican literature is already unfolding a history of its own. The sensationalist tenor of the 26 initial outburst has given way to a greater concern for the everyday lives of Puerto Rican working people. The growing diversity and sophistication of the movement is evident in the emergence of women writers and female perspectives, as in books like Sandra María Esteves's *Yerba buena* and Nicholasa Mohr's *Rituals of Survival*, and in the appearance of writers in other parts of the United States. Also of key importance is the ongoing use of an actively bilingual literary field. For it becomes clear that, in the literature as in the community, the switch from Spanish to English is by no means complete or smooth, and it certainly is not a sign of cultural accommodation. For all the young writers Spanish remains a key language-culture of reference even when not used, and some, like Tato Laviera, demonstrate full bilingual capacity in their writing. There also continues to be a Spanish-language literature by Puerto Ricans living here, some of which hovers between Nuyorican concerns and styles and those of contemporary Island literature. Such writers as Iván Silén and Victor Fragoso, like Jaime Carrero and Guillermo Cotto-Thorner before them, have served as important bridges between the two language poles of present-day Puerto Rican writing.

Thus, rather than abandoning one language in favor of another, contemporary Puerto Rican literature in the United States actually exhibits the full 27 range of bilingual and interlingual use. Like Mexican-American and other minority literatures, it cannot be understood and assessed on the basis of a strict English-language conceptualization of "American" literature, or of literary practice in general. Some of the best Nuyorican texts require knowledge of Spanish and English, which does not make them any less a part of American, or Puerto Rican, literature. And the choice and inclusiveness of a literary language is but one aspect of a broader process of cultural interaction between Puerto Ricans and the various nationalities they encounter in the United States.

By its Nuyorican stage Puerto Rican literature in the United States comes 28 to share the features of "minority" or noncanonical literatures of the United

States. Like them it is a literature of recovery and collective affirmation, and it is a literature of "mingling and sharing," of interaction and exchange with neighboring, complementary cultures. What stronger source, after all, for the emergence of Nuyorican literature than Afro-American literature and political culture? What more comparable a context of literary expression than Chicano writing of the same period?

Perhaps most distinctly among these literatures, though, Puerto Rican   29
writing today is a literature of straddling, a literature operative within and between two national literatures and marginal in both. In this respect Nuyorican writing may well come to serve as a model or paradigm for emerging literatures by other Caribbean groups in the United States, such as Dominicans, Haitians, and Jamaicans. Despite the sharp disconnections between Island- and United States–based traditions, and between stages of the literary history here, it is still necessary to talk about modern Puerto Rican literature as a whole and of the emigrant literature—including the Nuyorican—as an extension of manifestation of that national literature. This inclusion within, or integral association with, a different and in some ways opposing national culture stretches the notion of a pluralist American canon to the limit. Ethnic, religious, and racial diversity is one thing, but a plurality of nations and national languages within the American canon—that is a different and more serious issue. After all, if Tato Laviera and Nicholasa Mohr are eligible for canonical status, why not José Louis González or Julia de Burgos, or, for that matter, Manuel Zeno Gandía, the author of the great Puerto Rican novel *La charca*?

Yes, what about *La charca*? It's a fine novel; in fact, if it had been written   30
by an author from a "big" country, say France or Russia, or even Argentina or Mexico, it would probably be more widely admired and even held up as an example of late nineteenth-century realism. It was published in 1894, before the United States acquired the Island, and its plot is set several decades earlier, long before any significant relations had developed between the two countries. And yet, though it does not mention or refer to the United States, *La charca* is still, somehow, about America, a literary pre-sentiment of what contact with North American society had in store for Puerto Rico. The isolated mountain coffee plantation issues into the wider world of commerce and international dealings, represented in Puerto Rican history, and in Zeno Gandía's later novels, by the United States. Like Jose Martí, "Pachín" Marín, and other Latin American intellectuals of the time, Zeno Gandía anticipated the coming of the United States' values and power. Even at such a remove, with America's presence still but a metaphor, *La charca* touches the American canon and contributes impressively to the larger task of American literature. ◆

Works Cited

Binder, Wolfgang. *"Anglos are weird people for me"*: *Interviews with Chicanos and Puerto Ricans.* Berlin: John F. Kennedy-Institut für Nordamerikastudien at Freie Universität, 1979.

———. *Puerto Ricaner in New York: Volk zwischen zwei Kulturen.* Erlangen: Städtische Galerie, 1978.

Carrero, Jaime. *Jet neorriqueño: Neo-Rican Jet Liner.* San Germán: Universidad Interamericana, 1964.

———. *Pipo subway no sabe reir.* Río Piedras: Ediciones Puerto, 1973.

———. *Raquelo tiene un mensaje.* San Juan: Manuel Pareja, 1970.

Colón, Jesús. *A Puerto Rican in New York and Other Sketches.* New York: Mainstream, 1961.

Cotto-Thorner, Guillermo, *Trópico en Manhattan.* San Juan: Editorial Cordillera. 1960.

Diaz Valcárcel, Emilio. *Harlem todos los días.* México: Editorial Nueva Imagen, 1978.

Duany, Jorge. "Popular Music in Puerto Rico: Toward an Anthropology of Salsa." *Latin American Music Review* 5.2 (1984): 186–216.

Esteves, Sandra María. *Yerba buena.* Greenfield: Greenfield Review, 1980.

Gelfant, Blanche H. "Mingling and Sharing in American Literature: Teaching Ethnic Fiction." *College English* 43 (1981): 763–72.

González, José Luis. "La noche que volvimos a ser gente." *Mambru se fué a la guerra.* México: Mortiz, 1972. 117–34.

Lewis, Oscar, *La Vida: A Puerto Rican Family in the Culture of Poverty.* New York: Random, 1965.

Marín, Pachín. "Nueva York por dentro: Una faz de su vida bohemia." *La gaceta del pueblo* [1892?].

Mohr, Eugene. *The Nuyorican Experience: Literature of the Puerto Rican Minority.* Westport: Greenwood, 1982.

Mohr, Nicholasa. *Nilda.* New York: Harper, 1973.

———. *Rituals of Survival.* Houston: Arte Público, 1985.

Padró, José de Diego, *En Babia.* México: El Manuscripto de un Braquicéfalo, 1961.

Pietri, Pedro. *Puerto Rican Obituary.* New York: Monthly Review, 1973.

Rivera, Edward. *Family Installments.* New York: Penguin, 1983.

Rodríguez, Emilio Jorge. "Apuntes sobre la visión del emigrante en la narrative puertorriqueña." *Primer seminario sobre la situaction de las comunidades negra, chicana, cubana, india y puertorriqueña en Estados Unidos.* Havana: Editora Política, 1984. 445–85.

Sierra Berdecía, Fernando. *Esta noche juega el jóker.* San Juan: Biblioteco de Autores Puertorriqueños, 1939. San Juan: Instituto de Cultura Puertorriqueña, 1960.

Thomas, Piri. *Down These Mean Streets.* New York: Knopf, 1967.

Vega, Bernardo. *Memoirs of Bernardo Vega.* Ed. César Andreu Iglesias. Trans. Juan Flores. New York: Monthly Review, 1984.

Zeno Gandía, Manuel, *La charca.* Trans. Kal Wagenheim. Maplewood: Waterfront, 1984.

———. *El negocio.* Río Piedras: Editorial Edil, 1973.

———. *Los redentores. Obras completas.* Vol. 2. Río Piedras: Instituto de Cultura Puertorriqueña, 1973.

◆ Responding

1. Working individually or in a group, define "literary canon." What works are traditionally part of the American literary canon? What does Flores want to include?

2. Using examples from the readings and your own experience, argue for or against broadening the canon. For additional information, you might want to read the essay by David Mura in Chapter 9.

3. Outline the stages in the development of Puerto Rican literature that Flores defines in his article.

4. According to Flores, what are the characteristics of immigrant literature? Compare immigrant literature to what Flores calls "minority literature." How is contemporary Puerto Rican literature distinct from both? Write an essay agreeing or disagreeing with Flores when he says that Puerto Rican literature is "a literature operative within and between two national literatures and marginal in both. . . . This inclusion within, or integral association with, a different and in some ways opposing national culture stretches the notion of a pluralist American canon to the limit."

◆

C O N N E C T I N G

Critical Thinking and Writing

1. For many Puerto Ricans in New York, the Island continues to occupy an important place in their thoughts and dreams. Compare the different attitudes toward Puerto Rico held by the different characters in the readings.

2. People moving to a new country often have a difficult time adjusting because they speak a different language or dialect and have different customs or a different culture. Compare the experiences of European immigrants, such as the Italians, with the experiences of the Puerto Ricans in this chapter.

3. Many of the readings in this chapter describe situations in which workers are exploited or their opportunities limited. Write an essay arguing for or against the idea that much of that exploitation has been based on racism. You may use examples from other chapters of the text.

4. Write an essay defining what it means to be educated; illustrate your definition with examples from the readings and from your own observations. In your definition, does being educated include being "street smart" as well as "book

smart"? Consider basic skills learned in school and those learned through experience. For example, Piri Thomas's mother, although not formally educated, is well informed about her own culture, while Santos, who has a formal education, knows very little about his. The Boss in "A Soul Above Buttons," has practical knowledge but can't read and write.

5. Some of the families in this section support each other emotionally as well as economically. Using examples from the readings, write an essay discussing the importance of this support.

6. Many of the readings describe situations involving insider/outsider relationships. Write an essay discussing these relationships, using specific examples from the text.

7. Compare the working conditions of the *tabaqueros* with those of other immigrant groups, such as Chinese railroad workers. How do you account for the differences?

8. Most Puerto Rican immigrants settled in New York City. Speculate about the attraction of that particular large urban area as compared to that of a smaller town or a rural area. Focus on conditions and opportunities in each environment.

9. Using examples from this chapter, other readings in this book, and your own experience, write an essay discussing the role of language and culture in forging bonds within or between immigrant groups.

10. Design your own essay topic based on an issue in these readings that engaged your interest.

For Further Research

1. Research the current political situation in Puerto Rico. Consider the likelihood of statehood as well as other options available for the territory.

2. Investigate the current demographics of Puerto Ricans in the United States. How many people come to the continental United States each year? Where do they settle? What reasons do they have for leaving the island? Compare those reasons to those of other current immigrant groups—for example, those from Latin America.

◆

REFERENCES AND ADDITIONAL SOURCES

Acosta-Belén, Edna, and Barbara R. Sjostrom, eds. *The Hispanic Experience in the United States: Contemporary Issues and Perspectives*. New York: Praeger, 1988.

Centro de Estudios Puertorriqueños, Oral History Task Force. *Labor Migration under Capitalism: The Puerto Rican Experience*. New York: Monthly Review Press, 1979.

Cordasco, Francesco, and Eugene Bucchioni, eds. *The Puerto Rican Experience: A Sociological Textbook*. Tottowa, N.J.: Rowman and Littlefield, 1973.

———. *The Puerto Ricans, 1493–1973: A Chronology and Fact Book*. Dobbs Ferry, N.Y.: Oceana, 1973.

Dietz, James. *Economic History of Puerto Rico*. Princeton: Princeton University Press, 1986.

Fitzpatrick, Joseph P. *Puerto Rican Americans: The Meaning of Migration to the Mainland*. Englewood Cliffs, N.J.: Prentice-Hall, 1971.

Garcia-Passalacqua, Juan Manual. *Puerto Rico: Equality and Freedom at Issue*. New York: Praeger, 1984.

Hauberg, Clifford A. *Puerto Rico and the Puerto Ricans*. New York: Hippocrene Books, 1984.

Hernández Alvarez, José. *Return Migration to Puerto Rico*. Berkeley: Institute of International Studies, University of California, 1967.

Jennings, James, and Monte Rivera. *Puerto Rican Politics in Urban America*. Westport, Conn.: Greenwood, 1984.

Lopez, Adalberto, ed. *The Puerto Ricans: Their History, Culture and Society*. Cambridge, Mass.: Schenkman, 1981.

Mohr, Eugene V. *The Nuyorican Experience: Literature of the Puerto Rican Minority*. Westport, Conn.: Greenwood, 1982.

Morales Carrión, Arturo. *Puerto Rico: A Political and Cultural History*. New York: W.W. Norton, 1983.

Padilla, Elena. *Up from Puerto Rico*. New York: Columbia University Press, 1958.

Rodriguez, Clara E., et al., eds. *The Puerto Rican Struggle: Essays on Survival in the U.S.* Maplewood, N.J.: Waterfront, 1984.

Sanchez Korrol, Virginia E. *From Colonia to Community: The History of Puerto Ricans in New York City, 1917–1948*. Westport, Conn.: Greenwood, 1983.

Stevens-Arroyo, Anthony M. and Ana María Díaz Ramírez. "Puerto Ricans in the States" in *The Minority Report*, edited by A. G. Dworkin and R. J. Dworkin. 2nd edition. New York: Holt, Rinehart and Winston, pp. 196–232.

United States Commission on Civil Rights. *Puerto Ricans in the Continental United States: An Uncertain Future*. Washington, D.C.: GPO, 1976.

Weisskoff, Richard. *Factories and Food Stamps*. Baltimore: Johns Hopkins University Press, 1985.

Young Lords Party. *Palante: Young Lords Party*. New York: McGraw Hill, 1971.

American serviceman visits his parents in an Idaho internment camp. Even though his brother had been killed in the war, and he was fighting for America, his parents were still interned. (National Archives)

Chapter 5

JAPANESE AMERICANS
The Internment Experience

Detail of background photo, Heart Mountain, Wyoming, Japanese American internment camp, with tarpaper-covered barracks housing 10,000 citizens. (National Archives)

◆ SETTING THE HISTORICAL CONTEXT ◆

IN HER BOOK *Nisei Daughter*, Monica Sone quotes her brother's question: "Doesn't my citizenship mean a single blessed thing to anyone?" This question, rhetorical as it was, helps to dramatize the sense of exasperation and outrage felt by Japanese Americans when they learned that they would have to leave their homes and businesses and move to remote camps, ostensibly to protect national security. This forced resettlement, known as the Internment, followed the United States's declaration of war against Japan and affected both Japanese nationals and those persons of Japanese ancestry who were also American citizens. Many people, both within and outside the Japanese community, look back on this action, like the attack on Pearl Harbor itself, as an event that, in the words of Franklin Delano Roosevelt, "would live in infamy."

The Internment was not, of course, the first time that immigrants from Japan had suffered because of their race and country of origin. Unable to leave Japan until late in the nineteenth century because of prohibitions maintained by the Japanese government, the first groups of Japanese to immigrate found a country already reeling from mass immigration and reluctant to accept more foreigners. Exclusionists, including such influential people as the writer Jack London and Senator Henry Cabot Lodge, campaigned to have quotas set on those of non-European origin. Exclusionists sought to extend to the Japanese the Chinese Exclusion Acts of 1882 and 1902.

When that was unsuccessful, they pressured the federal government to negotiate restrictive quotas with the emperor of Japan. These negotiations resulted in the Gentlemen's Agreement, which was announced in 1908. The agreement stipulated how many Japanese would be allowed to immigrate to the United States each year; it also prohibited unskilled workers (a large percentage of those who would typically emigrate) from coming to America.

Once in the United States, Japanese immigrants faced discrimination in employment and education. Unions excluded them, and they were often prohibited from holding professional positions. School districts, such as those of San Francisco, attempted to segregate Japanese students from white students. Although segregation was ordered stopped in 1906 by President Roosevelt, who was concerned about its effect on the American government's relations with Japan, similar policies remained in effect in other communities as late as 1936, when they were declared unconstitutional.

During the period between 1910 and 1920, "protective" leagues, special interest groups motivated by racial bigotry and exaggerated economic fears, pressured the legislature to restrict the economic power of the Japanese even further. As a result of such pressure, the Alien Land Act, passed in 1913, prohibited Japanese immigrants from owning land or deeding it to their relatives and from leasing land for more than three years. Stricter legislation passed in 1920 prevented the Japanese from leasing agricultural land.

Unlike European immigrants, Japanese immigrants were prevented by law from becoming naturalized American citizens. Citing a 1790 law that restricted citizenship to whites, the courts and the Justice Department denied citizenship to both the Chinese (in 1882) and the Japanese (in 1906 and 1913). This racial requirement for naturalization was upheld by the Supreme Court as late as 1922, when the Court ruled that Takao Ozawa was ineligible for citizenship because of his race. In 1924 Congress passed the Reed Johnson Act, which allowed only those immigrants racially eligible for citizenship to enter the country; this act cut off immigration from Japan almost completely.

These legal and social restrictions affected the development of the Japanese American community before World War II in large part by determining the composition of that community. The first wave of immigration took place between 1890, when the emperor lifted his ban on emigration, and the U.S.-Japanese Gentlemen's Agreement of 1907. These immigrants were primarily unmarried, unskilled workers who planned to work abroad until they had earned enough money to return to Japan as successful and wealthy men. Those who were married often planned to settle in the United States and send to Japan for their wives. The immigrants who came after the signing of the Gentlemen's Agreement were primarily skilled workers who established themselves in business or in agriculture.

With the Reed Johnson Act of 1924, the shape of the community changed. Because no new Japanese immigrants were allowed to enter the country, a gap in age and culture developed between the dwindling Issei (first-generation immigrants, born in Japan) and the increasing Nisei (second-generation, those born in the United States). At the same time, the discrimination experienced in the larger society led the Japanese community to hold itself separate. As such it retained much of its cultural heritage and identity longer than most other immigrant groups. Children were taught the importance of hard work, obedience to authority, and self-sacrifice. They were taught Japanese language and culture in schools established and supported by their parents; many children were sent to Japan to complete their education.

Despite restrictive immigration, discrimination in employment, and legislation barring Japanese from land ownership, members of the Japanese community did find employment. Many worked in agriculture, commercial fishing, and canning, where their contributions to the economy became increasingly important. Japanese farmers were responsible for a large percentage of the berries and vegetables grown in California; this helped to provide a base for the dramatic population increase experienced during the first third of the twentieth century. Japanese involvement in commercial fishing and canning helped these industries to thrive in Southern California and throughout the Pacific Northwest. At the same time, other Japanese immigrants helped to establish an urban service economy. They worked in and later founded their own small restaurants, hotels, and shops, which primarily served the immigrant population, and in gardening and laundry services for those outside their own community. Although some immigrants, such as George Shima and Masajiro Furiya, were able to acquire great wealth as a result of wise investments and perseverance, many others prospered in less dramatic ways. They saved money and purchased property, putting the deeds in the names of their American-born children. Belief remained strong that hard work and academic achievement would lead to success.

This belief was tested when the United States entered World War II on December 8, 1941. Anti-Japanese sentiment among whites, less often expressed since the passage of the Reed Johnson Act, re-emerged. This sentiment affected not only the way in which individuals of Japanese descent were treated by the general public, but also the way in which these individuals, whether Japanese or American citizens, were treated as a group by the American government. Vocal special interest groups, as well as some members of Congress and of the American military, held the Japanese American community responsible for the Japanese government's surprise attack on Pearl Harbor, the American naval headquarters in Hawaii. Rumors circulated that Japanese immigrants, both in Hawaii and on the mainland, had been in communication with the Japanese military forces and that they had been involved in directing planes and in transmitting information to the Japanese forces. Moreover, early victories by the emperor's army in the Pacific made Americans fearful that the West Coast might be invaded.

When combined with the prevalent racial stereotypes of the period, these suspicions and fears caused Japanese Americans to be treated differently from German Americans and Italian Americans, even though the United States was also at war with Germany and Italy. Because some members of the military feared that Japanese Americans living on the West Coast could sabotage military installations, the military was able to pressure the executive branch of government to suspend many of their constitutional rights. Despite the strong protests of the United States attorney general, the government authorized extensive searches of private residences and businesses for anything that might be considered contraband. The homes of both Japanese immigrants and Japanese American citizens were searched, often in the middle of the night. As Monica Sone describes, few personal possessions were considered above suspicion; the presence of cameras or radios, Japanese newspapers, books, or magazines—or the total absence of such objects— made ordinary families the object of further government surveillance. Those who failed to answer questions to the authorities' satisfaction could be detained for further questioning. As a result, many Japanese and Japanese American heads of households—some of whom spoke little English—were rounded up and detained by the Federal Bureau of Investigation.

This time of search and seizure, painful as it was, was only a prelude to the more extensive violation of rights that members of the Japanese community experienced as the war continued. They found themselves subjected to verbal and physical abuse. Their homes and businesses were vandalized and sometimes destroyed. When the military, wary of Japanese living along the Pacific coast, asked them to move to areas farther inland, they were abused and threatened by the citizens in the inland areas. Understandably, only a small number of Japanese Americans volunteered for the program.

The military then asked President Franklin Roosevelt to begin a forced evacuation. General John DeWitt, an army officer with no combat experience but evidently a very strong anti-Asian bias, called for internment. On February 19, 1942, Roosevelt signed Executive Order 9066, which authorized the removal of certain people from military areas. DeWitt, who was given the authority to oversee the evacuation of the West Coast, stated that all persons of Japanese ancestry would be removed from that area "in the interest of military necessity." On March 18, Roosevelt established the War Relocation Authority (WRA) to handle the evacuation.

Those subject to the internment order—both Japanese immigrants and

Posting of Civilian Exclusion Order #5.

American citizens of Japanese descent, or, in the contemporary vernacular, "aliens" and "nonaliens"—were given only a few days to leave their homes and relocate in camps designated by the government as exclusion areas. Allowed to take only their bedding and a few suitcases, the Japanese were forced to sell their homes, businesses, and other property at great loss or to entrust them to fate or neighbors. After reporting to a local pick-up area, they were taken first by bus and then by train to one of ten internment camps, located in remote sections of California and Arizona, and, later, in Colorado, Utah, Idaho, and Arkansas.

Life in the camps was dismal. Dwellings consisted of hastily constructed barracks or other makeshift structures, such as recently cleared livestock exhibition halls. Barbed wire and watch towers marked the perimeter of the camps. The barracks offered little comfort and lacked adequate heat and privacy. Internees used some of their precious blankets to shield the windows from searchlights. They stood in line for meals, eating in communal kitchens where the food allotment was less than fifty cents per person per day. Their bathroom facilities were often latrines without running water. Internees were subject to curfews, monitoring, and arbitrary searches. There were usually meager "work opportunities" for adults and minimal education for children. This environment, combined with the internees' awareness that their rights were being violated, contributed to the disillusionment and restless despair described by those sent to the camps.

In 1943, one year after the internment order, the United States Army invited young male internees eighteen years old or older to serve in special units of the armed forces. When the army distributed loyalty questionnaires to all candidates and to the rest of the interned population, it found more than 17,000 men eligible for service. Many of these recruits went on to fight in the war, some earning medals for their courage. Other young men refused military service, feeling that they could not fight for a country that had refused to recognize their own rights as citizens. These people, called "No-no Boys," were segregated from the rest of the internees. Some renounced their citizenship.

In 1945 the Supreme Court ruled unanimously in the Endo case that the prolonged internment of Japanese nationals who posed no threat to the national security had been unconstitutional. This ruling brought the Internment to an end, but it was difficult for the Japanese American community, which had suffered so much, to feel much of a sense of vindication. When the internees returned from the camps, they found much of their property gone, often sold to pay back taxes. Their businesses and farms had often been dissolved or were in other hands. And in the larger society, prejudice against people of Japanese ancestry remained.

In recent years the American government has begun to acknowledge that the Internment was unjust. The Civil Liberties Act of 1988 awarded the 60,000 former internees alive on the day of signing $1.25 billion in reparations. In October 1990, Attorney General Dick Thornberg offered an apology and the first set of reparation checks to members of the Japanese community who had been interned during World War II. Speaking for the entire nation, President George Bush asserted, "We can never fully right the wrongs of the past . . . but we can take a clear stand for justice and recognize that serious injustices were done to Japanese Americans during World War II."

EXPLORING THE LITERARY AND
◆ CULTURAL CONTEXT ◆

The Internment tested an ideal and galvanized a community. Not only did it call into question the values on which the Japanese American community had built and maintained its identity, but it revealed how insubstantial American values were when fear and self-interest blinded their guardians. The questioning of values that resulted from the Internment gave rise to many works of fiction and nonfiction.

In "Pearl Harbor Echoes in Seattle," from *Nisei Daughter*, Monica Sone recalls, through a young woman's perspective, the reaction in the Japanese American community to the news that the United States was at war with Japan. The description explains how the family was affected by the government's searches of their property.

The excerpt from Jeanne Wakatsuki Houston's and James D. Houston's *Farewell to Manzanar* depicts life in the camps, and in her report we see family members in a daily struggle to adapt to a lack of privacy and personal liberty. We also see the struggle to maintain a sense of dignity and self-worth in a dehumanizing environment.

Two of the stories focus on the experience of internees who were asked to serve in the American armed forces. Toshio Mori's "Unfinished Message" tells the story of the bitter ironies experienced by a mother whose sons fight in the war. The excerpt from John Okada's novel *No-no Boy* contrasts those who were so hurt and humiliated at having their loyalty questioned that they renounced their U.S. citizenship and those who retained their loyalty.

For many Japanese Americans, the pain of the Internment did not end with the closing of the camps. The confusion and alienation that persisted well into the postwar period emerges dramatically in "Las Vegas Charley," by Hisaye Yamamoto. Janice Mirikitani expresses the hold that the past still has on a Japanese American born after World War II in her poem "We, the Dangerous."

In the essay "Roots," Ronald Takaki takes a contemporary view of the Internment and its consequences. In so doing he reveals the difficulty that many still face in attempting to come to terms with the internment.

BEGINNING: PRE-READING/WRITING

◆ *Imagine yourself in the following situation: A government agency has informed you that you must leave your home in seven days and go to an internment camp. You can take only two small suitcases and a bag of bedding with you. How do you react to what is happening? What will you do? What will you take with you and why? Share your choices with the class.*

Executive Order 9066, which was signed by President Franklin D. Roosevelt on February 19, 1942, gave the secretary of war the power to evacuate from specific military areas any residents who were considered to be risks to national security. Although the act did not mention any ethnic group, it was applied almost exclusively to Japanese Americans. Almost immediately after the order was signed, the military officer in charge ordered the evacuation of people of Japanese ancestry.

On March 18, Roosevelt established the War Relocation Authority (WRA) to take charge of this evacuation. The injustice of the Internment was not acknowledged by Congress until the 1980s, when it ordered that reparations be paid.

◆ JAPANESE RELOCATION ORDER ◆

February 19, 1942
(*Federal Register*, Vol. VII, No. 38)

Alarmed by the supposed danger of Japanese invasion of the Pacific coast after Pearl Harbor and under the apprehension that all persons of Japanese ancestry were a potential threat to the United States, the War Department persuaded the President to authorize the evacuation of some 112,000 West Coast Japanese, two-thirds of them American citizens to "relocation" centers. A Congressional Resolution of March 21, 1942, made it a misdemeanor "to knowingly enter, remain in, or leave prescribed military areas" contrary to the orders of the commanding officer of the area. This Act which, in perspective seems to have been wholly unnecessary, has been called by E. S. Corwin "the most drastic invasion of the rights of citizens of the U.S. by their own government that has thus far occurred in the history of our nation." See Doc. No. 547 and M. Grodzins, *Americans Betrayed.*

Executive Order
Authorizing the Secretary of War to Prescribe Military Areas

Whereas the successful prosecution of the war requires every possible protection against espionage and against sabotage to national-defense materials, national-defense premises, and national-defense utilities. . . . 1

Now, therefore, by virtue of the authority vested in me as President of the United States, and Commander in Chief of the Army and Navy, I hereby authorize and direct the Secretary of War, and the Military Commanders whom he may from time to time designate, whenever he or any designated Commander deems such action necessary or desirable, to prescribe military areas in such places and of such extent as he or the appropriate Military Commander may 2 determine, from which any or all persons may be excluded, and with respect to which, the right of any person to enter, remain in, or leave shall be subject to whatever restrictions the Secretary of War or the appropriate Military Commander may impose in his discretion. The Secretary of War is hereby authorized to provide for residents of any such area who are excluded therefrom, such transportation, food, shelter, and other accommodations as may be necessary, in the judgment of the Secretary of War or the said Military Commander, and until other arrangements are made, to accomplish the purpose of this order. The designation of military areas in any region or locality shall supersede designations of prohibited and restricted areas by the Attorney General under the Proclamations of December 7 and 8, 1941, and shall supersede the responsibility and authority of the Attorney General under the said Proclamations in respect of such prohibited and restricted areas.

3 I hereby further authorize and direct the Secretary of War and the said Military Commanders to take such other steps as he or the appropriate Military Commander may deem advisable to enforce compliance with the restrictions applicable to each Military area hereinabove authorized to be designated, including the use of Federal troops and other Federal Agencies, with authority to accept assistance of state and local agencies.

4 I hereby further authorize and direct all Executive Departments, independent establishments and other Federal Agencies, to assist the Secretary of War or the said Military Commanders in carrying out this Executive Order, including the furnishing of medical aid, hospitalization, food, clothing, transportation, use of land, shelter, and other supplies, equipment, utilities, facilities, and services. . . . ◆

FRANKLIN D. ROOSEVELT

◆ Responding

1. Explain the government's reasons for issuing this order.

2. How did the act directly or indirectly indicate that the Japanese would be forced to live in relocation centers?

3. Identify the powers given to the "appropriate military commander."

4. This order has been called "the most drastic invasion of the rights of citizens of the U.S. by their own government that has thus far occurred in the history of our nation" (E. S. Corwin). Explain this statement. Do you agree or disagree with it? Support your answer.

MONICA SONE

Monica Sone, born Kazuko Itoi in 1919, grew up in Seattle, Washington, where her family was in the hotel business until they were forced to evacuate. After the war she attended Hanover College and did graduate work in psychology at Case Western Reserve University.

In the following selection from her book Nisei Daughter *(1953), Sone recounts the changes in the country and in the Japanese American community after the attack on Pearl Harbor. The chapter also raises some uncomfortable questions about the relationship between national security and personal liberty during times of war.*

◆ PEARL HARBOR ECHOES IN SEATTLE ◆

On a peaceful Sunday morning, December 7, 1941, Henry, Sumi and I were at choir rehearsal singing ourselves hoarse in preparation for the annual Christmas recital of Handel's "Messiah." Suddenly Chuck Mizuno, a young University of Washington student, burst into the chapel, gasping as if he had sprinted all the way up the stairs.

"Listen, everybody!" he shouted. "Japan just bombed Pearl Harbor . . . in Hawaii! It's war!"

The terrible words hit like a blockbuster, paralyzing us. Then we smiled feebly at each other, hoping this was one of Chuck's practical jokes. Miss Hara, our music director, rapped her baton impatiently on the music stand and chided him, "Now Chuck, fun's fun, but we have work to do. Please take your place. You're already half an hour late."

But Chuck strode vehemently back to the door. "I mean it, folks, honest! I just heard the news over my car radio. Reporters are talking a blue streak. Come on down and hear it for yourselves."

With that, Chuck swept out of the room, a swirl of young men following in his wake. Henry was one of them. The rest of us stayed, rooted to our places like a row of marionettes. I felt as if a fist had smashed my pleasant little existence, breaking it into jigsaw puzzle pieces. An old wound opened up again, and I found myself shrinking inwardly from my Japanese blood, the blood of an enemy. I knew instinctively that the fact that I was an American by birthright was not going to help me escape the consequences of this unhappy war.

One girl mumbled over and over again, "It can't be, God, it can't be!" Someone else was saying, "What a spot to be in! Do you think we'll be considered Japanese or Americans?"

A boy replied quietly, "We'll be Japs, same as always. But our parents are enemy aliens now, you know."

A shocked silence followed. Henry came for Sumi and me. "Come on, let's go home," he said. 8

We ran trembling to our car. Usually Henry was a careful driver, but that morning he bore down savagely on the accelerator. Boiling angry, he shot us up Twelfth Avenue, rammed through the busy Jackson Street intersection, and rocketed up the Beacon Hill bridge. We swung violently around to the left of the Marine Hospital and swooped to the top of the hill. Then Henry slammed on the brakes and we rushed helter-skelter up to the house to get to the radio. Asthma skidded away from under our trampling feet. 9

Mother was sitting limp in the huge armchair as if she had collapsed there, listening dazedly to the turbulent radio. Her face was frozen still, and the only words she could utter were, "*Komatta neh, komatta neh.* How dreadful, how dreadful." 10

Henry put his arms around her. She told him she first heard about the attack on Pearl Harbor when one of her friends phoned her and told her to turn on the radio. 11

We pressed close against the radio, listening stiffly to the staccato outbursts of an excited reporter: "The early morning sky of Honolulu was filled with the furious buzzing of Jap Zero planes for nearly three hours, raining death and destruction on the airfields below. . . . A warship anchored beyond the Harbor was sunk. . . ." 12

We were switched to the White House. The fierce clack of teletype machines and the babble of voices surging in and out from the background almost drowned out the speaker's terse announcements. 13

With every fiber of my being I resented this war. I felt as if I were on fire. "Mama, they should never have done it," I cried. "Why did they do it? Why? Why?" 14

Mother's face turned paper white. "What do you know about it? Right or wrong, the Japanese have been chafing with resentment for years. It was bound to happen, one time or another. You're young, Ka-chan, you know very little about the ways of nations. It's not as simple as you think, but this is hardly the time to be quarreling about it, is it?" 15

"No, it's too late, too late!" and I let the tears pour down my face. 16

Father rushed home from the hotel. He was deceptively calm as he joined us in the living room. Father was a born skeptic, and he believed nothing unless he could see, feel and smell it. He regarded all newspapers and radio news with deep suspicion. He shook his head doubtfully. "It must be propaganda. With the way things are going now between America and Japan, we should expect the most fantastic rumors, and this is one of the wildest I've heard yet." But we noticed that he was firmly glued to the radio. It seemed as if the regular Sunday programs, sounding off relentlessly hour after hour on schedule, were trying to blunt the catastrophe of the morning. 17

The telephone pealed nervously all day as people searched for comfort from each other. Chris called, and I told her how miserable and confused I felt about the war. Understanding as always, Chris said, "You know how I feel 18 about you and your family, Kaz. Don't, for heaven's sake, feel the war is going to make any difference in our relationship. It's not your fault, nor mine! I wish to God it could have been prevented." Minnie called off her Sunday date with Henry. Her family was upset and they thought she should stay close to home instead of wandering downtown.

Late that night Father got a shortwave broadcast from Japan. Static sputtered, then we caught a faint voice, speaking rapidly in Japanese. Father sat unmoving as a rock, his head cocked. The man was talking about the war between Japan and America. Father bit his lips and Mother whispered to him anxiously, "It's true then, isn't it, Papa? It's true?" **19**

Father was muttering to himself, "So they really did it!" Now having heard the news in their native tongue, the war had become a reality to Father and Mother. **20**

"I suppose from now on, we'll hear about nothing but the humiliating defeats of Japan in the papers here," Mother said, resignedly. **21**

Henry and I glared indignantly at Mother, then Henry shrugged his shoulders and decided to say nothing. Discussion of politics, especially Japan versus America, had become taboo in our family for it sent tempers skyrocketing. Henry and I used to criticize Japan's aggressions in China and Manchuria while Father and Mother condemned Great Britain and America's superior attitude toward Asiatics and their interference with Japan's economic growth. During these arguments, we had eyed each other like strangers, parents against children. They left us with a hollow feeling at the pit of the stomach. **22**

Just then the shrill peel of the telephone cut off the possibility of a family argument. When I answered, a young girl's voice fluttered through breathily, "Hello, this is Taeko Tanabe. Is my mother there?" **23**

"No, she isn't, Taeko." **24**

"Thank you," and Taeko hung up before I could say another word. Her voice sounded strange. Mrs. Tanabe was one of Mother's poet friends. Taeko called three more times, and each time before I could ask her if anything was wrong, she quickly hung up. The next day we learned that Taeko was trying desperately to locate her mother because FBI agents had swept into their home and arrested Mr. Tanabe, a newspaper editor. The FBI had permitted Taeko to try to locate her mother before they took Mr. Tanabe away while they searched the house for contraband and subversive material, but she was not to let anyone else know what was happening. **25**

Next morning the newspapers fairly exploded in our faces with stories about the Japanese raids on the chain of Pacific islands. We were shocked to read Attorney General Biddle's announcement that 736 Japanese had been picked up in the United States and Hawaii. Then Mrs. Tanabe called Mother about her husband's arrest, and she said at least a hundred others had been taken from our community. Messrs. Okayama, Higashi, Sughira, Mori, Okada—we knew them all. **26**

"But why were they arrested, Papa? They weren't spies, were they?" **27**

Father replied almost curtly, "Of course not! They were probably taken 28 for questioning."

The pressure of war moved in on our little community. The Chinese 29 consul announced that all the Chinese would carry identification cards and wear "China" badges to distinguish them from the Japanese. Then I really felt left standing out in the cold. The government ordered the bank funds of all Japanese nationals frozen. Father could no longer handle financial transactions through his bank accounts, but Henry, fortunately, was of legal age so that business could be negotiated in his name.

In the afternoon President Roosevelt's formal declaration of war against 30 Japan was broadcast throughout the nation. In grave, measured words, he described the attack on Pearl Harbor as shameful, infamous. I writhed involuntarily. I could no more have escaped the stab of self-consciousness than I could have changed my Oriental features.

Monday night a complete blackout was ordered against a possible Japanese 31 air raid on the Puget Sound area. Mother assembled black cloths to cover the windows and set up candles in every room. All radio stations were silenced from seven in the evening till morning, but we gathered around the dead radio anyway, out of sheer habit. We whiled away the evening reading instructions in the newspapers on how to put out incendiary bombs and learning about the best hiding places during bombardments. When the city pulled its switches at blackout hour and plunged us into an ominous dark silence, we went to bed shivering and wondering what tomorrow would bring. All of a sudden there was a wild screech of brakes, followed by the resounding crash of metal slamming into metal. We rushed out on the balcony. In the street below we saw dim shapes of cars piled grotesquely on top of each other, their soft blue headlights staring helplessly up into the sky. Angry men's voices floated up to the house. The men were wearing uniforms and their metal buttons gleamed in the blue lights. Apparently two police cars had collided in the blackout.

Clutching at our bathrobes we lingered there. The damp winter night 32 hung heavy and inert like a wet black veil, and at the bottom of Beacon Hill, we could barely make out the undulating length of Rainier Valley, lying quietly in the somber, brooding silence like a hunted python. A few pinpoints of light pricked the darkness here and there like winking bits of diamonds, betraying the uneasy vigil of a tense city.

It made me positively hivey the way the FBI agents continued their raids 33 into Japanese homes and business places and marched the Issei men away into the old red brick immigration building, systematically and efficiently, as if they were stocking a cellarful of choice bottles of wine. At first we noted that the men arrested were those who had been prominent in community affairs, like Mr. Kato, many times president of the Seattle Japanese Chamber of Commerce, and Mr. Ohashi, the principal of our Japanese language school, or individuals whose business was directly connected with firms in Japan; but as time went on, it became less and less apparent why the others were included in these raids.

We wondered when Father's time would come. We expected momentarily 34
to hear strange footsteps on the porch and the sudden demanding ring of the
front doorbell. Our ears became attuned like the sensitive antennas of moths,
translating every soft swish of passing cars into the arrival of the FBI squad.

Once when our doorbell rang after curfew hour, I completely lost my 35
Oriental stoicism which I had believed would serve me well under the most
trying circumstances. No friend of ours paid visits at night anymore, and I was
sure that Father's hour had come. As if hypnotized, I walked woodenly to the
door. A mass of black figures stood before me, filling the doorway. I let out a
magnificent shriek. Then pandemonium broke loose. The solid rank fell apart
into a dozen separate figures which stumbled and leaped pell-mell away from
the porch. Watching the mad scramble, I thought I had routed the FBI agents
with my cry of distress. Father, Mother, Henry and Sumi rushed out to support
my wilting body. When Henry snapped on the porch light, one lone figure
crept out from behind the front hedge. It was a newsboy who, standing at a
safe distance, called in a quavering voice, "I . . . I came to collect for . . . for
the *Times*."

Shaking with laughter, Henry paid him and gave him an extra large tip 36
for the terrible fright he and his bodyguards had suffered at the hands of the
Japanese. As he hurried down the walk, boys of all shapes and sizes crawled
out from behind trees and bushes and scurried after him.

We heard all kinds of stories about the FBI, most of them from Mr. Yorita, 37
the grocer, who now took twice as long to make his deliveries. The war seemed
to have brought out his personality. At least he talked more, and he glowed,
in a sinister way. Before the war Mr. Yorita had been uncommunicative. He
used to stagger silently through the back door with a huge sack of rice over his
shoulders, dump it on the kitchen floor and silently flow out of the door as if
he were bored and disgusted with food and the people who ate it. But now
Mr. Yorita swaggered in, sent a gallon jug of soy sauce spinning into a corner,
and launched into a comprehensive report of the latest rumors he had picked
up on his route, all in chronological order. Mr. Yorita looked like an Oriental
Dracula, with his triangular eyes and yellow-fanged teeth. He had a mournfully
long sallow face and in his excitement his gold-rimmed glasses constantly slipped
to the tip of his long nose. He would describe in detail how some man had
been awakened in the dead of night, swiftly handcuffed, and dragged from out
of his bed by a squad of brutal, tight-lipped men. Mr. Yorita bared his teeth
menacingly in his most dramatic moments and we shrank from him instinctively.
As he backed out of the kitchen door, he would shake his bony finger at us
with a warning of dire things to come. When Mother said, "Yorita-san, you
must worry about getting a call from the FBI, too," Mr. Yorita laughed mod-
estly, pushing his glasses back up into place. "They wouldn't be interested in
anyone as insignificant as myself!" he assured her.

But he was wrong. The following week a new delivery boy appeared at 38
the back door with an airy explanation, "Yep, they got the old man, too, and
don't ask me why! The way I see it, it's subversive to sell soy sauce now."

The Matsuis were visited, too. Shortly after Dick had gone to Japan, Mr. 39
Matsui had died and Mrs. Matsui had sold her house. Now she and her daughter
and youngest son lived in the back of their little dry goods store on Jackson
Street. One day when Mrs. Matsui was busy with the family laundry, three
men entered the shop, nearly ripping off the tiny bell hanging over the door.
She hurried out, wiping sudsy, reddened hands on her apron. At best Mrs.
Matsui's English was rudimentary, and when she became excited, it deteriorated
into Japanese. She hovered on her toes, delighted to see new customers in her
humble shop. "Yes, yes, something you want?"

"Where's Mr. Matsui?" a steely-eyed man snapped at her. 40

Startled, Mrs. Matsui jerked her thumb toward the rear of the store and 41
said, "He not home."

"What? Oh, in there, eh? Come on!" The men tore the faded print curtain 42
aside and rushed into the back room. "Don't see him. Must be hiding."

They jerked open bedroom doors, leaped into the tiny bathroom, flung 43
windows open and peered down into the alley. Tiny birdlike Mrs. Matsui rushed
around after them. "No, no! Whatsamalla, whatsamalla!"

"Where's your husband! Where is he?" one man demanded angrily, fling- 44
ing clothes out of the closet.

"Why you mix 'em all up? He not home, not home." She clawed at the 45
back of the burly men like an angry little sparrow, trying to stop the holocaust
in her little home. One man brought his face down close to hers, shouting
slowly and clearly, "WHERE IS YOUR HUSBAND? YOU SAID HE WAS
IN HERE A MINUTE AGO!"

"Yes, yes, not here. *Mah, wakara nai hito da neh.* Such stupid men." 46

Mrs. Matsui dove under a table, dragged out a huge album and pointed 47
at a large photograph. She jabbed her gnarled finger up toward the ceiling,
saying, "Heben! Heben!"

The men gathered around and looked at a picture of Mr. Matsui's funeral. 48
Mrs. Matsui and her two children were standing by a coffin, their eyes cast
down, surrounded by all their friends, all of whom were looking down. The
three men's lips formed an "Oh." One of them said, "We're sorry to have
disturbed you. Thank you, Mrs. Matsui, and good-by." They departed quickly
and quietly.

Having passed through this baptism, Mrs. Matsui became an expert on 49
the FBI, and she stood by us, rallying and coaching us on how to deal with
them. She said to Mother, "You must destroy everything and anything Japanese
which may incriminate your husband. It doesn't matter what it is, if it's printed
or made in Japan, destroy it because the FBI always carries off those items for
evidence."

In fact all the women whose husbands had been spirited away said the 50
same thing. Gradually we became uncomfortable with our Japanese books,
magazines, wall scrolls and knickknacks. When Father's hotel friends, Messrs.
Sakaguchi, Horiuchi, Nishibue and a few others vanished, and their wives
called Mother weeping and warning her again about having too many Japanese

objects around the house, we finally decided to get rid of some of ours. We knew it was impossible to destroy everything. The FBI would certainly think it strange if they found us sitting in a bare house, totally purged of things Japanese. But it was as if we could no longer stand the tension of waiting, and we just had to do something against the black day. We worked all night, feverishly combing through bookshelves, closets, drawers, and furtively creeping down to the basement furnace for the burning. I gathered together my well-worn Japanese language schoolbooks which I had been saving over a period of ten years with the thought that they might come in handy when I wanted to teach Japanese to my own children. I threw them into the fire and watched them flame and shrivel into black ashes. But when I came face to face with my Japanese doll which Grandmother Nagashima had sent me from Japan, I rebelled. It was a gorgeously costumed Miyazukai figure, typical of the lady in waiting who lived in the royal palace during the feudal era. The doll was gowned in an elegant purple silk kimono with the long, sweeping hemline of its period and sashed with rich-embroidered gold and silver brocade. With its black, shining coiffed head bent a little to one side, its delicate pink-tipped ivory hand holding a red lacquer message box, the doll had an appealing, almost human charm. I decided to ask Chris if she would keep it for me. Chris loved and appreciated beauty in every form and shape, and I knew that in her hands, the doll would be safe and enjoyed.

Henry pulled down from his bedroom wall the toy samurai sword he had 51 brought from Japan and tossed it into the flames. Sumi's contributions to the furnace were books of fairy tales and magazines sent to her by her young cousins in Japan. We sorted out Japanese classic and popular music from a stack of records, shattered them over our knees and fed the pieces to the furnace. Father piled up his translated Japanese volumes of philosophy and religion and carted them reluctantly to the basement. Mother had the most to eliminate, with her scrapbooks of poems cut out from newspapers and magazines, and her private collection of old Japanese classic literature.

It was past midnight when we finally climbed upstairs to bed. Wearily 52 we closed our eyes, filled with an indescribable sense of guilt for having destroyed the things we loved. This night of ravage was to haunt us for years. As I lay struggling to fall asleep, I realized that we hadn't freed ourselves at all from fear. We still lay stiff in our beds, waiting.

Mrs. Matsui kept assuring us that the FBI would get around to us yet. 53 It was just a matter of time and the least Mother could do for Father was to pack a suitcase for him. She said that the men captured who hadn't been prepared had grown long beards, lived and slept in the same clothes for days before they were permitted visits from their families. So Mother dutifully packed a suitcase for Father with toilet articles, warm flannel pajamas, and extra clothes, and placed it in the front hall by the door. It was a personal affront, the way it stood there so frank and unabashedly. Henry and I said that it was practically a confession that Papa was a spy. "So please help yourself to him, Mr. FBI, and God speed you."

Mother was equally loud and firm, "No, don't anyone move it! No one 54 thought that Mr. Kato or the others would be taken, but they're gone now. Why should we think Papa's going to be an exception?"

Henry threw his hands up in the air and muttered about the odd ways 55 of the Japanese.

Every day Mrs. Matsui called Mother to check Father in; then we caught 56 the habit and started calling him at the hotel every hour on the hour until he finally exploded. "Stop this nonsense! I don't know which is more nerve-wracking, being watched by the FBI or by my family!"

When Father returned home from work, a solicitous family eased him 57 into his favorite armchair, arranged pillows behind his back, and brought the evening paper and slippers to him. Mother cooked Father's favorite dishes frenziedly, night after night. It all made Father very uneasy.

We had a family conference to discuss the possibility of Father and Mother's internment. Henry was in graduate school and I was beginning my second 58 year at the university. We agreed to drop out should they be taken and we would manage the hotel during our parents' absence. Every week end Henry and I accompanied Father to the hotel and learned how to keep the hotel books, how to open the office safe, and what kind of linen, paper towels, and soap to order.

Then a new menace appeared on the scene. Cries began to sound up and 59 down the coast that everyone of Japanese ancestry should be taken into custody. For years the professional guardians of the Golden West had wanted to rid their land of the Yellow Peril, and the war provided an opportunity for them to push their program through. As the chain of Pacific islands fell to the Japanese, patriots shrieked for protection from us. A Californian sounded the alarm: "The Japanese are dangerous and they must leave. Remember the destruction and the sabotage perpetrated at Pearl Harbor. Notice how they have infiltrated into the harbor towns and taken our best land."

He and his kind refused to be comforted by Edgar Hoover's special report 60 to the War Department stating that there had not been a single case of sabotage committed by a Japanese living in Hawaii or on the Mainland during the Pearl Harbor attack or after. I began to feel acutely uncomfortable for living on Beacon Hill. The Marine Hospital rose tall and handsome on our hill, and if I stood on the west shoulder of the Hill, I could not help but get an easily photographed view of the Puget Sound Harbor with its ships snuggled against the docks. And Boeing airfield, a few miles south of us, which had never bothered me before, suddenly seemed to have moved right up into my back yard, daring me to take just one spying glance at it.

In February, Executive Order No. 9066 came out, authorizing the War 61 Department to remove the Japanese from such military areas as it saw fit, aliens and citizens alike. Even if a person had a fraction of Japanese blood in him, he must leave on demand.

A pall of gloom settled upon our home. We couldn't believe that the 62 government meant that the Japanese-Americans must go, too. We had heard the clamoring of superpatriots who insisted loudly, "Throw the whole kaboodle out. A Jap's a Jap, no matter how you slice him. You can't make an American out of little Jap Junior just by handing him an American birth certificate." But we had dismissed these remarks as just hot blasts of air from an overheated patriot. We were quite sure that our rights as American citizens would not be violated, and we would not be marched out of our homes on the same basis as enemy aliens.

In anger, Henry and I read and reread the Executive Order. Henry   63
crumpled the newspaper in his hand and threw it against the wall. "Doesn't my citizenship mean a single blessed thing to anyone? Why doesn't somebody make up my mind for me? First they want me in the army. Now they're going to slap an alien 4-C on me because of my ancestry. What the hell!"

Once more I felt like a despised, pathetic two-headed freak, a Japanese   64
and an American, neither of which seemed to be doing me any good. The Nisei leaders in the community rose above their personal feelings and stated that they would co-operate and comply with the decision of the government as their sacrifice in keeping with the country's war effort, thus proving themselves loyal American citizens. I was too jealous of my recently acquired voting privilege to be gracious about giving in, and felt most unco-operative. I noticed wryly that the feelings about the Japanese on the Hawaiian Islands were quite different from those on the West Coast. In Hawaii, a strategic military outpost, the Japanese were regarded as essential to the economy of the island and powerful economic forces fought against their removal. General Delos Emmons, in command of Hawaii at the time, lent his authoritative voice to calm the fears of the people on the island and to prevent chaos and upheaval. General Emmons established martial law, but he did not consider evacuation essential for the security of the island.

On the West Coast, General, J. L. DeWitt of the Western Defense Com-   65
mand did not think martial law necessary, but he favored mass evacuation of the Japanese and Nisei. We suspected that pressures from economic and political interests who would profit from such a wholesale evacuation influenced this decision.

Events moved rapidly. General DeWitt marked off Western Washington,   66
Oregon, and all of California, and the southern half of Arizona as Military Area No. 1, hallowed ground from which we must remove ourselves as rapidly as possible. Unfortunately we could not simply vanish into thin air, and we had no place to go. We had no relatives in the east we could move in on. All our relatives were sitting with us in the forbidden area, themselves wondering where to go. The neighboring states in the line of exit for the Japanese protested violently at the prospect of any mass invasion. They said, very sensibly, that if the Coast didn't want the Japanese hanging around, they didn't either.

A few hardy families in the community liquidated their property, tied   67
suitcases all around their cars, and sallied eastward. They were greeted by signs in front of store windows, "Open season for Japs!" and "We kill rats and Japs

here." On state lines, highway troopers swarmed around the objectionable migrants and turned them back under governor's orders.

General DeWitt must have finally realized that if he insisted on voluntary 68 mass evacuation, hundreds and thousands of us would have wandered back and forth, clogging the highways and pitching tents along the roadside, eating and sleeping in colossal disorder. He suddenly called a halt to voluntary movement, although most of the Japanese were not budging an inch. He issued a new order, stating that no Japanese could leave the city, under penalty of arrest. The command had hatched another plan, a better one. The army would move us out as only the army could do it, and march us in neat, orderly fashion into assembly centers. We would stay in these centers only until permanent camps were set up inland to isolate us.

The orders were simple: 69

> Dispose of your homes and property. Wind up your businesses. Register the family. One seabag of bedding, two suitcases of clothing allowed per person. People in District #1 must report at 8th and Lane Street, 8 p.m. on April 28.

I wanted no part of this new order. I had read in the papers that the 70 Japanese from the state of Washington would be taken to a camp in Puyallup, on the state fairgrounds. The article apologetically assured the public that the camp would be temporary and that the Japanese would be removed from the fairgrounds and parking lots in time for the opening of the annual State Fair. It neglected to say where we might be at the time when those fine breeds of Holstein cattle and Yorkshire hogs would be proudly wearing their blue satin ribbons.

We were advised to pack warm, durable clothes. In my mind, I saw our 71 permanent camp sprawled out somewhere deep in a snow-bound forest, an American Siberia. I saw myself plunging chest deep in the snow, hunting for small game to keep us alive. I decided that one of my suitcases was going to hold nothing but vitamins from A to Z. I thought of sewing fur-lined hoods and parkas for the family. I was certain this was going to be a case of sheer animal survival.

One evening Father told us that he would lose the management of the 72 hotel unless he could find someone to operate it for the duration, someone intelligent and efficient enough to impress Bentley Agent and Company. Father said, "Sam, Joe, Peter, they all promised to stay on their jobs, but none of them can read or write well enough to manage the business. I've got to find a responsible party with experience in hotel management, but where?"

Sumi asked, "What happens if we can't find anyone?" 73

"I lose my business and my livelihood. I'll be saying good-by to a lifetime 74 of labor and all the hopes and plans I had for the family."

We sagged. Father looked at us thoughtfully, "I've never talked much 75 about the hotel business to you children, mainly because so much of it has been an uphill climb of work and waiting for better times. Only recently I was able to clear up the loans I took out years ago to expand the business. I was sure that in the next five or ten years I would be getting returns on my long-range investments, and I would have been able to do a lot of things eventually. . . . Send you through medical school," Father nodded to Henry, "and let Kazu and Sumi study anything they liked." Father laughed a bit self-consciously as he looked at Mother. "And when all the children had gone off on their own, I had planned to take Mama on her first real vacation, to Europe as well as Japan."

We listened to Father wide-eyed and wistful. It had been a wonderful, wonderful dream. [76]

Mother suddenly hit upon a brilliant idea. She said maybe the Olsens, our old friends who had once managed the Camden Apartments, might be willing to run a hotel. The Olsens had sold the apartment and moved to Aberdeen. Mother thought that perhaps Marta's oldest brother, the bachelor of the family, might be available. If he refused, perhaps Marta and her husband might consider the offer. We rushed excitedly to the telephone to make a long-distance call to the Olsens. After four wrong Olsens, we finally reached Marta. [77]

"Marta? Is this Marta?" [78]

"Yes, this is Marta." [79]

I nearly dove into the mouthpiece, I was so glad to hear her voice. Marta remembered us well and we exchanged news about our families. Marta and her husband had bought a small chicken farm and were doing well. Marta said, "I come from the farm ven I vas young and I like it fine. I feel more like home here. How's everybody over there?" [80]

I told her that we and all the rest of the Japanese were leaving Seattle soon under government order on account of the war. Marta gasped, "Everybody? You mean the Saitos, the Fujinos, Watanabes, and all the rest who were living at the Camden Apartments, too?" [81]

"Yes, they and everyone else on the West Coast." [82]

Bewildered, Marta asked where we were going, what we were going to do, would we ever return to Seattle, and what about Father's hotel. I told her about our business situation and that Father needed a hotel manager for the duration. Would she or any of her brothers be willing to accept such a job? There was a silence at the other end of the line and I said hastily, "This is a very sudden call, Marta. I'm sorry I had to surprise you like this, but we felt this was an emergency and . . ." [83]

Marta was full of regrets. "Oh, I vish we could do someting to help you folks, but my husband and I can't leave the farm at all. We don't have anyone here to help. We do all the work ourselves. Magnus went to Alaska last year. He has a goot job up there, some kind of war work. My other two brothers have business in town and they have children so they can't help you much." [84]

My heart sank like a broken elevator. When I said, "Oh . . ." I felt the family sitting behind me sink into a gloomy silence. Our last hope was gone. We finally said good-by, Marta distressed at not being able to help, and I apologizing for trying to hoist our problem on them. [85]

The next week end Marta and Karl paid us a surprise visit. We had not [86] seen them for nearly two years. Marta explained shyly, "It was such a nice day and we don't go novair for a long time, so I tole Karl, 'Let's take a bus into Seattle and visit the Itois.' "

We spent a delightful Sunday afternoon taking about old times. Mother 87 served our guests her best green tea and, as we relaxed, the irritating presence of war vanished. When it was time for them to return home, Marta's sparkling blue eyes suddenly filled. "Karl and I, we feel so bad about the whole ting, the war and everyting, we joost had to come out to see you and say 'good by.' God bless you. Maybe we vill see you again back home here. Anyvay, we pray for it."

Marta and Karl's warmth and sincerity restored a sense of peace into our 88 home, an atmosphere which had disappeared ever since Pearl Harbor. They served to remind us that in spite of the bitterness war had brought into our lives, we were still bound to our home town. Bit by bit, I remembered our happy past, the fun we had growing up along the colorful brash waterfront, swimming through the white-laced waves of Puget Sound, and lolling luxuriously on the tender green carpet of grass around Lake Washington from where we could see the slick, blue-frosted shoulders of Mount Rainier. There was too much beauty surrounding us. Above all, we must keep friends like Marta and Karl, Christine, Sam, Peter and Joe, all sterling products of many years of associations. We could never turn our faces away and remain aloof forever from Seattle. ◆

◆ Responding

1. Sone states that the internment of her family violated their rights as American citizens. Using examples from her autobiography and from other readings, such as the Bill of Rights, write an essay agreeing or disagreeing with her statement.

2. Have you ever felt that your rights were taken away unfairly by a social institution, family, or friend? Write a letter of protest to the individual or institution who you felt treated you unjustly.

3. Working individually or in a group, outline the changes that took place in the lives of the Sone family between the bombing of Pearl Harbor and the evacuation of the Japanese Americans.

4. Compare the attitudes and reactions of different members of the family toward the United States and Japan before and after Pearl Harbor, or before and after the evacuation order. Did the older generation have a markedly different attitude from that of the younger generation?

JEANNE WAKATSUKI HOUSTON
AND JAMES HOUSTON

Jeanne Wakatsuki Houston, who was born in California in 1934, lived in an internment camp in Manzanar, California, between 1942 and 1945. After the war she attended San Jose State University, where she earned her bachelor's degree in 1956, and the Sorbonne. She married James D. Houston in 1956, and together they wrote Farewell to Manzanar: A True Story of Japanese American Experience During and After the World War II Internment, *which was published in 1973. This book and the screenplay* Farewell to Manzanar *have been honored with the Humanities Prize, the Christopher Award, and the award of the National Women's Political Caucus.*

James D. Houston, who was born in 1933, earned his bachelor's degree from San Jose State in 1956 and his master's degree from Stanford University in 1962. He has taught writing at Cabrillo College, Stanford University, and the University of California at Santa Cruz. His other publications include Between Battles, Gig, *and* Voices of Man.

The selection that follows describes the atmosphere of the internment camp from a child's perspective. The chapter vividly portrays the regimented routine of the camp and its effect on those forced to live there.

◆ *From* **FAREWELL TO MANZANAR** ◆

In Spanish, Manzanar means "apple orchard." Great stretches of Owens Valley were once green with orchards and alfalfa fields. It has been a desert ever since its water started flowing south into Los Angeles, sometime during the twenties. But a few rows of untended pear and apple trees were still growing there when the camp opened, where a shallow water table had kept them alive. In the spring of 1943 we moved to block 28, right up next to one of the old pear orchards. That's where we stayed until the end of the war, and those trees stand in my memory for the turning of our life in camp, from the outrageous to the tolerable.

Papa pruned and cared for the nearest trees. Late that summer we picked the fruit green and stored it in a root cellar he had dug under our new barracks. At night the wind through the leaves would sound like the surf had sounded in Ocean Park, and while drifting off to sleep I could almost imagine we were still living by the beach.

Mama had set up this move. Block 28 was also close to the camp hospital. For the most part, people lived there who had to have easy access to it. Mama's connection was her job as dietician. A whole half of one barracks had fallen empty when another family relocated. Mama hustled us in there almost before they'd snapped their suitcases shut.

For all the pain it caused, the loyalty oath finally did speed up the reloca- 4
tion program. One result was a gradual easing of the congestion in the barracks.
A shrewd househunter like Mama could set things up fairly comfortably—by
Manzanar standards—if she kept her eyes open. But you had to move fast. As
soon as the word got around that so-and-so had been cleared to leave, there would
be a kind of tribal restlessness, a nervous rise in the level of neighborhood gossip
as wives jockeyed for position to see who would get the empty cubicles.

In Block 28 we doubled our living space—four rooms for the twelve of 5
us. Ray and Woody walled them with sheetrock. We had ceilings this time,
and linoleum floors of solid maroon. You had three colors to choose from—
maroon, black, and forest green—and there was plenty of it around by this
time. Some families would vie with one another for the most elegant floor
designs, obtaining a roll of each color from the supply shed, cutting it into
diamonds, squares, or triangles, shining it with heating oil, then leaving their
doors open so that passers-by could admire the handiwork.

Papa brought his still with him when we moved. He set it up behind the 6
door, where he continued to brew his own sake and brandy. He wasn't drinking
as much now, though. He spent a lot of time outdoors. Like many of the older
Issei men, he didn't take a regular job in camp. He puttered. He had been
working hard for thirty years and, bad as it was for him in some ways, camp
did allow him time to dabble with hobbies he would never had found time for
otherwise.

Once the first year's turmoil cooled down, the authorities started letting 7
us outside the wire for recreation. Papa used to hike along the creeks that
channeled down from the base of the Sierras. He brought back chunks of
driftwood, and he would pass long hours sitting on the steps carving myrtle
limbs into benches, table legs, and lamps, filling our rooms with bits of gnarled,
polished furniture.

He hauled stones in off the desert and built a small rock garden outside 8
our doorway, with succulents and a patch of moss. Near it he laid flat step-
pingstones leading to the stairs.

He also painted watercolors. Until this time I had not known he could 9
paint. He loved to sketch the mountains. If anything made that country hab-
itable it was the mountains themselves, purple when the sun dropped and so
sharply etched in the morning light the granite dazzled almost more than the
bright snow lacing it. The nearest peaks rose ten thousand feet higher than the
valley floor, with Whitney, the highest, just off to the south. They were important for all of us, but especially for the Issei. Whitney reminded Papa of
Fujiyama, that is, it gave him the same kind of spiritual sustenance. The tremendous beauty of those peaks was inspirational, as so many natural forms are
to the Japanese (the rocks outside our doorway could be those mountains in
miniature). They also represented those forces in nature, those powerful and
inevitable forces that cannot be resisted, reminding a man that sometimes he
must simply endure that which cannot be changed.

Subdued, resigned, Papa's life—all our lives—took on a pattern that would   10
hold for the duration of the war. Public shows of resentment pretty much spent
themselves over the loyalty oath crises. *Shikata ga nai* again became the motto,
but under altered circumstances. What had to be endured was the climate, the
confinement, the steady crumbling away of family life. But the camp itself had
been made livable. The government provided for our physical needs. My parents
and older brothers and sisters, like most of the internees, accepted their lot and
did what they could to make the best of a bad situation. "We're here," Woody
would say. "We're here, and there's no use moaning about it forever."

Gardens had sprung up everywhere, in the firebreaks, between the rows   11
of barracks—rock gardens, vegetable gardens, cactus and flower gardens. People
who lived in Owens Valley during the war still remember the flowers and lush
greenery they could see from the highway as they drove past the main gate.
The soil around Manzanar is alluvial and very rich. With water siphoned off
from the Los Angeles–bound aqueduct, a large farm was under cultivation just
outside the camp, providing the mess halls with lettuce, corn, tomatoes, eggplant,
string beans, horseradish, and cucumbers. Near Block 28 some of the men who
had been professional gardeners built a small park, with mossy nooks, ponds,
waterfalls, and curved wooden bridges. Sometimes in the evenings we could
walk down the raked gravel paths. You could face away from the barracks, look
past a tiny rapids toward the darkening mountains, and for a while not be a
prisoner at all. You could hang suspended in some odd, almost lovely land you
could not escape from yet almost didn't want to leave.

As the months at Manzanar turned to years, it became a world unto itself,   12
with its own logic and familiar ways. In time, staying there seemed far simpler
than moving once again to another, unknown place. It was as if the war were
forgotten, our reason for being there forgotten. The present, the little bit of
busywork you had right in front of you, became the most urgent thing. In such
a narrowed world, in order to survive, you learn to contain your rage and your
despair, and you try to re-create, as well as you can, your normality, some
sense of things continuing. The fact that America had accused us, or excluded
us, or imprisoned us, or whatever it might be called, did not change the kind
of world we wanted. Most of us were born in this country; we had no other
models. Those parks and gardens lent it an oriental character, but in most ways
it was a totally equipped American small town, complete with schools, churches,
Boy Scouts, beauty parlors, neighborhood gossip, fire and police departments,
glee clubs, softball leagues, Abbott and Costello movies, tennis courts, and
traveling shows. (I still remember an Indian who turned up one Saturday billing
himself as a Sioux chief, wearing bear claws and head feathers. In the firebreak
he sang songs and danced his tribal dances while hundreds of us watched.)

In our family, while Papa puttered, Mama made daily rounds to the mess   13
halls, helping young mothers with their feeding, planning diets for the various
ailments people suffered from. She wore a bright yellow, longbilled sun hat
she had made herself and always kept stiffly starched. Afternoons I would see

her coming from blocks away, heading home, her tiny figure warped by heat waves and that bonnet a yellow flower wavering in the glare.

In their disagreement over serving the country, Woody and Papa had 14 struck a kind of compromise. Papa talked him out of volunteering; Woody waited for the army to induct him. Meanwhile he clerked in the co-op general store. Kiyo, nearly thirteen by this time, looked forward to the heavy winds. They moved the sand around and uncovered obsidian arrowheads he could sell to old men in camp for fifty cents apiece. Ray, a few years older, played in the six-man touch football league, sometimes against Caucasian teams who would come in from Lone Pine or Independence. My sister Lillian was in high school and singing with a hillbilly band called The Sierra Stars—jeans, cowboy hats, two guitars, and a tub bass. And my oldest brother, Bill, led a dance band called The Jive Bombers—brass and rhythm, with cardboard fold-out music stands lettered J. B. Dances were held every weekend in one of the recreation halls. Bill played trumpet and took vocals on Glenn Miller arrangements of such tunes as *In the Mood, String of Pearls*, and *Don't Fence Me In*. He didn't sing *Don't Fence Me In* out of protest, as if trying quietly to mock the authorities. It just happened to be a hit song one year, and they all wanted to be an up-to-date American swing band. They would blast it out into recreation barracks full of bobbysoxed, jitterbugging couples:

> Oh, give me land, lots of land
> Under starry skies above,
> Don't fence me in.
> Let me ride through the wide
> Open country that I love . . .

Pictures of the band, in their bow ties and jackets, appeared in the high 15 school yearbook for 1943–1944, along with pictures of just about everything else in camp that year. It was called *Our World*. In its pages you see school kids with armloads of books, wearing cardigan sweaters and walking past rows of tarpapered shacks. You see chubby girl yell leaders, pompons flying as they leap with glee. You read about the school play, called *Growing Pains* ". . . the story of a typical American home, in this case that of the McIntyres. They see their boy and girl tossed into the normal awkward growing up stage, but can offer little assistance or direction in their turbulent course . . ." with Shoji Katayama as George McIntyre, Takudo Ando as Terry McIntyre, and Mrs. McIntyre played by Kazuko Nagai.

All the class pictures are in there, from the seventh grade through twelfth, 16 with individual head shots of seniors, their names followed by the names of the high schools they would have graduated from on the outside: Theodore Roosevelt, Thomas Jefferson, Herbert Hoover, Sacred Heart. You see pretty girls on bicycles, chicken yards full of fat pullets, patients back-tilted in dental chairs, lines of laundry, and finally, two large blowups, the first of a high tower with a searchlight, against a Sierra backdrop, the next a two-page endsheet showing a wide path that curves among rows of elm trees. White stones border the path. Two dogs are following an old woman in gardening clothes as she strolls along. She is in the middle distance, small beneath the trees, beneath the snowy peaks. It is winter. All the elms are bare. The scene is both stark and comforting. This path leads toward one edge of camp, but the wire is out of sight, or out of focus. The tiny woman seems very much at ease. She and her tiny dogs seem almost swallowed by the landscape, or floating in it.◆

◆ Responding

1. Describe or draw a picture of the camp at Manzanar. Share your work with the class.

2. Working individually or in a group, list the hardships of camp life. What would you find most intolerable?

3. Houston talks about "the turning of our life in camp, from the outrageous to the tolerable. . . . You try to re-create, as well as you can, your normality, some sense of things continuing." Discuss the strategies that people interned at Manzanar used to cope with their situation and make it bearable.

4. Houston writes, "The fact that America had accused us, or excluded us, or imprisoned us, or whatever it might be called, did not change the kind of world we wanted. Most of us were born in this country; we had no other models." Using evidence from the story, analyze the attitude of the internees at Manzanar to America and American ideas.

TOSHIO MORI

Toshio Mori, born in Oakland, California in 1910, lived from 1912 in San Leandro, California, where his parents ran a nursery business. He later attended the local public schools. During World War II, his family was interned at the Topaz Relocation Center in Utah, where Mori helped to found a newspaper and served as camp historian.

Mori's book Yokohama, California *(1949) was the first collection of short stories written by a Japanese American to be published in this country. It included an introduction by William Saroyan praising the work's originality. Mori's later work included a collection entitled* The Chauvinist and Other Stories *(1979) and the novel* The Woman from Hiroshima *(1979). He died in 1980.*

"Unfinished Messages," from Mori's second short story collection, explores some of the events experienced by his family during the war. Like the character in the story, Mori's brother was wounded in combat.

◆ UNFINISHED MESSAGE ◆

It was on a chilly May night in 1945 in the middle of Utah desert when my mother sharply called me. "I can't sleep tonight," she said. True, she had been fretting the past few nights, and I knew she was worried over her son at the Italian front. 1

I reassured her that everything would be all right. Hadn't he, I reasoned with her, come through without a scratch with a full year's service at the front, even with the 442nd Infantry Regiment? 2

"But I keep seeing Kazuo's face tonight," she said. "Each time I'm about to fall asleep his face keeps coming back." 3

I tried to calm her fears as best as I could. Nevertheless, she did not sleep that night. 4

The next night and the night following she slept fitfully more or less. Beneath her outward calm, however, she was under an ordeal only a mother could understand. "No news is good news. He's all right," I assured her. 5

A few days later we received a wire from the War Department that Kazuo had been seriously wounded. The news almost killed her. In the full medical report following we learned that he had a fractured skull but was resting peacefully. What struck me as odd was the day my brother was wounded. It was on May 5, the very night my mother was unable to sleep. 6

When we received word again, it was more cheerful. Kazuo was coming back on the hospital ship destined for home, and we were to decide the hospital nearest our home. We were still living in Topaz, Utah Relocation Center at the time, and the nearest available army hospital was the Fitzsimmons in Colorado. 7

"Let's have him transferred there so we can visit him as soon as he comes home," I said to Mother. 8

My mother would have none of it. "Do you think this is our real home? Our home is back in San Leandro, California. We'll be moving from here again, and Kazuo too will have to transfer. No, we'll go back and Kazuo can go to a hospital in California." 9

My mother couldn't get out of the camp soon enough. She counted the days when the next train to California would take us back home. In the meantime we learned that Kazuo was being transferred to DeWitt Army Hospital in Auburn, California. 10

On our trip home, our train stopped for a few minutes at Auburn, and our first urge was to get off the train and visit Kazuo. My mother stared toward the Auburn interiors. "It must be only a few miles from here. Here we are, so close to him and yet so far." 11

We heeded our good judgment and did not get off the train. "We must make ready our home. It must be in a mess. We must first go home and get busy cleaning the place. Our home must resemble our old home for Kazuo." 12

It took us two weeks to clean the house and settle down. My mother had to apply to the United States Attorney's office for a travel permit because she was an enemy alien and Japan and United States were still at war. Secure with a permit my mother accompanied me to Auburn. All the way on the bus to the hospital she nervously weighed the seriousness of Kazuo's actual condition. Are his legs all intact, are his hands there? she wondered. Can he see, is he normal mentally? It wasn't until she saw him in person did she feel relieved. He could see, his hands were usable, but his legs? Mother talked constantly on everything she could think of but his condition. Before long, she became aware of his actual condition. 13

In order to relieve ourselves of the hot valley air caught inside of the ward, my brother suggested sitting on the screened porch. It was when the ward boy saw my brother moving on the bed that he came to help him to his wheelchair. The ward boy bodily lifted him on the chair, and Mother saw my brother's spindly legs. He was unable to walk. 14

Afterwards, Mother asked me to inquire the doctor about Kazuo's condition. Will he ever walk? The doctor I talked to was not too hopeful, but I did not tell Mother. 15

"He says there's a fifty-fifty possibility that Kazuo will walk," I said to Mother. 16

Coming home, Mother said, "I'm worried over him. If I only could live long enough to see him fully recovered." 17

After another operation on his head, my brother was transferred to Letterman Hospital in San Francisco, making possible weekly visits for Mother and I. Each time we saw him, she would take me aside and ask, "Do you think he's much improved? Isn't he better?" 18

That Christmas my brother got a two week furlough and came home for 19 the first time since the war had started. I had to help him with his bath and toilet. My brother was confined to his wheelchair.

Time and again, Mother would ask me, "Will he ever walk again? I can't tell him that I worry over him." 20

Before my brother was released from the hospital, Mother died in her sleep on August 5, 1946. Although she complained of pains in the neck, we were totally unprepared for her death. Her doctor had previously diagnosed her symptoms as arthritis, but her death was sudden. 21

After her death our house became dark and silent. Even when my brother returned home for good in a wheelchair, the atmosphere was unchanged. We seemed to be companions in the dark. However, it changed one day. 22

As I sat quietly in the living room I heard a slight tapping on the window just above the divan where my mother had slept her last. When the taps repeated again, I went outside to check, knowing well that a stiff wind could move a branch of our lemon tree with a lemon or two tapping the wall of our house. There was no wind, no lemon near enough to reach the window. I was puzzled but did not confide in my brother when he joined me in the living room. 23

I had all but forgotten the incident when my brother and I were quietly sitting in the living room near the spot where our mother had passed away. For a while I was not conscious of the slight tapping on the window. When the repeated taps were loud enough to be heard clearly, I first looked at the window and then glanced at my brother. He too had heard the taps. 24

"Did you hear that?" I said. 25

My brother nodded. "Sure," he said. "Did you hear it too? I heard it the other day but I thought it was strange." 26

We looked at the window. There were no birds in sight, no lemons tapping. Then the taps repeated. After a few moments of silence I was about to comment when we heard the tapping again. This time I looked silently at my brother and on tiptoes approached the window. The tapping continued so I softly touched the window pane. The instant my fingers touched the glass, it stopped. 27

My brother and I looked at each other, silently aware that it must have been Mother calling our attention. At that instant I became conscious of the purpose of the mysterious taps. I couldn't help but recall Mother's words, "I can't stop worrying over you, my son." 28

The tappings stopped once and for all after that. We never heard it again after the message had reached us. 29

—1947

Epilogue

This story was written nearly thirty years ago. My brother is alive and well, raising a family in San Leandro, California. He is still paralyzed to this day.◆ 30

◆ Responding

1. Kazuo is a soldier fighting for the United States in World War II. Why does his mother need a travel permit to visit him? What justification might the government give for such restrictions? How might the Japanese American soldier respond? Discuss your own possible reaction to this situation.

2. Research the fighting record of Japanese American soldiers in World War II.

3. Do you believe that Kazuo's mother knew her son was in danger? Did she try to communicate with him from beyond the grave? What do you think the author believes? Present evidence from the text to support your opinion.

4. The author doesn't report the scene that takes place between the mother and the wounded son when they meet. Write your own version of that meeting.

JOHN OKADA

Born in Seattle, Washington, in 1923, John Okada served in the Army during World War II. After earning a bachelor's degree from the University of Washington and a master's degree from Columbia University, he worked as a reference librarian and a technical writer. He died of a heart attack in 1971. Although Okada did not enjoy great fame during his lifetime, he is now considered by many to be one of the most important Japanese American writers.

The following excerpt from No-no Boy, *first published in 1957, describes some of the conflicts within the Japanese community at the time of the war. In the passage, the main character begins to see how one's sense of loyalty is very often a function of one's position in society. He also discovers how people use both ideology and emotion to justify their decisions.*

◆ *From* **NO-NO BOY** ◆

"Ichiro." 1

He propped himself up on an elbow and looked at her. She had hardly 2 changed. Surely, there must have been a time when she could smile and, yet, he could not remember.

"Yeah?" 3

"Lunch is on the table." 4

As he pushed himself off the bed and walked past her to the kitchen, she 5 took broom and dustpan and swept up the mess he had made.

There were eggs, fried with soy sauce, sliced cold meat, boiled cabbage, 6 and tea and rice. They all ate in silence, not even disturbed once by the tinkling of the bell. The father cleared the table after they had finished and dutifully retired to watch the store. Ichiro had smoked three cigarettes before his mother ended the silence.

"You must go back to school." 7

He had almost forgotten that there had been a time before the war when 8 he had actually gone to college for two years and studiously applied himself to courses in the engineering school. The statement staggered him. Was that all there was to it? Did she mean to sit there and imply that the four intervening years were to be casually forgotten and life resumed as if there had been no four years and no war and no Eto who had spit on him because of the thing he had done?

"I don't feel much like going to school." 9

"What will you do?" 10

"I don't know." 11

"With an education, your opportunities in Japan will be unlimited. You must go and complete your studies." 12

"Ma," he said slowly, "Ma, I'm not going to Japan. Nobody's going to Japan. The war is over. Japan lost. Do you hear? Japan lost." 13

"You believe that?" It was said in the tone of an adult asking a child who is no longer a child if he really believed that Santa Claus was real. 14

"Yes, I believe it. I know it. America is still here. Do you see the great Japanese army walking down the streets? No. There is no Japanese army any more." 15

"The boat is coming and we must be ready." 16

"The boat?" 17

"Yes." She reached into her pocket and drew out a worn envelope. 18

The letter had been mailed from São Paulo, Brazil, and was addressed to a name that he did not recognize. Inside the envelope was a single sheet of flimsy, rice paper covered with intricate flourishes of Japanese characters. 19

"What does it say?" 20

She did not bother to pick up the letter. "To you who are a loyal and honorable Japanese, it is with humble and heartfelt joy that I relay this momentous message. Word has been brought to us that the victorious Japanese government is presently making preparations to send ships which will return to Japan those residents in foreign countries who have steadfastly maintained their faith and loyalty to our Emperor. The Japanese government regrets that the responsibilities arising from the victory compel them to delay in the sending of the vessels. To be among the few who remain to receive this honor is a gratifying tribute. Heed not the propaganda of the radio and newspapers which endeavor to convince the people with lies about the allied victory. Especially, heed not the lies of your traitorous countrymen who have turned their backs on the country of their birth and who will suffer for their treasonous acts. The day of glory is close at hand. The rewards will be beyond our greatest expectations. What we have done, we have done only as Japanese, but the government is grateful. Hold your heads high and make ready for the journey, for the ships are coming." 21

"Who wrote that?" he asked incredulously. It was like a weird nightmare. It was like finding out that an incurable strain of insanity pervaded the family, an intangible horror that swayed and taunted beyond the grasp of reaching fingers. 22

"A friend in South America. We are not alone." 23

"We *are* alone," he said vehemently. "This whole thing is crazy. You're crazy. I'm crazy. All right, so we made a mistake. Let's admit it." 24

"There has been no mistake. The letter confirms." 25

"Sure it does. It proves there's crazy people in the world besides us. If Japan won the war, what the hell are we doing here? What are you doing running a grocery store? It doesn't figure. It doesn't figure because we're all wrong. The minute we admit that, everything is fine. I've had a lot of time to 26 think about all this. I've thought about it, and every time the answer comes out the same. You can't tell me different any more."

She sighed ever so slightly. "We will talk later when you are feeling better." Carefully folding the letter and placing it back in the envelope, she returned it to her pocket. "It is not I who tell you that the ship is coming. It is in the letter. If you have come to doubt your mother—and I'm sure you do not mean it even if you speak in weakness—it is to be regretted. Rest a few days. Think more deeply and your doubts will disappear. You are my son, Ichiro." 27

No, he said to himself as he watched her part the curtains and start into the store. There was a time when I was your son. There was a time that I no longer remember when you used to smile a mother's smile and tell me stories about gallant and fierce warriors who protected their lords with blades of shining steel and about the old woman who found a peach in the stream and took it home and when her husband split it in half, a husky little boy tumbled out to fill their hearts with boundless joy. I was that boy in the peach and you were the old woman and we were Japanese with Japanese feelings and Japanese pride and Japanese thoughts because it was all right then to be Japanese and feel and think all the things that Japanese do even if we lived in America. Then there came a time when I was only half Japanese because one is not born in America and raised in America and taught in America and one does not speak and swear and drink and smoke and play and fight and see and hear in America among Americans in American streets and houses without becoming American and loving it. But I did not love enough, for you were still half my mother and I was thereby still half Japanese and when the war came and they told me to fight for America, I was not strong enough to fight you and I was not strong enough to fight the bitterness which made the half of me which was you bigger than the half of me which was America and really the whole of me that I could not see or feel. Now that I know the truth when it is too late and the half of me which was you is no longer there, I am only half of me and the half that remains is American by law because the government was wise and strong enough to know why it was that I could not fight for America and did not strip me of my birthright. But it is not enough to be American only in the eyes of the law and it is not enough to be only half an American and know that it is an empty half. I am not your son and I am not Japanese and I am not American. I can go someplace and tell people that I've got an inverted stomach and that I am an American, true and blue and Hail Columbia, but the army wouldn't have me because of the stomach. That's easy and I would do it, only I've got to convince myself first and that I cannot do. I wish with all my heart that I were Japanese or that I were American. I am neither and I blame you and I blame myself and I blame the world which is made up of many countries which fight with each other and kill and hate and destroy but not enough, so that they must kill and hate and destroy again and again and again. It is so easy and simple that I cannot understand it at all. And the reason I do not understand it is because I do not understand you who were the half of me that is no 28 more and because I do not understand what it was about that half that made me destroy the half of me which was American and the half which might have become the whole of me if I had said yes I will go and fight in your army because that is what I believe and want and cherish and love . . .

Defeatedly, he crushed the stub of a cigarette into an ash tray filled with 29 many other stubs and reached for the package to get another. It was empty and he did not want to go into the store for more because he did not feel much like seeing either his father or mother. He went into the bedroom and tossed and groaned and half slept.

Hours later, someone shook him awake. It was not his mother and it was not 30 his father. The face that looked down at him in the gloomy darkness was his brother's.

"Taro," he said softly, for he had hardly thought of him. 31

"Yeah, it's me," said his brother with unmistakable embarrassment. "I 32 see you got out."

"How've you been?" He studied his brother, who was as tall as he but 33 skinnier.

"Okay. It's time to eat." He started to leave. 34

"Taro, wait." 35

His brother stood framed in the light of the doorway and faced him. 36

"How've you been?" he repeated. Then he added quickly for fear of losing 37 him: "No, I said that before and I don't mean it the way it sounds. We've got things to talk about. Long time since we saw each other."

"Yeah, it's been a long time." 38

"How's school?" 39

"Okay." 40

"About through with high school?" 41

"Next June." 42

"What then? College?" 43

"No, army." 44

He wished he could see his face, the face of the brother who spoke to 45 him as though they were strangers—because that's what they were.

"You could get in a year or two before the draft," he heard himself saying 46 in an effort to destroy the wall that separated them. "I read where you can take an exam now and get a deferment if your showing is good enough. A fellow's got to have all the education he can get, Taro."

"I don't want a deferment. I want in." 47

"Ma know?" 48

"Who cares?" 49

"She won't like it." 50

"Doesn't matter." 51

"Why so strong about the army? Can't you wait? They'll come and get 52 you soon enough."

"That isn't soon enough for me." 53

"What's your reason?" 54

He waited for an answer, knowing what it was and not wanting to hear 55
it.

"Is it because of me? What I did?" 56

"I'm hungry," his brother said and turned into the kitchen. 57

His mother had already eaten and was watching the store. He sat opposite 58
his brother, who wolfed down the food without looking back at him. It wasn't
more than a few minutes before he rose, grabbed his jacket off a nail on the
wall, and left the table. The bell tinkled and he was gone.

"Don't mind him," said the father apologetically. "Taro is young and 59
restless. He's never home except to eat and sleep."

"When does he study?" 60

"He does not." 61

"Why don't you do something about it?" 62

"I tell him. Mama tells him. Makes no difference. It is the war that has 63
made them that way. All the people say the same thing. The war and the camp
life. Made them wild like cats and dogs. It is hard to understand."

"Sure," he said, but he told himself that he understood, that the reason 64
why Taro was not a son and not a brother was because he was young and
American and alien to his parents, who had lived in America for thirty-five
years without becoming less Japanese and could speak only a few broken words
of English and write it not at all, and because Taro hated that thing in his elder
brother which had prevented him from thinking for himself. And in his hate
for that thing, he hated his brother and also his parents because they had created
the thing with their eyes and hands and minds which had seen and felt and
thought as Japanese for thirty-five years in an America which they rejected as
thoroughly as if they had never been a day away from Japan. That was the
reason and it was difficult to believe, but it was true because he was the emptiness
between the one and the other and could see flashes of the truth that was true
for his parents and the truth that was true for his brother.

"Pa," he said. 65

"Ya, Ichiro." He was swirling a dishcloth in a pan of hot water and working 66
up suds for the dishes.

"What made you and Ma come to America?" 67

"Everyone was coming to America." 68

"Did you have to come?" 69

"No. We came to make money." 70

"Is that all?" 71

"Ya, I think that was why we came." 72

"Why to make money?" 73

"There was a man in my village who went to America and made a lot of 74
money and he came back and bought a big piece of land and he was very

comfortable. We came so we could make money and go back and buy a piece of land and be comfortable too."

"Did you ever think about staying here and not going back?" 75

"No." 76

He looked at his father, who was old and bald and washing dishes in a 77 kitchen that was behind a hole in the wall that was a grocery store. "How do you feel about it now?"

"About what?" 78

"Going back." 79

"We are going." 80

"When?" 81

"Oh, pretty soon." 82

"How soon?" 83

"Pretty soon." 84

There didn't seem to be much point in pursuing the questioning. He went 85 out to the store and got a fresh pack of cigarettes. His mother was washing down the vegetable stand, which stood alongside the entrance. Her thin arms swabbed the green-painted wood with sweeping, vigorous strokes. There was a power in the wiry, brown arms, a hard, blind, unreckoning force which coursed through veins of tough bamboo. When she had done her work, she carried the pail of water to the curb outside and poured it on the street. Then she came back through the store and into the living quarters and emerged once more dressed in her coat and hat.

"Come, Ichiro," she said, "we must go and see Kumasaka-san and Ashida- 86 san. They will wish to know that you are back."

The import of the suggested visits made him waver helplessly. He was 87 too stunned to voice his protest. The Kumasakas and the Ashidas were people from the same village in Japan. The three families had been very close for as long as he could recall. Further, it was customary among the Japanese to pay ceremonious visits upon various occasions to families of close association. This was particularly true when a member of one of the families either departed on an extended absence or returned from an unusually long separation. Yes, he had been gone a long time, but it was such a different thing. It wasn't as if he had gone to war and returned safe and sound or had been matriculating at some school in another city and come home with a sheepskin *summa cum laude*. He scrabbled at the confusion in his mind for the logic of the crazy business and found no satisfaction.

"Papa," his mother shouted without actually shouting. 88

His father hastened out from the kitchen and Ichiro stumbled in blind 89 fury after the woman who was only a rock of hate and fanatic stubbornness and was, therefore, neither woman nor mother.

They walked through the night and the city, a mother and son thrown 90 together for a while longer because the family group is a stubborn one and does not easily disintegrate. The woman walked ahead and the son followed and no word passed between them. They walked six blocks, then six more, and still another six before they turned in to a three-story frame building.

The Ashidas, parents and three daughters, occupied four rooms on the 91 second floor.

"Mama," screamed the ten-year-old who answered the knock, "Mrs. 92 Yamada."

A fat, cheerful-looking woman rushed toward them, then stopped, flushed 93 and surprised. "Ichiro-san. You have come back."

He nodded his head and heard his mother say, with unmistakable exul- 94 tation: "Today, Ashida-san. Just today he came home."

Urged by their hostess, they took seats in the sparsely furnished living 95 room. Mrs. Ashida sat opposite them on a straight-backed kitchen chair and beamed.

"You have grown so much. It is good to be home, is it not, Ichiro-san?" 96 She turned to the ten-year-old who gawked at him from behind her mother: "Tell Reiko to get tea and cookies."

"She's studying, Mama." 97

"You mustn't bother," said his mother. 98

"Go now, I know she is only listening to the radio." The little girl fled 99 out of the room.

"It is good to see you again, Ichiro-san. You will find many of your young 100 friends already here. All the people who said they would never come back to Seattle are coming back. It is almost like it was before the war. Akira-san— you went to school with him I think—he is just back from Italy, and Watanabe- san's boy came back from Japan last month. It is so good that the war is over and everything is getting to be like it was before."

"You saw the pictures?" his mother asked. 101

"What pictures?" 102

"You have not been to the Watanabes'?" 103

"Oh, yes, the pictures of Japan." She snickered. "He is such a serious 104 boy. He showed me all the pictures he had taken in Japan. He had many of Hiroshima and Nagasaki and I told him that he must be mistaken because Japan did not lose the war as he seems to believe and that he could not have been in Japan to take pictures because, if he were in Japan, he would not have been permitted to remain alive. He protested and yelled so that his mother had to tell him to be careful and then he tried to argue some more, but I asked him if he was ever in Japan before and could he prove that he was actually there and he said again to look at the pictures and I told him that what must really have happened was that the army only told him he was in Japan when he was someplace else, and that it was too bad he believed the propaganda. Then he got so mad his face went white and he said: 'How do you know you're you? Tell me how you know you're you!' If his mother had not made him leave the room, he might even have struck me. It is not enough that they must willingly take up arms against their uncles and cousins and even brothers and sisters, but they no longer have respect for the old ones. If I had a son and he had gone in the American army to fight Japan, I would have killed myself with shame."

"They know not what they do and it is not their fault. It is the fault of 105 the parents. I've always said that Mr. Watanabe was a stupid man. Gambling and drinking the way he does. I am almost ashamed to call them friends." Ichiro's mother looked at him with a look which said I am a Japanese and you are my son and have conducted yourself as a Japanese and I know no shame such as other parents do because their sons were not really their sons or they would not have fought against their own people.

He wanted to get up and dash out into the night. The madness of his 106 mother was in mutual company and he felt nothing but loathing for the gentle, kindly-looking Mrs. Ashida, who sat on a fifty-cent chair from Goodwill Industries while her husband worked the night shift at a hotel, grinning and bowing for dimes and quarters from rich Americans whom he detested, and couldn't afford to take his family on a bus ride to Tacoma but was waiting and praying and hoping for the ships from Japan.

Reiko brought in a tray holding little teacups and a bowl of thin, round 107 cookies. She was around seventeen with little bumps on her chest which the sweater didn't improve and her lips heavily lipsticked a deep red. She said "Hi" to him and did not have to say look at me, I was a kid when you saw me last but now I'm a woman with a woman's desires and a woman's eye for men like you. She set the tray on the table and gave him a smile before she left.

His mother took the envelope from São Paulo out of her dress pocket and 108 handed it to Mrs. Ashida.

"From South America." 109

The other woman snatched at the envelope and proceeded to read the 110 contents instantly. Her face glowed with pride. She read it eagerly, her lips moving all the time and frequently murmuring audibly. "Such wonderful news," she sighed breathlessly as if the reading of the letter had been a deep emotional experience. "Mrs. Okamoto will be eager to see this. Her husband, who goes out of the house whenever I am there, is threatening to leave her unless she gives up her nonsense about Japan. Nonsense, he calls it. He is no better than a Chinaman. This will show him. I feel so sorry for her."

"It is hard when so many no longer believe," replied his mother, "but 111 they are not Japanese like us. They only call themselves such. It is the same with the Teradas. I no longer go to see them. The last time I was there Mr. Terada screamed at me and told me to get out. They just don't understand that Japan did not lose the war because Japan could not possibly lose. I try not to hate them but I have no course but to point them out to the authorities when the ships come."

"It's getting late, Ma." He stood up, sick in the stomach and wanting 112 desperately to smash his way out of the dishonest, warped, and uncompromising world in which defeated people like his mother and the Ashidas walked their perilous tightropes and could not and would not look about them for having to keep their eyes fastened to the taut, thin support.

"Yes," his mother replied quickly, "forgive us for rushing, for you know 113 that I enjoy nothing better than a visit with you, but we must drop in for a while on the Kumasakas."

"Of course. I wish you could stay longer, but I know that there will be 114 plenty of opportunities again. You will come again, please, Ichiro-san?"

Mumbling thanks for the tea, he nodded evasively and hurried down the 115 stairs. Outside, he lit a cigarette and paced restlessly until his mother came out.

"A fine woman," she said without stopping. 116

He followed, talking to the back of her head: "Ma, I don't want to see 117 the Kumasakas tonight. I don't want to see anybody tonight. We'll go some other time."

"We won't stay long." 118

They walked a few blocks to a freshly painted frame house that was 119 situated behind a neatly kept lawn.

"Nice house," he said. 120

"They bought it last month." 121

"Bought it?" 122

"Yes." 123

The Kumasakas had run a dry-cleaning shop before the war. Business 124 was good and people spoke of their having money, but they lived in cramped quarters above the shop because, like most of the other Japanese, they planned someday to return to Japan and still felt like transients even after thirty or forty years in America and the quarters above the shop seemed adequate and sensible since the arrangement was merely temporary. That, he thought to himself, was the reason why the Japanese were still Japanese. They rushed to America with the single purpose of making a fortune which would enable them to return to their own country and live adequately. It did not matter when they discovered that fortunes were not for the mere seeking or that their sojourns were spanning decades instead of years and it did not matter that growing families and growing bills and misfortunes and illness and low wages and just plain hard luck were constant obstacles to the realization of their dreams. They continued to maintain their dreams by refusing to learn how to speak or write the language of America and by living only among their own kind and by zealously avoiding long-term commitments such as the purchase of a house. But now, the Kumasakas, it seemed, had bought this house, and he was impressed. It could only mean that the Kumasakas had exchanged hope for reality and, late as it was, were finally sinking roots into the land from which they had previously sought not nourishment but only gold.

Mrs. Kumasaka came to the door, a short, heavy woman who stood solidly 125 on feet planted wide apart, like a man. She greeted them warmly but with a sadness that she would carry to the grave. When Ichiro had last seen her, her hair had been pitch black. Now it was completely white.

In the living room Mr. Kumasaka, a small man with a pleasant smile, was 126 sunk deep in an upholstered chair, reading a Japanese newspaper. It was a comfortable room with rugs and soft furniture and lamps and end tables and pictures on recently papered walls.

"Ah, Ichiro, it is nice to see you looking well," Mr. Kumasaka struggled 127 out of the chair and extended a friendly hand. "Please, sit down."

"You've got a nice place," he said, meaning it. 128

"Thank you," the little man said. "Mama and I, we finally decided that 129 America is not so bad. We like it here."

Ichiro sat down on the sofa next to his mother and felt strange in this 130 home which he envied because it was like millions of other homes in America and could never be his own.

Mrs. Kumasaka sat next to her husband on a large, round hassock and 131 looked at Ichiro with lonely eyes, which made him uncomfortable.

"Ichiro came home this morning." It was his mother, and the sound of 132 her voice, deliberately loud and almost arrogant, puzzled him. "He has suffered, but I make no apologies for him or for myself. If he had given his life for Japan, I could not be prouder."

"Ma," he said, wanting to object but not knowing why except that her 133 comments seemed out of place.

Ignoring him, she continued, not looking at the man but at his wife, who 134 now sat with head bowed, her eyes emptily regarding the floral pattern of the carpet. "A mother's lot is not an easy one. To sleep with a man and bear a son is nothing. To raise the child into a man one can be proud of is not play. Some of us succeed. Some, of course, must fail. It is too bad, but that is the way of life."

"Yes, yes, Yamada-san," said the man impatiently. Then, smiling, he 135 turned to Ichiro: "I suppose you'll be going back to the university?"

"I'll have to think about it," he replied, wishing that his father was like 136 this man who made him want to pour out the turbulence in his soul.

"He will go when the new term begins. I have impressed upon him the 137 importance of a good education. With a college education, one can go far in Japan." His mother smiled knowingly.

"Ah," said the man as if he had not heard her speak. "Bobbie wanted to 138 go to the university and study medicine. He would have made a fine doctor. Always studying and reading, is that not so, Ichiro?"

He nodded, remembering the quiet son of the Kumasakas, who never 139 played football with the rest of the kids on the street or appeared at dances, but could talk for hours on end about chemistry and zoology and physics and other courses which he hungered after in high school.

"Sure, Bob always was pretty studious." He knew, somehow, that it was 140 not the right thing to say, but he added: "Where is Bob?"

His mother did not move. Mrs. Kumasaka uttered a despairing cry and 141 bit her trembling lips.

The little man, his face a drawn mask of pity and sorrow, stammered: 142
"Ichiro, you—no one has told you?"

"No. What? No one's told me anything." 143

"Your mother did not write you?" 144

"No. Write about what?" He knew what the answer was. It was in the 145
whiteness of the hair of the sad woman who was the mother of the boy named
Bob and it was in the engaging pleasantness of the father which was not really
pleasantness but a deep understanding which had emerged from resignation to
a loss which only a parent knows and suffers. And then he saw the picture on
the mantel, a snapshot, enlarged many times over, of a grinning youth in uniform
who had not thought to remember his parents with a formal portrait because
he was not going to die and there would be worlds of time for pictures and
books and other obligations of the living later on.

Mr. Kumasaka startled him by shouting toward the rear of the house: 146
"Jun! Please come."

There was the sound of a door opening and presently there appeared a 147
youth in khaki shirt and wool trousers, who was a stranger to Ichiro.

"I hope I haven't disturbed anything, Jun," said Mr. Kumasaka. 148

"No, it's all right. Just writing a letter." 149

"This is Mrs. Yamada and her son Ichiro. They are old family friends." 150

Jun nodded to his mother and reached over to shake Ichiro's hand. 151

The little man waited until Jun had seated himself on the end of the sofa. 152
"Jun is from Los Angeles. He's on his way home from the army and was good
enough to stop by and visit us for a few days. He and Bobbie were together.
Buddies—is that what you say?"

"That's right," said Jun. 153

"Now, Jun." 154

"Yes?" 155

The little man looked at Ichiro and then at his mother, who stared stonily 156
at no one in particular.

"Jun, as a favor to me, although I know it is not easy for you to speak of 157
it, I want you to tell us about Bobbie."

Jun stood up quickly. "Gosh, I don't know." He looked with tender 158
concern at Mrs. Kumasaka.

"It is all right, Jun. Please, just this once more." 159

"Well, okay." He sat down again, rubbing his hands thoughtfully over 160
his knees. "The way it happened, Bobbie and I, we had just gotten back to the
rest area. Everybody was feeling good because there was a lot of talk about the
Germans' surrendering. All the fellows were cleaning their equipment. We'd
been up in the lines for a long time and everything was pretty well messed up.
When you're up there getting shot at, you don't worry much about how crummy
your things get, but the minute you pull back, they got to have inspection. So,
we were cleaning things up. Most of us were cleaning our rifles because that's

HISAYE YAMAMOTO

Hisaye Yamamoto, born in Redondo Beach, California, in 1921, spent the war years interned with her family in Arizona. After the war she attended college and wrote for the Los Angeles Tribune. *Yamamoto also has published short stories in such journals as* The Kenyon Review, Amerasia Journal, The Partisan Review, Arizona Quarterly, *and* Counterpoint.

Like several of her other stories, "Las Vegas Charley" (1961) explores the consequences of the Internment. It considers the ways in which people's lives are still affected by the political and cultural choices made a generation ago.

◆ LAS VEGAS CHARLEY ◆

There are very few Japanese residing in Las Vegas proper, that glittering city 1
which represents, probably, the ultimate rebellion against the Puritan origins
of this singular country. A few Japanese families farm on the outskirts, but I
can't imagine what they grow there in that arid land where, as far as the eye
can see from a Greyhound bus (and a Scenicruiser it was, at that), there are
only sand, bare mountains, sagebrush, and more sand. Sometimes the families
come into town for shopping; sometimes they come for a feast of Chinese food,
because the Japanese regard Chinese cuisine as the height of gourmandism, to
be partaken of on special occasions, as after a wedding or a funeral.

But there are a handful of Japanese who live in the city itself, and they 2
do so because they cannot tear themselves away. They are victims of Las Vegas
fever, that practically incurable disease, and while they usually make their living
as waiters or dishwashers, their principal occupation, day after hopeful day, is
to try their luck at feeding those insatiable mechanical monsters which swallow
up large coins as though they were mere Necco wafers, or at blotting out, on
those small rectangular slips of paper imprinted with Chinese characters, the
few black words which may justify their whole existence.

The old Japanese that everyone knew as Charley (he did not mind being 3
called that—it was as good a name as any and certainly easier to pronounce
than Kazuyuki Matsumoto) was a dishwasher in a Chinese restaurant. His
employer, a most prosperous man named Dick Chew, owned several cafes in
the city, staffed by white waitresses and by relatives he had somehow arranged—
his money was a sharp pair of scissors that snipped rapidly through tangles of
red tape—to bring over from China. Mr. Chew dwelt, with his wife and children, in a fabulous stucco house which was a showplace (even the mayor had
come to the housewarming). He left most of the business in the hands of relatives
and went on many vacations. One year he had even gone as far as England, to
see London and the charms of the English countryside.

As for Charley, he worked ten hours a night, in five-hour shifts. He slept 4 a few hours during the day, in a dormitory with the Chinese kitchen employees; the rest of his free time was spent in places called the Boulder Club, the California Club, the Pioneer Club, or some such name meant to evoke the derring-do of the Old West. He belonged to the local culinary union, so his wages were quite satisfactory. His needs were few; sometimes he bought a new shirt or a set of underwear. But it never failed: at the end of each month, he was quite penniless.

Not that life was bleak for Charley, not at all. Each day was exciting,   5
fraught with the promise of sudden wealth. Why, one Japanese man who claimed to be eighty-five years old had won $25,000 on a keno ticket! And he had been there only a day or two, on a short holiday from Los Angeles. The Oriental octogenarian's beaming face (Charley decided the man had lied about his age; he looked to be more his own age—sixty-two or so) had been pictured on the front page of the *Las Vegas Sun*, and Charley had saved the whole newspaper, to take out and study now and then, in envy and hope.

And all the waitresses were nice to Charley, not only because Charley   6
was a conscientious dishwasher (better than those sloppy Chinese, they confided), but because he was usually good for the loan of a few dollars when their luck had been bad. The bartender was also very good to him; when he came off shift at six o'clock in the morning, tired to the bone, there was always waiting for him a free jigger or two of whiskey, which would ease his body and warm his spirit, reminding him sometimes of the small glass of *sake* he had been wont to sip, with an appetizer of pickled greens, just before supper, after a day's toil out in the fields. (But it seemed as though it had been another man, and not himself, who had once had a farm in Santa Maria, California, and a young wife to share his work and his bed.)

Then there had been the somewhat fearful time when the Army had   7
conducted those atom bomb tests in the Nevada desert. Everyone had talked about it; the whole town had been shaken by intermittent earthquakes, each accompanied by a weird flash of light that hovered over the whole town for a ghastly instant. It was during this time that Charley had been disconcerted by a tipsy soldier, who, after their first encounter, had searched out Charley time and again. Although Charley's command of pidgin English was not sufficient to take in every meaning of the soldier's message, he had understood that the man was most unhappy over having been chosen to push the button that had dropped the atomic bomb over Hiroshima.

Indeed, once, tears streaming down his cheeks, the soldier had grabbed   8
Charley by the shoulders and apologized for the heinous thing he had done to Charley's people. Then he had turned back to his drink, pounded the counter with one tight fist, and muttered, "But it was them or us, you understand, it was them or us!"

Charley had not said a word then. What was there to say? He could have   9
said he was not from Hiroshima, but from Kumamoto, that province whose natives are described as among the most amiable in all Japan, unless aroused,

and then they are considered the most dangerous. He could have said that the people of Kumamoto-*ken* had always regarded the people of Hiroshima-*ken* as being rather too parsimonious. But his English was not up to imparting such small talk, and he doubted, too, that information of this kind would have been of much interest to such a deeply troubled man.

So Charley was doubly relieved when the Army finally went away. The   10
soldier had revived a couple of memories which Charley had pushed far back in his mind. There had been that time, just after the war, when he had been a janitor in Los Angeles' Little Tokyo, and he had been walking down the sidewalk, just minding his own business. This white man had come out of nowhere, suddenly shoved Charley against a wall, and placed an open penknife against his stomach. "Are you Japanese or Chinese?" the man had demanded, and Charley had seen then that the man, middle-aged, red-faced, had been drinking. Charley had not said a word. What was there to say at such a startling time? "If you're Chinese, that's okay, but if you're Japanese . . . !" The man had moved the point of the penknife a little closer to Charley's stomach. Charley had remained silent, tense against the brick wall of the building. Then, after a few moments, possibly because he obtained no satisfaction, no argument, the man had closed his penknife and gone unsteadily on his way.

There had been a similar incident not long after, but Charley had talked   11
his way out of that one. Charley had just gotten off the streetcar when he bumped into a Mexican man about his own age. This man, who had also reeked of liquor, had grabbed his arm tightly and cursed him. "My boy, my Angel, he die in the war! You Japs keel him! Only nineteen years old, and you Japs keel him! I'm going to keel you!" But somehow a Mexican had not been as intimidating as a white man; hadn't he hired Mexicans once upon a time, been their boss, each summer when he and his wife had needed help with the harvesting of the vegetables?

"Mexicans, Japanese, long time good friends," Charley had answered.   12
"My boy die in the war, too. In Italy. I no hate Germans. No use."

Wonderingly, the Mexican had released his grip on Charley's arm. "Oh,   13
yeah?" he had asked, tilting his head.

The magic word had come to Charley's tongue. "*Verdad,*[1]" he had said.   14
"*Verdad.*"

So this man, too, had turned away and gone, staggering a bit from side   15
to side.

It was not long after that Charley, dismissed from his janitorial duties for   16
spending too much time in the pool hall down in the basement, had been sent by the Japanese employment agency to Las Vegas, where dishwashers were in great demand.

---

[1]True

It was like Paradise: the heavy silver dollars that were as common as 17
pennies; the daily anticipation of getting rich overnight; the rejoicing when a
fellow worker had a streak of luck and shared his good fortune with one and
all, buying presents all around (the suitcase under Charley's bed became full
of expensive neckties which were never used) and treating everyone to the drink
of his choice.

It was a far cry from Tomochi-machi, that small village of his birth in 18
the thirtieth year of the reign of the Emperor Meiji. The place had been known
in those days as Hara-machi, meaning wilderness, and it had been a lonely
backwoods, in a sector called Aza-Kashiwagawa, or Oakstream. Above his
father's tiny house had risen the peaks of Azame-yama and Karamata-dake;
beyond that mountains higher still. Below was Midori-kawa, Emerald Lake,
where abounded the troutlike fish called *ayu*. The mountains about were thick
with trees, the larger of them pine and redwood, and he had, as a small boy,
been regularly sent to bring down bundles of wood.

He still wore a deep purple scar on his leg from those days, and there 19
was a bitterness he could not help when he remembered why. A nail had lodged
deep in his leg, too deep to remove; the leg had swollen to a frightening size
and finally the nail had burst out with the pus. He could not forget that when
he was in agony from the pain and unable to walk, his mother (that good, quiet
woman) had asked, "Will you bring down one more load of wood from the
mountain?"

He had attended school for two or three years, but he was not much for 20
studying, so he had hired out as a baby sitter, going about his chores with some
damp baby strapped to his back. Older, he had worked on farms.

When he was twenty, he had ridden the *basha*, the horse-drawn carriage, 21
to the town of Kumamoto, from thence taken the train to Nagasaki, where he
had boarded the Shunryo-Maru as a steerage passenger bound for America,
that far land where, it was said, people had green hair and red eyes, and where
the streets were paved with gold.

In Santa Maria, friends who had preceded him there from his village had 22
helped him lease a small farm (Japanese were not allowed to buy property,
they told him—it was part of something called a Gentleman's Agreement between Japan and the United States). A couple of years later, his picture bride,
Haru, had joined him, and she had been a joy as refreshing as the meaning of
her name (Spring), hard-working, docile, eager to attend to his least wants.
Within the first year, she had presented him with a boy-child, whom they had
named Isamu, because he was the first.

What New Year celebrations they had held in this new land! Preparations had 23
begun about Christmastime, with relatives and friends gathering for the day-
long making of rice cakes. Pounds and pounds of a special glutinous rice, soaked
overnight in earthen vats, would be steamed in square wooden boxes, two or

three piled one atop the other, over an outside fire. The men would all tie handkerchiefs or towels about their heads, to absorb the sweat, then commence to clean out the huge wooden mortar, the tree trunk with a basin carved out at the top. One box of the steaming rice would be dumped into the basin; then the rhythmic pounding of the rice would begin, the men grunting exaggeratedly as they wielded the long-handled wooden mallets. Usually two men at a time would work on the rice, while one woman stood by with a pan of cold water. It was the woman's job to quickly dab water at the rice dough so it would not stick to the mortar or mallets, while the men did not once pause in their steady, alternate pounding.

The rest of the aproned women would be waiting at a long table spread   24
with befloured newspapers, and when the rice had become a soft lump of hot dough, it was thrown onto the table, where each woman would wring off a handful to pat into shape before placing it on a floured wooden tray. Some of the cakes would be plain, some filled with a sweet mealy jam made of an interminable boiling together of tiny, maroon Indian beans and sugar. There were not only white cakes; there were pink ones, made so during the pounding with a touch of vegetable coloring; green ones, made so during the steaming with the addition of dried seaweed; and yellow ones, which were green ones dusted with orangish bean flour.

But the main purpose of the work was to make the larger unsweetened   25
cakes which in tiers two or three high, one tier for each member of the family, topped with choice tangerines with the leafy stems left on, decorated the *hotoke-sama*, the miniature temple representing the Buddha which occupies a special corner in every Buddhist household. On New Year's morning, the cakes would be joined, reverently placed, by miniature bowls of rice and miniature cups of *sake*.

Sometimes, enough *mochi* was made to last almost throughout the whole   26
year, either preserved in water periodically changed, or cut into strips and dried. The sweet cakes would be eaten early, toasted on an asbestos pad over the tin winter stove (when done, the dark filling would burst out in a bubble); the soaked would be boiled and eaten plain with soy sauce or sugared bean flour, or made into dumplings with meat and vegetables. The dried flinty strips would be fried in deep oil until they became crisp, puffy confections which were sprinkled with sugar.

How rosy the men had grown during the cake-making, not only from   27
their exertions but from frequently repairing to the house for a taste of fresh *mochi* and a sip of *sake*. There would be impromptu singing above the sound of the slapping mallets; women chasing men with threatening, floury hands; and continuous shouted jokes with earthy references more often than not.

Then, on New Year's Eve, Haru would prepare the last meal of the year,   28
to be eaten just before midnight. This was *somen*, the very thin, grey, brown-flecked noodles, served with *tororo*, the slippery brown sauce of grated raw

yams. At the stroke of midnight, Kazuyuki Matsumoto (he was not Charley then) went outside with his shotgun and used up several shells, to bid appropriate farewell to the passing year.

On New Year's morning, dressed in brand-new clothing, Kazuyuki and Haru would, following tradition, eat that first breakfast of the New Year, the thick soup of fresh *mochi* dumplings, vegetables, tender strips of dried cuttlefish. It was also necessary to take, from tiny cups, token sips of hot mulled *sake*, poured from a small porcelain decanter shaped like a rosebud vase. 29

Then it was open house everywhere, for almost the whole week, and it was an insult not to accept token sips of hot *sake* at each house visited. Sometimes Kazuyuki Matsumoto was so polite that when they somehow arrived home, in that old topless Ford, Haru had to unlace his shoes, undress him, and tuck him in bed. 30

And the ritual was the same with each friend seen for the first time in the year, each solemn, prescribed greeting accompanied by deep, deep bows: 31

"*Akema-shite omedeto gozai-masu.*" (The old year has ended and the new begun—congratulations!) 32

"*Sakunen wa iro-iro o-sewa ni nari-mashite, arigato gozai-masu.*" (Thank you for the many favors of the past year.) 33

"*Konnen mo onegai itashi-masu.*" (Again this year, I give myself unto your care.) 34

What a mountain of food Haru had prepared on New Year's Eve, cooking till almost morning: bamboo shoots, stalks of pale green bog rhubarb, both taken from cans with Japanese labels; red and white fish galantines, fish rolls with burdock root centers, both of these delicacies purchased ready-made from the Japanese market; fried shrimp; fried chicken; thin slices of raw fish; gelatinous red and white agar-agar cakes, tasting faintly of peppermint; sweet Indian-bean cakes; dried herring roe soaked in soy sauce; vinegared rice rolls covered with thin sheets of dried seaweed and containing in the center thin strips of fried egg, canned eel, long strings of dried gourd, mushrooms, carrots, and burdock root—neatly sliced; triangles of fried bean curd filled with vinegared rice and chopped vegetables; sliced lotus root stems, which when bitten would stretch shimmering, cobwebby filaments from the piece in your mouth to the remnant between your chopsticks. The centerpiece was usually a huge red lobster, all appendages intact, or a red-gold seabream, resting on a bed of parsley on the largest and best platter in the house. 35

But that had been long, long ago. The young Japanese, the *Nisei*, were so Americanized now. While most of them still liked to eat their boiled rice, raw fish, and pickled vegetables, they usually spent New Year's Eve in some nightclub. Charley knew this because many of them came to Las Vegas, from as far away as San Francisco and Los Angeles, to inaugurate the New Year. 36

Then, abruptly, Haru, giving birth to the second boy, had died. He had 37 been a huge baby, almost ten pounds, and the midwife said Haru, teeth clenched, had held with all her might to the metal bed rods behind her head; and at long last, when the infant gargantua had emerged, she had asked, "Boy or girl?" The midwife had said, "It's a boy, a giant of a boy!" And Haru, answering, "Good . . . ," had closed her eyes and died.

Kazuyuki Matsumoto had sent his two small sons over to a cousin of Haru's, but this woman, with five older children of her own, had eventually, embarrassedly, confessed that her husband was complaining that the additional burden was too much, that the babies did not allow her enough time in the fields. So Kazuyuki had taken his sons to Japan, to Tomochi-machi, where his own mother had reluctantly accepted them. **38**

Returning to California, Kazuyuki had stopped farming on his own and worked for friends, for twenty cents an hour with room and board. Frugal, he sent most of his wages to Japan, where, at the favorable rate of exchange, his mother and father had been able to build a larger house and otherwise raise their standard of living, as well as their prestige in the sector. **39**

For several years, Kazuyuki had kept to this unvaried but rewarding way of life. Friends had shaken their heads over his truly self-sacrificing ways; he was admired as an exceptional fellow. **40**

But Kazuyuki, living in bunkhouses with the other seasonal workers, who were usually bachelors, gradually came to love the game of *hana-fuda*, flower cards, which relaxed him of evenings, giving him a more immediate pleasure to look forward to than taking a hot bath and going to bed. So the money orders to Japan became fewer and farther between before they had finally stopped. By that time, Kazuyuki had wandered the length of California, picking grapes in Fresno, peaches in Stockton, strawberries in Watsonville, flowers in San Fernando, cantaloupe in Imperial Valley, always ending his day and filling his Saturdays off with the shuffling and dealing of flower cards. **41**

His mother had written once in a while, in her unpunctuated *katakana*, unacknowledged (he was not one for writing letters) messages which nevertheless moved him to the core, saying that his sons were fine and bright, but that both she and his father were getting older and that they would like to see him once more before they died. When was he coming to visit them? Finally, his father had died during the New Year holidays; they had found him drunk, lying helplessly there on the steep path home after visiting friends in the village below. Since this had become a common event, they had merely carried him home and put him to bed. But this, as it happened, was the sleep from which he never awoke. **42**

Learning of this news, Kazuyuki has secretly wept. Like father, like son, the saying went, and it was true, it was true. He was as worthless, as *tsumara-nai*, as his father had in the end become. **43**

The shock had the effect of reforming him; he gave up flower cards and, within a couple of diligent years, had saved enough money to send for his boys. **44**

The wages had risen to fifty cents per hour with room and board; the rate of exchange had become even more favorable, so his few hundred American dollars had amounted to a considerable pile of yen.

With his sons by his side to assist him, he leased again a small farm, this   45
time in Orange County, but somehow things did not go well. They tried things like tomatoes and Italian squash. The vegetables flourished, but it seemed that since the man called Rusuberuto had been elected President of the United States, there had come into being a system called prorating, in which one had to go into town and get coupons which limited the number of boxes one could pick and send to market. This was intended to keep the prices up, to help the farmer. The smaller the farm, the fewer the coupons it was allotted, so it was a struggle. They lived on tomato soup and sliced Italian squash fried in batter—this was quite tasty, with soy sauce—and, of course, boiled rice, although the cost of a hundred-pound sack of Blue Rose had become amazing. During the winter, the fare was usually the thick yellow soup made by adding water to soy bean paste, and pickled vegetables.

At first, too, the relationship with his sons had been a source of distress.   46
They had expected wondrous things of America, not this drudgery, this poverty. Alien, too, to their father, they had done his bidding as though he were some lord and master who expected them to wash his feet. This had annoyed him and he had treated them sternly, too sternly. And both of them had been resentful of the fact that their contemporaries here, the *Nisei*, looked down upon them as *Kibei*,[2] for lacking English, as though there were rice hulls sticking to their hair.

As he had come to know them better, however, he saw that the two were   47
as different as grey and white. Isamu, now nineteen, was quick to pick up colloquial English, eager to learn how to drive the old pick-up truck, fascinated with the American movies which now and then they were able to afford, and his father perceived that he was ambitious, perhaps too ambitious, restless for the day when he could own a shining automobile and go on his way. Noriyuki, two years younger, was more like Haru, quiet, amiable, content to listen to the Japanese popular songs which he played over and over on the Victrola (he sang a nice baritone himself as he worked out in the fields), and he spoke nostalgically of his grandmother, the blue-green coolness of Midori-kawa, the green loveliness of the fields of rape and barley in the spring.

Then, after only a little more than a year together, had come the incredible   48
war, and the trio, along with all the other Japanese on the West Coast, had been notified that they would be sent to concentration camps. How uneasy they had been in those days, with government men coming in unannounced,

---

[2]Children born in the U.S. of Japaness immigrant parents who were sent to Japan for their education.

on three occasions, to inspect the small wooden house for evidence of sabotage. In their panic, they had burned all their Japanese magazines and records, hidden the *hotoke-sama*, buried the *judo* outfits and the *happi* coats the boys had brought with them from Japan. They had had to turn in their little Kodak (it had never been retrieved), lest they be tempted to photograph American military installations and transmit them secretly to Japan.

But the Arizona concentration camp, once they became accustomed to the heat and dust and mudstorms, was not too unbearable. In fact, Noriyuki, with his repertoire of current Japanese songs, became quite popular with even the *Nisei* girls, and he was in great demand for the amateur talent shows which helped illuminate that drab incarceration. Kazuyuki Matsumoto settled for a job as cook in one of the mess halls; Isamu immediately got a job driving one of the covered surplus Army trucks which brought supplies to these mess halls; and Noriyuki went to work with the men and women who were making adobe bricks for the school buildings which the government planned to build amidst the black tar-papered barracks. `49`

One day, a white officer, accompanied by a *Nisei* in uniform, came to recruit soldiers for the United States Army, and Isamu was among the few who unhesitatingly volunteered. He was sent to Mississippi, where an all-Japanese group from Hawaii and the mainland was being given basic training, and his regular letters to his father and brother indicated that he was, despite some reservations, satisfied with his decision. Once he was able to come on a furlough, and they saw that he was a new man, all (visible) trace of boy gone, with a certain burliness, a self-confidence that was willing to take on all comers. Then, after a silence, came small envelopes called V-Mail, which gave no indication of his whereabouts. Finally, he was able to tell them that he was in Italy, and he sent them sepia postcards of the ancient ruins of Rome. Almost on the heels of this packet, the telegram had come, informing them of the death in action of Pfc. Isamu Matsumoto; a later letter from his sergeant had filled in the details—it had occurred near a town called Grosseto; it had been an 88-millimeter shell; death had been (if it would comfort) instantaneous. `50`

Kazuyuki Matsumoto continued to cook in the mess hall and Noriyuki went on making adobe bricks. After the school buildings were completed— they turned out quite nicely—Noriyuki decided to attend classes in them. As he was intelligent and it was mostly a matter of translating his solid Japanese schooling into English, he skipped rapidly from one grade to the next, and although he never lost the accent which marked him as a *Kibei*, he was graduated from the camp high school with honors. `51`

By this time, Kazuyuki Matsumoto was on the road that would lead, inexorably, to Las Vegas. At first, in that all-Japanese milieu, he had taken courage and tried courting a *Nisei* spinster who worked as a waitress in the same mess hall. Once he had even dared to take her a gift of a bag of apples, bought at the camp canteen; but the woman already had her eye on a fellow-waiter `52` several years her junior. She refused the apples and proceeded to ensnare the younger man with a desperation which he was simply not equipped to combat. After this rejection, Kazuyuki Matsumoto had returned to his passion for flower cards. What else was there to do? He had tried passing the time, as some of the other men did, by making polished canes of mesquite and ironwood, by carving and enameling little birds and fish to be used as brooches, but he was not truly cut out for such artistic therapy. Flower cards were what beguiled—that occasional unbeatable combination of the four cards: the pink cherry blossoms in full, festive bloom; the black pines with the stork standing in between; the white moon rising in a red sky over the black hill; and the red-and-black crest symbolizing the paulownia tree in flower.

Then had come the day of decision. The government announced that all 53 Japanese wanting to return to Japan (with their American-born children) would be sent to another camp in northern California, to await the sailings of the Swedish *Gripsholm*. The removal was also mandatory for all young men of draft age who did not wish to serve in the United States Army and chose to renounce their American citizenship. Kazuyuki Matsumoto, busy with the cooking and absorbed in flower cards, was not too surprised when Noriyuki decided in favor of Japan. At least there would not be another son dead in Europe; the boy would be a comfort to his grandmother in her old age. As for himself, he would be quite content to remain in this camp the rest of his life—free food, free housing, friends, flower cards; what more could life offer? It was true that he had partially lost his hearing in one ear, from standing by those hot stoves on days of unbearable heat, but that was a small complaint. The camp hospital had provided free treatment, free medicines, free cottonballs to stuff in his bad ear. Kazuyuki Matsumoto was far from agreeing with one angry man who had one day, annoyed with a severe duststorm, shouted, "America is going to pay for every bit of this suffering! Taking away my farm and sending me to this hell! Japan will win the war, and then we'll see who puts who where!"

So Noriyuki was among those departing for Tule Lake, where, for a time, 54 he thoroughly enjoyed the pro-Japanese atmosphere, the freedom of shouting a *banzai* or two whenever he felt like it. Then, despite himself, he kept remembering a *Nisei* girl in that Arizona camp he thought he had been glad to leave behind. She had wept a little when he left. He recalled the habit she had of saying something amusing and then sticking out her tongue to lick a corner of her lip. He began to dream of her almost nightly. Once, he wired together and enameled with delicate colors a fragile corsage, fashioned of those tiny white seashells which one could harvest by the basketful in that region. This he sent on to her with a tender message. One morning his dormitory mates teased him, saying he had cried out in his sleep, clear as a bell, "Alice, Alice, don't leave me!" In English, too, they said. So, one day, Noriyuki, as Isamu had before him, volunteered for service in the Army of the United States. He spent most of his hitch in Colorado, as an instructor in the Japanese language, and ended up as a technical sergeant. Alice joined him there, and they were married in Denver one fine day in June.

Since the war had ended in the meantime, Noriyuki and Alice went to live in Los Angeles, where most of their camp friends had already settled, and Kazuyuki Matsumoto, already in Las Vegas, already Charley, received a monthly long-distance call from them, usually about six in the morning, because, as they said, they wanted to make sure he was still alive and kicking. 55

 Noriyuki was doing well as an assistant in the office of a landscape architect; Alice had first a baby girl, then another. Each birth was announced to Charley by telephone, and while he rejoiced, he was also made to feel worthless, because he was financially unable to send even a token gift of felicitations. 56

 But he would make up for it, he knew. One day his time would come, and he would return in triumph to Los Angeles, laden with gifts for Noriyuki (a wristwatch, probably), for Alice (she might like an ornate necklace, such as he had seen some of these rich women wear), and an armload of toys for the babies. 57

 But Charley began having trouble with his teeth, and he decided to take a short leave of absence in order to obtain the services of a good Japanese dentist in Los Angeles. He had to stay with Noriyuki and his family, and they, with no room for a houseguest, allowed him the use of the couch in the front room which could be converted into a bed at night. Charley, paid at the end of each month, had brought some money with him, so, at first, the reunion went quite well. After his visits to the dentist, who decided to remove first all the upper teeth, then all the lower, and then to fit him with plates, he remembered to bring back a gift-box of either the rice-cakes and bean confections of all shapes and colors known as *manju*, or of *o-sushi*, containing a miscellany of vinegared rice dolls and squares. He bought a musical jack-in-the-box for the older child, and a multi-colored rubber ball for the baby. After a while, the dentist asked for a hundred dollars as part payment, and Charley gave it to him, although this was about all he had left, except for the return bus ticket to Las Vegas. 58

 About the middle of his month in Los Angeles, Charley felt unwelcome, but there was no help for it. The dentist was not through with him. He could hear, from the sofa bed, the almost nightly reproaches, sometimes accompanied with weeping, that Noriyuki had to listen to. Since his hearing was not too good, he could not make out all that Alice said, but it seemed there was the problem of his napping on the couch and thus preventing her from having friends over during the day, of his turning on the television (and so loud) just when she wanted the children to take their nap, and just how long did that father of his intend to stay? Forever? 59

 Charley was crushed; it had never been his intention to hurt anyone, never once during his lifetime. The dentist, however, took his time; a month was up before he finally got around to inserting both plates, and he still wanted Charley 60 to return for three appointments, in order to insure the proper fit. But Charley ignored him and returned to Las Vegas, posthaste, to free Noriyuki and Alice from their burden.

Some days before he left, Alice, who was not at heart unkind, but irritable 61 from the daily care of two active youngsters and the requirement of having to prepare three separate meals (one for the babies, one for herself and husband, and a bland, soft diet for toothless Charley), had a heart-to-heart talk with her father-in-law. Noriyuki, patient, easygoing, had never mentioned the sorrows of his wife.

In halting Japanese, interspersed with the simplest English she could think 62 of, Alice begged Charley to mend his ways.

"You're not getting any younger," she told him. "What of the future, 63 when you're unable to work any longer? You're making a good salary; if you saved most of it, you wouldn't have to worry about who would take care of you in your old age. This *bakuchi* (gambling) is getting you nowhere. Why, you still owe the dentist two hundred dollars!"

Charley was ashamed. Every word she spoke was the truth. "You have 64 been so good to me," he said, "when I have been so *tsumara-nai*. I know I have been a lot of trouble to you."

There and then, they made a pact. Charley would send Alice at least a 65 hundred dollars a month; she would put it in the bank for him. When he retired, at sixty-five, he would be a man of substance. With his Social Security, he could visit Japan and see his mother again before she died. He might even stay on in Japan; at the rate of exchange, which was now about three thousand yen for ten American dollars, he could lead a most comfortable, even luxurious life.

But once in Las Vegas again, Charley could not keep to the pact. His 66 compulsion was more than he could deny; and Noriyuki, dunned by the dentist, felt obliged to pay the two hundred dollars which Charley owed. Alice was furious.

Then Charley's mother died, and Charley was filled with grief and guilt. 67 Those letters pleading for one more visit from her only son, her only child, of whom she had been so proud; those letters which he had not once answered. But he would somehow atone. When he struck it rich, he would go to Japan and buy a fine headstone for the spot under which her urn was buried. He would buy chrysanthemums (she had loved chrysanthemums) by the dozens to decorate the monument. It would make a lovely sight, to make the villagers sit up and take notice.

Charley's new teeth, handsome as they were (the waitresses were admir- 68 ing, saying they made him look ten years younger), were troublesome, too. Much too loose, they did not allow the consumption of solids. He had to subsist on rice smothered with gravy, soft-boiled eggs, soups. But at least he did not have to give up that morning pickup that the bartender still remembered him with. That whiskey was a marvel, warming his insides (especially welcome on chilly winter mornings), giving him a glow that made him surer than ever that one day he, too, would hit the jackpot of jackpots.

But Charley's health began to fail. His feet would swell and sometimes 69
he had to lean against the sink for support, in order to wash the endless platters, plates, dishes, saucers, cups, glasses, knives, forks, spoons, pots, and pans. Once, twice, he got so dizzy climbing the stairs to the dormitory that he almost blacked out, and, hearing him cry out, his Chinese roommates had to carry him the rest of the way to his bed.

One day Mr. Chew, coming to inspect, looked at Charley and said with 70
some concern, "What's the matter? You look bad." And Charley admitted that he had not been feeling up to snuff of late.

Mr. Chew then insisted that he go home to his son in Los Angeles, for a 71
short rest. That was what he probably needed.

By that time Charley was glad for the advice. He was so tired, so tired. 72
One of the waitresses called Noriyuki on the telephone and asked him to come after his father. Charley was pretty sick, she said; he could probably use a good vacation.

So Noriyuki, in his gleaming station wagon, which was only partly paid 73
for, sped to Las Vegas to fetch his father. Charley slept on and off during most of the long trip back.

The young Japanese doctor in Los Angeles shook his head when Charley 74
listed his symptoms. Charley thought it was his stomach; there was a sharp pain there sometimes, right between the ribs.

The young Japanese doctor said to Noriyuki, "When an *Issei* starts com- 75
plaining about his stomach, it's usually pretty serious." He meant there was the possibility of cancer. For some reason, possibly because of the eating of raw fish, Japanese are more prone to stomach cancer than other races.

But the pain in Charley's stomach turned out to be an ulcer. That was 76
not too bad. As for the swollen feet, that was probably an indication of hepatitis, serious but curable in time. Then, in the process of studying the routine X-rays, the doctor came upon a dismaying discovery. There was definite evidence of advanced cirrhosis of the liver.

"Cirrhosis of the liver?" said Noriyuki. "Doesn't that come from drinking? 77
My father gambled, but he didn't drink. He's no drunkard."

"Usually it comes from drinking. Your father says he did drink some 78
whiskey every day. And if his loose plates kept him from eating a good diet, that could do it, that could do it."

So Charley went to stay at the Japanese Hospital, where the excess fluid 79
in his abdomen could be drained periodically. He was put on a low-sodium diet, and the dietitian was in a quandary. A salt-free diet for a man who could not eat solids; there was very little she could plan for him, hardly any variety.

Subsequent X-rays showed up some dark spots on the lungs. The young 80
Japanese doctor shook his head again.

"It's hopeless," he said to Noriyuki. "That means cancer of the liver, 81
spreading to the lungs. He doesn't have much time left."

Noriyuki told Alice, who, relieved that the culinary union had provided 82
for insurance which would take care of the hospital bills, tried to console him.
"Who can understand these things?" she said. "Look at your mother—dead at
twenty-four, with so much to live for . . ."

Biting her lips, she stopped. She had said the wrong thing. Noriyuki, all 83
his life, under his surface serenity, had known guilt that his birth had been the
cause of his mother's death.

Thus Charley died, leaving a son, a daughter-in-law, two grandchildren. 84
Towards the end, his mind had wandered, because the medication for the
cirrhosis had drained him of potassium, and the pills prescribed to make up the
lack had not sufficed. There was a huge stack of sympathy cards from Las
Vegas, from the kitchen employees, the waitresses, the cashier, the sweet,
elderly lady-bookkeeper who had always helped Charley file his income tax
statements, a cab driver, and a few others who had come to accept Charley as
part of the Las Vegas scene. They even chipped in to wire him an enormous
floral offering.

The young Japanese doctor would not take his fee (the union insurance 85
had not provided for his services). "The worst mistake I made in my life was
becoming a doctor," he confided to Noriyuki. "Life is hell, nothing but hell."

"But you help people when they need help the most," Noriyuki tried to
tell him. "What could be more satisfying than that?"

"Yeah, and you see people die right in front of you, and there isn't a damn 87
thing you can do about it! Well, at least your father had a good time—he drank,
he gambled, he smoked. I don't do any of those things; all I do is work, work,
work. At least he enjoyed himself while he was alive."

And Noriyuki—who, without one sour word, had lived through a succes- 88
sion of conflicting emotions about his father—hate for rejecting him as a child;
disgust and exasperation over that weak moral fiber; embarrassment when people
asked what his father did for a living; and finally, something akin to compassion,
when he came to understand that his father was not an evil man, but only an
inadequate one with the most shining intentions, only one man among so many
who lived from day to day as best as they could, limited, restricted, by the
meager gifts Fate or God had doled out to them—could not quite agree. ◆

◆ Responding

1. The narrator introduces the main character as "the old Japanese that everyone
   knew as Charley (he did not mind being called that—it was as good a name
   as any and certainly easier to pronounce . . .)." Do you think that Yamamoto

would agree that the name change is unimportant? Discuss the relationship between a name and a person's sense of identity.

2. Working individually or in a group, summarize the main events of Charley's life. Using information from the introduction and other sources, discuss which of Charley's experiences represented the experiences of many Japanese immigrants and which were the result of his character.

3. Was Charley a victim of fate? What choices were made for him? What choices did he make?

4. What did Noriyuki finally understand about his father?

JANICE MIRIKITANI

Janice Mirikitani was born in Stockton, California. She received a bachelor's degree from the University of California, Los Angeles and did graduate study at San Francisco State University. Her poems have been published in several collections of Asian American literature. In addition, she has edited several volumes of literature, including Third World Woman *and* Ayumi: The Japanese American Anthology.

In the three poems that follow, Mirikitani uses vivid images to comment on the present and the past. "Desert Flower" and "For My Father" address issues of the past by noting the experiences and expectations of the speaker's parents. "We the Dangerous" combines images from the Internment and from the period after the Vietnam War to reflect on the suspicion and prejudices that still exist today.

◆ WE, THE DANGEROUS ◆

I swore
it would not devour me
I swore
it would not humble me
I swore
it would not break me.

      And they commanded we dwell in the desert
      Our children be spawn of barbed wire and barracks

We, closer to the earth,
squat, short thighed,
knowing the dust better.

      And they would have us make the garden
      Rake the grass to soothe their feet

We, akin to the jungle,
plotting with the snake,
tails shedding in civilized America.

      And they would have us skin their fish
      deft hands like blades/sliding back flesh/bloodless

We, who awake in the river
Ocean's child
Whale eater.

And they would have us strange scented women,
Round shouldered/strong and yellow/like the moon
to pull the thread to the cloth
to loosen their backs massaged in myth

We, who fill the secret bed,
the sweat shops
the laundries.

And they would dress us in napalm,
Skin shred to clothe the earth,
Bodies filling pock-marked fields.
Dead fish bloating our harbors.

We, the dangerous,
Dwelling in the ocean.
Akin to the jungle.
Close to the earth.

Hiroshima
Vietnam
Tule Lake

And yet we were not devoured.
And yet we were not humbled.
And yet we are not broken. ◆

◆ Responding

1. Plan a class choral reading of this poem. How would you divide it for different voices? Explain your reasons. What does the reading reveal about the differences among the "I," "we," and "they" of the poem?

2. Through whose eyes do we see the characteristics of "We, the Dangerous"? Would the poet agree that these are the characteristics of Japanese Americans,

or does she believe that they were stereotypes about Asians common during World War II?

3. Compare the effects of the opening and closing stanzas of the poem. How do you respond to the repetition of words and phrases? If you had to assign an emotion to the voice used by the poet, what would it be?

4. What is the relationship among Hiroshima, Vietnam, and Tule Lake? Why does the author include Hiroshima and Vietnam in a poem about the internment experience? From the evidence in the poem, who do you think the author believes is really dangerous?

◆ DESERT FLOWERS ◆

Flowers
faded
in desert wind.
No flowers grow
where dust winds blow
and rain is like
a dry heave moan.

> Mama, did you dream about that
> beau who would take you
> away from it all,
> who would show you
> in his '41 ford
> and tell you how soft
> your hands
> like the silk kimono
> you folded for the wedding?
> Make you forget
> about That place,
> the back bending
> wind that fell like a wall,
> drowned all your geraniums
> and flooded the shed
> where you tried to sleep
> away hyenas?
> And mama,
> bending in the candlelight

after lights out in barracks,
an ageless shadow
grows victory flowers
made from crepepaper,
shaping those petals
like the tears
your eyes bled.
Your fingers
knotted at knuckles
wounded, winding around wire stems
the tiny, sloganed banner:
    "america for americans."
Did you dream
of the shiny ford
(only always a dream)
ride your youth
like the wind
in the headless night?

Flowers
2¢ a dozen,
flowers for American Legions
worn like a badge
on america's lapel
made in post-concentration camps
by candlelight.
Flowers
watered
by the spit
of "no japs wanted here,"
planted in poverty
of postwar relocations,
plucked by victory's veterans.

    Mama, do you dream
    of the wall of wind
    that falls
    on your limbless desert,
    on stems
    brimming with petals/crushed
    crepepaper
    growing
    from the crippled
    mouth of your hand?

Your tears, mama,
have nourished us.
Your children
like pollen
scatter in the wind.◆

◆ Responding

1. Discuss the irony of Japanese Americans in internment camps making flowers for the American Legion.

2. In the second stanza, line 11, "That" is capitalized, but "america" in line 31 and in stanza 3, line 5, is not. Discuss possible reasons that the poet has defied conventional capitalization rules and what she may be trying to convey by doing so.

3. Mirikitani writes about her past. Write your own poem about a past event in your family or your culture that still influences your attitudes and behavior.

◆ FOR MY FATHER ◆

He came over the ocean
carrying Mr. Fuji on
his back / Tule Lake on his chest
hacked through the brush
of deserts
and made them grow
strawberries

　　　　　we stole berries
　　　　　from the stem
　　　　　we could not afford them
　　　　　for breakfast

his eyes held
nothing
as he whipped us
for stealing.

the desert had dried
his soul.

wordless
he sold
the rich,
full berries
to hakujin
whose children
pointed at our eyes

> they ate fresh
> strawberries
> on corn flakes.

Father,
i wanted to scream
at your silence.
Your strength
was a stranger
i could never touch.

iron
in your eyes
to shield
the pain
to shield desert-like wind
from patches
of strawberries
grown
from
tears.◆

◆ Responding

1. Mirikitani draws a verbal picture of her father's character and the events that shaped it. Working individually or in a group, use the clues from the poem to write a prose description of this man.

2. Discuss the attitude of the speaker toward her father. Use examples from the poem to support your points.

3. Write a poem or an essay that captures the essence of someone important to you.

REFLECTING A CRITICAL CONTEXT

RONALD TAKAKI

Ronald Takaki, who was born in 1939, is the grandson of Japanese immigrants who settled in Hawaii. He earned his bachelor's degree from the College of Wooster and his doctorate from the University of California at Berkeley, where he is currently a professor of ethnic studies. Takaki has written and edited several books on ethnic issues, including A Pro Slavery Crusade: Agitation to Open the African Slave Trade, Violence in the Black Imagination, Iron Cages: Plantation Life and Labor in Hawaii, *and* From Different Shores: Perspectives on Race and Ethnicity in America.

The excerpt that follows is from Takaki's most recent text, Strangers from a Different Shore: A History of Asian Americans *(1989). In the passage, the author reflects on the Internment from the perspective of forty years' distance. Takaki calls on the people victimized by the Internment to "break the silence" in which they have lived for too long.*

◆ ROOTS ◆

To confront the current problems of racism, Asian Americans know they must   1
remember the past and break its silence. This need was felt deeply by Japanese Americans during the hearings before the commission reviewing the issue of redress and reparations for Japanese Americans interned during World War II. Memories of the internment nightmare have haunted the older generation like ghosts. But the former prisoners have been unable to exorcise them by speaking out and ventilating their anger.

> When we were children,
> you spoke Japanese
> in lowered voices
> between yourselves.
>
> Once you uttered secrets
> which we should not know,
> were not to be heard by us.
> When you spoke
> of some dark secret,
> you would admonish us,
> "Don't tell it to anyone else."
>
> It was a suffocated vow of silence.

What we have come to know
yet cannot tell
lingers like voiceless ghosts
wandering in our memory
as though memory is
desert bleached by
years of cruel exile.

It is the language
the silence within myself
I cannot fill with words,
the sound of mournful music
distantly heard.[1]

"Stigmatized," the ex-internees have been carrying the "burden of shame" for over forty painful years. "They felt like a rape victim," explained Congressman Norman Mineta, a former internee of the Heart Mountain internment camp. "They were accused of being disloyal. They were the victims but they were on trial and they did not want to talk about it." But Sansei, or third-generation Japanese Americans, want their elders to tell their story. Warren Furutani, for example, told the commissioners that young people like himself had been asking their parents to tell them about the concentration camps and to join them in pilgrimages to the internment camp at Manzanar. "Why? Why!" their parents would reply defensively. "Why would you want to know about it? It's not important, we don't need to talk about it." But, Furutani continued, they need to tell the world what happened during those years of infamy.[2]

Suddenly, during the commission hearings, scores of Issei and Nisei came forward and told their stories. "For over thirty-five years I have been the stereotype Japanese American," Alice Tanabe Nehira told the commission. "I've kept quiet, hoping in due time we will be justly compensated and recognized for our years of patient effort. By my passive attitude, I can reflect on my past years to conclude that it doesn't pay to remain silent." The act of speaking out has enabled the Japanese-American community to unburden itself of years of anger and anguish. Sometimes their testimonies before the commission were long and the chair urged them to conclude. But they insisted the time was theirs. "Mr. Commissioner," protested poet Janice Mirikitani,

---

[1]Richard Oyama, poem published in *Transfer 38* (San Francisco, 1979), p. 43, reprinted in Elaine Kim, *Asian American Literature: An Introduction to the Writings and Their Social Context* (Philadelphia, 1982), pp. 308–309.

[2]Congressman Robert Matsui, speech in the House of Representatives on bill 442 for redress and reparations, September 17, 1987, *Congressional Record* (Washington, 1987), p. 7584; Congressman Norman Mineta, interview with author, March 26, 1988; Warren Furutani, testimony, reprinted in *Amerasia*, vol. 8, no. 2 (1981), p. 104.

So when you tell me my time is
up I tell you this.
Pride has kept my lips
pinned by nails,
my rage confined.
But I exhume my past
to claim this time.[3]

The former internees finally had spoken, and their voices compelled the   4
nation to redress the injustice of internment. In August 1988, Congress passed
a bill giving an apology and a payment of $20,000 to each of the survivors of
the internment camps. When President Ronald Reagan signed the bill into law,
he admitted that the United States had committed "a grave wrong," for during
World War II, Japanese Americans had remained "utterly loyal" to this country.
"Indeed, scores of Japanese Americans volunteered for our Armed Forces—
many stepping forward in the internment camps themselves. The 442nd Reg-
imental Combat Team, made up entirely of Japanese Americans, served with
immense distinction to defend this nation, their nation. Yet, back at home, the
soldiers' families were being denied the very freedom for which so many of the
soldiers themselves were laying down their lives." Then the president recalled
an incident that happened forty-three years ago. At a ceremony to award the
Distinguished Service Cross to Kazuo Masuda, who had been killed in action
and whose family had been interned, a young actor paid tribute to the slain
Nisei soldier. "The name of that young actor," remarked the president, who
had been having trouble saying the Japanese names, "—I hope I pronounce this
right—was Ronald Reagan." The time had come, the president acknowledged,
to end "a sad chapter in American history."[4]

Asian Americans have begun to claim their time not only before the   5
commission on redress and reparations but elsewhere as well—in the novels of
Maxine Hong Kingston and Milton Murayama, the plays of Frank Chin and
Philip Gotanda, the scholarly writings of Sucheng Chan and Elaine Kim, the
films of Steve Okazaki and Wayne Wang, and the music of Hiroshima and Fred
Houn. Others, too, have been breaking silences. Seventy-five-year-old Tomo
Shoji, for example, had led a private life, but in 1981 she enrolled in an acting
course because she wanted to try something frivolous and to take her mind off
her husband's illness. In the beginning, Tomo was hesitant, awkward on the
stage. "Be yourself," her teacher urged. Then suddenly she felt something surge
through her, springing from deep within, and she began to tell funny and also
sad stories about her life. Now Tomo tours the West Coast, a wonderful word-
smith giving one-woman shows to packed audiences of young Asian Americans.

---

[3]Alice Tanabe Nehira, testimony, reprinted in *Amerasia*, vol. 8, no. 2 (1981), p. 93; Janice Mirikitani,
"Breaking Silences," reprinted ibid., p. 109.
[4]"Text of Reagan's Remarks," reprinted in *Pacific Citizen*, August 19–26, 1988, p. 5; *San Francisco
Chronicle*, August 5 and 11, 1988.

"Have we really told our children all we have gone through?" she asks. Telling one of her stories, Tomo recounts: "My parents came from Japan and I was born in a lumber camp. One day, at school, my class was going on a day trip to a show, and I was pulled aside and told I would have to stay behind. All the white kids went." Tomo shares stories about her husband: "When I first met him, I thought, 'wow.' Oh, he was so macho! And he wanted his wife to be a good submissive wife. But then he married me." Theirs had been at times a stormy marriage. "Culturally we were different because he was Issei and I was American, and we used to argue a lot. Well, one day in 1942 right after World War II started he came home and told me we had to go to an internment camp. 'I'm not going to camp because I'm an American citizen,' I said to him. 'You have to go to camp, but not me.' Well you know what, that was one time my husband was right!" Tomo remembers the camp: "We were housed in barracks, and we had no privacy. My husband and I had to share a room with another couple. So we hanged a blanket in the middle of the room as a partition. But you could hear everything from the other side. Well, one night, while we were in bed, my husband and I got into an argument, and I dumped him out of the bed. The other couple thought we were making violent love." As she stands on the stages and talks stories excitedly, Tomo cannot be contained: "We got such good, fantastic stories to tell. All our stories are different."[5]

Today, young Asian Americans want to listen to these stories—to shatter images of themselves and their ancestors as "strangers" and to understand who they are as Asian Americans. "What don't you know?" their elders ask. Their question seems to have a peculiar frame: it points to the blank areas of collective memory. And the young people reply that they want "to figure out how the invisible world the emigrants built around [their] childhoods fit in solid America." They wanted to know more about their "no name" Asian ancestors. They want to decipher the signs of the Asian presence here and there across the landscape of America—railroad tracks over high mountains, fields of cane virtually carpeting entire islands, and verdant agricultural lands.   6

> Deserts to farmlands
> Japanese-American
> Page in history.[6]

They want to know what is their history and "what is the movies." They want to trace the origins of terms applied to them. "Why are we called 'Oriental'?" they question, resenting the appellation that has identified Asians as exotic, mysterious, strange, and foreign. "The word 'orient' simply means 'east.'   7

---

[5]Tomo Shoji, "Born Too Soon . . . It's Never Too Late: Growing Up Nisei in Early Washington," presentations at the University of California, Berkeley, September 19, 1987, and the Ohana Cultural Center, Oakland, California, March 4, 1988.

[6]Kingston, *The Woman Warrior*, p. 6; poem in Kazuo Ito, *Issei: A History of Japanese Immigrants in North America* (Seattle, 1973), p. 493.

So why are Europeans 'West' and why are Asians 'East'? Why did empire-minded Englishmen in the sixteenth century determine that Asia was 'east' of London? Who decided what names would be given to the different regions and peoples of the world? Why does 'American' usually mean 'white'?" Weary of Eurocentric history, young Asian Americans want their Asian ancestral lives in America chronicled, "given the name of a place." They have earned the right to belong to specific places like Washington, California, Hawaii, Punnene, Promontory Point, North Adams, Manzanar, Doyers Street. "And today, after 125 years of our life here," one of them insists, "I do not want just a home that time allowed me to have." Seeking to lay claim to America, they realize they can no longer be indifferent to what happened in history, no longer embarrassed by the hardships and humiliations experienced by their grandparents and parents.

> My heart, once bent and cracked, once
> ashamed of your China ways.
> Ma, hear me now, tell me your story
> again and again.[7]◆

---

[7]Kingston, *The Woman Warrior*, p. 6; Robert Kwan, "Asian v. Oriental: A Difference that Counts," *Pacific Citizen*, April 25, 1980; Sir James Augustus Henry Murry (ed.), *The Oxford English Dictionary* (Oxford, 1933); vol. 7, p. 200; Aminur Rahim, "Is Oriental an Occident?" in *The Asiandian*, vol. 5, no. 1, April 1983, p. 20; Shawn Wong, *Homebase* (New York, 1979), p. 111; Nellie Wong, "From a Heart of Rice Straw," in Nellie Wong, *Dreams in Harrison Railroad Park* (Berkeley, 1977), p. 41.

◆ Responding

1. Explain why Congressman Norman Mineta said that ex-internees have been " 'stigmatized'. . . carrying the 'burden of shame' for over forty painful years." What did the Japanese Americans feel ashamed about? Using information from the readings and your own knowledge of human nature, discuss the fact that though they were the victims of an injustice, they felt shame rather than anger. Does Japanese culture help explain this reaction, or are feelings of shame and guilt typical reactions of victims?

2. What caused Japanese Americans finally to break their silence about the Internment? Discuss the role of their stories in helping the younger generation understand themselves and their heritage.

3. Thinking about the connotations of names of ethnic groups, explain the role of names in forming group images and individual identities. Consider the effect on children of derogatory names.

4. Read David Mura's "Strangers in the Village" in Chapter 9. Compare his attitudes toward the history and literature studied in most American schools with the attitudes expressed by the young Asian Americans in this reading.

◆

CONNECTING

Critical Thinking and Writing

1. Reread the Internment Order. Why did the United States government think that the Japanese in America, including American citizens of Japanese descent, were a security risk? Did these reasons justify the government's actions? Many Japanese Americans, as well as others, have charged that the public's fears were based on racial prejudice. Write an essay supporting or refuting this charge.

2. Every character in the selections was influenced by the Internment. Compare the varying responses of two or more characters. Alternatively, write an essay classifying the range of responses.

3. Many of these readings deal with the issue of trying to adapt to a new culture while retaining your own. Write an essay comparing the responses to this challenge of at least two individuals in the readings in this and other chapters.

4. Language is often an important part of a person's identity. Compare the role of language in shaping the identity of at least two people in the readings in this and other chapters. For example, you might compare the significance of Sone's native Japanese to the significance of Mora's native Chicano Spanish.

5. Many of the readings in this text deal with the relationships between parents and children, old ways and new. Analyze the difficulties of communication that can develop between parents who were raised in one culture and children who are raised in another.

6. Being pulled between two cultures is a theme that recurs throughout this text. Write an essay discussing what it means to be bicultural. You can use examples from the text as well as from your own experience.

7. For many of these authors, loyalty is an important issue. To whom do you owe loyalty—your government, your parents, your friends? When loyalties conflict, who has priority?

8. Do your possessions define you? Describe the possessions that are most important to you and reveal most about your personality and history. Are the Sones defined by their possessions? What about the family being evicted in the excerpt from *The Invisible Man* in chapter 6?

9. Use the readings in this and other sections to illustrate how personal ambitions can come into conflict with cultural expectations.

10. Using your school library, research the history of the struggle of Japanese Americans to obtain justice for the wrongs done to them during the Internment. Read the 1988 newspaper articles reporting the effort to obtain an apology and reparations. What is the current status of reparations?

For Further Research

1. Research current laws protecting citizens' rights. Are there laws now that would prevent the internment of American citizens? What organizations work to protect individuals and groups? Are there enough safeguards in our currrent system? What is your evaluation? What suggestions for changes would you make?

2. Though their families and friends were in internment camps, many Japanese Americans enlisted in the army and fought for the United States in Europe. Some units were cited for exceptional bravery. Examine the war record of one of those units.

3. The treatment of German Americans during World War II was quite different from the treatment of Japanese Americans. After studying the opinions of historians, sociologists, politicians, and victims, write an essay about the reasons that account for the difference.

◆

REFERENCES AND ADDITIONAL SOURCES

Christgau, John. *Enemies: World War II Alien Internment*. Ames: Iowa State University Press, 1985.

Collins, Donald E. *Native American Aliens: Disloyalty and the Renunciation of Citizenship by Japanese Americans During World War II*. Westport, Conn.: Greenwood, 1985.

Daniels, Roger. *Concentration Camps: North American Japanese in the United States & Canada During World War II*. Melbourne, FL: Krieger, 1981.

Kim, Elaine. "Japanese American Portraits" in *Asian American Literature: An Introduction to the Writings and Their Social Context*. Philadelphia: Temple University Press, 1984.

Myer, Dillon S. *Uprooted Americans: The Japanese Americans and the War Relocation Authority during World War II*. Tucson: University of Arizona Press, 1972.

Takaki, Ronald. *Strangers from a Different Shore: A History of Asian Americans*. Boston: Little, Brown, 1989.

Uchida, Yoshiko. *Desert Exile: The Uprooting of a Japanese-American Family*. Seattle: University of Washington Press, 1982.

Wilson, Robert A., and Bill Hosokawa. *East to America: A History of the Japanese in the United States*. New York: Morrow, 1980.

Reverend Martin Luther King, Jr.
(© 1985 Bob Fitch/Black Star)

Detail of background photo, march from Selma to Montgomery, in summer of 1965. (© James H. Karales)

Chapter 6

AFRICAN AMERICANS
The Struggle for Civil Rights

*Freedom Riders' bus burned in Alabama in May, 1961.
(Courtesy,* The Birmingham News/
Birmingham Post-Herald*)*

◆ SETTING THE HISTORICAL CONTEXT ◆

IN GWENDOLYN BROOKS'S POEM "The Chicago Defender Sends a Man to Little Rock," the speaker begins by describing what might be considered a typical community of the late 1950s:

> In Little Rock the people bear
> Babes, and comb and part their hair
> And watch the want ads, put repair
> To roof and latch. While wheat toast burns
> A woman waters multiferns. . . .
>
> In Little Rock the people sing
> Sunday hymns like anything,
> Through Sunday pomp and polishing.
>
> And after testament and tunes,
> Some soften Sunday afternoons
> With lemon tea and Lorna Doones.

It becomes all the more inexplicable that this community, so "like people everywhere," behaved with unspeakable cruelty toward a group of African American students who, supported by the Supreme Court ruling against segregated schools, sought admission to the local high school. As the speaker of the poem, a reporter who was himself injured while covering the event, recounts:

> And true, they are hurling spittle, rock,
> Garbage and fruit in Little Rock.
> And I saw coiling storm a-writhe
> On bright madonnas. And a scythe
> Of men harassing brownish girls.
> (The bows and barrettes in the curls
> And braids declined away from joy.)
>
> I saw a bleeding brownish boy. . . .

In the poem, people who observe conventions of duty and civility when dealing with members of their own race, seem to think little of committing acts of brutality when dealing with people from another race.

In a literal sense, Brooks's poem has its grounding in the incidents of 1957, when a group of African American students attempted to attend Little Rock's formerly segregated Central High School. In another sense, the poem reflects the widely felt pain that compelled many African Americans, both adults and children, to enlist in the struggle for civil rights. This struggle involved the courts, the Congress, and the White House; it took place in offices, in churches, and in the streets; and it brought together people from different backgrounds who were willing to risk their social position, their safety, and their lives to bring to fulfillment the promise of equality.

For African Americans, the promise of America has been, in the words of Martin Luther King, Jr., "a promissory note" on which the nation has "defaulted." Brought to the United States in chains, they remained, a century after the Emancipation Proclamation, "crippled by the manacles of segregation and the chains of discrimination."

After the Emancipation Proclamation, three important amendments were added to the Constitution. The Thirteenth Amendment (1865) outlawed slavery throughout the nation, not just in the areas specified in the Emancipation Proclamation. The Fourteenth Amendment (1868) guaranteed all Americans due process of law, and the Fifteenth Amendment (1870) extended to African Americans the right to vote. Moreover, the Civil Rights Act of 1875 guaranteed all Americans equal access to public accommodations. As early as the 1880s, however, these acts were weakened because of inadequate enforcement by the federal government and the very narrow interpretation given them by the Supreme Court. Not only was the Civil Rights Act of 1875 rendered invalid because of lack of federal support, but the Supreme Court's rulings, which allowed private organizations and individuals to continue to discriminate on the basis of race, substantially weakened the constitutional amendments.

Throughout the period after Reconstruction, southern legislatures drafted laws circumventing and even nullifying the rights guaranteed to

African Americans under the Constitution. These "Jim Crow" laws were intended to keep public facilities segregated on the basis of color. African Americans were forced to ride in the back of buses, to drink from segregated drinking fountains, and even to step off sidewalks in order to make room for whites. More important, they were forced to attend segregated, inferior schools. They had no way to nullify these laws, because, despite the Fifteenth Amendment guarantees, they were systematically excluded from voting in many southern states by discriminatory poll taxes, "grandfather clauses" (which made the right to vote dependent on whether one's ancestors had voted), and literacy tests. As a part of the examination process, applicants were required both "to read and to interpret" sections from their state's constitution; by using oral exams, examiners were able to fail whomever they wished.

The situation in the North was only somewhat better. Although many states outlawed segregation, there were still private, unspoken agreements and economic and other barriers that prevented full integration. Few schools in the North, for example, were actually integrated, and as late as the 1940s restaurants in Chicago and other northern cities would serve African Americans only after being targeted by demonstrators. As the United States prepared to enter World War II, African Americans throughout the country were discriminated against both by defense industries, who would hire them only for janitorial and other low-status positions, and by the segregated armed forces.

King's "Letter from Birmingham Jail" notes that "privileged groups rarely give up their privileges voluntarily." For over a century, African Americans attempted to gain the rights guaranteed them by federal law but often denied them by local practice and tradition. In many places throughout the South there were sporadic demonstrations against discriminatory legislation and attempts to mobilize through boycott. The migration of large numbers of African Americans to the North helped create concentrated populations with a strengthened sense of political purpose. Organizations such as the NAACP and the National Urban League were founded, and their publications, begun during the Harlem Renaissance of the 1920s, announced a new political and cultural awakening. Yet the period around World War II witnessed an especially strong demand by African Americans for equal rights.

Much of the political action of the 1940s can be credited to the organizational talents of A. Philip Randolph, who, as editor of *The Messenger* and president of the Brotherhood of Sleeping Car Porters, had been politically active since the Harlem Renaissance. In 1940 Randolph enlisted 100,000 people to march on Washington to protest segregation in the government and discriminatory hiring practices in the defense industries. This group called off its march only after it had received a commitment to the cause of civil rights from President Franklin D. Roosevelt, embodied in Roosevelt's Executive Order 8802, which outlawed discrimination in defense industries and in government hiring. Later that year the government formed the Fair Employment Practices Commission. Full integration of the armed forces, however, was not accomplished until the Korean War of the 1950s.

During the 1950s, organizations such as the NAACP began to press for an end to segregated schools. Until this time the prevailing doctrine, derived from the Supreme Court decision in *Plessy* v. *Ferguson* in 1898, had allowed so-called separate but equal schools. Civil rights groups were encouraged, however, by the Court's 1946 ruling in *Sweatt* v. *Painter*, which, without overturning the ruling in *Plessy*, maintained that school districts had to be able to prove that separate facilities were indeed equal. It was in the 1954 case of *Brown* v. *The Board of Education of Topeka* that the doctrine of separate but equal was successfully challenged for the first time. Led by Thurgood Marshall (who later became a justice of the Supreme Court), the plaintiffs argued against the doctrine in *Plessy* on educational, psychological, and economic grounds. In a unanimous ruling, the Supreme Court reversed the *Plessy* decision, declaring that separate educational facilities were inherently unequal and therefore unconstitutional.

The *Brown* decision, important as it was, did not lead to the prompt elimination of racially segregated schools. Instead, many southerners protested against the ruling; others sought ways to evade or defer it. More than a hundred congressmen from southern states wrote a letter denouncing the decision, and several southern governors attempted to block its implementation. In 1957 Governor Orval Faubus ordered the Arkansas National Guard to prevent the court-ordered integration of Little Rock's Central High; after President Eisenhower forced him to rescind the order, an angry mob formed to take the guardsmen's place, and several African American students were severely beaten. In 1962, as James Meredith, aided by Medgar Evers and others from the NAACP, attempted to register at the University of Mississippi, Governor Ross Barnett made public statements predicting that violence would result from this attempt at desegregation; a mob subsequently began a riot, which was not put down until federal troops were sent to the scene. In 1963 Alabama's governor, George Wallace, stood in a doorway to bar two students from registering at the University of Alabama; it took the intervention of the Justice Department before the students were admitted. In other areas, parents were encouraged by school districts to send their children to private schools, which remained segregated. In Virginia, the public schools were closed and much of their property was given to private schools; as a result, many African American children were kept out of school for two years.

African Americans also had to demand their rights to public transportation. Although the Supreme Court had outlawed segregation in interstate transportation, most public transportation within individual southern states was segregated. African Americans, who paid the same fare as Caucasians, had to sit in the back of the bus; moreover, when there was a shortage of seats for whites, the black riders were expected to give up theirs. On December 5, 1955, Mrs. Rosa Parks protested this form of discrimination by refusing to give her seat to a white; her action, which led to her arrest and imprisonment, sparked the beginning of a thirteen-month boycott of the bus system, largely organized by Dr. Martin Luther King, Jr., president of the Southern Christian Leadership Conference. Although there had been earlier protests against this form of discrimination, including a boycott of a Louisiana bus system, the Montgomery boycott of 1955 was the first to meet with success. During the early 1960s, the Congress of Racial Equality organized groups of Freedom Riders—both African Americans and whites—

who rode buses in the South to protest continued illegal segregation in interstate transportation. Activists from this group also worked in the voter education and registration drives. In these protests and others, African Americans demonstrated the power of nonviolent direct action.

During the 1950s and early 1960s, African Americans continued to be refused service at the lunch counters of many department stores. Martin Luther King, Jr., expressed the grim irony of this daily humiliation in his "Letter from Birmingham Jail": "The nations of Asia and Africa are moving with jetlike speed toward gaining political independence while we still creep at horse and buggy pace toward gaining a cup of coffee at a lunch counter." Even before King wrote his letter, however, successful protests of these inequities had begun. In 1960, African American college students, members of the Student Nonviolent Coordinating Committee, sat in at a local lunch counter in Greensboro, North Carolina, manning the counters in shifts, occupying seats daily until they were finally served. The sit-in, inaugurated by four college freshmen, was repeated with success at lunch counters, libraries, swimming pools, theaters, and other public facilities throughout the South.

During the Easter shopping season of 1963, Martin Luther King, Jr., and the Southern Christian Leadership Conference led a large-scale boycott of Birmingham, Alabama, stores. Arrested for parading without a permit, and held in solitary confinement, King wrote his famous "Letter from Birmingham Jail," outlining the tenets of nonviolent direct action and answering those who criticized its use.

These protests for equality and equal opportunity on the local, state, and national levels culminated in the great March on Washington in August 1963. This march, which brought together over a quarter of a million people, has been called by Juan Williams "the largest demonstration for human rights in the history of the world." Organized to promote the passage of the Civil Rights Act, the march featured addresses by activists John Lewis and Bayard Rustin, among others, and Martin Luther King's now famous "I Have a Dream" speech. The major television and radio networks provided extensive coverage of the event. Finally passed in 1964, the Civil Rights Act was considered the furthest-reaching legislation in the nation's history. The Voting Rights Act, passed the following year, established federal offices in the South to aid in the registration of African American voters and to prevent abuses by registrars.

Each victory in the civil rights movement was achieved because black and white activists willingly risked their safety in the cause of equality. Those sitting in at lunch counters were subject to arrest and were often beaten; food, ammonia, and other substances were poured on them, and lighted cigarettes were ground into their backs. The homes, churches, and families of clergymen and other civil rights leaders were threatened and at times attacked. Freedom Riders traveling the South by bus were stoned and beaten; their buses burned by angry mobs. In Birmingham during the administration of Mayor Eugene "Bull" Connor, protesters—both adults and children—were met with firehoses and attack dogs and savagely beaten by police. In 1965, peaceful demonstrators marching through Selma, Alabama, were driven back by tear gas and attacked by officers of the sheriff's department, some riding horses. Such scenes, which were often televised, exposed the conditions to which African Americans were subjected in the South.

Many civil rights activists paid with their lives for their belief in freedom and equality. In 1963, Medgar Evers, the NAACP's Mississippi field secretary, who had helped James Meredith gain admission to the University of Mississippi, was gunned down in front of his home. A year later, also in Mississippi, three Freedom Riders—Andrew Goodman, Michael Schwerner, and James Chaney, two whites and an African American—disappeared. They had been investigating a church fire when they were apprehended by local authorities, turned over to a mob, tortured, and murdered. In 1968, while leading a strike of workers in Memphis, Martin Luther King, Jr. was assassinated.

The numerous and mounting pressures on the civil rights movement, the slow progress to equality, and the sometimes high price paid for small gains caused divisions in the movement and disagreements over methods. The nonviolent action advocated by the Southern Christian Leadership Conference and CORE was rejected by Stokely Carmichael and other

"All the News That's Fit to Print"

The New York Times.

LATE CITY EDITION

VOL. CXII.No. 38,237. NEW YORK, TUESDAY, OCTOBER 2, 1962. FIVE CENTS

3,000 TROOPS PUT DOWN MISSISSIPPI RIOTING AND SEIZE 200 AS NEGRO ATTENDS CLASSES; EX-GEN. WALKER IS HELD FOR INSURRECTION

SENATE REJECTS AID CUTS AND BAN ON HELP FOR REDS

Upholds Kennedy's Authority to Assist Nations That Do Business With Cuba

By FELIX BELAIR Jr.
Special to The New York Times

WASHINGTON, Oct. 1—The Senate decided for the Administration today in preliminary votes on the foreign aid appropriation bill, due for passage tomorrow.

It voted, 47 to 38, against cutting $785,000,000 from the $799,400,000 of military and economic aid funds that its Appropriations Committee restored to the bill the House had cut heavily.

The effect of the vote was to hold the appropriation at $4,422,800,000, as recommended by its Appropriations Committee. The Administration had requested the full amount of

PRISONERS ARE MARCHED TO ARMORY IN OXFORD: Army men escort a group of prisoners to National Guard Armory. The group had participated in a disturbance and was apprehended after the soldiers were ordered to fire at the feet of the rioters.

WALKER IS STOPPED BY TROOPS: Former Maj. Gen. Edwin A. Walker is detained by soldiers near the courthouse in Oxford. He was turned over to U.S. marshals and is being held in $100,000 bail on charges stemming from his role in Sunday's campus riots.

SHOTS QUELL MOB

Enrolling of Meredith Ends Segregation in State Schools

By CLAUDE SITTON
Special to The New York Times

OXFORD, Miss., Oct. 1—James H. Meredith, a Negro, enrolled in the University of Mississippi today and began classes as Federal troops and federalized units of the Mississippi National Guard quelled a 15-hour riot.

A force of more than 3,000 soldiers and guardsmen and 400 deputy United States marshals fired rifles and hurled tear-gas grenades to stop the violent demonstrations.

Throughout the day more troops streamed into Oxford. Tonight a force approaching 5,000 soldiers and guardsmen, along with the Federal marshals, maintained an uneasy peace in this town of 6,500 in the northern Mississippi hills.

[There were two flareups

Newspaper report of riots at University of Mississippi campus after James Meredith registered for classes. (© 1962 The New York Times)

African American leaders. Malcolm X, one of the most influential of these, questioned the achievements of the civil rights movement—"A desegregated cup of coffee, a theater, public toilets—the whole range of hypocritical 'integration' "—calling these concessions inadequate "atonement" for the nation's crimes against African Americans.

Despite many accomplishments, the ultimate goal of full equality of opportunity articulated by the leaders of the civil rights movement has yet to be achieved. Activists point to the higher rates of poverty, unemployment, infant mortality, and crime in African American communities than in the majority culture. Although African Americans now have greater opportunities to serve in public office and to participate in the political process, neither the government nor the private sector has been able to stop the deterioration of many American urban areas or counteract the extreme poverty of many rural areas. Despite the victories of the 1960s, African Americans in the 1990s still have to demand the right to join exclusive business and social clubs; Medgar Evers's murder is still unsolved; and cities from Brooklyn to Long Beach cannot escape the specter of racially motivated violence. The war against prejudice and injustice has not yet been fully won.

EXPLORING THE LITERARY AND
◆ CULTURAL CONTEXT ◆

The authors of the essays, fiction, and poetry that follow reflect on the events and significance of the struggle for civil rights during the 1950s and 1960s. They consider the environment of prejudice and injustice in America and the struggle to eliminate it. Many reveal the force of individual belief, leadership, and sacrifice in African Americans' struggle for the rights guaranteed them under the Constitution.

Ralph Ellison's novel *The Invisible Man* examines the experiences of a young man, first at school in the South and later as a migrant to the North, where he attempts to find work and a greater sense of dignity among the wider opportunities of the city. Although the first and probably best-known chapter of the book reveals the indignities to which the main character is subjected as a black child growing up in the South, the passage included here explores his reactions as an adult to a subtler, more pervasive form of cruelty. Seeing an elderly couple being evicted from their home, their possessions tossed into the snow, he must decide how to respond. Although they might seem inconsequential to others, many of the couple's possessions call to mind in the character a piece of the individual and collective history and make him feel connected to them; that a "dream book" is among the items thrown aside is not without its irony.

The relation between the dreams and ambitions of individuals and the broken promises of history is explored more explicitly in the writings of Martin Luther King, Jr. In "Letter from Birmingham Jail," King states forcefully the reasons that he and the members of his organization cannot be passive witnesses to prejudice and injustice but must vigorously protest when the promises of equal opportunity are not fulfilled. The letter relies on philosophical, theological, and historical arguments to make its point. King's "I Have a Dream" speech uses a rich network of metaphors and rhetorical structures reminiscent of both the Declaration of Independence and the Gettysburg Address to speak to Americans of their common heritage and the rights promised all.

Several readings consider the questions King raises about moral obligations versus legal duties and the distinction between just and unjust laws. Ellison's narrative describes the behavior of which people are capable when "just following orders"; the response of his main character in part dramatizes the "creative tension" between just and unjust laws described in King's essay.

The selection from Malcolm X's *Autobiography* explores the question of how to achieve justice with dignity. Other readings in the chapter consider the individual and group sacrifices made in the course of the civil rights movement. The excerpt from Juan Williams's *Eyes on the Prize* provides an overview of the struggle that engaged a generation. The chapter from James Farmer's *Lay Bare the Heart* explains what happened to three individuals—the murdered Freedom Riders Chaney, Goodman, and Schwerner. Gwendolyn Brooks pays tribute in her poems to other people of strength and vision—the children of Little Rock, Medgar Evers, and Malcolm X, all of whom suffered to ensure the survival of a dream for the future. In Brooks's words, each of these people, and many others in the civil rights movement, "leaned against tomorrow."

BEGINNING: PRE-READING/WRITING

◆ *Before reading the selections in this chapter, try to determine how much you actually know about the civil rights movement and its leaders by listing events that led up to and took place during the struggle for civil rights. Working with the class, construct a time line of significant events. As you read the selections and learn more about the civil rights movement, revise your time line as necessary.*

In 1954 the Supreme Court ruled that the school board of Topeka, Kansas, had violated the law when it had ordered children to attend racially segregated schools. In their unanimous decision, the justices said that segregation by race violated the constitutional guarantee of equal protection under the law. The Court reversed the earlier decision of Plessy v. Ferguson *(1896), which had permitted "separate but equal" schools.*

◆ *From* BROWN V. THE BOARD OF EDUCATION OF TOPEKA ◆

These cases come to us from the States of Kansas, South Carolina, Virginia, and Delaware. They are premised on different facts and different local conditions, but a common legal question justifies their consideration together in this consolidated opinion.

In approaching this problem, we cannot turn the clock back to 1868 when the Amendment was adopted, or even to 1896 when Plessy v. Ferguson was written. We must consider public education in the light of its full development and its present place in American life throughout the Nation. Only in this way can it be determined if segregation in public schools deprives these plaintiffs of the equal protection of the laws.

Today, education is perhaps the most important function of state and local governments. Compulsory school attendance laws and the great expenditures for education both demonstrate our recognition of the importance of education to our democratic society. It is required in the performance of our most basic public responsibilities, even service in the armed forces. It is the very foundation of good citizenship. Today it is a principal instrument in awakening the child to cultural values, in preparing him for later professional training, and in helping him to adjust normally to his environment. In these days, it is doubtful that any child may reasonably be expected to succeed in life if he is denied the opportunity of an education. Such an opportunity, where the state has undertaken to provide it, is a right which must be made available to all on equal terms.

We come then to the question presented: Does segregation of children in public schools solely on the basis of race, even though the physical facilities and other "tangible" factors may be equal, deprive the children of the minority group of equal educational opportunities? We believe that it does.

In Sweatt v. Painter, . . . in finding that a segregated law school for Negroes could not provide them equal educational opportunities, this Court relied in large part on "those qualities which are incapable of objective measurement but which make for greatness in a law school." In McLaurin v. Oklahoma State Regents, . . . the Court, in requiring that a Negro admitted to a white graduate school be treated like all other students, again resorted to intangible considerations: ". . . his ability to study, to engage in discussions and exchange views with other students, and, in general, to learn his profession." Such considerations apply with added force to children in grade and high schools. To separate them from others of similar age and qualifications solely because of their race generates a feeling of inferiority as to their status in the community that may affect their hearts and minds in a way unlikely ever to be undone. The effect of this separation on their educational opportunities was well stated by a finding in the Kansas case by a court which nevertheless felt compelled to rule against the Negro plaintiffs:

> Segregation of white and colored children in public schools has a detrimental effect upon the colored children. The impact is greater when it has the sanction of the law; for the policy of separating the races is usually interpreted as denoting the inferiority of the Negro group. A sense of inferiority affects the motivation of a child to learn. Segregation with the sanction of the law, therefore, has a tendency to retard the educational and mental development of Negro children and to deprive them of some of the benefits they would receive in a racially integrated school system.

Whatever may have been the extent of psychological knowledge at the time of Plessy v. Ferguson, this finding is amply supported by modern authority. Any language in Plessy v. Ferguson contrary to this finding is rejected.

We conclude that in the field of public education the doctrine of "separate but equal" has no place. Separate educational facilities are inherently unequal. Therefore, we hold that the plaintiffs and others similarly situated for whom the actions have been brought are, by reason of the segregation complained of, deprived of the equal protection of the laws guaranteed by the Fourteenth Amendment. . . . ◆

6

◆ Responding

1. Explain the significance of the Fourteenth Amendment to the Constitution.

2. List the reasons that the justices give to support their statement, "Today, education is perhaps the most important function of state and local governments." Which of these reasons do you think is most persuasive and important? Write an essay supporting your choice.

3. Working individually or in a group, define *segregation, de facto segregation*, and *separate but equal*. Discuss the ways in which these policies were implemented in many school systems.

4. Using arguments from the decision as well as from your own knowledge and experience, agree or disagree that "in the field of public education the doctrine of 'separate but equal' has no place." Consider whether the same arguments apply to private education.

RALPH ELLISON

Ralph Ellison, who was born in Oklahoma City, Oklahoma, in 1914, studied at the Tuskegee Institute in Alabama and served in the merchant marines during World War II. Since the war he has taught at several major universities, including the University of Chicago, UCLA, Yale, New York University, and Bard College. His publications include the novel Invisible Man *(1952), a collection of essays entitled* Shadow and Art *(1964), and essays, articles, and short stories in many periodicals.*

In the following excerpt from Invisible Man, *the narrator describes his feelings as he joins a group of people witnessing the eviction of an elderly couple. In its depiction of the couple's attempt to retain their dignity at this moment of crisis, the passage raises troubling questions about the nature of justice and leadership.*

◆ *From* INVISIBLE MAN ◆

The wind drove me into a side street where a group of boys had set a packing box afire. The gray smoke hung low and seemed to thicken as I walked with my head down and eyes closed, trying to avoid the fumes. My lungs began to pain; then emerging, wiping my eyes and coughing, I almost stumbled over it: It was piled in a jumble along the walk and over the curb into the street, like a lot of junk waiting to be hauled away. Then I saw the sullen-faced crowd, looking at a building where two white men were toting out a chair in which an old woman sat; who, as I watched, struck at them feebly with her fists. A motherly-looking old woman with her head tied in a handkerchief, wearing a man's shoes and a man's heavy blue sweater. It was startling: The crowd watched silently, the two white men lugging the chair and trying to dodge the blows and the old woman's face streaming with angry tears as she thrashed at them with her fists. I couldn't believe it. Something, a sense of foreboding, filled me, a quick sense of uncleanliness. 1

"Leave us alone," she cried, "leave us alone!" as the men pulled their heads out of range and sat her down abruptly at the curb, hurrying back into the building. 2

What on earth, I thought, looking about me. What on earth? The old woman sobbed, pointing to the stuff piled along the curb. "Just look what they doing to us. Just look," looking straight at me. And I realized that what I'd taken for junk was actually worn household furnishings. 3

"Just look at what they doing," she said, her teary eyes upon my face. 4

I looked away embarrassed, staring into the rapidly growing crowd. Faces were peering sullenly from the windows above. And now as the two men reappeared at the top of the steps carrying a battered chest of drawers, I saw 5 a third man come out and stand behind them, pulling at his ear as he looked out over the crowd.

"Shake it up, you fellows," he said, "shake it up. We don't have all day." 6

Then the men came down with the chest and I saw the crowd give way 7 sullenly, the men trudging through, grunting and putting the chest at the curb, then returning into the building without a glance to left or right.

"Look at that," a slender man near me said. "We ought to beat the hell 8 out of those paddies!"

I looked silently into his face, taut and ashy in the cold, his eyes trained 9 upon the men going up the steps.

"Sho, we ought to stop 'em," another man said, "but ain't that much nerve 10 in the whole bunch."

"There's plenty nerve," the slender man said. "All they need is someone 11 to set it off. All they need is a leader. You mean *you* don't have the nerve."

"Who me?" the man said. "Who me?" 12

"Yes, you." 13

"Just look," the old woman said, "just look," her face still turned toward 14 mine. I turned away, edging closer to the two men.

"Who are those men?" I said, edging closer. 15

"Marshals or something. I don't give a damn who they is." 16

"Marshals, hell," another man said. "Those guys doing all the toting ain't 17 nothing but trusties. Soon as they get through they'll lock 'em up again."

"I don't care who they are, they got no business putting these old folks 18 out on the sidewalk."

"You mean they're putting them out of their apartment?" I said. "They 19 can do that up *here?*"

"Man, where *you* from?" he said, swinging toward me. "What does it look 20 like they puttin' them out of, a Pullman car? They being evicted!"

I was embarrassed; others were turning to stare. I had never seen an 21 eviction. Someone snickered.

"Where did *he* come from?" 22

A flash of heat went over me and I turned. "Look, friend," I said, hearing 23 a hot edge coming into my voice. "I asked a civil question. If you don't care to answer, don't, but don't try to make me look ridiculous."

"Ridiculous? Hell, all scobos is ridiculous. Who the hell is you?" 24

"Never mind, I am who I am. Just don't beat up your gums at me," I 25 said, throwing him a newly acquired phrase.

Just then one of the men came down the steps with an armful of articles, 26 and I saw the old woman reach up, yelling, "Take your hands off my Bible!" And the crowd surged forward.

The white man's hot eyes swept the crowd. "Where, lady?" he said. "I 27 don't see any Bible."

And I saw her snatch the Book from his arms, clutching it fiercely and 28 sending forth a shriek. "They can come in your home and do what they want to you," she said. "Just come stomping in and jerk your life up by the roots! But this here's the last straw. They ain't going to bother with my Bible!"

The white man eyed the crowd. "Look, lady," he said, more to the rest 29 of us than to her, "I don't want to do this, I *have* to do it. They sent me up here to do it. If it was left to me, you could stay here till hell freezes over . . ."

"These white folks, Lord. These white folks," she moaned, her eyes turned 30 toward the sky, as an old man pushed past me and went to her.

"Hon, Hon," he said, placing his hand on her shoulder. "It's the agent, 31 not these gentlemen. He's the one. He says it's the bank, but you know he's the one. We've done business with him for over twenty years."

"Don't tell me," she said. "It's all the white folks, not just one. They all 32 against us. Every stinking low-down one of them."

"She's right!" a hoarse voice said. "She's right! They *all* is!" 33

Something had been working fiercely inside me, and for a moment I had 34 forgotten the rest of the crowd. Now I recognized a self-consciousness about them, as though they, we, were ashamed to witness the eviction, as though we were all unwilling intruders upon some shameful event; and thus we were careful not to touch or stare too hard at the effects that lined the curb; for we were witnesses of what we did not wish to see, though curious, fascinated, despite our shame, and through it all the old female, mind-plunging crying.

I looked at the old people, feeling my eyes burn, my throat tighten. The 35 old woman's sobbing was having a strange effect upon me—as when a child, seeing the tears of its parents, is moved by both fear and sympathy to cry. I turned away, feeling myself being drawn to the old couple by a warm, dark, rising whirlpool of emotion which I feared. I was wary of what the sight of them crying there on the sidewalk was making me begin to feel. I wanted to leave, but was too ashamed to leave, was rapidly becoming too much a part of it to leave.

I turned aside and looked at the clutter of household objects which the 36 two men continued to pile on the walk. And as the crowd pushed me I looked down to see looking out of an oval frame a portrait of the old couple when young, seeing the sad, stiff dignity of the faces there; feeling strange memories awakening that began an echoing in my head like that of a hysterical voice stuttering in a dark street. Seeing them look back at me as though even then in that nineteenth-century day they had expected little, and this with a grim, unillusioned pride that suddenly seemed to me both a reproach and a warning. My eyes fell upon a pair of crudely carved and polished bones, "knocking bones," used to accompany music at country dances, used in black-face minstrels; the flat ribs of a cow, a steer or sheep, flat bones that gave off a sound, when struck, like heavy castanets (had he been a minstrel?) or the wooden block of a set of drums. Pots and pots of green plants were lined in the dirty snow, certain to die of the cold; ivy, canna, a tomato plant. And in a basket I saw a straightening comb, switches of false hair, a curling iron, a card with silvery letters against a background of dark red velvet, reading "God Bless Our Home"; and scattered across the top of a chiffonier were nuggets of High John the Conqueror, the lucky stone; and as I watched the white men put down a basket in which I saw a whiskey bottle filled with rock candy and camphor, a small Ethiopian flag, a faded tintype of Abraham Lincoln, and the smiling image of a Hollywood star torn from a magazine. And on a pillow several badly cracked pieces of delicate china, a commemorative plate celebrating the St. Louis World Fair . . . I stood in a kind of daze, looking at an old folded lace fan studded with jet and mother-of-pearl.

The crowd surged as the white men came back, knocking over a drawer   37 that spilled its contents in the snow at my feet. I stooped and started replacing the articles: a bent Masonic emblem, a set of tarnished cuff links, three brass rings, a dime pierced with a nail hole so as to be worn about the ankle on a string for luck, an ornate greeting card with the message "Grandma, I love you" in childish scrawl; another card with a picture of what looked like a white man in black-face seated in the door of a cabin strumming a banjo beneath a bar of music and the lyric "Going back to my old cabin home"; a useless inhalant, a string of bright glass beads with a tarnished clasp, a rabbit foot, a celluloid baseball scoring card shaped like a catcher's mitt, registering a game won or lost years ago; an old breast pump with rubber bulb yellowed with age, a worn baby shoe and a dusty lock of infant hair tied with a faded and crumpled blue ribbon. I felt nauseated. In my hand I held three lapsed life insurance policies with perforated seals stamped "Void"; a yellowing newspaper portrait of a huge black man with the caption: MARCUS GARVEY[1] DEPORTED.

I turned away, bending and searching the dirty snow for anything missed   38 by my eyes, and my fingers closed upon something resting in a frozen footstep: a fragile paper, coming apart with age, written in black ink grown yellow. I read: FREE PAPERS. *Be it known to all men that my negro, Primus Provo, has been freed by me this sixth day of August, 1859. Signed: John Samuels. Macon* . . . I folded it quickly, blotting out the single drop of melted snow which glistened on the yellowed page, and dropped it back into the drawer. My hands were trembling, my breath rasping as if I had run a long distance or come upon a coiled snake in a busy street. *It has been longer than that, further removed in time,* I told myself, and yet I knew that it hadn't been. I replaced the drawer in the chest and pushed drunkenly to the curb.

But it wouldn't come up, only a bitter spurt of gall filled my mouth and   39 splattered the old folk's possessions. I turned and stared again at the jumble, no longer looking at what was before my eyes, but inwardly-outwardly, around a corner in the dark, far-away-and-long-ago, not so much of my own memory as of remembered words, of linked verbal echoes, images, heard even when not listening at home. And it was as though I myself was being dispossessed of

---

[1]Marcus Garvey (1887–1940), Jamaican-born Black Nationalist leader deported to Jamaica for mail fraud.

some painful yet precious thing which I could not bear to lose; something confounding, like a rotted tooth that one would rather suffer indefinitely than endure the short, violent eruption of pain that would mark its removal. And with this sense of dispossession came a pang of vague recognition: this junk, these shabby chairs, these heavy, old-fashioned pressing irons, zinc wash tubs with dented bottoms—all throbbed within me with more meaning than there should have been: *And why did I, standing in the crowd, see like a vision my mother hanging wash on a cold windy day, so cold that the warm clothes froze even before the vapor thinned and hung stiff on the line, and her hands white and raw in the skirt-swirling wind and her gray head bare to the darkened sky—why were they causing me discomfort so far beyond their intrinsic meaning as objects? And why did I see them now as behind a veil that threatened to lift, stirred by the cold wind in the narrow street?*

A scream, "I'm going in!" spun me around. The old couple were on the steps now, the old man holding her arm, the white men leaning forward above, and the crowd pressing me closer to the steps. 40

"You can't go in, lady," the man said. 41

"I want to pray!" she said. 42

"I can't help it, lady. You'll have to do your praying out here." 43

"I'm go'n in!" 44

"Not in here!" 45

"All we want to do is go in and pray," she said, clutching her Bible. "It ain't right to pray in the street like this." 46

"I'm sorry," he said. 47

"Aw, let the woman go in to pray," a voice called from the crowd. "You got all their stuff out here on the walk—what more do you want, blood?" 48

"Sure, let them old folks pray." 49

"That's what's wrong with us now, all this damn praying," another voice called. 50

"You don't go back, see," the white man said. "You were legally evicted." 51

"But all we want to do is go in an' kneel on the floor," the old man said. "We been living right here for over twenty years. I don't see why you can't let us go just for a few minutes . . ." 52

"Look, I've told you," the man said. "I've got my orders. You're wasting my time." 53

"We go'n in!" the woman said. 54

It happened so suddenly that I could barely keep up with it: I saw the old woman clutching her Bible and rushing up the steps, her husband behind her and the white man stepping in front of them and stretching out his arm. "I'll jug you," he yelled, "by God, I'll jug you!" 55

"Take your hands off that woman!" someone called from the crowd. 56

Then at the top of the stairs they were pushing against the man and I saw the old woman fall backwards, and the crowd exploded. 57

"Get that paddie sonofabitch!" 58

"He struck her!" a West Indian woman screamed into my ear. "The filthy 59
brute, he struck her!"

"Stand back or I'll shoot," the man called, his eyes wild as he drew a gun 60
and backed into the doorway where the two trusties stood bewildered, their
arms full of articles. "I swear I'll shoot. You don't know what you're doing,
but I'll shoot!"

They hesitated. "Ain't but six bullets in that thing," a little fellow called. 61
"Then what you going to do?"

"Yeah, you damn sho caint hide." 62

"I advise you to stay out of this," the marshal called. 63

"Think you can come up here and hit one of our women, you a fool." 64

"To hell with all this talk, let's rush that bastard!" 65

"You better think twice," the white man called. 66

I saw them start up the steps and felt suddenly as though my head would 67
split. I knew that they were about to attack the man and I was both afraid and
angry, repelled and fascinated. I both wanted it and feared the consequences,
was outraged and angered at what I saw and yet surged with fear; not for the
man or of the consequences of an attack, but of what the sight of violence might
release in me. And beneath it all there boiled up all the shock-absorbing phrases
that I had learned all my life. I seemed to totter on the edge of a great dark
hole.

"No, no," I heard myself yelling. "Black men! Brothers! Black Brothers! 68
That's not the way. We're law-abiding. We're a law-abiding people and a slow-
to-anger people."

Forcing my way quickly through the crowd, I stood on the steps facing 69
those in front, talking rapidly without thought but out of my clashing emotions.
"We're a law-abiding people and a slow-to-anger people . . ." They stopped,
listening. Even the white man was startled.

"Yeah, but we mad now," a voice called out. 70

"Yes, you're right," I called back. "We're angry, but let us be wise. Let 71
us, I mean let us not . . . Let us learn from that great leader whose wise action
was reported in the newspaper the other day . . ."

"What, mahn? Who?" a West Indian voice shouted. 72

"Come on! To hell with this guy, let's get that paddie before they send 73
him some help . . ."

"No, wait," I yelled. "Let's follow a leader, let's organize. *Organize*. We 74
need someone like that wise leader, you read about him, down in Alabama. He
was strong enough to choose to do the wise thing in spite of what he felt
himself . . ."

"Who, mahn? Who?" 75

This was it, I thought, they're listening, eager to listen. Nobody laughed. 76
If they laugh, I'll die! I tensed my diaphragm.

"That wise man," I said, "you read about him, who when that fugitive 77 escaped from the mob and ran to his school for protection, that wise man who was strong enough to do the legal thing, the law-abiding thing, to turn him over to the forces of law and order . . ."

"Yeah," a voice rang out, "yeah, so they could lynch his ass." 78

Oh, God, this wasn't it at all. Poor technique and not at all what I intended. 79

"He was a wise leader," I yelled. "He was within the law. Now wasn't 80 that the wise thing to do?"

"Yeah, he was wise all right," the man laughed angrily. "Now get out of 81 the way so we can jump this paddie."

The crowed yelled and I laughed in response as though hypnotized. 82

"But wasn't that the human thing to do? After all, he had to protect 83 himself because—"

"He was a handkerchief-headed rat!" a woman screamed, her voice boiling 84 with contempt.

"Yes, you're right. He was wise and cowardly, but what about us? What 85 are we to do?" I yelled, suddenly thrilled by the response. "Look at him," I cried.

"Yes, just look at him!" an old fellow in a derby called out as though 86 answering a preacher in church.

"And look at that old couple . . ." 87

"Yeah, what about Sister and Brother Provo?" he said. "It's an ungodly 88 shame!"

"And look at their possessions all strewn there on the sidewalk. Just look 89 at their possessions in the snow. How old are you, sir?" I yelled.

"I'm eighty-seven," the old man said, his voice low and bewildered. 90

"How's that? Yell so our slow-to-anger brethren can hear you." 91

"I'm *eighty-seven years old!*" 92

"Did you hear him? He's eighty-seven. Eighty-seven and look at all he's 93 accumulated in eighty-seven years, strewn in the snow like chicken guts, and we're a law-abiding, slow-to-anger bunch of folks turning the other cheek every day in the week. What are we going to do? What would you, what would I, what would he have done? *What is to be done?* I propose we do the wise thing, the law-abiding thing. Just look at this junk! Should two old folks live in such junk, cooped up in a filthy room? It's a great danger, a fire hazard! Old cracked dishes and broken-down chairs. Yes, yes, yes! Look at that old woman, some-body's mother, somebody's grandmother, maybe. We call them 'Big Mama' and they spoil us and—*you* know, *you* remember . . . Look at her quilts and broken-down shoes. I know she's somebody's mother because I saw an old breast pump fall into the snow, and she's somebody's grandmother, because I saw a card that read 'Dear Grandma' . . . But we're law-abiding . . . I looked into a basket and I saw some bones, not neckbones, but rib bones, knocking bones . . . This old couple used to dance . . . I saw—What kind of work do you do, Father?" I called.

"I'm a day laborer . . ." 94

"... A day laborer, you heard him, but look at his stuff strewn like 95
chitterlings in the snow . . . Where has all his labor gone? Is he lying?"

"Hell, no, he ain't lying." 96

"Naw, suh!" 97

"Then where did his labor go? Look at his old blues records and her pots 98
of plants, they're down-home folks, and everything tossed out like junk whirled
eighty-seven years in a cyclone. Eighty-seven years, and *poof!* like a snort in a
wind storm. Look at them, they look like my mama and my papa and my
grandma and grandpa, and I look like you and you look like me. Look at them
but remember that we're a wise, law-abiding group of people. And remember
it when you look up there in the doorway at that law standing there with his
forty-five. Look at him, standing with his blue steel pistol and his blue serge
suit. Look at him! You don't see just one man dressed in one blue serge suit,
or one forty-five, you see ten for every one of us, ten guns and ten warm suits
and ten fat bellies and ten million laws. *Laws*, that's what we call them down
South! Laws! And we're wise, and law-abiding. And look at this old woman
with her dog-eared Bible. What's she trying to bring off here? She's let her
religion go to her head, but we all know that religion is for the heart, not for
the head. 'Blessed are the pure in heart,' it says. Nothing about the poor in
head. What's she trying to do? What about the clear of head? And the clear of
eye, the ice-water-visioned who see too clear to miss a lie? Look out there at
her cabinet with its gaping drawers. Eighty-seven years to fill them, and full
of brick and brack, a bricabrac, and she wants to break the law . . . What's
happened to them? They're our people, your people and mine, your parents
and mine. What's happened to 'em?"

"I'll tell you!" a heavyweight yelled, pushing out of the crowd, his face 99
angry. "Hell, they been dispossessed, you crazy sonofabitch, get out the way!"

"Dispossessed?" I cried, holding up my hand and allowing the word to 100
whistle from my throat. "That's a good word, 'Dispossessed'! 'Dispossessed,'
eighty-seven years and dispossessed of what? They ain't *got* nothing, they caint
get nothing, they never *had* nothing. So who was dispossessed?" I growled.
"We're law-abiding. So who's being dispossessed? Can it be us? These old ones
are out in the snow, but we're here with them. Look at their stuff, not a pit to
hiss in, not a window to shout the news and us right with them. Look at them,
not a shack to pray in or an alley to sing the blues! They're facing a gun and
we're facing it with them. They don't want the world, but only Jesus. They
only want Jesus, just fifteen minutes of Jesus on the rug-bare floor . . . How
about it, Mr. Law? Do we get our fifteen minutes worth of Jesus? You got the
world, can we have our Jesus?"

"I got my orders, Mac," the man called, waving the pistol with a sneer. 101
"You're doing all right, tell 'em to keep out of this. This is legal and I'll shoot
if I have to . . ."

"But what about the prayer?" 102

"They don't go back!" 103

"Are you positive?"   104

"You could bet your life," he said.   105

"Look at him," I called to the angry crowd. "With his blue steel pistol   106
and his blue serge suit. You heard him, he's the law. He says he'll shoot us
down because we're a law-abiding people. So we've been dispossessed, and
what's more, he thinks he's God. Look up there backed against the post with
a criminal on either side of him. Can't you feel the cold wind, can't you hear
it asking, 'What did you do with your heavy labor? What did you do?' When
you look at all you haven't got in eighty-seven years you feel ashamed—"

"Tell 'em about it, brother," an old man interrupted. "It makes you feel   107
you ain't a man."

"Yes, these old folks had a dream book, but the pages went blank and it   108
failed to given them the number. It was called the Seeing Eye, The Great
Constitutional Dream Book, The Secrets of Africa, The Wisdom of Egypt—
but the eye was blind, it lost its luster. It's all cataracted like a cross-eyed
carpenter and it doesn't saw straight. All we have is the Bible and this Law
here rules that out. So where do we go? Where do we go from here, without
a pot—"

"We going after that paddie," the heavyweight called, rushing up the   109
steps.

Someone pushed me. "No, wait," I called.   110

"Get out the way now."   111

There was a rush against me and I fell, hearing a single explosion, back-   112
ward into a whirl of milling legs, overshoes, the trampled snow cold on my
hands. Another shot sounded above like a bursting bag. Managing to stand, I
saw atop the steps the fist with the gun being forced into the air above the
crowd's bobbing heads and the next instant they were dragging him down into
the snow; punching him left and right, uttering a low tense swelling sound of
desperate effort; a grunt that exploded into a thousand softly spat, hate-sizzling
curses. I saw a woman striking with the pointed heel of her shoe, her face a
blank mask with hollow black eyes as she aimed and struck, aimed and struck,
bringing spurts of blood, running along beside the man who was dragged to
his feet now as they punched him gauntlet-wise between them. Suddenly I saw
a pair of handcuffs arc gleaming into the air and sail across the street. A boy
broke out of the crowd, the marshal's snappy hat on his head. The marshal
was spun this way and that, then a swift tattoo of blows started him down the
street. I was beside myself with excitement. The crowd surged after him, milling
like a huge man trying to turn in a cubbyhole—some of them laughing, some
cursing, some intently silent.

"The brute struck that gentle woman, poor thing!" the West Indian woman   113
chanted. "Black men, did you ever see such a brute? Is he a gentleman, I ask
you? The brute! Give it back to him, black men. Repay the brute a thousandfold!
Give it back to him unto the third and fourth generations. Strike him, our fine

black men. Protect your black women! Repay the arrogant creature to the third
and fourth generations!"

"We're dispossessed," I sang at the top of my voice, "dispossessed and   114
we want to pray. Let's go in and pray. Let's have a big prayer meeting. But
we'll need some chairs to sit in . . . rest upon as we kneel. We'll need some
chairs!"

"Here's some chairs down here," a women called from the walk. "How   115
'bout taking in some chairs?"

"Sure," I called, "take everything. Take it all, hide that junk! Put it back   116
where it came from. It's blocking the street and the sidewalk, and that's against
the law. We're law-abiding, so clear the street of the debris. Put it out of sight!
Hide it, hide their shame! Hide *our* shame!

"Come on, men," I yelled, dashing down the steps and seizing a chair   117
and starting back, no longer struggling against or thinking about the nature of
my action. The others followed, picking up pieces of furniture and lugging it
back into the building.

"We ought to done this long ago," a man said.   118

"We damn sho should."   119

"I feel so good," a woman said, "I feel so *good!*"   120

"Black men, I'm proud of you," the West Indian woman shrilled. "Proud!"   121

We rushed into the dark little apartment that smelled of stale cabbage and   122
put the pieces down and returned for more. Men, women and children seized
articles and dashed inside shouting, laughing. I looked for the two trusties, but
they seemed to have disappeared. Then, coming down into the street, I thought
I saw one. He was carrying a chair back inside.

"So you're law-abiding too," I called, only to become aware that it was   123
someone else. A white man but someone else altogether.

The man laughed at me and continued inside. And when I reached the   124
street there were several of them, men and women, standing about, cheering
whenever another piece of furniture was returned. It was like a holiday. I didn't
want it to stop.

"Who are those people?" I called from the steps.   125

"What people?" someone called back.   126

"*Those,*" I said, pointing.   127

"You mean those ofays?"   128

"Yes, what do they want?"   129

"We're friends of the people," one of the white men called.   130

"Friends of what people?" I called, prepared to jump down upon him if   131
he answered, "*You* people."

"We're friends of *all* the common people," he shouted. "We came up to   132
help."

"We believe in brotherhood," another called.   133

"Well, pick up that sofa and come on," I called. I was uneasy about their   134 presence and disappointed when they all joined the crowd and starting lugging the evicted articles back inside. Where had I heard of them?

"Why don't we stage a march?" one of the white men called, going past.   135

"Why don't we march!" I yelled out to the sidewalk before I had time to   136
think.

They took it up immediately.   137

"Let's march . . ."   138

"It's a good idea."   139

"Let's have a demonstration . . ."   140

"Let's parade!"   141

I heard the siren and saw the scout cars swing into the block in the same   142
instant. It was the police! I looked into the crowd, trying to focus upon their
faces, hearing someone yell, "Here come the cops," and others answering, "Let
'em come!"

Where is all this leading? I thought, seeing a white man run inside the   143
building as the policemen dashed from their cars and came running up.

"What's going on here?" a gold-shield officer called up the steps.   144

It had become silent. No one answered.   145

"I said, what's going on here," he repeated. "You," he called, pointing   146
straight at me.

"We've . . . we've been clearing the sidewalk of a lot of junk," I called,   147
tense inside.

"What's that?" he said.   148

"It's a clean-up campaign," I called, wanting to laugh. "These old folks   149
had all their stuff cluttering up the sidewalk and we cleared the street . . ."

"You mean you're interfering with an eviction," he called, starting through   150
the crowd.

"He ain't doing nothing," a woman called from behind me.   151

I looked around, the steps behind were filled with those who had been   152
inside.

"We're all together," someone called, as the crowd closed in.   153

"Clear the streets," the officer ordered.   154

"That's what we were doing," someone called from back in the crowd.   155

"Mahoney!" he bellowed to another policeman, "send in a riot call!"   156

"What riot?" one of the white men called to him. "There's no riot."   157

"If I say there's a riot, there's a riot," the officer said. "And what are you   158
white people doing up here in Harlem?"

"We're citizens. We go anywhere we like."   159

"Listen! Here come some more cops!" someone called.   160

"Let them come!"   161

"Let the Commissioner come!"   162

It became too much for me. The whole thing had gotten out of hand.   163
What had I said to bring on all this? I edged to the back of the crowd on the

steps and backed into the hallway. Where would I go? I hurried up to the old couple's apartment. But I can't hide here, I thought, heading back for the stairs.

"No. You can't go that way," a voice said. 164

I whirled. It was a white girl standing in the door. 165

"What are you doing in here?" I shouted, my fear turning to feverish 166 anger.

"I didn't mean to startle you," she said. "Brother, that was quite a speech 167 you made. I heard just the end of it, but you certainly moved them to action . . ."

"Action," I said, "action—" 168

"Don't be modest, brother," she said, "I heard you." 169

"Look, Miss, we'd better get out of here," I said, finally controlling the 170 throbbing in my throat. "There are a lot of policemen downstairs and more coming."

"Oh, yes. You'd better go over the roof," she said. "Otherwise, someone 171 is sure to point you out."

"Over the roof?" 172

"It's easy. Just go up to the roof of the building and keep crossing until 173 you reach the house at the end of the block. Then open the door and walk down as though you've been visiting. You'd better hurry. The longer you remain unknown to the police, the longer you'll be effective."

Effective? I thought. What did she mean? And what was this "brother" 174 business?

"Thanks," I said, and hurried for the stairs. 175

"Good-bye," her voice rose fluidly behind me. I turned, glimpsing her 176 white face in the dim light of the darkened doorway.

I took the flight in a bound and cautiously opened the door, and suddenly 177 the sun flared bright on the roof and it was windy cold. Before me the low, snow-caked walls dividing the buildings stretched hurdle-like the long length of the block to the corner, and before me empty clotheslines trembled in the wind. I made my way through the wind-carved snow to the next roof and then to the next, going with swift caution. Planes were rising over an airfield far to the southeast, and I was running now and seeing all the church steeples rising and falling and stacks with smoke leaning sharp against the sky, and below in the street the sound of sirens and shouting. I hurried. Then, climbing over a wall I looked back, seeing a man hurrying after me, slipping, sliding, going over the low dividing walls of the roofs with puffing, bustling effort. I turned and ran, trying to put the rows of chimneys between us, wondering why he didn't yell "Halt!" or shout, or shoot. I ran, dodging behind an elevator housing, then dashing to the next roof, going down, the snow cold to my hands, knees striking, toes gripping, and up and running and looking back, seeing the short figure in black still running after. The corner seemed a mile away. I tried to count the number of roofs that bounced before me yet to be crossed. Getting to seven, I ran, hearing shouts, more sirens, and looking back and him still behind me, running in a short-legged scramble, still behind me as I tried to open the door of a building to go down and finding it stuck and running once more, trying to zig-zag in the snow and feeling the crunch of gravel underneath, and behind me still, as I swung over a partition and went brushing past a huge cote and arousing a flight of frantic white birds, suddenly as large as buzzards as they beat furiously against my eyes, dazzling the sun as they fluttered up and away and around in a furious glide and me running again and looking back and for a split second thinking him gone and once more seeing him bobbing after. Why doesn't he shoot? Why? If only it were like at home where I knew someone in *all* the houses, knew them by sight and by name, by blood and by background, by shame and pride, and by religion.

It was a carpeted hall and I moved down with pounding heart as a dog set up a terrific din within the top apartment. Then I moved quickly, my body like glass inside as I skipped downward off the edges of the stairs. Looking down the stairwell I saw pale light filtering through the door glass, far below. But what had happened to the girl, had she put the man on my trail? What was she doing there? I bounded down, no one challenging me, and I stopped in the vestibule, breathing deeply and listening for his hand upon the door above and brushing my clothing into order. Then I stepped into the street with a nonchalance copied from characters I had seen in the movies. No sound from above, not even the malicious note of the barking dog. ◆ 178

◆ Responding

1. The narrator in this selection says, "It was as though I myself was being dispossessed of some painful yet precious thing which I could not bear to lose." In an essay, explain why the narrator identifies with the couple being evicted and why he feels dispossessed.

2. Working as an individual or in a group, examine the events in this narrative chronologically and explain how each subsequent event escalates hostilities. Identify the interchanges that particularly move the onlookers to anger.

3. Compare the narrator's speech to the crowd to Marc Antony's speech to the crowd in Shakespeare's play *Julius Caesar*. What techniques do both speakers use to move people to action?

> Friends, Romans, countrymen, lend me your ears!
> I come to bury Caesar, not to praise him.
> The evil that men do lives after them,
> The good is oft interred with their bones;

So are they all, all honorable men),
Come I to speak of Caesar's funeral.
He was my friend, faithful and just to me;
But Brutus says he was ambitious,
And Brutus is an honorable man.
He hath brought many captives home to Rome,
Whose ransoms did the general coffers fill;
Did this in Caesar seem ambitious?
When that the poor have cried, Caesar hath wept;
Ambition should be made of sterner stuff:
Yet Brutus says he was ambitious,
And Brutus is an honorable man.
You all did see that on the Lupercal
I thrice presented him a kingly crown,
Which he did thrice refuse. Was this ambition?
Yet Brutus says he was ambitious,
And sure he is an honorable man.
I speak not to disprove what Brutus spoke,
But here I am to speak what I do know.
You all did love him once, not without cause;
What cause withholds you then to mourn for him?
O judgment! thou [art] fled to brutish beasts,
And men have lost their reason. Bear with me,
My heart is in the coffin there with Caesar,
And I must pause till it come back to me.

4. How do the narrator's feelings about his identity change during the course
   of this incident?

JAMES FARMER

James Farmer was born in Marshall, Texas, in 1920. He studied at Wiley College in Texas before pursuing graduate studies in religion at Howard University, where he earned a degree in divinity in 1941.

Even while attending school, Farmer was active in religious and civil rights groups, including the Christian Youth Movement, the National Council of Methodist Youth, and the Christian Youth Council of America. His involvement in civil rights led to his co-founding of the Congress of Racial Equality (CORE) in 1942, the first African American protest organization to adopt the methods of nonviolent resistance advocated by Gandhi. A year later, in a Chicago restaurant, Farmer organized the first successful sit-in demonstration. In 1961 CORE introduced the Freedom Ride to Alabama and Mississippi. After this period, Farmer worked as an adviser in the Johnson and Nixon administrations. He currently teaches and lectures on the civil rights movement. His publications include Freedom When? *(1965),* Lay Bare the Heart: The Autobiography of the Civil Rights Movement *(1986), and many magazine articles.*

The following chapter from Lay Bare the Heart *describes the ways in which peaceful demonstrators sometimes met with violence. The passage serves as a reminder that some civil rights workers made the ultimate sacrifice for their beliefs.*

◆ "TOMORROW IS FOR OUR MARTYRS" ◆

It had been a calm day in the office, if any days could be considered calm in the frenetic atmosphere in which we functioned. There had been no major crises; no mass arrests or calls for immediate bail money; no libel suits had been filed against any of our chapters; no scandals were threatening to erupt in the press; the sky had not fallen that day. Such tranquility was rare, particularly in the freedom summer of 1964 when CORE and SNCC had drawn hundreds of young volunteers into Mississippi, blanketing the state with voter registration workers.   1

I went home the evening of June 21, 1964, with a sense of well-being, cherishing the night of easy sleep that lay ahead.   2

Gretchen, now an old dog, labored to get on the bed and snuggle in her favorite spot on the pillows between Lula's head and mine. ("I always knew some bitch would come between us," Lula had once said.) At 3:00 A.M., the bedside phone rang. Cursing the intrusion, I growled hello into the receiver.   3

CORE's Mississippi field secretary, George Raymond, spoke into the   4 phone: "Jim, three of our guys, Schwerner, Goodman, and Chaney, are missing. They left Meridian yesterday afternoon to go over to the town of Philadelphia in Neshoba County to look at the ruins of the church where they had been teaching voter registration courses. You know that church was burned down a week ago. They were supposed to return by sundown, but they're not back yet. Can you come down right away?"

"Don't jump to conclusions, George," I said. "It's only been a few hours. Maybe they stopped to visit some friends for dinner and decided to take a nap before driving home."

"Face facts, Jim," Raymond shouted into the phone. "Our guys and gals don't just stop over and visit friends or take a nap without calling in. Those three are responsible guys; they wouldn't be nine hours late without calling us. That is, if they could call."

"Okay, I'll be on the next plane to Meridian," I said. "I'll call you back in a few minutes to let you know the time of arrival."

I wanted company going to Neshoba County, so I called Dick Gregory at his home in Chicago, waking him up. Before he answered the phone, I glanced at Lula and saw that she was wide awake, watching with no sign of emotion.

"Hey, big daddy," said Gregory. "What's happening?"

"Three of my guys are missing in Mississippi," I said.

After a brief silence, Gregory said, "Okay, I know you're going down there. I'll meet you there. What airport do I fly to?"

Meridian, though close to Neshoba County, was an island of relative sanity in Mississippi. At the airport when we arrived were a few dozen city policemen with rifles. They were there to ensure my safety. I was given a police escort to the small, unpretentious black hotel. Immediately, I was closeted with George Raymond; Mickey Schwerner's wife, Rita; and several other CORE people in Meridian.

It was early evening on the day after the disappearance, and still there was no word. We were certain our colleagues were dead. Rita, no more than five feet tall and less than a hundred pounds, was dry-eyed and rational. When Mickey had accepted the assignment, both of them were well aware of the risks. Mickey was a social worker from New York who had joined the CORE staff several months earlier. Rita intended to study law.

The local and state officials were showing no interest in locating the men or their bodies. We had alerted the FBI, but there was not yet any evidence of their involvement in the search. A nearby U.S. military unit had just been called in to search some of the swamps for bodies, but the results thus far were negative. The CORE car in which the men had been riding when last seen— a white Ford station wagon—had not been found.

As we discussed things that might be done to aid the search, Rita suggested that going through the ashes at the city dump where trash was burned might possibly yield some fragments of metal that could be identified as having belonged to one of the three men. Nothing more helpful than that came immediately to mind.

I told them that on the following morning, I intended to go into Phila- 16
delphia in Neshoba County to talk with Sheriff Lawrence Rainey and Deputy Sheriff Cecil Price about the disappearance of the men. Considering the racist reputation of the sheriff and his deputy, all agreed that one or both of them knew something about the disappearance of our friends.

George Raymond told us that Dick Gregory had called to say that he 17
would be joining me in Meridian early the next morning.

"Good," I said. "Let's time my trip to Philadelphia so that Dick can go 18
along with me."

Early the next morning, after Gregory's arrival, he and I sat in the small 19
hotel office on the ground floor with Raymond and one or two other CORE staffers. There was also a lieutenant of the Meridian City Police. Outside the building were several uniformed policemen and two squad cars, with others ready if needed.

The police official asked me what our plans were and I told him of my 20
intention to talk with Rainey and Price in their office. He let out a low whistle. "Farmer," he said, "you can't go over there. That's Neshoba County. That's real red-neck territory. We cain't protect you outside of Meridian."

"Lieutenant, we do appreciate the protection the city police is giving us 21
and we want to thank you for it. However, we're not asking for protection, and certainly not from the Meridian police, when we go into Neshoba County. Mr. Gregory and I will go to Neshoba County this morning to try to see the sheriff and his deputy. That is our right and our duty, and we intend to exercise it."

The lieutenant shook his head and then made a phone call to a Mr. 22
Snodgrass, head of the Mississippi State Police. I knew Snodgrass and had always respected him. He was a conscientious law enforcement officer and, I felt, a humane one. At the various marches and demonstrations CORE had held in Mississippi, when Snodgrass personally was present, I had felt a little more at ease.

This time, I could hear Snodgrass shouting over the phone from ten feet 23
away: "He can't go over there. They'll kill him in that place. We can't protect him."

The lieutenant handed me the phone. "Mr. Snodgrass wants to talk to 24
you."

Still shouting, Snodgrass said, "Farmer, don't go over there. That's one 25
of the worst red-neck areas in this state. They would just as soon kill you as look at you. We cannot protect you over there."

"Mr. Snodgrass, we have not asked for your protection. This is something 26
we have to do, protection or not."

"Okay, okay," Snodgrass replied. "What time are you going?" 27

"We're leaving here in about an hour and a half," I said and hung up. 28

We left Meridian in a caravan of five cars, with an escort of city police 29
cars. Dick Gregory and I were in the lead car. Our escort left us at the Meridian
city limits.

At the Neshoba County line, there was a roadblock with two sheriff's 30
cars and one unmarked vehicle. A hefty middle-aged man, stereotypical of the
"Negro-hating" southern sheriff of that day—chewing either a wad of tobacco
or the end of a cigar, I forget which—swaggered up to our lead car. He was
closely followed by an equally large but younger deputy sheriff.

The middle-aged man spoke to me: "Whut's yo' name?" 31

"James Farmer, and this gentleman is Mr. Dick Gregory, the entertainer 32
and social critic."

"Where yo' think you goin'?" 33

"Mr. Gregory and I are going to Philadelphia." 34

"Whut yo' gon' do there?" 35

"We are going to talk to Sheriff Rainey and Deputy Price." 36

"Whut yo' wanna talk ta them 'bout?" 37

"We are going to talk with them about the disappearance of three of the 38
staff members of the organization I head: Michael Schwerner, Andrew Goodman, and James Chaney."

"Well, Ah'm Sheriff Rainey and this heah's mah deputy, Deputy Price. 39
Y'all wanna talk ta us heah?"

"No. We want to talk to you in your office." 40

"Awright, folla me." 41

"Just a moment," I said, "let me pass the word back down the line that 42
we're all going to Philadelphia."

"Naw. Jus' you and this heah man can come," he said, pointing to Gregory. 43
"The rest of them boys'll have to wait heah."

I glanced at the unmarked car and saw that leaning against it was Mr. 44
Snodgrass, watching the scene closely.

Gregory and I followed Rainey and Price into town. Outside the court- 45
house were several hundred shirt-sleeved white men, standing with assorted
weapons in hand. Surrounding the courthouse, though, were state police with
rifles pointed at the crowd. State police also flanked the sidewalk leading to the
steps of the building.

Gregory and I followed Rainey and Price up those steps and into the 46
courthouse. We followed them to an elevator, and as the doors closed behind
us, we thought of the same thing simultaneously. We never should have gotten
into that box with those two men. They could have killed us and said that we
had jumped them and that they had to shoot us in self-defense. And there
would have been no witnesses. But it was too late now. We shrugged our
shoulders.

To our relief, the door opened on the second floor without event, and we 47
followed the two men down the hallway to an office at its end. Rainey introduced

the three men seated in that office as the city attorney of Philadelphia, the county attorney of Neshoba, and Mr. Snodgrass of the state police. Snodgrass merely nodded at the introduction, and looked sharply at the faces of the other men in the room.

Rainey cleared his throat and rasped, "Ah've got laryngitis or somethin'. This heah man will tall fer me." He was pointing at the county attorney. I nodded, but thought it strange that I had not noticed the impaired throat during our conversation at the roadblock.   48

The county attorney squinted his eyes, and said to me, "Well, we're all heah. What was it you wanted to talk to the sheriff and his deputy about?"   49

I told him that, as national director of CORE, I was charged with responsibility for the supervision of all members of the CORE staff. Three members of that staff had been missing for thirty-six hours. Mr. Gregory and I were there, I said, to try to find out what had happened to them and whether they were alive or dead. Specifically, I indicated I wanted to ask Deputy Price a question.   50

Price then sat upright in his seat. Deputy Price had given conflicting stories to the press, I pointed out. First, he had said he never saw the men, then he said he had arrested them and released them in the evening. I wanted to know the true story.   51

The attorney looked at Price and the deputy spoke: "Ah'll tell ya the God's truth. Ah did see them boys. I arrested them for speedin' and took them ta jail—"   52

"What time did you arrest them?" I said.   53

"It was about three or three-thirty. Yeah, closer to three-thirty when Ah arrested them. Ah kept them in jail till 'bout six-thirty or seven in the evenin'—"   54

"Why would you keep men in jail for three and a half hours for speeding?"   55

"Ah had to find out how much the justice of the peace was gonna fine them. The justice of the peace was not at home, so Ah had to wait till he got home. He fined them fifteen dollars. That colored boy, Chaney, who wuz drivin' the car, didn't have no fifteen dollars, but one of them Jew boys, Schwerner, had fifteen an' he paid the fine. Then, I took them boys out to the edge of town and put them in their car and they headed for Meridian. Ah sat in mah car and watched their taillights as long as Ah could see them. An' they were goin' toward Meridian. Then Ah turned around and came back into town, and that was the last Ah seen of them boys. Now, that's the God's truth."   56

"At this moment," I said, "I have about fifteen young men waiting at the county line. They are friends and coworkers of Mickey Schwerner, Jim Chaney, and Andy Goodman. They want to join in the search for their missing colleagues."   57

"What would they do? Where would they look?" the county attorney asked, rather anxiously, I felt. Could it have been he thought we might have gotten some clue as to where the bodies could be found?   58

"They would look anywhere and everywhere that bodies could be hidden 59
or disposed of—in the woods, the swamps, the rivers, whatever."

"No!" he said. "We can't let them go out there by themselves without 60
any supervision."

"Oh, they'll be supervised," I replied. "I'll go with them." 61

"And I'll be with them, too," Gregory added. 62

"No, no! I can't let you do that. This is private property all around heah 63
and the owners could shoot you for trespassing. We don't want anything to
happen to you down here," he said.

"Something already *has* happened to three of our brothers. I'll take my 64
chances," I said.

"No, these swamps around here are very dangerous," the attorney said. 65
"They've got water moccasins, rattlesnakes, copperheads, and everything else
in them. Like I said, we don't want anything to happen to you. We won't allow
you to do it."

"Then," I said, "I have another question. We heard over the car radio 66
coming here that the car in which the men were riding, that white Ford station
wagon, has been found burned out on the other side of town, the opposite side
from Meridian. That automobile belonged to the organization I serve as national
director, and I want to look at what is left of it."

"No," said the county lawyer emphatically. "We can't let you do that 67
either. You might destroy fingerprints or some other evidence that will be useful
to Sheriff Rainey or Deputy Price in solving this crime—if there has been a
crime. You know, those boys may have decided to go up north or someplace
and have a short vacation. They'll probably be coming back shortly."

Dick Gregory, who had shown masterful restraint thus far, rose to his 68
feet. He began speaking to the assembled men, pointing his finger at them,
looking at each one with sharp eyes, and speaking with an even sharper tongue.
He made it clear that he thought someone there knew much more about the
disappearance of the three men than was being told. He said that we were not
going to let this matter rest but were going to get to the bottom of it, and the
guilty persons were going to pay for their crimes.

I felt this was neither the time nor the place to have a showdown with 69
Rainey and Price. Yet, I was struggling with my own feelings. I was not Christ.
I was not Gandhi. I was not King. I wanted to kill those men—not with bullets,
but with my fingers around their throats, squeezing tighter as I watched life
ebb from their eyes.

Back in Meridian, I called a meeting of the CORE staff and summer volunteers. 70
Our embattled southern staff evidenced little of the black/white tension so
prevalent in the North. At the meeting, I announced that I wanted two volunteers for an extraordinarily important and dangerous mission. The qualifications for the volunteers were that they had to be black, male, and young. I
wanted them to slip into Philadelphia in Neshoba County in the dead of night,

not going by the main highway but by side routes. They would very quietly disappear into the black community of Philadelphia, see a minister, and ask if he could find a family for them to stay with.

They would have to do all they could to keep the officials from knowing   71
that they were there or of their mission. I believed that the black community would take them in, for that is an old tradition among blacks—the extended family. They would have to try not to be conspicuous, but to disappear into the woodwork, so to speak, until they were trusted by the blacks in Philadelphia.

In all probability, George Raymond and I believed, some person or per-   72
sons in the black community knew what had happened to the three men. Someone in that community always does, but no one would tell the FBI or any city or state officials, for fear of retribution.

When accepted and trusted, our men were to begin asking discreet ques-   73
tions. When any information was secured, they were to communicate that to me. If they did so by phone, it was to be from a phone booth and not the same one each time. If by letter, the message should be mailed from another town, and without a return address on the envelope. If they had any reason to believe that Rainey or Price knew of their presence or mission, they were to contact me immediately by phone.

Practically all hands went up. Everyone wanted to go. When George   74
Raymond and I selected two, most others felt let down and angry.

The two volunteers left the meeting, packed small suitcases, and surrep-   75
titiously moved into Philadelphia. It was about two weeks before I began getting reports. Those reports from eyewitnesses of various parts of the tragedy indicated a clear scenario, the stage for which had been set by an earlier report from another source.

A black maid in Meridian had told us of overhearing a phone call from   76
a black Meridian man who was speaking in an open telephone booth. The man allegedly fingered the three young CORE men. The maid, of course, did not know to whom the call was made, but we suspected it was either to Sheriff Rainey or Deputy Price. The caller said that the three guys, two Jews and one colored, were in a white '62 Ford station wagon. He also gave the license number of the car. He said the three had just left Meridian, heading for Philadelphia.

The scenario as told to the CORE volunteers by various eyewitnesses was   77
as follows: when Schwerner, Goodman, and Chaney entered Philadelphia, they were trailed by Deputy Price, who kept his distance. When they stopped at the charred ruins of the small black church on the other side of town, Price parked at a distance and watched them. As they got back into the car to drive on, Deputy Price, according to the witnesses, closed in on them.

James Chaney, who was driving the car, saw Price in his rearview mirror   78
and, knowing Price's reputation as a "nigger killer," sped up.

Price then shot a tire on the Ford wagon and it came to a halt. The men   79 were arrested and taken to jail, as Price had said. Also, as the deputy had told us, he took them out of jail about sundown, but there the similarity between the deputy's story and fact seemed to end.

He took them to the other side of town, not the Meridian side, and turned 80 them over to a waiting mob in a vacant field. The three men were pulled into the field and pushed beneath a large tree. There, members of the mob held Schwerner and Goodman while the other mobsters beat Chaney without mercy. He was knocked down, stomped, kicked, and clubbed. Schwerner broke away from his captives and tried to help Chaney. He was then clubbed once on the head and knocked unconscious. Seconds later, he revived and was again held by members of the mob while the beating of Chaney continued.

By this time Chaney appeared dead, and the beating stopped. Members 81 of the mob huddled, and then Deputy Price, who was also in the group, went back to his car and drove away. The mob remained there, holding Schwerner and Goodman and looking at the prone form of Chaney on the ground.

A little while later, Price returned and said something to the members of 82 the mob. They then dragged Schwerner and Goodman and Chaney's body to a car and threw them into it. The car drove off.

The latter scene was allegedly witnessed by two blacks crossing different 83 corners of the field at about the same time, on the way to church for a prayer meeting.

We turned this information over to the FBI. 84

It was weeks later—August fifth—when I received a call from Deke DeLoach, 85 then assistant to the director at FBI headquarters in Washington, D.C.

DeLoach said, "Mr. Farmer, since Schwerner, Goodman, and Chaney 86 were members of your staff, I wanted you to be the first to know. We have found the bodies. An informant told us to look under a fake dam. We drove in a bulldozer and with the first scoop of earth uncovered the three bodies. Though they were badly decomposed, there was every evidence that Chaney had received the most brutal beating imaginable. It seemed that every bone in his body was broken. He was beaten to death. Each of the other two was shot once in the heart."

Months later, on October 3, 1964, the FBI arrested a group of men and 87 charged them with conspiracy to violate the civil rights of the dead trio—the only charge available to the federal government, since murder is a state charge. Mississippi never charged them with murder.

Among those arrested and convicted of conspiracy, in addition to Deputy 88 Price, was a minister of the gospel. When he prayed to his God, did he feel remorse? Or had he silenced the still, small voice within his soul?

Evil societies always kill their consciences. 89

We, who are the living, possess the past. Tomorrow is for our 90 martyrs. ◆

◆ Responding

1. Describe the circumstances in which Farmer says, "I was not Christ. I was not Gandhi. I was not King." Why was it especially hard for him to practice nonviolence at that moment? Using your own knowledge, speculate about what arguments Christ, Gandhi, or King might present for turning the other cheek.

2. Using examples from the reading or from your own experience, write an essay explaining the phrase "Evil societies always kill their consciences."

3. Members of the African American community possessed information about the murder of Chaney, Schwerner, and Goodman but didn't come forward immediately. Working in a group, discuss why having such information would be dangerous. What difficulties would African Americans have had in getting the information to someone they could trust?

4. Farmer implies that the three civil rights workers were "fingered" by an African American. What might explain such a betrayal? Why might some members of the African American community cooperate with a Caucasian sheriff?

5. Members of CORE and other groups—both African American and Caucasian—who went to the South to register voters willingly risked their lives. Does such idealism exist in America today? Support your position, using examples from the readings, current events, or personal feelings and experiences.

MARTIN LUTHER KING, JR.

Martin Luther King, Jr., the son, grandson, and greatgrandson of Baptist ministers, was born in Atlanta, Georgia in 1929. After graduating from Morehouse College in 1951, he earned a doctorate from Boston University in 1955. In that year he also led the Montgomery bus boycott; two years later he founded the Southern Christian Leadership Conference (SCLC). During this time and throughout the 1960s, King worked vigorously to organize and promote boycotts and voter registration drives in the South. Because of the leadership and self-sacrifice he displayed on behalf of the civil rights movement, he received the 1964 Nobel Prize for Peace, the youngest person ever to receive this honor. King was assassinated in 1968.

Among his most important writings are "Letter from Birmingham Jail" (1963); and the "I Have a Dream" speech, delivered at the Lincoln Memorial on August 28, 1963, at the climax of the famous March on Washington. In both these works King describes the chain of broken promises that made the demonstrations and boycotts necessary. At the same time, the author goes beyond merely listing his grievances to depict in strong images his dreams for the future.

◆ LETTER FROM BIRMINGHAM JAIL* ◆

April 16, 1963

MY DEAR FELLOW CLERGYMEN:

While confined here in the Birmingham city jail, I came across your recent statement calling my present activities "unwise and untimely." Seldom do I pause to answer criticism of my work and ideas. If I sought to answer all the criticisms that cross my desk, my secretaries would have little time for anything other than such correspondence in the course of the day, and I would have no time for constructive work. But since I feel that you are men of genuine good will and that your criticisms are sincerely set forth, I want to try to answer your statement in what I hope will be patient and reasonable terms.

I think I should indicate why I am here in Birmingham, since you have

*Author's Note: This response to a published statement by eight fellow clergymen from Alabama (Bishop C. C. J. Carpenter, Bishop Joseph A. Durick, Rabbi Hilton L. Grafman, Bishop Paul Hardin, Bishop Holan B. Harmon, the Reverend George M. Murray, the Reverend Edward V. Ramage and the Reverend Earl Stallings) was composed under somewhat constricting circumstances. Begun on the margins of the newspaper in which the statement appeared while I was in jail, the letter was continued on scraps of writing paper supplied by a friendly Negro trusty, and concluded on a pad my attorneys were eventually permitted to leave me. Although the text remains in substance unaltered, I have indulged in the author's prerogative of polishing it for publication.

been influenced by the view which argues against "outsiders coming in." I have the honor of serving as president of the Southern Christian Leadership Conference, an organization operating in every southern state, with headquarters in Atlanta, Georgia. We have some eighty-five affiliated organizations across the South, and one of them is the Alabama Christian Movement for Human Rights. Frequently we share staff, educational and financial resources with our affiliates. Several months ago the affiliate here in Birmingham asked us to be on call to engage in a nonviolent direct-action program if such were deemed necessary. We readily consented, and when the hour came we lived up to our promise. So I, along with several members of my staff, am here because I was invited here. I am here because I have organizational ties here.

But more basically, I am in Birmingham because injustice is here. Just as the prophets of the eighth century B.C. left their villages and carried their "thus saith the Lord" far beyond the boundaries of their home towns, and just as the Apostle Paul left his village of Tarsus and carried the gospel of Jesus Christ to the far corners of the Greco-Roman world, so am I compelled to carry the gospel of freedom beyond my own home town. Like Paul, I must constantly respond to the Macedonian call for aid.   3

Moreover, I am cognizant of the interrelatedness of all communities and states. I cannot sit idly by in Atlanta and not be concerned about what happens in Birmingham. Injustice anywhere is a threat to justice everywhere. We are caught in an inescapable network of mutuality, tied in a single garment of destiny. Whatever affects one directly, affects all indirectly. Never again can we afford to live with the narrow, provincial "outside agitator" idea. Anyone who lives inside the United States can never be considered an outsider anywhere within its bounds.   4

You deplore the demonstrations taking place in Birmingham. But your statement, I am sorry to say, fails to express a similar concern for the conditions that brought about the demonstrations. I am sure that none of you would want to rest content with the superficial kind of social analysis that deals merely with effects and does not grapple with underlying causes. It is unfortunate that demonstrations are taking place in Birmingham, but it is even more unfortunate that the city's white power structure left the Negro community with no alternative.   5

In any nonviolent campaign there are four basic steps: collection of the facts to determine whether injustices exist; negotiation; self-purification; and direct action. We have gone through all these steps in Birmingham. There can be no gainsaying the fact that racial injustice engulfs this community. Birmingham is probably the most thoroughly segregated city in the United States. Its ugly record of brutality is widely known. Negroes have experienced grossly unjust treatment in the courts. There have been more unsolved bombings of Negro homes and churches in Birmingham than in any other city in the nation. These are the hard, brutal facts of the case. On the basis of these conditions,   6

Negro leaders sought to negotiate with the city fathers. But the latter consistently refused to engage in good-faith negotiation.

Then, last September, came the opportunity to talk with leaders of Birmingham's economic community. In the course of the negotiations, certain promises were made by the merchants—for example, to remove the stores' humiliating racial signs. On the basis of these promises, the Reverend Fred Shuttlesworth and the leaders of the Alabama Christian Movement for Human Rights agreed to a moratorium on all demonstrations. As the weeks and months went by, we realized that we were the victims of a broken promise. A few signs, briefly removed, returned; the others remained. 7

As in so many past experiences, our hopes had been blasted, and the shadow of deep disappointment settled upon us. We had no alternative except to prepare for direct action, whereby we would present our very bodies as a means of laying our case before the conscience of the local and the national community. Mindful of the difficulties involved, we decided to undertake a process of self-purification. We began a series of workshops on nonviolence, and we repeatedly asked ourselves: "Are you able to accept blows without retaliating?" "Are you able to endure the ordeal of jail?" We decided to schedule our direct-action program for the Easter season, realizing that except for Christmas, this is the main shopping period of the year. Knowing that a strong economic-withdrawal program would be the by-product of direct action, we felt that this would be the best time to bring pressure to bear on the merchants for the needed change. 8

Then it occurred to us that Birmingham's mayoral election was coming up in March, and we speedily decided to postpone action until after election day. When we discovered that the Commissioner of Public Safety, Eugene "Bull" Connor, had piled up enough votes to be in the run-off, we decided again to postpone action until the day after the run-off so that the demonstrations could not be used to cloud the issues. Like many others, we waited to see Mr. Connor defeated, and to this end we endured postponement after postponement. Having aided in the community need, we felt that our direct-action program could be delayed no longer. 9

You may well ask: "Why direct action? Why sit-ins, marches and so forth? Isn't negotiation a better path?" You are quite right in calling for negotiation. Indeed, this is the very purpose of direct action. Nonviolent direct action seeks to create such a crisis and foster such a tension that a community which has constantly refused to negotiate is forced to confront the issue. It seeks so to dramatize the issue that it can no longer be ignored. My citing the creation of tension as part of the work of the nonviolent-resister may sound rather shocking. But I must confess that I am not afraid of the word "tension." I have earnestly opposed violent tension, but there is a type of constructive, nonviolent tension which is necessary for growth. Just as Socrates felt that it was necessary to create a tension in the mind so that individuals could rise from the bondage of 10 myths and half-truths to the unfettered realm of creative analysis and objective appraisal, so must we see the need for nonviolent gadflies to create the kind of tension in society that will help men rise from the dark depths of prejudice and racism to the majestic heights of understanding and brotherhood.

The purpose of our direct-action program is to create a situation so crisis-packed that it will inevitably open the door to negotiation. I therefore concur with you in your call for negotiation. Too long has our beloved Southland been bogged down in a tragic effort to live in monologue rather than dialogue. 11

One of the basic points in your statement is that the action that I and my associates have taken in Birmingham is untimely. Some have asked: "Why didn't you give the new city administration time to act?" The only answer that I can give to this query is that the new Birmingham administration must be prodded about as much as the outgoing one, before it will act. We are sadly mistaken if we feel that the election of Albert Boutwell as mayor will bring the millennium to Birmingham. While Mr. Boutwell is a much more gentle person than Mr. Connor, they are both segregationists, dedicated to maintenance of the status quo. I have hope that Mr. Boutwell will be reasonable enough to see the futility of massive resistance to desegregation. But he will not see this without pressure from devotees of civil rights. My friends, I must say to you that we have not made a single gain in civil rights without determined legal and nonviolent pressure. Lamentably, it is an historical fact that privileged groups seldom give up their privileges voluntarily. Individuals may see the moral light and voluntarily give up their unjust posture; but, as Reinhold Niebuhr has reminded us, groups tend to be more immoral than individuals. 12

We know through painful experience that freedom is never voluntarily given by the oppressor; it must be demanded by the oppressed. Frankly, I have yet to engage in a direct-action campaign that was "well timed" in the view of those who have not suffered unduly from the disease of segregation. For years now I have heard the word "Wait!" It rings in the ear of every Negro with piercing familiarity. This "Wait" has almost always meant "Never." We must come to see, with one of our distinguished jurists, that "justice too long delayed is justice denied." 13

We have waited for more than 340 years for our constitutional and God-given rights. The nations of Asia and Africa are moving with jetlike speed toward gaining political independence, but we still creep at horse-and-buggy pace toward gaining a cup of coffee at a lunch counter. Perhaps it is easy for those who have never felt the stinging darts of segregation to say, "Wait." But when you have seen vicious mobs lynch your mothers and fathers at will and drown your sisters and brothers at whim; when you have seen hate-filled policemen curse, kick and even kill your black brothers and sisters; when you see the vast majority of your twenty million Negro brothers smothering in an airtight cage of poverty in the midst of an affluent society; when you suddenly find your tongue twisted and your speech stammering as you seek to explain to your six-year-old daughter why she can't go to the public amusement park 14 that has just been advertised on television, and see tears welling up in her eyes when she is told that Funtown is closed to colored children, and see ominous clouds of inferiority beginning to form in her little mental sky, and see her beginning to distort her personality by developing an unconscious bitterness toward white people; when you have to concoct an answer for a five-year-old son who is asking: "Daddy, why do white people treat colored people so mean?"; when you take a cross-country drive and find it necessary to sleep night after night in the uncomfortable corners of your automobile because no motel will accept you; when you are humiliated day in and day out by nagging signs reading "white" and "colored"; when your first name becomes "nigger," your middle name becomes "boy" (however old you are) and your last name becomes "John," and your wife and mother are never given the respected title "Mrs."; when you are harried by day and haunted by night by the fact that you are a Negro, living constantly at tiptoe stance, never quite knowing what to expect next, and are plagued with inner fears and outer resentments; when you are forever fighting a degenerating sense of "nobodiness"—then you will understand why we find it difficult to wait. There comes a time when the cup of endurance runs over, and men are no longer willing to be plunged into the abyss of despair. I hope, sirs, you can understand our legitimate and unavoidable impatience.

You express a great deal of anxiety over our willingness to break laws. 15 This is certainly a legitimate concern. Since we so diligently urge people to obey the Supreme Court's decision of 1954 outlawing segregation in the public schools, at first glance it may seem rather paradoxical for us consciously to break laws. One may well ask: "How can you advocate breaking some laws and obeying others?" The answer lies in the fact that there are two types of laws: just and unjust. I would be the first to advocate obeying just laws. One has not only a legal but a moral responsibility to obey just laws. Conversely, one has a moral responsibility to disobey unjust laws. I would agree with St. Augustine that "an unjust law is no law at all."

Now, what is the difference between the two? How does one determine 16 whether a law is just or unjust? A just law is a man-made code that squares with the moral law or the law of God. An unjust law is a code that is out of harmony with the moral law. To put it in the terms of St. Thomas Aquinas: An unjust law is a human law that is not rooted in eternal law and natural law. Any law that uplifts human personality is just. Any law that degrades human personality is unjust. All segregation statutes are unjust because segregation distorts the soul and damages the personality. It gives the segregator a false sense of superiority and the segregated a false sense of inferiority. Segregation, to use the terminology of the Jewish philosopher Martin Buber, substitutes an "I–it" relationship for an "I–thou" relationship and ends up relegating persons to the status of things. Hence segregation is not only politically, economically and sociologically unsound, it is morally wrong and sinful. Paul Tillich has said that sin is separation. Is not segregation an existential expression of man's tragic separation, his awful estrangement, his terrible sinfulness? Thus it is that I can urge men to obey the 1954 decision of the Supreme Court, for it is morally right; and I can urge them to disobey segregation ordinances, for they are morally wrong.

Let us consider a more concrete example of just and unjust laws. An unjust law is a code that a numerical or power majority group compels a minority group to obey but does not make binding on itself. This is *difference* made legal. By the same token, a just law is a code that a majority compels a minority to follow and that it is willing to follow itself. This is *sameness* made legal.

Let me give another explanation. A law is unjust if it is inflicted on a minority that, as a result of being denied the right to vote, had no part in enacting or devising the law. Who can say that the legislature of Alabama which set up that state's segregation laws was democratically elected? Throughout Alabama all sorts of devious methods are used to prevent Negroes from becoming registered voters, and there are some counties in which, even though Negroes constitute a majority of the population, not a single Negro is registered. Can any law enacted under such circumstances be considered democratically structured?

Sometimes a law is just on its face and unjust in its application. For instance, I have been arrested on a charge of parading without a permit. Now, there is nothing wrong in having an ordinance which requires a permit for a parade. But such an ordinance becomes unjust when it is used to maintain segregation and to deny citizens the First-Amendment privilege of peaceful assembly and protest.

I hope you are able to see the distinction I am trying to point out. In no sense do I advocate evading or defying the law, as would the rabid segregationist. That would lead to anarchy. One who breaks an unjust law must do so openly, lovingly, and with a willingness to accept the penalty. I submit that an individual who breaks a law that conscience tells him is unjust, and who willingly accepts the penalty of imprisonment in order to arouse the conscience of the community over its injustice, is in reality expressing the highest respect for law.

Of course, there is nothing new about this kind of civil disobedience. It was evidenced sublimely in the refusal of Shadrach, Meshach and Abednego to obey the laws of Nebuchadnezzar, on the ground that a higher moral law was at stake. It was practiced superbly by the early Christians, who were willing to face hungry lions and the excruciating pain of chopping blocks rather than submit to certain unjust laws of the Roman Empire. To a degree, academic freedom is a reality today because Socrates practiced civil disobedience. In our own nation, the Boston Tea Party represented a massive act of civil disobedience.

We should never forget that everything Adolf Hitler did in Germany was "legal" and everything the Hungarian freedom fighters did in Hungary was "illegal." It was "illegal" to aid and comfort a Jew in Hitler's Germany. Even so, I am sure that, had I lived in Germany at the time, I would have aided and comforted my Jewish brothers. If today I lived in a Communist country where certain principles dear to the Christian faith are suppressed, I would openly advocate disobeying that country's antireligious laws.

I must make two honest confessions to you, my Christian and Jewish 23
brothers. First, I must confess that over the past few years I have been gravely disappointed with the white moderate. I have almost reached the regrettable conclusion that the Negro's great stumbling block in his stride toward freedom is not the White Citizen's Counciler or the Ku Klux Klanner, but the white moderate, who is more devoted to "order" than to justice; who prefers a negative peace which is the absence of tension to a positive peace which is the presence of justice; who constantly says: "I agree with you in the goal you seek, but I cannot agree with your methods of direct action"; who paternalistically believes he can set the timetable for another man's freedom; who lives by a mythical concept of time and who constantly advises the Negro to wait for a "more convenient season." Shallow understanding from people of good will is more frustrating than absolute misunderstanding from people of ill will. Lukewarm acceptance is much more bewildering than outright rejection.

I had hoped that the white moderate would understand that law and order 24
exist for the purpose of establishing justice and that when they fail in this purpose they become the dangerously structured dams that block the flow of social progress. I had hoped that the white moderate would understand that the present tension in the South is a necessary phase of the transition from an obnoxious negative peace, in which the Negro passively accepted his unjust plight, to a substantive and positive peace, in which all men will respect the dignity and worth of human personality. Actually, we who engage in nonviolent direct action are not the creators of tension. We merely bring to the surface the hidden tension that is already alive. We bring it out in the open, where it can be seen and dealt with. Like a boil that can never be cured so long as it is covered up but must be opened with all its ugliness to the natural medicines of air and light, injustice must be exposed, with all the tension its exposure creates, to the light of human conscience and the air of national opinion before it can be cured.

In your statement you assert that our actions, even though peaceful, must 25
be condemned because they precipitate violence. But is this a logical assertion? Isn't this like condemning a robbed man because his possession of money precipitated the evil act of robbery? Isn't this like condemning Socrates because his unswerving commitment to truth and his philosophical inquiries precipitated the act by the misguided populace in which they made him drink hemlock? Isn't this like condemning Jesus because his unique God-consciousness and never-ceasing devotion to God's will precipitated the evil act of crucifixion? We must come to see that, as the federal courts have consistently affirmed, it is wrong to urge an individual to cease his efforts to gain his basic constitutional rights because the quest may precipitate violence. Society must protect the robbed and punish the robber.

I had also hoped that the white moderate would reject the myth concerning   26
time in relation to the struggle for freedom. I have just received a letter from
a white brother in Texas. He writes: "All Christians know that the colored
people will receive equal rights eventually, but it is possible that you are in too
great a religious hurry. It has taken Christianity almost two thousand years to
accomplish what it has. The teachings of Christ take time to come to earth."
Such an attitude stems from a tragic misconception of time, from the strangely
irrational notion that there is something in the very flow of time that will
inevitably cure all ills. Actually, time itself is neutral; it can be used either
destructively or constructively. More and more I feel that the people of ill will
have used time much more effectively than have the people of good will. We
will have to repent in this generation not merely for the hateful words and
actions of the bad people but for the appalling silence of the good people. Human
progress never rolls in on wheels of inevitability; it comes through the tireless
efforts of men willing to be co-workers with God, and without this hard work,
time itself becomes an ally of the forces of social stagnation. We must use time
creatively, in the knowledge that the time is always ripe to do right. Now is the
time to make real the promise of democracy and transform our pending
national elegy into a creative psalm of brotherhood. Now is the time to lift our
national policy from the quicksand of racial injustice to the solid rock of human
dignity.

You speak of our activity in Birmingham as extreme. At first I was rather   27
disappointed that fellow clergymen would see my nonviolent efforts as those
of an extremist. I began thinking about the fact that I stand in the middle of
two opposing forces in the Negro community. One is a force of complacency,
made up in part of Negroes who, as a result of long years of oppression, are
so drained of self-respect and a sense of "somebodiness" that they have adjusted
to segregation; and in part of a few middle-class Negroes who, because of a
degree of academic and economic security and because in some ways they profit
by segregation, have become insensitive to the problems of the masses. The
other force is one of bitterness and hatred, and it comes perilously close to
advocating violence. It is expressed in the various black nationalist groups that
are springing up across the nation, the largest and best-known being Elijah
Muhammad's Muslim movement. Nourished by the Negro's frustration over
the continued existence of racial discrimination, this movement is made up of
people who have lost faith in America, who have absolutely repudiated Christianity, and who have concluded that the white man is an incorrigible "devil."

I have tried to stand between these two forces, saying that we need emulate   28
neither the "do-nothingism" of the complacent nor the hatred and despair of
the black nationalist. For there is the more excellent way of love and nonviolent
protest. I am grateful to God that, through the influence of the Negro church,
the way of nonviolence became an integral part of our struggle.

If this philosophy had not emerged, by now many streets of the South   29
would, I am convinced, be flowing with blood. And I am further convinced

that if our white brothers dismiss as "rabble-rousers" and "outside agitators" those of us who employ nonviolent direct action, and if they refuse to support our nonviolent efforts, millions of Negroes will, out of frustration and despair, seek solace and security in black-nationalist ideologies—a development that would inevitably lead to a frightening racial nightmare.

Oppressed people cannot remain oppressed forever. The yearning for freedom eventually manifests itself, and that is what has happened to the American Negro. Something within has reminded him of his birthright of freedom, and something without has reminded him that it can be gained. Consciously or unconsciously, he has been caught up by the *Zeitgeist*, and with his black brothers of Africa and his brown and yellow brothers of Asia, South America and the Caribbean, the United States Negro is moving with a sense of great urgency toward the promised land of racial justice. If one recognizes this vital urge that has engulfed the Negro community, one should readily understand why public demonstrations are taking place. The Negro has many pent-up resentments and latent frustrations, and he must release them. So let him march; let him make prayer pilgrimages to the city hall; let him go on freedom rides—and try to understand why he must do so. If his repressed emotions are not released in nonviolent ways, they will seek expression through violence; this is not a threat but a fact of history. So I have not said to my people: "Get rid of your discontent." Rather, I have tried to say that this normal and healthy discontent can be channeled into the creative outlet of nonviolent direct action. And now this approach is being termed extremist.

But though I was initially disappointed at being categorized as an extremist, as I continued to think about the matter I gradually gained a measure of satisfaction from the label. Was not Jesus an extremist for love: "Love your enemies, bless them that curse you, do good to them that hate you, and pray for them which despitefully use you, and persecute you." Was not Amos an extremist for justice: "Let justice roll down like waters and righteousness like an ever-flowing stream." Was not Paul an extremist for the Christian gospel: "I bear in my body the marks of the Lord Jesus." Was not Martin Luther an extremist: "Here I stand; I cannot do otherwise, so help me God." And John Bunyan: "I will stay in jail to the end of my days before I make a butchery of my conscience." And Abraham Lincoln: "This nation cannot survive half slave and half free." And Thomas Jefferson: "We hold these truths to be self-evident, that all men are created equal . . ." So the question is not whether we will be extremists, but what kind of extremists we will be. Will we be extremists for hate or for love? Will we be extremists for the preservation of injustice or for the extension of justice? In that dramatic scene on Calvary's hill three men were crucified. We must never forget that all three were crucified for the same crime—the crime of extremism. Two were extremists for immorality, and thus fell below their environment. The other, Jesus Christ, was an extremist for love, truth and goodness, and thereby rose above his environment. Perhaps the South, the nation and the world are in dire need of creative extremists.

I had hoped that the white moderate would see this need. Perhaps I was too optimistic; perhaps I expected too much. I suppose I should have realized that few members of the oppressor race can understand the deep groans and passionate yearnings of the oppressed race, and still fewer have the vision to see that injustice must be rooted out by strong, persistent and determined action. I am thankful, however, that some of our white brothers in the South have grasped the meaning of this social revolution and committed themselves to it. They are still all too few in quantity, but they are big in quality. Some—such as Ralph McGill, Lillian Smith, Harry Golden, James McBride Dabbs, Ann Braden and Sarah Patton Boyle—have written about our struggle in eloquent and prophetic terms. Others have marched with us down nameless streets of the South. They have languished in filthy, roach-infested jails, suffering the abuse and brutality of policemen who view them as "dirty nigger-lovers." Unlike so many of their moderate brothers and sisters, they have recognized the urgency of the moment and sensed the need for powerful "action" antidotes to combat the disease of segregation. 32

Let me take note of my other major disappointment. I have been so greatly disappointed with the white church and its leadership. Of course, there are some notable exceptions. I am not unmindful of the fact that each of you has taken some significant stands on this issue. I commend you, Reverend Stallings, for your Christian stand on this past Sunday, in welcoming Negroes to your worship service on a nonsegregated basis. I commend the Catholic leaders of this state for integrating Spring Hill College several years ago. 33

But despite these notable exceptions, I must honestly reiterate that I have been disappointed with the church. I do not say this as one of those negative critics who can always find something wrong with the church. I say this as a minister of the gospel, who loves the church; who was nurtured in its bosom; who has been sustained by its spiritual blessings and who will remain true to it as long as the cord of life shall lengthen. 34

When I was suddenly catapulted into the leadership of the bus protest in Montgomery, Alabama, a few years ago, I felt we would be supported by the white church. I felt that the white ministers, priests and rabbis of the South would be among our strongest allies. Instead, some have been outright opponents, refusing to understand the freedom movement and misrepresenting its leaders; all too many others have been more cautious than courageous and have remained silent behind the anesthetizing security of stained-glass windows. 35

In spite of my shattered dreams, I came to Birmingham with the hope that the white religious leadership of this community would see the justice of our cause and, with deep moral concern, would serve as the channel through which our just grievances could reach the power structure. I had hoped that each of you would understand. But again I have been disappointed. 36

I have heard numerous southern religious leaders admonish their worshipers to comply with a desegregation decision because it is the law, but I have longed to hear white ministers declare: "Follow this decree because integration 37 is morally right and because the Negro is your brother." In the midst of blatant injustices inflicted upon the Negro, I have watched white churchmen stand on the sideline and mouth pious irrelevancies and sanctimonious trivialities. In the midst of a mighty struggle to rid our nation of racial and economic injustice, I have heard many ministers say: "Those are social issues, with which the gospel has no real concern." And I have watched many churches commit themselves to a completely otherworldly religion which makes a strange, un-Biblical distinction between body and soul, between the sacred and the secular.

I have traveled the length and breadth of Alabama, Mississippi and all   38
the other southern states. On sweltering summer days and crisp autumn mornings I have looked at the South's beautiful churches with their lofty spires pointing heavenward. I have beheld the impressive outlines of her massive religious-education buildings. Over and over I have found myself asking: "What kind of people worship here? Who is their God? Where were their voices when the lips of Governor Barnett dripped with words of interposition and nullification? Where were they when Governor Wallace gave a clarion call for defiance and hatred? Where were their voices of support when bruised and weary Negro men and women decided to rise from the dark dungeons of complacency to the bright hills of creative protest?"

Yes, these questions are still in my mind. In deep disappointment I have   39
wept over the laxity of the church. But be assured that my tears have been tears of love. There can be no deep disappointment where there is not deep love. Yes, I love the church. How could I do otherwise? I am in the rather unique position of being the son, the grandson and the great-grandson of preachers. Yes, I see the church as the body of Christ. But, oh! How we have blemished and scarred the body through social neglect and through fear of being nonconformists.

There was a time when the church was very powerful—in the time when   40
the early Christians rejoiced at being deemed worthy to suffer for what they believed. In those days the church was not merely a thermometer that recorded the ideas and principles of popular opinion; it was a thermostat that transformed the mores of society. Whenever the early Christians entered a town, the people in power became disturbed and immediately sought to convict the Christians for being "disturbers of the peace" and "outside agitators." But the Christians pressed on, in the conviction that they were "a colony of heaven," called to obey God rather than man. Small in number, they were big in commitment. They were too God-intoxicated to be "astronomically intimidated." By their effort and example they brought an end to such ancient evils as infanticide and gladiatorial contests.

Things are different now. So often the contemporary church is a weak,   41
ineffectual voice with an uncertain sound. So often it is an archdefender of the status quo. Far from being disturbed by the presence of the church, the power structure of the average community is consoled by the church's silent—and often even vocal—sanction of things as they are.

But the judgment of God is upon the church as never before. If today's church does not recapture the sacrificial spirit of the early church, it will lose its authenticity, forfeit the loyalty of millions, and be dismissed as an irrelevant social club with no meaning for the twentieth century. Every day I meet young people whose disappointment with the church has turned into outright disgust.   42

Perhaps I have once again been too optimistic. Is organized religion too inextricably bound to the status quo to save our nation and the world? Perhaps I must turn my faith to the inner spiritual church, the church within the church, as the true *ekklesia* and the hope of the world. But again I am thankful to God that some noble souls from the ranks of organized religion have broken loose from the paralyzing chains of conformity and joined us as active partners in the struggle for freedom. They have left their secure congregations and walked the streets of Albany, Georgia, with us. They have gone down the highways of the South on tortuous rides for freedom. Yes, they have gone to jail with us. Some have been dismissed from their churches, have lost the support of their bishops and fellow ministers. But they have acted in the faith that right defeated is stronger than evil triumphant. Their witness has been the spiritual salt that has preserved the true meaning of the gospel in these troubled times. They have carved a tunnel of hope through the dark mountain of disappointment.   43

I hope the church as a whole will meet the challenge of this decisive hour. But even if the church does not come to the aid of justice, I have no despair about the future. I have no fear about the outcome of our struggle in Birmingham, even if our motives are at present misunderstood. We will reach the goal of freedom in Birmingham and all over the nation, because the goal of America is freedom. Abused and scorned though we may be, our destiny is tied up with America's destiny. Before the pilgrims landed at Plymouth, we were here. Before the pen of Jefferson etched the majestic words of the Declaration of Independence across the pages of history, we were here. For more than two centuries our forebears labored in this country without wages; they made cotton king; they built the homes of their masters while suffering gross injustice and shameful humiliation—and yet out of a bottomless vitality they continued to thrive and develop. If the inexpressible cruelties of slavery could not stop us, the opposition we now face will surely fail. We will win our freedom because the sacred heritage of our nation and the eternal will of God are embodied in our echoing demands.   44

Before closing I feel impelled to mention one other point in your statement that has troubled me profoundly. You warmly commended the Birmingham police force for keeping "order" and "preventing violence." I doubt that you would have so warmly commended the police force if you had seen its dogs sinking their teeth into unarmed, nonviolent Negroes. I doubt that you would so quickly commend the policemen if you were to observe their ugly and inhuman treatment of Negroes here in the city jail; if you were to watch them push and curse old Negro women and young Negro girls; if you were to see them slap and kick old Negro men and young boys; if you were to observe   45 them, as they did on two occasions, refuse to give us food because we wanted to sing our grace together. I cannot join you in your praise of the Birmingham police department.

It is true that the police have exercised a degree of discipline in handling the demonstrators. In this sense they have conducted themselves rather "nonviolently" in public. But for what purpose? To preserve the evil system of segregation. Over the past few years I have consistently preached that nonviolence demands that the means we use must be as pure as the ends we seek. I have tried to make clear that it is wrong to use immoral means to attain moral ends. But now I must affirm that it is just as wrong, or perhaps even more so, to use moral means to preserve immoral ends. Perhaps Mr. Connor and his policemen have been rather nonviolent in public, as was Chief Pritchett in Albany, Georgia, but they have used the moral means of nonviolence to maintain the immoral end of racial injustice. As T. S. Eliot has said: "The last temptation is the greatest treason: To do the right deed for the wrong reason." 46

I wish you had commended the Negro sit-inners and demonstrators of Birmingham for their sublime courage, their willingness to suffer and their amazing discipline in the midst of great provocation. One day the South will recognize its real heroes. They will be the James Merediths, with the noble sense of purpose that enables them to face jeering and hostile mobs, and with the agonizing loneliness that characterizes the life of the pioneer. They will be old, oppressed, battered Negro women, symbolized in a seventy-two-year-old woman in Montgomery, Alabama, whose rose up with a sense of dignity and with her people decided not to ride segregated buses, and who responded with ungrammatical profundity to one who inquired about her weariness: "My feets is tired, but my soul is at rest." They will be the young high school and college students, the young ministers of the gospel and a host of their elders, courageously and nonviolently sitting in at lunch counters and willingly going to jail for conscience' sake. One day the South will know that when these disinherited children of God sat down at lunch counters, they were in reality standing up for what is best in the American dream and for the most sacred values in our Judaeo-Christian heritage, thereby bringing our nation back to those great wells of democracy which were dug deep by the founding fathers in their formulation of the Constitution and the Declaration of Independence. 47

Never before have I written so long a letter. I'm afraid it is much too long to take your precious time. I can assure you that it would have been much shorter if I had been writing from a comfortable desk, but what else can one do when he is alone in a narrow jail cell, other than write long letters, think long thoughts and pray long prayers? 48

If I have said anything in this letter that overstates the truth and indicates an unreasonable impatience, I beg you to forgive me. If I have said anything that understates the truth and indicates my having a patience that allows me to settle for anything less than brotherhood, I beg God to forgive me. 49

I hope this letter finds you strong in the faith. I also hope that circum- 50 stances will soon make it possible for me to meet each of you, not as an integrationist or a civil-rights leader but as a fellow clergyman and a Christian brother. Let us all hope that the dark clouds of racial prejudice will soon pass away and the deep fog of misunderstanding will be lifted from our fear-drenched communities, and in some not too distant tomorrow the radiant stars of love and brotherhood will shine over our great nation with all their scintillating beauty.

Yours for the cause of Peace and Brotherhood,

MARTIN LUTHER KING, JR. ◆

51

◆ Responding

1. Write an essay agreeing or disagreeing with the following statement: "Injustice anywhere is a threat to justice everywhere. We are caught in an inescapable network of mutuality, tied in a single garment of destiny. Whatever affects one directly, affects all indirectly."

2. Argue for or against the following proposition: ". . . an individual who breaks a law that conscience tells him is unjust, and who willingly accepts the penalty of imprisonment in order to arouse the conscience of the community over its injustice, is in reality expressing the highest respect for law."

3. Working individually or in a group, discuss the reasons that Dr. King was in jail if he was fighting injustice.

4. In your opinion, has the hope that Dr. King expressed in the last paragraph of the letter been realized? Support your position with examples from your reading, experience, or television news reports or special programs.

◆ I HAVE A DREAM ◆

Five score years ago, a great American, in whose symbolic shadow we stand today, signed the Emancipation Proclamation. This momentous decree came as a great beacon of light of hope to millions of Negro slaves who had been seared in the flames of withering injustice. It came as a joyous daybreak to end the long night of their captivity.

But one hundred years later, the Negro still is not free. One hundred years later, the life of the Negro is still sadly crippled by the manacles of segregation and the chains of discrimination.

One hundred years later, the Negro lives on a lonely island of poverty in the midst of a vast ocean of material prosperity. One hundred years later, the Negro is still languished in the corners of American society and finds himself an exile in his own land. So we have come here today to dramatize a shameful condition.

In a sense we have come to our nation's capital to cash a check. When the architects of our republic wrote the magnificent words of the Constitution and the Declaration of Independence, they were signing a promissory note to which every American was to fall heir. This note was a promise that all men, yes, black men as well as white men, would be granted the unalienable rights of life, liberty, and the pursuit of happiness.

It is obvious today that America has defaulted on this promissory note insofar as her citizens of color are concerned. Instead of honoring this sacred obligation, America has given the Negro people a bad check; which has come back marked "insufficient funds."

But we refuse to believe that the bank of justice is bankrupt. We refuse to believe that there are insufficient funds in the great vaults of opportunity of this nation. So we have come to cash this check—a check that will give us upon demand the riches of freedom and the security of justice.

We have also come to this hallowed spot to remind America of the fierce urgency of now. This is no time to engage in the luxury of cooling off or to take the tranquilizing drug of gradualism. Now is the time to make real the promises of democracy. Now is the time to rise from the dark and desolate valley of segregation to the sunlit path of racial justice. Now is time to lift our nation from the quick sands of racial injustice and to the solid rock of brotherhood. Now is the time to make justice a reality for all of God's children.

It would be fatal for the nation to overlook the urgency of the movement and to underestimate the determination of the Negro. This sweltering summer of the Negro's legitimate discontent will not pass until there is an invigorating autumn of freedom and equality. Nineteen sixty-three is not an end but a beginning. Those who hope that the Negro needed to blow off steam and will now be content will have a rude awakening if the nation returns to business as usual.

There will be neither rest nor tranquility in America until the Negro is 9
granted his citizenship rights. The whirlwinds of revolt will continue to shake
the foundations of our nation until the bright day of justice emerges.

But there is something that I must say to my people who stand on the 10
warm threshold which leads into the palace of justice. In the process of gaining
our rightful place we must not be guilty of wrongful deeds.

Let us not seek to satisfy our thirst for freedom by drinking from the cup 11
of bitterness and hatred. We must forever conduct our struggle on the high
plane of dignity and discipline. We must not allow our creative protest to
degenerate into physical violence. Again and again we must rise to the majestic
heights of meeting physical force with soul force.

The marvelous new militancy which has engulfed the Negro community 12
must not lead us to a distrust of all white people, for many of our white brothers,
as evidenced by their presence here today, have come to realize that their destiny
is tied up with our destiny and they have come to realize that their freedom is
inextricably bound to our freedom. This offense we share, mounted to storm
the battlements of injustice, must be carried forth by a bi-racial army. We
cannot walk alone.

And as we walk, we must make the pledge that we shall always march 13
ahead. We cannot turn back. There are those who are asking the devotees of
civil rights, "When will you be satisfied?" We can never be satisfied as long as
the Negro is the victim of the unspeakable horrors of police brutality.

We can never be satisfied as long as our bodies, heavy with fatigue of 14
travel, cannot gain lodging in the motels of the highways and the hotels of the
cities. We cannot be satisfied as long as the Negro's basic mobility is from a
smaller ghetto to a larger one.

We can never be satisfied as long as our children are stripped of their 15
selfhood and robbed of their dignity by signs stating "for whites only." We
cannot be satisfied as long as a Negro in Mississippi cannot vote and a Negro
in New York believes he has nothing for which to vote. No, we are not satisfied,
and we will not be satisfied until justice rolls down like waters and righteousness
like a mighty stream.

I am not unmindful that some of you have come here out of excessive 16
trials and tribulation. Some of you have come fresh from narrow jail cells. Some
of you have come from areas where your quest for freedom left you battered
by the storms of persecution and staggered by the winds of police brutality.
You have been the veterans of creative suffering. Continue to work with the
faith that unearned suffering is redemptive.

Go back to Mississippi; go back to Alabama; go back to South Carolina; 17
go back to Georgia; go back to Louisiana; go back to the slums and ghettoes of
the Northern cities, knowing that somehow this situation can, and will, be
changed. Let us not wallow in the valley of despair.

So I say to you, my friends, that even though we must face the difficulties 18 of today and tomorrow, I still have a dream. It is a dream deeply rooted in the American dream that one day this nation will rise up and live out the true meaning of its creed—we hold these truths to be self-evident, that all men are created equal.

I have a dream that one day on the red hills of Georgia, sons of former 19 slaves and sons of former slave-owners will be able to sit down together at the table of brotherhood.

I have a dream that one day, even the state of Mississippi, a state sweltering 20 with the heat of injustice, sweltering with the heat of oppression, will be transformed into an oasis of freedom and justice.

I have a dream my four little children will one day live in a nation where they 21 will not be judged by the color of their skin but by content of their character. I have a dream today!

I have a dream that one day, down in Alabama, with its vicious racists, 22 with its governor having his lips dripping with the words of interposition and nullification, that one day, right there in Alabama, little black boys and black girls will be able to join hands with little white boys and white girls as sisters and brothers. I have a dream today!

I have a dream that one day every valley shall be exalted, every hill and 23 mountain shall be made low, the rough places shall be made plain, and the crooked places shall be made straight and the glory of the Lord will be revealed and all flesh shall see it together.

This is our hope. This is the faith that I go back to the South with. 24

With this faith we will be able to bear out of the mountain of despair a 25 stone of hope. With this faith we will be able to transform the jangling discords of our nation into a beautiful symphony of brotherhood.

With this faith we will be able to work together, to pray together, to 26 struggle together, to go to jail together, to stand up for freedom together, knowing that we will be free one day. This will be the day when all of God's children will be able to sing with new meaning "my country 'tis of thee; sweet land of liberty; of thee I sing; land where my fathers died, land of the pilgrim's pride; from every mountain side, let freedom ring." And if America is to be a great nation, this must become true.

So let freedom ring from the prodigious hilltops of New Hampshire. 27

Let freedom ring from the mighty mountains of New York. 28

Let freedom ring from the heightening Alleghenies of Pennsylvania. 29

Let freedom ring from the snow-capped Rockies of Colorado. 30

Let freedom ring from the curvaceous slopes of California. 31

But not only that. 32

Let freedom ring from Stone Mountain of Georgia. 33

Let freedom ring from Lookout Mountain of Tennessee. 34

Let freedom ring from every hill and molehill of Mississippi, from every 35 mountainside, let freedom ring.

[handwritten marginalia: Taken from color & builds up to everyone.]

And when we allow freedom to ring, when we let it ring from every   36
village and hamlet, from every state and city, we will be able to speed up that
day when all of God's children—black men and white men, Jews and Gentiles,
Catholics and Protestants—will be able to join hands and to sing in the words
of the old Negro spiritual, "Free at last, free at last; thank God Almighty, we
are free at last." ◆

◆ Responding

1. Working individually or in a group, locate the parts of the speech in which
   King gives advice to his followers. Summarize that advice and discuss how
   it exemplifies his philosophy of nonviolent resistance to injustice.

2. Working with the rest of the class, develop a list of criteria for effective
   political speeches. Watch a videotape of King delivering this speech, or have
   someone read the speech aloud. Consider the speech in light of your criteria
   and evaluate its effectiveness.

3. Since "I Have a Dream" is a speech and not an essay, Dr. King must make
   sure his audience understands his message immediately, because they won't
   have the opportunity to refer to the text. Analyze the techniques he uses to
   build a cumulative oral argument.

4. Discuss the current status of African Americans in the United States. Argue
   whether or not King's dream of an America where "all men are created equal"
   has become a reality.

MALCOLM X

*Malcolm X was born Malcolm Little in Omaha, Nebraska, in 1925. When
the author was only six years old, his father was murdered—apparently by
members of the Ku Klux Klan. He left school in the eighth grade and became
involved in crime; he was imprisoned for burglary and larceny in 1946.
While in prison, Malcolm X studied the teachings of Mohammed and became
a Black Muslim minister; he also changed his name to Malcolm X in order
to eliminate his slave name. After his release from prison in 1952, he worked
first as an evangelist for the Nation of Islam, and later as the leader of the
Muslim Mosque and the Organization of Afro-American Unity. He also
became a major spokesman for the Black separatist movement. In 1965, he
was assassinated.*

Alex P. Haley, with whom Malcolm X collaborated on his Autobiography *(1965) was born in Ithaca, New York in 1921. He served as a journalist
in the coast guard for twenty years before beginning work as a freelance writer
in 1959. His most famous work,* Roots *(1976), won a Pulitzer Prize.*

This excerpt from Malcolm X's Autobiography *examines the injustices
endured by African Americans and takes issue with those who rely on non-
violence as a means of obtaining equality.*

◆ *From* **THE AUTOBIOGRAPHY
OF MALCOLM X** ◆

1965

I must be honest. Negroes—Afro-Americans—showed no inclination to rush   1
to the United Nations and demand justice for themselves here in America. I
really had known in advance that they wouldn't. The American white man has
so thoroughly brainwashed the black man to see himself as only a domestic
"civil rights" problem that it will probably take longer than I live before the
Negro sees that the struggle of the American black man is international.

And I had known too, that Negroes would not rush to follow me into the   2
orthodox Islam which had given me the insight and perspective to see that
the black men and white men truly could be brothers. America's Negroes—
especially older Negroes—are too indelibly soaked in Christianity's double standard of oppression.

So, in the "public invited" meetings which I began holding each Sunday   3
afternoon or evening in Harlem's well-known Audubon Ballroom, as I addressed
predominantly non-Muslim Negro audiences, I did not immediately attempt
to press the Islamic religion, but instead to embrace all who sat before me:

"—not Muslim, nor Christian, Catholic, nor Protestant . . . Baptist nor   4
Methodist, Democrat nor Republican, Mason nor Elk! I mean the black people
of America—and the black people all over this earth! Because it is as this
collective mass of black people that we have been deprived not only of our civil
rights, but even of our human rights, the right to human dignity. . . ."

On the streets, after my speeches, in the faces and the voices of the people   5
I met—even those who would pump my hands and want my autograph—I
would feel the wait-and-see attitude. I would feel—and I understood—their
uncertainty about where I stood. Since the Civil War's "freedom," the black
man has gone down so many fruitless paths. His leaders, very largely, had
failed him. The religion of Christianity had failed him. The black man was
scarred, he was cautious, he was apprehensive.

I understood it better now than I had before. In the Holy World, away   6
from America's race problem, was the first time I ever had been able to think
clearly about the basic divisions of white people in America, and how their
attitudes and their motives related to, and affected Negroes. In my thirty-nine
years on this earth, the Holy City of Mecca had been the first time I had ever
stood before the Creator of All and felt like a complete human being.

In that peace of the Holy World—in fact, the very night I have mentioned   7
when I lay awake surrounded by snoring brother pilgrims—my mind took me
back to personal memories I would have thought were gone forever . . . as far
back, even, as when I was just a little boy, eight or nine years old. Out behind
our house, out in the country from Lansing, Michigan, there was an old, grassy
"Hector's Hill," we called it—which may still be there. I remembered there in
the Holy World how I used to lie on top of Hector's Hill, and look up at the
sky, at the clouds moving over me, and daydream, all kinds of things. And
then, in a funny contrast of recollections, I remembered how years later, when
I was in prison, I used to lie on my cell bunk—this would be especially when
I was in solitary: what we convicts called "The Hole"—and I would picture
myself talking to large crowds. I don't have any idea why such previsions came
to me. But they did. To tell that to anyone then would have sounded crazy.
Even I didn't have, myself, the slightest inkling. . . .

In Mecca, too, I had played back for myself the twelve years I had spent   8
with Elijah Muhammad[1] as if it were a motion picture. I guess it would be
impossible for anyone ever to realize fully how complete was my belief in Elijah
Muhammad. I believed in him not only as a leader in the ordinary *human* sense,
but also I believed in him as a *divine* leader. I believed he had no human
weaknesses or faults, and that, therefore, he could make no mistakes and that
he could do no wrong. There on a Holy World hilltop, I realized how very

---

[1]Elijah Mohammed (1896–1975), a leader of the Black Muslim faith in the U.S. Malcolm X began
corresponding with him soon after his conversion.

dangerous it is for people to hold any human being in such esteem, especially to consider anyone some sort of "divinely guided" and "protected" person.

My thinking had been opened up wide in Mecca. In the long letters I 9 wrote to friends, I tried to convey to them my new insights into the American black man's struggle and his problems, as well as the depths of my search for truth and justice.

"I've had enough of someone else's propaganda," I had written to these 10 friends. "I'm for truth, no matter who tells it. I'm for justice, no matter who it is for or against. I'm a human being first and foremost, and as such I'm for whoever and whatever benefits humanity *as a whole*."

Largely, the American white man's press refused to convey that I was 11 now attempting to teach Negroes a new direction. With the 1964 "long, hot summer" steadily producing new incidents, I was constantly accused of "stirring up Negroes." Every time I had another radio or television microphone at my mouth, when I was asked about "stirring up Negroes" or "inciting violence," I'd get hot.

"It takes no one to stir up the sociological dynamite that stems from the 12 unemployment, bad housing, and inferior education already in the ghettoes. This explosively criminal condition has existed for so long, it needs no fuse; it fuses itself; it spontaneously combusts from within itself. . . ."

They called me "the angriest Negro in America." I wouldn't deny that 13 charge. I spoke exactly as I felt. "I *believe* in anger. The Bible says there is a *time* for anger." They called me a "teacher, a fomentor of violence." I would say point blank, "That is a lie. I'm not for wanton violence, I'm for justice. I feel that if white people were attacked by Negroes—if the forces of law prove unable, or inadequate, or reluctant to protect those whites from those Negroes—then those white people should protect and defend themselves from those Negroes, using arms if necessary. And I feel that when the law fails to protect Negroes from whites' attack, then those Negroes should use arms, if necessary, to defend themselves."

"Malcolm X Advocates Armed Negroes!" 14

What was wrong with that? I'll tell you what was wrong. I was a black 15 man talking about physical defense against the white man. The white man can lynch and burn and bomb and beat Negroes—that's all right: "Have patience" . . . "The customs are entrenched" . . . "Things are getting better."

Well, I believe it's a crime for anyone who is being brutalized to continue 16 to accept that brutality without doing something to defend himself. If that's how "Christian" philosophy is interpreted, if that's what Gandhian philosophy teaches, well, then, I will call them criminal philosophies.

I tried in every speech I made to clarify my new position regarding white 17 people—"I don't speak against the sincere, well-meaning, good white people. I have learned that there *are* some. I have learned that not all white people are racists. I am speaking against and my fight is against the white *racists*. I firmly believe that Negroes have the right to fight against these racists, by any means that are necessary."

But the white reporters kept wanting me linked with that word "violence." I doubt if I had one interview without having to deal with that accusation. 18

"I *am* for violence if non-violence means we continue postponing a solution to the American black man's problem—just to *avoid* violence. I don't go for non-violence if it also means a delayed solution. To me a delayed solution is a non-solution. Or I'll say it another way. If it must take violence to get the black man his human rights in this country, I'm *for* violence exactly as you know the Irish, the Poles, or Jews would be if they were flagrantly discriminated against. I am just as they would be in that case, and they would be for violence—no matter what the consequences, no matter who was hurt by the violence." 19

White society *hates* to hear anybody, especially a black man, talk about the crime the white man has perpetrated on the black man. I have always understood that's why I have been so frequently called "a revolutionist." It sounds as if *I* have done some crime! Well, it may be the American black man does need to become involved in a *real* revolution. The word for "revolution" in German is *Umwälzung*. What it means is a complete overturn—a complete change. The overthrow of King Farouk in Egypt and the succession of President Nasser is an example of a true revolution. It means the destroying of an old system, and its replacement with a new system. Another example is the Algerian revolution, led by Ben Bella; they threw out the French who had been there over 100 years. So how does anybody sound talking about the Negro in America waging some "revolution"? Yes, he is condemning a system—but he's not trying to overturn the system, or to destroy it. The Negro's so-called "revolt" is merely an asking to be *accepted* into the existing system! A *true* Negro revolt might entail, for instance, fighting for separate black states within this country—which several groups and individuals have advocated, long before Elijah Muhammad came along. 20

When the white man came into this country, he certainly wasn't demonstrating any "non-violence." In fact, the very man whose name symbolizes non-violence here today has stated: 21

"Our nation was born in genocide when it embraced the doctrine that the original American, the Indian, was an inferior race. Even before there were large numbers of Negroes on our shores, the scar of racial hatred had already disfigured colonial society. From the sixteenth century forward, blood flowed in battles over racial supremacy. We are perhaps the only nation which tried as a matter of national policy to wipe out its indigenous population. Moreover, we elevated that tragic experience into a noble crusade. Indeed, even today we have not permitted ourselves to reject or to feel remorse for this shameful episode. Our literature, our films, our drama, our folklore all exalt it. Our children are still taught to respect the violence which reduced a red-skinned people of an earlier culture into a few fragmented groups herded into impoverished reservations." 22

"Peaceful coexistence!" That's another one the white man has always   23
been quick to cry. Fine! But what have been the deeds of the white man?
During his entire advance through history, he has been waving the banner
of Christianity . . . and carrying in his other hand the sword and the flint-
lock.

You can go right back to the very beginning of Christianity. Catholicism,   24
the genesis of Christianity as we know it to be presently constituted, with its
hierarchy, was conceived in Africa—by those whom the Christian church calls
"The Desert Fathers." The Christian church became infected with racism when
it entered white Europe. The Christian church returned to Africa under the
banner of the Cross—conquering, killing, exploiting, pillaging, raping, bullying,
beating—and teaching white supremacy. This is how the white man thrust
himself into the position of leadership of the world—through the use of naked
physical power. And he was totally inadequate spiritually. Mankind's history
has proved from one era to another that the true criterion of leadership is
spiritual. Men are attracted by spirit. By power, men are *forced*. Love is engendered by spirit. By power, anxieties are created.

I am in agreement one hundred per cent with those racists who say that   25
no government laws ever can *force* brotherhood. The only true world solution
today is governments guided by true religion—of the spirit. Here in race-torn
America, I am convinced that the Islam religion is desperately needed, particularly by the American black man. The black man needs to reflect that he has
been America's most fervent Christian—and where has it gotten him? In fact,
in the white man's hands, in the white man's interpretation . . . where has
Christianity brought this *world?*

It has brought the non-white two-thirds of the human population to re-   26
bellion. Two-thirds of the human population today is telling the one-third
minority white man, "Get out!" And the white man is leaving. And as he leaves,
we see the non-white peoples returning in a rush to their original religions,
which had been labeled "pagan" by the conquering white man. Only one religion—Islam—had the power to stand and fight the white man's Christianity
for a *thousand years!* Only Islam could keep white Christianity at bay.

The Africans are returning to Islam and other indigenous religions. The   27
Asians are returning to being Hindus, Buddhists and Muslims.

As the Christian Crusade once went East, now the Islamic Crusade is   28
going West. With the East—Asia—closed to Christianity, with Africa rapidly
being converted to Islam, with Europe rapidly becoming un-Christian, generally
today it is accepted that the "Christian" civilization of America—which is prop-
ping up the white race around the world—is Christianity's remaining strongest
bastion.

Well, if *this* is so—if the so-called "Christianity" now being practiced in   29
America displays the best that world Christianity has left to offer—no one in
his right mind should need any much greater proof that very close at hand is
the *end* of Christianity.

Are you aware that some Protestant theologians, in their writings, are 30
using the phrase "post-Christian era"—and they mean *now?*

And what is the greatest single reason for this Christian church's failure? 31
It is its failure to combat racism. It is the old "You sow, you reap" story. The
Christian church sowed racism—blasphemously; now it reaps racism.

Sunday mornings in this year of grace 1965, imagine the "Christian con- 32
science" of congregations guarded by deacons barring the door to black would-
be worshipers, telling them, "You can't enter *this* House of God!"

Tell me, if you can, a sadder irony than that St. Augustine, Florida—a 33
city named for the black African saint who saved Catholicism from heresy—
was recently the scene of bloody race riots.

I believe that God now is giving the world's so-called "Christian" white 34
society its last opportunity to repent and atone for the crimes of exploiting and
enslaving the world's non-white peoples. It is exactly as when God gave Pharaoh
a chance to repent. But Pharaoh persisted in his refusal to give justice to those
whom he oppressed. And, we know, God finally destroyed Pharaoh.

Is white America really sorry for her crimes against the black people? 35
Does white America have the capacity to repent—and to atone? Does the
capacity to repent, to atone, exist in a majority, in one-half, in even one-third
of American white society?

Many black men, the victims—in fact most black men—would like to be 36
able to forgive, to forget, the crimes.

But most American white people seem not to have it in them to make any 37
serious atonement—to do justice to the black man.

Indeed, how *can* white society atone for enslaving, for raping, for un- 38
manning, for otherwise brutalizing *millions* of human beings, for centuries? What
atonement would the God of Justice demand for the robbery of the black people's
labor, their lives, their true identities, their culture, their history—and even
their human dignity?

A desegregated cup of coffee, a theater, public toilets—the whole range 39
of hypocritical "integration"—these are not atonement.

After a while in America, I returned abroad—and this time, I spent 40
eighteen weeks in the Middle East and Africa.

The world leaders with whom I had private audiences this time included 41
President Gamal Abdel Nasser, of Egypt; President Julius K. Nyerere, of Tan-
zania; President Nnamoi Azikiwe, of Nigeria; Osagyefo Dr. Kwame Nkrumah,
of Ghana; President Sekou Touré, of Guinea; President Jomo Kenyatta, of Kenya;
and Prime Minister Dr. Milton Obote, of Uganda.

I also met with religious leaders—African, Arab, Asian, Muslim, and non- 42
Muslim. And in all of these countries, I talked with Afro-Americans and whites
of many professions and backgrounds.

An American white ambassador in one African country was Africa's most 43
respected American ambassador: I'm glad to say that this was told to me by

one ranking African leader. We talked for an entire afternoon. Based on what I had heard of him, I had to believe him when he told me that as long as he was on the African continent, he never thought in terms of race, that he dealt with human beings, never noticing their color. He said he was more aware of language differences than of color differences. He said that only when he returned to America would he become aware of color differences.

I told him, "What you are telling me is that it isn't the American white *man* who is a racist, but it's the American political, economic, and social *atmosphere* that automatically nourishes a racist psychology in the white man." He agreed.

44

We both agreed that American society makes it next to impossible for humans to meet in America and not be conscious of their color differences. And we both agreed that if racism could be removed, America could offer a society where rich and poor could truly live like human beings.

45

That discussion with the ambassador gave me a new insight—one which I like: that the white man is *not* inherently evil, but America's racist society influences him to act evilly. The society has produced and nourishes a psychology which brings out the lowest, most base part of human beings.

46

I had a totally different kind of talk with another white man I met in Africa—who, to me, personified exactly what the ambassador and I had discussed. Throughout my trip, I was of course aware that I was under constant surveillance. The agent was a particularly obvious and obnoxious one; I am not sure for what agency, as he never identified it, or I would say it. Anyway, this one finally got under my skin when I found I couldn't seem to eat a meal in the hotel without seeing him somewhere around watching me. You would have thought I was John Dillinger or somebody.

47

I just got up from my breakfast one morning and walked over to where he was and I told him I knew he was following me, and if he wanted to know anything, why didn't he ask me. He started to give me one of those too-lofty-to-descend-to-you attitudes. I told him then right to his face he was a fool, that he didn't know me, or what I stood for, so that made him one of those people who let somebody else do their thinking; and that no matter what job a man had, at least he ought to be able to think for himself. That stung him; he let me have it.

48

I was, to hear him tell it, anti-American, un-American, seditious, subversive, and probably Communist. I told him that what he said only proved how little he understood about me. I told him that the only thing the F.B.I., the C.I.A., or anybody else could ever find me guilty of, was being open-minded. I said I was seeking for the truth, and I was trying to weigh—objectively—everything on its own merit. I said what I was against was strait-jacketed thinking, and strait-jacketed societies. I said I respected every man's right to believe whatever his intelligence tells him is intellectually sound, and I expect everyone else to respect my right to believe likewise. ◆

49

◆ Responding

1. Clarify Malcolm X's position on nonviolence and on the appropriate use of violence. Respond to his statement that "when the law fails to protect Negroes from whites' attack, then those Negroes should use arms, if necessary, to defend themselves."

2. Working individually or in a group, list Malcolm X's criticisms of the Christian church. Do you think his charges are valid?

3. Discuss Malcolm X's solution to the problems of the "black man" around the world. Consider the strengths and weaknesses of that solution.

4. Argue in support of or against the position stated in the following passage: "It's the American political, economic, and social *atmosphere* that automatically nourishes a racist psychology in the white man. . . . American society makes it next to impossible for humans to meet in America and not be conscious of their color differences."

GWENDOLYN BROOKS

The poet Gwendolyn Brooks was born in Topeka, Kansas, in 1917. After graduating from Wilson Junior College, she worked as a book reviewer for The New York Times *and the* New York Herald Tribune. *During the late 1930s she joined the NAACP; she has remained active in the civil rights movement since that time. Her publications include* A Street in Bronzeville *(1945),* Annie Allen *(1949),* The Bean Eaters *(1960),* Selected Poems *(1963),* In the Mecca *(1968), and* Family Pictures *(1970). Brooks's work has been awarded the prize of the American Academy of Arts and Letters (1946), Guggenheim Fellowships (1946 and 1947), and the Pulitzer Prize for Poetry (1950). In 1968 Brooks was named the poet laureate of Illinois. In that post, as writer in residence at several universities, and as distinguished professor of the arts at the City College of New York, she has worked to make young people more aware of their talents as writers.*

The first two poems included here explore the civil rights and separatist movements by focusing on two important leaders of the 1960s, Medgar Evers and Malcolm X. The other poem, "The Chicago Defender Sends a Man to Little Rock," explores the effects of prejudice and injustice on the children who were its victims.

◆ THE CHICAGO DEFENDER SENDS A MAN TO LITTLE ROCK ◆

FALL, 1957

In Little Rock the people bear
Babes, and comb and part their hair
And watch the want ads, put repair
To roof and latch. While wheat toast burns
A woman waters multiferns.

Time upholds or overturns
The many, tight, and small concerns.

In Little Rock the people sing
Sunday hymns like anything,
Through Sunday pomp and polishing.

And after testament and tunes,
Some soften Sunday afternoons
With lemon tea and Lorna Doones.

I forecast
And I believe
Come Christmas Little Rock will cleave
To Christmas tree and trifle, weave,
From laugh and tinsel, texture fast.

In Little Rock is baseball; Barcarolle.
That hotness in July . . . the uniformed figures raw and
    implacable
And not intellectual,
Batting the hotness or clawing the suffering dust.
The Open Air Concert, on the special twilight green . . .
When Beethoven is brutal or whispers to lady-like air.
Blanket-sitters are solemn, as Johann troubles to lean
To tell them what to mean. . . .

There is love, too, in Little Rock. Soft women softly
Opening themselves in kindness,
Or, pitying one's blindness,
Awaiting one's pleasure
In azure
Glory with anguished rose at the root. . . .
To wash away old semi-discomfitures.
They re-teach purple and unsullen blue.
The wispy soils go. And uncertain
Half-havings have they clarified to sures.

In Little Rock they know
Not answering the telephone is a way of rejecting life,
That it is our business to be bothered, is our business
To cherish bores or boredom, be polite
To lies and love and many-faceted fuzziness.

I scratch my head, massage the hate-I-had.
I blink across my prim and pencilled pad.
The saga I was sent for is not down.
Because there is a puzzle in this town.
The biggest News I do not dare
Telegraph to the Editor's chair:
"They are like people everywhere."

The angry Editor would reply
In hundred harryings of Why.

And true, they are hurling spittle, rock,
Garbage and fruit in Little Rock.
And I saw coiling storm a-writhe
On bright madonnas. And a scythe
Of men harassing brownish girls.
(The bows and barrettes in the curls
And braids declined away from joy.)

I saw a bleeding brownish boy. . . .

The lariat lynch-wish I deplored.

The loveliest lynchee was our Lord. ◆

◆ Responding

1. Why does the poem begin with the date "Fall, 1957"? Is it necessary to know about the events in Little Rock in order to understand the poem? What else does the poet expect her audience to know?

2. Describe the speaker. Who is he? For whom does he work? Is he white or black? How does he feel about what is happening?

3. Working individually or in a group, describe the people to whom the poet refers. Do they include the entire population of Little Rock?

4. Describe a time when you or someone you know became aware of an incident of injustice. What response did you or your friend have? Did you try to rectify what you felt was wrong? Were you successful or unsuccessful?

◆ MEDGAR EVERS ◆

For Charles Evers

The man whose height his fear improved he
arranged to fear no further. The raw
intoxicated time was time for better birth or
a final death.

Old styles, old tempos, all the engagement of
the day—the sedate, the regulated fray—
the antique light, the Moral rose, old guests,
tight whistlings from the past, the mothballs
in the Love at last our man forswore.

Medgar Evers annoyed confetti and assorted
brands of businessmen's eyes.

The shows came down: to maxims and surprise.
And palsy.

Roaring no rapt arise-ye to the dead, he
leaned across tomorrow. People said that
he was holding clean globes in his hands. ◆

◆ Responding

1. After reading the poem, research the events that made Medgar Evers a public figure and write a brief biography of him. Read the poem again after completing your research. In an essay, discuss the ways in which your additional knowledge changed your response to the poem.

2. In a brief essay, explain what you think Brooks means when she says Evers "leaned across tomorrow."

3. Write your own tribute to an important person in the public eye or in your own life.

◆ MALCOLM X ◆

For Dudley Randall

Original.
Ragged-round.
Rich-robust.

He had the hawk-man's eyes.
We gasped. We saw the maleness.
The maleness raking out and making guttural the air
and pushing us to walls.

And in a soft and fundamental hour
a sorcery devout and vertical
beguiled the world.

He opened us—
who was a key,

who was a man. ◆

◆ Responding

1. Why does Brooks call Malcolm X "original"? Use information from your
   own knowledge or from other reading to support your answer.

2. Working individually or in a group, discuss the characteristics associated
   with "maleness." How does Brooks use the term in this poem?

3. Discuss the poet's attitude toward her subject. Support your opinions with
   evidence from the poem.

REFLECTING A CRITICAL CONTEXT

JUAN WILLIAMS

Juan Williams, born in Panama in 1954, earned a bachelor's degree from Haverford College in 1976. Since that time he has worked as a reporter and columnist for the Washington Post. *His work has won several awards, including honors from the Washington-Baltimore New Guild, the Education Writers of America, and* Washingtonian. *Williams's book* Eyes on the Prize: America's Civil Rights Years, 1954–1965 *(1987) formed the basis of two PBS television series of the same name.*

The following selection, taken from the conclusion of Williams's book, assesses the effects of the civil rights movement on the executive and judicial branches of government and on the public at large.

◆ *From* **E Y E S   O N   T H E   P R I Z E** ◆

Securing the Voting Rights was a major victory for the civil rights movement. But it was only one part of the larger struggle for dignity, equality, and justice. Segregation lingered in many spheres, black unemployment remained disproportionately high, and violence still flared against black men, women, and children. But with the passage of the Voting Rights Act, black citizens had at last gained access to one of the most potent tools of democracy. Black voters throughout the nation began to elect people of color to such public offices as mayor, state legislator, and congressional representative. Those officials began to serve constituencies that finally included people of all races.

By the summer following the bill's passage, 9,000 blacks in Dallas County, Alabama, had registered to vote. Sheriff Jim Clark was voted out of office. Over the next decade, as more black people throughout the South began to register and vote, segregationists lost seats of local power. At the state level, progress was much slower. Governors Orval Faubus of Arkansas and George Wallace of Alabama remained in office for several more terms. Nationally, senators James Eastland of Mississippi and Strom Thurmond of South Carolina held their posts for many years. But even these once-ardent segregationists eventually found it politically prudent to soften their rhetoric and seek black support. Joseph Smitherman, still Selma's mayor at this writing, was elected to six consecutive terms of office. He says that in the last election he gained as much as eighty percent of the black vote.

The voting power of blacks also affected federal appointments. President Kennedy named Thurgood Marshall to a United States circuit court of appeals in 1961. In 1965 President Johnson selected Marshall as his solicitor general and two years later asked him to serve as the nation's first black justice of the Supreme Court. In 1966 Johnson appointed the nation's first black cabinet member, Robert Weaver, to the position of secretary of the Department of Housing and Urban Development. President Jimmy Carter appointed Andrew Young to the position of United Nations ambassador. Young went on to become the mayor of Atlanta, while Unita Blackwell became mayor of Mayersville, Mississippi—a state with more black elected officials than any other. By 1984, black mayors had been elected in 255 cities.

The North was also affected by the increased participation of blacks in the electoral process. In 1966, Edward W. Brooke of Massachusetts became the first black elected to the United States Senate. The next year, Carl B. Stokes became the first black mayor of a major city when he won that office in Cleveland. Tom Bradley won Los Angeles' mayoral seat in 1973, and former SNCC worker Marion Barry was elected mayor of Washington, D.C., in 1979. In 1983, Harold Washington became Chicago's chief executive.

Few people in the movement believed that morality could be controlled by legislation. But expecting things to change without the force of law would be treating freedom like a gift subject to the generosity of the giver, and not a right due each American citizen. Securing legislation was a crucial step in making the country more democratic. Voting, access to public accommodations, and an equal education were no longer matters of local largess; they were matters of law.

Over a period of ten years, the civil rights movement not only dramatically altered the nation, but also transformed a race. Black people who had lived under oppression for 300 years gained a new sense of dignity and power and a truer sense of citizenship. White people were changed as well; after an unquestioned acceptance of a segregated society, many examined how they treated their black neighbors and went on to accept civil rights as human rights. But changing the hearts and minds of most white people would take more than legislation. After the Selma march, the assassination of Malcolm X, and the signing of the Voting Rights Act, a new sense of injustice began to burn in northern cities.

The movement's emphasis shifted from the moral imperatives that had garnered support from the nation's moderates—issues such as the right to vote and the right to a decent education—to issues whose moral rightness was not as readily apparent: job and housing discrimination, Johnson's war on poverty, and affirmative action. The movement tackled these varied issues in many different ways, from black nationalism, black power, and even a call for full-scale revolution to a continuation of marches, protests, court battles, and sit-ins. Nonviolence was no longer the only tool for change; many blacks had seen too many murders, too many betrayals. The built-up anger expressed itself in the 1965 riots in Watts and Harlem, and later in Chicago, Detroit, and many other cities. Violence fractured the movement's widespread moral support. The split in the coalition between white liberals and black activists, seen in an early stage at the 1964 Democratic Convention, widened dramatically.

But the violent events of later years and the many new directions of the civil rights movement cannot obscure the remarkable accomplishments wrought by the men and women, black and white, who in ten short years rewove the fabric of American society. The decade spanning the *Brown* decision of 1954 and the Voting Rights Act of 1965 saw more social change, more court decisions, and more legislation in the name of civil rights than any decade in our nation's history. Those changes were forced by millions of Americans who, with a sense of service and justice, kept their eyes on the prize of freedom.

> "I know one thing we did right
> was the day we started to fight
> Keep your eyes on the prize,
> hold on, hold on." ◆

◆ Responding

1. Restate Williams's reasons for thinking that the Voting Rights Act was highly influential and significant.

2. Argue for or against the idea that though morality cannot be controlled by legislation, the passage of laws can gradually change attitudes.

3. Working individually or in a group, discuss the shift in focus that took place in the civil rights movement after 1965. List the civil rights issues that seem most important today. Share your list with the class.

◆

C O N N E C T I N G

Critical Thinking and Writing

1. The theme of injustice runs through many of the selections in this book. Choose an individual or an ethnic group and write an essay about how they suffered as the victims of injustice.

2. Many of the readings in this text describe people's responses to injustice. Discuss the ways in which one or more groups mentioned in the readings have tried to gain acceptance and equal treatment.

3. Using examples from this book or from your own knowledge and experience, write an essay comparing Farmer's reflection that "Evil societies always kill their consciences" with King's statement that "groups tend to be more immoral than individuals."

4. Watch the 1989 film *Mississippi Burning*, which tells the story of the murders of Schwerner, Chaney, and Goodman, and compare its account of events with Farmer's. Some social and film critics were very unhappy with the movie version. Read reviews by both black and white critics and summarize their comments. Write your own review of the film, considering the reviews you have read and Farmer's essay.

5. Apply King's argument in defense of breaking an unjust law to a current issue. Present the case both for and against such an action. Be sure to consider the restrictions King placed on the lawbreaker.

6. Write about a time when you or someone you know was torn between a violent and a nonviolent reaction to a situation. What choice did you or your friend make? Was it the more effective solution? Why or why not?

7. See Spike Lee's film *Do the Right Thing* and compare the circumstances surrounding the conflict in the film with the situation described by Ellison. What was the origin of the conflict in these two cases? Should we view these disturbances as civil disobedience or as criminal activity?

8. Compare the ideologies, goals, and tactics of Martin Luther King, Jr., and Malcolm X.

9. Discuss the parallels between the Black Power movement and the Red Power movement discussed in chapter 8.

10. Compare the living and working conditions, education, and political activity of an African American living in Montgomery, Alabama, in 1965 and today. Research and describe the role of specific legislation in effecting changes in living conditions for African Americans in the South.

11. A landmark decision, *Brown* v. *The Board of Education of Topeka* led to many social changes in both the North and the South. Using evidence from the readings as well as your own knowledge and experience, write an essay describing how desegregation affected the school experience of both African American and Caucasian children in the North or the South.

12. Compare the issues that were important to African Americans during the Harlem Renaissance with those issues that were important to African Americans in the 1960s. Consider which issues changed, if any, and in what way.

13. Using information from your reading in this text and elsewhere, argue that a nonviolent restructuring of society is or is not possible.

For Further Research

1. Many of the selections in this chapter focus on the role of men in the civil rights movement—specifically leadership and status positions. Research and describe the role that women played in the movement.

2. Investigate the history of civil disobedience, both in America and elsewhere in the world. Select a country such as India or South Africa and compare nonviolent protest there with the nonviolent civil rights movement in the United States.

3. Research the contributions of major civil rights figures such as Martin Luther King, Jr., James Farmer, and Malcolm X. Compare their methods and discuss their relative successes and failures.

◆

REFERENCES AND ADDITIONAL SOURCES

Bates, Daisy. *The Long Shadow of Little Rock*. Little Rock: University of Arkansas Press, 1987.

Branch, Taylor. *Parting the Waters: America in the King Years, 1954–63*. New York: Simon and Schuster, 1988.

Brooks, Thomas R. *Walls Come Tumbling Down: A History of the Civil Rights Movement, 1940–1970*. Englewood Cliffs, N.J.: Prentice-Hall, 1974.

Buchanan, A. Russell. *Black Americans in World War II*. Claremont, CA: Regina Books, 1977.

Clark, B. Kenneth. *The Negro Protest*. Boston: Beacon, 1963.

Clark, Septima. *Echo in My Soul*. New York: Dutton, 1962.

Farmer, James. *Lay Bare the Heart: The Autobiography of the Civil Rights Movement*. New York: New American Library, 1986.

Franklin, John Hope. *From Slavery to Freedom: A History of Negro Americans*. New York: Knopf, 1979.

Friedman, Lawrence M. *A History of American Law*. 2nd ed. New York: Simon and Schuster (Touchstone), 1986.

Holt, Thomas C. "Afro Americans," *Harvard Encyclopedia of American Ethnic Groups*. Cambridge: Harvard University Press, 1980.

Jones, Jacqueline. *Labor of Love, Labor of Sorrow: Black Women, Work & the Family from Slavery to the Present*. New York: Random, 1986.

Kluger, Richard. *Simple Justice: The History of Brown v. Board of Education and Black America's Struggle for Equality*. New York: Knopf, 1976.

Malcolm X. *Malcolm X Speaks*. Edited by Goerge Breitman. New York: Path Press, 1976.

Moody, Anne. *Coming of Age in Mississippi*. New York: Dell, 1980.

Oates, Stephen B. *Let the Trumpet Sound: The Life of Martin Luther King, Jr*. New York: New American Library, 1988.

Smythe, Mabel M. *The Black American Reference Book*. Englewood Cliffs, N.J.: Prentice-Hall, 1976.

Williams, Juan. *Eyes on the Prize: America's Civil Rights Years, 1954–65*. New York: Penguin, 1988.

Woodward, C. Vann. *The Strange Career of Jim Crow*. 3d rev. ed. New York: Oxford University Press, 1974.

César Chávez addressing United Farmworkers Union members. (© Victor Aleman)

Frida Kahlo, Self-Portrait of the Borderline Between Mexico and the United States, *1932. Oil on metal, 11 3/4″ × 13 1/2″. (Collection of Mr. and Mrs. Manuel Reyero/photo courtesy Christie's, New York)*

Chapter **7**

CHICANOS
Negotiating Economic and Cultural Boundaries

Contemporary santero, *seller of
religious objects, Nambe, New Mexico.
(© Nancy Hunter Warren)*

*Village of El Cerrito, New Mexico. Isolated by high mesas and miles
of dirt roads, it has retained many of its early characteristics.
(© Nancy Hunter Warren)*

♦ SETTING THE HISTORICAL CONTEXT ♦

IN HIS POEM "I Am Joaquín," Rodolfo Gonzales writes of the need to establish an identity within a collective experience:

> My fathers
>   have lost the economic battle
> and won
>   the struggle of cultural survival . . .
> And now I must choose
>   between the paradox
>   of the victory of the spirit
> [and] the sterilization of the soul
> and a full stomach.

Gonzales depicts the Chicano people as struggling with irreconcilable, opposing goals: to enjoy economic success in the majority culture is to gain "a full stomach" but to lose one's soul. For the poet, the struggle to maintain cultural identity, to survive as a culture, requires a process of retreat and separation:

> I withdraw to the safety
> within the circle of life
> MY OWN PEOPLE

In this withdrawal, the poet finds his own reason for being.

When it was first published in 1967, "I am Joaquín" was considered a very influential poem. Its author, Rodolfo "Corky" Gonzales, was himself a leader in the demonstrations for Chicano rights throughout the Southwest. In a larger sense, the poem helped to dramatize the struggle for dignity and cultural awareness in which many Chicanos were engaged during the late 1960s and early 1970s. They sought "the victory of the spirit" to which Gonzalez refers within the collective *raza*, the ideal of Aztlán.

To search for Aztlán, the mythic homeland of the Aztec peoples, is to seek one's identity in the civilizations of the Mexican Indians that had shaped the Southwest and Mesoamerica centuries before the arrival of the Spanish conquistadors. Among these native peoples—the Mayans, the Pueblo, and the Aztecs—the Mayans of Yucatán and Central America were considered the most sophisticated. They established a network of cities, a system of mathematics, and a calendar as accurate as the Gregorian calendar used in the United States today but predating it by a thousand years. The Pueblos of the Southwest, who emerged as a culture around A.D. 500, were known for their pottery and weaving. The Aztec civilization of central Mexico had many urban centers and was known for its use of astronomy, its system of barter and exchange, and its military prowess; it also set up alliances with other native tribes. A polytheistic culture, it relied on human sacrifice to appease the anger of its deities. Although the classic Mayan culture had disappeared by the time the conquistadors reached the continent in the 1500s, the Pueblo and Aztec civilizations were still flourishing.

Spanish explorers were attracted to this territory for several reasons. Explorers and adventurers such as Hernán Cortés and Francisco Vásquez de Coronado sought labor, natural resources, and the promise of the Seven Cities of Gold. When he arrived in continental Yucatán in search of laborers, Cortés was treated well by the Mayas, whose legends taught them to be wary of "bearded strangers." He was given Malinche, an Aztec noblewoman who had been sold into slavery, as a translator and mistress. Within two years, however, Cortés conquered Moctezuma's Aztec empire and had claimed its territory and minerals for the Spanish. In Chicano culture, therefore, "la Malinche" has come to signify a betrayal. In many Mexican American works, *la Malinche* symbolizes one who sacrifices cultural affiliation for advancement within the larger society. Recently, Chicano writers have reconsidered these views of Malinche, challenging them as prejudices of a traditional patriarchal culture.

The period of Spanish conquest and settlement is recorded in eye-witness histories, such as those by Bernal Díaz del Castillo and Bartholomé de las Casas. Explorers and missionaries had strategic, economic, and cultural motives for settling the area. Strategists sought a protective buttress for Mexican territory farther south. Those looking for wealth for themselves or for the Spanish crown were drawn by the area's minerals and other natural resources. Missionaries felt a moral obligation to convert the native population to Catholicism.

Historians offer conflicting views of the role of the Spanish explorers and missionaries in the economic and cultural development of the Southwest. Some credit the missionaries with educating native peoples about methods of irrigation and planting or ascribe to the intermarriage of explorers and Native Americans the formation of the *mestizo* (mixed) culture. Other historians view the Spanish expeditions as having primarily deleterious effects on the native population. They point to the large numbers of Native Americans who perished after the arrival of the Spanish, both from diseases against which they had no immunity and from brutal forced labor. Exploitative labor systems were sanctioned and even perpetuated by some church officials. It was the missionary Bartholomé de las Casas, however, who chronicled the abuse of the native population in a protest written to the Spanish government. Unfortunately, this protest had little effect.

Spanish settlements extended throughout the area that now comprises Texas, New Mexico, Arizona, and California. Despite the success of the hacienda system in California, the rest of the viceroyalty of Nueva España remained sparsely populated by Novohispanos. The Spanish and, later, the Mexican government (after it had declared independence from Spain in 1821) tried to address the problem by offering *norteamericanos* grants of property and livestock to establish settlements in certain parts of the territory. After the discovery of mineral reserves and good fur-trapping areas, the population increased dramatically. In the Austin Colony (now in Texas), for example, the population of *norteamericanos* increased during the 1820s from 300 families to more than 25,000 people.

In addition to economic factors, political considerations also affected the settlement of the territory. Many people who had property claims in what is now Texas owned slaves, a violation of Mexican law; they were eager to secede from Mexico and have their territory admitted to the United States as a "slave state." An additional factor during the first part of the nineteenth century was that many Americans subscribed to the doctrine of Manifest Destiny—the destiny of the United States to settle the entire American continent. Other peoples, even those whose claims on the land has predated those of the Americans, were often viewed as obstacles to achieving this objective. Coupled with the discovery of gold in California, this doctrine helped to determine the fate of the southwest territory.

Euro-American settlers in both Texas and California revolted against Mexico. Texas, declaring its independence from Mexico, established itself as a republic in 1836 and immediately sought annexation by the United States. In California, Euro-American settlers led by John Charles Frémont and others moved against Mexican authorities and established the Bear Flag Republic. These hostilities led to the United States-Mexican War in 1846 and, after two years of bitter fighting, the defeat of Mexican military forces. When it signed the Treaty of Guadalupe Hidalgo in 1848, Mexico gave up all claims to Texas and ceded to the United States government much of the territory that now comprises Arizona, New Mexico, Utah, Nevada, and California, in exchange for $15 million. The treaty gave those living in the territory the choice of remaining there as American citizens or leaving for Mexico. All citizens living in the area were guaranteed property rights and the freedom to choose their own language, religion, and culture.

For many Chicanos, the Treaty of Guadalupe Hidalgo represents a turning point in relations between Mexico and the United States. Because of the treaty, Mexico lost approximately half its territory to those to whom it had once granted generous settlement rights. However, ties of culture and tradition remained firm. For this reason, many Chicanos regard the border between Mexico and the United States as arbitrary and irrelevant.

Immigration laws notwithstanding, the migration of people across the border, which is caused by economic and political conditions in Mexico, began long before the United States-Mexican War and continues unabated to the present day. A great influx of immigrants, for example, occurred during the period between 1910 and 1920 as a result of the Mexican Revolution. Yet it could also be said that it is the demands of the American economy that actually determine the fate of these workers. During labor shortages migrants are tolerated, even encouraged; indeed, many service industries in the Southwest depend for their survival on this cheap labor. When the U.S.

economy slumps, however, and the demand for jobs by the white population increases, restrictions against Mexican migrant workers are more rigorously enforced. During the early years of the Great Depression, for example, more than 500,000 Mexicans or people of Mexican descent—one third of the Chicano population—were deported or repatriated to Mexico; many were United States citizens.

In addition to enduring an uncertain legal status, migrant workers in the Southwest have suffered as well from substandard working conditions. This group of workers, responsible for much of the labor needed to build the railroads, work the mines, and cultivate the fields, enjoyed few of the safeguards that Euro-American workers took for granted on the job. Mexicans were often forced to work long hours without breaks for wages far below the minimum wage given to other workers. Frequently they had to house their families in primitive shacks, without electricity or indoor plumbing, for months on end while they did their seasonal labor. The economic power of landowners, combined with the workers' frequent migrations and their marginal legal status, slowed movements for unionizing and collective bargaining.

Despite a long history of political and labor activism, therefore, conditions changed slowly. During the 1960s and 1970s, César Chávez and his followers drew the country's attention to the farmworkers' struggle by leading *huelgas*, or strikes, against the growers. In addition, the group organized a boycott of California grapes, the largest such boycott in American history. These combined actions led to the recognition of the United Farm Workers Union and contracts for its members. Using boycotts, strikes, and hunger strikes, the group continues to work for the rights of farmworkers despite declining membership. Recently they have protested the exposure of field workers to potentially carcinogenic pesticides. The migrant workers in industry have fared less well; despite recent efforts at immigration reform, many people still work long hours in the modern equivalent of the nineteenth-century "sweat shop."

The recent history of the Southwest suggests that it is not only the migrant workers whose rights have been ignored. Despite the rights guaranteed by the Treaty of Guadalupe Hidalgo and the Constitution of the United States, the Chicano community has suffered discrimination and sometimes violence at the hands of the larger society. The Texas Rangers, that state's principal law enforcement officers, became notorious for their cruel and arbitrary treatment of people of Mexican descent; some historians claim that there were more lynchings of Mexicans in the Southwest than of blacks in the South. Despite guarantees of freedom of language, Chicano children in California were routinely segregated from Anglo children during the nineteenth century, and only twenty years ago were punished for speaking Spanish.

Beginning in the 1950s and intensifying during the 1960s and 1970s, Chicanos began to assert their rights as citizens. Organizations such as the Mexican American Political Association and MECHA (Movimiento Estudiantíl Chicano de Aztlán) were founded to represent the interests of Chicano constituents. Striking students in cities such as Los Angeles demanded that Chicanos be given more say in the kind of education they received, and students and other activists organized the Chicano Moratorium to protest the war in Vietnam. The Mexican American Legal Defense and Education Fund was established to provide legal assistance for people defending their civil rights.

Alongside this political activism there developed a heightened cultural awareness. The term *Chicano*, which became popular during this time, dramatized the sense of self-definition that was critical to the movement. The word embodied an attempt to move beyond the hyphenated appellation Mexican-American to a term that strongly and directly suggested ethnic identity and pride. The Chicano Renaissance, as this movement was often called, used literature, music, and art to signal a rebirth of cultural identity and to convey the strength derived from the Chicano heritage.

Today the Chicano community continues to face many struggles, both external and internal. It has entered the national debates over sexism, affirmative action, immigrant reform, the status of the undocumented worker, bilingual education programs, and English-only initiatives. Yet many Chicanos feel a sense of self-definition and self-assertion. In the words of Joaquín, "The odds are great/but my spirit is strong . . . [and] I shall endure."

Exploring the Literary and
◆ Cultural Context ◆

The works in this chapter reflect the sense of discovery that accompanied the Chicano Renaissance, and the emergence of the Chicano voice in American literature. Our first selection is from José Antonio Villarreal's novel *Pocho*. The novel relates the life of Juan Rubio—his involvement in the Mexican Revolution, escape into Mexico, and eventual migration to California—and his son Richard's maturation as a first generation Mexican American. The chapter selected depicts the uneasy relationship between education and cultural heritage. Richard tries to balance cultural and personal identity, as well as family and social expectations, in determining the role education can play in helping him achieve his goals.

Chicano writers explore not only personal but also social issues and tensions—particularly the life and struggles of migrant workers, which have engendered many works in fiction, nonfiction, and poetry. The migrants struggle is represented in this chapter by several readings. César Chávez's first-person account of his early days as a labor organizer reveals both his sense of identity with and his commitment to the farmworkers he tries to help. Tómas Rivera's "Christmas Eve" provides testimony of a different kind—and from a different perspective. Rivera, who grew up in a family of migrant workers, explores psychological effects of this life on a wife and mother.

The two poets included in the chapter both address, from differing viewpoints, the strengths and struggles of Chicano farm workers. In "Napa, California," Ana Castillo pays tribute to the farmworkers and reflects on the cycle of their lives—of all lives—in which one day follows another, while "the land . . . waits for us." The two poems by Pat Mora explore the human, personal dimension behind the cold, bureaucratic designations "Legal Alien" and "Illegal Alien."

Sabine Ulibarrí's semi-autobiographical short stories reflect upon life in the small New Mexico town where the author grew up. In "My Grandmother Smoked Cigars," he uses a strong female character to depict the importance of both family and tradition. Moreover, the story illustrates the importance of orally-transmitted legends and tales in forming and preserving family and cultural heritage.

The cultural permeation of the border figures in Arturo Islas's chapter from *Migrant Souls*. In this story, the characters who are fully at ease on both sides of the border feel tension when they attempt to cross it.

The themes of female strength and of a community solidarity that transcend political borders underlie Sandra Cisneros's story, "Woman Hollering Creek." Cleófilas, the main character, content in the traditional female roles as daughter, sister, wife, and mother, seeks strength from within and from the surrounding community to help her solve her problem.

In the final essay, Héctor Calderón examines Chicano heritage from personal experience. For Calderón, the importance of preserving heritage goes beyond the writing of cultural history. By writing and reflecting on experience Chicanos can come to terms with the border and assert control over their identity.

BEGINNING: PRE-READING/WRITING

◆ *Working individually or in a group, list examples of Mexican culture that you encounter in your daily life. Consider the following:*

Food:

Clothing:

Language:

Architecture:

Holidays:

Art:

Music:

Share your examples with the class and discuss the ways in which Mexican culture enriches American culture.

---

*T*he Treaty of Guadalupe Hidalgo, ratified in 1848, brought an end to the Mexican-American War. As a part of the treaty, Mexico ceded to the United States much of the territory now referred to as the American Southwest, with the understanding that Mexican nationals living in the territory would be guaranteed their rights to property, religion, and liberty. However, the specific provisions guarding these rights were never passed by the U.S. Congress. The excerpt below shows the treaty as passed by Congress, followed by the original version of Article IX and the excised Article X.

◆ *From* THE TREATY OF GUADALUPE HIDALGO ◆

Articles 8–15

Article VIII

Mexicans now established in territories previously belonging to Mexico, and which remain for the future within the limits of the United States, as defined by the present treaty, shall be free to continue where they now reside, or to remove at any time to the Mexican Republic, retaining the property which they possess in the said territories, or disposing thereof, and removing the proceeds wherever they please, without their being subjected, on this account, to any contribution, tax or charge whatever.

Those who shall prefer to remain in the said territories, may either retain the title and rights of Mexican citizens, or acquire those of citizens of the United States. But they shall be under the obligation to make their election within one year from the date of the exchange of ratifications of this treaty: and those who shall remain in the said territories, after the expiration of that year, without having declared their intention to retain the character of Mexicans, shall be considered to have elected to become citizens of the United States.

In the said territories, property of every kind, now belonging to Mexicans, not established there, shall be inviolably respected. The present owners, the heirs of these, and all Mexicans who may hereafter acquire said property by contract, shall enjoy with respect to it, guarantees equally ample as if the same belonged to citizens of the United States.

Article IX

The Mexicans who, in the territories aforesaid, shall not preserve the character of citizens of the Mexican Republic, conformably with what is stipulated in the

Reprinted from Hunter Miller, ed., *Treaties and Other International Acts of the United States of America*, Vol. 5 (Washington, D.C.: Government Printing Office, 1937).

preceding article, shall be incorporated into the Union of the United States and be admitted, at the proper time (to be judged of by the Congress of the United States) to the enjoyment of all the rights of citizens of the United States according to the principles of the Constitution; and in the mean time shall be maintained and protected in the free enjoyment of their liberty and property, and secured in the free exercise of their religion without restriction.

[*One of the amendments of the Senate struck out Article 10.*]

Article XI

Considering that a great part of the territories which, by the present Treaty, are to be comprehended for the future within the limits of the United States, is now occupied by savage tribes, who will hereafter be under the exclusive control of the Government of the United States, and whose incursions within the territory of Mexico would be prejudicial in the extreme; it is solemnly agreed that all such incursions shall be forcibly restrained by the Government of the United States, whensoever this may be necessary; and that when they cannot be prevented, they shall be punished by the said Government, and satisfaction for the same shall be exacted; all in the same way, and with equal diligence and energy, as if the same incursions were meditated or committed within its own territory against its own citizens.

It shall not be lawful, under any pretext whatever, for any inhabitant of the United States, to purchase or acquire any Mexican or any foreigner residing in Mexico, who may have been captured by Indians inhabiting the territory of either of the two Republics, nor to purchase or acquiring horses, mules, cattle or property of any kind, stolen within Mexican territory by such Indians.

And, in the event of any person or persons, captured within Mexican Territory by Indians, being carried into the territory of the United States, the Government of the latter engages and binds itself in the most solemn manner, so soon as it shall know of such captives being within its territory, and shall be able so to do, through the faithful exercise of its influence and power, to rescue them and return them to their country, or deliver them to the agent or representative of the Mexican Government. The Mexican Authorities will, as far as practicable, give to the Government of the United States notice of such captures; and its agent shall pay the expenses incurred in the maintenance and transmission of the rescued captives; who, in the mean time, shall be treated with the utmost hospitality by the American authorities at the place where they may be. But if the Government of the United States, before receiving such notice from Mexico, should obtain intelligence through any other channel, of the existence of Mexican captives within its territory, it will proceed forthwith to effect their release and delivery to the Mexican agent, as above stipulated.

For the purpose of giving to these stipulations the fullest possible efficacy, thereby affording the security and redress demanded by their true spirit and intent, the Government of the United States will now and hereafter pass, without unnecessary delay, and always vigilantly enforce, such laws as the nature of the subject may require. And finally, the sacredness of this obligation shall never be lost sight of by the said Government, when providing for the removal of the Indians from any portion of the said territories, or for its being settled by citizens of the United States; but on the contrary special care shall then be taken not to place its Indian occupants under the necessity of seeking new homes, by committing those invasions which the United States have solemnly obliged themselves to restrain.

Article XII

In consideration of the extension acquired by the boundaries of the United States, as defined in the fifth Article of the present Treaty, the Government of the United States engages to pay to that of the Mexican Republic the sum of fifteen Millions of Dollars.

Immediately after this treaty shall have been duly ratified by the Government of the Mexican Republic, the sum of three millions of dollars shall be paid to the said Government by that of the United States at the city of Mexico, in the gold or silver coin of Mexico. The remaining twelve millions of dollars shall be paid at the same place and in the same coin, in annual instalments of three millions of dollars each, together with interest on the same at the rate of six per centum per annum. This interest shall begin to run upon the whole sum of twelve millions, from the day of the ratification of the present treaty by the Mexican Government, and the first of the instalments shall be paid at the expiration of one year from the same day. Together with each annual instalment, as it falls due, the whole interest accruing on such instalment from the beginning shall also be paid.

Article XIII

The United States engage moreover, to assume and pay to the claimants all amounts now due them, and those hereafter to become due, by reason of the claims already liquidated and decided against the Mexican Republic, under the conventions between the two Republics severally concluded on the eleventh day of April eighteen hundred and thirty-nine, and on the thirtieth day of January eighteen hundred and forty-three: so that the Mexican Republic shall be absolutely exempt for the future, from all expense whatever on account of the said claims.

Article XIV

The United States do furthermore discharge the Mexican Republic from all claims of citizens of the United States, not heretofore decided against the Mexican Government, which may have arisen previously to the date of the signature of this treaty: which discharge shall be final and perpetual, whether the said claims be rejected or be allowed by the Board of Commissioners provided for in the following Article, and whatever shall be the total amount of those allowed.

Article XV

The United States, exonerating Mexico from all demands on account of the claims of their citizens mentioned in the preceding Article, and considering them entirely and forever cancelled, whatever their amount may be, undertake to make satisfaction for the same, to an amount not exceeding three and one quarter millions of Dollars. To ascertain the validity and amount of those claims, a Board of Commissioners shall be established by the Government of the United States, whose awards shall be final and conclusive: provided that in deciding upon the validity of each claim, the board shall be guided and governed by the principles and rules of decision prescribed by the first and fifth Articles of the unratified convention, concluded at the City of Mexico on the twentieth day of November, one thousand eight hundred and forty-three; and in no case shall an award be made in favour of any claim not embraced by these principles and rules.

    If, in the opinion of the said Board of Commissioners, or of the claimants, any books, records or documents in the possession or power of the Government of the Mexican Republic, shall be deemed necessary to the just decision of any claim, the Commissioners or the claimants, through them, shall, within such period as Congress may designate, make an application in writing for the same, addressed to the Mexican Minister for Foreign Affairs, to be transmitted by the Secretary of State of the United States; and the Mexican Government engages, at the earliest possible moment after the receipt of such demand, to cause any of the books, records or documents, so specified, which shall be in their possession or power (or authenticated Copies or extracts of the same) to be transmitted to the said Secretary of State, who shall immediately deliver them over to the said Board of Commissioners: provided that no such application shall be made, by, or at the instance of, any claimant, until the facts which it is expected to prove by such books, records or documents, shall have been stated under oath or affirmation.

Articles 9 and 10 Before Senate Amendment

Article IX

The Mexicans who, in the territories aforesaid, shall not preserve the character of citizens of the Mexican Republic, conformably with what is stipulated in the preceding Article, shall be incorporated into the Union of the United States, and admitted as soon as possible, according to the principles of the Federal Constitution, to the enjoyment of all the rights of citizens of the United States. In the mean time, they shall be maintained and protected in the enjoyment of their liberty, their property, and the civil rights now vested in them according to the Mexican laws. With respect to political rights, their condition shall be on an equality with that of the inhabitants of the other territories of the United States; and at least equally good as that of the inhabitants of Louisiana and the Floridas, when these provinces, by transfer from the French Republic and the Crown of Spain, became territories of the United States.

The same most ample guaranty shall be enjoyed by all ecclesiastics and religious corporations or communities, as well in the discharge of the offices of their ministry, as in the enjoyment of their property of every kind, whether individual or corporate. This guaranty shall embrace all temples, houses and edifices dedicated to the Roman Catholic worship; as well as all property destined to its support, or to that of schools, hospitals and other foundations for charitable or beneficent purposes. No property of this nature shall be considered as having become the property of the American Government, or as subject to be, by it, disposed of or diverted to other uses.

Finally, the relations and communication between the Catholics living in the territories aforesaid, and their respective ecclesiastical authorities shall be open, free and exempt from all hindrance whatever, even although such authorities should reside within the limits of the Mexican Republic, as defined by this treaty; and this freedom shall continue, so long as a new demarcation of ecclesiastical districts shall not have been made, conformably with the laws of the Roman Catholic Church.

Article X

All grants of land made by the Mexican Government or by the competent authorities, in territories previously appertaining to Mexico, and remaining for the future within the limits of the United States, shall be respected as valid, to the same extent that the same grants would be valid, if the said territories had remained within the limits of Mexico. But the grantees of lands in Texas, put in possession thereof, who, by reason of the circumstances of the country since the beginning of the troubles between Texas and the Mexican Government, may have been prevented from fulfilling all the conditions of their grants, shall be under the obligation to fulfill the said conditions within the periods limited in the same respectively; such periods to be now counted from the date of the exchange of ratifications of this treaty: in default of which the said grants shall not be obligatory upon the State of Texas, in virtue of the stipulations contained in this Article.

The foregoing stipulation in regard to grantees of land in Texas, is extended to all grantees of land in the territories aforesaid, elsewhere than in Texas, put in possession under such grants; and, in default of the fulfillment of the conditions of any such grant, within the new period, which, as is above stipulated, begins with the day of the exchange of ratifications of this treaty, the same shall be null and void.

The Mexican Government declares that no grant whatever of lands in Texas has been made since the second day of March one thousand eight hundred and thirty-six; and that no grant whatever of lands in any of the territories aforesaid has been made since the thirteenth day of May one thousand eight hundred and forty-six. ◆

◆ Responding

1. Determine which parts of the United States were originally settled by Mexico. How did they become American territory?

2. Discuss the effects of the Treaty of Guadalupe Hidalgo on Mexicans living in the disputed area. What rights were they guaranteed? What did they have to give up?

JOSÉ ANTONIO VILLARREAL

José Antonio Villarreal, born in Los Angeles in 1924, spent part of his childhood working with his parents in migrant labor camps in northern California. After serving in the navy during World War II, he earned his bachelor's degree from the University of California, Berkeley in 1950 and pursued graduate studies at Berkeley and UCLA. His works include the novels Pocho *(1959),* The Fifth Horseman *(1974), and* Clemente Cha-cón *(1984), as well as numerous essays and short stories published in journals. Villarreal settled in Mexico and became a Mexican citizen in 1970.*

In a 1974 interview in The Bilingual Review, *Villarreal related his feelings about his heritage: "I believed [in 1959] as I do now that our parents who came from Mexico, whether they intended to remain here or not, were American pioneers and just as important to the development of America as the pioneers who beat their way across the prairies, the western European immigrants, the black slaves and the first English who came here."*

The following excerpt is from Pocho, *a novel based loosely on the author's own experiences growing up in the Santa Clara Valley. As the selection describes the main character's disagreements with his mother, it explores some of the ways that personal ambition can conflict with familial obligation. Moreover, it asks readers to consider the effects of cultural heritage and formal education on the narrator's sense of identity.*

♦ *From* **POCHO** ♦

He had been asking her questions again, and she was a little angry. She always became quiet when he asked her things. Suddenly she sat down and pulled him onto her lap. She held his head against her breasts, and her heart was beating through her dress loudly. She talked but she would not let him move his head to see her face.

"Look, little son," she said. "Many times I do not answer you when you ask me things, and other times I simply talk about something else. Sometimes this is because you ask things that you and I should not be talking about, but most of the time it is because I am ashamed that I do not know what you ask. You see, we are simple people, your father and I. We did not have the education, because we came from the poorest class of people in México. Because I was raised by the Spanish people, I was taught to read and write. I even went to school for a time, but your father did not, and it was only because, from the time he was a small boy, he decided he would never be a peón, that he taught himself to read and write. But that is all we can do, read and write. We cannot teach you the things that you want us to teach you. And I am deeply ashamed that we are going to fail in a great responsibility—we cannot guide you, we

1

2

cannot select your reading for you, we cannot even talk to you in your own language.

"No, let me finish telling you. Already I can see that books are your life. We cannot help you, and soon we will not even be able to encourage you, because you will be obliged to work. We could not afford to spare you to go to school even if there was a way for you to do it, and there is a great sadness in our hearts."   3

"But my father wants me to go to school. Always he tells me that, and he never takes me out of school to work, the way the other men do with their children," said Richard.   4

"I know. But he talks aloud to drown out the thoughts in his head and the knowledge in his heart. Inside, he knows that it is inevitable that you will have to go to work soon, for you are the only boy in the family, and when you are in the secondary school, maybe it will be the end of your education."   5

Her words frightened him, because she was so sure of what she was saying, and he knew that she was telling him this to save him from heartbreak at some later time; then he thought of a thing that gave him hope. "I will finish the secondary, Mamá. Of that I am sure—as long as we live in town. My father cannot take me out of school until I become of age, and I will be too young. Then, after that, things might be different and I can continue on. Anyway, the girls can help out."   6

"What you say is true about the secondary school, but we cannot expect help from the girls much longer. They are growing up, and soon they will begin to marry. Their business and their responsibility will be with their husbands and their husbands' families."   7

"But they are young girls yet." He refused to be discouraged. "They will not possibly marry soon."   8

"Young? I was carrying your sister Concha when I was younger than she is now. No, my son, I know what I am telling you is true. Your father talks about you being a lawyer or a doctor when we return to México, but he knows that you will be neither and that we will never leave this place."   9

"But that was in México," he said. "In México, women marry young, but here we are Americans and it is different. Take the case of my teachers who are twenty-five or almost thirty years old and they have not married!"   10

"That is different," she explained patiently, "for they are cotorronas and will never marry. Here in your country, teachers are all cotorronas. They are not allowed to marry."   11

"Why?"   12

"I do not know. Maybe it is because parents do not want married women to have such intimate relationships with their children. I do not know."   13

How silly! he thought. *Mothers* are married, and what is more intimate than a child and its mother? But he did not say this to her, because his thoughts suddenly switched into English, and it occurred to him that his mother always followed rules and never asked the why of them. He had known this but had   14 never honestly accepted it, because it seemed such a loss to him to accept the fact that his mother was not infallible. And yet in a sense she was right, for Miss Crane and Miss Broughton and two or three others were close to seventy and were still called "Miss."

Back in Spanish, he remembered what she had just said about the profes-   15
sions, and knew that she wanted that for him and the family more than any other thing, with the possible exception of the priesthood, and, of course, that was impossible, because he was the only son and his father would undoubtedly shoot himself if his only son became a priest. He could almost hear his father say, when she timidly sought his reaction to such a possibility, "Make nuns of all the females if that will make you happy—let the boy be, for he is on earth for other things!" And Richard smiled that he would be spared that, at least. Then he suddenly felt a responsibility so heavy as to be a physical pressure, and first he became sad that his lot was a dictate and that his parents believed so strongly in the destiny, and then he was angry that traditions could take a body and a soul—for he had a soul; of that he was certain—and mold it to fit a pattern. He spoke out then, but not in anger, saying things he sensed but did not really understand, an uncomprehending child with the strong desire to have a say in his destiny, with the willful words of a child but with the knowledge and fear that his thoughts could not possibly come true.

"Then perhaps it is just as well that I cannot go on to school," he said.   16
"For I do not intend to be a doctor or a lawyer or anything like that. If I were to go to school only to learn to work at something, then I would not do it. I would just work in the fields or in the cannery or something like that. My father would be disappointed in me if I did get an education, so it does not matter. When the time comes, I will do what I have to do."

She was surprised at his words, and she knew then that though she could   17
understand him better than most people, she would never really get to know him.

"But all this reading, my son," she asked. "All this studying—surely it is   18
for something? If you could go to the university, it would be to learn how you could make more money than you would make in the fields or the cannery. So you can change our way of living somewhat, and people could see what a good son we had, and it would make us all something to respect. Then, when you married and began your family, you would have a nice home and could be assured that you would be able to afford an education for your children."

He was disappointed and tried to keep the bitterness from his voice, but   19
could not quite succeed. "And I am supposed to educate my children so that they can change my way of living and they theirs, and so on? Ah, Mamá! Try to understand me. I want to learn, and that is all. I do not want to be something—I *am*. I do not care about making a lot of money and about what people think and about the family in the way you speak. I have to learn as much as I can, so that *I* can live . . . learn for *me*, for *myself*— Ah, but I cannot explain to you, and you would not understand me if I could!"

Whatever bond they had shared for a while was now gone. The magic of   20
the moment was broken, and she talked to him once again as his superior, and
her voice had that old trace of impersonal anger. "But that is wrong, Richard,"
she said. "That kind of thinking is wrong and unnatural—to have that kind of
feeling against the family and the custom. It is as if you were speaking against
the Church."

They were standing now, and she moved to the table where the masa   21
was, and began to roll out tortillas. He tried to make her see him in his way.
"Mamá, do you know what happens to me when I read? All those hours that
I sit, as you sometimes say, 'ruining my eyes'? If I do ruin them, it would be
worth it, for I do not need eyes where I go then. I travel, Mamá. I travel all
over the world, and sometimes out of this whole universe, and I go back in
time and again forward. I do not know I am here, and I do not care. I am
always thinking of you and my father except when I read. Nothing is important
to me then, and I even forget that I am going to die sometime. I know that I
have so much to learn and so much to see that I cannot possibly have enough
time to do it all, for the Mexican people are right when they say that life is
only a breath. I do not know that I will find time to make a family, for the
important thing is that I must learn, Mamá! Cannot you understand that?"

"I have told you I understand very little. I know only that you are blas-   22
phemous and you want to learn more in order to be more blasphemous still—
if that is possible. I know that we cannot live in a dream, because everything
else around us is real."

"But that is exactly what I mean, Mamá. Everything does not necessarily   23
have to be real. Who said that everything has to be real, anyway?"

She was perplexed, because she had got into a discussion in spite of her   24
ignorance, yet she was intelligent enough to find her only answer. "I do not
know, but I would say God said so. Yes, God must have said so, because He
says everything. When you think of Him in the way you should, you will find
the answers to any question you might have."

"It is too late for that, because I cannot believe everything that He says   25
or said." He was deeply sorry that he must hurt her. He tried to ease her
feelings, but was certain that in the end he would hurt her more. "You know,
Mamá, it is partly because of that that I need to learn. I believe in God, Mamá—
I believe in the Father, the Son, and the Holy Ghost, but I do not believe
everything I am told about Him. Last year I tried to reach Him, to talk to Him
about it. I used to go out into the orchards or the meadows and concentrate
and concentrate, but I never saw Him or heard His voice or that of one of His
angels. And I was scared, because if He willed it so, I knew that the earth
would open and it would swallow me up because I dared to demand explanations
from Him. And yet I wanted so desperately to know that I found courage to
do it. Then, after a long time that I did this, I stopped and tried to find Him
in church, because I would be safer there; He would not destroy a churchful

of people just because of me. But I never saw Him or heard Him. Then, one day, I knew that indeed He *could* destroy the church, because if He could do the best thing in the world, He could also do the most evil thing in the world. Who am I, I thought, to dare bring out that which is cruel in Him? He *is* cruel, you know, Mamá, but I believe in Him just the same. If I learn enough, I may sometime learn how to talk to Him. Some people do. You yourself have told me of miracles."

His mother looked at him as if he were not her son. She was frightened, and he thought she wanted to send him away, but she was his mother and loved him, and therefore she conquered her fear and held him and cried, "I have really lost you, my son! You are the light of my life and I have already lost you," she said. In spite of himself, his mother's tears always made him cry, and they rocked in each other's arms. "For a moment, I thought that I had given birth to the Devil in a little angel's body, and I knew that I could not bear the child I carry now in my womb. It will be born dead, I thought to myself—but only for a moment did I think that, my son. Forgive me, little one! Forgive me!" 26

His fear made him half believe that he was the Devil incarnate. Later, when his new sister was delivered stillborn and his mother almost died, he was griefstricken with the knowledge that he was to blame. 27

So now I have added murder and almost matricide to my evilness, he thought in his heart, but his mind knew that the tragedy had in no way been his fault. The senile midwife who worked the neighborhood was as much to blame as his mother, who obstinately refused to go to the hospital because of a certainty the doctor would be a man and would look at her private parts.◆ 28

◆ Responding

1. This reading presents two views of education. Richard argues, "If I were to go to school only to learn to work at something, then I would not do it." His mother responds, "If you could go to the university, it would be to learn how you could make more money than you would make in the fields or the cannery." Discuss the merits of each point of view.

2. What do you think Richard will be doing in ten years? Do you think he will quit school, or will he finish his education? Write a story about Richard that takes place ten years after this episode ends.

3. Several value systems come into conflict in this story. Working individually or in a group, list the values of Richard, his mother, his father, and their

community. Compare your list with those of other classmates and discuss how values shape behavior and what possible conflicts between family members can arise.

4. Richard's parents want him to have a better life than they have. Would your parents like your life to be different from theirs? In what ways? How do your wishes and plans for your future differ from theirs? How do you and your parents cope with these differences?

CÉSAR CHÁVEZ

César Chávez is best known as the founder of the United Farm Workers Union. Born in San Jose, California, in 1927, to a family of migrant workers, he experienced firsthand the deplorable working conditions of seasonal laborers. During the mid 1960s and early 1970s his union organized boycotts of California table grapes and non-union lettuce. During the 1980s the union focused attention on the use of dangerous pesticides in the fields, documenting and publicizing the extraordinary number of miscarriages and cancerous tumors occurring among farmworkers exposed to these chemicals.

In the essay that follows, first published in Ramparts *magazine in 1966, Chávez talks about his early involvement in the farmworkers' cause. In describing his attempt to obtain support from various community groups, the essay suggests the special demands that leadership makes on an individual. It also explores the ways in which public and private identities sometimes reinforce each other—and sometimes come into conflict.*

◆ THE ORGANIZER'S TALE ◆

It really started for me 16 years ago in San Jose, California, when I was working on an apricot farm. We figured he was just another social worker doing a study of farm conditions, and I kept refusing to meet with him. But he was persistent. Finally, I got together some of the rough element in San Jose. We were going to have a little reception for him to teach the *gringo* a little bit of how we felt. There were about 30 of us in the house, young guys mostly. I was supposed to give them a signal—change my cigarette from my right hand to my left, and then we were going to give him a lot of hell. But he started talking and the more he talked, the more wide-eyed I became and the less inclined I was to give the signal. A couple of guys who were pretty drunk at the time still wanted to give the *gringo* the business, but we got rid of them. This fellow was making a lot of sense, and I wanted to hear what he had to say.

His name was Fred Ross, and he was an organizer for the Community Service Organization (CSO) which was working with Mexican-Americans in the cities. I became immediately really involved. Before long I was heading a voter registration drive. All the time I was observing the things Fred did, secretly, because I wanted to learn how to organize, to see how it was done. I was impressed with his patience and understanding of people. I thought this was a tool, one of the greatest things he had.

It was pretty rough for me at first. I was changing and had to take a lot of ridicule from the kids my age, the rough characters I worked with in the fields. They would say, "Hey, big shot. Now that you're a *politico*, why are you working here for 65 cents an hour?" I might add that our neighborhood had the highest percentage of San Quentin graduates. It was a game among the *pachucos* in the sense that we defended ourselves from outsiders, although inside the neighborhood there was not a lot of fighting.

After six months of working every night in San Jose, Fred assigned me   4
to take over the CSO chapter in Decoto. It was a tough spot to fill. I would suggest something, and people would say, "No, let's wait till Fred gets back," or "Fred wouldn't do it that way." This is pretty much a pattern with people, I discovered, whether I was put in Fred's position, or later, when someone else was put in my position. After the Decoto assignment I was sent to start a new chapter in Oakland. Before I left, Fred came to a place in San Jose called the Hole-in-the-Wall and we talked for half an hour over coffee. He was in a rush to leave, but I wanted to keep him talking; I was scared of my assignment.

There were hard times in Oakland. First of all, it was a big city and I'd   5
get lost every time I went anywhere. Then I arranged a series of house meetings. I would get to the meeting early and drive back and forth past the house, too nervous to go in and face the people. Finally I would force myself to go inside and sit in a corner. I was quite thin then, and young, and most of the people were middle-aged. Someone would say, "Where's the organizer?" And I would pipe up, "Here I am." Then they would say in Spanish—these were very poor people and we hardly spoke anything but Spanish—"Ha! This *kid*?" Most of them said they were interested, but the hardest part was to get them to start pushing themselves, on their own initiative.

The idea was to set up a meeting and then get each attending person to   6
call his own house meeting, inviting new people—a sort of chain letter effect. After a house meeting, I would lie awake going over the whole thing, playing the tape back, trying to see why people laughed at one point, or why they were for one thing and against another. I was also learning to read and write, those late evenings. I had left school in the 7th grade after attending 67 different schools, and my reading wasn't the best.

At our first organizing meeting we had 368 people: I'll never forget it   7
because it was very important to me. You eat your heart out; the meeting is called for 7 o'clock and you start to worry about 4. You wait. Will they show up? Then the first one arrives. By 7 there are only 20 people, you have everything in order, you have to look calm. But little by little they filter in and at a certain point you know it will be a success.

After four months in Oakland, I was transferred. The chapter was be-   8
ginning to move on its own, so Fred assigned me to organize the San Joaquin Valley. Over the months I developed what I used to call schemes or tricks—now I call them techniques—of making initial contacts. The main thing in convincing someone is to spend time with him. It doesn't matter if he can read, write or even speak well. What is important is that he is a man and second, that he has shown some initial interest. One good way to develop leadership is to take a man with you in your car. And it works a lot better if you're doing the driving; that way you are in charge. You drive, he sits there, and you talk.

These little things were very important to me; I was caught in a big game by then, figuring out what makes people work. I found that if you work hard enough you can usually shake people into working too, those who are concerned. You work harder and they work harder still, up to a point and then they pass you. Then, of course, they're on their own.

I also learned to keep away from the established groups and so-called 9 leaders, and to guard against philosophizing. Working with low-income people is very different from working with the professionals, who like to sit around talking about how to play politics. When you're trying to recruit a farmworker, you have to paint a little picture, and then you have to color the picture in. We found out that the harder a guy is to convince, the better leader or member he becomes. When you exert yourself to convince him, you have his confidence and he has good motivation. A lot of people who say OK right away wind up hanging around the office, taking up the workers' time.

During the McCarthy era in one Valley town, I was subjected to a lot of 10 redbaiting. We had been recruiting people for citizenship classes at the high school when we got into a quarrel with the naturalization examiner. He was rejecting people on the grounds that they were just parroting what they learned in citizenship class. One day we had a meeting about it in Fresno, and I took along some of the leaders of our local chapter. Some redbaiting official gave us a hard time, and the people got scared and took his side. They did it because it seemed easy at the moment, even though they knew that sticking with me was the right thing to do. It was disgusting. When we left the building they walked by themselves ahead of me as if I had some kind of communicable disease. I had been working with these people for three months and I was very sad to see that. It taught me a great lesson.

That night I learned that the chapter officers were holding a meeting to 11 review my letters and printed materials to see if I really was a Communist. So I drove out there and walked right in on their meeting. I said, "I hear you've been discussing me, and I thought it would be nice if I was here to defend myself. Not that it matters that much to you or even to me, because as far as I'm concerned you are a bunch of cowards." At that they began to apologize. "Let's forget it," they said. "You're a nice guy." But I didn't want apologies. I wanted a full discussion. I told them I didn't give a damn, but that they had to learn to distinguish fact from what appeared to be a fact because of fear. I kept them there till two in the morning. Some of the women cried. I don't know if they investigated me any further, but I stayed on another few months and things worked out.

This was not an isolated case. Often when we'd leave people to themselves 12 they would get frightened and draw back into their shells where they had been all the years. And I learned quickly that there is no real appreciation. Whatever you do, and no matter what reasons you may give to others, you do it because you want to see it done, or maybe because you want power. And there shouldn't be any appreciation, understandably. I know good organizers who were destroyed, washed out, because they expected people to appreciate what they'd done. Anyone who comes in with the idea that farmworkers are free of sin and that the growers are all bastards, either has never dealt with the situation or is an idealist of the first order. Things don't work that way.

For more than 10 years I worked for the CSO. As the organization grew, we found ourselves meeting in fancier and fancier motels and holding expensive conventions. Doctors, lawyers and politicians began joining. They would get elected to some office in the organization and then, for all practical purposes, leave. Intent on using the CSO for their own prestige purposes, these "leaders," many of them, lacked the urgency we had to have. When I became general director I began to press for a program to organize farmworkers into a union, an idea most of the leadership opposed. So I started a revolt within the CSO. I refused to sit at the head table at meetings, refused to wear a suit and tie, and finally I even refused to shave and cut my hair. It used to embarrass some of the professionals. At every meeting I got up and gave my standard speech: we shouldn't meet in fancy motels, we were getting away from the people, farmworkers had to be organized. But nothing happened. In March of '62 I resigned and came to Delano to begin organizing the Valley on my own. 13

By hand I drew a map of all the towns between Arvin and Stockton—86 of them, including farming camps—and decided to hit them all to get a small nucleus of people working in each. For six months, I traveled around, planting an idea. We had a simple questionnaire, a little card with space for name, address and how much the worker thought he ought to be paid. My wife, Helen, mimeographed them, and we took our kids for two or three day jaunts to these towns, distributing the cards door-to-door and to camps and groceries. 14

Some 80,000 cards were sent back from eight Valley counties. I got a lot of contacts that way, but I was shocked at the wages the people were asking. The growers were paying $1 and $1.15, and maybe 95 per cent of the people thought they should be getting only $1.25. Sometimes people scribbled messages on the cards: "I hope to God we win" or "Do you think we can win?" or "I'd like to know more." So I separated the cards with the pencilled notes, got in my car and went to those people. 15

We didn't have any money at all in those days, none for gas and hardly any for food. So I went to people and started asking for food. It turned out to be about the best thing I could have done, although at first it's hard on your pride. Some of our best members came in that way. If people give you their food, they'll give you their hearts. Several months and many meetings later we had a working organization, and this time the leaders were the people. 16

None of the farmworkers had collective bargaining contracts, and I thought it would take ten years before we got that first contract. I wanted desperately to get some color into the movement, to give people something they could identify with, like a flag. I was reading some books about how various leaders discovered what colors contrasted and stood out the best. The Egyptians had found that a red field with a white circle and a black emblem in the center 17 crashed into your eyes like nothing else. I wanted to use the Aztec eagle in the center, as on the Mexican flag. So I told my cousin Manuel, "Draw an Aztec eagle." Manuel had a little trouble with it, so we modified the eagle to make it easier for people to draw.

The first big meeting of what we decided to call the National Farm Workers Association was held in September 1962, at Fresno, with 287 people. We had our huge red flag on the wall, with paper tacked over it. When the time came, Manuel pulled a cord ripping the paper off the flag and all of a sudden it hit the people. Some of them wondered if it was a Communist flag, and I said it probably looked more like a neo-Nazi emblem than anything else. But they wanted an explanation. So Manuel got up and said, "When that damn eagle flies—that's when the farmworkers' problems are going to be solved."

One of the first things I decided was that outside money wasn't going to organize people, at least not in the beginning. I even turned down a grant from a private group—$50,000 to go directly to organize farmworkers—for just this reason. Even when there are no strings attached, you are still compromised because you feel you have to produce immediate results. This is bad, because it takes a long time to build a movement, and your organization suffers if you get too far ahead of the people it belongs to. We set the dues at $42 a year per family, really a meaningful dues, but of the 212 we got to pay, only 12 remained by June of '63. We were discouraged at that, but not enough to make us quit.

Money was always a problem. Once we were facing a $180 gas bill on a credit card I'd got a long time ago and was about to lose. And we *had* to keep that credit card. One day my wife and I were picking cotton, pulling bolls, to make a little money to live on. Helen said to me, "Do you put all this in the bag, or just the cotton?" I thought she was kidding and told her to throw the whole boll in so that she had nothing but a sack of bolls at the weighing. The man said, "Whose sack is this?" I said, well, my wife's, and he told us we were fired. "Look at all that crap you brought in," he said. Helen and I started laughing. We were going anyway. We took the $4 we had earned and spent it at a grocery store where they were giving away a $100 prize. Each time you shopped they'd give you one of the letters of M-O-N-E-Y or a flag: you had to have M-O-N-E-Y plus the flag to win. Helen had already collected the letters and just needed the flag. Anyway, they gave her the ticket. She screamed, "A flag? I don't believe it," ran in and got the $100. She said "Now we're going to eat steak." But I said no, we're going to pay the gas bill. I don't know if she cried, but I think she did.

It was rough in those early years. Helen was having babies and I was not there when she was at the hospital. But if you haven't got your wife behind you, you can't do many things. There's got to be peace at home. So I did, I think, a fairly good job of organizing her. When we were kids, she lived in Delano and I came to town as a migrant. Once on a date we had a bad experience about segregation at a movie theater, and I put up a fight. We were together then, and still are. I think I'm more of a pacifist than she is. Her father, Fabela, was a colonel with Pancho Villa in the Mexican Revolution. Sometimes she gets angry and tells me, "These scabs—you should deal with them sternly," and I kid her, "It must be too much of that Fabela blood in you."

The movement really caught on in '64. By August we had a thousand members. We'd had a beautiful 90-day drive in Corcoran, where they had the Battle of the Corcoran Farm Camp 30 years ago, and by November we had assets of $25,000 in our credit union, which helped to stabilize the membership. I had gone without pay the whole of 1963. The next year the members voted me a $40 a week salary, after Helen had to quit working in the fields to manage the credit union.

Our first strike was in May of '65, a small one but it prepared us for the big one. A farmworker from McFarland named Epifanio Camacho came to see me. He said he was sick and tired of how people working the roses were being treated, and he was willing to "go the limit." I assigned Manuel and Gilbert Padilla to hold meetings at Camacho's house. The people wanted union recognition, but the real issue, as in most cases when you begin, was wages. They were promised $9 a thousand, but they were actually getting $6.50 and $7 for grafting roses. Most of them signed cards giving us the right to bargain for them. We chose the biggest company, with about 85 employees, not counting the irrigators and supervisors, and we held a series of meetings to prepare the strike and call the vote. There would be no picket line; everyone pledged on their honor not to break the strike.

Early on the first morning of the strike, we sent out 10 cars to check the people's homes. We found lights in five or six homes and knocked on the doors. The men were getting up and we'd say, "Where are you going?" They would dodge, "Oh, uh . . . I was just getting up, you know." We'd say, "Well, you're not going to work, are you?" And they'd say no. Dolores Huerta, who was driving the green panel truck, saw a light in one house where four rose-workers lived. They told her they were going to work, even after she reminded them of their pledge. So she moved the truck so it blocked their driveway, turned off the key, put it in her purse and sat there alone.

That morning the company foreman was madder than hell and refused to talk to us. None of the grafters had shown up for work. At 10:30 we started to go to the company office, but it occurred to us that maybe a woman would have a better chance. So Dolores knocked on the office door, saying, "I'm Dolores Huerta from the National Farm Workers Association." "Get out!" the man said, "you Communist. Get out!" I guess they were expecting us, because as Dolores stood arguing with him the cops came and told her to leave. She left.

For two days the fields were idle. On Wednesday they recruited a group of Filipinos from out of town who knew nothing of the strike, maybe 35 of them. They drove through escorted by three sheriff's patrol cars, one in front, one in the middle and one at the rear with a dog. We didn't have a picket line, but we parked across the street and just watched them go through, not saying

22

23

24

25

26

a word. All but seven stopped working after half an hour, and the rest had quit by mid-afternoon.

The company made an offer the evening of the fourth day, a package deal that amounted to a 120 per cent wage increase, but no contract. We wanted to hold out for a contract and more benefits, but a majority of the rose-workers wanted to accept the offer and go back. We are a democratic union so we had to support what they wanted to do. They had a meeting and voted to settle. Then we had a problem with a few militants who wanted to hold out. We had to convince them to go back to work, as a united front, because otherwise they would be canned. So we worked—Tony Orendain and I, Dolores and Gilbert, Jim Drake and all the organizers—knocking on doors till two in the morning, telling people, "You have to go back or you'll lose your job." And they did. They worked.

Our second strike, and our last before the big one at Delano, was in the grapes at Martin's Ranch last summer. The people were getting a raw deal there, being pushed around pretty badly. Gilbert went out to the field, climbed on top of a car and took a strike vote. They voted unanimously to go out. Right away they started bringing in strikebreakers, so we launched a tough attack on the labor contractors, distributed leaflets portraying them as really low characters. We attacked one—Luis Campos—so badly that he just gave up the job, and he took 27 of his men out with him. All he asked was that we distribute another leaflet reinstating him in the community. And we did. What was unusual was that the grower would talk to us. The grower kept saying, "I can't pay. I just haven't got the money." I guess he must have found the money somewhere, because we were asking $1.40 and we got it.

We had just finished the Martin strike when the Agricultural Workers Organizing Committee (AFL-CIO) started a strike against the grape growers, DiGiorgio, Schenley liquors and small growers, asking $1.40 an hour and 25 cents a box. There was a lot of pressure from our members for us to join the strike, but we had some misgivings. We didn't feel ready for a big strike like this one, one that was sure to last a long time. Having no money—just $87 in the strike fund—meant we'd have to depend on God knows who.

Eight days after the strike started—it takes time to get 1,200 people together from all over the Valley—we held a meeting in Delano and voted to go out. I asked the membership to release us from the pledge not to accept outside money, because we'd need it now, a lot of it. The help came. It started because of the close, and I would say even beautiful relationship that we've had with the Migrant Ministry for some years. They were the first to come to our rescue, financially and in every other way, and they spread the word to other benefactors.

We had planned, before, to start a labor school in November. It never happened, but we have the best labor school we could ever have, in the strike. The strike is only a temporary condition, however. We have over 3,000 members spread out over a wide area, and we have to service them when they have problems. We get letters from New Mexico, Colorado, Texas, California, from farmworkers saying, "We're getting together and we need an organizer." It kills you when you haven't got the personnel and resources. You feel badly about not sending an organizer because you look back and remember all the difficulty you had in getting two or three people together, and here *they're* together. Of course, we're training organizers, many of them younger than I was when I started in CSO. They can work 20 hours a day, sleep four, and be ready to hit it again; when you get to 39 it's a different story.

The people who took part in the strike and the march have something 32 more than their material interest going for them. If it were only material, they wouldn't have stayed on the strike long enough to win. It is difficult to explain. But it flows out in the ordinary things they say. For instance, some of the younger guys are saying, "Where do you think's going to be the next strike?" I say, "Well, we have to win in Delano." They say, "We'll win, but where do we go next?" I say, "Maybe most of us will be working in the fields." They say, "No, I don't want to go and work in the fields. I want to organize. There are a lot of people that need our help." So I say, "You're going to be pretty poor then, because when you strike you don't have much money." They say they don't care about that.

And others are saying, "I have friends who are working in Texas. If we 33 could only help them." It is bigger, certainly, than just a strike. And if this spirit grows within the farm labor movement, one day we can use the force that we have to help correct a lot of things that are wrong in this society. But that is for the future. Before you can run, you have to learn to walk.

There are vivid memories from my childhood—what we had to go through 34 because of low wages and the conditions, basically because there was no union. I suppose if I wanted to be fair I could say that I'm trying to settle a personal score. I could dramatize it by saying that I want to bring social justice to farmworkers. But the truth is that I went through a lot of hell, and a lot of people did. If we can even the score a little for the workers then we are doing something. Besides, I don't know any other work I like to do better than this. I really don't, you know.◆

◆ Responding

1. Identify what Chávez learned that helped him become a labor organizer.

2. Research the McCarthy era. What does Chávez mean when he says he was "subjected to a lot of redbaiting"?

3. Chávez says, "Whatever you do, and no matter what reasons you may give to others, you do it because you want to see it done, or maybe because you want power." Agree or disagree with this statement. Use examples from the essay to support your argument.

4. Review the philosophy, focus, and methods of the organization Chávez founded. Discuss the advantages and disadvantages of his method of going directly to the people.

◆ L A   N O C H E   B U E N A ◆

La noche buena se aproximaba y la radio igualmente que la comioneta de la   1
bocina que anunciaba las películas del Teatro Ideal parecían empujarla con
canción, negocio y bendición. Faltaban tres días para la noche buena cuando
doña María se decidió comprarles algo a sus niños. Esta sería la primera vez
que les compraría juguetes. Cada año se proponía a hacerlo pero siempre terminaba diciéndose que no, que no podían. Su esposo de todas maneras les traía
dulces y nueces a cada uno así que racionalizaba que en realidad no les faltaba
nada. Sin embargo cada navidad preguntaban los niños por sus juguetes. Ella
siempre los apaciguaba con lo de siempre. Les decía que se esperaran hasta el
seis de enero, el día de los reyes magos y así para cuando se llegaba ese día ya
hasta se les había olvidado todo a los niños. También había notado que sus hijos
apreciaban menos y menos la venida de don Chon la noche de navidad cuando
venía con el costal de naranjas y nueces.

> —Pero, ¿por qué a nosotros no nos trae nada Santo Clos?
> —¿Cómo que no? ¿Luego cuando viene y les trae naranjas y nueces?
> —No, pero ése es don Chon.
> —No, yo digo lo que siempre aparece debajo de la máquina de coser.
> —Ah, eso lo trae papá, apoco cree que no sabemos. ¿Es que no somos buenos
> como los demás?

TOMÁS RIVERA

Tomás Rivera was born in Crystal City, Texas, in 1935, the child of migrant workers who had emigrated from Mexico. He spent his childhood working on farms from Texas to the Midwest. Rivera earned a bachelor's degree from Southwest Texas State University in 1964, as well as a master's degree in educational administration and a doctorate in Romance languages and literature from the University of Oklahoma.

From 1957 until his death in 1984, Rivera held several university teaching and administrative positions in Texas and California. In 1980 he was named chancellor of the University of California at Riverside; he was the youngest person and the first member of a minority group to earn this position. Tomás Rivera died in 1984, at the age of forty-eight.

Rivera's most famous work, Y no se lo trago la tiera (. . . And the Earth Did Not Part, *1969) examines the experience of a migrant family. While most of the book's chapters focus on the thoughts of a young boy, the excerpted chapter centers on the reactions of the family's mother. As it describes the townspeople's treatment of this woman, the passage asks us to consider the ways in which economic and political issues can affect both families and individual lives.*

◆ CHRISTMAS EVE ◆

Christmas Eve was approaching. The radio as well as the loudspeaker on the pickup truck that advertised the movies for the Teatro Ideal seemed to draw it closer with songs, business, and prayers. It was three days before Christmas when doña María decided to buy something for her children. This would be the first time that she had bought toys for them. She planned to do it every year, but she always wound up convincing herself that they could not afford it. Her husband brought candies and nuts for each one of them, so she rationalized that they weren't missing anything. Still, every Christmas day the children would ask for their toys. She always placated them with the same story. She would tell them to wait until the sixth of January, the day of the Reyes Magos. By the time the day arrived the children had completely forgotten about toys. She had also noticed that her children appreciated less and less each year the visit by don Chon with his sack of oranges and nuts.

> "But why doesn't Santa Claus bring us anything?"
> "What do you mean? What about the oranges and nuts that he brings you?"
> "No, that's don Chon who brings them."
> "No, I mean what is always left under the sewing machine."
> "Oh, father brings that, don't think we don't know. Aren't we as good as the other children?"

—Sí, sí son buenos, pero . . . pues espérense hasta el día de los reyes magos. Ese es el día en que de veras vienen los juguetes y los regalos. Allá en México no viene Santo Clos sino los reyes magos. Y no vienen hasta el seis de enero. Así que ése sí es el mero día.

—Pero, lo que pasa es que se les olvida. Porque a nosotros nunca nos han dado nada ni en la noche buena ni en el día de los reyes magos.

—Bueno, pero a lo mejor esta vez sí.

—Pos sí, ojalá.

Por eso se decidió comprarles algo. Pero no tenían dinero para gastar en juguetes. Su esposo trabajaba casi las diez y ocho horas lavando platos y haciendo de comer en un restaurante. No tenía tiempo de ir al centro para comprar juguetes. Además tenían que alzar cada semana para poder pagar para la ida al norte. Ya les cobraban por los niños aunque fueran parados todo el camino hasta Iowa. Así que les costaba bastante para hacer el viaje. De todas maneras le propuso a su esposo esa noche, cuando llegó bien cansado del trabajo, que les compraran algo.

—Fíjate, viejo, que los niños quieren algo para crismes.

—¿Y luego las naranjas y las nueces que les traigo?

—Pos sí, pero ellos quieren juguetes. Ya no se conforman con comida. Es que están más grandes y ven más.

—No necesitan nada.

—¿A poco tú no tenías juguetes cuando eras niño?

—Sabes que yo mismo los hacía de barro—caballitos, soldaditos. . . .

—Pos sí, pero aquí es distinto, como ven muchas cosas . . . ándale vamos a comprarles algo . . . yo misma voy al Kres.

—¿Tú?

—Sí, yo.

—¿No tienes miedo ir al centro? ¿Te acuerdas allá en Wilmar, Minesóra, cómo te perdiste en el centro? ¿'Tas segura que no tienes miedo?

—Sí, sí me acuerdo pero me doy ánimo. Yo voy. Ya me estuve dando ánimo todo el día y estoy segura que no me pierdo aquí. Mira, salgo a la calle. De aquí se ve la hielería. Son cuatro cuadras nomás, según me dijo doña Regina. Luego cuando llegue a la hielería volteo a la derecha y dos cuadras más y estoy en el centro. Allí está el Kres. Luego salgo del Kres, voy hacia la hielería y volteo para esta calle y aquí me tienes.

—De veras que no estaría difícil. Pos sí. Bueno, te voy a dejar dinero sobre la mesa cuando me vaya por la mañana. Pero tienes cuidado, vieja, en estos días hay mucha gente en el centro.

Era que doña María nunca salía de casa sola. La única vez que salía era cuando iba a visitar a su papá y a su hermana quienes vivían en la siguiente cuadra. Sólo iba a la iglesia cuando había difuntito y a veces cuando había boda. Pero iba siempre con su esposo así que nunca se fijaba por donde iba. También su esposo le traía siempre todo. El era el que compraba la comida y la ropa. En realidad no conocía el centro aun estando solamente a seis cuadras de su casa. El camposanto quedaba por el lado opuesto al centro, la iglesia también

"Yes, of course you are, but why don't you wait until the day of the Reyes Magos. That's really the day when toys and other gifts should be given. In Mexico it isn't Santa Claus who brings toys, but the Reyes Magos. And they don't come until the sixth of January. So, you see, that is the real day."

"But what happens is that you forget all about it. We've never received anything either on Christmas Eve or on the day of the Reyes Magos."

"Well, maybe this time you will."

"Yes, I really hope so."

She decided to buy something for them. But she didn't have any money to spend on toys. Her husband worked almost eighteen hours washing dishes and cooking in a restaurant. He didn't have time to go downtown to buy toys. Furthermore, every week they had to save some money to pay for the trip north. They had to pay the children's fare even if they had to stand up all the way to Iowa. It was very expensive for them to make the trip. In spite of all this, that night when her husband arrived tired from work she suggested that they buy something for them.

"Look, viejo, the children would like something for Christmas."

"What about the oranges and nuts that I bring them?"

"Well, yes, but they want toys. They won't settle for food. They're older now, and they are aware of more things."

"They're not in need of anything."

"Don't tell me you didn't have any toys when you were a child."

"You know, I used to make them myself, out of clay. I'd make little horses, little soldiers. . . ."

"Well, yes, but it's different here since they see many things . . . come on, let's go buy something for them . . . I'll go to Kress myself."

"You?"

"Yes, me."

"Aren't you afraid to go downtown? Don't you remember what happened in Wilmar, Minnesota, when you got lost downtown? Are you sure you're not afraid?"

"Yes, yes, I remember, but I'll try to get up my courage. I'll go. I've been building up courage all day and I'm sure that I won't get lost. Look, all I have to do is go out to the street. I can see the ice plant from here. It's only four blocks away, according to doña Regina. When I get to the ice plant I'll turn right and two blocks more I'll be downtown. Kress is right there. Then I leave Kress, head toward the ice plant, turn into this street and here I am."

"It really won't be difficult at all. Alright, I'll leave you some money on the table when I leave in the morning. But be careful, vieja, there are a lot of people in town these days."

The fact was that doña María never went out of the house by herself. The only time she left the house was when she visited her father and her sister who lived a block away. She went to church only when someone passed away or sometimes when there was a wedding. But she always went with her husband, so she never noticed where she was going. Also, her husband always brought

quedaba por ese rumbo. Pasaban por el centro sólo cuando iban de pasada para San Antonio o cuando iban o venían del norte. Casi siempre era de madrugada o de noche. Pero ese día traía ánimo y se preparó para ir al centro.

El siguiente día se levantó, como lo hacía siempre, muy temprano y ya cuando había despachado a su esposo y a los niños recogió el dinero de sobre la mesa y empezó a prepararse para ir al centro. No le llevó mucho tiempo.

> —Yo no sé por qué soy tan miedosa yo, Dios mío. Si el centro está solamente a seis cuadras de aquí. Nomás me voy derechito y luego volteo a la derecha al pasar los traques. Luego, dos cuadras, y allí está el Kres. De allá para acá ando las dos cuadras, y luego volteo a la izquierda y luego hasta que llegue aquí otra vez. Dios quiera y no me vaya a salir algún perro. Al pasar los traques que no vaya a venir un tren y me pesque en medio . . . Ojalá y no me salga un perro . . . Ojalá y no venga un tren por los traques.

La distancia de su casa al ferrocarril la anduvo rapidamente. Se fue en medio de la calle todo el trecho. Tenía miedo andar por la banqueta. Se le hacía que la mordían los perros o que alguien la cogia. En realidad solamente había un perro en todo el trecho y la mayor parte de la gente ni se dio cuenta de que iba al centro. Ella, sin embargo, seguía andando por en medio de la calle y tuvo suerte de que no pasara un solo mueble si no no hubiera sabido que hacer. Al llegar al ferrocarril le entró el miedo. Oía el movimiento y el pitido de los trenes y esto la desconcertaba. No se animaba a cruzar los rieles. Parecía que cada vez que se animaba se oía el pitido de un tren y se volvía a su lugar. Por fin venció el miedo, cerró los ojos y pasó sobre los rieles. Al pasar se le fue quitando el miedo. Volteó a la derecha.

Las aceras estaban repletas de gente y se le empezaron a llenar los oídos de ruido, un ruido que después de entrar no quería salir. No reconocía a nadie en la banqueta. Le entraron ganas de regresarse pero alguien la empujó hacia el centro y los oídos se le llenaban más y más de ruido. Sentía miedo y más y más se le olvidaba la razón por la cual estaba allí entre el gentío. En medio de dos tiendas donde había una callejuela se detuvo para recuperar el ánimo un poco y se quedó viendo un rato a la gente que pasaba.

> —Dios mío, ¿qué me pasa? Ya me empiezo a sentir como me sentí en Wilmar. Ojalá y no me vaya a sentir mal. A ver. Para allá queda la hielería. No, para allá. No, Dios mío, ¿qué me pasa? A ver. Venía andando de allá para acá. Así que queda para allá. Mejor me hubiera quedado en casa. Oiga, perdone usted, ¿dónde está el Kres, por favor? . . . Gracias.

Se fue andando hasta donde le habían indicado y entró. El ruido y la apretura de la gente era peor. Le entró más miedo y ya lo único que quería era salirse de la tienda pero ya no veía la puerta. Sólo veía cosas sobre cosas, gente sobre gente. Hasta oía hablar a las cosas. Se quedó parada un rato viendo vacíamente a lo que estaba enfrente de ella. Era que ya no sabía los nombres de las cosas. Unas personas se le quedaban viendo unos segundos otras solamente la empujaban para un lado. Permaneció así por un rato y luego empezó a andar

everything to her. He was the one who brought food and clothing. In reality she had never been downtown even though it was just six blocks away from her house. The cemetery was in the opposite direction from the downtown area, as was the church. They crossed the downtown area only when they were on their way to San Antonio or when they were on their way back from up north. Somehow it was always at dawn or during the night. But that day she had built up her courage and she got ready to go downtown.

The following day she got up very early, as she always did, and after she had sent off her husband and the children she picked up the money from the table and started to ready herself to go downtown. It didn't take her very long.

4

> "I don't know why I'm so timid, my God. Downtown is only six blocks away. I just go straight and I turn right when I cross the tracks. Then two blocks and there is Kress. On the way back I walk two blocks and then I turn left and then straight home. God willing I won't meet any dogs on the way. I'll be careful when I cross the tracks, or a train might come along and catch me in the middle of the tracks . . . I hope I don't meet any dogs . . . I hope there is no train."

Rapidly she walked the distance from her house to the railroad tracks. The entire distance she walked along the middle of the street. She was afraid to walk on the sidewalk. She was afraid of being bitten by dogs or of being accosted by someone. Actually there was only one dog along the entire route, and most of the people didn't even notice that she was going downtown. However, she kept on walking in the middle of the street, lucky that not a single car came along, otherwise she would not have known what to do. As she approached the railroad track she became afraid. She could hear movements and the whistles of the trains, and this unsettled her. She didn't dare cross the tracks. It seemed as though every time she built up enough courage to do so she heard a train whistle and she retreated. Finally she overcame her fear, closed her eyes and crossed the tracks. Her fear left her as she crossed the tracks. She turned to her right.

5

The streets were full of people and her ears became crowded with noise that once inside refused to leave. She didn't recognize anyone on the sidewalk. She felt the urge to go home, but someone pushed her toward downtown as more and more noises crowded into her ears. She was afraid. More and more she was forgetting the reason for being there among so many people. To regain her courage she stopped in an alley that separated two stores and for a while she looked at the people who passed by.

6

> "My God, what's wrong with me? I'm beginning to feel the same way I felt in Wilmar. I hope I don't get sick. Let's see. The ice plant is in that direction. No, it's this other way. No, my God, what's happening to me? Let's see. I came from that direction toward here, so, it's in that direction. I should have stayed at home. Excuse me, can you tell me where Kress is, please? . . . Thank you."

She walked to the place that was pointed out to her and she went in. The noise was worse and the crowd was thicker. She became even more afraid and

7

de nuevo. Reconoció unos juguetes y los echó en su bolsa, luego vio una cartera y también la echó a la bolsa. De pronto ya no oía el ruido de la gente aunque sí veía todos los movimientos de sus piernas, de sus brazos, de la boca, de sus ojos. Pero no oía nada. Por fin preguntó que dónde quedaba la puerta, la salida. Le indicaron y empezó a andar hacia aquel rumbo. Empujó y empujó gente hasta que llegó a empujar la puerta y salió.

Apenas había estado unos segundos en la acera tratando de reconocer **8** dónde estaba, cuando sintió que alguien la cogió fuerte del brazo. Hasta la hicieron que diera un gemido.

—Here she is . . . these damn people, always stealing something, stealing. I've been watching you all along. Let's have that bag.
—¿Pero . . . ?

Y ya no oyó nada por mucho tiempo. Sólo vio que el cemento de la acera **9** se vino a sus ojos y que una piedrita se le metió en el ojo y le calaba mucho. Sentía que la estiraban de los brazos y aun cuando la voltearon boca arriba veía a todos muy retirados. Se veía a sí misma. Se sentía hablar pero ni ella sabía lo que decía pero sí se veía mover la boca. También veía puras caras desconocidas. Luego vio al empleado con la pistola en la cartuchera y le entró un miedo terrible. Fue cuando se volvió a acordar de sus hijos. Le empezaron a salir las lágrimas y lloró. Luego ya no supo nada. Sólo se sentía andar en un mar de gente. Los brazos la rozaban como si fueran olas.

—De a buena suerte que mi compadre andaba por allí. El fue el que me fue a avisar al restaurante. ¿Cómo te sientes?
—Yo creo que estoy loca, viejo.
—Por eso te pregunté que si no te irías a sentir mal como en Wilmar.
—¿Qué va a ser de mis hijos con una mamá loca? Con una loca que ni siquiera sabe hablar ni ir al centro.
—De todos modos, fui a traer al notario público. Y él fue el que fue conmigo a la cárcel. El le explicó todo al empleado. Que se te había volado la cabeza. Y que te daban ataques de nervios cuando andabas entre mucha gente.
—¿Y si me mandan a un manicomio? Yo no quiero dejar a mis hijos. Por favor, viejo, no vayas a dejar que me manden, que no me lleven. Mejor no hubiera ido al centro.
—Pos nomás quédate aquí dentro de la casa y no te salgas del solar. Que al cabo no hay necesidad. Yo te traigo todo lo que necesites. Mira, ya no llores, ya no llores. No, mejor llora, para que te desahogues. Les voy a decir a los muchachos que ya no te anden fregando con Santo Clos. Les voy a decir que no hay para que no te molesten con eso ya.
—No, viejo, no seas malo. Díles que si no les trae nada en noche buena que es porque les van a traer algo los reyes magos.
—Pero . . . Bueno, como tú quieras. Yo creo que siempre lo mejor es tener esperanzas.

Los niños que estaban escondidos detrás de la puerta oyeron todo pero **10** no comprendieron muy bien. Y esperaron el día de los reyes magos como todos los años. Cuando llegó y pasó aquel día sin regalos no preguntaron nada.◆

the only thing she wanted to do was to leave the store but she couldn't find the door. She only saw things piled on top of things, people piled on top of people. She could even hear the different things speak. She stood there for a while, emptily looking at what was in front of her. She could no longer remember the names of things. A few people stared at her for a second or so, others shoved her aside. She remained fixed in that position for a while and then started to walk again. She was able to make out some toys and she put them in her shopping bag; then she saw a wallet and put that in her shopping bag, too. Suddenly the noise of the crowd stopped, even though she could still see all the movements of their legs, their arms, their mouths and their eyes. But she couldn't hear anything. She finally asked where the door was, the way out. They pointed it out to her and she began to walk in that direction. She pushed and pushed people aside until finally she was pushing on the door and went out.

She had been outside only for a few seconds, on the sidewalk, trying to   8
get her bearings when she felt someone grab her strongly by the arm. The force with which she was seized forced a moan out of her.

> "Here she is . . . these damn people, always stealing something, always stealing. I've been watching you all along. Let's have that bag."
> "But . . . ?"

And she didn't hear anything else for a long time. She only saw the   9
sidewalk cement rush to her eyes and a small pebble lodge in her eye and felt its irritation. She felt someone pull her arms, and when she was turned face up the people appeared elongated in shape. She looked at herself. She was aware that she was speaking but not even she understood what she was saying, even though she could see her lips move. Also, all the faces that she saw were unfamiliar to her. She then saw the store guard with a gun in his holster and she became terrified. It was then that she remembered her children. Tears rolled out and she cried. Then everything went blank. She was only aware of walking in a sea of people. Their arms touched her like ocean waves.

> "It was a good thing my compadre was around. He was the one who rushed over to the restaurant with the news. How do you feel?"
> "I think I'm insane, viejo."
> "That's why I asked if you thought you might get sick as you did in Wilmar."
> "What will become of my children with an insane mother like me? With an insane woman who can't even express herself nor go downtown?"
> "I brought along the notary public just in case. He was the one who went with me to the jailhouse. He explained everything to the guard, that your thoughts became confused. And that you became very nervous when you were in a crowd."
> "What if they send me to the insane asylum? I don't want to leave my children alone. Please, viejo, don't let them send me; don't let them take me. I shouldn't have gone downtown."
> "Well, just stay here in the house and don't leave the yard. There is no need for you to go out anyway. I'll bring everything you need. Look, don't cry, don't cry. Well, maybe you should cry, it will ease your pain. I'm going to tell the boys

not to bother you anymore about Santa Claus. I'll tell them there is no Santa Claus so they won't bother you with that anymore."

"No, viejo, don't be mean. Tell them that if they didn't get anything for Christmas it's because the Reyes Magos will bring them something."

"But . . . well, whatever you say. I guess it's always best to have hope."

The children, who had been hiding behind the door, heard everything   10 even though they didn't understand too well. And they waited the coming of the Reyes Magos just as they did every year. When that day arrived and there were no gifts they didn't question anything.◆

◆ Responding

1. Discuss Rivera's attitude toward doña María. Is he sympathetic or unsympathetic? How does he try to get the reader to share his viewpoint?

2. Have you ever been afraid to do something or tried to do something that was very threatening and failed in the attempt? How did you feel about yourself? Did you try again? How does doña María feel about her attempt to go to the store? Do you think she will try again?

3. What is the attitude of the person who stops doña María outside the store? What do this person's comments reveal about attitudes toward the migrant community?

4. Pretend that you are one of the following people in the crowd around doña María: a local banker, the store owner, the guard, a friend, a migrant worker, one of doña María's children, a local reporter, a reporter from a large metropolitan area, a civil rights worker. Write a letter to a friend or a letter to the editor of the local paper about the incident.

ANA CASTILLO

Born in Chicago in 1953, Ana Castillo earned a bachelor's degree from Northwestern University in 1975. In addition to serving as a reviewer for and associate editor of Third Woman Magazine *and the co-editor of* Humanizarte Magazine, *she has contributed poems and short stories to several anthologies and literary journals, among them* The Third Woman *and* Woman of Her Word. *Her publications include the poetry collections* Otro Canto *(1977),* The Invitation *(1979),* Women Are Not Roses *(1984), and* My Father Was a Toltec *(1988), as well as the novels* The Mixquiahuala Letters *(1986) and* Sapognia *(1989). Castillo has been the recipient of several grants and awards, including a grant from the National Endowment for the Arts.*

In Castillo's poems, the struggle of the migrant workers provides a focal point for reflecting on the relationship between labor and dignity. "Napa, California," for example, considers the people's attitudes toward their leader and the reasons they follow him.

◆ NAPA, CALIFORNIA ◆

Dedicado al Sr. Chávez, sept. '75

We pick
the bittersweet grapes
at harvest
one
  by
    one
with leather worn hands
      as they pick
        at our dignity
        and wipe our pride
        away
        like the sweat we wipe
        from our sun-beaten brows
        at midday

In fields
  so vast
  that our youth seems
  to pass before us
  and we have grown
  very
    very
      old
        by dusk . . .
        (bueno pues, ¿qué vamos a hacer, Ambrosio?
        ¡bueno pues, seguirle, comparde, seguirle!
        ¡Ay, Mama!
        Sí pues, ¿qué vamos a hacer, compadre?
        ¡Seguirle, Ambrosio, seguirle!)[1]
We pick
  with a desire
  that only survival
  inspires
While the end
  of each day only brings
  a tired night
  that waits for the sun
  and the land
  that in turn waits
  for us . . . ◆

◆ Responding

1. Understanding a poem often means understanding the poem's references to events and people. Research the title and dedication of this poem. Why did the poet choose "Napa," "Sr. Chávez," and "sept. '75"? Reflect on the role of titles and the information they provide the reader. What might some alternate titles for this poem be? What response might these titles produce in a reader?

---

[1]Well then, what are we going to do, Ambrosio?
Well then, follow him, my good friend, follow him!
Mama!
Yes, well, what are we going to do, friend?
Follow him, Ambrosio, follow him!

2. Who is the "we" in the poem? What information does the poem give you about these people?

3. Copy one stanza of the poem into conventional prose sentences. How is the effect different? Discuss the reasons why the poet may have written the stanzas in the form she did.

4. Reread the translation of the Spanish text. Why do you think the author includes several lines in Spanish? How did you react when you first read these lines?

◆ MILAGROS ◆

Morenita clara
ojos grandes,
like those
      painted on
             four for a dollar prints.
             of shaggy pups
             and ragged dolls—

hung up
    on the
          bedroom walls
          where her baby sleeps.

Milagros
talks about
the importance
of her education,
the state of affairs
on the island,
her husband—
who doesn't speak
English . . .
but that's okay.
They're going back home again anyway—
Someday
As she talks of these things,

you smile
    just to watch
        her beautiful face
            shine
like her tropical sun:
Only a childhood memory
these days . . .
        When the ambition of a degree
        is taking the form of a dream . . .
        Another baby on the way,
        (Well, her husband never did like
        the idea of this college business
        anyway . . .)

These days are getting shorter.
The nights keep getting longer.
The kitchen clock starts ticking
                louder . . .

Milagros has no time to talk,
            her rice may overcook.

But just before
she turns away
you catch that look:
        painted on four for a dollar prints
        of shaggy pups and ragged dolls
        hung up on the bedroom walls
Where her
    baby
        sleeps. ◆

◆ Responding

1. Do you think Milagros's dreams of going back home and getting an education will come true? What do you think the poet believes?

2. Compare the treatment of the repeated line "where her baby sleeps." What do you think the poet may be trying to suggest by changing the format? Do you respond to the line differently at each repetition? How?

3. Milagros's husband doesn't appear in the poem, but we hear about him. What clues does the poem give us about his attitudes toward the United States, the role of women, and the family?

4. Who is Milagros talking to? Working in a group, describe the speaker and write a scenario explaining who this person is and what his or her relationship is to Milagros.

PAT MORA

Although Pat Mora now lives in the Midwest, she incorporates much of the heritage of her native Southwest in her writing. Born in El Paso, Texas, she earned her bachelor's degree from Texas Western College in 1963 and her master's degree from the University of Texas at El Paso in 1967. Since the late 1960s she has worked in the academic and cross-cultural fields, first by teaching English and later by working in university administration. In 1986 she was awarded a Kellogg National Fellowship to study cultural conservation issues. In addition to contributing poetry to numerous journals and anthologies, Mora has published two collections of poems, Chants *(1984) and* Borders *(1986), which have received several awards.*

The following two poems, from Chants, *explore the effect of economic and cultural boundaries in allowing each speaker to articulate her feelings.*

◆ ILLEGAL ALIEN ◆

Socorro, you free me
to sit in my yellow kitchen
waiting for a poem
while you scrub and iron.

Today you stand before me
holding cleanser and sponge
and say you can't sleep at night.
"My husband's fury is a fire.
His fist can burn.
We don't fight with words
on that side of the Rio Grande."

Your eyes fill. I want
to comfort you, but my arms
feel heavy, unaccustomed
to healing grown-up bodies.

I offer foolish questions
when I should hug you hard,
when I should dry your eyes, my sister,
sister because we are both women,
both married, both warmed
by Mexican blood.

It is not cool words you need
but soothing hands.
My plastic band-aid doesn't fit
your hurt.
I am the alien here.◆

◆ Responding

1. What relationship do the two women in the poem have? What does the relationship mean to the speaker? What images in the poem help the reader to understand the poet's attitude toward the narrator and Socorro?

2. Imagine that Socorro has written to one of the following people for help in dealing with her physically-abusive husband: her mother, a social worker, "Dear Abby," a religious leader, an administrator of a shelter for battered women. Write a reply from the point of view of that person.

3. We know what the speaker has to say, but not what Socorro is thinking. Working with a partner, each taking one role, write a dialogue between Socorro and the speaker. Share your dialogue with your classmates.

4. What bond does being "women, both married, both warmed by Mexican blood" create between the two people in the poem? Does it make them responsible to each other for comfort and guidance?

◆ LEGAL ALIEN ◆

Bi-lingual. Bi-cultural,
able to slip from "How's life?"
to *"Me'stan volviendo loca,"*
able to sit in a paneled office
drafting memos in smooth English,
able to order in fluent Spanish
at a Mexican restaurant,
American but hyphenated,
viewed by Anglos as perhaps exotic,
perhaps inferior, definitely different,
viewed by Mexicans as alien.
(their eyes say, "You may speak
Spanish but you're not like me")
an American to Mexicans
a Mexican to Americans
a handy token
sliding back and forth
between the fringes of both worlds
by smiling
by masking the discomfort
of being pre-judged
Bi-laterally.◆

◆ Responding

1. Is "legal alien" a contradiction in terms? What does the speaker mean when she calls herself a legal alien?

2. The speaker believes that being bicultural means that you aren't really accepted by either culture. Do you agree or disagree? Support your position by referring to the poem, other readings in the text, or your experience.

3. Tell about a time when you or someone you know felt torn between two traditions, two sets of beliefs, or two cultures.

4. Working individually or in a group, list the advantages and disadvantages of being bicultural in the United States today. Compare notes with the class. Write an essay presenting your conclusions.

◆ MI ABUELA FUMABA PUROS ◆

Según entiendo, mi abuelo era un tipazo. Se cuentan muchas cosas de él. 1
Algunas respetables, otras no tanto. Una de las últimas va como sigue. Que
volviendo de Tierra Amarilla a Las Nutrias, después de copas y cartas, ya en
su coche ligero con sus caballos bien trotadores, ya en su caballo criollo, solía
quitarse el sombrero, colgarlo en un poste, sacar la pistola y dirigirse al tieso
caballero de su invención.

—Dime, ¿Quién es el más rico de todas estas tierras? 2
Silencio. 3
—Pues toma. 4
Disparo. Saltaban astillas del poste o aparecía un agujero en el sombrero. 5
—¿Quién es el más hombre de por acá? 6
Silencio. 7
—Pues, toma. 8
Otra vez lo mismo. Era buen tirador. Más preguntas de la misma índole, 9
acentuadas con balazos. Cuando el majadero madero entraba en razón y le daba
las contestaciones que mi abuelo quería oír, terminaba el ritual y seguía su
camino, cantando o tarareando una canción sentimental de la época. Allá en el
pueblo se oía el tiroteo sin que nadie se preocupara. No faltaba quien dijera
con una sonrisa, "Allá está don Prudencio haciendo sus cosas."

Claro que mi abuelo tenía otros lados (el plural es intencionado) que no 10

SABINE ULIBARRÍ

*Sabine Ulibarrí was born in Santa Fe, New Mexico, in 1919 and raised
in Tierra Amarilla. After serving in the air force and being awarded the
Distinguished Flying Cross during World War II, he earned his bachelor's
and master's degrees from the University of New Mexico in 1947 and 1949
and his doctorate from UCLA in 1958. In addition to writing several critical
essays and two volumes of poetry, Ulibarrí has published two collections of
short stories,* Tierra Amarilla *(1964) and* Mi abuela fumaba puros *(My
Grandma Smoked Cigars) (1977). Both these collections reflect the humor
of the environment—the kinds of minor misunderstandings that enliven small-
town life.*

*"My Grandma Smoked Cigars" is the title work of Ulibarrí's second
collection of stories. In narrating this tale about his childhood, the speaker
gives us a sense of the importance of personal memories to one's sense of identity
and pride. At the same time, in showing his grandmother's role in keeping
the family together, he reflects on the implications of a matriarchal family
structure.*

◆ MY GRANDMA SMOKED CIGARS ◆

The way I've heard it, my grandfather was quite a guy. There are many stories 1
about him. Some respectable, others not quite. One of the latter goes as follows.
That returning from Tierra Amarilla to Las Nutrias, after cups and cards,
sometimes on his buggy with its spirited trotters, sometimes on his *criollo* horse,
he would take off his hat, hang it on a fence post, pull out his six-gun and
address himself to the stiff gentleman of his own invention.

"Tell me, who is the richest man in all these parts?" 2

Silence. 3

"Well then, take this." 4

A shot. Splinters flew out of the post or a hole appeared in the hat. 5

"Who's the toughest man around here?" 6

Silence. 7

"Well then, take this." 8

The same thing happened. He was a good shot. More questions of the 9
same kind, punctuated with shots. When the sassy post learned his lesson and
gave my grandfather the answers he wanted to hear, the ritual ended, and he
went on his way, singing or humming some sentimental song of the period.
The shooting was heard back in the town without it bothering anyone. Someone
was sure to say with a smile, "There's don Prudencio doing his thing."

Of course my grandfather had other sides (the plural is intended) that are 10

interesan en este relato. Fue ente cívico, social, y político, y padre de familias (el plural tiene segunda intención). Lo que ahora me importa es hacer constar que mi pariente fue un tipazo: pendenciero, atrevido y travieso.

Murió de una manera misteriosa, o quizás vergonzosa. Nunca he podido 11
sacar en limpio qué tranvía tomó para el otro mundo mi distinguido antecedente. Acaso ese caballero de palo con el sombrero calado, de las afrentas del hidalgo de Las Nutrias, le dió un palo mortal. Hidalgo era—y padre de más de cuatro.

Yo no lo conocí. Cuando me presenté en ese mundo con mis credenciales 12
de Turriaga, ya él había entregado los suyos. Me figuro que allá donde esté estará haciéndoles violento y apasionado amor a las mujeres salvadas—o perdidas, según el caso. Esto es si mi abuela no ha logrado encontrarlo por esos mundos del trasmundo.

No creo que él y mi abuela tuvieran un matrimonio idílico en el sentido 13
de las novelas sentimentales donde todo es dulzura, suavidad y ternura. Esos son lujos, acaso decadencias, que no pertenecían a ese mundo violento, frecuentemente hostil, del condado de Río Arriba a fines del siglo pasado. Además las recias personalidades de ambos lo habrían impedido. Sí creo que fueron muy felices. Su amor fue una pasión que no tuvo tiempo de convertirse en costumbre o en simple amistad. Se amaron con mutuo respeto y miedo, entre admiración y rabias, entre ternura y bravura. Ambos eran hijos de su tierra y su tiempo. Había tanto que hacer. Labrar una vida de una frontera inhospitalaria. Criar unos cachorros rebeldes y feroces. Su vida fue una cariñosa y apasionada guerra sentimental.

Todo esto lo digo como preámbulo para entrar en materia: mi abuela. Son 14
tantos y tan gratos los recuerdos que guardo de ella. Pero el primero de todos es un retrato que tengo colgado en sitio de honor en la sala principal de mi memoria.

Tenía sus momentos en que acariciaba su soledad. Se apartaba de todos 15
y todos sabían que valía más apartarse de ella.

Siempre la ví vestida de negro. Blusa de encajes y holanes en el frente. 16
Falda hasta los tobillos. Todo de seda. Delantal de algodón. Zapatos altos. El cabello apartado en el centro y peinado para atrás, liso y apretado, con un chongo (moño) redondo y duro atrás. Nunca la ví con el cabello suelto.

Era fuerte. Fuerte como ella sola. A través de los años en tantas peripecias, 17
grandes y pequeñas tragedias, accidentes y problemas, nunca la ví torcerse o doblarse. Era seria y formal fundamentalmente. De modo que una sonrisa, un complido o una caricia de ella eran monedas de oro que se apreciaban y se guardaban de recuerdo para siempre. Monedas que ella no despilfarraba.

El rancho era negocio grande. La familia era grande y problemática. Ella 18
regía su imperio con mano firme y segura. Nunca hubo duda adonde iban sus asuntos ni quién llevaba las riendas.

Ese primer recuerdo: el retrato. La veo en este momento en el alto de la 19
loma como si estuviera ante mis ojos. Silueta negra sobre fondo azul. Recta, alta y esbelta. El viento de la loma pegándole la ropa al cuerpo delante, perfilando

not relevant to this narrative. He was a civic, social and political figure and a family man twice over. What I want to do now is stress the fact that my relative was a real character: quarrelsome, daring and prankish.

He died in a mysterious way, or perhaps even shameful. I've never been 11 able to find out exactly what streetcar my distinguished antecedent took to the other world. Maybe that wooden gentleman with his hat pulled over his eyes, the one who suffered the insults of the hidalgo of Las Nutrias, gave him a woody and mortal whack. An hidalgo he was—and a father of more than four.

I never knew him. When I showed up in this world to present my Turriaga 12 credentials, he had already turned his in. I imagine that wherever he is he's making violent and passionate love to the ladies who went to heaven—or hell, depending . . . That is if my grandmother hasn't caught up with him in those worlds beyond the grave.

I don't think he and my grandmother had an idyllic marriage in the man- 13 ner of sentimental novels where everything is sweetness, softness and tenderness. Those are luxuries, perhaps decadences, that didn't belong in that violent world, frequently hostile, of Río Arriba County at the end of the past century. Furthermore, the strong personalities of both would have prevented it. I do believe they were very happy. Their love was a passion that didn't have time to become a habit or just friendship. They loved each other with mutual respect and fear, something between admiration and fury, something between tenderness and toughness. Both were children of their land and their times. There was so much to do. Carve a life from an unfriendly frontier. Raise their to do. Carve a life from an unfriendly frontier. Raise their rebellious and fe- rebellious and ferocious cubs. Their life was an affectionate and passionate sentimental war.

I say all of this as a preamble in order to enter into my subject: my 14 grandmother. I have so many and so gratifying memories of her. But the first one of all is a portrait that hangs in a place of honor in the parlor of my memory.

She had her moments in which she caressed her solitude. She would go 15 off by herself, and everyone knew it was best to leave her alone.

She always dressed in black. A blouse of lace and batiste up front. A skirt 16 down to her ankles. All silk. A cotton apron. High shoes. Her hair parted in the middle and combed straight back, smooth and tight, with a round and hard bun in the back. I never saw her hair loose.

She was strong. As strong as only she could be. Through the years, in 17 so many situations, small and big tragedies, accidents and problems, I never saw her bend or fold. Fundamentally, she was serious and formal. So a smile, a compliment or a caress from her were coins of gold that were appreciated and saved as souvenirs forever. Coins she never wasted.

The ranch was big business. The family was large and problematic. She 18 ran her empire with a sure and firm hand. Never was there any doubt about where her affairs were going nor who held the reins.

That first memory: the portrait. I can see her at this moment as if she 19

sus formas, una por una. La falda y el chal aleteando agitados detrás. Los ojos puestos no sé donde. Los pensamientos fijos en no sé qué. Estatua animada. Alma petrificada.

Mi abuelo fumaba puros. El puro era el símbolo y la divisa del señor 20 feudal, del patrón. Cuando alguna vez la regalaba un puro al mayordomo o a alguno de los peones por impulso o como galardón por algo bien hecho, era de ver la transfiguración de los tíos. Chupar ese tabaco era beber de las fuentes de la autoridad. El puro daba categoría.

Dicen que cuando el abuelo murió la abuela encendía puros y los ponía 21 en los ceniceros por toda la casa. El aroma del tabaco llenaba la casa. Esto le daba a la viuda la ilusión de que su marido todavía andaba por la casa. Un sentimentalismo y romanticismo difíciles de imaginar antes.

Al pasar el tiempo, y después de tanto encender puros, parece que al fin 22 le entró el gusto. Mi abuela empezó a fumar puros. Al anochecer, todos los días, después de la comida, cuando los quehaceres del día habían terminado, se encerraba en su cuarto, se sentaba en su mecedora y encendía su puro.

Allí pasaba su largo rato. Los demás permanecíamos en la sala haciendo 23 vida de familia como si nada. Nadie se atrevió nunca a interrumpir su arbitraria y sagrada soledad. Nadie nunca hizo alusión a su extraordinaria costumbre.

El puro que antes había sido símbolo de autoridad ahora se había con- 24 vertido en instrumento afectivo. Estoy convencido que en la soledad y el silencio, con el olor y el sabor del tabaco, allí en el humo, mi abuela establecía alguna mística comunicación con mi abuelo. Creo que allí, a solas, se consiguió el matrimonio idílico, lleno de ternura, suavidad y dulzura, que no fue posible mientras él vivía. Sólo bastaba verle la cara enternecida y transfigurada a la abuelo cuando volvía a nosotros de esa extraña comunión, ver el cariño y mimo con que nos trataba a nosotros los niños.

Allí mismo, y en las mismas condiciones, se hicieron las decisiones, se 25 tomaron las determinaciones, que rigieron el negocio, que dirigieron a la familia. Allí, al sol o a la sombra de un viejo amor, ahora un eterno amor, se forjó la fuerza espiritual que mantuvo a mi abuela recta, alta y esbelta, una animada mujer de piedra, frente a los vientos y tormentas de su vida cabal y densa.

Cuando mis padres se casaron construyeron su casa al lado de la vieja 26 casona solariega. Yo crecí en la ventosa loma en el centro del valle de Las Nutrias, con los pinos en todos los horizontes, el arroyo lleno de nutrias, *boquinetes* y truchas, el chamizal lleno de conejos y coyotes, ganado en todas partes, ardillas y tecolotes en las caballerizas.

Crecí al lado y la distancia de mi abuela, entre tierno amor y reverente 27 temor.

Cuando yo tenía ocho años se decidió en la familia que nos mudaríamos 28 a Tierra Amarilla para que yo y mis hermanitos asistiéramos a la escuela. Todavía me arden los surcos que me dejaron las lágrimas en la cara y todavía recuerdo su sabor salado el día que abandonamos a mi abuela recta, alta y esbelta, agitando su pañuelo, con el viento en la frente en la loma en el fondo del valle.

were before my eyes. A black silhouette on a blue background. Straight, tall and slender. The wind of the hill cleaving her clothes to her body up front, outlining her forms, one by one. Her skirt and her shawl flapping in the wind behind her. Her eyes fixed I don't know where. Her thoughts fixed on I don't know what. An animated statue. A petrified soul.

My grandfather smoked cigars. The cigar was the symbol and the badge   20
of the feudal lord, the *patrón*. When on occasion he would give a cigar to the foreman or to one of the hands on impulse or as a reward for a task well done, the transfiguration of those fellows was something to see. To suck on that tobacco was to drink from the fountains of power. The cigar gave you class.

They say that when my grandfather died my grandmother would light   21
cigars and place them on ashtrays all over the house. The aroma of the tobacco filled the house. This gave the widow the illusion that her husband was still around. A sentimentalism and romanticism difficult to imagine before.

As time went on, and after lighting many a cigar, a liking for the cigars   22
seemed to sneak up on her. She began to smoke the cigars. At nightfall, every day, after dinner, when the tasks of the day were done, she would lock herself in her room, sit in her rocker and light her cigar.

She would spend a long time there. The rest of us remained in the living   23
room playing the family role as if nothing were amiss. No one ever dared interrupt her arbitrary and sacred solitude. No one ever mentioned her unusual custom.

The cigar that had once been a symbol of authority had now become an   24
instrument of love. I am convinced that in the solitude and in the silence, with the smell and taste of the tobacco, there in the smoke, my grandmother established some kind of mystical communication with my grandfather. I think that there, all alone, that idyllic marriage, full of tenderness, softness and sweetness was attained, not possible while he lived. It was enough to see the soft and transfigured face of the grandmother when she returned to us from her strange communion, to see the affection and gentleness with which she treated us kids.

Right there, and in those conditions, the decisions were made, the posi-   25
tions were taken that ran the business, that directed the family. There in the light or in the shade of an old love, now an eternal love, the spiritual strength was forged that kept my grandmother straight, tall and slender, a throbbing woman of stone, facing the winds and storms of her full life.

When my parents married they built their home next to the old family   26
house. I grew up on the windy hill in the center of the valley of Las Nutrias, with pine trees on all the horizons, with the stream full of beaver, trout and suckers, the sagebrush full of rabbits and coyotes, stock everywhere, squirrels and owls in the barn.

I grew up alongside my grandmother and far away from her, between   27
tender love and reverent fear.

When I was eight years old, it was decided in the family that we should   28
move to Tierra Amarilla so that my brothers and I could attend school. The

En Tierra Amarilla yo fui un antisocial. Habiendo crecido solo, yo no 29
sabía jugar con otros niños. Jugaba con mis perros. A pesar de esto me fue bien
en la escuela y un día llegué a los quince años, más o menos adaptado a mis
circunstancias.

Un día de invierno nos preparamos todos para ir a Las Nutrias. Todos 30
con mucha ilusión. Ir a visitar a la abuela siempre era un acontecimiento. La
familia iría conmigo en el automóvil. Mi padre seguiría con los trineos y los
peones. Se trataba de ir a cortar postes.

Todo el camino cantamos. Es decir, hasta que llegamos a donde se aparta 31
el camino. Había mucha nieve. La carretera estaba barrida pero el caminito a
Las Nutrias no.

Le puse cadenas al coche y nos lanzamos a ese mar blanco. Ahora callados 32
y aprehensivos. Pronto nos atascamos. Después de mucha pala y mucho empujar
seguimos, sólo para volvernos a atascar más allá, una y otra vez.

Estábamos todos vencidos y congelados y el día se nos iba. Por fin subimos 33
la ladera y salimos del pinar de donde se divisaba la casa de mi abuela. Nos
volvimos a atascar. Esta vez no hubo manera de sacar el coche. Mi madre y los
niños siguieron a pie, abriéndose camino por dos pies y medio de nieve blanda.
Mi hermano Roberto iba tirando un pequeño trinco con mi hermanita Carmen.
Ya estaba oscureciendo. Un viaje de nueve millas nos había tomado casi todo
el día.

Pronto vino Juan Maes, el mayordomo, con un tiro de caballos y me llevó 34
arrastrando hasta la casa.

Apenas había entrado y estaba deshelándome, mi madre me había sacado 35
ropa seca para que me pusiera, cuando vimos las luces de un coche en el pinar.
Lo vimos acercarse lentamente, vacilando a ratos. Era más fácil ahora, ya el
camino estaba abierto.

Era mi tío Juan Antonio. Al momento que entró todos supimos que traía 36
muy malas noticias. Hubo un silencio espantoso. Nadie dijo nada. Todos mu
dos y tiesos como muñecos de madera en una escena grotesca.

Mi madre rompió el silencio con un desgarrador "¡Alejandro!" 37

Mi tío asintió con la cabeza. 38

—¿Qué pasó?—Era mi abuela. 39

—Alejandro. Un accidente. 40

—¿Qué pasó? 41

—Un disparo accidental. Estaba limpiando el rifle. Se le fue un tiro. 42

—¿Cómo está? 43

—Está mal, pero saldrá bien. 44

Todos supimos que mentía, que mi padre estaba muerto. En la cara se le 45
veía. Mi madre lloraba desaforadamente, en punto de ponerse histérica. Nosotros la abrazábamos, todos llorando. Mi tío con el sombrero en la mano sin
saber qué hacer. Había venido otro hombre con él. Nadie le había hecho caso.

Entonces entró mi abuela en acción. Ni una sola lágrima. La voz firme. 46
Los ojos espadas que echaban rayos. Tomó control total de la situación.

furrows the tears left on my face still burn, and I still remember their salty taste the day we left my straight, tall and slender grandmother, waving her handkerchief, with the wind on her face on the hill in the center of the valley.

In Tierra Amarilla I was antisocial. Having grown up alone, I didn't know 29 how to play with other children. I played with my dogs instead. In spite of this I did all right in school, and one day I was fifteen years old, more or less adapted to my circumstances.

One winter day we got ready to go to Las Nutrias. All with a great deal 30 of anticipation. To visit my grandmother was always an event. The family would go with me in the car. My father with the sleigh and the hired hands. It was a matter of cutting fence posts.

We sang all the way. That is until we had to leave the highway. There 31 was a lot of snow. The highway had been cleared, but the little road to Las Nutrias hadn't.

I put chains on the car, and we set out across the white sea. Now we 32 were quiet and apprehensive. We soon got stuck. After a lot of shoveling and much pushing we continued, only to get stuck again farther on, again and again.

We were all exhausted and cold, and the day was drifting away. Finally 33 we climbed the hill and came out of the pine grove from where we could see my grandmother's house. We got stuck again. This time there was no way of pulling the car out. My mother and the children continued on foot, opening their way through two and a half feet of soft snow. My brother Roberto pulled my sister Carmen on a small sled. It was getting dark. A trip of nine miles had taken us all day.

Juan Maes, the foreman quickly came with a team of horses and pulled 34 me home.

I had barely come in and was warning up. My mother had brought me 35 dry clothes, when we saw the lights of a car in the pine grove. We saw it approach slowly, hesitating from time to time. It was easier now; the road was now open.

It was my uncle Juan Antonio. The moment he came in we all knew he 36 had bad news. There was a frightening silence. No one said a word. Everyone silent and stiff like wooden figures in a grotesque scene.

My mother broke the silence with a heartbreaking "Alejandro!" 37
My uncle nodded. 38
"What happened?" It was my grandmother. 39
"Alejandro. An accident." 40
"What happened?" 41
"An accidental shot. He was cleaning a rifle. The gun went off." 42
"How is he?" 43
"Not good, but he'll pull through." 44
We all knew he was lying, that my father was dead. We could see it in 45 his face. My mother was crying desperately, on the verge of becoming hysterical. We put our arms around her, crying. My uncle with his hat in his hands not

Entró en una santa ira contra mi padre. Le llamó ingrato, sinvergüenza,   47
indino (indigno), mal agradecido. Un torrente inacabable de insultos. Una furia
soberbia. Entretanto tomó a mi madre en sus brazos y la mecía y la acariciaba
como a un bebé. Mi madre se entregó y poco a poco se fue apaciguando. También
nosotros. La abuela que siempre habló poco, esa noche no dejó de hablar.

Yo no comprendí entonces. Sentí un fuerte resentimiento. Quise defender   48
a mi padre. No lo hice porque a mi abuela no la contradecía nadie. Mucho
menos yo. Es que ella comprendió muchas cosas.

La situación de mi madre rayaba en la locura. Había que hacer algo. La   49
abuela creó una situación dramática tan violenta que nos obligó a todos, a mi
madre especialmente, a fijarnos en ella y distraernos de la otra situación hasta
poder acostumbrarnos poco a poco a la tragedia. No dejó de hablar para no
dejar un solo intersticio por donde podría meterse la desesperación. Hablando,
hablando, entre arrullos e injurias consiguió que mi madre, en su estado vulnerable, se quedara dormida a las altas horas de la madrugada. Como tantas
veces, la abuela había dominado la realidad difícil en que vivió.

Comprendió otra cosa. Que a mi padre no se le iban disparos accidentales.   50
Las dificultades para enterrarlo en sagrado confirmaron el instinto infalible de
la dama y dueña de Las Nutrias. Todo afirmó el talento y vivencias de la madre
del Clan Turrriaga.

Pasaron algunos años. Ya yo era profesor. Un día volvímos a visitar a la   51
abuela. Veníamos muy contentos. Ya lo he dicho, visitarla era un acontecimiento. Las cosas habían cambiado mucho. Con la muerte de mi padre la abuela
se deshizo de todo el ganado. Con el ganado se fueron los peones. Sólo la
acompañaban y la cuidaban Rubel y su familia.

Cuando nos apartamos de la carretera y tomamos el poco usado y muy   52
ultrajado camino lleno de las acostumbradas zanjas la antigua ilusión nos em-
bargaba. De pronto vimos una columna de humo negro que se alzaba más allá
de la loma. Mi hermana gritó:

—¡La casa de mi granma!   53

—No seas tonta. Estarán quemando hierbas, o chamizas o basura.   54

Eso dije pero me quedó el recelo. Pisé el acelerador fuerte.   55

Cuando salimos del pinar vimos que sólo quedaban los escombros de la   56
casa de la abuela. Llegué a matacaballo. La encontramos rodeada de las pocas
cosas que se pudieron salvar. Rodeada también de todos los vecinos de los
ranchos de toda la región que acudieron cuando vieron el humo.

No sé qué esperaba, pero no me sorprendió hallarla dirigiendo todas las   57
actividades, dando órdenes. Nada de lágrimas, nada de quejumbres, nada le
lamentos.

—Dios da y Dios quita, mi hijito. Bendito sea su dulce nombre.   58

Yo sí me lamenté. Las arañas de cristal, deshechas. Los magníficos juegos   59
de mesas y aguamaniles con sobres de mármol, los platones y jarrones que había
en cada dormitorio, destruídos. Los muebles, traídos desde Kansas, hechos

knowing what to do. Another man had come with him. No one had noticed him.

That is when my grandmother went into action. Not a single tear. Her voice steady. Her eyes two flashing spears. She took complete control of the situation.   46

She went into a holy fury against my father. She called him ungrateful, shameless, unworthy. An inexhaustible torrent of insults. A royal rage. In the meantime she took my mother in her arms and rocked her and caressed her like a baby. My mother submitted and settled down slowly. We did too. My grandmother who always spoke so little did not stop talking that night.   47

I didn't understand then. I felt a violent resentment. I wanted to defend my father. I didn't because no one ever dared to talk back to my grandmother. Much less me. The truth is that she understood many things.   48

My mother was on the verge of madness. Something had to be done.   49

My grandmother created a situation, so violent and dramatic, that it forced us all, my mother especially, to fix our attention on her and shift it away from the other situation until we could get used to the tragedy little by little. She didn't stop talking in order not to allow a single aperture through which despair might slip in. Talking, talking, between abuse and lullaby, she managed that my mother, in her vulnerable state, fall asleep in the wee hours of the morning. As she had done so many times in the past, my grandmother had dominated the harsh reality in which she lived.   50

She understood something else. That my father didn't fire a rifle accidentally. The trouble we had to bury him on sacred ground confirmed the infallible instinct of the lady and mistress of Las Nutrias. Everything confirmed the talent and substance of the mother of the Turriaga clan.   51

The years went by. I was now a professor. One day we returned to visit the grandmother. We were very happy. I've said it before, visiting her was an event. Things had changed a great deal. With the death of my father, my grandmother got rid of all the stock. The ranch hands disappeared with the stock. Rubel and his family were the only ones who remained to look after her. 52

When we left the highway and took the little used and much abused road full of the accustomed ruts, the old memories took possession of us. Suddenly we saw a column of black smoke rising beyond the hill. My sister shouted.   53

"Grandma's house!"   54

"Don't be silly. They must be burning weeds, or sage brush, or trash."   55
I said this but apprehension gripped me. I stepped hard on the gas.

When we came out of the pine grove, we saw that only ruins remained of the house of the grandmother. I drove like a madman. We found her surrounded by the few things that were saved. Surrounded also by neighbors of all the ranches in the region who rushed to help when they saw the smoke.   56

I don't know what I expected but it did not surprise me to find her directing all the activities, giving orders. No tears, no whimpers, no laments.   57

carbón. Las colchas de encaje, de crochet, bordadas. Los retratos, las fotos, los recuerdos de la familia.

Ironía de ironías. Había un frasco de agua bendita en la ventana del desván. 60 Los rayos del sol, penetrando a través del agua, lo convirtieron en una lupa, se concentró el calor y el fuego en un solo punto e incendiaron los papeles viejos que había allí. Y se quemaron todos los santos, las reliquias y relicarios, el altar al Santo Niño de Atocha, las ramas del Domingo de Ramos. Toda la protección celestial se quemó.

Esa noche nos recogimos en la casa que antes había sido nuestra. Me 61 pareció mi abuela más pequeña, un poco apagada, hasta un poco dócil, "Lo que tú quieras, mi hijito." Esto me entristeció.

Después de la cena mi abuela desapareció. La busqué aprehensivo. La 62 encontré donde bien me habría sospechado. En la punta de la loma. Perfilada por la luna. El viento en la frente. La falda agitándos en el viento. La ví crecer. Y fue como antes era: recta, alta y esbelta.

Ví encenderse la brasa de su puro. Estaba con mi abuelo, el travieso, 63 atrevido y pendenciero. Allí se harían las decisiones, se tomarían las determinaciones. Estaba recobrando sus fuerzas espirituales. Mañana sería otro día pero mi abuela seguiría siendo la misma. Y me alegré.◆

"God gives and God takes away, my son. Blessed be His Holy Name." 58

I did lament. The crystal chandeliers, wrecked. The magnificent sets of 59
tables and washstands with marble tops. The big basins and water jars in every
bedroom, destroyed. The furniture brought from Kansas, turned to ashes. The
bedspreads of lace, crochet, embroidery. The portraits, the pictures, the memories of a family.

Irony of ironies. There was a jar of holy water on the window sill in the 60
attic. The rays of the sun, shining through the water, converted into a mag-
nifying glass. The heat and the fire concentrated on a single spot and set on
fire some old papers there. And all of the saints, the relics, the shrines, the
altar to the Santo Niño de Atocha, the palms of Palm Sunday, all burned up.
All of the celestial security went up in smoke.

That night we gathered in what had been our old home. My grandmother 61
seemed smaller to me, a little subdued, even a little docile: "Whatever you say,
my son." This saddened me.

After supper my grandmother disappeared. I looked for her apprehen- 62
sively. I found her where I could very well have suspected. At the top of the
hill. Profiled by the moon. The wind in her face. Her skirt flapping in the
wind. I saw her grow. And she was what she had always been: straight, tall
and slender.

I saw the ash of her cigar light up. She was with my grandfather, the 63
wicked one, the bold one, the quarrelsome one. Now the decisions would be
made, the positions would be taken. She was regaining her spiritual strength.
Tomorrow would be another day, but my grandmother would continue being
the same one. And I was happy.◆

◆ Responding

1. Ulibarrí's verbal portrait of his grandmother draws on significant details that
   reveal her personality and character. Working individually or in a group,
   review the information he gives and compile a list of his grandmother's
   character traits. Compare your list with those of other groups.

2. Ulibarrí's grandmother had a special significance in his life. Write a character
   sketch of someone you admire who has influenced you. Through your selection of details, try to illustrate and dramatize why you regard this person
   as a good role model.

3. Write an essay supporting Ulibarrí's statement that his grandmother "had dominated the harsh reality in which she lived."

4. Write an essay arguing that the grandmother is both very dominating and very sentimental. Support your argument with evidence from the reading.

ARTURO ISLAS

Arturo Islas was born in El Paso, Texas, in 1938. He earned his bachelor's, master's, and doctoral degrees from Stanford University, where he has served on the faculty since 1970 and is currently a professor of English. In addition to contributing several essays, short stories, poems, and reviews to literary journals, Islas has published two novels, The Rain God *(1984) and* Migrant Souls *(1988). He has been awarded the Woodrow Wilson Fellowship (1963–64), the Howard Foundation Fellowship (1973–74), the Carnegie Mellon Faculty Award (1974), and the Dinkelspiel Award for Outstanding Service to Undergraduate Education (1976).*

The following excerpt, from Migrant Souls, *uses the backdrop of the Thanksgiving holiday celebration to examine issues of heritage and cultural tradition. As it explores the relationship between names and cultural values, it asks us to consider the ways in which some cultural traditions seem to carry greater weight than others.*

◆ *From* MIGRANT SOULS ◆

After the war, their mother took to raising chickens and pigeons in order to save money. Josie saw their neighbors enjoying life and thought that her mother had gone crazy. Eduviges had even bought a live duck from God knows where and kept it until the Garcias next door began complaining about all the racket it made at night. Josie and Serena had become attached to it, so much so that when it appeared piecemeal in a *mole poblano,* both of them refused to eat it. 1

"It's too greasy," Josie said, holding back her tears and criticizing her mother's cooking instead. 2

"Then let your sisters have your portion. Eat the beans," Sancho said from behind the hunting magazine that was his bible. 3

"I don't want it," Serena said, her tears falling unchecked. "Poor don Pato. He didn't make that much noise. The Garcias are louder than he ever was." 4

Ofelia was dutifully, even happily, chewing away. "I think he's delicious," she said. 5

Josie glared at her and held her hands tightly under the table and away from the knife next to her plate. In her mind, she was dumping its contents into Ofelia's lap. 6

Eduviges stared at her husband until the silence made him glance up from his magazine. "Well," she said, "if your little darlings won't eat what I raise, slaughter, and cook with my own hands, let them live on beans. I know Josie likes chicken well enough. And pigeon stew. From now on, she can do the killing before she eats them. Let's see how she likes it." 7

And then speaking to Josie directly, she added, "This is not a restaurant, 8 young lady. You have to eat what I serve you. And that's that." She said nothing to Serena, who was blowing her nose loudly into a paper napkin and not glaring at her in an accusing way.

"Leave her alone," Sancho said, meaning Josie. "The child liked that dumb 9 duck, that's all. She doesn't have to eat him if she doesn't want to." These words caused Josie to leave the table in tears, followed by Serena, now struck by another fit of weeping. Ofelia kept eating and asked that her sisters' portions be passed to her.

"Of course, darling," Eduviges said. Sancho returned to his magazine. 10

In their bedroom, Josie and Serena held each other until they stopped 11 crying. "I'll never forgive her for killing him," Josie said.

"Oh, Josie, don't say that. I was crying because of the way you were 12 looking at Ofelia and Mother. We can always get another duck."

After don Pato's transformation, their mother stuck to chickens and pi- 13 geons. Atoning for her harshness toward Josie, she cooked omelets and looked the other way whenever Serena slipped Josie a piece of chicken. But for Thanksgiving in 1947, Eduviges, in a fit of guilt, decided to bake a turkey with all the trimmings. She had memorized the recipes in the glossy American magazines while waiting her turn at the Safeway checkout counter.

Because the girls were in public school and learning about North American 14 holidays and customs, Eduviges thought her plan would please them. It did and even Josie allowed her mother to embrace her in that quick, embarrassed way she had of touching them. As usual, Sancho had no idea why she was going to such lengths preparing for a ritual that meant nothing to him.

"I don't see why we can't have the enchiladas you always make," he said. 15 "I don't even like turkey. Why don't you let me bring you a nice, fat pheasant from the Chihuahua mountains? At least it'll taste like something. Eating turkey is going to turn my girls into little *gringos*. Is that what you want?"

"Oh, Daddy, please! Everybody else is going to have turkey." The girls, 16 wearing colored paper headdresses they had made in art class, were acting out the Pocahontas story and reciting from "Hiawatha" in a hodgepodge of Indian sentiment that forced Sancho to agree in order to keep them quiet.

"All right, all right," he said, "Just stop all the racket, please. And Serena, 17 *querida*, don't wear that stuff outside the house or they'll pick you up and send you to a reservation. That would be okay with me, but your mother wouldn't like it."

Serena and Josie gave each other knowing glances. "They" were the *migra*, 18 who drove around in their green vans, sneaked up on innocent dark-skinned people, and deported them. Their neighbor down the block—Benito Cruz, who was lighter-skinned than Serena and did not look at all like an Indian—had been picked up three times already, detained at the border for hours, and then released with the warning that he was to carry his identification papers at all times. That he was an American citizen did not seem to matter to the immigration officers.

The Angel children were brought up on as many deportation stories as 19
fairy tales and family legends. The latest border incident had been the discovery
of twenty-one young Mexican males who had been left to asphyxiate in an
airtight boxcar on their way to pick cotton in the lower Rio Grande Valley.

When they read the newspaper articles about how the men died, both 20
Josie and Serena thought of the fluttering noises made by the pigeons their
mother first strangled and then put under a heavy cardboard box for minutes
that seemed eternal to the girls. They covered their ears to protect their souls
from the thumping and scratching noises of the doomed birds.

Even their mother had shown sympathy for the Mexican youths, especially 21
when it was learned that they were not from the poorest class. "I feel very bad
for their families," she said, "Their mothers must be in agony."

What about their fathers? Josie felt like asking but did not. Because of the 22
horror she imagined they went through, Josie did not want to turn her own
feelings for the young men into yet another argument with her mother about
"wetbacks" or about who did and did not "deserve" to be in the United States.

In the first semester of seventh grade, Josie had begun to wonder why 23
being make-believe North American Indians seemed to be all right with their
mother. "Maybe it was because those Indians spoke English," Josie said to
Serena. Mexican Indians were too close to home and the truth, and the way
Eduviges looked at Serena in her art class getup convinced Josie she was on the
right track.

That year on the Saturday before Thanksgiving, their mother and father 24
took them across the river in search of the perfect turkey. Sancho borrowed
his friend Tacho Morales' pickup and they drove down the valley to the Zaragoza
crossing. It was closer to the ranch where Eduviges had been told the turkeys
were raised and sold for practically nothing. Josie and Serena sat in the front
seat of the pickup with their father. Eduviges and Ofelia followed them in the
Chevy in case anything went wrong.

Sancho was a slower, more patient driver than their mother, who turned 25
into a speed demon with a sharp tongue behind the wheel. More refined than
her younger sisters, Ofelia was scandalized by every phrase that came out of
Eduviges' mouth when some sorry driver from Chihuahua or New Mexico got
in her way.

"Why don't they teach those imbecilic cretins how to drive?" she said 26
loudly in Spanish, window down and honking. Or, "May all your teeth fall
out but one and may that ache until the day you die" to the man who pulled
out in front of her without a signal.

Grateful that her mother was being good for once and following slowly 27
and at a safe distance behind the pickup, Ofelia dozed, barely aware of the clear
day so warm for November. Only the bright yellow leaves of the cottonwood

trees reminded her that it was autumn. They clung to the branches and vibrated in the breeze, which smelled of burning mesquite and Mexican alders. As they followed her father away from the mountains and into the valley, Ofelia began to dream they were inside one of Mama Chona's Mexican blue clay bowls, suspended in midair while the sky revolved around them.

To Josie and Serena, it seemed their father was taking forever to get to where they were going. "Are we there yet?" they asked him until he told them that if they asked again, he would leave them in the middle of nowhere and not let their mother rescue them. The threat only made them laugh more and they started asking him where the middle of nowhere was until he, too, laughed with them. 28

"The middle of nowhere, smart alecks, is at the bottom of the sea and so deep not even the fish go there," Sancho said, getting serious about it. 29

"No, no," Serena said, "It's in the space between two stars and no planets around." 30

"I already said the middle of nowhere is in Del Sapo, Texas," Josie said, not wanting to get serious. 31

"I know, I know. It's in the Sahara Desert where not even the tumbleweeds will grow," their father said. 32

"No, Daddy. It's at the top of Mount Everest." Serena was proud of the B she had gotten for her report on the highest mountain in the world. They fell silent and waited for Josie to take her turn. 33

"It's here," Josie said quietly and pointed to her heart. 34

"Oh, for heaven's sake, Josie, don't be so dramatic. You don't even know what you are saying," Serena said. Their father changed the subject. 35

When they arrived at the ranch, he told Eduviges and the girls that the worst that could happen on their return was that the turkey would be taken away from them. But the girls, especially, must do and say exactly as he instructed them. 36

Their mother was not satisfied with Sancho's simple directions and once again told them about the humiliating body search her friend from New Mexico, *la señora* Moulton, had been subjected to at the Santa Fe Street bridge. She had just treated her daughter Ethel and her granddaughters, Amy and Mary Ann, to lunch at the old Central Cafe in Juarez. When *la señora* had been asked her citizenship, she had replied in a jovial way, "Well, what do I look like, sir?" 37

They made her get out of the car, led her to a special examining cell, ordered her to undress, and made her suffer unspeakable mortifications while her relatives waited at least four hours in terror, wondering if they would ever see her again or be allowed to return to the country of their birth. Then, right on cue, Josie and Serena said along with Eduviges, "And they were Anglos and blond!" 38

While their parents were bargaining for the bird, the girls looked with awe upon the hundreds of adult turkeys kept inside four large corrals. As they 39 walked by each enclosure, one of the birds gobbled and the rest echoed its call until the racket was unbearable. Serena was struck by an attack of giggles.

"They sure are stupid," Josie said in Spanish to their Mexican guide. 40

"They really are," he said with a smile. "When it rains, we have to cover 41 the coops of the younger ones so they won't drown." He was a dark red color and very shy. Josie liked him instantly.

"How can they drown?" Serena asked him. "The river is nowhere near 42 here. Does it flood?"

"No," the young man said, looking away from them. "Not from the Rio 43 Bravo. From the rain itself. They stretch their necks, open their beaks wide and let it pour in until they drown. They keel over all bloated. That's how stupid they are." He bent his head back and showed them as they walked by an enclosure. "Gobble, gobble," the guide called and the turkeys answered hysterically.

Josie and Serena laughed all the way back to the pickup. Ofelia had not 44 been allowed to join them because of the way their mother thought the guide was looking at her. She was dreaming away in the backseat of the Chevy while their father struggled to get the newly bought and nervous turkey into a slatted crate. Eduviges was criticizing every move he made. At last, the creature was in the box and eerily silent.

"Now remember, girls," Sancho said, wiping his face, "I'll do all the 45 talking at the bridge. You just say 'American' when the time comes. Not another word, you hear? Think about Mrs. Moulton, Josie," He gave her a wink.

The turkey remained frozen inside the crate. Sancho lifted it onto the 46 pickup, covered it with a yellow plastic tablecloth they used on picnics, and told Serena to sit on top of it with her back against the rear window.

"Serena," he said, "I'd hate to lose you because of this stupid bird, but 47 if you open your mouth except to say 'American,' I won't be responsible for what happens. Okay?" He kissed her on the cheek as if in farewell forever, Josie thought, looking at them from the front seat. She was beginning to wish they had not begged so successfully for a traditional North American ceremony. Nothing would happen to Ofelia, of course. She was protected in their mother's car and nowhere near the turkey. Josie felt that Serena was in great peril and made up her mind to do anything to keep her from harm.

On the way to the bridge, Josie made the mistake of asking her father if 48 they were aliens. Sancho put his foot on the brake so hard that Eduviges almost rear-ended the truck. He looked at Josie very hard and said, "I do not ever want to hear you use that word in my presence again. About anybody. We are not aliens. We are American citizens of Mexican heritage. We are proud of both countries and have never and will never be that word you just said to me."

"Well," Josie said. Sancho knew she was not afraid of him. He pulled the 49 truck away from the shoulder and signaled for his wife to continue following them. "That's what they call Mexican people in all the newspapers. And Kathy

Jarvis at school told me real snotty at recess yesterday that we were nothing but a bunch of resident aliens."

After making sure Eduviges was right behind them, Sancho said in a 50 calmer, serious tone, "Josie, I'm warning you. I do not want to hear those words again. Do you understand me?"

"I'm only telling you what Kathy told me. What did she mean? Is she 51 right?"

"Kathy Jarvis is an ignorant little brat. The next time she tells you that, 52 you tell her that Mexican and Indian people were in this part of the country long before any *gringos*, Europeans (he said 'Yurrup-beans') or anyone else decided it was theirs. That should shut her up. If it doesn't, tell her those words are used by people who think Mexicans are not human beings. That goes for the newspapers, too. They don't think anyone is human." She watched him look straight ahead, then in the rearview mirror, then at her as he spoke.

"Don't you see, Josie? When people call Mexicans those words, it makes 53 it easier for them to deport or kill them. Aliens come from outer space." He paused. "Sort of like your mother's family, the blessed Angels, who think they come from heaven. Don't tell her I said that."

Before he made that last comment, Josie was impressed by her father's 54 tone. Sancho seldom became that passionate in their presence about any issue. He laughed at the serious and the pompous and especially at religious fanatics.

During their aunt Jesus Maria's visits, the girls and their cousins were 55 sent out of the house in the summer or to the farthest room away from the kitchen in the winter so that they would not be able to hear her and Sancho arguing about God and the Church. Unnoticed, the children sneaked around the house and crouched in the honeysuckle under the kitchen window, wide open to the heat of July. In horror and amusement, they listened to Jesus Maria tell Sancho that he would burn in hell for all eternity because he did not believe in an afterlife and dared to criticize the infallibility of the Pope.

"It's because they're afraid of dying that people make up an afterlife to 56 believe in," Sancho said.

"That's not true. God created Heaven, Hell, and Purgatory before He 57 created man. And you are going to end up in Hell if you don't start believing what the Church teaches us." Jesus Maria was in her glory defending the teachings of Roman Catholicism purged by the fires of the Spanish Inquisition.

"Oh, Jessie—" he began. 58

"Don't call me that. My name is Jesus Maria and I am proud of it." She 59 knew the children were listening.

"Excuse me, Jesus Maria," he said with a flourish. "I just want to point 60 out to you that it's hotter here in Del Sapo right now than in hell." He saw her bristle but went on anyway. "Haven't you figured it out yet? This is hell and heaven and purgatory right here. How much worse, better, or boring can the afterlife be?" Sancho was laughing at his own insight.

"If you are going to start joking about life-and-death matters, I simply 61 won't talk about anything serious with you again," their aunt said. They knew she meant it. "I, like the Pope, am fighting for your everlasting soul, Sancho. If I did not love you because you are my sister's husband, I would not be telling you these things."

"Thank you, Jessie. I appreciate your efforts and love. But the Pope is only a man. He is not Christ. Don't you read history? All most popes have cared about is money and keeping the poor in rags so that they can mince about in gold lamé dresses." 62

"Apostate!" their aunt cried. 63

"What's that?" Serena whispered to Josie. 64

"I don't know but it sounds terrible. We'll look it up in the dictionary as soon as they stop." They knew the arguing was almost over when their aunt began calling their father names. Overwhelmed by the smell of the honeysuckle, the children ran off to play kick the can. Later, when Josie looked up the word "apostate," she kept its meaning to herself because she knew that Serena believed in an afterlife and would be afraid for her father. 65

That one word affected her father more than another was a mystery to Josie. She loved words and believed them to be more real than whatever they described. In her mind, she, too, suspected that she was an apostate but, like her father, she did not want to be an alien. 66

"All right, Daddy, I promise I won't say that word again. And I won't tell Mother what you said about the Angels." 67

They were now driving through the main streets of Juarez, and Sancho was fighting to stay in his lane. "God, these Mexicans drive like your mother," he said with affection. 68

At every intersection, young Indian women with babies at their breast stretched out their hands. Josie was filled with dread and pity. One of the women knocked on her window while they waited for the light to change. She held up her baby and said, "*Señorita, por favor. Dinero para el niño.*" Her hair was black and shiny and her eyes as dark as Josie's. The words came through the glass in a muted, dreamlike way. Silent and unblinking, the infant stared at Josie. She had a quarter in her pocket. 69

"Don't roll down the window or your mother will have a fit," Sancho said. He turned the corner and headed toward the river. The woman and child disappeared. Behind them, Eduviges kept honking almost all the way to the bridge. 70

"I think it was blind," Josie said. Her father did not answer and looked straight ahead. 71

The traffic leading to the declaration points was backed up several blocks, and the stop-and-go movement as they inched their way to the American side was more than Josie could bear. She kept looking back at Serena, who sat like a *Virgen de Guadalupe* statue on her yellow plastic-covered throne. 72

Knowing her sister, Josie was certain that Serena was going to free the turkey, jump out of the truck with it, gather up the beggarly women and 73 children, and disappear forever into the sidestreets and alleys of Juarez. They drove past an old Indian woman, her long braids silver gray in the sun, begging in front of Curley's Club. And that is how Josie imagined Serena years from that day—an ancient and withered creature, bare feet crusted with clay, too old to recognize her little sister. The vision made her believe that the middle of nowhere was exactly where she felt it was. She covered her chest with her arms.

"What's the matter? Don't tell me you're going to be sick," her father said. 74

"No. I'm fine. Can't you hurry?" 75

Seeing the fear in her face, Sancho told her gently that he had not yet figured out how to drive through cars without banging them up. Josie smiled and kept her hands over her heart. 76

When they approached the border patrolman's station, the turkey began gobbling away. "Oh, no," Josie cried and shut her eyes in terror for her sister. 77

"Oh, shit," her father said. "I hate this god-damned bridge." At that moment, the officer stuck his head into the pickup and asked for their citizenship. 78

"American," said Sancho. 79

"American," said Josie. 80

"Anything to declare? Any liquor or food?" he asked in an accusing way. While Sancho was assuring him that there was nothing to declare, the turkey gobbled again in a long stream of high-pitched gurgles that sent shivers up and down Josie's spine. She vowed to go into the cell with Serena when the search was ordered. 81

"What's that noise?" the patrolman wanted to know. Sancho shrugged and gave Josie and then the officer a look filled with the ignorance of the world. 82

Behind them, Serena began gobbling along with the bird and it was hard for them to tell one gobble from the another. Their mother pressed down on the horn of the Chevy and made it stick. Eduviges was ready to jump out of the car and save her daughter from a fate worse than death. In the middle of the racket, the officer's frown was turning into anger and he started yelling at Serena. 83

"American!" she yelled back and gobbled. 84

"What have you got there?" The officer pointed to the plastic-covered crate. 85

"It's a turkey," Serena shouted. "It's American, too." She kept gobbling along with the noise of the horn. Other drivers had begun honking with impatience. 86

The patrolman looked at her and yelled, "Sure it is! Don't move," he shouted toward Sancho. 87

Eduviges had opened the hood and was pretending not to know what to do. Rushing toward the officer, she grabbed him by the sleeve and pulled him away from the pickup. Confused by the din, he made gestures that Sancho took as permission to drive away. "Relax, *señora*. Please let go of my arm." 88

In the truck, Sancho was laughing like a maniac and wiping the tears and 89
his nose on his sleeve. "Look at that, Josie. The guy is twice as big as your
mother."

She was too scared to laugh and did not want to look. Several blocks into 90
South Del Sapo, she was still trembling. Serena kept on gobbling in case they
were being followed by the *migra* in unmarked cars.

Fifteen minutes later, Eduviges and Ofelia caught up with them on Ala- 91
meda Street. Sancho signaled his wife to follow him into the vacant lot next to
Don Luis Leal's Famous Tex-Mex Diner. They left the turkey unattended and
silent once more.

"Dumb bird," Sancho said. With great ceremony, he treated them to 92
menudo and *gorditas* washed down with as much Coca-Cola as they could
drink. ◆

◆ Responding

1. Compare the mother's attitudes toward American Indians and Mexican Indians. Why might someone find her statements ironic? Do you think her
views are widespread in American society?

2. Explain Sancho's reaction to the term "alien." How does he define the term,
and why is it so offensive to him? Write an essay explaining why his reaction
is or is not excessive. Or write an essay speculating about Sancho's reaction
to Mora's poems "Legal Alien" and "Illegal Alien"?

3. Working individually or in a group, list examples of the bicultural aspects
of the Angel family's lifestyle. Discuss the advantages and disadvantages of
being bicultural.

4. Taking the turkey over the border can be viewed as humorous, serious, or
even frightening, depending on your point of view. Imagine you are one of
the characters in the story and report the incident to a friend.

5. "The Angel children were brought up on as many deportation stories as fairy
tales and family legends." Discuss the possible psychological effects of such
stories on young children.

SANDRA CISNEROS

*Born in Chicago in 1954, the poet and short story writer Sandra Cisneros
earned her bachelor's degree from Loyola University of Chicago in 1976 and
her master's degree from the University of Iowa Writers Workshop in 1978.
While teaching at the Latino Youth Alternative High School and working
as a counselor in the Educational Opportunities Program at Loyola University
of Chicago during the early 1980s, she also served as an artist-in-residence
for the Illinois Arts Council, leading poetry workshops for younger students.
During the mid-1980s Cisneros held teaching and administrative positions
in Texas, teaching creative writing at the Austin Women's Peace House,
serving as an artist-in-the-schools, and directing the Guadalupe Cultural
Arts Center in San Antonio. Since 1988 she has been a guest writer in
residence at the University of California at Berkeley, the University of
California at Irvine, and the University of Michigan. In addition to contributing essays, fiction, and poetry to numerous journals, Cisneros has published two volumes of poetry,* Bad Boys *(1980) and* My Wicked Ways
(1987), and the fictional work The House on Mango Street *(1984).
Her writing has earned her numerous fellowships and awards, among them
the Roberta Holloway Lectureship at the University of California at Berkeley
(1988), two National Endowment for the Arts Creative Writing Fellowships
(1982 and 1988), and the Before Columbus Book Award (1985).*

*"Woman Hollering Creek," from a new collection of Cisneros's short stories
(forthcoming), explores the way in which one character looks for strength in
other people and in herself when she needs to make changes in her life.*

◆ WOMAN HOLLERING CREEK ◆

The day Don Serafín gave Juan Pedro Martínez Sánchez permission to take   1
Cleófilas Enriqueta DeLeón Hernández as his bride, across her father's threshold, over several miles of dirt road and several miles of paved, over one border
and beyond to a town four hours from the Rio Grande in the E.E.U.U., did
he divine already the morning his daughter would raise her hand over her eyes,
look south, and dream of returning to the chores that never ended, six good-
for-nothing brothers, and one old man's complaints.

He had said, after all, in the hubbub of parting: I am your father, I will   2
never abandon you. He *had* said that, hadn't he, when he hugged and then let
her go. But at the moment Cleófilas was busy looking for Chela, her maid of
honor, to fulfill their bouquet conspiracy. She would not remember her father's
parting words until three years had passed since holding that ragged face in her
hands. I am your father, I will never abandon you.

Only now that she was a mother, now when she and Juan Pedrito sat by   3 the creek's edge, did she remember. When a man and a woman love each other, how sometimes that love sours. But a parent's love for a child, a child's for its parents, was another thing entirely.

This is what Cleófilas thought evenings when Juan Pedro did not come 4 home, and she lay on her side of the bed listening to the hollow roar of the interstate, a distant dog barking, the pecan trees rustling like ladies in stiff petticoats—shh-shh-shh, shh-shh-shh, soothing her to sleep.

In the town where she grew up, there isn't very much to do except accompany 5 the aunts and godmothers to the house of one or the other to play cards. Or walk to the cinema to see this week's film again speckled and with one hair quivering annoyingly on the screen. Or to the center of town to order a milkshake that will appear in a day and a half as a pimple on her backside. Or to the girlfriend's house to watch the latest telenovela episode and try to copy the way the women comb their hair, wear their make-up.

But what Cleófilas has been waiting for, has been whispering and sighing 6 and giggling for, has been anticipating since she was old enough to lean against the window displays of gauze and butterflies and lace, is passion. Not the kind on the cover of the ¡Alarma! magazines, mind you, where the lover is photo-graphed with the bloody fork she used to salvage her good name. But passion in its purest crystalline essence. The kind the books and songs and telenovelas describe when one finds, finally, the great love of one's life, and does whatever one can, must do, at whatever the cost. Tú o Nadie. You or No One. The title of the current favorite telenovela. The beautiful Lucía Méndez having to put up with all kinds of hardships of the heart, separation and betrayal, and loving, always loving no matter what, because *that* is the most important thing, and did you see Lucía Méndez on the Bayer aspirin commercials, wasn't she lovely? Does she dye her hair do you think? Cleófilas is going to go to the farmacia and buy a hair rinse because her girlfriend Chela will apply it, it's not that difficult at all. Because you didn't watch last night's episode when Lucía con-fessed she loved him more than anyone in her life. In her life! And she sings the song "You or No One" in the beginning and end of the show. Tú o Nadie. Somehow one ought to live one's life like that, don't you think? You or no one. Because to suffer for love is good. The pain all sweet somehow, in the end.

Seguin. She had liked the sound of it. Far away and lovely. Not like 7 Monclova, Coahuila. Ugly.

Seguín, Tejas. A nice sterling ring to it. The tinkle of money. She would 8 get to wear outfits like the women on the tele, like Lucía Méndez. And have a lovely house, and wouldn't Chela be jealous.

And yes, they will drive all the way to Laredo to get her wedding dress. 9 That's what they say. Because Juan Pedro wants to get married right away, without a long engagement since he can't take off too much time from work. He has a very important position in Seguin with, with . . . a beer company I think. Or was it tires? Yes, he has to be back. So they will get married in the spring when he can take off work, and then they will drive off in his new pickup—did you see it?—to their new home in Seguin. Well, not exactly new, but they're going to repaint the house. You know newlyweds. New paint and new furniture. Why not? He can afford it. And later on add maybe a room or two for the children. May they be blessed with many. Well, you'll see. Cleófilas has always been so good with her sewing machine. A little whirr, whirr, whirr of the machine and ¡zas! Miracles. She's always been so clever that girl. Poor thing. And without even a mama to advise her on things like her wedding night. Well, may God help her. What with a father with a head like a burro, and those six clumsy brothers. Well, what do you think. Yes, I'm going to the wedding. Of course! The dress I want to wear just needs to be altered a teensy bit to bring it up to date. See, I saw a new style last night that I thought would suit me. Did you watch last night's episode of "And the Rich Also Cry"? Well, did you notice the dress the mother was wearing.

La mujer gritando. Such a funny name for such a lovely arroyo. Though no one could say whether the woman had hollered from anger or pain. The natives only knew the arroyo one crossed on the way to San Antonio, and then once again on the way back, was called Woman Hollering, a name no one from these parts questioned, little less understood. Pues, allá de los Indios, quien sabe— who knows, the townspeople shrugged, because it was of no concern to their lives how this trickle of water received its curious name. 10

What do you want to know for? Trini the laundromat attendant asked in the same gruff Spanish she always used whenever she gave Cleófilas change or yelled at her for something. First for putting too much soap in the machines. Later, for sitting on a washer. And still later, after Juan Pedrito was born, for not understanding that in this country you cannot let your baby walk around with no diaper and his pee-pee hanging out, it wasn't nice, entiendes? Pues. 11

How could Cleófilas explain to a woman like this why the name Woman Hollering fascinated her. Well, there was no sense talking to Trini. 12

On the other hand there were the neighbor ladies, one on either side of the house they rented near the arroyo. The woman Soledad on the left, the woman Dolores on the right. 13

The neighbor lady Soledad liked to call herself a widow though how she came to be one was a mystery. Her husband had either died, or run away with an ice house floozie, or simply had gone out for cigarettes one afternoon and never come back. It was hard to say which since Soledad, as a rule, didn't mention him. 14

In the other house lives la señora Dolores, kind and very sweet, but her house smelled too much of incense and candles from the altars that burned continuously in memory of two sons who had died in the last war and one husband who had died shortly after from grief. The neighbor lady Dolores divided her time between the memory of these men and her garden, famous 15 for its sunflowers—so tall they had to be supported with broom handles and old boards; red red cockscombs, fringed and bleeding a thick menstrual color; and, especially, roses whose sad scent reminded Cleófilas of the dead. Each Sunday la señora Dolores clipped the most beautiful of these flowers and arranged them on three modest headstones at the Seguin cemetery.

The neighbor ladies, Soledad, Dolores, they might've known once the name of the arroyo before it turned English but they did not know now. They were too busy remembering the men who had left either through choice or circumstance and would never come back. 16

Pain or rage, Cleófilas wondered when she drove over the bridge the first time as a newlywed and Juan Pedro had pointed it out. La mujer gritando, he had said, and she had laughed. Such a funny name for a creek so pretty and full of happily ever after. 17

The first time she had been so surprised she didn't cry out nor try to defend herself. She had always said she would strike back if a man, any man, were to touch her. 18

But when the moment came, and he slapped her once, and then again, and again, until the lip split and bled an orchid of blood, she didn't fight back, she didn't break into tears, she didn't run away as she imagined she might when she saw such things in the telenovelas. 19

In her own home her parents had never raised a hand to each other nor to their children. Although she admitted she may have been brought up a little leniently as an only daughter—la consentida, the princess—there were some things she would never tolerate. Ever. 20

Instead, when it happened the first time, when they were barely man and wife, she had been so stunned, it left her speechless, motionless, numb. She had done nothing but reach up to the heat on her mouth and stare at the blood on her hand as if even then she didn't understand. 21

She could think of nothing to say, said nothing. Just stroked the dark curls of the man who wept and would weep like a child, his tears of repentance and shame, this time and each. 22

The men at the ice house. From what she can tell, from the times during her first year when still a newlywed she is invited and accompanies her husband, sits mute beside their conversation, waits and sips a beer until it grows warm, twists a paper napkin into a knot, then another into a fan, one into a rose, nods her head, smiles, yawns, politely grins, laughs at the appropriate moments, leans against her husband's sleeve, tugs at his elbow, and finally becomes good at predicting where the talk will lead. 23

From this Cleófilas concludes each is nightly trying to find the truth lying at the bottom of the glass like a gold doubloon on the sea bottom. They want to tell each other what they want to tell themselves. But what is bumping like a helium balloon at the ceiling of the brain never finds its way out. It bubbles 24 and rises, it gurgles in the throat, it rolls across the surface of the tongue, and erupts from the lips—a belch.

If they are lucky, there are tears at the end of the long night. At any given   25
moment, the fists try to speak. They are dogs chasing their own tail before lying down to sleep, trying to find a way, a route, an out, and—finally—get some peace.

In the morning sometimes before he opens his eyes. Or after they have finished   26
loving. Or at times when he is simply across from her at the table putting pieces of food into his mouth and chewing. Cleófilas thinks, this is the man I have waited my whole life for.

Not that he isn't a good man. She has to remind herself why she loves   27
him when she changes the baby's Pampers, or when she mops the bathroom floor, or tries to make the curtains for the doorways without doors, or whiten the linen. Or wonder a little when he kicks the refrigerator and says he hates this shitty house and is going out where he won't be bothered with the baby's howling and her suspicious questions, and her requests to fix this and this and this because if she had any brains in her head she'd realize he's been up before the rooster earning his living to pay for the food in her belly and the roof over her head and would have to wake up again early the next day so why can't you just leave me in peace, woman.

He is not very tall, no, and he doesn't look like the men on the telenovelas.   28
His face still scarred from acne. And he has a bit of a belly from all the beer he drinks. Well, he's always been husky.

This man who farts and belches and snores as well as laughs and kisses   29
and holds her. Somehow this husband whose whiskers she finds each morning in the sink, whose shoes she must air each evening on the porch, this husband who cuts his fingernails in public, laughs loudly, curses like a man, and demands each course of dinner be served on a separate plate like at his mother's, as soon as he gets home, on time or late, and who doesn't care at all for music or telenovelas or romance or roses or the moon floating pearly over the arroyo, or through the bedroom window for that matter, shut the blinds and go back to sleep, this man, this father, this rival, this keeper, this lord, this master, this husband till kingdom come.

Slender like a hair. A washed cup set back on the shelf wrong side up. Her   30
lipstick, and body talc, and hair brush all arranged in the bathroom a different way.

No. Her imagination. The house the same as always. Nothing.   31

Coming home from the hospital with her new son, her husband. Some-   32
thing comforting in discovering her house slippers beneath the bed, the faded housecoat where she left it on the bathroom hook. Her pillow. Their bed.

Sweet sweet homecoming. Sweet as the scent of face powder in the air,   33
jasmine, sticky liquor.

Smudged fingerprint on the door. Crushed cigarette in a glass. Wrinkle 34
in the brain crumpling to a crease.

Sometimes she thinks of her father's house. But how could she go back there? 35
What a disgrace. What would the neighbors say? Coming home like that with
one baby on her hip and one in the oven. Where's your husband?

The town of gossips. The town of dust and despair. Which she has traded 36
for this town of gossips. This town of dust, despair. Houses further apart
perhaps, though no more privacy because of it. No leafy zocalo in the center
of the town, though the murmur of talk is clear enough all the same. No huddled
whispering on the church steps each Sunday. Because here the whispering
begins at sunset at the ice house instead.

This town with its silly pride for a bronze pecan the size of a baby carriage 37
in front of the city hall. T.V. repair shop, drug store, hardware, dry cleaners,
chiropractor's, liquor store, bail bonds, empty storefront and nothing, nothing,
nothing of interest. Nowhere one could walk to any rate. Because the towns
here are built so that you have to depend on husbands. Or you stay home. Or
you drive. If you're rich enough to own, allowed to drive, your own car.

There is no place to go. Unless one counts the neighbor ladies. Soledad 38
on one side, Dolores on the other. Or the creek.

Don't go out there after dark, mi'jita. Stay near the house. No es bueno 39
para la salud. Mala suerte. Bad luck. Mal aire. You'll get sick and the baby too.
You'll catch a fright wandering about in the dark, and then you'll see how right
we were.

The stream sometimes only a muddy puddle in the summer, though now 40
in the springtime, because of the rains, a good-size alive thing, a thing with a
voice all its own, all day and all night calling in its high, silver voice. Is it La
Llorona, the weeping woman? La Llorona who drowned her own children.
Perhaps La Llorona is the one they named the creek after, she thinks, remembering all the stories she learned as a child.

La Llorona calling to her. She is sure of it. Cleófilas sets the baby's Donald 41
Duck blanket on the grass. Listens. The day sky turning to night. The baby
pulling up fistfuls of grass and laughing. La Llorona. Wonders if something as
quiet as this drives a woman to the darkness under the trees.

What she needs is . . . and made a gesture as if to yank a woman's buttocks to 42
his groin. Maximiliano the foul-smelling fool from across the road said this and
set the men laughing, but Cleófilas just muttered *grosero* and went on washing
dishes.

She knew he said it not because it was true, but more because it was he 43
who needed to sleep with a woman, instead of drinking each night at the ice
house and stumbling home alone.

Maximiliano who was said to have killed his wife in an ice house brawl 44
when she came at him with a mop. I had to shoot, he had said, she was armed.

Their laughter outside the kitchen window. Her husband's, his friends'. 45
Manolo, Beto, Efrain, el Perico. Maximiliano.

Was Cleófilas just exaggerating as her husband always said? It seemed the 46
newspapers were full of such stories. This woman found on the side of the
interstate. This one pushed from a moving car. This one's cadaver, this one
unconscious, this one beaten blue. Her ex-husband, her husband, her lover,
her father, her brother, her uncle, her friend, her co-worker. Always. The
same grisly news in the pages of the dailies, She dunked a glass under the soapy
water for a moment—shivered.

He had thrown a book. Hers. From across the room. A hot welt across the 47
cheek. She could forgive that. But what stung more was the fact it was *her*
book, a love story by Corin Tellado, what she loved most now that she lived
in the U.S., without a television set, without the telenovelas.

Except now and again when her husband was away and she could manage 48
it, the few episodes glimpsed at the neighbor lady Soledad's house because
Dolores didn't care for that sort of thing, though Soledad was often kind enough
to retell what had happened on what episode of "Maria de Nadie," the poor
Argentine country girl who had the ill fortune of falling in love with the beautiful
son of the Arrocha family, the very family she worked for, whose roof she slept
under and whose floors she vacuumed, while in that same house, with the
dustbrooms and floor cleaners as witnesses, the square-jawed Juan Carlos Arrocha had uttered words of love, I love you, Maria, listen to me, mi querida,
but it was she who had to say no, no, we are not of the same class, and remind
him it was not in his place nor hers to fall in love, while all the while her heart
was breaking, can you imagine.

Cleófilas thought her life would have to be like that, like a telenovela, 49
only now the episodes got sadder and sadder. And there were no commercials
in between for comic relief. And no happy ending in sight. She thought this
when she sat with the baby out by the creek behind the house. Cleófilas de . . . ?
But somehow she would have to change her name to Topazio, or Yesenia,
Cristal, Adriana, Stefania, Andrea, something more poetic than Cleófilas.
Everything happened to women with names like jewels. But what happened to
Cleófilas? Nothing. But a crack in the face.

Because the doctor has said so. She has to go. To make sure the new baby is 50
alright, so there won't be any problems when he's born, and the appointment
card says next Tuesday. Could he please take her. And that's all.

No, she won't mention it. She promises. If the doctor asks she can say 51
she fell down the front steps or slipped when she was out in the back yard,
slipped out back, she could tell him that. She has to go back next Tuesday,
Juan Pedro, please, for the new baby. For their child.

She could write to her father and ask maybe for money, just a loan, for 52 the new baby's medical expenses. Well then if he'd rather she didn't. All right, she won't. Please don't anymore. Please don't. She knows it's difficult saving money with all the bills they have, but how else are they going to get out of debt with the truck payments. And after the rent and the food and the electricity and the gas and the water and the who-knows-what, well, there's hardly anything left. But please, at least for the doctor visit. She won't ask for anything else. She has to. Why is she so anxious? Because.

Because she is going to make sure the baby is not turned around backwards 53 this time to split her down the center. Yes. Next Tuesday at 5:30. I'll have Juan Pedrito dressed and ready. But those are the only shoes he has. I'll polish them, and we'll be ready. As soon as you come from work. We won't make you ashamed.

Felice? It's me, Graciela. 54

No, I can't talk louder. I'm at work. 55

Look, I need kind of a favor. There's a patient, a lady here who's got a 56 problem.

Well, wait a minute. Are you listening to me or what? 57

I can't talk real loud 'cause her husband's in the next room. 58

Well, would you just listen. 59

I was going to do this sonogram on her—she's pregnant, right?—and she 60 just starts crying on me. Hijole, Felice! This poor lady's got black-and-blue marks all over. I'm not kidding.

From her husband. Who else? Another one of those brides from across 61 the border. And her family's all in Mexico.

Shit. You think they're going to help her? Give me a break. This lady 62 doesn't even speak English. She hasn't been allowed to call home or write or nothing. That's why I'm calling you.

She needs a ride. 63

Not to Mexico, you goof. Just to the Greyhound. In San Anto. 64

No, just a ride. She's got her own money. All you'd have to do is drop 65 her off in San Antonio on your way home. Come on, Felice. Please? If we don't help her, who will? I'd drive her myself, but she needs to be on that bus before her husband gets home from work. What do you say?

I don't know. Wait. 66

Right away she says. Tomorrow even. 67

Well, if tomorrow's no good for you . . . 68

It's a date, Felice. Thursday. At the Cash N Carry off I-80. Noon. She'll 69 be ready.

Oh, and her name's Cleófilas. 70

I don't know. One of those Mexican saints I guess. A martyr or something. 71

Cleófilas. C-L-E-O-F-I-L-A-S. Cle. O. Fi. Las. Write it down. 72

Thanks, Felice, When her kid's born she'll name her after us, right? 73

Yeah, you got it. A regular soap opera sometimes. Que vida, comadre. 74
Bueno bye.

All morning that flutter of half fear, half doubt. At any moment Juan Pedro 75
might appear in the doorway. On the street. At the Cash N Carry. Like in the
dreams she dreamed.

There was that to think about, yes, until the woman in the pickup drove 76
up. Then there wasn't time to think about anything but the pickup pointed
towards San Antonio. Put your bags in the back and get in.

But when they drove across the arroyo, the driver opened her mouth and 77
let out a yell as loud as any mariachi. Which startled not only Cleófilas, but
Juan Pedrito as well.

Pues, look how cute. I scared you two, right? Sorry. Should've warned 78
you. Every time I cross that bridge I do that. Because of the name, you know.
Woman Hollering. Pues, I holler. She said this in a Spanish pocked with English
and laughed. Did you ever notice, Felice continued, how nothing around here
is named after a woman. Really. Unless she's the Virgin. I guess you're only
famous if you're a virgin. She was laughing again.

That's why I like the name of that arroyo. Makes you want to holler like 79
Tarzan, right?

Everything about this woman, this Felice, amazed Cleófilas. The fact that 80
she drove a pickup. A pickup mind you, but when Cleófilas asked if it was her
husband's, she said she didn't have a husband. The pickup was hers. She herself
had chosen it. She herself was paying for it.

I used to have a Pontiac Sunbird. But those cars are for viejas. Pussy cars. 81
Now this here is a *real* car.

What kind of talk was that coming from a woman, Cleófilas thought. But 82
then again, Felice was like no woman she'd ever met. Can you imagine. When
we crossed the arroyo she just started yelling like a crazy, she would say later
to her father and brothers. Just like that. Who would've thought.

Who would've? Pain or rage perhaps but not a hoot like the one Felice 83
had just let go. Makes you want to holler like Tarzan, Felice had said.

Then Felice began laughing again, but it wasn't Felice laughing. It was 84
gurgling out of her own throat, a long ribbon of laughter, like water. ◆

◆ Responding

1. Compare Cleófilas's situation and Graciela's response to it with Socorro's
   situation and the speaker's response in Mora's poem "Illegal Alien."

2. Why does Cleófilas think that "Felice was like no woman she'd ever met"? Is that observation a compliment or a criticism? Explain Cleófilas's attitude toward Felice.

3. Analyze the appeal of the *telenovelas* for Cleófilas. If her story appeared on a soap opera, how might the ending differ? Write an alternate ending for the story, and discuss it with the class. In an essay, explain which ending you like best and why.

4. Cleófilas acts to remove herself and her child from a dangerous situation. Write about a time when you or someone you know or have read about took a risk to make a bad situation better.

REFLECTING A CRITICAL CONTEXT

HÉCTOR CALDERÓN

Héctor Calderón was born in the California border town of Calexico in 1945. He earned undergraduate degrees from UCLA (1968) and California State University of Los Angeles (1972), a master's degree from the University of California at Irvine (1975), and a doctorate in Latin American literature and comparative literature from Yale University (1981). He has taught at Stanford, UCLA, and Yale, and is currently associate professor of Hispanic studies and Chicano studies at Scripps College. Calderón has published numerous articles in his field and is the author of Conciencia y lenguaje en el "Quijote" y "El obsceno pájaro de la noche" *(1987), and he is coeditor of* Criticism in the Borderlands: Studies in Chicano Literature, Culture and Ideology *(forthcoming). Currently he is at work on* Contemporary Chicano Narrative: A Tradition and Its Forms.

The following essay was written specifically for this book in 1990. Here Calderón uses his childhood experiences of growing up in a California border town as a backdrop for exploring Chicano heritage.

◆ REINVENTING THE BORDER ◆

I

The creators of borders . . . are . . . great pretenders. They post their projects in the world with the sturdiest available signs and hope that conventions (or, in the instance of California, a language law) will keep them in place. But even as the first stakes are driven, the earth itself, in all its intractable shiftiness, moves toward displacement.[1]

For the first eighteen years of my life the border, the line or *la línea*, was a daily presence. From the north end of the Imperial Valley in Brawley, Highway 98 winds down past agricultural fields and several cities—Imperial, El Centro, and Heber—to arrive eventually at the very limits of the American Southwest at the border, at Calexico, California. I, who grew up on Highway 98, also Imperial Avenue, four blocks from *la línea*, would rather think of the border

---

[1]Houston A. Baker, Jr., "LimIts of the Border." (unpublished)

not as a limit but as both a cultural and a historical crossroads; for Calexico, like no other border town I know, has a mirror held up to it in Mexicali, Baja California. Both cities have been historical and cultural reflections of each other; both the same, yet quite different.

Calexico began in the 1890s as an encampment for laborers in a water 2
diversion project that was to transform an area of the Sonora desert into one of the most productive agricultural regions of both the United States and Mexico. Mexicali, which had been an early extension of Calexico, rapidly outgrew its sister city. By the 1950s, and throughout my childhood, Calexico remained a dusty border town of eleven thousand, while Mexicali, the capital of Baja California del Norte, was a thriving (as only Mexican cities can thrive), tumultuous city of one hundred thousand. Nowadays, Calexico boasts a population of twenty-two thousand; I would wager that the population of Mexicali and its surrounding valleys is close to one million, with both its economy and its population boosted by assembly plants, *maquiladoras*, built since 1968 by U.S. companies on the Mexican side under the Border Industrial Program.

Both cities, ingeniously named around 1900 by a Mr. L. M. Holt, are, 3
in fact, a single economic entity separated by a fence constructed in this century. Commercial traffic has flowed more or less freely across the border. Many Mexican families from Calexico, including mine, would "cross the line" into Mexicali three or four days of the week, whether to visit relatives, to shop or dine, or to seek any number of professional or medical services. The Mexicali upper crust would frequent our Calexico stores, while the lower class would compete with us for jobs as clerks, domestics, and, most important of all, agricultural workers. At 4:00 A.M. the sleeping border town would awaken, and the Calexico downtown, the four blocks on Second Street, would be busier than at any other time of the day with both foot and auto traffic on the way to "The Hole," *el hoyo*. At El Hoyo, labor contractors and their hawkers awaited men, women, and children, in summer taking them as far north as Indio to harvest Thompson seedless grapes and in winter as near as the outskirts of Holtville or El Centro to pick carrots or lettuce. The Imperial Valley, you see, has a year-around growing season; it is where the "sun spends the winter"; it is also where migrant worker families would return from northern California, from as far as Napa and California's central valley, to work on winter crops.

During the 1940s and '50s in this poor, working-class town, we were 4
reminded of both what we were and what we were not. To the Euro-American minority of ranchers, shopkeepers, clerks, teachers, and government officials, we were not real Americans: we were foreigners, Mexicans. To our brothers and sisters on the other side of the line, we were *pochos*: inauthentic, Americanized Mexicans, identifiable by our mutilated pachuco Spanish and our dress, "con lisas y tramados y calcos siempre bien shiniados."[2] I grew up *mestizo* and

---

[2] With *lisas* and *tramados* and always well-shined shoes. *Lisas* are a special type of loose fitting, long sleeve shirt worn buttoned to the neck. *Tramados* are baggy khaki pants.

rascuachi, impure and lower class, in Calecia (Calexico) and Chikis (Mexicali), listening with my family to Spanish-language radio on XECL, enjoying the African rhythms of the mambo and chachachá; the great big bands of Luis Alcaraz and Pérez Prado; the German-influenced Banda de Sinaloa; the border *corridos* and *norteña* polkas sung by the Alegres de Terán; the national idols of mariachi music, Jorge Negrete, Pedro Infante, Lola Beltrán, José Alfredo Jiménez, Amalia Mendoza; the romantic ballads composed by Agustín Lara interpreted by the Trío Los Panchos, Pedro Vargas, or Toña la Negra. Fridays were reserved for the Aztec Theatre, where we both laughed and cried to Mexican films by the exiled Spanish director Luis Buñuel or starring the Mexican national hero Cantinflas.

Many of our daily and seasonal activities were still dictated by Mexican oral and cultural traditions handed down to our family by our grandmother. Before we acquired a television set, our grandmother would narrate tales every night. However, our world was rapidly changing. The alternative to the Mexican radio station, XECL, was the appropriately named KROP of Brawley, on which we listened to R&B and rockabilly as they became rock 'n roll. We danced to James Brown, Little Richard, Chuck Berry, Laverne Baker, Buddy Holly and Ritchie Valens, the Platters, doo-wop, and Elvis and the Everlys—even Hank Williams and Patsy Cline on the "West Side of Your Hit Parade." We really hit the big time when the Ike and Tina Turner Revue came to the El Centro National Guard Armory and Little Richard played at the Mexicali Gimnasio. And yes, the Cisco Kid was a friend of mine.

This multicultural lens through which we viewed our world certainly made us "Mexicans" different from Euro-American Calexicans. However, in school we were told, assured, that we were white, Spanish, descendents of the conquistadors. Many years later, as I read my birth certificate, I think about how much our world has changed, for my race in 1945 was identified as white. But despite this, and even though we were legal citizens and should have been treated equally, we attended school in segregated classrooms. We were still, after all, foreigners, the children of Mexicans who had arrived in large numbers in the first decades of this century to play a significant role as agricultural laborers in a region that was undergoing a major economic transformation. My parents arrived shortly after the Mexican Revolution.[3] My mother belonged to a migrant worker family that traveled up and down California's central valley; my father, like all the males in his family, worked for the Southern Pacific Railroad.

These ethnic and class contradictions come back to me as I recall our most important annual festive occasion: the parade and pageant known as the Calexico Desert Cavalcade. Begun in the Depression years to boost the morale of the

---

[3]Mexican Revolution of 1910.

border community, the pageant was the invention of a Mrs. Keller, who had the support of the editor of the Calexico *Chronicle*, the local newspaper, and of the president of the Chamber of Commerce and representatives of the city's service clubs. This reenactment of California's past began, in the words of the organizing committee, "with the stout-hearted pioneers who brought God and civilization to the Southwest." My fourth-grade experience is especially memorable: dressed like all my classmates as a Plains Indian in feathers and buckskin, I fell in behind the gallant Juan Bautista de Anza and kindly, black-robed padres as we paraded past our two important side-by-side architectural landmarks, the neo-Spanish Hotel de Anza and the mission-like Our Lady of Guadalupe Catholic Church, on our way to Monterrey in Alta California. That de Anza did not establish a Mexican settlement in the area in 1775 was not important to some Calexicans. Actually, de Anza had the more important task of establishing an overland route from what is now southern Arizona to Alta California, a task made easier by existing Native American trails. It also did not matter to the Cavalcade organizers that their activities made no sense given the cultural, historical, and economic realities of this overwhelmingly Mexican town. The Cavalcade probably made no sense either to Mrs. Yokum, Pete Emmett, or Lucille, our African American neighbors, or to Mar Chan, our corner grocer.

We in the Southwest were never so different from our friends and relatives 8 across the border in Mexico as when we asserted this, our Spanish heritage. Though biologically and culturally we were indistinct from one another—we were all Mexican *mestizos*—we had different national cultural heritages and ideologies imposed from above by educators, civic leaders, and government officials. Just a short distance across the border, buildings and monuments bore the names of Mexican revolutionary leaders like Obregón and Cárdenas. Not Spanish, but Native American culture had been purified into their norm of the classic after the Mexican Revolution of 1910. From José Vasconcelos's *La raza cósmica* (*The Cosmic Race*) of 1926 to Octavio Paz's *El laberinto de la soledad* (*The Labyrinth of Solitude*) of 1949, Native American culture was not only Mexico's historical base, but also its possibility for the future. In the idealized Mexican historical drama, Cuauhtémoc, Fallen Eagle, the last Aztec emperor, became the nation's hero, and Cortés, Spanish conqueror, became the archvillain. These different popular and intellectual traditions reveal why, until the Chicano movement of the 1960s, one side of the border was "Spanish" and the other "Mexican," although we shared the same Mexican-*mestizo* culture.

II

Perhaps the single most influential agent of Euro-American cultural domina- 9 tion was Charles F. Lummis, whose lifelong activities and writings changed the image of a region, Mexican America, that had been acquired through military conquest some thirty-six years prior to his arrival in Sante Fe, New

Mexico, in 1884. In 1925, three years before his death, Lummis boasted in *Mesa, Cañon and Pueblo*, that he had been the first to apply the generic name "Southwest," or more specifically, "Spanish Southwest," to the million square miles that include New Mexico, Arizona, southern California, and parts of Colorado, Utah, and Texas. In a span of nine years, from 1891 to 1899, Lummis published eleven books, changing what was a physical and cultural desert into a land internationally known for its seductive natural and cultural attractions. Though in truth an amateur inclined toward self-promotion and melodramatic and hyperbolic writing, Lummis became the founder of the "Southwest genre," recognized by both professionals and the popular media as the undisputed authority on the history, anthropology, and folklore of the Southwest.

In the West, Lummis discovered for his readers a culture much like that 10 of the fictional characters and settings of romantic literature. Unlike the East, the West had an authentic folk culture of simple and picturesque, yet dignified, souls still existing in a pastoral or agricultural mode of production undisturbed by the modern world. So taken was Lummis by the alien culture he encountered that he adopted it as his own; he learned Spanish, took on the name of Don Carlos, and was fond of posing for photographs in Spanish, Western, Apache, and Navajo attire. He was a promoter of "Spanish" architecture and established the Landmarks Club to revive the California missions. He founded the Southwest Museum in Los Angeles to house his collections of Native American artifacts.

Like other foreigners who make native culture their own, however, Lum- 11 mis also had a conservative and patronizing side. He was intent on writing only about the most folkloric and romantic elements of Native American and *mestizo* culture. Thus in his first books, *A New Mexico David* (1891) and *The Land of Poco Tiempo* (1893), Lummis reveals his attraction to courtly dons, beautiful, dark-eyed Spanish señoritas, innocent Indian children, kind Mexican peons, witches, liturgical feast days, medieval-style penitents, haciendas, burros, carretas, and sunshine. Charmed by his "child-hearted" Spanish, Lummis became an apologist for the Spanish conquest of the Americas. His early book, *The Spanish Pioneers* (1893), is a history of the heroic padres and gallant Spaniards who brought God and civilization to the Americas.

Of course, the past was not just a romance, and the present was more 12 than Mexicans resting against adobe. This strategy of glorifying the past ignored the historical fact that the land upon which Lummis set foot in 1884 was conquered Mexican territory. For Lummis, it was as if Spain had become the United States without centuries of racial and cultural mixture. Yet Lummis's view of the conquest and colonization of Arizona, California, New Mexico, and Texas as the golden age of Hispanic culture in the Southwest became a standard interpretation of Euro-American and Hispanic academic scholarship early in the twentieth century, and it continues to flourish in the popular imagination in literature, mass media images and Hollywood films and in the celebrations of Spanish fiesta days throughout the Southwest.

III

But what about the cultural changes during the viceroyalty of New Spain and   13
the young Mexican nation? These changes created new American cultural traditions throughout the years from the conquest of Mexico in 1521 to the establishment of Santa Fe in 1610 and down to the growth of Arizona, California,
New Mexico, and Texas in the twentieth century. On these issues virtually
nothing was written in the United States until the reinvention of the border
from a Chicano perspective. I am referring to Américo Paredes's ground-break-
ing study in 1958, *"With His Pistol in His Hand": A Border Ballad and Its Hero*.
As the title indicates, the book is a study of folk balladry along the Texas lower
Rio Grande border, from the two Laredos in the north to Brownsville and
Matamoros on the Gulf of Mexico. As a work of scholarship—it was Paredes's
doctoral dissertation, presented in 1956 to the English department at the University of Texas at Austin—it did not differ from traditional studies. The author
established a theory of genesis for border balladry, tracing its development from
its origins in the Spanish *romance* to the Texas-Mexican *corrido*. But the book
was more than this; it was a highly conscious, imaginative act of resistance that
established for Chicanos a definition for the border, which is to say, not as a
line but as Greater Mexico, a historically determined geopolitical zone of military, cultural, and linguistic conflict. For me, when I came upon Paredes's
book by accident as a student at UCLA in 1965, it was the answer to the
silencing of our voices, the stereotyping of our culture, and the reification of
our history that resulted from the Southwest genre.

It is difficult to describe the complexity of Parades's study. It is a hybrid   14
form, blurring the boundaries between genres and disciplines; it is part history,
anthropology, folklore, and fiction. It is a reconstruction of the history of the
lower Río Grande Valley from Spanish colonization in 1749 to the displacement
of a Mexican ranching culture by large-scale farming in the 1930s and '40s to
the migrant worker culture of the post–World War II era. A graduate student
at Austin faced up to the myth of the Texas Rangers and the white supremacist
attitudes of Texas scholar Walter Prescott Webb, who had written in *The Texas
Rangers* (1936) that Mexican blood "was no better than ditch water." Paredes
dared to utter the unspeakable: that the development of a Texas-Mexican pastoral mode of production, a ranching culture, that had emerged from the mixture
of Spanish and Native American elements and was beginning to extend up from
the Rio Grande to the Nueces River, was cut short in 1836 and 1848 by a
"restless and acquisitive people, exercising the rights of conquest."

"With His Pistol in His Hand" is also a theory of culture by a native   15
anthropologist who understood that culture is not necessarily consensual but
conflictual. Given the current temper of anthropological studies, in which the
question of the objective gaze of the observer is being displaced by the acknowledgment of the institutional and political situation of the discipline, Paredes
was ahead of his time. He turned his scholarly attention to the voices of his
people, to the *corridos*, the ballads, that he had heard as a child, and chose to

study the "Corrido de Gregorio Cortez," the ballad of a Texas-Mexican vaquero who in 1901 had been wrongly accused of killing an Anglo sheriff. Unlike earlier scholars, Paredes studied the oral tradition in its context, to understand how it had developed. According to Paredes, after 1836 the Spanish *romance* developed into the *corrido* as a result of the border conflicts that became its dominant theme: the protagonist of the *corrido* defends his rights with his pistol in his hand. Other border heroes preceded and followed Cortez: Juan Nepomuceno Cortina, from Brownsville, who led a rebellion in 1859; Catarino Garza, of Brownsville-Matamoros, who was probably the first to rise up against the Mexican dictator Porfirio Diaz in 1890; and Aniceto Pizaña, who led a 1915 rebellion against the state of Texas.

While most critics of Chicano literature have focused their attention on Gregorio Cortez as the complete and legitimate Texas-Mexican persona whose life of struggle was worthy of being told, I would rather think of Paredes as the writer who made the Chicano genre possible. After poking fun at the biased scholarship of his "objective" colleagues at the University of Texas in Chapter I, "The Country," the Texas-Mexican trickster Paredes disappears in Chapter II, "The Legend of Gregorio Cortez," giving way to a third-person plural narrative, told in the anonymous voices of the elders of the tribe who gather at night to tell the legend. Paredes transcribes and translates a group storytelling performance, so that, through his individual talents and inventive energy as a writer, the interests of the community are represented. As the elders relive the exploits of Gregorio Cortez, in a retelling spiced with humor and linguistic jokes, the hero becomes the embodiment of the cultural values that developed during a history of conflict and resistance. In Chapter IV, "The Hero's Progress," Paredes returns to this storytelling situation, explaining that the legend as it appears in Chapter II is his own creation; he put together those parts that seemed to him furthest removed from fact and the most revealing of folk attitudes. This narrative stance, with its folkloric, anthropological, and historical elements, seems to me the inner form of much of Chicano literature, from Tomás Rivera's *y no se lo tragó la tierra/And the Earth Did Not Part* (1971) and Rolando Hinojosa's *Klail City Death Trip Series* (1973–1989) to Sandra Cisneros's *The House on Mango Street* and Gloria Anzaldúa's *Borderlands/La Frontera: The New Mestiza* (1987). 16

IV

Whenever Chicanas or Chicanos write on behalf of their community, the border has always loomed in the background. This is true whether it is a real historical or cultural crossing back and forth between the United States and Mexico or a crossing of more symbolic barriers, as in confronting issues of racism and language, gender, sexual, and class differences. These issues found their way to paper in the early work of Jovita González (1930), Américo Paredes (1958), 17 and Ernesto Galarza (1964), and also appear in the work of the writers of the Chicano movement selected for this volume.

Given these scholarly and creative traditions and the national and inter- 18 national preoccupation with the question of the border, it is not surprising that the Chicana lesbian activist Gloria Anzaldúa in her *Borderlands/La Frontera: The New Mestiza* (1987) should combine an autobiographical account with a reconceptualization of the border. Hers is a new historical and metaphorical version. For her, borders are established to protect what is "ours" from danger, from the "alien," because they are also places inhabited by what is forbidden. For those in power, border zones, are inhabited by Chicanos, African Americans, Native Americans, Asian Americans, mulattos, *mestizos*, gays, lesbians, "wetbacks," illegals—in short, all those who are judged to be illegitimate. To sum up in another way, borders are those spaces, both geographical and conceptual, where the contradictions of power and repression, resistance and rebellion, are painfully visible.

To really know border zones, one has to overcome barriers, to be *atra-* 19 *vesada*, a border-crosser. Anzaldúa is a border writer who lives her contradictions at various levels. She is no longer a quiet woman. She speaks out and confronts her own Texas-Mexican patriarchal and heterosexist culture. She writes in both English and Spanish to find her own voice and rejects any linguistic inferiority imposed by nationalists from both sides of the border. As she explains, Chicano language was invented to communicate realities and values belonging to a border zone.

Like Paredes before her, Anzaldúa retells the history of Anglo-Texan 20 domination of the Río Grande border; however, she bears witness to land fraud and usurpation suffered by both of her grandmothers. As she matured through the decade of the fifties, she saw her borderlands parcelled out for the benefit of U.S. companies. Like other Texas-Mexican families displaced from their ancestral homeland, the Anzaldúas became sharecroppers. The transformation of the Río Grande Valley did not stop at *la línea*. Nowadays, observes Anzaldúa, U.S. companies (RCA, Fairchild, Litton, Zenith, Motorola, among others) control the border economy through their assembly plants, the *maquiladoras*, whose workforces are mostly women. These new industrial forces have displaced older rural social and cultural structures.

V

Anzaldúa's account should be inserted within a new historical problematic along 21 the border: The dividing lines between north and south, First and Third World, are being effaced even as I write. We are witnessing dramatic demographic changes in the West and Southwest, and in northern Mexico, that will play a decisive role in the development of Chicano-Latino culture. Since the 1950s the population of major Mexican border towns, from Tijuana, on the Pacific Ocean, to Matamoros, on the Gulf of Mexico, has more than quadrupled, because women, men, and children from Mexico, Central America, and the Caribbean are flocking to these cities as points of entry into the United States, to work in U.S. assembly plants on the Mexican side, or to take advantage of a growing international business and tourist trade. As if in a García Márquez tale, one of the largest flea markets in the Southwest has sprung up in an empty field on the outskirts of Calexico. The promise of inexpensive U.S. products offered by Asian entrepreneurs from Los Angeles draws Mexican nationals from isolated areas, who must travel days to reach Calexico. I heard from a touring Japanese family that some street vendors in Tijuana now speak Japanese. I imagine similar border crossings occur in Texas, New Mexico, and Arizona.

This multicultural world will have its effect on Mexico. Because of U.S. 22 cultural and economic influence (U.S. assembly plants are now being constructed in the interior of Mexico), we hear from a frank Mexican historian that every Mexican national is a potential Chicano. Similar phenomena are occurring on the northern side of the border. California, we are told, is fast becoming a Third World state; soon after the year 2000, the Euro-American population will reach minority status. In the late 1970s, I taught as a substitute teacher in a Hollywood elementary school whose administrators had to deal with fifteen different languages. I have even heard that there exists in Los Angeles a community of Mexicans who speak their native *quiché* Maya. A recent concert of Filipino popular music in a white suburb of Los Angeles drew 10,000. It is therefore not surprising to read reports that if current population trends and birthrates continue, California will experience a complete reversal from its 1945 ratio of whites to nonwhites. Thus, a centuries-old border culture with new social and economic realities, extending from San Francisco in the West and Chicago in the Midwest to Mexico, Central America, and the Caribbean, is reasserting itself on the U.S. national scene.

However, we should not be totally celebratory of a multicultural United 23 States. To understand the economic realities of the expanding border zone, we should also be aware that the gap between privileged and underprivileged along the border and in this country—including Chicanos and millions of Mexicans and other Latino and Third World groups—has never been greater. There exists the real possibility that some regions of this country, especially California, like the Third World countries in Latin America and, indeed, South Africa, will be composed of a ruling minority and an underprivileged majority. Although these political and economic problems will not be solved in the very near future, it is true at this moment that we can no longer ignore the centuries old Mexican-*mestizo* presence in the Southwest. ◆

◆ Responding

1. Explain what Calderón means when he says "we were reminded of both what we were and what we were not."

2. Discuss the way in which Lummis romanticized the Southwest. Compare his version of history with the presentations in the other readings in this chapter.

3. Define *border*. Compare your definition with Calderón's.

4. Calderón reports that many of his daily and seasonal activities as a child were "dictated by Mexican oral and written tradition, handed down to our family by our grandmother." Write an essay about the influence of cultural or family traditions on your childhood.

◆

CONNECTING

Critical Thinking and Writing

1. Analyze the role that economic realities play in the lives of the characters in this section. How do their financial situations limit or restrict their choices?

2. Examine the economic realities faced by the early immigrants, Native Americans, or any other group, and compare them with those of Chicanos in the 1940s and 1950s.

3. Compare the conflicts caused by biculturalism experienced by the narrator of "Legal Alien" and Ichiro in *No-no Boy*.

4. A variety of women characters appear in this chapter. Choose two and compare their ways of coping with life's challenges. Alternatively, classify the women according to the way they respond to difficult situations. What elements might account for these different responses? Consider the characters' personalities, social circumstances, education, and economic situations.

5. Compare the images of the traditional roles of men and women that emerge from the readings in this chapter. Which characters conform and which rebel against these roles?

6. Using information from the readings, identify gender roles in two particular cultures during a specific period, such as Chicanos in the 1940s and 1950s, Jews in the late 1800s, or Japanese in the 1930s and 1940s, and compare them to

each other. Alternatively, identify gender roles in one group during a specific period and compare them to gender roles in that group in the present.

7. For many of the characters in this section, education is the way to a better life. What difficulties do they encounter as they pursue their education? Analyze the barriers to education that faced Chicanos in the 1950s.

8. Compare barriers that Chicanos faced in the 1950s with the problems faced by other groups, such as early immigrants, Japanese Americans during World War II, or blacks before desegregation. What barriers still exist today that might prevent people from getting an education in spite of their desire to do so? Write an essay presenting the problems and suggesting solutions.

9. Many of the older people portrayed in these stories are bewildered by the changes that are taking place around them, though some accept change more easily than others. Compare the different ways in which the older people in the readings adjust to life in America.

10. Adjusting to a new country means adjusting to a new culture and often a new language. For older people such an adjustment is often difficult, while younger people frequently adapt more quickly. This can cause conflict between the new values the children hold and the traditional values retained by their parents. Write an essay illustrating the difficulties that arise within families when children begin to move away from the beliefs of their parents. Use examples from this and other sections of the text.

11. Working in a group, generate a list of essay questions based on issues raised in this chapter. Share your list with the class. Choose one question and answer it in an essay.

For Further Research

1. Research the current situation of migrant workers. Who are they? What are their working conditions? What organizations support them? What is their legal status?

2. Research the Chicano Moritorium Movement.

3. Explore the concept of La Raza and its implications for various Chicano communities.

◆

REFERENCES AND ADDITIONAL SOURCES

Bruce-Novoa, Juan D. *Chicano Authors: Inquiry by Interview*. Austin: University of Texas Press, 1980.

———. *Chicano Poetry: A Response to Chaos*. Austin: University of Texas Press, 1982.

Calderón, Héctor. "At the Crossroads of History, on the Borders of Change: Chicano Literary Studies Past, Present and Future," in *Left Politics and the Literary Profession*. 1990, pp. 211–235. Edited by M. Bella Mirabella and Leonnard J. Davis. New York: Columbia University Press, 1990, pp. 211–235.

Castro, Tony. *Chicano Power: The Emergence of the Mexican American*. New York: Saturday Review, 1974.

Durán, Livie Isauro, and H. Russell Bernard. *Introduction to Chicano Studies: A Reader*. New York: Macmillan, 1973.

Garlarza, Ernesto. *Merchants of Labor: The Mexican Bracero Story*. Charlotte and Santa Barbara: McNally and Loftin, 1964.

McWilliams, Carey. *North from Mexico: The Spanish Speaking People of the United States*. Westport, Conn.: Greenwood, 1969.

Meier, Matt S., and Feliciano Rivera. *The Chicanos: A History of Mexican Americans*. New York: Hill and Wang, 1972.

Moquin, Wayne, and Charles Van Doren, eds. *A Documentary History of the Mexican Americans*. New York: Praeger, 1971.

Paredes, Raymund. "The Evolution of Chicano Literature," in Baker, Houston A., Jr., ed. *Three American Literatures: Essays in Chicano, Native American, and Asian-American Literature for Teachers of American Literature*. New York: Modern Language Association of America, 1982.

Rendon, Armando. *Chicano Manifesto*. New York: Collier-Macmillan, 1971.

Samora, Julian, and Patricia Simon. *A History of the Mexican-American People*. Notre Dame, Ill.: University of Notre Dame Press, 1977.

Servin, Manuel P. *An Awakened Minority: The Mexican Americans*. New York: Macmillan, 1974.

Tatum, Charles M. *Chicano Literature*. Boston: Twayne, 1982.

*Stickball, a popular South-
eastern Native American
game, is one of the oldest
games in the world.
(Courtesy Choctaw
Community News)*

*Thanksgiving celebrated by
Native Americans occupying
Alcatraz Island off
San Francisco, 1969.
(© AP/Wide World Photos)*

Chapter 8

NATIVE AMERICANS
Pride and Cultural Heritage

Detail of background photo, Anasazi ruins, Arizona.
(© 1982 Jonathon A. Meyers)

◆ SETTING THE HISTORICAL CONTEXT ◆

IN JAMES WELCH'S POEM "Plea to Those Who Matter," the speaker dramatizes pressure on Native Americans to assimilate with the majority culture:

> Don't ignore me. I'll build my face a different way,
> a way to make you know that I am no longer
> proud, my name not strong enough to stand alone.
> If I lie and say you took me for a friend,
> patched together in my thin bones,
> will you help me be cunning and noisy as the wind?

The poem suggests, through its irony, some of the ways in which Native Americans have been asked to exchange their pride and identity for an image held by the majority culture. To obtain property and mineral rights belonging to Native Americans, Euro-Americans have often coerced tribes into signing treaties against their best interests and then refused to honor the terms of these agreements. In the interest of acculturation, the majority culture has penalized those natives who attempted to retain their cultural identity. Native Americans, in recent years, however, have had somewhat greater success fighting for what is legally and morally their own.

The history of Native Americans and their relations to the federal and state governments is a very complex subject. Their community comprises, in the words of the Supreme Court, many "distinct and independent communities," each with separate linguistic and cultural systems, and in many cases separate dealings with the state and federal governments of the United States. We cannot recount all of these histories here, but we will describe some crucial events from the period of the United States' rapid western expansion in the nineteenth century to the emergence of a Native American rights movement in the twentieth century.

The history of relations between the federal government and the Native American peoples has been dictated largely by the government's growing desire for land. The property claims and terms of earlier treaties were often ignored as a result. The Indian Relocation Act of 1830 provides a dramatic illustration of this principle. Passed by Congress at the request of President

Andrew Jackson, this act gave the executive branch of government vast powers to order native peoples living east of the Mississippi River to relocate in a designated Indian territory that would be set up in the West. Those who relocated often did so at great personal suffering; anguish, starvation, disease, and death plagued the Cherokees on the "Trail of Tears," a forced relocation from Georgia to Oklahoma in 1838 through harsh winter conditions. In turn they were promised that they would be allowed to live in their new area "in perpetuity." With the increase in Euro-American settlers during the westward expansion of the late nineteenth century, however, there was even greater pressure on the land; the guarantee that Native Americans would be able to keep their land was not honored.

In Welch's poem, the speaker asserts, "I have plans to burn my drum/move out and civilize my hair," an illustration of the assault on Native Americans' ways of life, which also began in the nineteenth century. Through the establishment of the Bureau of Indian Affairs in 1824 and the passage of legislation such as the Dawes Allotment Act of 1887 and the Curtis Act of 1898, the federal government attempted to alter tribal customs and values. Reservations were created, and Native Americans were forced to abandon their traditional nomadic way of life and to create an agrarian culture on the much smaller lands allotted them. Tribal governments were dissolved and replaced with federally-appointed administrators, whose task it was to "civilize" the Native Americans; laws were passed to prevent Native Americans from exercising tribal customs and religion. Children were often taken from their parents and sent to foster parents and boarding schools in distant states, where they were required to adopt the language and culture of Euro-Americans. Until the 1930s, Native Americans had to obtain permission to leave their reservations; those living in Arizona and New Mexico remained disfranchised until the late 1940s.

Between 1930 and 1945 the status of Native American peoples improved marginally. The Bureau of Indian Affairs instituted reforms providing greater autonomy; the Indian Reorganization Act (1934), for example, gave tribes greater control over their property and funds as well as the administration of programs for education, health, and welfare. Many of these reforms were undermined during the 1950s, however, when the federal government adopted a termination policy designed to dissolve the reservations, relocate their residents, and allocate private property— all largely without the consent of the people affected. Administered by Dillon S. Myer, who had run the Japanese American internment camps during World War II, the termination policy eroded tribal authority and reduced Native Americans' control of land, since much of their former reservation territory was signed over to whites.

The termination policy was renounced by the Kennedy administration, which took office in 1960. Relations between the federal government and Native American groups changed to reflect the growing appreciation among the American people of the values of pluralism. The government promised to help Native Americans preserve their cultural heritage and to negotiate directly any changes in treaties or contracts. There was also growing awareness that governmental policies toward Native Americans could not be imposed from without, as had typically been done in the past, but had to be based on the initiative and cooperation of those affected.

Native Americans had protested their treatment by the United States government since the time of Tecumseh, a Shawnee chief and Indian organizer who died in 1813. It was not until the 1960s, however, that Native American groups began to be recognized by the government. In 1961, the American Indian Chicago Conference, a meeting of more than 450 delegates from 90 tribes, issued a formal Declaration of Indian Purpose, reaffirming the resolve of Native Americans to have a voice in their own destiny. The conference called for the abandonment of the termination policy, the establishment of broad educational programs to help Native Americans make use of their own resources, and the reorganization of the federal government's Bureau of Indian Affairs to allow for more local control. At the same time, the Task Force on Indian Affairs, established by the Kennedy admin- istration, recommended industrial development, vocational training and employment placement, loan funds, protection of the rights of off-reservation Native Americans, and improved educational facilities to help Native Americans achieve greater self-sufficiency.

One of the priorities for the new efforts was the alleviation of the extreme poverty on many tribal reservations. Many Native Americans were able to take advantage of the Economic Opportunity Act of 1964, part of the war on poverty initiated by the Kennedy administration and carried forward by the administration of President Lyndon B. Johnson. This act stressed local initiative, encouraging the poor to take an active part in planning and administering programs. Tribal governments were quick to set up community action programs.

A further step toward helping Native Americans achieve equal opportunity occurred when the Civil Rights Act of 1968 was extended to protect their rights. While this law limited the powers of tribal governments, it did guarantee that the freedom from discrimination and civil rights violations accorded by the Constitution would be fully applied to Native Americans.

In 1968, President Johnson created the National Council on Indian Opportunity. This council, chaired by Vice President Hubert Humphrey, emphasized Native American leadership and initiative in solving their own problems. Despite progress, however, many Native Americans, still fearing a policy of termination, distrusted the federal government. Even though President Johnson appointed the first Native American commissioner of Indian affairs in a hundred years, Robert J. Bennett, an Oneida, the government could not gain the complete confidence of the tribes.

While some Native Americans waited for the government to act on the promises of the Civil Rights Act, others took more direct action. Activitists from a militant group called Red Power, after the Black Power movement, occupied Alcatraz Island in San Francisco Bay in 1969 and attempted to convert it into a Native American cultural and educational center. Although this project was ultimately abandoned, the occupation came to symbolize Native American unity, since the leaders called themselves All Tribes. Other protests followed, among them the 1972 Trail of Broken Treaties, an occupation of the Bureau of Indian Affairs building in Washington, D.C., and a 1972 march on Washington organized by the American Indian Movement (AIM). To call attention to the continuing problems faced by Native Americans, AIM in 1973 seized the village of Wounded Knee on the

Pine Ridge Reservation in South Dakota—the site of the final large-scale massacre of Native Americans by U.S. military forces, in 1890. The occupation, condemned by many Native Americans, lasted for more than seventy days.

The government continued to move toward a policy of Native American self-determination without termination. Under President Richard Nixon, procedural changes improved the relationship between the tribes and the government. Nixon's team on Indian affairs gained the trust and support of Native Americans by renouncing the termination policy and restoring sacred lands. The passage of the Alaska Native Claims Settlement Act of 1971 granted Alaskan Native Americans legal title to 40 million acres of land and restored to tribal status the previously terminated Menominees. During this period the Native American community assumed control of some federal programs and began administering their own public schools.

Relations between the federal government and the tribes continued to improve during the Carter administration. The position of commissioner of Indian affairs was elevated to the assistant secretary level, and legislation further guaranteeing the rights of Native Americans and other native peoples was passed, giving Native Americans increased hopes for the future.

Native Americans remaining on reservations were still concerned about education and family issues, however. The government schools, they felt, did not meet the varying educational and cultural needs of the different tribes. With increasing interest in tradition and the "old ways," there arose a need for an educational system that would validate tribal culture and would train a new generation of children to carry on their heritage. Another serious problem was the high rate of adoption of Native American children by non-Native American families. Approximately one-quarter of all Native American children were taken from their families and placed in foster or adoptive homes because the Bureau of Indian Affairs or state social workers had judged their own homes unsuitable. In 1978, Congress passed the American Indian Child Welfare Act to protect the interests of these children and their families.

Today Native Americans no longer live solely on reservations. Since

World War II, steady numbers have migrated to the cities, where they have generally attained higher incomes, occupational status, levels of education, and better housing than those remaining on reservations. The combined impact of losing the support of the tribe as an extended family and the conflicts between the traditional way of life and urban ways, however, has contributed to the rise of alcoholism, crime, and mental illness among urban Native Americans. But these changes have also led to the establishment of Native American centers in many cities to help urban Native Americans to survive socially and economically.

After many years of eroding autonomy, Native Americans have used legal action and a renewed regard for their own culture to strengthen tradition, hope, and pride in their communities. Tribes today want to work toward becoming economically self-sufficient, maintaining sovereignty on their reservations, and dealing effectively with the United States govern- ment. They also want to find ways to include all Native Americans in the decision-making processes that will determine their future. Above all, Native Americans want to make sure that they do not lose the traditions that have defined their tribal identities for generations.

EXPLORING THE LITERARY AND
◆ CULTURAL CONTEXT ◆

In essays, fiction, and poetry, many Native American authors have reflected on the ways in which their history and their cultural heritage relate to contemporary tribal and personal identities. Each of the selections that follows explores aspects of that history and its effects on everyday life.

A good deal of the Native American's history with the United States government involves a series of broken territorial promises and forced assimilation. The Removal Act was but one example of the federal govern- ment's attempt to deny Native Americans a voice in their future. And as Kenneth Lincoln points out in his essay from *Native American Renaissance*, efforts to assimilate Native Americans into the majority culture have been almost as destructive as efforts to remove or eliminate them.

Policies of assimilation evoke powerful and sometimes poignant responses in fiction and poetry. One policy, begun in the late nineteenth century, removed many Native American children from their family homes; Leslie Marmon Silko makes one such event compellingly real in her story "Lullaby." James Welch's poem "A Plea to Those Who Matter" responds with bitter, mocking irony to federal policies of forced relocation and cultural control imposed on many of the tribes for over a century.

While some of the selections examine the ways in which one can come to terms with history, others reflect upon events and traditions of the past to suggest ways in which Native American culture and traditions can blend with modern life. In her essay "Where I Come From Is Like This," Paula Gunn Allen expresses the desire of Native American women to redefine themselves and "reconcile traditional tribal definitions of women with industrial and postindustrial non-Indian definitions." Rather than rejecting the past and tribal identity as limiting, she considers ways to integrate them into her present life. The excerpt from Louise Erdrich's novel *Love Medicine* takes a wry approach to the effort to integrate the Native American tradition with the perspective of mainstream culture. And the excerpt from N. Scott Momaday's *House Made of Dawn* relates the merging of the Native American and Christian religions.

Native Americans, long forced to remain silent about their heritage and conform to forced relocations and assimilation, are finally able to reflect upon their own heritages, their true identities. The pride in tribal traditions, fully resurgent in recent decades, is well served by their writers, who renew and extend their cultures to future generations.

BEGINNING: PRE-READING/WRITING

◆ *Critics charge that Native Americans have often been stereotyped in films and on television as vicious savages or romanticized innocents. Working individually or in a group, list the general characteristics attributed to Native Americans in early Westerns, specific television series, and commercials. Has the portrayal changed over time? If so, in what ways? As you read the chapter, compare these depictions with those by Native American authors.*

Characteristics

Men	*Film*	*Television*	*Commericals*
Physical appearance			
Personality			
Character traits			
Behavior			
Clothing			
Work			
Hobbies			

Women	*Film*	*Television*	*Commercials*
Physical appearance			
Personality			
Character traits			
Behavior			
Clothing			
Work			
Hobbies			

*T*he Indian Removal Act of 1830, passed during Andrew Jackson's admin-istration, gave the president authority to transfer to the western territories any Indian tribes living in the East. The law dissolved tribal governments, but guaranteed that Native Americans would hold the new territories "in perpetuity"—a promise soon forgotten. The passage of this bill led to the forced relocation of 1838. Because of the suffering it caused, the journey from the east to the so-called Indian Territories of the West is often called the "Trail of Tears."

◆ *From* **THE INDIAN REMOVAL ACT** ◆

CHAP. CXLVIII.—*An Act to provide for an exchange of lands with the Indians residing in any of the states or territories, and for their removal west of the river Mississippi.*

Be it enacted by the Senate and House of Representatives of the United States of America, in Congress assembled, That it shall and may be lawful for the President of the United States to cause so much of any territory belonging to the United States, west of the river Mississippi, not included in any state or organized territory, and to which the Indian title has been extinguished, as he may judge necessary, to be divided into a suitable number of districts, for the reception of such tribes or nations of Indians as may choose to exchange the lands where they now reside, and remove there; and to cause each of said districts to be so described by natural or artificial marks, as to be easily distinguished from every other.

SEC. 2. *And be it further enacted,* That it shall and may be lawful for the President to exchange any or all of such districts, so to be laid off and described, with any tribe or nation of Indians now residing within the limits of any of the states or territories, and with which the United States have existing treaties, for the whole or any part or portion of the territory claimed and occupied by such tribe or nation, within the bounds of any one or more of the states or territories, where the land claimed and occupied by the Indians, is owned by the United States, or the United States are bound to the state within which it lies to extinguish the Indian claim thereto.

SEC. 3. *And be it further enacted,* That in the making of any such exchange or exchanges, it shall and may be lawful for the President solemnly to assure the tribe or nation with which the exchange is made, that the United States will forever secure and guaranty to them, and their heirs or successors, the country so exchanged with them; and if they prefer it, that the United States will cause a patent or grant to be made and executed to them for the same: *Provided always,* That such lands shall revert to the United States, if the Indians become extinct, or abandon the same.

SEC. 4. *And be it further enacted*, That if, upon any of the lands now occupied by the Indians, and to be exchanged for, there should be such improvements as add value to the land claimed by any individual or individuals of such tribes or nations, it shall and may be lawful for the President to cause such value to be ascertained by appraisement or otherwise, and to cause such ascertained value to be paid to the person or persons rightfully claiming such improvements. And upon the payment of such valuation, the improvements so valued and paid for, shall pass to the United States, and possession shall not afterwards be permitted to any of the same tribe. 4

SEC. 5. *And be it further enacted*, That upon the making of any such exchange as is contemplated by this act, it shall and may be lawful for the President to cause such aid and assistance to be furnished to the emigrants as may be necessary and proper to enable them to remove to, and settle in, the country for which they may have exchanged; and also, to give them such aid and assistance as may be necessary for their support and subsistence for the first year after their removal. 5

SEC. 6. *And be it further enacted*, That it shall and may be lawful for the President to cause such tribe or nation to be protected, at their new residence, against all interruption or disturbance from any other tribe or nation of Indians, or from any other person or persons whatever. 6

SEC. 7. *And be it further enacted*, That it shall and may be lawful for the President to have the same superintendence and care over any tribe or nation in the country to which they may remove, as contemplated by this act, that he is now authorized to have over them at their present places of residence: *Provided*, That nothing in this act contained shall be construed as authorizing or directing the violation of any existing treaty between the United States and any of the Indian tribes. 7

SEC. 8. *And be it further enacted*, That for the purpose of giving effect to the provisions of this act, the sum of five hundred thousand dollars is hereby appropriated, to be paid out of any money in the treasury, not otherwise appropriated. 8

APPROVED, May 28, 1830.◆

◆ Responding

1. Working individually or in a group, paraphrase and list the provisions of the Act. Share your list with the class and discuss what the provisions meant to the people affected.

2. Discuss the government's assumptions about the future of Native Americans implicit in the document. Support your opinions with evidence from the Act.

3. Research the myth of the "vanishing American." Using evidence from the Act, argue that the legislators who wrote this bill did or did not give credence to this myth.

N. Scott Momaday

N. Scott Momaday was born in Lawton, Oklahoma, in 1934, of Kiowa and Cherokee parentage. As a child he lived on New Mexican reservations where his parents taught school. He received his bachelor's degree from the University of New Mexico in 1958 and later earned a master's degree and a doctorate from Stanford University, where he studied with Yvor Winters. After teaching literature at the University of California at Santa Barbara, New Mexico State University, the University of Calfiornia at Berkeley, and Stanford University, he joined the faculty of the University of Arizona, where he is currently professor of English.

In addition to editing American Indian Authors, *Momaday has published several volumes of poetry, fiction, and an autobiography which focuses on Native American culture. These works include* Journey of Tai-Me *(1968),* The Way to Rainy Mountain *(1969),* The House Made of Dawn *(1969),* Angle of Geese and Other Poems *(1974), and* The Names: A Memoir *(1976). Momaday's writing has won him awards and fellowships from the National Academy of American Poets, the Whitney Foundation, the Guggenheim Foundation, the Fulbright Foundation, and the National Institute of Arts and Letters; his first novel,* House Made of Dawn, *was awarded the Pulitzer prize for fiction in 1969.*

The following chapter from House Made of Dawn *depicts the central character's encounter with organized religion while he is living away from the reservation in urban Los Angeles. The sermon presented at the Holiness Pan-Indian Rescue Mission illustrates the blending of themes amd images from Christian and Native American traditions. At the same time it considers different attitudes towards language and religion in the Euro-American and Native American traditions.*

◆ JANUARY 26 ◆

There is a small silversided fish that is found along the coast of southern California. In the spring and summer it spawns on the beach during the first three hours after each of the three high tides following the highest tide. These fishes come by the hundreds from the sea. They hurl themselves upon the land and writhe in the light of the moon, the moon, the moon; they writhe in the light of the moon. They are among the most helpless creatures on the face of the earth. Fishermen, lovers, passers-by catch them up in their bare hands.

The Priest of the Sun lived with his disciple Cruz on the first floor of a two-story red-brick building in Los Angeles. The upstairs was maintained as a storage facility by the A. A. Kaul Office Supply Company. The basement was a kind of church. There was a signboard on the wall above the basement steps, encased in glass. In neat, movable white block letters on a black field it read:

LOS ANGELES
HOLINESS PAN-INDIAN RESCUE MISSION
Rev. J. B. B. Tosamah, Pastor & Priest of the Sun
Saturday 8:30 P.M.
"The Gospel According to John"
Sunday 8:30 P.M.
"The Way to Rainy Mountain"
Be kind to a white man today

The basement was cold and dreary, dimly illuminated by two 40-watt   3
bulbs which were screwed into the side walls above the dais. This platform was made out of rough planks of various woods and dimensions, thrown together without so much as a hammer and nails; it stood seven or eight inches above the floor, and it supported the tin firebox and the crescent altar. Off to one side was a kind of lectern, decorated with red and yellow symbols of the sun and moon. In back of the dais there was a screen of purple drapery, threadbare and badly faded. On either side of the aisle which led to the altar there were chairs and crates, fashioned into pews. The walls were bare and gray and streaked with water. The only windows were small, rectangular openings near the ceiling, at ground level; the panes were covered over with a thick film of coal oil and dust, and spider webs clung to the frames or floated out like smoke across the room. The air was heavy and stale; odors of old smoke and incense lingered all around. The people had filed into the pews and were waiting silently.

Cruz, a squat, oily man with blue-black hair that stood out like spines   4
from his head, stepped forward on the platform and raised his hands as if to ask for the quiet that already was. Everyone watched him for a moment; in the dull light his skin shone yellow with sweat. Turning slightly and extending his arm behind him, he said, "The Right Reverend John Big Bluff Tosamah."

There was a ripple in the dark screen; the drapes parted and the Priest   5
of the Sun appeared, moving shadow-like to the lectern. He was shaggy and awful-looking in the thin, naked light: big, lithe as a cat, narrow-eyed, suggesting in the whole of his look and manner both arrogance and agony. He wore black like a cleric; he had the voice of a great dog:

" '*In principio erat Verbum.*' Think of Genesis. Think of how it was before   6
the world was made. There was nothing, the Bible says. 'And the earth was without form, and void; and darkness was upon the face of the deep.' It was dark, and there was nothing. There were no mountains, no trees, no rocks, no rivers. There was nothing. But there was darkness all around, and in the darkness something happened. *Something happened!* There was a single sound. Far away in the darkness there was a single sound. Nothing made it, but it was there; and there was no one to hear it, but it was there. It was there, and there was nothing else. It rose up in the darkness, little and still, almost nothing in

itself—like a single soft breath, like the wind arising; yes, like the whisper of
the wind rising slowly and going out into the early morning. But there was no
wind. There was only the sound, little and soft. It was almost nothing in itself,
the smallest seed of sound—but it took hold of the darkness and there was light;
it took hold of the stillness and there was motion forever; it took hold of the
silence and there was sound. It was almost nothing in itself, a single sound, a
word—a word broken off at the darkest center of the night and let go in the
awful void, forever and forever. And it was almost nothing in itself. It scarcely
was; but it was, and everything began."

Just then a remarkable thing happened. The Priest of the Sun seemed   7
stricken; he let go of his audience and withdrew into himself, into some strange
potential of himself. His voice, which had been low and resonant, suddenly
became harsh and flat; his shoulders sagged and his stomach protruded, as if
he had held his breath to the limit of endurance; for a moment there was a look
of amazement, then utter carelessness in his face. Conviction, caricature, cal-
lousness: the remainder of his sermon was a going back and forth among these.

"Thank you so much, Brother Cruz. Good evening, blood brothers and   8
sisters, and welcome, welcome. Gracious me, I see lots of new faces out there
tonight. *Gracious me!* May the Great Spirit—can we knock off that talking in
the back there?—be with you always.

" 'In the beginning was the Word.' I have taken as my text this evening   9
the almighty Word itself. Now get this: "There was a man sent from God,
whose name was John. The same came for a witness, to bear witness of the
Light, that all men through him might believe.' Amen, brothers and sisters,
Amen. And the riddle of the Word, 'In the beginning was the Word. . . .' Now
what do you suppose old John *meant* by that? That cat was a preacher, and,
well, you know how it is with preachers; he had something big on his mind.
Oh my, it was big; it was the *Truth*, and it was heavy, and old John hurried
to set it down. And in his hurry he said too much. 'In the beginning was the
Word, and the Word was with God, and the Word was God.' It was the Truth,
all right, but it was more than the Truth. The Truth was overgrown with fat,
and the fat was God. The fat was *John's* God, and God stood between John
and the Truth. Old John, see, he got up one morning and caught sight of the
Truth. It must have been like a bolt of lightning, and the sight of it made him
blind. And for a moment the vision burned on in back of his eyes, and he knew
what it was. In that instant he saw something he had never seen before and
would never see again. That was the instant of revelation, inspiration, Truth.
And old John, he must have fallen down on his knees. Man, he must have been
shaking and laughing and crying and yelling and praying—all at the same time—
and he must have been drunk and delirious with the Truth. You see, he had
lived all his life waiting for that one moment, and it came, and it took him by
surprise, and it was gone. And he said, 'In the beginning was the Word. . . .'
And, man, right then and there he should have stopped. There was nothing
more to say, but he went on. He had said all there was to say, everything, but
he went on. 'In the beginning was the Word. . . .' Brothers and sisters, *that*

was the Truth, the whole of it, the essential and eternal Truth, the bone and blood and muscle of the Truth. But he went on, old John, because he was a preacher. The perfect vision faded from his mind, and he went on. The instant passed, and then he had nothing but a memory. He was desperate and confused, and in his confusion he stumbled and went on. 'In the beginning was the Word, and the Word was with God, and the Word was God.' He went on to talk about Jews and Jerusalem, Levites and Pharisees, Moses and Philip and Andrew and Peter. Don't you see? Old John *had* to go on. That cat had a whole lot at stake. He couldn't let the Truth alone. He couldn't see that he had come to the end of the Truth, and he went on. He tried to make it bigger and better than it was, but instead he only demeaned and encumbered it. He made it soft and big with fat. He was a preacher, and he made a complex sentence of the Truth, two sentences, three, a paragraph. He made a sermon and theology of the Truth. He imposed his idea of God upon the everlasting Truth. 'In the beginning was the Word. . . .' And that is all there was, and it was enough.

"Now, brothers and sisters, old John was a white man, and the white 10 man has his ways. Oh gracious me, he has his ways. He talks about the Word. He talks through it and around it. He builds upon it with syllables, with prefixes and suffixes and hyphens and accents. He adds and divides and multiplies the Word. And in all of this he subtracts the Truth. And, brothers and sisters, you have come here to live in the white man's world. Now the white man deals in words, and he deals easily, with grace and sleight of hand. And in his presence, here on his own ground, you are as children, mere babes in the woods. You must not mind, for in this you have a certain advantage. A child can listen and learn. The Word is sacred to a child.

"My grandmother was a storyteller; she knew her way around words. She 11 never learned to read and write, but somehow she knew the good of reading and writing; she had learned how to listen and delight. She had learned that in words and in language, and there only, she could have whole and consummate being. She told me stories, and she taught me how to listen. I was a child and I listened. She could neither read nor write, you see, but she taught me how to live among her words, how to listen and delight. 'Storytelling; to utter and to hear . . .' And the simple act of listening is crucial to the concept of language, more crucial even than reading and writing, and language in turn is crucial to human society. There is proof of that, I think, in all the histories and prehistories of human experience. When that old Kiowa woman told me stories, I listened with only one ear. I was a child, and I took the words for granted. I did not know what all of them meant, but somehow I held on to them; I remembered them, and I remember them now. The stories were old and dear; they meant a great deal to my grandmother. It was not until she died that I knew how *much* they meant to her. I began to think about it, and then I knew. When she told me those old stories, something strange and good and powerful was going on. I was a child, and that old woman was asking me to come directly into the presence of her mind and spirit; she was taking hold of my imagination, giving me to share in the great fortune of her wonder and delight. She was asking me to go with her to the confrontation of something that was sacred and eternal. It was a timeless, *timeless* thing; nothing of her old age or of my childhood came between us.

"Children have a greater sense of the power and beauty of words than 12 have the rest of us in general. And if that is so, it is because there occurs—or reoccurs—in the mind of every child something like a reflection of all human experience. I have heard that the human fetus corresponds in its development, stage by stage, to the scale of evolution. Surely it is no less reasonable to suppose that the waking mind of a child corresponds in the same way to the whole evolution of human thought and perception.

"In the white man's world, language, too—and the way in which the white 13 man thinks of it—has undergone a process of change. The white man takes such things as words and literatures for granted, as indeed he must, for nothing in his world is so commonplace. On every side of him there are words by the millions, an unending succession of pamphlets and papers, letters and books, bills and bulletins, commentaries and conversations. He has diluted and multiplied the Word, and words have begun to close in upon him. He is sated and insensitive; his regard for language—for the Word itself—as an instrument of creation has diminished nearly to the point of no return. It may be that he will perish by the Word.

"But it was not always so with him, and it is not so with you. Consider 14 for a moment that old Kiowa woman, my grandmother, whose use of language was confined to speech. And be assured that her regard for words was always keen in proportion as she depended upon them. You see, for her words were medicine; they were magic and invisible. They came from nothing into sound and meaning. They were beyond price; they could neither be bought nor sold. And she never threw words away.

"My grandmother used to tell me the story of Tai-me, of how Tai-me 15 came to the Kiowas. The Kiowas were a sun dance culture, and Tai-me was their sun dance doll, their most sacred fetish; no medicine was ever more powerful. There is a story about the coming of Tai-me. This is what my grandmother told me:

> Long ago there were bad times. The Kiowas were hungry and there was no food. There was a man who heard his children cry from hunger, and he began to search for food. He walked four days and became very weak. On the fourth day he came to a great canyon. Suddenly there was thunder and lightning. A Voice spoke to him and said, "Why are you following me? What do you want?" The man was afraid. The thing standing before him had the feet of a deer, and its body was covered with feathers. The man answered that the Kiowas were hungry. "Take me with you," the Voice said, "and I will give you whatever you want." From that day Tai-me has belonged to the Kiowas.

"Do you see? There, far off in the darkness, something happened. Do 16 you see? Far, far away in the nothingness something happened. There was a voice, a sound, a word—and everything began. The story of the coming of Tai-me has existed for hundreds of years by word of mouth. It represents the oldest and best idea that man has of himself. It represents a very rich literature, which, because it was never written down, was always but one generation from extinction. But for the same reason it was cherished and revered. I could see that reverence in my grandmother's eyes, and I could hear it in her voice: It was that, I think, that old Saint John had in mind when he said, 'In the beginning was the Word. . . .' But he went on. He went on to lay a scheme about the Word. He could find no satisfaction in the simple fact that the Word was; he had to account for it, not in terms of that sudden and profound insight, which must have devastated him at once, but in terms of the moment afterward, which was irrelevant and remote; not in terms of his imagination, but only in terms of his prejudice.

"Say this: 'In the beginning was the Word. . . .' There was nothing. There 17 was *nothing!* Darkness. There was darkness, and there was no end to it. You look up sometimes in the night and there are stars; you can see all the way to the stars. And you begin to know the universe, how awful and great it is. The stars lie out against the sky and do not fill it. A single star, flickering out in the universe, is enough to fill the mind, but it is nothing in the night sky. The darkness looms around it. The darkness flows among the stars, and beyond them forever. In the beginning that is how it was, but there were no stars. There was only the dark infinity in which nothing was. And something happened. At the distance of a star something happened, and everything began. The Word did not come into being, but *it was*. It did not break upon the silence, but *it was older than the silence and the silence was made of it.*

"Old John caught sight of something terrible. The thing standing before 18 him said, 'Why are you following me? What do you want?' And from that day the Word has belonged to us, who have heard it for what it is, who have lived in fear and awe of it. In the Word was the beginning; '*In the beginning was the Word. . . .*' "

The Priest of the Sun appeared to have spent himself. He stepped back 19 from the lectern and hung his head, smiling. In his mind the earth was spinning and the stars rattled around in the heavens. The sun shone, and the moon. Smiling in a kind of transport, the Priest of the Sun stood silent for a time while the congregation waited to be dismissed.

"Good night," he said, at last, "and get yours."◆

◆ Responding

1. The signboard on the building where the Priest of the Sun gives his sermon reads "Holiness Pan-Indian Rescue Mission." Using information from the introduction to the chapter, define Pan-Indian and explain why that term

would have been unusual before 1960. What changes in attitudes does it reflect?

2. Write an essay discussing the cultural conflicts that Native Americans face in trying to adopt Christianity while retaining their own religion.

3. Explain the ways in which the Priest of the Sun believes the white man's use of "the Word" differs from the Kiowas'. Use examples from the reading and your own knowledge to illustrate the differences. Write an essay or a journal entry agreeing or disagreeing with the Priest's conclusions.

4. Are stories an important way of transmitting knowledge in your family, or among friends? Tell a story that teaches a cultural lesson.

LESLIE MARMON SILKO

The poet, novelist, and short story writer Leslie Marmon Silko was born in 1948 of Laguna parentage. After earning a bachelor's degree from the University of New Mexico and attending law school, she devoted herself to writing, focusing primarily on Native American themes. In addition to contributing work to literary journals and collections, Silko has published a poetry collection, Laguna Woman *(1974); the novel* Ceremony *(1977); and a poetry and short story collection,* The Storyteller *(1981). She has been honored with grants from the National Endowment for the Arts (1974) and the MacArthur Foundation (1983), as well as with the* Chicago Review *poetry prize (1974) and the Pushcart prize for poetry (1977).*

"Lullaby," from Silko's collection The Storyteller, *describes a Native American woman as she confronts government authorities, whose language she cannot understand, and comes to terms with the decisions they force upon her. At the same time, the story asks us to consider the ways in which language and power can be interconnected.*

◆ LULLABY ◆

The sun had gone down but the snow in the wind gave off its own light. It came in thick tufts like new wool—washed before the weaver spins it. Ayah reached out for it like her own babies had, and she smiled when she remembered how she had laughed at them. She was an old woman now, and her life had become memories. She sat down with her back against the wide cottonwood tree, feeling the rough bark on her back bones; she faced east and listened to the wind and snow sing a high-pitched Yeibechei song. Out of the wind she felt warmer, and she could watch the wide fluffy snow fill in her tracks, steadily, until the direction she had come from was gone. By the light of the snow she could see the dark outline of the big arroyo a few feet away. She was sitting on the edge of Cebolleta Creek, where in the springtime the thin cows would graze on grass already chewed flat to the ground. In the wide deep creek bed where only a trickle of water flowed in the summer, the skinny cows would wander, looking for new grass along winding paths splashed with manure. 1

Ayah pulled the old Army blanket over her head like a shawl. Jimmie's blanket—the one he had sent to her. That was a long time ago and the green wool was faded, and it was unraveling on the edges. She did not want to think about Jimmie. So she thought about the weaving and the way her mother had done it. On the tall wooden loom set into the sand under a tamarack tree for shade. She could see it clearly. She had been only a little girl when her grandma gave her the wooden combs to pull the twigs and burrs from the raw, freshly washed wool. And while she combed the wool, her grandma sat beside her, 2 spinning a silvery strand of yarn around the smooth cedar spindle. Her mother worked at the loom with yarns dyed bright yellow and red and gold. She watched them dye the yarn in boiling black pots full of beeweed petals, juniper berries, and sage. The blankets her mother made were soft and woven so tight that rain rolled off them like birds' feathers. Ayah remembered sleeping warm on cold windy nights, wrapped in her mother's blankets on the hogan's sandy floor.

The snow drifted now, with the northwest wind hurling it in gusts. It 3 drifted up around her black overshoes—old ones with little metal buckles. She smiled at the snow which was trying to cover her little by little. She could remember when they had no black rubber overshoes; only the high buckskin leggings that they wrapped over their elkhide moccasins. If the snow was dry or frozen, a person could walk all day and not get wet; and in the evenings the beams of the ceiling would hang with lengths of pale buckskin leggings, drying out slowly.

She felt peaceful remembering. She didn't feel cold any more. Jimmie's 4 blanket seemed warmer than it had ever been. And she could remember the morning he was born. She could remember whispering to her mother, who was sleeping on the other side of the hogan, to tell her it was time now. She did not want to wake the others. The second time she called to her, her mother stood up and pulled on her shoes; she knew. They walked to the old stone hogan together, Ayah walking a step behind her mother. She waited alone, learning the rhythms of the pains while her mother went to call the old woman to help them. The morning was already warm even before dawn and Ayah smelled the bee flowers blooming and the young willow growing at the springs. She could remember that so clearly, but his birth merged into the births of the other children and to her it became all the same birth. They named him for the summer morning and in English they called him Jimmie.

It wasn't like Jimmie died. He just never came back, and one day a dark 5 blue sedan with white writing on its doors pulled up in front of the boxcar shack where the rancher let the Indians live. A man in a khaki uniform trimmed in gold gave them a yellow piece of paper and told them that Jimmie was dead. He said the Army would try to get the body back and then it would be shipped to them; but it wasn't likely because the helicopter had burned after it crashed. All of this was told to Chato because he could understand English. She stood inside the doorway holding the baby while Chato listened. Chato spoke English like a white man and he spoke Spanish too. He was taller than the white man and he stood straighter too. Chato didn't explain why; he just told the military man they could keep the body if they found it. The white man looked bewildered; he nodded his head and he left. Then Chato looked at her and shook his head, and then he told her, "Jimmie isn't coming home anymore," and when he spoke, he used the words to speak of the dead. She didn't cry then, but she hurt inside with anger. And she mourned him as the years passed, when a horse fell with Chato and broke his leg, and the white rancher told them he wouldn't pay Chato until he could work again. She mourned Jimmie because he would have worked for his father then; he would have saddled the big bay horse and ridden the fence lines each day, with wire cutters and heavy gloves, fixing the breaks in the barbed wire and putting the stray cattle back inside again.

She mourned him after the white doctors came to take Danny and Ella   6
away. She was at the shack alone that day they came. It was back in the days before they hired Navajo women to go with them as interpreters. She recognized one of the doctors. She had seen him at the children's clinic at Cañoncito about a month ago. They were wearing khaki uniforms and they waved papers at her and a black ball-point pen, trying to make her understand their English words. She was frightened by the way they looked at the children, like the lizard watches the fly. Danny was swinging on the tire swing on the elm tree behind the rancher's house, and Ella was toddling around the front door, dragging the broomstick horse Chato made for her. Ayah could see they wanted her to sign the papers, and Chato had taught her to sign her name. It was something she was proud of. She only wanted them to go, and to take their eyes away from her children.

She took the pen from the man without looking at his face and she signed   7
the papers in three different places he pointed to. She stared at the ground by their feet and waited for them to leave. But they stood there and began to point and gesture at the children. Danny stopped swinging. Ayah could see his fear. She moved suddenly and grabbed Ella into her arms; the child squirmed, trying to get back to her toys. Ayah ran with the baby toward Danny; she screamed for him to run and then she grabbed him around his chest and carried him too. She ran south into the foothills of juniper trees and black lava rock. Behind her she heard the doctors running, but they had been taken by surprise, and as the hills became steeper and the cholla cactus were thicker, they stopped. When she reached the top of the hill, she stopped to listen in case they were circling around her. But in a few minutes she heard a car engine start and they drove away. The children had been too surprised to cry while she ran with them. Danny was shaking and Ella's little fingers were gripping Ayah's blouse.

She stayed up in the hills for the rest of the day, sitting on a black lava   8
boulder in the sunshine where she could see for miles all around her. The sky was light blue and cloudless, and it was warm for late April. The sun warmth relaxed her and took the fear and anger away. She lay back on the rock and watched the sky. It seemed to her that she could walk into the sky, stepping through clouds endlessly. Danny played with little pebbles and stones, pretending they were birds' eggs and then little rabbits. Ella sat at her feet and dropped fistfuls of dirt into the breeze, watching the dust and particles of sand intently. Ayah watched a hawk soar high above them, dark wings gliding; hunting or only watching, she did not know. The hawk was patient and he circled all afternoon before he disappeared around the high volcanic peak the Mexicans called Guadalupe.

Late in the afternoon, Ayah looked down at the gray boxcar shack with   9 the paint all peeled from the wood; the stove pipe on the roof was rusted and crooked. The fire she had built that morning in the oil drum stove had burned out. Ella was asleep in her lap now and Danny sat close to her, complaining that he was hungry; he asked when they would go to the house. "We will stay up here until your father comes," she told him, "because those white men were chasing us." The boy remembered then and he nodded at her silently.

If Jimmie had been there he could have read those papers and explained   10
to her what they said. Ayah would have known then, never to sign them. The doctors came back the next day and they brought a BIA policeman with them. They told Chato they had her signature and that was all they needed. Except for the kids. She listened to Chato sullenly; she hated him when he told her it was the old woman who died in the winter, spitting blood; it was her old grandma who had given the children this disease. "They don't spit blood," she said coldly. "The whites lie." She held Ella and Danny close to her, ready to run to the hills again. "I want a medicine man first," she said to Chato, not looking at him. He shook his head. "It's too late now. The policeman is with them. You signed the paper." His voice was gentle.

It was worse than if they had died: to lose the children and to know that   11
somewhere, in a place called Colorado, in a place full of sick and dying strangers, her children were without her. There had been babies that died soon after they were born, and one that died before he could walk. She had carried them herself, up to the boulders and great pieces of the cliff that long ago crashed down from Long Mesa; she laid them in the crevices of sandstone and buried them in fine brown sand with round quartz pebbles that washed down the hills in the rain. She had endured it because they had been with her. But she could not bear this pain. She did not sleep for a long time after they took her children. She stayed on the hill where they had fled the first time, and she slept rolled up in the blanket Jimmie had sent her. She carried the pain in her belly and it was fed by everything she saw: the blue sky of their last day together and the dust and pebbles they played with; the swing in the elm tree and the broomstick horse choked life from her. The pain filled her stomach and there was no room for food or for her lungs to fill with air. The air and the food would have been theirs.

She hated Chato, not because he let the policeman and doctors put the   12
screaming children in the government car, but because he had taught her to sign her name. Because it was like the old ones always told her about learning their language or any of their ways: it endangered you. She slept alone on the hill until the middle of November when the first snows came. Then she made a bed for herself where the children had slept. She did not lie down beside Chato again until many years later, when he was sick and shivering and only her body could keep him warm. The illness came after the white rancher told Chato he was too old to work for him anymore, and Chato and his old woman should be out of the shack by the next afternoon because the rancher had hired new people to work there. That had satisfied her. To see how the white man

repaid Chato's years of loyalty and work. All of Chato's fine-sounding English talk didn't change things.

It snowed steadily and the luminous light from the snow gradually diminished 13 into the darkness. Somewhere in Cebolleta a dog barked and other village dogs joined with it. Ayah looked in the direction she had come, from the bar where Chato was buying the wine. Sometimes he told her to go on ahead and wait; and then he never came. And when she finally went back looking for him, she would find him passed out at the bottom of the wooden steps to Azzie's Bar. All the wine would be gone and most of the money too, from the pale blue check that came to them once a month in a government envelope. It was then that she would look at his face and his hands, scarred by ropes and the barbed wire of all those years, and she would think, this man is a stranger; for forty years she had smiled at him and cooked his food, but he remained a stranger. She stood up again, with the snow almost to her knees, and she walked back to find Chato.

It was hard to walk in the deep snow and she felt the air burn in her 14 lungs. She stopped a short distance from the bar to rest and readjust the blanket. But this time he wasn't waiting for her on the bottom step with his old Stetson hat pulled down and his shoulders hunched up in his long wool overcoat.

She was careful not to slip on the wooden steps. When she pushed the 15 door open, warm air and cigarette smoke hit her face. She looked around slowly and deliberately, in every corner, in every dark place that the old man might find to sleep. The bar owner didn't like Indians in there, especially Navajos, but he let Chato come in because he could talk Spanish like he was one of them. The men at the bar stared at her, and the bartender saw that she left the door open wide. Snowflakes were flying inside like moths and melting into a puddle on the oiled wood floor. He motioned to her to close the door, but she did not see him. She held herself straight and walked across the room slowly, searching the room with every step. The snow in her hair melted and she could feel it on her forehead. At the far corner of the room, she saw red flames at the mica window of the old stove door; she looked behind the stove just to make sure. The bar got quiet except for the Spanish polka music playing on the jukebox. She stood by the stove and shook the snow from her blanket and held it near the stove to dry. The wet wool smell reminded her of new-born goats in early March, brought inside to warm near the fire. She felt calm.

In past years they would have told her to get out. But her hair was white 16 now and her face was wrinkled. They looked at her like she was a spider crawling slowly across the room. They were afraid; she could feel the fear. She looked at their faces steadily. They reminded her of the first time the white people brought her children back to her that winter. Danny had been shy and hid behind the thin white woman who brought them. And the baby had not known her until Ayah took her into her arms, and then Ella had nuzzled close to her as she had when she was nursing. The blonde woman was nervous and kept looking at a dainty gold watch on her wrist. She sat on the bench near the small window and watched the dark snow clouds gather around the mountains; she was worrying about the unpaved road. She was frightened by what she saw inside too: the strips of venison drying on a rope across the ceiling and the children jabbering excitedly in a language she did not know. So they stayed for only a few hours. Ayah watched the government car disappear down the road and she knew they were already being weaned from these lava hills and from this sky. The last time they came was in early June, and Ella stared at her the way the men in the bar were now staring. Ayah did not try to pick her up; she smiled at her instead and spoke cheerfully to Danny. When he tried to answer her, he could not seem to remember and he spoke English words with the Navajo. But he gave her a scrap of paper that he had found somewhere and carried in his pocket; it was folded in half, and he shyly looked up at her and said it was a bird. She asked Chato if they were home for good this time. He spoke to the white woman and she shook her head. "How much longer?" he asked, and she said she didn't know; but Chato saw how she stared at the boxcar shack. Ayah turned away then. She did not say good-bye.

She felt satisfied that the men in the bar feared her. Maybe it was her face and the way she held her mouth with teeth clenched tight, like there was nothing anyone could do to her now. She walked north down the road, searching for the old man. She did this because she had the blanket, and there would be no place for him except with her and the blanket in the old adobe barn near the arroyo. They always slept there when they came to Cebolleta. If the money and the wine were gone, she would be relieved because then they could go home again; back to the old hogan with a dirt roof and rock walls where she herself had been born. And the next day the old man could go back to the few sheep they still had, to follow along behind them, guiding them, into dry sandy arroyos where sparse grass grew. She knew he did not like walking behind old ewes when for so many years he rode big quarter-horses and worked with cattle. But she wasn't sorry for him; he should have known all along what would happen.   17

There had not been enough rain for their garden in five years; and that was when Chato finally hitched a ride into the town and brought back brown boxes of rice and sugar and big tin cans of welfare peaches. After that, at the first of the month they went to Cebolleta to ask the postmaster for the check; and then Chato would go to the bar and cash it. They did this as they planted the garden every May, not because anything would survive the summer dust, but because it was time to do this. The journey passed the days that smelled silent and dry like the caves above the canyon with yellow painted buffaloes on their walls.   18

He was walking along the pavement when she found him. He did not stop or turn around when he heard her behind him. She walked beside him and she   19 noticed how slowly he moved now. He smelled strong of woodsmoke and urine. Lately he had been forgetting. Sometimes he called her by his sister's name and she had been gone for a long time. Once she had found him wandering on the road to the white man's ranch, and she asked him why he was going that way; he laughed at her and said, "You know they can't run that ranch without me," and he walked on determined, limping on the leg that had been crushed many years before. Now he looked at her curiously, as if for the first time, but he kept shuffling along, moving slowly along the side of the highway. His gray hair had grown long and spread out on the shoulders of the long overcoat. He wore the old felt hat pulled down over his ears. His boots were worn out at the toes and he had stuffed pieces of an old red shirt in the holes. The rags made his feet look like little animals up to their ears in snow. She laughed at his feet; the snow muffled the sound of her laugh. He stopped and looked at her again. The wind had quit blowing and the snow was falling straight down; the southeast sky was beginning to clear and Ayah could see a star.

"Let's rest awhile," she said to him. They walked away from the road   20
and up the slope to the giant boulders that had tumbled down from the red sandrock mesa throughout the centuries of rainstorms and earth tremors. In a place where the boulders shut out the wind, they sat down with their backs against the rock. She offered half of the blanket to him and they sat wrapped together.

The storm passed swiftly. The clouds moved east. They were massive   21
and full, crowding together across the sky. She watched them with the feeling of horses—steely blue-gray horses startled across the sky. The powerful haunches pushed into the distances and the tail hairs streamed white mist behind them. The sky cleared. Ayah saw that there was nothing between her and the stars. The light was crystalline. There was no shimmer, no distortion through earth haze. She breathed the clarity of the night sky; she smelled the purity of the half moon and the stars. He was lying on his side with his knees pulled up near his belly for warmth. His eyes were closed now, and in the light from the stars and the moon, he looked young again.

She could see it descend out of the night sky: an icy stillness from the   22
edge of the thin moon. She recognized the freezing. It came gradually, sinking snowflake by snowflake until the crust was heavy and deep. It had the strength of the stars in Orion, and its journey was endless. Ayah knew that with the wine he would sleep. He would not feel it. She tucked the blanket around him, remembering how it was when Ella had been with her; and she felt the rush so big inside her heart for the babies. And she sang the only song she knew to sing for babies. She could not remember if she had ever sung it to her children, but she knew that her grandmother had sung it and her mother had sung it:

> The earth is your mother,
>   she holds you.
> The sky is your father,
>   he protects you.

Sleep,
sleep.
Rainbow is your sister,
    she loves you.
The winds are your brothers,
    they sing to you.
Sleep,
sleep.
We are together always
We are together always
There never was a time
when this
was not so.◆

◆ Responding

1. Working with a partner, write a dialogue between Ayah and the doctor who comes to take away her children. If he spoke her language, what argument would he use to convince her to consent to having the children taken away for treatment? How would she respond?

2. Chato ends his life destitute, spending his government checks on alcohol. Discuss the causes of his difficulties. In your opinion, who is responsible for his problems?

3. Explain Ayah's attitude toward life and death, illustrating your explanation with examples from the text.

4. The action takes place "back in the days before they hired Navajo women to go with them as interpreters." Ayah loses her children because she doesn't speak English and can't read the paper she is given to sign. In a journal entry, describe your reactions to these tragic events, or tell about a time when you or someone you know was in a situation in which lack of understanding of language or customs created great difficulties.

JAMES WELCH

A poet of Blackfeet and Gros Ventre heritage, James Welch was born in Browning, Montana, in 1940. After growing up on Montana's Blackfeet and Fort Belknap reservations, he earned a bachelor's degree from the University of Montana. Welch's writing includes the novels Winter in the Blood *(1974) and* The Death of Jim Loney *(1979) and the poetry collection* Riding the Earthboy 40 *(1971). He has received several awards, including a grant from the National Endowment for the Arts; in 1970 he was named to the NEA's literature panel.*

The two poems that follow, from Riding the Earthboy 40, *explore issues of tradition and identity, and the social pressures that threaten them from both outside and within the culture.*

◆ PLEA TO THOSE WHO MATTER ◆

You don't know I pretend my dumb.
My songs often wise, my bells could chase
the snow across these whistle-black plains.
Celebrate. The days are grim. Call your winds
to blast these bundled streets and patronize
my past of poverty and 4-day feasts.

Don't ignore me. I'll build my face a different way,
a way to make you know that I am no longer
proud, my name not strong enough to stand alone.
If I lie and say you took me for a friend,
patched together in my thin bones,
will you help me be cunning and noisy as the wind?

I have plans to burn my drum, move out
and civilize this hair. See my nose? I smash it
straight for you. These teeth? I scrub my teeth
away with stones. I know you help me now I matter.
And I—I come to you, head down, bleeding from my smile,
happy for the snow clean hands of you, my friends.◆

◆ Responding

1. Identify and describe the speaker in the poem. According to the poem, who are "the ones who matter"? How is the speaker willing to change to please them?

2. Explain the attitude of the poet toward the speaker. Does he approve or disapprove of the speaker's behavior? Support your opinion by citing examples from the poem.

3. Working individually or with a partner, write a dialogue between the speaker and an Indian rights activist.

◆ R I D I N G   T H E   E A R T H B O Y   4 0   ◆

Earthboy: so simple his name
should ring a bell for sinners.
Beneath the clowny hat, his eyes
so shot the children called him
dirt, Earthboy farmed this land
and farmed the sky with words.

The dirt is dead. Gone to seed
his rows become marker to a grave
vast as anything but dirt.
Bones should never tell a story
to a bad beginner. I ride
romantic to those words,

those foolish claims that he
was better than dirt, or rain
that bleached his cabin
white as bone. Scattered in the wind
Earthboy calls me from my dream:
Dirt is where the dreams must end.◆

◆ **Responding**

1. Who is the speaker in this poem and what attitude does he have toward the Earthboy? What additional information might enrich your reading of the poem?

2. What do you think the speaker means when he says "Earthboy calls me from my dream: Dirt is where the dreams must end"?

LOUISE ERDRICH

Louise Erdrich, who is of Chippewa and German ancestry, was born in Little Falls, Minnesota, in 1954. After spending much of her youth on the North Dakota reservation where her father taught school, she received a bachelor's degree from Dartmouth College in 1976, and a master's degree from Johns Hopkins University in 1977. In addition to contributing to the Atlantic Monthly, Chicago *magazine, the* Kenyon Review, *and the* North American Review, *Erdrich has published the poetry collection* Jacklight *(1984), as well as the novels* Love Medicine *(1984) and* The Beet Queen *(1986). Her work has earned her the National Book Critics' Circle Award (1984) and the O. Henry Award (1985).*

In the following selection the young narrator, Lipsha Morrissey, describes his attitudes toward his extended family and the healing touch that he believes he has been given. The narrative provides a commentary not only on the Chippewa culture but on the culture beyond the Chippewa community.

◆ *From* **LOVE MEDICINE** ◆

Lipsha Morrissey

I never really done much with my life, I suppose. I never had a television. Grandma Kashpaw had one inside her apartment at the Senior Citizens, so I used to go there and watch my favorite shows. For a while she used to call me the biggest waste on the reservation and hark back to how she saved me from my own mother, who wanted to tie me in a potato sack and throw me in a slough. Sure, I was grateful to Grandma Kashpaw for saving me like that, for raising me, but gratitude gets old. After a while, stale. I had to stop thanking her. One day I told her I had paid her back in full by staying at her beck and call. I'd do anything for Grandma. She knew that. Besides, I took care of Grandpa like nobody else could, on account of what a handful he'd gotten to be.

But that was nothing. I know the tricks of mind and body inside out without ever having trained for it, because I got the touch. It's a thing you got to be born with. I got secrets in my hands that nobody ever knew to ask. Take Grandma Kashpaw with her tired veins all knotted up in her legs like clumps of blue snails. I take my fingers and I snap them on the knots. The medicine flows out of me. The touch. I run my fingers up the maps of those rivers of veins or I knock very gentle above their hearts or I make a circling motion on their stomachs, and it helps them. They feel much better. Some women pay me five dollars.

I couldn't do the touch for Grandpa, though. He was a hard nut. You know, some people fall right through the hole in their lives. It's invisible, but they come to it after time, never knowing where. There is this woman here, Lulu Lamartine, who always had a thing for Grandpa. She loved him since she was a girl and always said he was a genius. Now she says that his mind got so full it exploded.

How can I doubt that? I know the feeling when your mental power builds up too far. I always used to say that's why the Indians got drunk. Even statistically we're the smartest people on the earth. Anyhow with Grandpa I couldn't hardly believe it, because all my youth he stood out as a hero to me. When he started getting toward second childhood he went through different moods. He would stand in the woods and cry at the top of his shirt. It scared me, scared everyone, Grandma worst of all. 4

Yet he was so smart—do you believe it?—that he *knew* he was getting foolish. 5

He said so. He told me that December I failed school and came back on the train to Hoopdance. I didn't have nowhere else to go. He picked me up there and he said it straight out: "I'm getting into my second childhood." And then he said something else I still remember: "I been chosen for it. I couldn't say no." So I figure that a man so smart all his life—tribal chairman and the star of movies and even pictured in the statehouse and on cans of snuff—would know what he's doing by saying yes. I think he was called to second childhood like anybody else gets a call for the priesthood or the army or whatever. So I really did not listen too hard when the doctor said this was some kind of disease old people got eating too much sugar. You just can't tell me that a man who went to Washington and gave them bureaucrats what for could lose his mind from eating too much Milky Way. No, he put second childhood on himself. 6

Behind those songs he sings out in the middle of Mass, and back of those stories that everybody knows by heart, Grandpa is thinking hard about life. I know the feeling. Sometimes I'll throw up a smokescreen to think behind. I'll hitch up to Winnipeg and play the Space Invaders for six hours, but all the time there and back I will be thinking some fairly deep thoughts that surprise even me, and I'm used to it. As for him, if it was just the thoughts there wouldn't be no problem. Smokescreen is what irritates the social structure, see, and Grandpa has done things that just distract people to the point they want to throw him in the cookie jar where they keep the mentally insane. He's far from that, I know for sure, but even Grandma had trouble keeping her patience once he started sneaking off to Lamartine's place. He's not supposed to have his candy, and Lulu feeds it to him. That's *one* of the reasons why he goes. 7

Grandma tried to get me to put the touch on Grandpa soon after he began stepping out. I didn't want to, but before Grandma started telling me again what a bad state my bare behind was in when she first took me home, I thought I should at least pretend. 8

I put my hands on either side of Grandpa's head. You wouldn't look at him and say he was crazy. He's a fine figure of a man, as Lamartine would say, with all his hair and half his teeth, a beak like a hawk, and cheeks like the 9 blades of a hatchet. They put his picture on all the tourist guides to North Dakota and even copied his face for artistic paintings. I guess you could call him a monument all of himself. He started grinning when I put my hands on his templates, and I knew right then he knew how come I touched him. I knew the smokescreen was going to fall.

And I was right: just for a moment it fell. 10

"Let's pitch whoopee," he said across my shoulder to Grandma. 11

They don't use that expression much around here anymore, but for damn 12 sure it must have meant something. It got her goat right quick.

She threw my hands off his head herself and stood in front of him, 13 overmatching him pound for pound, and taller too, for she had a growth spurt in middle age while he had shrunk, so now the length and breadth of her surpassed him. She glared up and spoke her piece into his face about how he was off at all hours tomcatting and chasing Lamartine again and making a damn old fool of himself.

"And you got no more whoopee to pitch anymore anyhow!" she yelled 14 at last, surprising me so my jaw just dropped, for us kids all had pretended for so long that those rustling sounds we heard from their side of the room at night never happened. She sure had pretended it, up till now, anyway. I saw that tears were in her eyes. And that's when I saw how much grief and love she felt for him. And it gave me a real shock to the system. You see I thought love got easier over the years so it didn't hurt so bad when it hurt, or feel so good when it felt good. I thought it smoothed out and old people hardly noticed it. I thought it curled up and died, I guess. Now I saw it rear up like a whip and lash.

She loved him. She was jealous. She mourned him like the dead. 15

And he just smiled into the air, trapped in the seams of his mind. 16

So I didn't know what to do. I was in a laundry then. They was like 17 parents to me, the way they had took me home and reared me. I could see her point for wanting to get him back the way he was so at least she could argue with him, sleep with him, not be shamed out by Lamartine. She'd always love him. That hit me like a ton of bricks. For one whole day I felt this odd feeling that cramped my hands. When you have the touch, that's where longing gets you. I never loved like that. It made me feel all inspired to see them fight, and I wanted to go out and find a woman who I would love until one of us died or went crazy. But I'm not like that really. From time to time I heal a person all up good inside, however when it comes to the long shot I doubt that I got staying power.

And you need that, staying power, going out to love somebody. I knew 18 this quality was not going to jump on me with no effort. So I turned my thoughts back to Grandma and Grandpa. I felt her side of it with my hands and my tangled guts, and I felt his side of it within the stretch of my mentality. He had gone out to lunch one day and never came back. He was fishing in the middle of Lake Turcot. And there was big thoughts on his line, and he kept throwing them back for even bigger ones that would explain to him, say, the meaning of how we got here and why we have to leave so soon. All in all, I could not see myself treating Grandpa with the touch, bringing him back, when the real part of him had chose to be off thinking somewhere. It was only the rest of him that stayed around causing trouble, after all, and we could handle most of it without any problem.

Besides, it was hard to argue with his reasons for doing some things. Take Holy Mass. I used to go there just every so often, when I got frustrated mostly, because even though I know the Higher Power dwells everyplace, there's something very calming about the cool greenish inside of our mission. Or so I thought, anyway. Grandpa was the one who stripped off my delusions in this matter, for it was he who busted right through what Father Upsala calls the sacred serenity of the place.   19

We filed in that time. Me and Grandpa. We sat down in our pews. Then the rosary got started up pre-Mass and that's when Grandpa filled up his chest and opened his mouth and belted out them words.   20

HAIL MARIE FULL OF GRACE.   21

He had a powerful set of lungs.   22

And he kept on like that. He did not let up. He hollered and he yelled them prayers, and I guess people was used to him by now, because they only muttered theirs and did not quit and gawk like I did. I was getting red-faced, I admit. I give him the elbow once or twice, but that wasn't nothing to him. He kept on. He shrieked to heaven and he pleaded like a movie actor and he pounded his chest like Tarzan in the Lord I Am Not Worthies. I thought he might hurt himself. Then after a while I guess I got used to it, and that's when I wondered: how come?   23

So afterwards I out and asked him. "How come? How come you yelled?"   24

"God don't hear me otherwise," said Grandpa Kashpaw.   25

I sweat. I broke right into a little cold sweat at my hairline because I knew this was perfectly right and for years not one damn other person had noticed it. God's been going deaf. Since the Old Testament, God's been deafening up on us. I read, see. Besides the dictionary, which I'm constantly in use of, I had this Bible once. I read it. I found there was discrepancies between then and now. It struck me. Here God used to raineth bread from clouds, smite the Phillipines, sling fire down on red-light districts where people got stabbed. He even appeared in person every once in a while. God used to pay attention, is what I'm saying.   26

Now there's your God in the Old Testament and there is Chippewa Gods as well. Indian Gods, good and bad, like tricky Nanabozho or the water monster, Missepeshu, who lives over in Lake Turcot. That water monster was the last God I ever heard to appear. It had a weakness for young girls and grabbed one of the Blues off her rowboat. She got to shore all right, but only after this monster had its way with her. She's an old lady now. Old Lady Blue. She still won't let her family fish that lake.   27

Our Gods aren't perfect, is what I'm saying, but at least they come around. 28
They'll do a favor if you ask them right. You don't have to yell. But you do
have to know, like I said, how to ask in the right way. That makes problems,
because to ask proper was an art that was lost to the Chippewas once the
Catholics gained ground. Even now, I have to wonder if Higher Power turned
it back, if we got to yell, or if we just don't speak its language.

I looked around me. How else could I explain what all I had seen in my 29
short life—King smashing his fist in things, Gordie drinking himself down to
the Bismarck hospitals, or Aunt June left by a white man to wander off in the
snow. How else to explain the times my touch don't work, and farther back,
to the old-time Indians who was swept away in the outright germ warfare and
dirty-dog killing of the whites. In those times, us Indians was so much kindlier
than now.

We took them in. 30

Oh yes, I'm bitter as an old cutworm just thinking of how they done to 31
us and doing still.

So Grandpa Kashpaw just opened my eyes a little there. Was there any 32
sense relying on a God whose ears was stopped? Just like the government? I
says then, right off, maybe we got nothing but ourselves. And that's not much,
just personally speaking. I know I don't got the cold hard potatoes it takes to
understand everything. Still, there's things I'd like to do. For instance, I'd like
to help some people like my Grandpa and Grandma Kashpaw get back some
happiness within the tail ends of their lives.

I told you once before I couldn't see my way clear to putting the direct 33
touch on Grandpa's mind, and I kept my moral there, but something soon
happened to make me think a little bit of mental adjustment wouldn't do him
and the rest of us no harm.

It was after we saw him one afternoon in the sunshine courtyard of the 34
Senior Citizens with Lulu Lamartine. Grandpa used to like to dig there. He
had his little dandelion fork out, and he was prying up them dandelions right
and left while Lamartine watched him.

"He's scratching up the dirt, all right," said Grandma, watching Lamartine 35
watch Grandpa out the window.

Now Lamartine was about half the considerable size of Grandma, but 36
you would never think of sizes anyway. They were different in an even more
noticeable way. It was the difference between a house fixed up with paint and
picky fence, and a house left to weather away into the soft earth, is what I'm
saying. Lamartine was jacked up, latticed, shuttered, and vinyl sided, while
Grandma sagged and bulged on her slipped foundations and let her hair go the
silver gray of rain-dried lumber. Right now, she eyed the Lamartine's pert
flowery dress with such a look it despaired me. I knew what this could lead to
with Grandma. Alternating tongue storms and rock-hard silences was hard on
a man, even one who didn't notice, like Grandpa. So I went fetching him.

But he was gone when I popped through the little screen door that   37
led out on the courtyard. There was nobody out there either, to point which
way they went. Just the dandelion fork quibbling upright in the ground.
That gave me an idea. I snookered over to the Lamartine's door and I listened in first, then knocked. But nobody. So I went walking through the
lounges and around the card tables. Still nobody. Finally it was my touch that
led me to the laundry room. I cracked the door. I went in. There they were.
And he was really loving her up good, boy, and she was going hell for leather.
Sheets was flapping on the lines above, and washcloths, pillowcases, shirts
was also flying through the air, for they was trying to clear out a place for
themselves in a high-heaped but shallow laundry cart. The washers and the
dryers was all on, chock full of quarters, shaking and moaning. I couldn't
hear what Grandpa and the Lamartine was billing and cooing, and they couldn't
hear me.

I didn't know what to do, so I went inside and shut the door.   38

The Lamartine wore a big curly light-brown wig. Looked like one of them   39
squeaky little white-people dogs. Poodles they call them. Anyway, that wig is
what saved us from the worse. For I could hardly shout and tell them I was in
there, no more could I try and grab him. I was trapped where I was. There
was nothing I could really do but hold the door shut. I was scared of somebody
else upsetting in and really getting an eyeful. Turned out though, in the heat
of the clinch, as I was trying to avert my eyes you see, the Lamartine's curly
wig jumped off her head. And if you ever been in the midst of something and
had a big change like that occur in someone, you can't help know how it
devastates your basic urges. Not only that, but her wig was almost with a life
of its own. Grandpa's eyes were bugging at the change already, and swear to
God if the thing didn't rear up and pop him in the face like it was going to
start something. He scrambled up, Grandpa did, and the Lamartine jumped
up after him all addled looking. They just stared at each other, huffing and
puffing, with quizzical expression. The surprise seemed to drive all sense completely out of Grandpa's mind.

"The letter was what started the fire," he said. "I never would have done   40
it."

"What letter?" said the Lamartine. She was stiff-necked now, and elegant,   41
even bald, like some alien queen. I gave her back the wig. The Lamartine
replaced it on her head, and whenever I saw her after that, I couldn't help
thinking of her bald, with special powers, as if from another planet.

"That was a close call," I said to Grandpa after she had left.   42

But I think he had already forgot the incident. He just stood there all   43
quiet and thoughtful. You really wouldn't think he was crazy. He looked like
he was just about to say something important, explaining himself. He said
something, all right, but it didn't have nothing to do with anything that made
sense.

He wondered where the heck he put his dandelion fork. That's when I   44
decided about the mental adjustment.

Now what was mostly our problem was not so much that he was not all there,   45
but that what was there of him often hankered after Lamartine. If we could
put a stop to that, I thought, we might be getting someplace. But here, see,
my touch was of no use. For what could I snap my fingers at to make him
faithful to Grandma? Like the quality of staying power, this faithfulness was
invisible. I know it's something that you got to acquire, but I never known
where from. Maybe there's no rhyme or reason to it, like my getting the touch,
and then again maybe it's a kind of magic.

It was Grandma Kashpaw who thought of it in the end. She knows things.   46
Although she will not admit she has a scrap of Indian blood in her, there's no
doubt in my mind she's got some Chippewa. How else could you explain the
way she'll be sitting there, in front of her TV story, rocking in her armchair
and suddenly she turns on me, her brown eyes hard as lake-bed flint.

"Lipsha Morrissey," she'll say, "you went out last night and got drunk."   47

How did she know that? I'll hardly remember it myself. Then she'll say   48
she just had a feeling or ache in the scar of her hand or a creak in her shoulder.
She is constantly being told things by little aggravations in her joints or by her
household appliances. One time she told Gordie never to ride with a crazy
Lamartine boy. She had seen something in the polished-up tin of her bread
toaster. So he didn't. Sure enough, the time came we heard how Lyman and
Henry went out of control in their car, ending up in the river. Lyman swam
to the top, but Henry never made it.

Thanks to Grandma's toaster, Gordie was probably spared.   49

Someplace in the blood Grandma Kashpaw knows things. She also re-   50
members things, I found. She keeps things filed away. She's got a memory like
them video games that don't forget your score. One reason she remembers so
many details about the trouble I gave her in early life is so she can flash back
her total when she needs to.

Like now. Take the love medicine. I don't know where she remembered   51
that from. It came tumbling from her mind like an asteroid off the corner of
the screen.

Of course she starts out by mentioning the time I had this accident in   52
church and did she leave me there with wet overhalls? No she didn't. And ain't
I glad? Yes I am. Now what you want now, Grandma?

But when she mentions them love medicines, I feel my back prickle at   53
the danger. These love medicines is something of an old Chippewa specialty.
No other tribe has got them down so well. But love medicines is not for the
layman to handle. You don't just go out and get one without paying for it.
Before you get one, even, you should go through one hell of a lot of mental
condensation. You got to think it over. Choose the right one. You could really
mess up your life grinding up the wrong little thing.

So anyhow, I said to Grandma I'd give this love medicine some thought.   54
I knew the best thing was to go ask a specialist like Old Man Pillager, who
lives up in a tangle of bush and never shows himself. But the truth is I was
afraid of him, like everyone else. He was known for putting the twisted mouth
on people, seizing up their hearts. Old Man Pillager was serious business, and
I have always thought it best to steer clear of that whenever I could. That's
why I took the powers in my own hands. That's why I did what I could.

I put my whole mentality to it, nothing held back. After a while I started   55
to remember things I'd heard gossiped over.

I heard of this person once who carried a charm of seeds that looked like   56
baby pearls. They was attracted to a metal knife, which made them powerful.
But I didn't know where them seeds grew. Another love charm I heard about
I couldn't go along with, because how was I suppose to catch frogs in the act,
which it required. Them little creatures is slippery and fast. And then the
powerfullest of all, the most extreme, involved nail clips and such. I wasn't
anywhere near asking Grandma to provide me all the little body bits that this
last love recipe called for. I went walking around for days just trying to think
up something that would work.

Well I got it. If it hadn't been the early fall of the year, I never would   57
have got it. But I was sitting underneath a tree one day down near the school
just watching people's feet go by when something tells me, look up! Look up!
So I look up, and I see two honkers, Canada geese, the kind with little masks
on their faces, a bird what mates for life. I see them flying right over my head
naturally preparing to land in some slough on the reservation, which they
certainly won't get off of alive.

It hits me, anyway. Them geese, they mate for life. And I think to myself,   58
just what if I went out and got a pair? And just what if I fed some part—say
the goose heart—of the female to Grandma and Grandpa ate the other heart?
Wouldn't that work? Maybe it's all invisible, and then maybe again it's magic.
Love is a stony road. We know that for sure. If it's true that the higher feelings
of devotion get lodged in the heart like people say, then we'd be home free. If
not, eating goose heart couldn't harm nobody anyway. I thought it was worth
my effort, and Grandma Kashpaw thought so, too. She had always known a
good idea when she heard one. She borrowed me Grandpa's gun.

So I went out to this particular slough, maybe the exact same slough I   59
never got thrown in by my mother, thanks to Grandma Kashpaw, and I hunched
down in a good comfortable pile of rushes. I got my gun loaded up. I ate a few
of these soft baloney sandwiches Grandma made me for lunch. And then I
waited. The cattails blown back and forth above my head. Them stringy blue
herons was spearing up their prey. The thing I know how to do best in this
world, the thing I been training for all my life, is to wait. Sitting there and
and sitting there was no hardship on me. I got to thinking about some funny
things that happened. There was this one time that Lulu Lamartine's little blue
tweety bird, a paraclete, I guess you'd call it, flown up inside her dress and

got lost within there. I recalled her running out into the hallway trying to yell something, shaking. She was doing a right good jig there, cutting the rug for sure, and the thing is it *never* flown out. To this day people speculate where it went. They fear she might perhaps of crushed it in her corsets. It sure hasn't ever yet been seen alive. I thought of funny things for a while, but then I used them up, and strange things that happened started weaseling their way into my mind.

I got to thinking quite naturally of the Lamartine's cousin named Wrist-   60
watch. I never knew what his real name was. They called him Wristwatch because he got his father's broken wristwatch as a young boy when his father passed on. Never in his whole life did Wristwatch take his father's watch off. He didn't care if it worked, although after a while he got sensitive when people asked what time it was, teasing him. He often put it to his ear like he was listening to the tick. But it was broken for good and forever, people said so, at least that's what they thought.

Well I saw Wristwatch smoking in his pickup one afternoon and by nine   61
that evening he was dead.

He died sitting at the Lamartine's table, too. As she told it, Wristwatch   62
had just eaten himself a good-size dinner and she said would he take seconds on the hot dish when he fell over to the floor. They turnt him over. He was gone. But here's the strange thing: when the Senior Citizen's orderly took the pulse he noticed that the wristwatch Wristwatch wore was now working. The moment he died the wristwatch started keeping perfect time. They buried him with the watch still ticking on his arm.

I got to thinking. What if some gravediggers dug up Wristwatch's casket   63
in two hundred years and that watch was still going? I thought what question they would ask and it was this: Whose hand wound it?

I started shaking like a piece of grass at just the thought.   64

Not to get off the subject or nothing. I was still hunkered in the slough.   65
It was passing late into the afternoon and still no honkers had touched down. Now I don't need to tell you that the waiting did not get to me, it was the chill. The rushes was very soft, but damp. I was getting cold and debating to leave, when they landed. Two geese swimming here and there as big as life, looking deep into each other's little pinhole eyes. Just the ones I was looking for. So I lifted Grandpa's gun to my shoulder and I aimed perfectly, and *blam! Blam!* I delivered two accurate shots. But the thing is, them shots missed. I couldn't hardly believe it. Whether it was that the stock had warped or the barrel got bent someways, I don't quite know, but anyway them geese flown off into the dim sky, and Lipsha Morrissey was left there in the rushes with evening fallen and his two cold hands empty. He had before him just the prospect of another day of bone-cracking chill in them rushes, and the thought of it got him depressed.

Now it isn't my style, in no way, to get depressed.   66

So I said to myself, Lipsha Morrissey, you're a happy S.O.B. who could   67 be covered up with weeds by now down at the bottom of this slough, but instead you're alive to tell the tale. You might have problems in life, but you still got the touch. You got the power, Lipsha Morrissey. Can't argue that. So put your mind to it and figure out how not to be depressed.

I took my advice. I put my mind to it. But I never saw at the time how   68
my thoughts led me astray toward a tragic outcome none could have known. I ignored all the danger, all the limits, for I was tired of sitting in the slough and my feet were numb. My face was aching. I was chilled, so I played with fire. I told myself love medicine was simple. I told myself the old superstitions was just that—strange beliefs. I told myself to take the ten dollars Mary MacDonald had paid me for putting the touch on her arthritis joint, and the other five I hadn't spent from winning bingo last Thursday. I told myself to go down to the Red Owl store.

And here is what I did that made the medicine backfire. I took an evil   69
shortcut. I looked at birds that was dead and froze.

All right. So now I guess you will say, "Slap a malpractice suit on Lipsha   70
Morrissey."

I heard of those suits. I used to think it was a color clothing quack doctors   71
had to wear so you could tell them from the good ones. Now I know better that it's law.

As I walked back from the Red Owl with the rock-hard, heavy turkeys,   72
I argued to myself about malpractice. I thought of faith. I thought to myself that faith could be called belief against the odds and whether or not there's any proof. How does that sound? I thought how we might have to yell to be heard by Higher Power, but that's not saying it's not *there*. And that is faith for you. It's belief even when the goods don't deliver. Higher Power makes promises we all know they can't back up, but anybody ever go and slap an old malpractice suit on God? Or the U.S. government? No they don't. Faith might be stupid, but it gets us through. So what I'm heading at is this. I finally convinced myself that the real actual power to the love medicine was not the goose heart itself but the faith in the cure.

I didn't believe it, I knew it was wrong, but by then I had waded so far   73
into my lie I was stuck there. And then I went one step further.

The next day, I cleaned the hearts away from the paper packages of   74
gizzards inside the turkeys. Then I wrapped them hearts with a clean hankie and brung them both to get blessed up at the mission. I wanted to get official blessings from the priest, but when Father answered the door to the rectory, wiping his hands on a little towel, I could tell he was a busy man.

"Booshoo, Father," I said. "I got a slight request to make of you this   75
afternoon."

"What is it?" he said.   76

"Would you bless this package?" I held out the hankie with the hearts   77
tied inside it.

He looked at the package, questioning it. 78

"It's turkey hearts," I honestly had to reply. 79

A look of annoyance crossed his face. 80

"Why don't you bring this matter over to Sister Martin," he said. "I have 81
duties."

And so, although the blessing wouldn't be as powerful, I went over to 82
the Sisters with the package.

I rung the bell, and they brought Sister Martin to the door. I had her as 83
a music teacher, but I was always so shy then. I never talked out loud. Now,
I had grown taller than Sister Martin. Looking down, I saw that she was not
feeling up to snuff. Brown circles hung under her eyes.

"What's the matter?" she said, not noticing who I was. 84

"Remember me, Sister?" 85

She squinted up at me. 86

"Oh yes," she said after a moment. "I'm sorry, you're the youngest of the 87
Kashpaws. Gordie's brother."

Her face warmed up. 88

"Lipsha," I said, "that's my name." 89

"Well, Lipsha," she said, smiling broad at me now, "what can I do for 90
you?"

They always said she was the kindest-hearted of the Sisters up the hill, 91
and she was. She brought me back into their own kitchen and made me take
a big yellow wedge of cake and a glass of milk.

"Now tell me," she said, nodding at my package. "What have you got 92
wrapped up so carefully in those handkerchiefs?"

Like before, I answered honestly. 93

"Ah," said Sister Martin. "Turkey hearts." She waited. 94

"I hoped you could bless them." 95

She waited some more, smiling with her eyes. Kind-hearted though she 96
was, I began to sweat. A person could not pull the wool down over Sister
Martin. I stumbled through my mind for an explanation, quick, that wouldn't
scare her off.

"They're a present," I said, "for Saint Kateri's statue." 97

"She's not a saint yet." 98

"I know," I stuttered on, "in the hopes they will crown her." 99

"Lipsha," she said, "I never heard of such a thing." 100

So I told her. "Well the truth is," I said, "it's a kind of medicine." 101

"For what?" 102

"Love." 103

"Oh Lipsha," she said after a moment, "you don't need any medicine. 104
I'm sure any girl would like you exactly the way you are."

I just sat there. I felt miserable, caught in my pack of lies. 105

"Tell you what," she said, seeing how bad I felt, "my blessing won't make 106
any difference anyway. But there is something you can do."

I looked up at her, hopeless. 107

"Just be yourself." 108

I looked down at my plate. I knew I wasn't much to brag about right 109
then, and I shortly became even less. For as I walked out the door I stuck my
fingers in the cup of holy water that was sacred from their touches. I put my
fingers in and blessed the hearts, quick, with my own hand.

I went back to Grandma and sat down in her little kitchen at the Senior Citizens. 110
I unwrapped them hearts on the table, and her hard agate eyes went soft. She
said she wasn't even going to cook those hearts up but eat them raw so their
power would go down strong as possible.

I couldn't hardly watch when she munched hers. Now that's true love. I 111
was worried about how she would get Grandpa to eat his, but she told me she'd
think of something and don't worry. So I did not. I was supposed to hide off
in her bedroom while she put dinner on a plate for Grandpa and fixed up the
heart so he'd eat it. I caught a glint of the plate she was making for him. She
put that heart smack on a piece of lettuce like in a restaurant and then attached
to it a little heap of boiled peas.

He said down. I was listening in the next room. 112

She said, "Why don't you have some mash potato?" So he had some mash 113
potato. Then she gave him a little piece of boiled meat. He ate that. Then she
said, "Why you didn't never touch your salad yet. See that heart? I'm feeding
you it because the doctor said your blood needs building up."

I couldn't help it, at that point I peeked through a crack in the door. 114

I saw Grandpa picking at that heart on his plate with a certain look. He 115
didn't look appetized at all, is what I'm saying. I doubted our plan was going
to work. Grandma was getting worried, too. She told him one more time,
loudly, that he had to eat that heart.

"Swallow it down," she said. "You'll hardly notice it." 116

He just looked at her straight on. The way he looked at her made me 117
think I was going to see the smokescreen drop a second time, and sure enough
it happened.

"What you want me to eat this for so bad?" he asked her uncannily. 118

Now Grandma knew the jig was up. She knew that he knew she was 119
working medicine. He put his fork down. He rolled the heart around his saucer
plate.

"I don't want to eat this," he said to Grandma. "It don't look good." 120

"Why it's fresh grade-A," she told him. "One hundred percent." 121

He didn't ask percent what, but his eyes took on an even more warier 122
look.

"Just go on and try it," she said, taking the salt shaker up in her hand. 123
She was getting annoyed. "Not tasty enough? You want me to salt it for you?"
She waved the shaker over his plate.

"All right, skinny white girl!" She had got Grandpa mad. Oopsy-daisy, 124 he popped the heart into his mouth. I was about to yawn loudly and come out of the bedroom. I was about ready for this crash of wills to be over, when I saw he was still up to his old tricks. First he rolled it into one side of his cheek. "Mmmmm," he said. Then he rolled it into the other side of his cheek. "Mmmmmmm," again. Then he stuck his tongue out with the heart on it and put it back, and there was no time to react. He had pulled Grandma's leg once too far. Her goat was got. She was so mad she hopped up quick as a wink and slugged him between the shoulderblades to make him swallow.

Only thing is, he choked. 125

He choked real bad. A person can choke to death. You ever sit down at 126 a restaurant table and up above you there is a list of instructions what to do if something slides down the wrong pipe? It sure makes you chew slow, that's for damn sure. When Grandpa fell off his chair better believe me that little graphic illustrated poster fled into my mind. I jumped out the bedroom. I done everything within my power that I could do to unlodge what was choking him. I squeezed underneath his ribcage. I socked him in the back. I was desperate. But here's the factor of decision: he wasn't choking on the heart alone. There was more to it than that. It was other things that choked him as well. It didn't seem like he wanted to struggle or fight. Death came and tapped his chest, so he went just like that. I'm sorry all through my body at what I done to him with that heart, and there's those who will say Lipsha Morrissey is just excusing himself off the hook by giving song and dance about how Grandpa gave up.

Maybe I can't admit what I did. My touch had gone worthless, that is 127 true. But here is what I seen while he lay in my arms.

You hear a person's life will flash before their eyes when they're in danger. 128 It was him in danger, not me, but it was *his* life come over me. I saw him dying, and it was like someone pulled the shade down in a room. His eyes clouded over and squeezed shut, but just before that I looked in. He was still fishing in the middle of Lake Turcot. Big thoughts was on his line and he had half a case of beer in the boat. He waved at me, grinned, and then the bobber went under.

Grandma had gone out of the room crying for help. I bunched my force 129 up in my hands and I held him. I was so wound up I couldn't even breathe. All the moments he had spent with me, all the times he had hoisted me on his shoulders or pointed into the leaves was concentrated in that moment. Time was flashing back and forth like a pinball machine. Lights blinked and balls hopped and rubber bands chirped, until suddenly I realized the last ball had gone down the drain and there was nothing. I felt his force leaving him, flowing out of Grandpa never to return. I felt his mind weakening. The bobber going under in the lake. And I felt the touch retreat back into the darkness inside my body, from where it came.

One time, long ago, both of us were fishing together. We caught a big 130 old snapper what started towing us around like it was a motor. "This here fishline is pretty damn good," Grandpa said. "Let's keep this turtle on and see where he takes us." So we rode along behind that turtle, watching as from time to time it surfaced. The thing was just about the size of a washtub. It took us all around the lake twice, and as it was traveling, Grandpa said something as a joke. "Lipsha," he said, "we are glad your mother didn't want you because we was always looking for a boy like you who would tow us around the lake."

"I ain't no snapper. Snappers is so stupid they stay alive when their head's chopped off," I said. 131

"That ain't stupidity," said Grandpa. "Their brain's just in their heart, like yours is." 132

When I looked up, I knew the fuse had blown between my heart and my mind and that a terrible understanding was to be given. 133

Grandma got back into the room and I saw her stumble. And then she went down too. It was like a house you can't hardly believe has stood so long, through years of record weather, suddenly goes down in the worst yet. It makes sense, is what I'm saying, but you still can't hardly believe it. You think a person you know has got through death and illness and being broke and living on commodity rice will get through anything. Then they fold and you see how fragile were the stones that underpinned them. You see how instantly the ground can shift you thought was solid. You see the stop signs and the yellow dividing markers of roads you traveled and all the instructions you had played according to vanish. You see how all the everyday things you counted on was just a dream you had been having by which you run your whole life. She had been over me, like a sheer overhang of rock dividing Lipsha Morrissey from outer space. And now she went underneath. It was as though the banks gave way on the shores of Lake Turcot, and where Grandpa's passing was just the bobber swallowed under by his biggest thought, her fall was the house and the rock under it sliding after, sending half the lake splashing up to the clouds. 134

Where there was nothing. 135

You play them games never knowing what you see. When I fell into the dream alongside of both of them I saw that the dominions I had defended myself from anciently was but delusions of the screen. Blips of light. And I was scot-free now, whistling through space. 136

I don't know how I come back. I don't know from where. They was slapping my face when I arrived back at Senior Citizens and they was oxygenating her. I saw her chest move, almost unwilling. She sighed the way she would when somebody bothered her in the middle of a row of beads she was counting. I think it irritated her to no end that they brought her back. I knew from the way she looked after they took the mask off, she was not going to forgive them disturbing her restful peace. Nor was she forgiving Lipsha Morrissey. She had been stepping out onto the road of death, she told the children later at the funeral. I asked was there any stop signs or dividing markers on the road, but she clamped her lips in a vise the way she always done when she was mad. 137

Which didn't bother me. I knew when things had cleared out she wouldn't 138 have no choice. I was not going to speculate where the blame was put for Grandpa's death. We was in it together. She had slugged him between the shoulders. My touch had failed him, never to return.

All the blood children and the took-ins, like me, came home from Min- 139
neapolis and Chicago, where they had relocated years ago. They stayed with friends on the reservation or with Aurelia or slept on Grandma's floor. They were struck down with grief and bereavement to be sure, every one of them. At the funeral I sat down in the back of the church with Albertine. She had gotten all skinny and ragged haired from cramming all her years of study into two or three. She had decided that to be a nurse was not enough for her so she was going to be a doctor. But the way she was straining her mind she didn't look too hopeful. Her eyes were bloodshot from driving and crying. She took my hand. From the back we watched all the children and the mourners as they hunched over their prayers, their hands stuffed full of Kleenex. It was someplace in that long sad service that my vision shifted. I began to see things different, more clear. The family kneeling down turned to rocks in a field. It struck me how strong and reliable grief was, and death. Until the end of time, death would be our rock.

So I had perspective on it all, for death gives you that. All the Kashpaw 140
children had done various things to me in their lives—shared their folks with me, loaned me cash, beat me up in secret—and I decided, because of death, then and there I'd call it quits. If I ever saw King again, I'd shake his hand. Forgiving somebody else made the whole thing easier to bear.

Everybody saw Grandpa off into the next world. And then the Kashpaws 141
had to get back to their jobs, which was numerous and impressive. I had a few beers with them and I went back to Grandma, who had sort of got lost in the shuffle of everybody being sad about Grandpa and glad to see one another.

Zelda had sat beside her the whole time and was sitting with her now. I 142
wanted to talk to Grandma, say how sorry I was, that it wasn't her fault, but only mine. I would have, but Zelda gave me one of her looks of strict warning as if to say, "I'll take care of Grandma. Don't horn in on the women."

If only Zelda knew, I thought, the sad realities would change her. But of 143
course I couldn't tell the dark truth.

It was evening, late. Grandma's light was on underneath a crack in the door. 144
About a week had passed since we buried Grandpa. I knocked first but there wasn't no answer, so I went right in. The door was unlocked. She was there but she didn't notice me at first. Her hands were tied up in her rosary, and her gaze was fully absorbed in the easy chair opposite her, the one that had always been Grandpa's favorite. I stood there, staring with her, at the little green nubs in the cloth and plastic armrest covers and the sad little hair-tonic stain he had made on the white doily where he laid his head. For the life of me I couldn't figure what she was staring at. Thin space. Then she turned.

"He ain't gone yet," she said. 145

Remember that chill I luckily didn't get from waiting in the slough? I got 146
it now. I felt it start from the very center of me, where fear hides, waiting to
attack. It spiraled outward so that in minutes my fingers and teeth were shaking
and clattering. I knew she told the truth. She seen Grandpa. Whether or not
he had been there is not the point. She had *seen* him, and that meant anybody
else could see him, too. Not only that but, as is usually the case with these
here ghosts, he had a certain uneasy reason to come back. And of course
Grandma Kashpaw had scanned it out.

I sat down. We sat together on the couch watching his chair out of the 147
corner of our eyes. She had found him sitting in his chair when she walked in
the door.

"It's the love medicine, my Lipsha," she said. "It was stronger than we 148
thought. He came back even after death to claim me to his side."

I was afraid. "We shouldn't have tampered with it," I said. She agreed. 149
For a while we sat still. I don't know what she thought, but my head felt
screwed on backward. I couldn't accurately consider the situation, so I told
Grandma to go to bed. I would sleep on the couch keeping my eye on Grandpa's
chair. Maybe he would come back and maybe he wouldn't. I guess I feared the
one as much as the other, but I got to thinking, see, as I lay there in darkness,
that perhaps even through my terrible mistakes some good might come. If
Grandpa did come back, I thought he'd return in his right mind. I could talk
with him. I could tell him it was all my fault for playing with power I did not
understand. Maybe he'd forgive me and rest in peace. I hoped this. I calmed
myself and waited for him all night.

He fooled me though. He knew what I was waiting for, and it wasn't 150
what he was looking to hear. Come dawn I heard a blood-splitting cry from
the bedroom and I rushed in there. Grandma turnt the lights on. She was sitting
on the edge of the bed and her face looked harsh, pinched-up, gray.

"He was here," she said. "He came and laid down next to me in bed. 151
And he touched me."

Her heart broke down. She cried. His touch was so cold. She laid back 152
in bed after a while, as it was morning, and I went to the couch. As I lay there,
falling asleep, I suddenly felt Grandpa's presence and the barrier between us
like a swollen river. I felt how I had wronged him. How awful was the place
where I had sent him. Behind the wall of death, he'd watched the living eat
and cry and get drunk. He was lonesome, but I understood he meant no harm.

"Go back," I said to the dark, afraid and yet full of pity. "You got to be 153
with your own kind now," I said. I felt him retreating, like a sigh, growing
less. I felt his spirit as it shrunk back through the walls, the blinds, the brick
courtyard of Senior Citizens. "Look up Aunt June," I whispered as he left.

I slept late the next morning, a good hard sleep allowing the sun to rise and 154
warm the earth. It was past noon when I awoke. There is nothing, to my mind,
like a long sleep to make those hard decisions that you neglect under stress of

wakefulness. Soon as I woke up that morning, I saw exactly what I'd say to Grandma. I had gotten humble in the past week, not just losing the touch but getting jolted into the understanding that would prey on me from here on out. Your life feels different on you, once you greet death and understand your heart's position. You wear your life like a garment from the mission bundle sale ever after—lightly because you realize you never paid nothing for it, cherishing because you know you won't ever come by such a bargain again. Also you have the feeling someone wore it before you and someone will after. I can't explain that, not yet, but I'm putting my mind to it.

"Grandma," I said, "I got to be honest about the love medicine." 155

She listened. I knew from then on she would be listening to me the way 156 I had listened to her before. I told her about the turkey hearts and how I had them blessed. I told her what I used as love medicine was purely a fake, and then I said to her what my understanding brought me.

"Love medicine ain't what brings him back to you, Grandma. No, it's 157 something else. He loved you over time and distance, but he went off so quick he never got the chance to tell you how he loves you, how he doesn't blame you, how he understands. It's true feeling, not no magic. No supermarket heart could have brung him back."

She looked at me. She was seeing the years and days I had no way of 158 knowing, and she didn't believe me. I could tell this. Yet a look came on her face. It was like the look of mothers drinking sweetness from their children's eyes. It was tenderness.

"Lipsha," she said, "you was always my favorite." 159

She took the beads off the bedpost, where she kept them to say at night, 160 and she told me to put out my hand. When I did this, she shut the beads inside of my fist and held them there a long minute, tight, so my hand hurt. I almost cried when she did this. I don't really know why. Tears shot up behind my eyelids, and yet it was nothing. I didn't understand, except her hand was so strong, squeezing mine.

The earth was full of life and there were dandelions growing out the window, 161 thick as thieves, already seeded, fat as big yellow plungers. She let my hand go. I got up. "I'll go out and dig a few dandelions," I told her.

Outside, the sun was hot and heavy as a hand on my back. I felt it flow 162 down my arms, out my fingers, arrowing through the ends of the fork into the earth. With every root I prized up there was return, as if I was kin to its secret lesson. The touch got stronger as I worked through the grassy afternoon. Uncurling from me like a seed out of the blackness where I was lost, the touch spread. The spiked leaves full of bitter mother's milk. A buried root. A nuisance people dig up and throw in the sun to wither. A globe of frail seeds that's indestructible.◆

◆ Responding

1. Lipsha Morrissey describes human behavior by comparing it to things he sees in the world around him. Find some of his descriptions and discuss what they tell you about his daily life. Replace some of his descriptions with ones of your own that reflect your understanding of human behavior.

2. The Catholic Church and the Chippewas' traditional beliefs make up a great deal of Lipsha's worldview. Give some examples from the story that show how each influences his thinking and behavior and the ways in which he combines the two.

3. Explain why Lipsha views the U.S. government as a "Higher Power" or God.

4. Grandpa Kashpaw's death gives Lipsha a new understanding of life, death, and love. Using examples from the reading, discuss the changes that take place in his understanding of life's milestones.

Paula Gunn Allen

The novelist, essayist, and poet Paula Gunn Allen was born in 1939 in Cubero, New Mexico, of Laguna-Sioux and Lebanese-Jewish ancestry. She holds a doctorate from the University of New Mexico. In addition to serving as editor for Studies in American Indian Literature *(1983), she has published a novel,* The Woman Who Owned the Shadows *(1983), a book-length study,* The Sacred Hoop: Recovering the Feminine in American Indian Traditions *(1986), and five volumes of poetry. In addition, she has been awarded a grant for creative writing from the National Endowment for the Arts and a fellowship for Native American Studies from University of California at Los Angeles.*

"Where I Come from Is Like This," from The Sacred Hoop, *explores connections between ethnic identity and feminist ideology by tracing some of the stories that comprised the Native American oral tradition Allen was exposed to as a child.*

◆ WHERE I COME FROM IS LIKE THIS ◆

I

Modern American Indian women, like their non-Indian sisters, are deeply engaged in the struggle to redefine themselves. In their struggle they must reconcile traditional tribal definitions of women with industrial and postindustrial non-Indian definitions. Yet while these definitions seem to be more or less mutually exclusive, Indian women must somehow harmonize and integrate both in their own lives.

An American Indian woman is primarily defined by her tribal identity. In her eyes, her destiny is necessarily that of her people, and her sense of herself as a woman is first and foremost prescribed by her tribe. The definitions of woman's roles are as diverse as tribal cultures in the Americas. In some she is devalued, in others she wields considerable power. In some she is a familial/clan adjunct, in some she is as close to autonomous as her economic circumstances and psychological traits permit. But in no tribal definitions is she perceived in the same way as are women in western industrial and postindustrial cultures.

In the west, few images of women form part of the cultural mythos, and these are largely sexually charged. Among Christians, the madonna is the female prototype, and she is portrayed as essentially passive: her contribution is simply that of birthing. Little else is attributed to her and she certainly possesses few of the characteristics that are attributed to mythic figures among Indian tribes.

This image is countered (rather than balanced) by the witch-goddess/whore characteristics designed to reinforce cultural beliefs about women, as well as western adversarial and dualistic perceptions of reality.

The tribes see women variously, but they do not question the power of femininity. Sometimes they see women as fearful, sometimes peaceful, sometimes omnipotent and omniscient, but they never portray women as mindless, helpless, simple, or oppressed. And while the women in a given tribe, clan, or band may be all these things, the individual woman is provided with a variety of images of women from the interconnected supernatural, natural, and social worlds she lives in.

As a half-breed American Indian woman, I cast about in my mind for negative images of Indian women, and I find none that are directed to Indian women alone. The negative images I do have are of Indians in general and in fact are more often of males than of females. All these images come to me from non-Indian sources, and they are always balanced by a positive image. My ideas of womanhood, passed on largely by my mother and grandmothers, Laguna Pueblo women, are about practicality, strength, reasonableness, intelligence, wit, and competence. I also remember vividly the women who came to my father's store, the women who held me and sang to me, the women at Feast Day, at Grab Days, the women in the kitchen of my Cubero home, the women I grew up with; none of them appeared weak or helpless, none of them presented herself tentatively. I remember a certain reserve on those lovely brown faces; I remember the direct gaze of eyes framed by bright-colored shawls draped over their heads and cascading down their backs. I remember the clean cotton dresses and carefully pressed hand-embroidered aprons they always wore; I remember laughter and good food, especially the sweet bread and the oven bread they gave us. Nowhere in my mind is there a foolish woman, a dumb woman, a vain woman, or a plastic woman, though the Indian women I have known have shown a wide range of personal style and demeanor.

My memory includes the Navajo woman who was badly beaten by her Sioux husband; but I also remember that my grandmother abandoned her Sioux husband long ago. I recall the stories about the Laguna woman beaten regularly by her husband in the presence of her children so that the children would not believe in the strength and power of femininity. And I remember the women who drank, who got into fights with other women and with the men, and who often won those battles. I have memories of tired women, partying women, stubborn women, sullen women, amicable women, selfish women, shy women, and aggressive women. Most of all I remember the women who laugh and scold and sit uncomplaining in the long sun on feast days and who cook wonderful food on wood stoves, in beehive mud ovens, and over open fires outdoors.

Among the images of women that come to me from various tribes as well as my own are White Buffalo Woman, who came to the Lakota long ago and brought them the religion of the Sacred Pipe which they still practice; Tinotzin the goddess who came to Juan Diego to remind him that she still walked the hills of her people and sent him with her message, her demand and her proof to the Catholic bishop in the city nearby. And from Laguna I take the images of Yellow Woman, Coyote Woman, Grandmother Spider (Spider Old Woman), who brought the light, who gave us weaving and medicine, who gave us life. Among the Keres she is known as Thought Woman who created us all and who keeps us in creation even now. I remember Iyatiku, Earth Woman, Corn Woman, who guides and counsels the people to peace and who welcomes us home when we cast off this coil of flesh as huskers cast off the leaves that wrap the corn. I remember Iyatiku's sister, Sun Woman, who held metals and cattle, pigs and sheep, highways and engines and so many things in her bundle, who went away to the east saying that one day she would return.

II

Since the coming of the Anglo-Europeans beginning in the fifteenth century, the fragile web of identity that long held tribal people secure has gradually been weakened and torn. But the oral tradition has prevented the complete destruction of the web, the ultimate disruption of tribal ways. The oral tradition is vital; it heals itself and the tribal web by adapting to the flow of the present while never relinquishing its connection to the past. Its adaptability has always been required, as many generations have experienced. Certainly the modern American Indian woman bears slight resemblance to her forebears—at least on superficial examination—but she is still a tribal woman in her deepest being. Her tribal sense of relationship to all that is continues to flourish. And though she is at times beset by her knowledge of the enormous gap between the life she lives and the life she was raised to live, and while she adapts her mind and being to the circumstances of her present life, she does so in tribal ways, mending the tears in the web of being from which she takes her existence as she goes. 8

My mother told me stories all the time, though I often did not recognize them as that. My mother told me stories about cooking and childbearing; she told me stories about menstruation and pregnancy; she told me stories about gods and heroes, about fairies and elves, about goddesses and spirits; she told me stories about the land and the sky, about cats and dogs, about snakes and spiders; she told me stories about climbing trees and exploring the mesas; she told me stories about going to dances and getting married; she told me stories about dressing and undressing, about sleeping and waking; she told me stories about herself, about her mother, about her grandmother. She told me stories about grieving and laughing, about thinking and doing; she told me stories about school and about people; about darning and mending; she told me stories about turquoise and about gold; she told me European stories and Laguna stories; she told me Catholic stories and Presbyterian stories; she told me city stories and country stories; she told me political stories and religious stories. She told me stories about living and stories about dying. And in all of those stories she told me who I was, who I was supposed to be, who I came from, and who would follow me. In this way she taught 9 me the meaning of the words she said, that all life is a circle and everything has a place within it. That's what she said and what she showed me in the things she did and the way she lives.

Of course, through my formal, white, Christian education, I discovered   10
that other people had stories of their own—about women, about Indians, about fact, about reality—and I was amazed by a number of startling suppositions that others made about tribal customs and beliefs. According to the un-Indian, non-Indian view, for instance, Indians barred menstruating women from cer- emonies and indeed segregated them from the rest of the people, consigning them to some space specially designed for them. This showed that Indians considered menstruating women unclean and not fit to enjoy the company of decent (nonmenstruating) people, that is, men. I was surprised and confused to hear this because my mother had taught me that white people had strange attitudes toward menstruation: they thought something was bad about it, that it meant you were sick, cursed, sinful, and weak and that you had to be very careful during that time. She taught me that menstruation was a normal oc- currence, that I could go swimming or hiking or whatever else I wanted to do during my period. She actively scorned women who took to their beds, who were incapacitated by cramps, who "got the blues."

As I struggled to reconcile these very contradictory interpretations of   11
American Indians' traditional beliefs concerning menstruation, I realized that the menstrual taboos were about power, not about sin or filth. My conclusion was later borne out by some tribes' own explanations, which, as you may well imagine, came as quite a relief to me.

The truth of the matter as many Indians see it is that women who are at   12
the peak of their fecundity are believed to possess power that throws male power totally out of kilter. They emit such force that, in their presence, any male-owned or -dominated ritual or sacred object cannot do its usual task. For instance, the Lakota say that a menstruating woman anywhere near a yuwipi man, who is a special sort of psychic, spirit-empowered healer, for a day or so before he is to do his ceremony will effectively disempower him. Conversely, among many if not most tribes, important ceremonies cannot be held without the presence of women. Sometimes the ritual woman who empowers the ceremony must be un- married and virginal so that the power she channels is unalloyed, unweakened by sexual arousal and penetration by a male. Other ceremonies require tumes- cent women, others the presence of mature women who have borne children, and still others depend for empowerment on postmenopausal women. Women may be segregated from the company of the whole band or village on certain occa- sions, but on certain occasions men are also segregated. In short, each ritual de- pends on a certain balance of power, and the positions of women within the phases of womanhood are used by tribal people to empower certain rites. This does not derive from a male-dominant view; it is not a ritual observance imposed on women by men. It derives from a tribal view of reality that distinguishes tribal people from feudal and industrial people.

Among the tribes, the occult power of women, inextricably bound to our   13
hormonal life, is thought to be very great; many hold that we possess innately
the blood-given power to kill—with a glance, with a step, or with a judicious
mixing of menstrual blood into somebody's soup. Medicine women among the
Pomo of California cannot practice until they are sufficiently mature; when
they are immature, their power is diffuse and is likely to interfere with their
practice until time and experience have it under control. So women of the tribes
are not especially inclined to see themselves as poor helpless victims of male
domination. Even in those tribes where something akin to male domination was
present, women are perceived as powerful, socially, physically, and meta-
physically. In times past, as in times present, women carried enormous burdens
with aplomb. We were far indeed from the "weaker sex," the designation that
white aristocratic sisters unhappily earned for us all.

I remember my mother moving furniture all over the house when she   14
wanted it changed. She didn't wait for my father to come home and help—she
just went ahead and moved the piano, a huge upright from the old days, the
couch, the refrigerator. Nobody had told her she was too weak to do such
things. In imitation of her, I would delight in loading trucks at my father's
store with cases of pop or fifty-pound sacks of flour. Even when I was quite
small I could do it, and it gave me a belief in my own physical strength that
advancing middle age can't quite erase. My mother used to tell me about the
Acoma Pueblo women she had seen as a child carrying huge ollas (water pots)
on their heads as they wound their way up the tortuous stairwell carved into
the face of the "Sky City" mesa, a feat I tried to imitate with books and tin
buckets. ("Sky City" is the term used by the Chamber of Commerce for the
mother village of Acoma, which is situated atop a high sandstone table mountain.)
I was never very successful, but even the attempt reminded me that I was
supposed to be strong and balanced to be a proper girl.

Of course, my mother's Laguna people are Keres Indian, reputed to be   15
the last extreme mother-right people on earth. So it is no wonder that I got
notably nonwhite notions about the natural strength and prowess of women.
Indeed, it is only when I am trying to get non-Indian approval, recognition,
or acknowledgment that my "weak sister" emotional and intellectual ploys get
the better of my tribal woman's good sense. At such times I forget that I just
moved the piano or just wrote a competent paper or just completed a financial
transaction satisfactorily or have supported myself and my children for most
of my adult life.

Nor is my contradictory behavior atypical. Most Indian women I know   16
are in the same bicultural bind: we vacillate between being dependent and
strong, self-reliant and powerless, strongly motivated and hopelessly insecure.
We resolve the dilemma in various ways: some of us party all the time; some
of us drink to excess; some of us travel and move around a lot; some of us land
good jobs and then quit them; some of us engage in violent exchanges; some of

us blow our brains out. We act in these destructive ways because we suffer
from the societal conflicts caused by having to identify with two hopelessly
opposed cultural definitions of women. Through this destructive dissonance we
are unhappy prey to the self-disparagement common to, indeed demanded of,
Indians living in the United States today. Our situation is caused by the exi-
gencies of a history of invasion, conquest, and colonization whose searing marks
are probably ineradicable. A popular bumper sticker on many Indian cars
proclaims: "If You're Indian You're In," to which I always find myself adding
under my breath, "Trouble."

III

No Indian can grow to any age without being informed that her people were   17
"savages" who interfered with the march of progress pursued by respectable,
loving, civilized white people. We are the villains of the scenario when we are
mentioned at all. We are absent from much of white history except when we
are calmly, rationally, succinctly, and systematically dehumanized. On the few
occasions we are noticed in any way other than as howling, bloodthirsty beings,
we are acclaimed for our noble quaintness. In this definition, we are exotic
curios. Our ancient arts and customs are used to draw tourist money to state
coffers, into the pocketbooks and bank accounts of scholars, and into support
of the American-in-Disneyland promoters' dream.

As a Roman Catholic child I was treated to bloody tales of how the savage   18
Indians martyred the hapless priests and missionaries who went among them
in an attempt to lead them to the one true path. By the time I was through
high school I had the idea that Indians were people who had benefited mightily
from the advanced knowledge and superior morality of the Anglo-Europeans.
At least I had, perforce, that idea to lay beside the other one that derived from
my daily experience of Indian life, an idea less dehumanizing and more accurate
because it came from my mother and the other Indian people who raised me.
That idea was that Indians are a people who don't tell lies, who care for their
children and their old people. You never see an Indian orphan, they said. You
always know when you're old that someone will take care of you—one of your
children will. Then they'd list the old folks who were being taken care of by
this child or that. No child is ever considered illegitimate among the Indians,
they said. If a girl gets pregnant, the baby is still part of the family, and the
mother is too. That's what they said, and they showed me real people who
lived according to those principles.

Of course the ravages of colonization have taken their toll; there are or-   19
phans in Indian country now, and abandoned, brutalized old folks; there are
even illegitimate children, though the very concept still strikes me as absurd.
There are battered children and neglected children, and there are battered wives
and women who have been raped by Indian men. Proximity to the "civilizing"

effects of white Christians has not improved the moral quality of life in Indian country, though each group, Indian and white, explains the situation differently. Nor is there much yet in the oral tradition that can enable us to adapt to these inhuman changes. But a force is growing in that direction, and it is helping Indian women reclaim their lives. Their power, their sense of direction and of self will soon be visible. It is the force of the women who speak and work and write, and it is formidable.

Through all the centuries of war and death and cultural and psychic   20
destruction have endured the women who raise the children and tend the fires, who pass along the tales and the traditions, who weep and bury the dead, who are the dead, and who never forget. There are always the women, who make pots and weave baskets, who fashion clothes and cheer their children on at powwow, who make fry bread and piki bread, and corn soup and chili stew, who dance and sing and remember and hold within their hearts the dream of their ancient peoples—that one day the woman who thinks will speak to us again, and everywhere there will be peace. Meanwhile we tell the stories and write the books and trade tales of anger and woe and stories of fun and scandal and laugh over all manner of things that happen every day. We watch and we wait.

My great-grandmother told my mother: Never forget you are Indian. And   21
my mother told me the same thing. This, then, is how I have gone about remembering, so that my children will remember too.◆

◆ Responding

1. Allen asserts that "In the west, few images of women form part of the cultural mythos." Working individually or in a group, compare the way an American Indian woman is defined by her tribe with the way a woman is defined by Western civilization. Summarize the most important differences and share these with the class. Write an essay or a journal entry agreeing or disagreeing with Allen's depiction of Western women's roles in their culture.

2. How are women's and men's roles defined in your culture? Compare current roles for men and women with those in your mother's and your grandmother's time.

3. Allen talks about the power of the oral tradition—the family stories passed down to her from her mother. Using examples from the reading, discuss the role of tradition in preserving a culture. Consider the stories or traditions that have been passed down in your family. Do your stories tell you, as Allen's told her, "who I was, who I was supposed to be, whom I came from,

and who would follow me"? Write or tell one of your own important family stories.

4. According to Allen, "no Indian can grow to any age without being informed that her people were 'savages' who interfered with the march of progress pursued by respectable, loving, civilized white people." Consider the source or impetus behind such messages. What effects might such a portrayal have on a Native American's sense of identity and self-esteem?

REFLECTING   A   CRITICAL   CONTEXT

Kenneth Lincoln

Kenneth Lincoln, born in Lubbock, Texas, in 1943, received his bachelor's degree from Stanford University and his master's degree and doctorate from Indiana University. As a faculty member in the English department at the University of California at Los Angeles since 1969, Lincoln has participated actively in the American Indian Studies Program, serving as a faculty adviser, member of the core faculty, and chair of the master's program; he has also served as an adviser to the Northern Plains Indian Consortium, developing American Indian studies programs in six liberal arts colleges and the reservations adjacent to them. His publications on Native American issues include the book-length study Native American Renaissance *as well as essays, critical articles, and reviews in the* American Indian Quarterly, Southwest Review, *and* MELUS (Multi-Ethnic Literature of the United States). *Lincoln has also served as editor of the* American Indian Culture and Research Journal *and a member of the MELUS editorial board.*

The following chapter from Native American Renaissance *outlines some of the characteristics of Native American traditions and the ways in which they have often been misunderstood by Euro-Americans.*

◆ **"OLD   LIKE   HILLS,   LIKE   STARS"** ◆

"I do not know how many there are of these songs of mine," Orpingalik told   1
Knud Rasmussen among the Netsilik Eskimo. "Only I know that they are many, and that all in me is song. I sing as I draw breath."[1] Vital as breath itself, the oral literatures of native cultures lie deeply rooted in America. Radically diverse languages, life styles, ecologies, and histories have survived more than forty thousand years "native" to America. Perhaps the people can be imagined even farther back, "older than men can ever be—old like hills, like stars," Black Elk dreams his tribal ancestors.[2] Origin myths speak of ancient emergence from this land.

An introductory review of Indian history, known to some, obscure for   2
many, sets a necessary background for discussing the literature. By official count, three hundred and fifteen "tribes" remain in the United States, where once four to eight million people composed five hundred distinct cultures speaking as many languages.[3] The working definition of "Indian," though criteria vary from region to region, is minimally a quarter blood and tribal membership.

Roughly seven hundred thousand Native Americans survive as full-bloods or "bloods," to use the reservation idiom, mixed-bloods whose parents derive from different tribes, and half-bloods or "breeds" with one non-Indian parent. Another half million or more blooded Indian people live as whites. Over half of the Indian population now lives off the fifty-three million acres of federal reservation lands.

Whether an Alaskan Tlingit fishing village of forty extended kin, or the Navajo "nation" of one hundred and forty thousand Diné in Arizona, Utah, and New Mexico, each tribe can be traditionally defined through a native language, an inherited place, and a historical set of traditions. Their oral literatures are made up from a daily speech, a teaching folklore, a ritual sense of ceremony and religion, a heritage passed on generation to generation in songs, legends, morality plays, healing rites, event-histories, social protocol, jokes, spiritual rites of passage, and vision journeys to the sacred world. These cultural traditions evolved before the Old World "discovered" the New World. Many have survived changing circumstances and remain strong today. The distinguished Nobel poet, Jorge Luis Borges, for years taught "American Literature" beginning with George Cronyn's anthology, *The Path on the Rainbow* (1918), noting that native literature in translation "surprises by its contemplative perception of the visual world, its delicacy, its magic, and its terseness."[4]

Given their diversities, Native American peoples acknowledge specific and common inheritance of the land. They celebrate ancestral ties. They share goods and responsibilities, observe natural balances in the world, and idealize a biological and spiritual principle of reciprocation.[5] Personal concerns lead into communal matters. Black Elk opens his life story, a remembered history that is carried on not as autobiography but tribal history, as follows: "It is the story of all life that is holy and is good to tell, and of us two-leggeds sharing in it with the four-leggeds and the wings of the air and all green things; for these are children of one mother and their father is one Spirit."[6]

Literatures, in this sense, do not separate from the daily contexts of people's lives; the spoken, sung, and danced language binds the people as the living text of tribal life. "Firmly planted. Not fallen from on high: sprung up from below," Octavio Paz, the Mexican poet, says of native arts. The voiced word, like the handmade object, the right-told tale, the well-shaped poem, speaks of "a mutually shared physical life" (Octavio Paz, *In Praise of Hands*), not as icon, commodity, or art for its own precious sake. Words move among things in usable beauty. "A glass jug, a wicker basket, a coarse muslin huipil, a wooden serving dish: beautiful objects, not despite their usefulness but because of it."[7]

The many native peoples with ancient tenure in America remain as varied as the land itself—forest, prairie, river, valley, seacoast, mountain, tundra, desert, and cliff-dwelling peoples. They have lived as farmers, food gatherers, fishermen, and hunters inseparable from the land. Their cultures and histories differ as widely as terrain and climate, flora and fauna; but all native tribes look back to indigenous time on this "turtle land," as Iroquois origin myths envision the continent, unified in an ancient ancestral heritage. The Hopi village of Old Oraibi, on the third mesa in northern Arizona, has stood for at least eight hundred and fifty years. Canyon de Chelly, on the Navajo reservation near the Four Corners area, has been occupied continuously for two and one half thousand years. In contrast, the landscape east of the Mississippi carries slim living evidence of once powerful tribes who settled the forests. Among many others, the Powhatans saved Jamestown colony with gifts of green corn in the first severe winter of 1607. Until the 1830s the Five Civilized Tribes (Cherokee, Choctaw, Chickasaw, Creek, and Seminole) inhabited the Southeast and adapted successfully to new ways. In Colonial America the Ohio River and Great Lakes tribes lived along a western frontier, and "at the forest's edge" the Iroquois Confederacy treated as equal powers with the Confederation of United States in the eighteenth century.

What Indians gave in the exchanges between immigrants and natives is   7
not so much remembered as what was taken from them, primarily the richest lands—fertile valleys for farming, mountains rifted with minerals, grazing lands for stock, coastal fishing shores, river passages, forests of game. The Indians' intimate knowledge of American ecology rescued many pilgrims and pioneers from hardship, or even death, in a continent the newcomers viewed as "wilderness." Indian cultivations such as beans, maize, squash, hickory, pecan, pumpkin, and sweet potatoes fed the new Americans; Indian skills in gathering native foods saved settlers from their own agricultural failures (the first Thanksgiving of 1621, for example, where Indians and pilgrims ate, among other foods, corn and eel). Indian expertise in hunting secured the bounty of the animal food pack of America—turkey, deer, buffalo, rabbit, salmon, sturgeon, shellfish, among hundreds of other game. Indians contributed over a third of the medicines we now use synthetically, 220 drugs in the National Formulary, according to Virgil Vogel's native pharmacopoeia—astringents, cathartics, childbirth medicines, febrifuges, vermifuges, emetics, poisons, antibiotics, diabetes remedy, and contraceptives, including quinine, cocaine, tobacco, and techniques of birth control.

Native Americans showed uneasy settlers a love and regard for the living   8
land, premised on coexisting in harmony with its demands. Native governments, such as the Iroquois Confederacy, set models for new political experiments in representative democracy and tribal alliances; it was of no small significance to Franklin, Jefferson, and Washington that Iroquois meant "We-the-People." Indians gave names for rivers, mountains, lakes, cities, counties, streets, and over half the states. And they believed in the bonding and animating powers of words—to invoke and actualize the world through a language of experience. Words were not notational labels or signs, visually affixed to a blank page for material transaction: words were beings in themselves, incantatory, with spirits and bodies. Stories, songs, visions, and names lived empirically in the world, and people could seek them for power, identity, beauty, peace, and survival.

The many treaties and speeches spanning three centuries of white contact   9
represent the first recorded Indian literatures. The precision and eloquence of
Indian oratory highlight these first American "chronicle plays," Constance Rourke
observes.[8] The Indians "spoke as free men to free men," Lawrence Wroth notes,
"or often indeed as kings speaking to kings."[9] For over two hundred years
ceaseless invasion and even military defeat could not dislodge the Indian spirit
of rightful place in America. Fleeing seventeen hundred miles into the bitter
winter of 1877, Chief Joseph finally had to surrender the Nez Percé. He grieved
with dignity:

> My people, some of them, have run away to the hills and have no blankets, no
> food. No one knows where they are—perhaps they are freezing to death. I want
> to have time to look for my children and see how many of them I can find. Maybe
> I shall find them among the dead. Hear me, my chiefs, I am tired. My heart is
> sad and sick. From where the sun now stands I will fight no more forever.[10]

The people could be killed or captured or "reserved," but not defeated. In 1883
Sitting Bull told reservation bureaucrats:

> I am here by the will of the Great Spirit, and by His will I am a chief. My heart
> is red and sweet, and I know it is sweet, because whatever passes near me puts
> out its tongue to me; and yet you men have come here to talk with us, and you
> say you do not know who I am. I want to tell you that if the Great Spirit has
> chosen anyone to be the chief of this country, it is myself. [Senate Report #283][11]

While fighting to preserve their own cultural integrity, Indians survived   10
national policies of removal, starvation, warfare, and genocide. The Indian
Bureau was first established under the War Department in 1824. Within its
boundaries the United States warred against native peoples and guaranteed
political settlements for military alliances, the sale of lands, acquiescence to the
reservation system, and the surrender of mineral rights. Vine Deloria discusses
the 389 broken treaties in *Of Utmost Good Faith*, the opening words of the
Northwest Ordinance of 1787, the first treaty signed by George Washington
in the Continental Congress:

> The utmost good faith shall always be observed toward the Indians, their lands
> and property shall never be taken from them without their consent; and in their
> property, rights, and liberty, they shall never be invaded or disturbed, unless in
> just and lawful wars authorized by Congress; but laws founded in justice and
> humanity shall from time to time be made, for preventing wrongs being done to
> them, and for preserving peace and friendship with them.[12]

"They were chasing us now," Black Elk remembers of the nineteenth century,
"because we remembered and they forgot."[13]

Beginning in the 1830s many Indian cultures were "removed" to the "Great   11
American Desert" west of the Mississippi, despite the acculturative success of
the Five Civilized Tribes. This forced migration was more a diaspora under

presidential decree and military escort. Andrew Jackson promised the Eastern tribes:

> Say to them as friends and brothers to listen to their father, and their friend. Where they now are, they and my white children are too near to each other to live in harmony and peace. . . . Beyond the great River Mississippi . . . their father has provided a country large enough for them all, and he advises them to move to it. There their white brothers will not trouble them, and they will have no claim to the land, and they can live upon it, they and all their children, as long as grass grows and waters run.[14]

Already settled in the West, the Plains Indians resisted the intrusion. They militarily protested encroachment from Eastern tribes shoved west and an invasion by land-grabbing, gold-searching, buffalo-slaughtering, treaty-violating white immigrants who brought with them the railroad, guns, plows, fences, plagues, alcohol, and the Bible. The West wasn't wild until the whites came, Indians complained. They lived at home in land earlier considered by whites deserted.

The "Indian Wars" lasted from the 1860s to the Wounded Knee Massacre [12] in 1890. From 1881 to 1883 the government employed marksmen to slaughter the remaining two and a half million buffalo, once fifteen million in 1700, the life-support of the plains tribes.[15] The seasonal migrations of mid-American Indians, following the game, were disrupted forever. Soldiers herded the survivors onto reserves of waste land, issued "citizen's dress" of coat and trousers, and ordered the "savages" to "civilize." The secretary of the interior commented in 1872 on killing the buffalo to starve Indians onto reservations: "A few years of cessation from the chase will tend to unfit them for their former mode of life, and they will be the more readily led into new directions, toward industrial pursuits and peaceful habits."[16]

The transition did not take place so easily or soon; over a hundred years [13] later many Indian peoples are still caught between cultures, living the worst conditions of both. Their lands contain half the uranium and one-third the strip mine coal in the United States (the coal alone worth perhaps a trillion dollars), and yet some reservations suffer the worst hardship in America—incomes at half the poverty level, five years average schooling, the highest national alcoholism and suicide rates, substandard housing and social services, infant mortality, tuberculosis, and diabetes in multiples beyond any other minority in the country, resulting in an average lifespan of forty-four years.[17] For all the positive collaborations between Indians and newcomers to America, there runs a deeply bitter history, inherited for better or worse by "native" American writers.

The national myth of civilizing a virgin land, Fitzgerald's "green breast [14] of the new world" in *The Great Gatsby*, has been revised by the historian Francis Jennings in *The Invasion of America*: "The American land was more like a widow than a virgin. Europeans did not find a wilderness here; rather, however involuntarily, they made one. . . . The so-called settlement of America was a *re*settlement, a reoccupation of a land made waste by the diseases and demoralization introduced by the newcomers."[18] It is an old and shameful wound, still open—a story largely fabled in the popular mind and seldom taught honestly in American schools, a history of murder and cultural suppression and displacement from native lands. This last grievance, still active, is most commonly dramatized in the Long March of the Five Civilized Tribes when over a third of the people died on forced relocation to Oklahoma. Asked his age by a census taker in 1910, the old Creek, Itshas Harjo, answered with a memory purely elegiac:

> I have passed through many days and traveled a long way,
> the shadows have fallen all about me and I
> can see but dimly.
> But my mind is clear and my memory has not failed me.
> I cannot count the years I have lived.
> All that I know about my age is that I was old enough
>   to draw the bow
> and kill squirrels at the time of the second emigration of the
> Creeks and Cherokees from the old country under
> the leadership of Chief Cooweescoowee.
> I was born near Eufaula, Alabama, and left there
> when about fifteen years of age and the trip
> took about a year,
> for the peaches were green when we left Alabama and the
> wild onions plentiful here when we arrived.[19]

Despite the poetry of such natural observation, Indian traditions were dismissed as barbaric and pagan. The Commissioner of Indian Affairs stated in 1889:

> The Indians must conform to "the white man's ways," peaceably if they will, forcibly if they must. They must adjust themselves to their environment, and conform their mode of living substantially to our civilization. This civilization may not be the best possible, but it is the best the Indian can get. They cannot escape it, and must either conform to it or be crushed by it.[20]

Children "kidnapped" into government boarding schools, as Indians saw it, were ridiculed for their Indian names, stripped of their tribal dress, denied their customs, and punished for speaking native tongues. Eventually their elders were shamed from belief in the ancestral spirit world, animal totems, and vision powers, a speaking landscape sacredly interdependent with the people. Culture after culture, beginning with Cortez's destruction of Tenochtitlan in 1521, witnessed deicide as conquered tribes were forced to abandon their own beliefs and buckle to Christianity.

A more insidious oppression threatens Indians today under melting-pot policies of assimilation, direct and indirect coercion of tribes to adapt to mainstream American culture. The disastrous "termination" policies of the 1950s are currently being revived in congressional bills to abrogate treaties; and "when someone says 'termination,' " writes an anthropologist of the Montana Blackfeet, "the Indians hear 'extermination.' "[21] America's most diverse minorities of Native Americans hold the status, independently, of "domestic dependent nations" (Supreme Court Justice John Marshall's opinion of 1831), that is, nations within a nation whose members are legally entrusted "wards" of the federal government, yet remain "sovereign," and occupy separate land salvaged from the one hundred and forty million acres allotted under the 1887 Dawes Act.[22] Indians are legally cast as children who cannot grow up and answer prodigally to the Great White Father.

Historical irony notwithstanding, traditional native literatures celebrate spiritual and worldly harmonies. Yet there is a danger of misdirected romanticism, fueled by pastoral myths of the noble savage and nostalgic regression to the Garden of Eden. Indians and non-Indians alike tend to gloss contemporary reservation life and visions of the-way-things-used-to-be. America still fails to see the Native American as an individual with a tribal, human identity, directed by a history that informs the present. "To be an Indian in modern American society," Vine Deloria writes in *Custer Died for Your Sins*, "is in a very real sense to be unreal and ahistorical."[23]   17

The transparent "Indian," a film and fictional stereotype, lingers more as a silhouette—the only minority figure anonymously enshrined on our currency, the "Indian-head" nickel, now an artifact. And the true history of national Indian affairs shapes an oftentimes bitter resistance to "the American way." Dr. D. H. Lawrence wrote in *Studies in Classic American Literature* (1923):   18

> The desire to extirpate the Indian. And the contradictory desire to glorify him. Both are rampant still, to-day.
> The bulk of the white people who live in contact with the Indian to-day would like to see this Red brother exterminated; not only for the sake of grabbing his land, but because of the silent, invisible, but deadly hostility between the spirit of the two races. The minority of whites intellectualize the Red Man and laud him to the skies. But this minority of whites is mostly a high-brow minority with a big grouch against its own whiteness.[24]

When America catches the shadow of native peoples on its money and names professionally competitive teams the Warriors, the Indians, the Redskins, or the Aztecs (not to mention a Pontiac automobile, the Winnebago recreation vehicle, or "Geronimo!" as a battle cry), the stereotype surely reaches down through a sentimental myth of the noble savage into "the bloody loam" of national history. The Indian warrior, who has been warred against, refracts an image that covers several million lives destroyed or violently "removed" from their native earth.[25] And today, there seem "so few of them left," Frederick Turner observes in his *North American Indian Reader*, "so far away from the centers of population."[26] This, too, is open to dispute, since Native Americans represent the fastest growing minorities in America. Indians have doubled in population between 1950 and 1970, and more than half now live in cities.

If the people are proportionately few in number, they remain many in   19
ancient diversities and stand mythically large in the national consciousness. We would do well to appreciate their literatures as origins of native cultural history in America. Here lies the seedbed for a renaissance in American literature.◆

1. Knud Rasmussen, *Across Arctic America: Narrative of the Fifth Thule Expedition* (London and New York: G. P. Putnam's Sons, 1927), p. 164. [Author's note]

2. John Neihardt, trans., *Black Elk Speaks* (1932; New York: Pocket, 1972), p. 21. [Author's note]

3. I use Vine Deloria's figure of 315 culturally functional tribes in the United States today (*Custer Died for Your Sins: An Indian Manifesto*, [New York: Macmillan, 1969], p. 13). As a Standing Rock Sioux, former president of the National Congress of American Indians and legal counsel for Indian affairs, Deloria is in a position to arbitrate figures that vary from two hundred to six hundred extant "tribes." *Wassaja* 7 (January–February 1979) published a Federal Register list of 280 "tribal reservation entities" having a government-to-government relationship with the United States and another 40 Indian groups petitioning for federal acknowledgment through the Bureau of Indian Affairs (February 1979).

The statistics for aboriginal population are even less firm. Harold E. Driver cites Kroeber (1934, 1939) with the lowest estimate of 4,200,000 for North America in 1492 and Dobyns (1966) with about 60,000,000 for America. Driver revises the figures to estimate perhaps 30,000,000 for the continent. *Indians of North America*, 2d rev. ed. (1961; Chicago: University of Chicago Press, 1969), pp. 63–64. Dobyns' most liberal estimates are ten to twelve milion people north of the Rio Grande, roughly two thousand cultures speaking a thousand languages. Henry F. Dobyns, "Estimating Aboriginal American Population: An Appraisal of Techniques with a New Hemispheric Estimate," *Current Anthropology* 7 (1966), 414. In response to this controversy over numbers, Alfonso Ortiz, the Tewa anthropologist, wrote me that "no responsible anthropologist known to me believes that there were several thousand aboriginal cultures in Native America north of the Rio Grande, nor were there a thousand languages spoken. Five hundred languages and as many cultures is a commonly agreed estimate. On population eight million is the most liberal estimate with any following at all. True, the figures keep getting revised upward slowly as retrieval and sampling techniques improve, but until they do even more, anything beyond what I cite is at best conjectural" (25 January 1979). [Author's note]

4. Jorge Luis Borges, "The Oral Poetry of the Indians," in *Literature of the American Indians: Views and Interpretations*, ed. Abraham Chapman (New York: New American Library, 1975), p. 277. [Author's note]

5. Barre Toelken speaks of "sacred reciprocation" in "Seeing with a Native Eye: How Many Sheep Will It Hold?" in *Seeing with a Native Eye: Essays On Native American Religion*, ed. Walter Holden Capps (New York: Harper and Row, 1976), p. 17. [Author's note]

6. Niehardt, *Black Elk Speaks*, p. 1. [Author's note]

7. Octavio Paz, *In Praise of Hands: Contemporary Crafts of the World*, published in conjunction with the first World Crafts Exhibition held at the Ontario Science Center in Toronto (Greenwich, Conn.: New York Graphic Society, 1974). [Author's note]

8. Constance Rourke, "The Indian Background of American Theatricals" in Chapman, p. 257. [Author's note]

9. Lawrence C. Wroth, "The Indian Treaty as Literature" in Chapman, p. 327. Peter Nabokov's *Native American Testimony* is the best anthology of American Indian Speeches (New York: Harper and Row, 1978). Michael K. Foster examines Iroquois "speech events" still current in *From Earth to Beyond the Sky: An Ethnographic Approach to Four Longhouse Iroquois Speech Events* (Ottawa: National Museums of Canada, 1974). [Author's note]

10. Margot Astrov, ed., *American Indian Prose and Poetry*, originally published in 1946 as *The Winged Serpent* (New York: Capricorn, 1962), p. 87. [Author's note]

11. Dee Brown, *Bury My Heart at Wounded Knee* (New York: Holt, Rinehart, and Winston, 1970), p. 424. [Author's note]

12. D'Arcy McNickle, *Native American Tribalism: Indian Survivals and Renewals* (1973; reprint ed., New York: Oxford University Press, 1979), p. 51. [Author's note]

13. Neihardt, *Black Elk Speaks*, p. 112. [Author's note]

14. McNickle, *Native American Tribalism*, p. 72. [Author's note]

15. See Francis Haines, *The Buffalo* (New York: Crowell, 1970) Tom McHugh, *The Time of the Buffalo* (New York: Knopf, 1972): and Jerry N. McDonald, *North American Bison: Their Classfication and Evolution* (Berkeley, Los Angeles, London: University of California Press, 1981). [Author's note]

16. Edward S. Curtis, *The North American Indian: The Indian of the United States and Alaska*, 3 (New York: Johnson, 1970), p. 11. [Author's note]

17. Howell Raines, "American Indians Struggling for Power and Identity," *New York Times Magazine*, 11 February 1979; Edgar S. Cahn, *Our Brother's Keeper: The Indian in White America* (Washington, D.C.: World Publishing, 1969). [Author's note]

18. Francis Jennings, *The Invasion of America: Indians, Colonialism, and the Cant of Conquest* (Chapel Hill: University of North Carolina Press, 1975), p. 30. [Author's note]

19. William Brandon, ed., *The Magic World: American Indian Songs and Poems* (New York: Morrow, 1971), p. 115. [Author's note]

20. T. J. Morgan, Commissioner of Indian Affairs, to the Secretary of the Interior, 1 October 1889 in Chapman, p. 16. [Author's note]

21. Malcolm McFee, *Modern Blackfeet: Montanans on a Reservation* (New York: Holt, Rinehart, and Winston, 1972), p. 64. [Author's note]

22. See Vine Deloria's argument for a pan-Indian political coalition based on a separate land base and tribal sovereignty in *Custer Died for Your Sins.* [Author's note]

23. Ibid., p. 2. [Author's note]

24. D. H. Lawrence, "Fenimore Cooper's White Novels" in *Studies in Classic American Literature*, 2d ed. (1923; New York: Viking, 1966), p. 36. [Author's note]

25. Williams first wrote on American violence as a mythic act of regeneration soaked into "the bloody loam" of the country's history (*In the American Grain*, 2d ed. 1923; New York: New Directions, 1956). Richard Slotkin has developed a "myth-poeic" reading of American cultural archetypes through a study of colonial and frontier literary history (*Regeneration Through Violence: The Mythology of the American Frontier, 1600–1860* [Middletown, Conn.: Wesleyan University Press, 1973]). New studies on Indian sterotyping and image-making are revising old myths about civilization and savagery: among many recent statements see Hugh Honour, *The New Golden Land: European Images of America from the Discoveries to the Present Time* (New York: Random House, 1975), Wilcomb E. Washburn, *The Indian in America* (New York: Harper and Row, 1975), Frederick W. Turner III, Introduction to *The Portable North American Indian Reader* (1973; New York: Penguin, 1977) and *Beyond Geography: The Western Spirit Against the Wilderness* (New York: Viking, 1980), and Fredi Chiapelli et al., eds., *First Images of America: The Impact of the New World on the Old*, 2 vols. (Berkeley, Los Angeles, London: University of California Press, 1976). [Author's note]

26. Frederick W. Turner III, *The Portable North American Reader*, p. 9. [Author's note]

◆ Responding

1. Define a tribe. Lincoln identifies characteristics accepted by all Native American tribes in spite of their diversity. Describe these features.

2. Working individually or in a group, list the contributions of Native Americans to new immigrants. Share the list with the class and discuss how much of the information is new to you. What are the implications of this history?

3. Review the characteristics and contributions of Native Americans mentioned in the essay. Compare them with the image currently presented by the media.

4. Lincoln says that "Indians gave names for rivers, mountains, lakes, cities, counties, streets, and over half the states. And they believed in the bonding and animating powers of words—to invoke and actualize the world through a language of experience. Words were not notational labels or signs . . . words were beings in themselves, incantatory, with spirits and bodies." With the class, think of examples of Native American names. How do these names reflect Native American beliefs?

◆

CONNECTING

Critical Thinking and Writing

1. Critics have called the period during which the readings in this chapter were written the Native American Renaissance. Define *renaissance*. How do these readings exemplify a renaissance?

2. Compare the Native American Renaissance with the Harlem Renaissance, described in the readings in Chapter 3. What do the two periods have in common? Does each deserve to be called a renaissance?

3. Lincoln's essay discusses pressure on Native Americans to assimilate into mainstream society and culture. Describe ways in which the pressures felt by Native Americans are different from and similar to those experienced by early twentieth-century European immigrants, or by another immigrant group.

4. For many groups, tradition shapes understanding of the present. Using the readings in this chapter and your own experience, describe occasions when traditional beliefs have helped individuals solve problems or have created problems.

5. The earth itself is an important force in Native American culture. Write an essay describing the role of the earth in the life of one or more of the characters in these readings.

6. Compare Lipsha Morrissey's understanding and acceptance of events at the end of the story "Love Medicine" with Ayah's understanding at the end of "Lullaby." What aspects of their response are based on the teachings of their cultures? What might be considered universal? What aspects might be attributable to differences in personality or experience?

7. Allen describes Native American women as caught in a "bicultural bind"

and as acting in "destructive ways because we suffer from the societal conflicts caused by having to identify with two hopelessly opposed cultural definitions of women." Explain those conflicting definitions and the ways in which the women in these selections deal successfully or unsuccessfully with the dilemmas.

8. Storytelling and the oral tradition are an important part of many cultures. Momaday refers to " 'storytelling: to utter and to hear . . .' and the simple act of listening [as] crucial to the concept of language, more crucial even than reading and writing, and language in turn is crucial to human society." Discuss the importance of storytelling within a particular culture and support your points with examples from some of the readings in this text. Alternatively, compare the role of storytelling in Native American culture with that in another culture, such as the Chinese.

9. Using examples from the reading, explain what Lincoln means when he says that "they believed in the bonding and animating powers of words—to invoke and actualize the world through a language of experience."

10. In the story "Lullaby," Ayah expresses the point of view that contact with mainstream culture is dangerous when she says, "Learning their language or any of their ways: it endangered you." Explain her fears and compare her feelings and actions with characters in other readings. What compromise do you think might exist between a position that advocates total isolation from mainstream culture and one that accepts total loss of native culture? How could such a compromise be implemented?

11. Lincoln says that when thinking about Native Americans, " there is a danger of misdirected romanticism, fueled by pastoral myths of the noble savage and nostalgic regression to the Garden of Eden." Refer to the pre-reading assignment and review the characteristics the media currently attribute to Native Americans. Now that you have read the selections in this chapter, discuss the accuracy of these portrayals. Are they romanticized?

For Further Research

1. Research the life of a Native American leader such as Black Elk, Chief Joseph, or Geronimo. Read novels and watch films about events in that person's life; then compare the portrayals in the two forms of biography.

2. Many Native Americans still live on reservations. Study the political, social, and economic structure of the reservation.

3. More than half of Native Americans now live in cities. Research their social and economic situation. What factors cause people to leave the reservation? How successful are they in integrating into mainstream culture within urban areas? Are they able to live in cities and maintain their culture?

◆

REFERENCES AND ADDITIONAL SOURCES

Axtell, James. *The European & the Indian: Essays in the Ethnohistory of Colonial North America*. New York: Oxford University Press, 1961.

Debo, Angie. *A History of the Indians of the United States*. Vol. 106. The Civilizations of the American Indian series. Norman, OK: University of Oklahoma Press, 1984.

Deloria, Vine, Jr. *Custer Died for Your Sins: An American Manifesto*. Norman: University of Oklahoma Press, 1988.

———— and Clifford M. Lytle. *American Indians, American Justice*. Austin: University of Texas Press, 1983.

Fixico, Donald L. *Termination and Relocation: Federal Indian Policy, 1945–1960*. Albuquerque: University of New Mexico Press, 1986.

Hagan William T., Rev. ed. *The Indian in American History*. (AHA pamphlet 240) Washington, D.C.: American Historical Association, 1985.

Hobson, Geary, ed. *The Remembered Earth. An Anthology of Contemporary Native American Literature*. Albuquerque: University of New Mexico Press, 1981.

Larson, Charles. *American Indian Fiction*. Albuquerque: University of New Mexico Press, 1978.

McNickle, D'Arcy. *Native American Tribalism*. New York: Oxford University Press, 1973.

Mitchell, Lee C. *Witnesses to a Vanishing America: The Nineteenth-Century Response*. Princeton: Princeton University Press, 1987.

Neihardt, John G. *Black Elk Speaks: Being the Life Story of a Holy Man of the Ogala Sioux*. Lincoln: University of Nebraska Press, 1961.

Niatum, Duane, ed. *Carriers of the Dream Wheel*. New York: Harper & Row, 1975.

Oswalt, Wendell H. *This Land Was Theirs*. Mountainview, CA: Mayfield Pub., 1973.

Prucha, Francis P. *The Great Father: The United States Government and the American Indians*. Lincoln: University of Nebraska Press, 1984.

Rosen, Charles. *The Man to Send the Rain Clouds*. New York: Vintage, 1975.

Sturtevant, William C., and Washburn, Wilcomb E., eds. *History of Indian-White Relations*. Vol. 4. Handbook of North American Indians series. Washington, D.C.: Smithsonian, 1989.

Thernstrom, Stephen, et al., ed. "American Indians" in *Harvard Encyclopedia of American Ethnic Groups*. Cambridge, Mass.: Harvard University Press, 1980.

Tyler, S. Lyman. *A History of Indian Policy*. Washington, D.C.: Government Printing Office, 1973.

Vogel, Virgil J. *This Country Was Ours: A Documentary History of the American Indian*. New York: Harper, 1972.

Vietnamese boat people on the way to Hong Kong, 1979. (© 1979 Magnus Bartlett/Woodfin Camp and Associates)

Mariél boat-lift, 1980. (© 1980 Richard Sobol/Stock Boston)

Chapter 9

CONTEMPORARY VOICES
Diversity and Renewal

*Detail of background photo, two hundred sixty–nine im-
migrants take the oath of citizenship aboard the battleship
U.S.S. Massachusetts at Fall River, Massachusetts,
in 1976. (© AP/Wide World Photos)*

◆ Setting the Historical Context ◆

THE NOTION OF AMERICA as a land of renewal and opportunity for the oppressed is as old as the country itself. Author Mark Mathabane expresses his delight at escaping the apartheid of South Africa in his autobiography *Kaffir Boy in America*:

> I had finally set foot in *the* America. I felt the difference between South Africa and America instantly. The air seemed pervaded with freedom and hope and opportunity. Every object seemed brighter, newer, more modern, fresher, the people appeared better dressed, more intelligent, richer, warmer, happier, and full of energy—despite the profound impersonality of the place.

The ironic tone of this passage illustrates the immigrant's naive expectations and anticipates his later disillusionment. While Mathabane is no longer forced to use segregated facilities, college students tell him that they "prefer" to room with persons of their own race. While he takes a profound interest in American things, he discovers that the students he meets have very limited knowledge of or interest in events outside of their own country.

Earlier chapters in this book have explored the experiences and writings of many who, seeking political and religious freedoms or economic opportunity, came to America with similar expectations. They too found conflicts between the United States' traditional identity and its response to the multicultural reality. The Chinese immigrants of the nineteenth century, for example, sought economic opportunity in the Gold Mountain, but were confronted with the bitter reality of racism and long, hard labor. Nevertheless they pursued their dreams, building the transcontinental railroads and establishing their culture in San Francisco, Boston, New York, and many other cities. European immigrants who succeeded, exemplified by the family in Anzia Yezierska's "The Fat of the Land," call into question the high price of success and its effect on traditional family values.

Following World War II, persons from a growing number of nations sought political, religious, or economic refuge in the United States. Among these groups were Europeans displaced by the war, including many survivors of the Holocaust. Refugees from communist rule in China, the Soviet Union,

Eastern Europe, and Greece sought political asylum in the late 1940s and early 1950s. During the 1960s, many Cubans took *vuelos de libertad* (flights of freedom) to escape the regime of Fidel Castro; the Mariél boat-lift of the late 1970s allowed other Cubans, some of whom had been imprisoned for political and other crimes, to leave their homeland. Communist victory and the fall of Saigon in 1975 led many Vietnamese to flee their homeland. Central Americans sought an escape from dictatorial regimes and the death squads that allowed the governments to force their wills upon the people. And blacks in South Africa sought refuge from the discrimination and brutality that characterize apartheid.

In response to these demands, the United States government has passed a series of laws to increase quotas for some groups and to provide asylum for others. The President has also issued executive orders to ease restrictions in special cases. During the late 1940s, for example, President Franklin D. Roosevelt ordered immigration quotas to be increased for persons fleeing political persecution. The Truman administration granted new immigration privileges to so-called Displaced Persons. The Refuge Relief Act of 1953, passed by Congress during the Eisenhower administration, allowed for the admission of refugees, such as those fleeing the repression taking place in Hungary at the time. Special allowance was also made in the 1970s to accommodate the Vietnamese "boat people" and the Mariél Refugees from Cuba.

Those who have entered the country illegally, but who feel that they are victims of political persecution, have sometimes been given refuge as well. The Immigration and Naturalization Act of 1980, for example, outlines a procedure whereby those persons who fear for their lives can seek amnesty from deportation. Nonetheless, because of legislation dating back to the Cold War era, immigrants are still subject to deportation even after they have become American citizens. Many immigration policy experts contend that the enforcement and administration of immigration laws—with their continued focus on foreign policy toward the country of origin rather than the applicant's personal situation—are often arbitrary and unfair.

It is amidst this conflict between the country's promise as a land of opportunity and its failure to fulfill those promises that the readings in this chapter find their place. The authors' voices reflect both the hope and frustration which comprise the contemporary American experience.

EXPLORING THE LITERARY AND
◆ CULTURAL CONTEXT ◆

The dream of a better life continues in the contemporary writings in this chapter. Each author emerged from a different historical and cultural context, voicing different perspectives on the American dream—the hope and the disillusionment. Some write from immediate perspectives, while others reflect on history. But all forge identity and awareness in large measure through an understanding of their historical context. And writing that history gives all people, especially those formerly silenced, a new sense of control, a new key to understanding. For this reason many of the chapter's readings display a firm resolve to make others aware of the conditions left behind in their homelands, to keep the past alive for the sake of the future.

Achieving a clear sense of identity is the focus of the passage from Cynthia Ozick's novella. We hear the voice of Rosa, a survivor of the Holocaust, as she attempts to cope with what she has endured. For Rosa, the key to coping is to refuse to accept other people's versions of her experience, to learn instead to write her own history, to assert control over how her history will be recorded.

For several of the authors, taking control of their lives means first leaving the country of oppression. The excerpt from Tran Van Dihn's novel deals with the Vietnamese boat people—in this case a true-life story of a group of intellectuals who flee the repressive communist regime. Oscar Hijuelos's novel offers a broader perspective, as early Cuban émigrés help family members to escape the Castro regime and pursue the American dream. The author contrasts one family that realizes that dream with another that fails.

The poem of José Alejandro Romero depicts the Salvadorans' attempt to flee their oppressive regime, only to be massacred crossing the river to freedom. Romero's poetic language is very immediate: it forces us, along with the refugees, into the river of blood.

Gert Jacobson, Anywhere Europe, *a memorial to Holocaust victims.*

The chapter from Mark Mathabane's novel presents a comparative examination of the culture of apartheid in which he was raised and the culture of the American South, where he is arriving for college. The writer himself had suffered the daily indignities of separate facilities for people of color and nighttime police raids, and had witnessed the beating of his parents. Yet Mathabane refuses to become complacent and uncritical in his new environment. He immediately remarks on the "profound impersonality" of America, and notes subtle details such as the preponderance of whites on the covers of magazines at an airport newsstand.

While Mathabane writes from an immediate perspective, other authors have the advantage of a more reflective, historical perspective. Mike Rose takes a historical perspective. Born in this country of immigrant parents, he reflects on his family's hopes as he contrasts late-nineteenth- and early-twentieth-century advertisements proclaiming America a place where "prosperity was a way of life" and California "a paradise" with the reality of the poverty and isolation his family experienced in the Los Angeles of the 1950s. The problematic issue of heritage and identity raised in Alice Walker's "Everyday Use" emerges not only from the history of a single family, but also from the collective experience of African Americans—a history of three hundred years of slavery and the generations of segregation that followed. Mura raises this issue of collective responsibility both in the context of the Internment and through the kinship of knowledge and suffering.

BEGINNING: PRE-READING/WRITING

◆ *Throughout its history, the United States has often been a haven for citizens of other countries who are looking for improved political and economic conditions. Working individually or in a group, speculate about what recent political and economic situations in other countries might make citizens of certain countries choose to emigrate. Discuss why they might come to the United States, the possible problems of immigrating here, and the difficulties they would face once they arrive.*

---

*S*ome people immigrate to this country for political and religious reasons. In fleeing their repressive governments, they fear for their lives if they are denied entry to our country and are forced to return to their homelands. This section of the Immigration and Naturalization Act outlines the procedures whereby individuals can apply for political asylum. If asylum is denied, the applicant may appeal the decision, first to the Immigration Court and then to the Board of Immigration Appeals. In rare cases, the appeal process has been taken as far as the Supreme Court.

◆ *From* IMMIGRATION AND NATIONALITY ACT OF 1980 ◆

Asylum Procedure

SEC. 208. [8 U.S.C. 1158] (a) The Attorney General shall establish a procedure for an alien physically present in the United States or at a land border or port of entry, irrespective of such alien's status, to apply for asylum, and the alien may be granted asylum in the discretion of the Attorney General if the Attorney General determines that such alien is a refugee within the meaning of section 101(a)(42)(A).

(b) Asylum granted under subsection (a) may be terminated if the Attorney General, pursuant to such regulations as the Attorney General may prescribe, determines that the alien is no longer a refugee within the meaning of section 101(a)(42)(A) owing to a change in circumstances in the alien's country of nationality or, in the case of an alien having no nationality, in the country in which the alien last habitually resided.

(c) A spouse or child (as defined in section 101(b)(1) (A), (B), (C), (D), or (E)) of an alien who is granted asylum under subsection (a) may, if not otherwise eligible for asylum under such subsection, be granted the same status as the alien if accompanying, or following to join, such alien.

Adjustment of Status of Refugees

SEC. 209. [8 U.S.C. 1159] (a)(1) Any alien who has been admitted to the United States under section 207—

(A) whose admission has not been terminated by the Attorney General pursuant to such regulations as the Attorney General may prescribe,

(B) who has been physically present in the United States for at least one year, and

(C) who has not acquired permanent resident status,

shall, at the end of such year period, return or be returned to the custody of the Service for inspection and examination for admission to the United States as an immigrant in accordance with the provisions of sections 235, 236, and 237.

(2) Any alien who is found upon inspection and examination by an immigration officer pursuant to paragraph (1) or after a hearing before a special inquiry officer to be admissible (except as otherwise provided under subsection (c)) as an immigrant under this Act at the time of the alien's inspection and examination shall, notwithstanding any numerical limitation specified in this Act, be regarded as lawfully admitted to the United States for permanent residence as of the date of such alien's arrival into the United States. ◆

◆ Responding

1. Explain the provisions of the asylum regulations in your own words. If you were writing the law, how would you define *refugee*?

2. Write about the experience of someone you know or have read, studied, or heard about, who has sought asylum in the United States. What circumstances caused this person to leave his or her country? How do you think the circumstances of immigration affected his or her adjustment?

3. What do you think the United States's immigration policy should be? Who should be granted asylum? Choose a recent historical event such as the Tiananmen Square massacre and discuss whether the U.S. should give asylum to participants in that event.

CYNTHIA OZICK

Born in New York in 1928, Cynthia Ozick received her bachelor's degree from New York University in 1949 and her master's degree from Ohio State University in 1950. After teaching writing at New York University for a year, she devoted herself to writing full time. Since 1966 she has published both fiction and essays, including the novel Trust *(1966),* The Pagan Rabbi and Other Stories *(1971),* Bloodshed and Three Novellas *(1976),* Leviathan: Five Fictions *(1981),* Art and Ardor *(1983),* Metaphor and Memory *(1988), and* The Shawl: A Story and Novella *(1989).*

The following excerpt from the novella "Rosa," published in The Shawl, *uses the personal history of a Holocaust survivor to reflect on the narrator's individual and collective identity. At issue is not only the speaker's ability to remember but also her need to reinterpret, and to come to terms with, her past.*

◆ *From* **T H E   S H A W L** ◆

Department of Clinical Social Pathology
University of Kansas–Iowa

April 17, 1977

Dear Ms. Lublin:

Though I am not myself a physician, I have lately begun to amass survivor   1
data as rather a considerable specialty. To be concrete: I am presently working
on a study, funded by the Minew Foundation of the Kansas–Iowa Institute for
Humanitarian Context, designed to research the theory developed by Dr. Arthur
R. Hidgeson and known generally as Repressed Animation. Without at this stage
going into detail, it may be of some preliminary use to you to know that investigations so far reveal an astonishing generalized minimalization during any extended period of stress resulting from incarceration, exposure, and malnutrition.
We have turned up a wide range of neurological residues (including, in some cases,
acute cerebral damage, derangement, disorientation, premature senility, etc.), as
well as hormonal changes, parasites, anemia, thready pulse, hyperventilation, etc.;
in children especially, temperatures as high as 108°, ascitic fluid, retardation,
bleeding sores on the skin and in the mouth, etc. What is remarkable is that these
are all *current conditions* in survivors and their families.

Disease, disease! Humanitarian Context, what did it mean? An excitement   2
over other people's suffering. They let their mouths water up. Stories about
children running blood in America from sores, what muck. Consider also the

special word they used: *survivor*. Something new. As long as they didn't have to say *human being*. It used to be *refugee*, but by now there was no such creature, no more refugees, only survivors. A name like a number—counted apart from the ordinary swarm. Blue digits on the arm, what difference? They don't call you a woman anyhow. *Survivor*. Even when your bones get melted into the grains of the earth, still they'll forget *human being*. Survivor and survivor and survivor; always and always. Who made up these words, parasites on the throat of suffering!

> For some months teams of medical paraphrasers have been conducting interviews with survivors, to contrast current medical paraphrase with conditions found more than three decades ago, at the opening of the camps. This, I confess, is neither my field nor my interest. My own concern, both as a scholar of social pathology and as a human being . . .

3

Ha! For himself it was good enough, for himself he didn't forget this word *human being!*

4

> . . . is not with medical nor even with psychological aspects of survivor data.

5

Data. Drop in a hole!

6

> What particularly engages me for purposes of my own participation in the study (which, by the way, is intended to be definitive, to close the books, so to speak, on this lamentable subject) is what I can only term the "metaphysical" side of the Repressed Animation (R.A.). It begins to be evident that prisoners gradually came to Buddhist positions. They gave up craving and began to function in terms of non-functioning, i.e., non-attachment. The Four Noble Truths in Buddhist thought, if I may remind you, yield a penetrating summary of the fruit of craving: pain. "Pain" in this view is defined as ugliness, age, sorrow, sickness, despair, and, finally, birth. Non-attachment is attained through the Eightfold Path, the highest stage of which is the cessation of all human craving, the loftiest rapture, one might say, of consummated indifference.

7

> It is my hope that these speculations are not displeasing to you. Indeed, I further hope that they may even attract you, and that you would not object to joining our study by means of an in-depth interview to be conducted by me at, if it is not inconvenient, your home. I should like to observe survivor syndroming within the natural setting.

8

Home. Where, where?

9

> As you may not realize, the national convention of the American Association of Clinical Social Pathology has this year, for reasons of fairness to our East Coast members, been moved from Las Vegas to Miami Beach. The convention will take place at a hotel in your vicinity about the middle of next May, and I would be deeply grateful if you could receive me during that period. I have noted via a New York City newspaper (we are not so provincial out here as some may think!)

10

your recent removal to Florida; consequently you are ideally circumstanced to make a contribution to our R.A. study. I look forward to your consent at your earliest opportunity.

Very sincerely yours,
James W. Tree, Ph.D.

Drop in a hole! Disease! It comes from Stella, everything! Stella saw what 11 this letter was, she could see from the envelope—Dr. Stella! Kansas–Iowa Clinical Social Pathology, a fancy hotel, this is the cure for the taking of a life! Angel of Death!

With these university letters Rosa had a routine: she carried the scissors 12 over to the toilet bowl and snipped little bits of paper and flushed. In the bowl going down, the paper squares whirled like wedding rice.

But this one: drop in a hole with your Four Truths and your Eight Paths 13 together! Non-attachment! She threw the letter into the sink; also its crowded envelope ("Please forward," Stella's handwriting instructed, pretending to be American, leaving out the little stroke that goes across the 7); she lit a match and enjoyed the thick fire. Burn, Dr. Tree, burn up with your Repressed Animation! The world is full of Trees! The world is full of fire! Everything, everything is on fire! Florida is burning!

Big flakes of cinder lay in the sink: black foliage, Stella's black will. Rosa 14 turned on the faucet and the cinders spiraled down and away. Then she went to the round oak table and wrote the first letter of the day to her daughter, her healthy daughter, her daughter who suffered neither from thready pulse nor from anemia, her daughter who was a professor of Greek philosophy at Co-lumbia University in New York City, a stone's throw—the philosophers' stone that prolongs life and transmutes iron to gold—from Stella in Queens!

Magda, my Soul's Blessing [Rosa wrote]:

Forgive me, my yellow lioness. Too long a time since the last writing. Strangers 15 scratch at my life; they pursue, they break down the bloodstream's sentries. Always there is Stella. And so half a day passes without my taking up my pen to speak to you. A pleasure, the deepest pleasure, home bliss, to speak in our own language. Only to you. I am always having to write to Stella now, like a dog paying respects to its mistress. It's my obligation. She sends me money. She, whom I plucked out of the claws of all those Societies that came to us with bread and chocolate after the liberation! Despite everything, they were selling sectarian ideas; collecting troops for their armies. If not for me they would have shipped Stella with a boatload of orphans to Palestine, to become God knows what, to live God knows how. A field worker jabbering Hebrew. It would serve her right. Americanized airs. My father was never a Zionist. He used to call himself a "Pole by right." The Jews, he said, didn't put a thousand years of brains and blood into Polish soil in order to have to prove themselves to anyone. He was the wrong sort of idealist, maybe, but he had the instincts of a natural nobleman. I could laugh at that now—the whole business—but I don't, because I feel too vividly what he was, how substantial, how not given over to any light-mindedness whatever. He had Zionist friends in his youth. Some left Poland early and lived. One is a bookseller in Tel Aviv. He specializes in foreign texts and periodicals. My poor little father. It's only history—an ad hoc instance of it, you might say—that made the Zionist answer. My father's ideas were more logical. He was a Polish patriot on a temporary basis, he said, until the time when the nation should lie down beside nation like the lily and the lotus. He was at bottom a prophetic creature. My mother, you know, published poetry. To you all these accounts must have the ring of pure legend.

Even Stella, who *can* remember, refuses. She calls me a parable-maker. She   16 was always jealous of you. She has a strain of dementia, and resists you and all other reality. Every vestige of former existence is an insult to her. Because she fears the past she distrusts the future—it, too, will turn into the past. As a result she has nothing. She sits and watches the present roll itself up into the past more quickly than she can bear. That's why she never found the one thing she wanted more than anything, an American husband. I'm immune to these pains and panics. Motherhood—I've always know this—is a profound distraction from philosophy, and all philosophy is rooted in suffering over the passage of time. I mean the *fact* of motherhood, the physiological fact. To have the power to create another human being, to be the instrument of such a mystery. To pass on a whole genetic system. I don't believe in God, but I believe, like the Catholics, in mystery. My mother wanted so much to convert; my father laughed at her. But she was attracted. She let the maid keep a statue of the Virgin and Child in the corner of the kitchen. Sometimes she used to go in and look at it. I can even remember the words of a poem she wrote about the heat coming up from the stove, from the Sunday pancakes—

> Mother of God, how you shiver
> in these heat-ribbons!
> Our cakes rise to you
> and in the trance of His birthing
> you hide.

Something like that. Better than that, more remarkable. Her Polish was very dense. You had to open it out like a fan to get at all the meanings. She was exceptionally modest, but she was not afraid to call herself a symbolist.

I know you won't blame me for going astray with such tales. After all, you're   17 always prodding me for these old memories. If not for you, I would have buried them all, to satisfy Stella. Stella Columbus! She thinks there's such a thing as the New World. Finally—at last, at last—she surrenders this precious vestige of your sacred babyhood. Here it is in a box right next to me as I write. She didn't take the trouble to send it by registered mail! Even though I told her and told her. I've thrown out the wrapping paper, and the lid is plastered down with lots of Scotch tape. I'm not hurrying to open it. At first my hunger was unrestrained and I couldn't wait, but nothing is nice now. I'm saving you; I want to be serene. In a state of agitation one doesn't split open a diamond. Stella says I make a relic of you. She has no heart. It would shock you if I told you even one of the horrible games I'm made to play with her. To soothe her dementia, to keep her quiet, I pretend you died. Yes! It's true! There's nothing, however crazy, I wouldn't say to her to tie up her tongue. She slanders. Everywhere there are slanders, and sometimes—my bright lips, my darling!—the slanders touch even you. My purity, my snowqueen!

I'm ashamed to give an example. Pornography. What Stella, that pornographer, 18 has made of your father. She thieves all the truth, she robs it, she steals it, the robbery goes unpunished. She lies, and it's the lying that's rewarded. The New World! That's why I smashed up my store! Because here they make up lying theories. University people do the same: they take human beings for specimens. In Poland there used to be justice; here they have social theories. Their system inherits almost nothing from the Romans, that's why. Is it a wonder that the lawyers are no better than scavengers who feed on the droppings of thieves and liars? Thank God you followed your grandfather's bent and studied philosophy and not law.

Take my word for it, Magda, your father and I had the most ordinary lives— 19 by "ordinary" I mean respectable, gentle, cultivated. Reliable people of refined reputation. His name was Andrzej. Our families had status. Your father was the son of my mother's closest friend. She was a converted Jew married to a Gentile: you can be a Jew if you like, or a Gentile, it's up to you. You have a legacy of choice, and they say choice is the only true freedom. We were engaged to be married. We would have been married. Stella's accusations are all Stella's own excretion. Your father was not a German. I was forced by a German, it's true, and more than once, but I was too sick to conceive. Stella has a naturally pornographic mind, she can't resist dreaming up a dirty sire for you, an S.S. man! Stella was with me the whole time, she knows just what I know. They never put me in their brothel either. Never believe this, my lioness, my snowqueen! No lies come out of me to you. You are pure. A mother is the source of consciousness, of conscience, the ground of being, as philosophers say. I have no falsehoods for you. Otherwise I don't deny some few tricks: the necessary handful. To those who don't deserve the truth, don't give it. I tell Stella what it pleases her to hear. My child, perished. Perished. She always wanted it. She was always jealous of you. She has no heart. Even now she believes in my loss of you: and you a stone's throw from her door in New York! Let her think whatever she thinks; her mind is awry, poor thing; in me the strength of your being consumes my joy. Yellow blossom! Cup of the sun!

What a curiosity it was to hold a pen—nothing but a small pointed stick, 20 after all, oozing its hieroglyphic puddles: a pen that speaks, miraculously, Polish. A lock removed from the tongue. Otherwise the tongue is chained to the teeth and the palate. An immersion into the living language: all at once this cleanliness, this capacity, this power to make a history, to tell, to explain. To retrieve, to reprieve!

To lie. ◆

◆ Responding

1. Rosa calls writing "this capacity, this power to make a history, to tell, to explain. To retrieve, to reprieve! To lie." Explain how her letter to Magda, the child who perished in the Holocaust, does all of these things. Discuss why and to whom Rosa is lying.

2. Write an essay agreeing or disagreeing that events can be rewritten by individuals or by groups to distort history. Support your argument with incidents from the story, your own experience, or your knowledge of current events.

3. Dr. Tree asks Rosa to participate in his study of survivors. Working individually or in a group, discuss why Rosa is so angry at his letter and write the response she might send him. How do you think you would feel in her situation?

4. Discuss the ethical issues involved in studies of victims of tragedies. What benefits might result from such studies? What harmful effects might they produce? How would you balance the knowledge that can be gained with the victim's right to privacy?

TRAN VAN DINH

Tran Van Dinh was born in Hué, Vietnam, in 1923. After emigrating, he became a faculty member of Temple University's College of Arts and Sciences. He has subsequently published several studies on international issues.

Tran's novel, Blue Dragon, White Tiger: A Tet Story *(1983), one of the first published in English by a Vietnamese writer living in the United States, has its basis in fact. As the author explains in the preface, "Most of the characters in this novel are real people. . . . Obviously I have changed their situations, but I have not modified their essential positions in the drama."*

The excerpt that follows recounts the emigration from Vietnam of Tran Van Minh, a figure closely related to the author, and twenty other intellectuals. At the same time, the story's plot conveys a sense of the dangers experienced by the "boat people" as they make their way to a new life.

◆ TRUCE IN HEAVEN, PEACE ON EARTH ◆

Minh looked at the sea beyond. It was bluer than it had been on any other day of the whole journey. He imagined that a majestic Blue Dragon surged from the depths of the blue sea and with his ivory claws took all of them to the Isle of the Eastern Ocean where there would be no frontiers to cross or politics to tear people down.

The sky wasn't as clear as the day before. Isolated mountain-shaped white clouds began to appear. They brought to his memory a line by the famed Chinese Tang poet, Tu Fu:

> In the sky, a cloud appeared as a white cloth
> Suddenly, it turned into a bluish dog.

Minh didn't see any bluish dog. The white clouds now converged to take the form of a huge attacking tiger. A cold wind blew. Minh smelt the odor of dead fish. He heard Thai voices but could not understand what they were saying. A motorboat appeared suddenly alongside the junk, with three bronze-skinned men on board.

The tallest among them pointed a machine gun at Minh and asked loudly, "Vietnamese fleeing Communists?"

"Yes," Minh said, his teeth clenched. Before he could ask them if they were Thai Navy patrolmen, the man with the machine gun ordered his two revolver-carrying followers to jump over to Minh's boat. One fired a shot in the air. "Thai bandits!" Minh shouted.

But it was too late. The bandits lined everyone up on the deck. While the machinegunner stood guard over the victims, his two aides searched all corners of the boat. They took one submachine gun that Don had had neither time nor the chance to use. Then all three searched the Vietnamese, who lowered their heads more in shame and anger than in fear. From the Chinese merchant they took gold ingots that were hung on his shoulders under his T-shirt. They stripped Trang of the brand new hundred-dollar bills that had been sewn so carefully under his coat, as well as removing his watch. Then the tall bandit took Xuan aside and led her down into the cabin.

Minh could hear Xuan's metallic voice screaming at the Thai bandit in Vietnamese as she struggled furiously. The attacker shouted in Thai, "Devil, stubborn woman, submit to me! You dare to try to kill me by biting my testicles? Submit or you'll soon see your ancestors in the depth of the sea!" 7

A deadly silence followed. About five minutes later the bandit emerged, his hands stained with blood, his face scratched, carrying Xuan's broken body. Laughing, he threw it into the blue water. He jumped back into his motorboat with his two accomplices and in a few seconds they had all disappeared into the white cloud-covered horizon. 8

Minh looked at the sky with imploring eyes. Indeed, the White Tiger cloud had now been transformed into an advancing bluish dog. 9

The sky darkened. The wind blew stronger and colder. Winter seemed to descend on the New Spring operation. Everybody wept and sobbed. For the next twelve hours, they all lay on the deck, numb with the misfortune that had befallen them. No one ate anything, no one said anything. 10

Late the next afternoon Trang called the passengers together. 11

"My friends," he said, "despite our misfortune we have reached our goal. We'll be in Chantaburi no later than five o'clock. I have told you that the Prime Minister of Thailand is an old friend of our dear friend and brother, Doctor Minh. With your approval, I shall ask him to be our representative to the Thai authorities. We can celebrate the Tet's eve in Chantaburi, but I think it would be proper that we do so on our boat which is, according to international law, Vietnamese territory." 12

With the end of their journey in sight, the passengers seemed to have forgotten the nightmarish incident that had engulfed them in sorrow and despair the day before. They applauded Trang's announcement, and Minh was asked to speak. 13

"I shall never forget, as long as I live, our boat family. I shall do everything I can to help all of you settle in the new lands of freedom, either in Thailand or America. Obviously, the situation here is very favorable to us because of my connection with the Prime Minister, but one always has to be careful about politics in Thailand. The Prime Minister reached power through a *coup d'état*, and there could be a counter-coup at any time. When we arrive there, I'll contact the Prime Minister and see what his attitude to us will be." His short speech ended with several rounds of applause. 14

Early in the evening the junk lowered its anchor off Chantaburi. Operation 15

New Spring had come to an end. A police motorboat met the refugees. In Thai Minh asked the police officer to take him to the local army commander. Within half an hour, Minh and the police lieutenant were at the office of Colonel Amneuy Luksanand, commanding officer of the 25th Royal Thai Infantry Regiment. Minh explained the situation, reported the bandits' attack, and requested that he be allowed to contact the Prime Minister, his old friend Chamni. The colonel politely invited Minh to wait while he phoned Bangkok.

Minh was admiring a pot of blooming orchids when the colonel entered the living room.   16

"Professor, the Prime Minister is on the line. You can use the phone in my office."   17

Minh picked up the receiver. "Hello, Mr. Prime Minister. Congratulations."   18

"Stop it, Minh, I'm still Chamni, your old friend."   19

"But I'm now a boat person without a country, a wandering soul, as we say in Vietnamese."   20

"Forget about your boat and your wandering soul. You can stay in Thailand as long as you wish, as my government's guest. Thailand is now your country. Buddha will protect you. I'll have the colonel bring you to Bangkok tonight so you can have a good rest and we can meet for breakfast tomorrow. As for your compatriot boat people, how many of them are there?"   21

"Nineteen, including me."   22

"They'll be given special consideration by the Ministry of Interior, but in the meantime they'll have to stay in a refugee camp. I'm sorry about that, but I can't change all the laws even as a Prime Minister. I have to leave for a meeting now. I'll see you tomorrow. Sleep well, my dear friend."   23

"Thank you and goodnight, Mr. Prime Minister."   24

The colonel invited Minh to have dinner with him before his trip to Bangkok by helicopter. Minh explained that because it was Tet's eve, he preferred to eat with his compatriots. The colonel quickly proposed that the whole group be invited along to a Chinese restaurant. They accepted the invitation but they had no appetite: Minh had warned them before dinner that they would be temporarily sent to a refugee camp. ◆   25

◆ Responding

1. Research the history of the boat people of Vietnam. Working in a group, share the information you have gathered and explore one of the following issues:

   a. the boat people's reasons for leaving Vietnam.

   b. typical conditions aboard the boats

   c. their reception in Thailand

    d. conditions in the refugee camps
    e. their reception in the United States
Share your conclusions with the class.

2. Explain why the Vietnamese on the boat might have "lowered their heads more in shame and anger than in fear" during the attack by bandits.

3. Imagine having to flee your home and country at a moment's notice. Write an essay or a journal entry discussing your feelings at such a time.

OSCAR HIJUELOS

Oscar Hijuelos was born in New York in 1951 of Cuban parentage. After earning his bachelor's and master's degrees from the City College of the City University of New York in 1975 and 1976, he worked in advertising, finally devoting himself to writing full time in 1984. His writing, which includes the novels Our House in the Lost World *(1983) and* The Mambo Kings Play Songs of Love *(1989) as well as several short stories, has earned him several awards, among them a National Endowment for the Arts Creative Writing Fellowship (1985), an American Academy in Rome Fellowship in Literature (1985), and the Pulitzer Prize for fiction (1990).*

"Visitors, 1965," from Our House in the Lost World, *reflects the experiences of some Cuban émigrés living in the United States. In this chapter the narrator explains the community's reactions to news of Fidel Castro's victory. The text's references to the overthrow of Batista, the Bay of Pigs invasion, and the rationing system help to provide the novel with a sense of historical context. At the same time, the narrative explores the ways in which such events are connected to each person's sense of personal and collective identity.*

◆ VISITORS, 1965 ◆

1

Down in the cool basement of the hotel restaurant, Alejo Santinio looked over a yellowed newspaper clipping dating back to 1961. He had not looked at it recently, although in the past had always been proud to show it to visitors. And why? Because it was a brief moment of glory. In the newspaper picture Alejo and his friend Diego were in their best dress whites standing before a glittering cart of desserts. Beside them was a fat, cheery beaming face, the Soviet premier Nikita Khrushchev, who was attending a luncheon in his honor at the hotel.

Alejo always told the story: The governor and mayor were there with the premier, who had "great big ears and a bright red nose." The premier had dined on a five-course meal. The waiters and cooks, all nervous wrecks, had fumbled around in the kitchen getting things into order. But outside they managed an orderly composed appearance. After the meal had been served, the cooks drew lots to see who would wheel out the dessert tray. Diego and Alejo won.

Alejo put on his best white uniform and apron and waited in the foyer, chainsmoking nervously, while, outside, news reporters fired off their cameras and bodyguards stood against the walls, watching. Alejo and Diego did not say anything. Alejo was bewildered by the situation: Only in America could a worker get so close to a fat little guy with enormous power. These were the days of the new technology: mushroom-cloud bombs and satellites and missiles. And there he was, a hick from a small town in Cuba, slicked up by America, thinking, "If only my old compañeros could see me now! and my sisters and Mercedes."

When the time came, they went to the freezer, filled up shiny bowls with ice cream, brought out the sauces and hot fudge, and loaded them all onto a dessert cart. Alejo was in charge of cherries. They went out behind the maître d' and stood before the premier's table. They humbly waited as the smiling premier looked over the different cakes, tarts, pies, fruits, sauces, and ice creams. Through a translator the premier asked for a bowl of chocolate and apricot ice cream topped with hot fudge, cocoanut, and a high swirl of fresh whipped cream. This being served, Alejo picked out the plumpest cherry from a bowl and nimbly placed it atop the dessert.   4

Delighted, the premier whispered to the translator, who said, "The premier wishes to thank you for this masterpiece."   5

As Diego and Alejo bowed, lightbulbs and cameras flashed all around them. They were ready to wheel the cart back when the premier rose from the table to shake Diego's and Alejo's hands. Then through the translator he asked a few questions. To Alejo: "And where do you come from?"   6

"Cuba," Alejo answered in a soft voice.   7

"Oh yes, Cuba," the premier said in halting English. "I would like to go there one day, Cuba." And he smiled and patted Alejo's back and then rejoined the table. A pianist, a violinist, and a cellist played a Viennese waltz.   8

Afterward reporters came back into the kitchen to interview the two cooks, and the next morning the *Daily News* carried a picture of Alejo, Diego, and Khrushchev with a caption that read: DESSERT CHEFS CALL RUSKY PREMIER HEAP BIG EATER! It made them into celebrities for a few weeks. People recognized Alejo on the street and stopped to talk with him. He even went on a radio show in the Bronx. The hotel gave him a five-dollar weekly raise, and for a while Alejo felt important, and then it played itself out and became the yellowed clipping, stained by grease on the basement kitchen wall.   9

In Alejo's locker Khrushchev turned up again, on the cover of a *Life* magazine. He was posed, cheek against cheek, with the bearded Cuban premier Fidel Castro. "What was going to happen in Cuba?" Alejo wondered. He shook his head. "How could Cuba have gone 'red'?" It had been more than six years since the fall of Batista on New Year's Eve, 1958, the year of getting rid of the evil in Cuba, and now Alejo and Mercedes were going to sponsor the arrival of Aunt Luisa, her daughters, and a son-in-law, Pedro. They were coming to the United States via *un vuelo de la libertad*, or freedom flight, as the U.S. military airplane trips from Havana to Miami were called. Khrushchev was going to eat up Cuba like an ice cream sundae. Things had gotten out of hand, bad enough for Luisa, who had loved her life in Holguín, to leave. Gone were   10 the days of the happy-go-lucky Cubans who went on jaunts to Miami and New York to have a high time ballroom hopping; gone were the days when Cubans came to the States to make money and see more of the world. Now Cubans were leaving because of Khrushchev's new pal, Fidel Castro, the Shit, as some Cubans called him.

2

Alejo had supported Castro during the days of the revolution. He had raised   11
money for the pro-Castro Cubans in Miami by hawking copies of the *Sierra Maestra* magazine to pals on the street. This magazine was printed in Miami by pro-Castro Cubans and was filled with pictures of tortured heroes left on the streets or lying in the lightless mortuary rooms with their throats cut and their heads blood-splattered. They were victims of the crooked Batista regime, and now it was time for Batista and his henchmen to go! Alejo was not a political creature, but he supported the cause, of course, to end the injustices of Batista's rule. When someone brought him a box of Cuban magazines to sell, Alejo went down on Amsterdam Avenue and sold them to friends. Alejo always carried one of those magazines in his pocket, and he was persuasive, selling them. In his soft calm voice he would say, "Come on, it's only a dollar and for the cause of your countrymen's freedom!" And soon he would find himself inviting all the buyers back to his apartment, where they sat in the kitchen drinking and talking about what would save the world: "An honest man with a good heart, out of greed's reach," was the usual consensus. Political talk about Cuba always led to nostalgic talk, and soon Alejo's friends would soften up and bend like orchid vines, glorying in the lost joys of childhood. Their loves and regrets thickened in the room in waves, until they began singing along with their drinking and falling down. With their arms around each other and glasses raised, they toasted Fidel as "the hope for the future."

Alejo and Mercedes had been happy with the success of the revolution.   12
The day Castro entered Havana they threw a party with so much food and drink that the next morning people had to cross into the street to get around the stacks of garbage bags piled on the sidewalk in front of the building. Inside, people were sprawled around everywhere. There were sleepers in the kitchen and in the hall, sleepers in the closet. There was a *dudduhduh* of a skipping needle over a phonograph record. A cat that had come in through the window from the alley was going around eating leftover scraps of food.

Soon the papers printed that famous picture of Castro entering Havana   13
with his cowboy-looking friend, Camilio Cienfuegos, on a tank. They were like Jesus and John the Baptist in a Roman epic movie. The *Sierra Maestra* magazine would later feature a centerfold of Castro as Jesus Christ with his hair long and golden brown, almost fiery in a halo of light. And for the longest time Cubans, Alejo and Mercedes among them, referred to Castro with great reverence and love, as if he were a saint.

In a few years, however, kids in the street started to write slogans like 14
Castro eats big bananas! The New York press ran stories about the Castro visit to New York. Alejo and Hector stood on the corner one afternoon, watching his motorcade speed uptown to a Harlem hotel. There, the press said, Castro's men killed their own chickens and ate them raw. Castro even came to give a talk at the university. Alejo and Hector were among a crowd of admirers that clustered around him to get a look. Castro was very tall for a Cuban, six-feet-two. He was wearing a long raincoat and took sips from a bottle of Pepsi-Cola. He listened to questions intently, liked to smile, and kept reaching out to shake hands. He also signed an occasional autograph. He was, the newspapers said, unyielding in his support of the principles of freedom.

In time Castro announced the revolutionary program. Alejo read the *El* 15
Diario accounts intently while Mercedes wandered around the apartment asking, "What's going to happen to my sisters?" By 1962, after the Bay of Pigs invasion and the beginning of the Cuban ration-card programs, an answer to her question came in the form of letters. Standing by the window Mercedes would read the same letter over and over again, sighing and saying out loud, "Oh my Lord! They are so unhappy!"

"Ma, what's going on?" Hector would ask her. 16

"Things are very bad. The Communists are very bad people. Your aunts 17
have nothing to eat, no clothes to wear, no medicine. The Communists go around taking things away from people! And if you say anything they put you in jail!"

Mercedes's stories about the new life in Cuba made Hector think of a 18
house of horrors. In his sleep he pictured faceless, cowled abductors roaming the streets of Holguín in search of victims to send to brainwashing camps. He pictured the ransacking of old mansions, the burning of churches, deaths by firing squads. He remembered back many years and saw the door of Aunt Luisa's house on Arachoa Street, and then he imagined guards smashing that door open to search Luisa's home.

All the news that came into the house in those letters fed such visions: 19
"Ai, Hector, do you remember your cousin Paco? He has been sent to prison for a year, and all he did was get caught with a pound of sugar under his shirt!" A year later: "Oh your poor cousin Paco! He just came out of prison and now my sister can hardly recognize him. Listen to what Luisa says: 'He has lost most of his hair and is as thin as a skeleton with yellowed, jaundiced skin. He has aged twenty years in one.' " Another letter: "Dear sister, the headaches continue. Everything is upside down. You can't even go to church these days without someone asking, 'Where are you going?' Everyone in the barrio watches where you go. No one has any privacy. If you are not in the Party then you're no good. Many of them are Negroes, and now that they have the power, they are very bad to us. I don't know how long we can endure these humiliations. We hope for Castro's fall." Another letter: "Dear sister, last week your niece Maria was kicked out of dental school, and do you know what for? Because she

wouldn't recite 'Hail Lenin!' in the mornings with the other students. I went to argue with the headmaster of the school, but there was nothing I could do. On top of that, poor Rina's roof was hit by lightning but she can't get the materials to fix it. When it rains the floors are flooded—all because she is not in the Party. . . . As usual I ask for your prayers and to send us whatever you can by way of clothing, food and medicine. Aspirins and penicillin are almost impossible to find these days, as are most other things. I know I'm complaining to you, but if you were here, you would understand. With much love, Luisa."

To help her sisters, Mercedes went from apartment to apartment asking   20
neighbors for any clothing they might not need. These clothes were packed into boxes and sent down to Cuba at a cost of fifty dollars each. Mercedes paid for this out of her own pocket. She had been working at night cleaning in a nursery school since the days of Alejo's illness. Alejo too contributed. He came home with boxes of canned goods and soap and toothpaste from the hotel and he bought such items as rubbing alcohol, aspirins, mercurochrome, iodine, Tampax, Q-Tips, cotton, and toilet paper to send to Cuba.

"The world is going to the devil," Mercedes would say to Alejo as she   21
packed one of the boxes. "Imagine having to use old newspapers for toilet paper! The Russians are the new masters, they have everything, but what do Luisa and Rina have? Nothing!"

Of the family, Mercedes was the most outspoken about the revolution.   22
Alejo was very quiet in his views. He didn't like Castro, or, for that matter, Khrushchev. But he would never argue with a friend about politics. He was always more concerned about keeping his friendships cordial. To please two different sets of neighbors he subscribed to both the *Daily Worker* and the *Republican Eagle*. He read neither of them, but still would nod emphatically whenever he came upon these neighbors in the hallway and they bombarded him with their philosophies. "Certainly," Alejo would say to them, "why don't you come inside and have a drink with me?" When there was a gathering of visitors with different points of view, Alejo used liquor to keep the wagging tongues in line. Get them drunk and make them happy, was his motto.

But Mercedes didn't want to hear about Fidel Castro from anyone, not   23
even from Señor Lopez, a union organizer and good friend of the family who lived in the building. He would come to the apartment to recount the declines in illiteracy, prostitution, and malnutrition in Cuba. "No more of this!" he would declare, showing Mercedes and Alejo and Hector a picture from *La Bohemia* of a decrepit old Negro man dying in bed, with bloated stomach, festering sores on his limbs, and a long gray worm literally oozing out of his navel. "You won't see this anymore now that Castro is in power!"

"And what about the decent people who supported Castro in the first   24
place, and who now have nothing but troubles?" she would ask.

"Mercita, the revolution is the will of the majority of the Cuban people!"   25

"You mean the people who were the good-for-nothings?"   26

"No, the people who had nothing because they were allowed nothing."   27

"Oh yes? And what about my family?"   28

"Mercita, use your brains. I don't like to put it this way, but as the saying   29
goes, 'To make an omelet you have to break a few eggs.' "

"My family are not eggs! If you like eggs so much, why don't you go   30
down to Cuba and live there? Chickens have more to eat than what you would
get. Go there and see what freedom is like!"

By 1965 it was becoming clear that Castro was not going to fall from   31
power. Cubans who had been hoping for a counterrevolution were now growing
desperate to leave. Luisa and her family were among them. One evening an
errand boy from the corner drugstore knocked at the door. There was a call
from Cuba. Mercedes and Hector hurried down the hill. The called was Aunt
Luisa. Her sad voice was so far away, interrupted by sonic hums and clicking
static echoes. It sounded like the voices of hens reciting numbers in Spanish.
With the jukebox going, it was a wonder that Luisa's voice could be heard over
mountains and rivers and across the ocean.

"How is it over there now?" Mercedes asked.   32

"It's getting worse here. There are too many headaches. We want to leave.   33
Pedro, Virginia's husband, lost his mechanic's shop. There is no point in our
staying."

"Who wants to come?"   34

"Me, Pedro, Virginia, and Maria."   35

"And what about Rina?"   36

"She is going to stay for the time being with Delores and her husband."   37
Delores was Rina's daughter. She had a doctorate in pedagogy that made her
a valuable commodity in those days of literacy programs. "Delores has been
appointed to a government post and she is too afraid to refuse the Party, for
fear they will do something to Rina or to her husband. But we will come. I
have the address of the place where you must write for the sponsorship papers.
We've already put our name on the government waiting list. When our name
reaches the top of the list we'll be able to go."

The only other way was to fly either to Mexico or Spain, but at a cost of   38
two thousand dollars per person to Mexico, three thousand dollars per person
to Spain. The family did not have that kind of money.

Mercedes then gave Hector the telephone. He listened to his aunt's soft   39
voice, saying, "We will be with you soon, and you will know your family again.
Pray for us so that we will be safe." Her voice sounded weak. There was
clicking, like a plug being pulled. Perhaps someone was listening in the courthouse, where the call was being made.

Luisa spoke with Mercedes for another minute, and then their time was   40
up and Mercedes and Hector returned home.

Alejo took care of the paperwork. He wrote to immigration authorities in   41
Miami for their visas and for the special forms that would be mailed out by
him, approved by the U.S. Immigration Department, and sent to Cuba.

In February 1966 Luisa and her daughters and son-in-law left Cuba. First   42 they waited in front of the house on Arachoa Street in Holguín, where they had all been living, for the army bus that would take them on the ten-hour journey west to Havana. When they arrived at the José Marti Airport, they waited in a wire-fenced compound. A Cuban official went over their papers and had them stand in line for hours before they boarded the military transport jet to America.

On the day that Alejo looked at the clipping of Khrushchev again, they   43
received word that Luisa and her daughters and a son-in-law were coming, and a sort of shock wave of apprehension and hope passed through them.

3

For Hector the prospect of Aunt Luisa's arrival stirred up memories. He began   44
to make a conscious effort to be "Cuban," and yet the very idea of *Cubanness* inspired fear in him as if he would grow ill from it, as if micróbios would be transmitted by the very mention of the word *Cuba*. He was a little perplexed because he also loved the notion of Cuba to an extreme. In Cuba there were so many pleasant fragrances, like the smell of Luisa's hair and the damp clay ground of the early morning. Cuba was where Mercedes had once lived a life of style and dignity and happiness. And it was the land of happy courtship with Alejo and the land where men did not fall down. Hector was tired of seeing Mercedes cry and yell. He was tired of her moroseness and wanted the sadness to go away. He wanted the apartment to be filled with beams of sunlight, like in the dream house of Cuba.

He was sick at heart for being so Americanized, which he equated with   45
being fearful and lonely. His Spanish was unpracticed, practically nonexistent. He had a stutter, and saying a Spanish word made him think of drunkenness. A Spanish sentence wrapped around his face, threatened to peel off his skin and send him falling to the floor like Alejo. He avoided Spanish even though that was all he heard at home. He read it, understood it, but he grew paralyzed by the prospect of the slightest conversation.

"Hablame en espanol!" Alejo's drunken friends would challenge him. But   46
Hector always refused and got lost in his bedroom, read *Flash* comic books. And when he was around the street Ricans, they didn't want to talk Spanish with Whitey anyway, especially since he was not getting high with them, just getting drunk now and then, and did not look like a hood but more like a goody-goody, round-faced mama's boy: a dark dude, as they used to say in those days.

Even Horacio had contempt for Hector. Knowing that Hector was nervous   47
in the company of visitors, he would instigate long conversations in Spanish. When visiting men would sit in the kitchen speaking about politics, family, and Cuba, Horacio would play the patrón and join them, relegating Hector to the side, with the women. He had disdain for his brother and for the ignorance Hector represented. He was now interested in "culture." He had returned from England a complete European who listened to Mozart instead of diddy-bop

music. His hair was styled as carefully as Beau Brummell's. His wardrobe consisted of English tweed jackets and fine Spanish shoes; his jewelry, his watches, his cologne, everything was very European and very far from the gutter and the insecurity he had left behind. As he put it, "I'm never going to be fuckin' poor again."

He went around criticizing the way Mercedes kept house and cooked, the 48 way Alejo managed his money (buying everything with cash and never on credit) and the amounts of booze Alejo drank. But mostly he criticized Hector. The day he arrived home from the Air Force and saw Hector for the first time in years, his face turned red. He could not believe his eyes. Hector was so fat that his clothes were bursting at the seams, and when Hector embraced him, Horacio shook his head and said, "Man, I can't believe this is my brother."

And now the real Cubans, Luisa and her daughters and son-in-law, were 49 coming to find out what a false life Hector led. Hector could not sleep at night, thinking of it. He tried to remember his Spanish, but instead of sentences, pictures of Cuba entered into his mind. But he did not fight this. He fantasized about Cuba. He wanted the pictures to enter him, as if memory and imagination would make him more of a man, a Cuban man.

The day before Luisa arrived he suddenly remembered his trip to Cuba 50 with Mercedes and Horacio in 1954. He remembered looking out the window of the plane and seeing fire spewing from the engines on the wing. To Cuba. To Cuba. Mercedes was telling him a story when the plane abruptly plunged down through some clouds and came out into the night air again. Looking out the window he saw pearls in the ocean and the reflection of the moon in the water. For a moment he saw a line of three ships, caravels with big white sails like Columbus's ships, and he tugged at Mercedes's arm. She looked but did not see them. And when he looked again, they were gone.

Hector tried again for a genuine memory. Now he saw Luisa's house on 51 Arachoa Street, the sun a haze bursting through the trees.

"Do you remember a cat with one eye in Cuba?" he asked Horacio, who 52 was across the room reading *Playboy* magazine.

"What?" he said with annoyance. 53

"In Cuba, wasn't there a little cat who used to go in and out of the shadows 54 and bump into things? You know, into the steps and into the walls, because it only had one eye. And then Luisa would come out and feed it bits of meat?"

"You can't remember anything. Don't fool yourself," he replied. 55

But Hector could not stop himself. He remembered bulldozers tearing 56 up the street and that sunlight again, filtering through the flower heads, and flamingos of light on the walls of the house. He remembered the dog with the pathetic red dick running across the yard. Then he remembered holding an enormous, trembling white sunhat. His grandmother, Doña Maria, was sitting nearby in a blue-and-white dotted dress, and he took the sunhat to show her. But it wasn't a sunhat. It was an immense white butterfly. "¡Ai, que linda!" Doña Maria said. "It's so pretty, but maybe we should let the poor thing go."

And so Hector released the butterfly and watched it rise over the house and float silently away.

Then he saw Doña Maria, now dead, framed by a wreath of orchids in the yard, kissing him—so many kisses, squirming kisses—and giving advice. She never got over leaving Spain for Cuba and would always remain a proud Spaniard. "Remember," she had told Hector. "You're Spanish first and then Cuban." **57**

He remembered sitting on the cool steps to Luisa's kitchen and watching the road where the bulldozers worked. A turtle was crawling across the yard, and iguanas were licking up the sticky juice on the kitchen steps. Then he heard Luisa's voice: "Come along, child," she called. "I have something for you." And he could see her face again through the screen door, long and wistful. **58**

Inside, she had patted Hector's head and poured him a glass of milk. Cuban milk alone was sour on the tongues of children, but with the Cuban magic potion, which she added, it was the most delicious drink Hector ever tasted. With deep chocolate and nut flavors and traces of orange and mango, the bitter with the sweet, the liquid went down his throat, so delicious. "No child, drink that milk," Luisa said. "Don't forget your *tia*. She loves you." **59**

Then a bam! bam! came from the television and Hector could hear voices of neighbors out in the hallway. No, he wasn't used to hearing Luisa's niceties anymore, and he couldn't remember what was in the milk, except that it was Cuban, and then he wondered what he would say to his aunt and cousins, whether he would smile and nod his head or hide as much as possible, like a turtle on a hot day. **60**

4

It was late night when a van pulled up to the building and its four exhausted passengers stepped onto the sidewalk. Seeing the arrival from the window, Mercedes was in a trance for a moment and then removed her apron and ran out, almost falling down the front steps, waving her arms and calling, "Aaaaiiii, aaaaiiii, aaaaiiii! Oh my God! My God! My God," and giving many kisses. Alejo followed and hugged Pedro. The female cousins waited humbly, and then they began kissing Mercedes and Alejo and Hector and Horacio, their hats coming off and teeth chattering and hair getting all snarled like ivy on an old church . . . kisses, kisses, kisses . . . into the warm lobby with its deep, endless mirrors and the mailbox marked *Delgado/Santinio*. The female cousins, like china dolls, were incredibly beautiful, but struck dumb by the snow and the new world, silent because there was something dreary about the surroundings. They were thinking Alejo had been in this country for twenty years, and yet what did he have? But no one said this. They just put hands on hands and gave many kisses and said, "I can't believe I'm seeing you here." They were all so skinny and exhausted-looking, Luisa, Virginia, Maria, and Pedro. They came holding cloth bags with all their worldly possessions: a few crucifixes, a **61** change of clothing, aspirins given to them at the airport, an album of old photographs, prayer medals, a Bible, a few Cuban coins from the old days, and a throat-lozenge tin filled with some soil from Holguín, Oriente province, Cuba.

After kissing and hugging them Alejo took them into the kitchen where they almost died: There was so much of everything! Milk and wine and beer, steaks and rice and chicken and sausages and ham and plantains and ice cream and black bean soup and Pepsi-Cola and Hershey chocolate bars and almond nougat, and popcorn and Wise potato chips and Jiffy peanut butter, and rum and whiskey, marshmallows, spaghetti, flan and pasteles and chocolate cake and pie, more than enough to make them delirious. And even though the walls were cracked and it was dark, there was a television set and a radio and lightbulbs and toilet paper and pictures of the family and crucifixes and toothpaste and soap and more.   62

It was "Thank God for freedom and bless my family" from Luisa's mouth, but her daughters were more cautious. Distrusting the world, they approached everything timidly. In the food-filled kitchen Alejo told them how happy he was to have them in his house, and they were happy because the old misery was over, but they were still without a home and in a strange world. Uncertainty showed in their faces.   63

Pedro, Virginia's husband, managed to be the most cheerful. He smoked and talked up a storm about the conditions in Cuba and the few choices the Castro government had left to them. Smoking thick, black cigars, Horacio and Alejo nodded and agreed, and the conversation went back and forth and always ended with "What are you going to do?"   64

"Work until I have something," was Pedro's simple answer.   65

It was such a strong thing to say that Hector, watching from the doorway, wanted to be like Pedro. And from time to time, Pedro would look over and wink and flash his Victor Mature teeth.   66

Pedro was about thirty years old and had been through very bad times, including the struggle in 1957 and 1958 to get Castro into power. But wanting to impress Hector with his cheeriness, Pedro kept saying things in English to Hector like, "I remember Elvis Presley records. Do you know *You're My Angel Baby*?" And Hector would not even answer that. But Pedro would speak on, about the brave Cubans who got out of Cuba in the strangest ways. His buddy back in Holguín stole a small airplane with a few friends and flew west to Mexico, where they crash-landed their plane on a dirt road in the Yucatán. He ended up in Mexico City, where he found work in the construction business. He was due in America soon and would one day marry Maria, who wanted a brave man. These stories only made Hector more and more silent.   67

As for his female cousins, all they said to him was: "Do you want to eat?" or "Why are you so quiet?" And sometimes Horacio answered for him, saying: "He's just dumb when it comes to being Cuban."   68

Aunt Luisa, with her good heart, really didn't care what Hector said or   69 didn't say. Each time she encountered him in the morning or the afternoons, she would take his face between her hands and say, "Give me a kiss and say 'Tia, I love you.' " And not in the way Alejo used to, falling off a chair and with his eyes desperate, but sweetly. Hector liked to be near Luisa with her sweet angelic face.

He felt comfortable enough around Aunt Luisa to begin speaking to her.   70 He wasn't afraid because she overflowed with warmth. One day while Aunt Luisa was washing dishes, Hector started to think of her kitchen in Cuba. He remembered the magic Cuban drink.

"Auntie," he asked her. "Do you remember a drink that you used to make   71 for me in the afternoons in Cuba? What was it? It was the most delicious chocolate but with Cuban spices."

She thought about it. "Chocolate drink in the afternoon? Let me see . . ."   72 She wiped a plate clean in the sink. She seemed perplexed and asked, "And it was chocolate?"

"It was Cuban chocolate. What was it?"   73

She thought on it again and her eyes grew big and she laughed, slapping   74 her knee. "Ai, bobo. It was Hershey syrup and milk!"

After that he didn't ask her any more questions. He just sat in the living   75 room listening to her tell Mercedes about her impressions of the United States. For example, after she had sat out on the stoop or gazed out the window for a time, she would make a blunt declaration: "There are a lot of airplanes in the sky." But usually when Mercedes and Luisa got to talking, they drifted toward the subject of spirits and ghosts. When they were little girls spiritualism was very popular in Cuba. All the little girls were half mediums, in those days. And remembering this with great laughter, Luisa would say, "If only we could have seen what would happen to Papa! Or that Castro would turn out to be so bad!"

"Yes, Papa, that would have been something," Mercedes answered with   76 wide hopeful eyes. "But Castro is something else. What could a few people do about him?"

"Imagine if you're dead in Cuba," said Luisa, "and you wake up to that   77 mess. What would you do?"

"I would go to Miami, or somewhere like that."   78

"Yes, and you would go on angel wings."   79

It was Luisa's ambition to ignore America and the reality of her situation   80 completely. So she kept taking Mercedes back to the old days: "You were such a prankster, so mischievous! You couldn't sit down for a moment without being up to something. Poor Papa! What he had to do with you!" And then, turning to Hector, she would add, "Look at your Mama. This innocent over here was the fright of us all. She was always imagining things. Iguanas, even little baby iguanas, were dragons. A rustle in the bushes was ghosts of fierce Indians looking for their bones!" She laughed. "There are ghosts, but not as many as she saw. She was always in trouble with Papa. He was very good to her but also strict. But his punishments never stopped your mother. My, but she was a fresh girl!"

When she wasn't talking to Mercedes, Luisa watched the Spanish channel 81 on the television, or ate, or prayed. Pedro went out with Alejo and Horacio, looking for work. Maria and Virginia helped with the housecleaning and the cooking, and then they studied their books. They were very quiet, like felines, moving from one spot to another without a sound. Sometimes everyone went out to the movies; Alejo paid for it. Or they all went downtown to the department stores to buy clothing and other things they needed. Again, Alejo paid for everything, angering Mercedes, for whom he bought nothing.

"I know you're trying to be nice to my family, but remember we don't 82 have money."

Still, he was generous with them, as if desperate to keep Luisa and her 83 daughters in the apartment. Their company made him as calm and happy as a mouse. Nothing pleased Alejo more than sitting at the head of the dinner table, relishing the obvious affection that Luisa and her daughters and son-in-law felt for him. At meals Alejo would make toast after toast to their good health and long life, drink down his glass of rum or whiskey quickly, and then fill another and drink that and more. Mercedes always sat quietly wondering, "What does my sister really think of me for marrying him?" while Hector waited for Alejo suddenly to fall off his chair, finally showing his aunt and cousins just who the Santinios really were.

One night Alejo fell against the table and knocked down a big stack of 84 plates. The plates smashed all around Alejo, who was on the floor. Hector scrambled to correct everything before Virginia and Maria and Pedro came to look. He scrambled to get Alejo up before they saw him. He pulled with all his strength, the way he and Horacio used to, but Alejo weighed nearly three hundred pounds. As the cousins watched in silence, Hector wished he could walk through the walls and fly away. He thought that now they would know one of his secrets, that the son is like the father. He tried again to pull Alejo up and had nearly succeeded when Pedro appeared and, with amazing strength, wrapped his arms around Alejo's torso and heaved him onto a chair with one pull.

Hector hadn't wanted them to see this, because then they might want to 85 leave and the apartment would be empty of Pedro and Luisa and her daughters, those fabulous beings. He didn't want them to see the dingy furniture and the cracking walls and the cheap decorative art, plaster statues, and mass-produced paintings. He didn't want them to see that he was an element in this world, only as good as the things around him. He wanted to be somewhere else, be someone else, a Cuban . . . And he didn't want the family perceived as the poor relations with the drunk father. So he tried to laugh about Alejo and eventually went to bed, leaving Luisa and Pedro and his cousins still standing in the hall. Eventually, they did move away. Virginia and Maria found work in a factory in Jersey City, and Pedro came home one evening with news that he had landed a freight dispatcher's job in an airport. Just like that. He had brought home a big box of pastries, sweet cakes with super-sweet cream, chocolate eclairs, honey-drenched cookies with maraschino cherries in their centers.

As Alejo devoured some of these, he said to Pedro, "Well, that's good. You're lucky to have such good friends here. Does it pay you well?" 86

Pedro nodded slightly and said, "I don't know, it starts out at seven thousand dollars a year, but it will get better." 87

Alejo also nodded, but he was sick because after twenty years in the same job he did not make that much, and this brought down his head and made him yawn. He got up and went to his bedroom where he fell asleep. 88

A few months later, they were ready to rent a house in a nice neighborhood in Jersey. The government had helped them out with some emergency funds. ("We never asked the government for even a penny," Mercedes kept saying to Alejo.) Everyone but Luisa was bringing home money. They used that money to buy furniture and to send Virginia to night computer school taught by Spanish instructors. Instead of being cramped up in someone else's apartment with rattling pipes and damp plaster walls that seemed ready to fall in, they had a three-story house with a little yard and lived near many Cubans who kept the sidewalks clean and worked hard, so their sick hearts would have an easier time of it. 89

Hector was bereft at their leaving, but more than that he was astounded by how easily they established themselves. One day Pedro said, "I just bought a car." On another, "I just got a color TV." In time they would be able to buy an even larger house. The house would be filled with possessions: a dishwasher, a washing machine, radios, a big stereo console, plastic-covered velour couches and chairs, electric clocks, fans, air conditioners, hair dryers, statues, crucifixes, lamps and electric-candle chandeliers, and more. One day they would have enough money to move again, to sell the house at a huge profit and travel down to Miami to buy another house there. They would work like dogs, raise children, prosper. They did not allow the old world, the past, to hinder them. They did not cry but walked straight ahead. They drank but did not fall down. Pedro even started a candy and cigarette business to keep him busy in the evenings, earning enough money to buy himself a truck. 90

"Qué bueno," Alejo would say. 91

"This country's wonderful to new Cubans," Mercedes kept repeating. But then she added, "They're going to have everything, and we . . . what will we have?" And she would go about sweeping the floor or preparing chicken for dinner. She would say to Alejo, "Doesn't it hurt you inside?" 92

Alejo shrugged. "No, because they have suffered in Cuba." 93

He never backed off from that position and always remained generous to them, even after their visits became less frequent, even when they came only 94 once a year. And when Pedro tried to repay the loans, Alejo always waved the money away. By this time Virginia was pregnant, so Alejo said, "Keep it for the baby."

"You don't want the money?" 95

"Only when you don't need it. It's important for you to have certain things 96
now."

But Mercedes stalked around the apartment, screaming, "What about the 97
pennies I saved? What about us?" ◆

◆ Responding

1. Compare Alejo and Mercedes's attitudes toward the Cuban revolution before and after Castro came to power. What would they say to supporters of the revolution, such as their neighbor Señor Lopez?

2. What is Horacio's definition of *culture*? Compare his definition with other meanings.

3. Hector is "sick at heart for being so Americanized, which he [equates] with being fearful and lonely." Using examples from the reading, explain the ways in which he is Americanized. Compare his feelings about America with his feelings about Cuba. What does Cuba seem to represent to him?

4. Why is Mercedes angry? Compare the situation of the immigrants arriving in 1965 with that of immigrants who arrived twenty years earlier. Why do you think Pedro and his family become prosperous while Alejo and his family remain poor? Using information from the reading and your own knowledge, speculate about each family's reception in the new country.

JOSÉ ALEJANDRO ROMERO

José Alejandro Romero, a Salvadoran émigré now living in New England, has witnessed and attempted to protest against the repression and barbarism of El Salvador's right-wing dictatorship. Some of his poetry reflects on the suffering of that country. It is within this context of repression that Romero places the incident at Sumpul, where six hundred men, women, and children were massacred—while a few nursing mothers watched horrified from the shore. As the author explains, "Sumpul is a river dividing El Salvador and Honduras. On May 14, 1980, peasants fleeing to Honduras were pursued by the Salvadoran army for many days. Reaching Sumpul and what they believed would be safety, they faced on the other side the hostile Honduran army. While most of the people were in the middle of the river, which was at that point about 100 meters wide, the two armies opened fire, shooting until everyone in the water was dead. No sign of life remained, only the water mixed with the blood of the dead."

In the poem that follows, the river Sumpul becomes a mirror, for it reflects the pain of those who were helpless witnesses to the massacre, and those whose bodies have found no other grave.

◆ SUMPUL ◆

The afternoon has fallen into black dust,
and from the dust emerges death.
In the red river we swam, desperate to live.
We splashed in its waters and then,
bruised, we were floated by them.
From the river the massacred body arose.
Sumpul drowned in blood,
Sumpul deafened by the shots,
river turned red,
river swollen with anguish,
witnessing river, your hidden heart
containing the anonymous screams of martyrs—
of children, tender shoots,
of mothers, fruiting trees
and old ones ancient oaks.
Facing you is Yankee torture,
murderous sounds and the growl of the dog,
splattering this universe with shrapnel,
splitting open pregnant stars,
slashing the face of the peasant.

Beast, take note:
the worker's face will carry this scar.

River,
We seek your water made holy by force,
and with it anoint our arms,
with reddened eyes.
In a single, slaughtered droplet we watch
the sun, its hopeful yellow;
in its yellow is a future,
a victory, a triumph, a people.
In your winding current
We seek the wide and war-injured reflection of the people
confronting a vast machine;
their last words cursing despotism
their words like weapons, their body a shield,
their ideals, pure light.

I want to respond to the screams of the people,
to fixed eyes shooting off hatred,
to hoist your spirit in the fighting flag of guns.
I salute you with each shot aimed at the enemy
I swear to remember you in our future land,
and in the sky brimming with stars,
and in the first maize field of winter,
and in the waters of every river where I live. ◆

◆ Responding

1. Explain in your own words what the river has witnessed.

2. How would you describe the speaker in the poem? What is the speaker's situation?

3. The author uses poetry to express his feelings about an important event in his country's history. Write a poem about a place or event that is particularly meaningful to you.

MARK MATHABANE

Mark Mathabane was born in 1960 in South Africa, where his family suffered under apartheid, the forced segregation of the races. Because he had learned to play tennis well during his childhood, Mathabane was able to impress the American professional tennis star Stan Smith, who became his sponsor. With Smith's help, Mathabane received an athletic scholarship to a small college in the United States, and thereby escaped from the oppressive regime in his homeland.

Mathabane has recounted some of his experiences growing up in South Africa and emigrating in two books, Kaffir Boy *(1986) and* Kaffir Boy in America *(1989). The first work, which depicts the author's childhood of poverty and oppression, describes night raids by police, beatings, and other atrocities endured by the family. The second book, from which the following excerpt is taken, describes Mathabane's adjustment to life in the United States. Here the author recounts his difficulty in explaining his circumstances to a black separatist. Racial, historical, and other perspectives are at work as the narrator, who has just arrived from South Africa, tries to provide a context for the different attitudes he encounters.*

◆ I LEAVE SOUTH AFRICA ◆

The plane landed at Atlanta's International Airport the afternoon of September 17, 1978. I double-checked the name and description of Dr. Killion's friend who was to meet me. Shortly after the plane came to a standstill at the gate, and I was stashing Dr. Killion's letter into my totebag, I felt a tap on my shoulder, and turning met the steady and unsettling gaze of the Black Muslim. 1

"Are you from Africa?" he asked as he offered to help me with my luggage. 2

"Yes." I wondered how he could tell. 3

"A student?" 4

"Yes." We were aboard a jumbo jet, almost at the back of it. From the throng in front it was clear that it would be some time before we disembarked, so we fell into conversation. He asked if it was my first time in the United States and I replied that it was. He spoke in a thick American accent. 5

"Glad to meet you, brother," he said. We shook hands. "My name is Nkwame." 6

"I'm Mark," I said, somewhat intimidated by his aspect. 7

"Mark is not African," he said coolly. "What's your African name, brother?" 8

"Johannes." 9

"That isn't an African name either." 10

I was startled by this. How did he know I had an African name? I hardly 11 used it myself because it was an unwritten rule among black youths raised in the ghettos to deny their tribal identity and affiliation, and that denial applied especially to names. But I didn't want to offend this persistent stranger, so I gave it to him. "Thanyani."

"What does it stand for?" 12

How did he know that my name stood for something? I wondered in 13
amazement. My worst fears were confirmed. Black Americans did indeed possess the sophistication to see through any ruse an African puts up. Then and there I decided to tell nothing but the truth.

"The wise one," I said, and quickly added, "but the interpretation is not 14
meant to be taken literally, sir."

We were now headed out of the plane. He carried my tennis rackets. 15

"The wise one, heh," he mused. "You Africans sure have a way with 16
names. You know," he went on with great warmth, "one of my nephews is named after a famous African chief. Of the Mandingo tribe, I believe. Ever since I saw 'Roots' I have always wanted to know where my homeland is."

I found this statement baffling for I thought that as an American his 17
homeland was America. I did not know about "Roots."

"Which black college in Atlanta will you be attending, Thanyani?" he 18
asked. "You will be attending a black college, I hope?"

Black colleges? I stared at him. My mind conjured up images of the dismal 19
tribal schools I hated and had left behind in the ghetto. My God, did such schools exist in America?

"No, sir," I stammered. "I won't be attending school in Atlanta. I'm 20
headed for Limestone College in South Carolina."

"Is Limestone a black college?" 21

"No, sir," I said hastily. 22

"What a pity," he sighed. "You would be better off at a black college." 23

I continued staring at him. 24

He went on. "At a black college," he said with emphasis, "you can meet 25
with your true brothers and sisters. There's so much you can teach them about the true Africa and the struggles of our people over there. And they have a lot to teach you about being black in America. And, you know, there are lots of black colleges in the South."

I nearly fainted at this revelation. Black schools in America? Was I hearing 26
things or what? I almost blurted out that I had attended black schools all my life and wanted to have nothing to do with them. But instead I said, "Limestone College is supposed to be a good college, too, sir. It's integrated."

"That don't mean nothing," he snapped. "Integrated schools are the worst 27
places for black folks. I thought you Africans would have enough brains to know that this integration business in America is a fraud. It ain't good for the black mind and culture. Integration, integration," he railed. "What good has integration done the black man? We've simply become more dependent on the

white devil and forgotten how to do things for ourselves. Also, no matter how integrated we become, white folks won't accept us as equals. So why should we break our backs trying to mix with them, heh? To them we will always be niggers."

I was shaken by his outburst. I longed to be gone from him, especially since he had drawn me aside in the corridor leading toward customs. The Black Muslim must have realized that I was a complete stranger to him, that his bitter tone terrified and confused me, for he quickly recollected himself and smiled.

"Well, good luck in your studies, brother," he said, handing me my rackets. "By the way, where in Africa did you say you were from? Nigeria?"

"No. South Africa."

"South what!" he said.

"South Africa," I repeated. "That place with all those terrible race problems. Where black people have no rights and are being murdered every day."

I expected my statement to shock him; instead he calmly said, "You will find a lot of South Africa in this country, brother. Keep your eyes wide open all the time. Never let down your guard or you're dead. And while you're up there in South Carolina, watch out for the Ku Klux Klan. That's their home. And don't you ever believe that integration nonsense."

He left. I wondered what he meant by his warning. I stumbled my way to customs. There was a long queue and when my turn came the white, somber-faced immigration official, with cropped reddish-brown hair, seemed transformed into an Afrikaner bureaucrat. I almost screamed. He demanded my passport. After inspecting it, he asked to see my plane ticket. I handed it to him.

"It's a one-way ticket," he said.

"Yes, sir. I couldn't afford a return ticket," I answered, wondering what could be wrong.

"Under the student visa regulations you're required to have a return ticket," he said icily. "Otherwise how will you get back home? You intend returning home after your studies, don't you?"

"Yes, sir."

"Then you ought to have a return ticket."

I remained silent.

"Do you have relatives or a guardian in America?"

I speedily handed him a letter from Stan Smith, along with several completed immigration forms indicating that he had pledged to be my legal guardian for the duration of my stay in the States. The immigration official inspected the documents, then left his cubicle and went to consult his superior. I trembled at the thought that I might be denied entry into the United States. But the one-way ticket, which created the impression that I was coming to America for good, was hardly my fault. Having had no money to purchase a ticket of my own, I had depended on the charity of white friends, and I was in no position to insist that they buy me a return ticket. The immigration official came back. He stamped my passport and welcomed me to the United States. I almost fell on my knees and kissed the hallowed ground.

"Welcome to America, Mark," a tall, lean-faced white man greeted me as   43
I came out of customs. It was Dr. Waller.

His kind voice and smiling face, as he introduced himself and asked me   44
if I had a good flight, raised my spirits. As we walked toward the baggage claim area I stared at everything about me with childlike wonder. I scarcely believed I had finally set foot in *the* America. I felt the difference between South Africa and America instantly. The air seemed pervaded with freedom and hope and opportunity. Every object seemed brighter, newer, more modern, fresher, the people appeared better dressed, more intelligent, richer, warmer, happier, and full of energy—despite the profound impersonality of the place.

"I would like to use the lavatory," I told Dr. Waller.   45

"There should be one over there." He pointed to a sign ahead which read   46
RESTROOMS. "I'll wait for you at the newsstand over there."

When I reached the restroom I found it had the sign MEN in black and   47
white on it. Just before I entered I instinctively scoured the walls to see if I had missed the other more important sign: BLACKS ONLY or WHITES ONLY, but there was none. I hesitated before entering: this freedom was too new, too strange, too unreal, and called for the utmost caution. Despite what I believed about America, there still lingered in the recesses of my mind the terror I had suffered in South Africa when I had inadvertently disobeyed the racial etiquette, like that time in Pretoria when I mistakenly boarded a white bus, and Granny had to grovel before the irate redneck driver, emphatically declare that it was an insanity "not of the normal kind" which had made me commit such a crime, and to appease him proceeded to wipe, with her lovely tribal dress, the steps where I had trod. In such moments of doubt such traumas made me mistrust my instincts. I saw a lanky black American with a mammoth Afro enter and I followed. I relieved myself next to a white man and he didn't die.

The black American washed his hands and began combing his Afro. I   48
gazed at his hair with wonder. In South Africa blacks adored Afros and often incurred great expense cultivating that curious hairdo, in imitation of black Americans. Those who succeeded in giving their naturally crinkly, nappy, and matted hair, which they loathed, that buoyant "American" look were showered with praise and considered handsome and "glamorous," as were those who successfully gave it the permanent wave or jerry-curl, and bleached their faces white with special creams which affected the pigmentation.

I remember how Uncle Pietrus, on my father's side, a tall, athletic, hand-   49
some man who earned slave wages, was never without creams such as Ambi to bleach his face, and regularly wore a meticulously combed Afro greased with Brylcreem. Many in the neighborhood considered him the paragon of manly beauty, and women were swept away by his "American" looks.

From time to time he proudly told me stories of how, in the center of 50
Johannesburg, whites who encountered black men and women with bleached
faces, Afros, or straightened hair, and clad in the latest fashion from America,
often mistook them for black Americans and treated them as honorary whites.
A reasonable American accent made the masquerade almost foolproof. So for
many blacks there were these incentives to resemble black Americans, to adopt
their mannerisms and life-styles. And the so-called Coloureds (mixed race), with
their naturally lighter skin and straightened hair, not only frequently took
advantage of this deception but often passed for whites. But they were rarely
secure in their false identity. And in their desperation to elude discovery and
humiliation at being subjected to fraudulent race-determining tests like the
pencil test (where the authorities run a pencil through one's hair: if the pencil
slides smoothly through, one gets classified white; if it gets tangled, that's
"positive" proof of being black), they often adopted racist attitudes toward blacks
more virulent than those of the most racist whites.

I had sense enough to disdain the practice of whitening one's skin. I 51
considered it pathetic and demeaning to blacks. As for the companies which
manufactured these popular creams, they are insidiously catering to a demand
created by over three hundred years of white oppression and domination. During that traumatic time the black man's culture and values were decimated in
the name of civilization, and the white man's culture and values, trumpeted as
superior, became the standards of intelligence, excellence, and beauty.

I left the bathroom and rejoined Dr. Waller at the newsstand. I found 52
him reading a magazine.

"There's so much to read here," I said, running my eyes over the news- 53
papers, magazines, and books. Interestingly, almost all had white faces on the
cover, just as in South Africa.

"Yes," replied Dr. Waller. 54

I was shocked to see pornography magazines, which are banned in South 55
Africa, prominently displayed. The puritan and Calvinistic religion of the Af-
rikaners sought to purge South African society of "influences of the devil" and
"materials subversive to the state and public morals" by routinely banning and
censoring not only books by writers who challenged the status quo, but also
publications like *Playboy.*

"So many black people fly in America," I said. 56

"A plane is like a car to many Americans," said Dr. Waller. 57

"To many of my people cars are what planes are to Americans." 58

At the baggage-claim area I saw black and white people constantly rubbing 59
shoulders, animatedly talking to one another, and no one seemed to mind.
There were no ubiquitous armed policemen.

"There truly is no apartheid here," I said to myself. "This is indeed the 60
Promised Land."

I felt so happy and relieved that for the first time the tension that went 61
with being black in South Africa left me. I became a new person.◆

◆ Responding

1. Analyze the misunderstandings between Mark and the Black Muslim he meets during the flight to the United States. How do the differences in their backgrounds lead to these misunderstandings?

2. The Black Muslim says, "What good has integration done the black man? We've simply become more dependent on the white devil and forgotten how to do things for ourselves. Also, no matter how integrated we become, white folks won't accept us as equals. So why should we break our backs trying to mix with them, heh?" Agree or disagree with this statement, supporting your argument with evidence from this reading and your own knowledge and experience.

3. Working individually or in a group, list the differences in life situations, freedom, and opportunity for blacks in South Africa and blacks in America.

JESSICA HAGEDORN

Born in the Philippines in 1949, the writer Jessica Hagedorn has reflected on the experiences of immigrants to America in her poetic, fictional, and dramatic works. In addition to contributing poetry to the Third Woman *and the* Yardbird Reader, *she has published work in several journals, including the* Seattle Review. *Her book-length publications include a collection of poetry, prose, and short fiction entitled* Dangerous Music *(1975) and the novel* Dogeaters *(1990). Moreover, Hagedorn has composed multimedia pieces, which have been performed by such groups as the Public Theater in New York. Her work has won her several grants and awards from the MacDowell Colony, the Center for American Culture Studies at Columbia University, and the New York State Council on the Arts, among others.*

In "Luna Moth," from Dogeaters, *the narrator describes her experiences visiting her home in the Philippines after living abroad for some time. As she depicts the melancholy state of her environment, her disillusionment reflects the feelings of many refugees who find themselves settled in neither their native nor their adopted homelands.*

◆ LUNA MOTH ◆

My mother begins painting shortly after her fiftieth birthday. Except for occasional drawing lessons with Horacio, she has had no formal training in art and is ignorant of its history. She paints and paints; with furious energy, she covers immense canvases with slashes of red, black, yellow, and mauve. She uses the same colors in different combinations. "My bleeding bouquets," she calls them. She moves into Raul's now empty room and converts it into her bedroom-studio. My father acts as if everything were normal, even when Uncle Agustin says, "Your wife has slapped you in the face."   1

Without warning, she cheerfully announces she is sending me to school in America and moving there with me for an indefinite period. I am ecstatic, at first. Everyone else is stunned. My father cannot stop her—my mother has inherited money from her father and pays for our passage to America. We settle first in New York, then Boston. I convince myself I am not homesick, and try not to bring up my father or brother when I speak. My mother actually sells a few paintings. The months turn into years. "Are we going to stay here forever?" I finally ask her. She looks surprised. "I don't know about you, but I love the cold weather. Go back to Manila if you want. Tell Raul I miss him more than he could ever imagine." She smiles one of her cryptic smiles. "But he'll have to visit me here if he wants to see me—" her voice trails off.   2

Raul writes me letters in red ink, polite letters quoting from the Scriptures and inquiring about my health. He achieves local fame as a spiritualist healer and   3 preaches to his followers in the countryside. Erlinda and the children follow close behind, his loyal family of believers. He distances himself from the rest of the Gonzagas, who are ashamed of his newfound fundamentalist Christian ministry. Only Pucha, of all people, visits him regularly. She writes me notes on Hallmark greeting cards:

> *Oye, prima—que ba, when are you coming back? Tonyboy asked about you, I saw him at SPORTEX boy he still looks grate! I think he left his wife you dont know her shes a forinner from Austria or Australia you know he told me you really broke his heart when you left plus you never answered any of his letters,* pobrecito naman! *WOW! I saw Raul yesterday at that new apt of his I brought him new clothes for the kids, theres so many! Erlinda's pregnant again. I didnt stay two long, he was in one of his moods you know how Raul gets. Hes always complaineing you dont write anybody and its true. Write him, okay? And send your mother my regards I hope shes not mad at me. Thanks be to God my parents are okay. Uncle Esteban had another operation, in case you didnt here. Mommie says HELLO! She and Papi had* merienda *with your father last Sunday. Mikeys getting married. AT LAST. Why dont you come to the wedding?*
>
> *Love & prayers,*
> *PUCHA*

When I finally come home to Manila to visit, my father warns me not to bother visiting our old house. "You'll be disappointed. Memories are always better." Smiling apologetically, he tells me reality will diminish the grandeur of my childhood image of home. I take his picture with my new camera, which later falls in the swimming pool by accident. The camera is destroyed, along with my roll of film. I decide to visit our old house in Mandaluyong anyway, borrowing a car from Mikey. Pucha goes with me; she loves riding around in cars and doesn't need any excuse. "After that, let's go to the Intercon Hotel and have a drink," she says, a gleam of mischief in her eyes. "Put on some makeup," she bosses me, "you look tired." I laugh. Pucha is up to her old tricks. She applies thick coats of blue eyeshadow on her heavy eyelids, studying her face in the mirror with rapt concentration.

My father is right. The house with its shuttered windows looks smaller than I remember, and dingy. The once lush and sprawling garden is now a forlorn landscape of rocks, weeds, and wild ferns. The bamboo grove has been cut down. "Let's go," Pucha whispers, impatient and uninterested. An old man with bright eyes introduces himself as Manong Tibo, the caretaker. He unlocks door after door for us, pulling aside cobwebs, warning us to be careful. Rotting floorboards creak under the weight of our footsteps. "My bedroom," I say to the old man, who nods. I am overwhelmed by melancholy at the sight of the empty room. A frightened mouse dashes across the grimy tiled floor. Pucha jumps back and screams, clutching and pinching my arm. "Let's go," she pleads. "Wait outside. I'll be there soon," I say, trying to conceal my irritation. I am relieved finally to be alone, in this desolate house with only Manong for company. He studies me with his bright eyes. "You live in America?" His niece is a nurse in San Francisco, California, he tells me with pride. Someday, he hopes she'll send for him.

I stay another hour, walking in and out of the dusty rooms in a kind of stupor. The shutters in the windows of the kitchen, Pacita's kingdom, are hanging from their hinges. The gas stove and refrigerator are gone. "Thieves," Manong shrugs, when I ask him. Broken glass is scattered on the floor. He tells me the house will be torn down within the month and a complex of offices built in its place. The property and the squatters' land adjoining it have been bought by the Alacran corporation, Intercoco.

I say good-bye and thank the old man. "See you in America!" Manong Tibo says, waving farewell. Pucha is slumped down in the front seat of the car, irritated, hot, and sweaty. "I wouldn't do this for anyone but you," she grumbles without looking at me, then peers into the rearview mirror. "Look at my makeup!" She gives me an accusing look. I slide into the driver's seat, fighting back tears. Suddenly, I grab her hand. She stares at me, puzzled. "Are you okay?" It seems an eternity, but I pull myself together. Pucha hands me her lace handkerchief, drenched in perfume. "Watch out when you blow your nose—okay, *prima*?" She teases. She squeezes my hand, uncomfortable with our display of affection. I start the car, turning to look at her before we drive away. "I really love you," I say, to her utter amazement.

My cousin will find happiness with a man, once and for all. He is a stranger to us, a modest man from a modest family, someone we never knew in our childhood. The Gonzagas breathe a collective sigh of relief. Pucha lives with her new husband, childless and content; she never leaves Manila.

My *Lola* Narcisa lives to be a very old woman. She is the main reason for my frequent visits to Manila; I dread not being there when she dies.

I return to North America. I save all Raul's letters, along with my father's cordial birthday telegrams and Pucha's gossipy notes, in a large shopping bag labeled FAMILY. I move to another city, approximately five thousand miles away from where my mother lives and paints. We talk on the phone once a week. I am anxious and restless, at home only in airports. I travel whenever I can. My belief in God remains tentative. I have long ago stopped going to church. I never marry.

In my recurring dream, my brother and I inhabit the translucent bodies of nocturnal moths with curved, fragile wings. We are pale green, with luminous celadon eyes, fantastic and beautiful. In dream after dream, we are drawn to the same silent tableau: a mysterious light glowing from the window of a deserted, ramshackle house. The house is sometimes perched on a rocky abyss, or on a dangerous cliff overlooking a turbulent sea. The meaning is simple and clear, I think. Raul and I embrace our destiny: we fly around in circles, we swoop and dive in effortless arcs against a barren sky, we flap and beat our wings in our futile attempts to reach what surely must be heaven. ◆

◆ Responding

1. Speculate on the reasons for the narrator's initial enthusiasm about going to live in America and what might have made her unhappy once she was living there. Do you think the family she left behind or the culture she encounters is responsible?

2. When the speaker returns to Manila for a visit, her father warns her against visiting her old house, saying, "You'll be disappointed. Memories are always better." In what ways are her memories different from reality? Write an essay agreeing or disagreeing with her father's opinion. Support your argument with examples from the reading or from your own experience.

3. The narrator conveys some of her pain when she says, "I am anxious and restless, at home only in airports." She seems to belong nowhere. Write a journal entry about a time when you or someone you know felt uncomfortable or out of place in a new situation.

4. Compare the narrator's feelings of dislocation and disorientation with the feelings of any of the other immigrants you have read about in this text.

MIKE ROSE

Mike Rose was born in Altoona, Pennsylvania, in 1944, the son of immigrants from southern Italy, and grew up in south Los Angeles. Beginning as a marginalized student, he eventually became a nationally-known expert on language, literacy, and the teaching of writing. After spending part of high school on the vocational track, he attended Loyola University of Los Angeles, earning his bachelor's degree in 1966. He subsequently earned master's degrees from the University of Southern California and the University of California at Los Angeles, and a doctorate in educational psychology from UCLA, where he is currently associate director of Writing Programs. His publications, which examine issues of literacy and education, have earned him numerous awards from the National Council of Teachers of English, the National Academy of Education, and the McDonnell Foundation, among others.

Rose's most recent book, Lives on the Boundary: The Struggles and Achievements of America's Underprepared *(1989), uses knowledge gained through both personal experience and research to suggest the ways in which teachers and schools can do a better job of educating their students. In the chapter that follows, the author recalls his experiences during his early years in south Los Angeles.*

◆ *From* **LIVES ON THE BOUNDARY** ◆

Between 1880 and 1920, well over four million Southern Italian peasants immigrated to America. Their poverty was extreme and hopeless—twelve hours of farm labor would get you one lira, about twenty cents—so increasing numbers of desperate people booked passage for the United States, the country where, the steamship companies claimed, prosperity was a way of life. My father left Naples before the turn of the century; my mother came with her mother from Calabria in 1921. They met in Altoona, Pennsylvania, at the lunch counter of Tom and Joe's, a steamy diner with twangy-voiced waitresses and graveyard stew.

For my mother, life in America was not what the promoters had told her father it would be. She grew up very poor. She slept with her parents and brothers and sisters in one room. She had to quit school in the seventh grade to care for her sickly younger brothers. When her father lost his leg in a railroad accident, she began working in a garment factory where women sat crowded at their stations, solitary as penitents in a cloister. She stayed there until her marriage. My father had found a freer route. He was closemouthed about his past, but I know that he had been a salesman, a tailor, and a gambler; he knew people in the mob and had, my uncles whisper, done time in Chicago. He went through a year or two of Italian elementary school and could write a few words—those necessary to scribble measurements for a suit—and over the years developed a quiet urbanity, a persistence, and a slowly debilitating arteriosclerosis.

When my father proposed to my mother, he decided to open a spaghetti house, a venture that lasted through the war and my early years. The restaurant collapsed in bankruptcy in 1951 when Altoona's major industry, the Pennsylvania Railroad, had to shut down its shops. My parents managed to salvage seven hundred dollars and, on the advice of the family doctor, headed to California, where the winters would be mild and where I, their seven-year-old son, would have the possibility of a brighter future. 3

At first we lived in a seedy hotel on Spring Street in downtown Los Angeles, but my mother soon found an ad in the *Times* for cheap property on the south side of town. My parents contacted a woman named Mrs. Jolly, used my mother's engagement ring as a down payment, and moved to 9116 South Vermont Avenue, a house about one and one-half miles northwest of Watts. The neighborhood was poor, and it was in transition. Some old white folks had lived there for decades and were retired. Younger black families were moving up from Watts and settling by working-class white families newly arrived from the South and the Midwest. Immigrant Mexican families were coming in from Baja. Any such demographic mix is potentially volatile, and as the fifties wore on, the neighborhood would be marked by outbursts of violence. 4

I have many particular memories of this time, but in general these early years seem a peculiar mix of physical warmth and barrenness: a gnarled lemon tree, thin rugs, a dirt alley, concrete in the sun. My uncles visited a few times, and we went to the beach or to orange groves. The return home, however, left the waves and spray, the thick leaves and split pulp far in the distance. I was aware of my parents watching their money and got the sense from their conversations that things could quickly take a turn for the worse. I started taping pennies to the bottom of a shelf in the kitchen. 5

My father's health was bad, and he had few readily marketable skills. Poker and pinochle brought in a little money, and he tried out an idea that had worked in Altoona during the war: He started a "suit club." The few customers he could scare up would pay two dollars a week on a tailor-made suit. He would take the measurements and send them to a shop back East and hope for the best. My mother took a job at a café in downtown Los Angeles, a split shift 9:00 to 12:00 and 5:00 to 9:00, but her tips were totaling sixty cents a day, so she quit for a night shift at Coffee Dan's. This got her to the bus stop at one in the morning, waiting on the same street where drunks were urinating and hookers were catching the last of the bar crowd. She made friends with a Filipino cook who would scare off the advances of old men aflame with the closeness of taxi dancers. In a couple of years, Coffee Dan's would award her a day job at the counter. Once every few weeks my father and I would take a bus downtown and visit with her, sitting at stools by the window, watching the animated but silent mix of faces beyond the glass. 6

My father had moved to California with faint hopes about health and a 7
belief in his child's future, drawn by that far edge of America where the sun
descends into green water. What he found was a city that was warm, verdant,
vast, and indifferent as a starlet in a sports car. Altoona receded quickly, and
my parents must have felt isolated and deceived. They had fallen into the abyss
of paradise—two more poor settlers trying to make a go of it in the City of the
Angels.

Let me tell you about our house. If you entered the front door and turned right 8
you'd see a small living room with a couch along the east wall and one along
the west wall—one couch was purple, the other tan, both bought used and both
well worn. A television set was placed at the end of the purple couch, right at
arm level. An old Philco radio sat next to the TV, its speaker covered with
gold lamé. There was a small coffee table in the center of the room on which
sat a murky fishbowl occupied by two listless guppies. If, on entering, you
turned left you would see a green Formica dinner table with four chairs, a cedar
chest given as a wedding present to my mother by her mother, a painted statue
of the Blessed Virgin Mary, and a black trunk. I also had a plastic chaise longue
between the door and the table. I would lie on this and watch television.

A short hallway leading to the bathroom opened on one side to the kitchen 9
and, on the other, to the bedroom. The bedroom had two beds, one for me
and one for my parents, a bureau with a mirror, and a chest of drawers on
which we piled old shirt boxes and stacks of folded clothes. The kitchen held
a refrigerator and a stove, small older models that we got when our earlier (and
newer) models were repossessed by two silent men. There was one white
wooden chair in the corner beneath wall cabinets. You could walk in and through
a tiny pantry to the backyard and to four one-room rentals. My father got most
of our furniture from a secondhand store on the next block; he would tend the
store two or three hours a day as payment on our account.

As I remember it, the house was pretty dark. My mother kept the blinds 10
in the bedroom drawn—there were no curtains there—and the venetian blinds
in the living room were, often as not, left closed. The walls were bare except
for a faded picture of Jesus and a calendar from the *Altoona Mirror*. Some paper
carnations bent out of a white vase on the television. There was a window on
the north side of the kitchen that had no blinds or curtains, so the sink got good
light. My father would methodically roll up his sleeves and show me how to
prepare a sweet potato or avocado seed so it would sprout. We kept a row of
them on the sill above the sink, their shoots and vines rising and curling in the
morning sun.

The house was on a piece of land that rose about four feet up from heavily 11
trafficked Vermont Avenue. The yard sloped down to the street, and three
steps and a short walkway led up the middle of the grass to our front door.
There was a similar house immediately to the south of us. Next to it was
Carmen's Barber Shop. Carmen was a short, quiet Italian who, rumor had it,

had committed his first wife to the crazy house to get her money. In the afternoons, Carmen could be found in the lot behind his shop playing solitary catch, flinging a tennis ball high into the air and running under it. One day the police arrested Carmen on charges of child molesting. He was released but became furtive and suspicious. I never saw him in the lot again. Next to Carmen's was a junk store where, one summer, I made a little money polishing brass and rewiring old lamps. Then came a dilapidated real estate office, a Mexican restaurant, an empty lot, and an appliance store owned by the father of Keith Grateful, the streetwise, chubby boy who would become my best friend.

12   Right to the north of us was a record shop, a barber shop presided over by old Mr. Graff, Walt's Malts, a shoe repair shop with a big Cat's Paw decal in the window, a third barber shop, and a brake shop. It's as I write this that I realize for the first time that three gray men could have had a go at your hair before you left our street.

13   Behind our house was an unpaved alley that passed, just to the north, a power plant the length of a city block. Massive coils atop the building hissed and cracked through the day, but the doors never opened. I used to think it was abandoned—feeding itself on its own wild arcs—until one sweltering afternoon a man was electrocuted on the roof. The air was thick and still as two firemen—the only men present—brought down a charred and limp body without saying a word.

14   The north and south traffic on Vermont was separated by tracks for the old yellow trolley cars, long since defunct. Across the street was a huge garage, a tiny hot dog stand run by a myopic and reclusive man named Freddie, and my dreamland, the Vermont Bowl. Distant and distorted behind thick lenses, Freddie's eyes never met yours; he would look down when he took your order and give you your change with a mumble. Freddie slept on a cot in the back of his grill and died there one night, leaving tens of thousands of dollars stuffed in the mattress.

15   My father would buy me a chili dog at Freddie's, and then we would walk over to the bowling alley where Dad would sit at the lunch counter and drink coffee while I had a great time with pinball machines, electric shooting galleries, and an ill-kept dispenser of cheese corn. There was a small, dark bar abutting the lanes, and it called to me. I would devise reasons to walk through it: " 'Scuse me, is the bathroom in here?" or "Anyone see my dad?" though I can never remember my father having a drink. It was dark and people were drinking and I figured all sorts of mysterious things were being whispered. Next to the Vermont Bowl was a large vacant lot overgrown with foxtails and dotted with car parts, bottles, and rotting cardboard. One day Keith heard that the police had found a human head in the brush. After that we explored the lot periodically, coming home with stickers all the way up to our waists. But we didn't find a thing. Not even a kneecap.

16   When I wasn't with Keith or in school, I would spend most of my day

with my father or with the men who were renting the one-room apartments behind our house. Dad and I whiled away the hours in the bowling alley, watching TV, or planting a vegetable garden that never seemed to take. When he was still mobile, he would walk the four blocks down to St. Regina's Grammar School to take me home to my favorite lunch of boiled wieners and chocolate milk. There I'd sit, dunking my hot dog in a jar of mayonnaise and drinking my milk while Sheriff John tuned up the calliope music on his "Lunch Brigade." Though he never complained to me, I could sense that my father's health was failing, and I began devising child's ways to make him better. We had a box of rolled cotton in the bathroom, and I would go in and peel off a long strip and tape it around my jaw. Then I'd rummage through the closet, find a sweater of my father's, put on one of his hats—and sneak around to the back door. I'd knock loudly and wait. It would take him a while to get there. Finally, he'd open the door, look down, and quietly say, "Yes, Michael?" I was disappointed. Every time. Somehow I thought I could fool him. And, I guess, if he had been fooled, I would have succeeded in redefining things: I would have been the old one, he much younger, more agile, with strength in his legs.

The men who lived in the back were either retired or didn't work that much, so one of them was usually around. They proved to be, over the years, an unusual set of companions for a young boy. Ed Gionotti was the youngest of the lot, a handsome man whose wife had run off and who spoke softly and never smiled. Bud Hall and Lee McGuire were two out-of-work plumbers who lived in adjacent units and who weekly drank themselves silly, proclaiming in front of God and everyone their undying friendship or their unequivocal hatred. Old Cheech was a lame Italian who used to hobble along grabbing his testicles and rolling his eyes while he talked about the women he claimed to have on a string. There was Lester, the toothless cabbie, who several times made overtures to me and who, when he moved, left behind a drawer full of syringes and burnt spoons. Mr. Smith was a rambunctious retiree who lost his nose to an untended skin cancer. And there was Mr. Berryman, a sweet and gentle man who eventually left for a retirement hotel only to be burned alive in an electrical fire. 17

Except for Keith, there were no children on my block and only one or two on the immediate side streets. Most of the people I saw day to day were over fifty. People in their twenties and thirties working in the shoe shop or the garages didn't say a lot; their work and much of what they were working for drained their spirits. There were gang members who sauntered up from Hoover Avenue, three blocks to the east, and occasionally I would get shoved around, but they had little interest in me either as member or victim. I was a skinny, bespectacled kid and had neither the coloring nor the style of dress or carriage that marked me as a rival. On the whole, the days were quiet, lazy, lonely. The heat shimmering over the asphalt had no snap to it; time drifted by. I would lie on the couch at night and listen to the music from the record store or from Walt's Malts. It was new and quick paced, exciting, a little dangerous (the church had condemned Buddy Knox's "Party Doll"), and I heard in it a 18 deep rhythmic need to be made whole with love, or marked as special, or released in some rebellious way. Even the songs about lost love—and there were plenty of them—lifted me right out of my socks with their melodious longing:

> Came the dawn,
> and my heart and her love and the night
> were gone.
> But I know I'll never forget
> her kiss in the moonlight Oooo . . .
> such a kiss Oooo Oooo such a night . . .

In the midst of the heat and slow time the music brought the promise of its origins, a promise of deliverance, a promise that, if only for a moment, life could be stirring and dreamy.

But the anger and frustration of South Vermont could prove too strong 19 for music's illusion; then it was violence that provided deliverance of a different order. One night I watched as a guy sprinted from Walt's to toss something on our lawn. The police were right behind, and a cop tackled him, smashing his face into the sidewalk. I ducked out to find the packet: a dozen glassine bags of heroin. Another night, one August midnight, an argument outside the record store ended with a man being shot to death. And the occasional gang forays brought with them some fated kid who would fumble his moves and catch a knife.

It's popular these days to claim you grew up on the streets. Men tell 20 violent tales and romanticize the lessons violence brings. But, though it was occasionally violent, it wasn't the violence in South L.A. that marked me, for sometimes you can shake that ugliness off. What finally affected me was subtler, but more pervasive: I cannot recall a young person who was crazy in love or lost in work or one old person who was passionate about a cause or an idea. I'm not talking about an absence of energy—the street toughs and, for that fact, old Cheech had energy. And I'm not talking about an absence of decency, for my father was a thoughtful man. The people I grew up with were retired from jobs that rub away the heart or were working hard at jobs to keep their lives from caving in or were anchorless and in between jobs and spouses or were diving headlong into a barren tomorrow: junkies, alcoholics, and mean kids walking along Vermont looking to throw a punch. I developed a picture of human existence that rendered it short and brutish or sad and aimless or long and quiet with rewards like afternoon naps, the evening newspaper, walks around the block, occasional letters from children in other states. When, years later, I was introduced to humanistic psychologists like Abraham Maslow and Carl Rogers, with their visions of self-actualization, or even Freud with his sober dictum about love and work, it all sounded like a glorious fairy tale, a magical account of a world full of possibility, full of hope and empowerment. Sindbad and Cinderella couldn't have been more fanciful. ◆

◆ Responding

1. Compare Rose's neighborhood with the place where you grew up. In your description, include the opportunities and role models available to him and to you.

2. Rose characterizes his parents as "two more poor settlers trying to make a go of it in the City of the Angels." Compare the myth of California with the realities encountered by Rose's parents.

3. Rose says, "What finally affected me was subtler, but more persuasive: I cannot recall a young person who was crazy in love or lost in work or one old person who was passionate about a cause or an idea. . . . The people I grew up with were retired from jobs that rub away the heart or were working hard at jobs to keep their lives from caving in . . . junkies, alcoholics, and mean kids walking along Vermont [Avenue] looking to throw a punch. I developed a picture of human existence that rendered it short and brutish or sad and aimless. . . ." What are the possible psychological and social effects on a child of growing up in such a neighborhood? This kind of environment can severely limit a young person's opportunities for academic and economic success, yet, in spite of his background, Rose achieved academic success. What factors do you think counter the effects of environment?

ALICE WALKER

Alice Walker, born in the small town of Eatonsville, Georgia, in 1944, attended Spelman College and Sarah Lawrence College, where she received her bachelor's degree in 1965. During the 1960s and early 1970s she worked for voter registration in the South and welfare rights in New York, in addition to teaching literature and African American studies at several universities. Among her numerous publications are the collections of stories In Love and in Trouble *(1973) and* You Can't Keep a Good Woman Down *(1982), the novel* The Color Purple *(1982), the essay collection* In Search of Our Mothers' Gardens *(1983), and several volumes of poetry. Walker's critical and editorial projects have included a book-length study of Langston Hughes's poetry and* I Love Myself When I Am Laughing: A Zora Neale Hurston Reader.

"Everyday Use," from In Love and in Trouble, *examines the relationship between personal and collective history by showing how members of the same family can disagree about the meaning of the word* heritage *and the use to which it is put.*

◆ E V E R Y D A Y U S E ◆

for your grandmamma

I will wait for her in the yard that Maggie and I made so clean and wavy yesterday afternoon. A yard like this is more comfortable than most people know. It is not just a yard. It is like an extended living room. When the hard clay is swept clean as a floor and the fine sand around the edges lined with tiny, irregular grooves, anyone can come and sit and look up into the elm tree and wait for the breezes that never come inside the house.

Maggie will be nervous until after her sister goes: she will stand hopelessly in corners, homely and ashamed of the burn scars down her arms and legs, eying her sister with a mixture of envy and awe. She thinks her sister has held life always in the palm of one hand, that "no" is a word the world never learned to say to her.

You've no doubt seen those TV shows where the child who has "made it" is confronted, as a surprise, by her own mother and father, tottering in weakly from backstage. (A pleasant surprise, of course: What would they do if parent and child came on the show only to curse out and insult each other?) On TV mother and child embrace and smile into each other's faces. Sometimes the mother and father weep, the child wraps them in her arms and leans across the table to tell how she would not have made it without their help. I have seen these programs.

Sometimes I dream a dream in which Dee and I are suddenly brought   4
together on a TV program of this sort. Out of a dark and soft-seated limousine
I am ushered into a bright room filled with many people. There I meet a smiling,
gray, sporty man like Johnny Carson who shakes my hand and tells me what
a fine girl I have. Then we are on the stage and Dee is embracing me with tears
in her eyes. She pins on my dress a large orchid, even though she has told me
once that she thinks orchids are tacky flowers.

In real life I am a large, big-boned woman with rough, man-working   5
hands. In the winter I wear flannel nightgowns to bed and overalls during the
day. I can kill and clean a hog as mercilessly as a man. My fat keeps me hot
in zero weather. I can work outside all day, breaking ice to get water for washing;
I can eat pork liver cooked over the open fire minutes after it comes steaming
from the hog. One winter I knocked a bull calf straight in the brain between
the eyes with a sledge hammer and had the meat hung up to chill before nightfall.
But of course all this does not show on television. I am the way my daughter
would want me to be: a hundred pounds lighter, my skin like an uncooked
barley pancake. My hair glistens in the hot bright lights. Johnny Carson has
much to do to keep up with my quick and witty tongue.

But that is a mistake. I know even before I wake up. Who ever knew a   6
Johnson with a quick tongue? Who can even imagine me looking a strange white
man in the eye? It seems to me I have talked to them always with one foot
raised in flight, with my head turned in whichever way is farthest from them.
Dee, though. She would always look anyone in the eye. Hesitation was no part
of her nature.

"How do I look, Mama?" Maggie says, showing just enough of her thin body   7
enveloped in pink skirt and red blouse for me to know she's there, almost hidden
by the door.

"Come out into the yard," I say.   8

Have you ever seen a lame animal, perhaps a dog run over by some careless   9
person rich enough to own a car, sidle up to someone who is ignorant enough
to be kind to him? That is the way my Maggie walks. She has been like this,
chin on chest, eyes on ground, feet in shuffle, ever since the fire that burned
the other house to the ground.

Dee is lighter than Maggie, with nicer hair and a fuller figure. She's a   10
woman now, though sometimes I forget. How long ago was it that the other
house burned? Ten, twelve years? Sometimes I can still hear the flames and
feel Maggie's arms sticking to me, her hair smoking and her dress falling off
her in little black papery flakes. Her eyes seemed stretched open, blazed open
by the flames reflected in them. And Dee. I see her standing off under the
sweet gum tree she used to dig gum out of; a look of concentration on her face
as she watched the last dingy gray board of the house fall in toward the red-
hot brick chimney. Why don't you do a dance around the ashes? I'd wanted to
ask her. She had hated the house that much.

I used to think she hated Maggie, too. But that was before we raised the   11 money, the church and me, to send her to Augusta to school. She used to read to us without pity; forcing words, lies, other folks' habits, whole lives upon us two, sitting trapped and ignorant underneath her voice. She washed us in a river of make-believe, burned us with a lot of knowledge we didn't necessarily need to know. Pressed us to her with the serious way she read, to shove us away at just the moment, like dimwits, we seemed about to understand.

Dee wanted nice things. A yellow organdy dress to wear to her graduation from high school; black pumps to match a green suit she'd made from an old suit somebody gave me. She was determined to stare down any disaster in her efforts. Her eyelids would not flicker for minutes at a time. Often I fought off the temptation to shake her. At sixteen she had a style of her own: and knew what style was. 12

I never had an education myself. After second grade the school was closed down. Don't ask me why: in 1927 colored asked fewer questions than they do now. Sometimes Maggie reads to me. She stumbles along good-naturedly but can't see well. She knows she is not bright. Like good looks and money, quickness passed her by. She will marry John Thomas (who has mossy teeth in an earnest face) and then I'll be free to sit here and I guess just sing church songs to myself. Although I never was a good singer. Never could carry a tune. I was always better at a man's job. I used to love to milk till I was hooked in the side in '49. Cows are soothing and slow and don't bother you, unless you try to milk them the wrong way. 13

I have deliberately turned my back on the house. It is three rooms, just like the one that burned, except the roof is tin; they don't make shingle roofs any more. There are no real windows, just some holes cut in the sides, like the portholes in a ship, but not round and not square, with rawhide holding the shutters up on the outside. This house is in a pasture, too, like the other one. No doubt when Dee sees it she will want to tear it down. She wrote me once that no matter where we "choose" to live, she will manage to come see us. But she will never bring her friends. Maggie and I thought about this and Maggie asked me, "Mama, when did Dee ever *have* any friends?" 14

She had a few. Furtive boys in pink shirts hanging about on washday after school. Nervous girls who never laughed. Impressed with her, they worshiped the well-turned phrase, the cute shape, the scalding humor that erupted like bubbles in lye. She read to them. 15

When she was courting Jimmy T she didn't have much time to pay to us, but turned all her faultfinding power on him. He *flew* to marry a cheap city girl from a family of ignorant flashy people. She hardly had time to recompose herself. 16

When she comes I will meet—but there they are! 17

Maggie attempts to make a dash for the house, in her shuffling way, but I stay her with my hand. "Come back here," I say. And she stops and tries to dig a well in the sand with her toe. 18

It is hard to see them clearly through the strong sun. But even the first   19
glimpse of leg out of the car tells me it is Dee. Her feet were always neat-
looking, as if God himself had shaped them with a certain style. From the other
side of the car comes a short, stocky man. Hair is all over his head a foot long
and hanging from his chin like a kinky mule tail. I hear Maggie suck in her
breath. "Uhnnnh," is what it sounds like. Like when you see the wriggling end
of a snake just in front of your foot on the road. "Uhnnnh."

Dee next. A dress down to the ground, in this hot weather. A dress so   20
loud it hurts my eyes. There are yellows and oranges enough to throw back
the light of the sun. I feel my whole face warming from the heat waves it throws
out. Earrings gold, too, and hanging down to her shoulders. Bracelets dangling
and making noises when she moves her arm up to shake the folds of the dress
out of her armpits. The dress is loose and flows, and as she walks closer, I like
it. I hear Maggie go "Uhnnnh" again. It is her sister's hair. It stands straight
up like the wool on a sheep. It is black as night and around the edges are two
long pigtails that rope about like small lizards disappearing behind her ears.

"Wa-su-zo-Tean-o!" she says, coming on in that gliding way the dress   21
makes her move. The short stocky fellow with the hair to his navel is all grinning
and he follows up with "Asalamalakim, my mother and sister!" He moves to
hug Maggie but she falls back, right up against the back of my chair. I feel her
trembling there and when I look up I see the perspiration falling off her chin.

"Don't get up," says Dee. Since I am stout it takes something of a push.   22
You can see me trying to move a second or two before I make it. She turns,
showing white heels through her sandals, and goes back to the car. Out she
peeks next with a Polaroid. She stoops down quickly and lines up picture after
picture of me sitting there in front of the house with Maggie cowering behind
me. She never takes a shot without making sure the house is included. When
a cow comes nibbling around the edge of the yard she snaps it and me and
Maggie *and* the house. Then she puts the Polaroid in the back seat of the car,
and comes up and kisses me on the forehead.

Meanwhile Asalamalakim is going through motions with Maggie's hand.   23
Maggie's hand is as limp as a fish, and probably as cold, despite the sweat, and
she keeps trying to pull it back. It looks like Asalamalakim wants to shake hands
but wants to do it fancy. Or maybe he don't know how people shake hands.
Anyhow, he soon gives up on Maggie.

"Well," I say. "Dee."   24

"No, Mama," she says. "Not 'Dee,' Wangero Leewanika Kemanjo!"   25

"What happened to 'Dee'?" I wanted to know.   26

"She's dead," Wangero said. "I couldn't bear it any longer, being named   27
after the people who oppress me."

"You know as well as me you was named after your aunt Dicie," I said.   28
Dicie is my sister. She named Dee. We called her "Big Dee" after Dee was
born.

"But who was *she* named after?" asked Wangero.   29

"I guess after Grandma Dee," I said.   30

"And who was she named after?" asked Wangero.   31

"Her mother," I said, and saw Wangero was getting tired. "That's about   32
as far back as I can trace it," I said. Though, in fact, I probably could have
carried it back beyond the Civil War through the branches.

"Well," said Asalamalakim, "there you are."   33

"Uhnnnh," I heard Maggie say.   34

"There I was not," I said, "before 'Dicie' cropped up in our family, so 35
why should I try to trace it that far back?"

He just stood there grinning, looking down on me like somebody inspect- 36
ing a Model A car. Every once in a while he and Wangero sent eye signals over
my head.

"How do you pronounce this name?" I asked.   37

"You don't have to call me by it if you don't want to," said Wangero.   38

"Why shouldn't I?" I asked. "If that's what you want us to call you, we'll 39
call you."

"I know it might sound awkward at first," said Wangero.   40

"I'll get used to it," I said. "Ream it out again."   41

Well, soon we got the name out of the way. Asalamalakim had a name   42
twice as long and three times as hard. After I tripped over it two or three times
he told me to just call him Hakim-a-barber. I wanted to ask him was he a
barber, but I didn't really think he was, so I didn't ask.

"You must belong to those beef-cattle peoples down the road," I said.   43
They said "Asalamalakim" when they met you, too, but they didn't shake hands.
Always too busy: feeding the cattle, fixing the fences, putting up salt-lick
shelters, throwing down hay. When the white folks poisoned some of the herd
the men stayed up all night with rifles in their hands. I walked a mile and a
half just to see the sight.

Hakim-a-barber said, "I accept some of their doctrines, but farming and 44
raising cattle is not my style." (They didn't tell me, and I didn't ask, whether
Wangero (Dee) had really gone and married him.)

We sat down to eat and right away he said he didn't eat collards and pork 45
was unclean. Wangero, though, went on through the chitlins and corn bread,
the greens and everything else. She talked a blue streak over the sweet potatoes.
Everything delighted her. Even the fact that we still used the benches her daddy
made for the table when we couldn't afford to buy chairs.

"Oh, Mama!" she cried. Then turned to Hakim-a-barber. "I never knew   46
how lovely these benches are. You can feel the rump prints," she said, running
her hands underneath her and along the bench. Then she gave a sigh and her
hand closed over Grandma Dee's butter dish. "That's it!" she said. "I knew
there was something I wanted to ask you if I could have." She jumped up from
the table and went over in the corner where the churn stood, the milk in it
clabber by now. She looked at the churn and looked at it.

"This churn top is what I need," she said. "Didn't Uncle Buddy whittle it out of a tree you all used to have?" 47

"Yes," I said. 48

"Uh huh," she said happily. "And I want the dasher, too." 49

"Uncle Buddy whittle that, too?" asked the barber. 50

Dee (Wangero) looked up at me. 51

"Aunt Dee's first husband whittled the dash," said Maggie so low you almost couldn't hear her. "His name was Henry, but they called him Stash." 52

"Maggie's brain is like an elephant's," Wangero said, laughing. "I can use the churn top as a centerpiece for the alcove table," she said, sliding a plate over the churn, "and I'll think of something artistic to do with the dasher." 53

When she finished wrapping the dasher the handle stuck out. I took it for a moment in my hands. You didn't even have to look close to see where hands pushing the dasher up and down to make butter had left a kind of sink in the wood. In fact, there were a lot of small sinks; you could see where thumbs and fingers had sunk into the wood. It was beautiful light yellow wood, from a tree that grew in the yard where Big Dee and Stash had lived. 54

After dinner Dee (Wangero) went to the trunk at the foot of my bed and started rifling through it. Maggie hung back in the kitchen over the dishpan. Out came Wangero with two quilts. They had been pieced by Grandma Dee and then Big Dee and me had hung them on the quilt frames on the front porch and quilted them. One was in the Lone Star pattern. The other was Walk Around the Mountain. In both of them were scraps of dresses Grandma Dee had worn fifty and more years ago. Bits and pieces of Grandpa Jarrell's Paisley shirts. And one teeny faded blue piece, about the size of a penny matchbox, that was from Great Grandpa Ezra's uniform that he wore in the Civil War. 55

"Mama," Wangero said sweet as a bird. "Can I have these old quilts?" 56

I heard something fall in the kitchen, and a minute later the kitchen door slammed. 57

"Why don't you take one or two of the others?" I asked. "These old things was just done by me and Big Dee from some tops your grandma pieced before she died." 58

"No," said Wangero. "I don't want those. They are stitched around the borders by machine." 59

"That'll make them last better," I said. 60

"That's not the point," said Wangero. "These are all pieces of dresses Grandma used to wear. She did all this stitching by hand. Imagine!" She held the quilts securely in her arms, stroking them. 61

"Some of the pieces, like those lavender ones, come from old clothes her mother handed down to her," I said, moving up to touch the quilts. Dee (Wangero) moved back just enough so that I couldn't reach the quilts. They already belonged to her. 62

"Imagine!" she breathed again, clutching them closely to her bosom. 63

"The truth is," I said, "I promised to give them quilts to Maggie, for when she marries John Thomas."   64

She gasped like a bee had stung her.   65

"Maggie can't appreciate these quilts!" she said. "She'd probably be backward enough to put them to everyday use."   66

"I reckon she would," I said. "God knows I been saving 'em for long enough with nobody using 'em. I hope she will!" I didn't want to bring up how I had offered Dee (Wangero) a quilt when she went away to college. Then she had told me they were old-fashioned, out of style.   67

"But they're *priceless!*" she was saying now, furiously; for she has a temper. "Maggie would put them on the bed and in five years they'd be in rags. Less than that!" "She can always make some more," I said. "Maggie knows how to quilt."   68

Dee (Wangero) looked at me with hatred. "You just will not understand. The point is these quilts, *these* quilts!"   69

"Well," I said, stumped. "What would *you* do with them?"   70

"Hang them," she said. As if that was the only thing you *could* do with quilts.   71

Maggie by now was standing in the door. I could almost hear the sound her feet made as they scraped over each other.   72

"She can have them, Mama," she said, like somebody used to never winning anything, or having anything reserved for her. "I can 'member Grandma Dee without the quilts."   73

I looked at her hard. She had filled her bottom lip with checkerberry snuff and it gave her face a kind of dopey, hangdog look. It was Grandma Dee and Big Dee who taught her how to quilt herself. She stood there with her scarred hands hidden in the folds of her skirt. She looked at her sister with something like fear but she wasn't mad at her. This was Maggie's portion. This was the way she knew God to work.   74

When I looked at her like that something hit me in the top of my head and ran down to the soles of my feet. Just like when I'm in church and the spirit of God touches me and I get happy and shout. I did something I never had done before: hugged Maggie to me, then dragged her on into the room, snatched the quilts out of Miss Wangero's hands and dumped them into Maggie's lap. Maggie just sat there on my bed with her mouth open.   75

"Take one or two of the others," I said to Dee.   76

But she turned without a word and went out to Hakim-a-barber.   77

"You just don't understand," she said, as Maggie and I came out to the car.   78

"What don't I understand?" I wanted to know.   79

"Your heritage," she said. And then she turned to Maggie, kissed her, and said, "You ought to try to make something of yourself, too, Maggie. It's really a new day for us. But from the way you and Mama still live you'd never know it."   80

She put on some sunglasses that hid everything above the tip of her nose 81
and her chin.

Maggie smiled; maybe at the sunglasses. But a real smile, not scared. After 82
we watched the car dust settle I asked Maggie to bring me a dip of snuff. And
then the two of us sat there just enjoying, until it was time to go in the house
and go to bed. ◆

◆ Responding

1. The mother believes that Dee is ashamed of her house, saying, "No doubt
   when Dee sees it she will want to tear it down." Yet when Dee arrives she
   immediately wants to photograph it. What explains her changed attitude to
   the house and its contents?

2. Dee accuses her mother of not understanding their heritage. Heritage means
   something very different to these women. Compare their definitions. Then,
   using those definitions, argue that either Maggie or Dee should have the
   quilt.

3. The story is told from the point of view of the mother. Retell it from the
   point of view of one of the other characters.

4. Objects from the past can often be meaningful reminders of tradition and
   family. What important objects in the story might represent the family's
   experience as blacks in America? Describe an object owned by your family
   that represents an important event in your family's history and in your
   cultural heritage.

REFLECTING A CRITICAL CONTEXT

DAVID MURA

David Mura, who was born in Great Lakes, Illinois, in 1952, received his bachelor's degree from Grinnell College and later did graduate work at the University of Minnesota. He is currently a candidate for a master's in fine arts at Vermont College of Norwich. A poet, nonfiction writer, and critic, Mura has published After We Lost Our Way *(1989), which was honored in the National Poetry Series Contest, and* Turning Japanese: Memoirs of a Sansei *(forthcoming), as well as several essays. His work has won him a Jerome Literary Travel Grant, a grant from the National Endowment for the Arts, and two Bush Fellowships.*

"Strangers in the Village," first published in the Graywolf collection Multicultural Literacy: Opening the American Mind, *explores the ways in which people of color have attempted to come to terms with personal and collective experiences of exclusion and discrimination.*

◆ STRANGERS IN THE VILLAGE ◆

Recently, in *The Village Voice*, a number of articles were devoted to the issue of race in America. Perhaps the most striking article, "Black Women, White Kids: A Tale of Two Worlds," was about Black women in New York City who take care of upper-middle-class and upper-class white children. Merely by describing the situation of these Black women and recording their words, the article pointed out how race and class affects these women's lives: "As the nanny sits in the park watching a tow-haired child play, her own kids are coming home from school; they will do their homework alone and make dinner."

None of the white people who employed these nannies seemed at all cognizant of the contradictions of this description. Instead the whites seemed to view the Black nannies as a natural facet of their lives, an expected privilege. Yet, on another less-conscious level, the whites appeared to have misgivings that they could not express. One of the nannies, named Bertha, talked about how she objected to the tone of voice her employer, Barbra, used: "You wait a minute here, Barbra. I'm not a child," Bertha would tell Barbra, "I can talk to you any way I want. This is a free country, it's not a commie country." Every time Bertha and Barbra have an argument, Barbra buys Bertha presents: "She bought me shoes, a beautiful blouse, a Mother's Day present . . . she's a very generous person. She's got a good heart." But Bertha doesn't really like the presents. "It always made me feel guilty. To tell you the truth about it, I never had too many people give me presents, so it just made me feel bad.

"Another reason we don't get along," Bertha continues, "is she's always 3
trying to figure me out. See, I'm a very complicated person. I'm a very moody
person . . . I'm independent. I figure I can deal with it myself. And we would
sit there, I could just feel her eyes on me, and I'd have to get up and leave the
room . . . She just wants you to be satisfied with her all the time . . . She
wants me to tell her I love you. I just can't."

The author of the article says that sometimes Barbra seems to want love 4
and sometimes she seems to want forgiveness. "But perhaps for most white
people, a black person's affection can never mean more than an act of absolution
for historical and collective guilt, an affection desired not because of how one
feels about that particular person but because that person is black."

As a middle-class third-generation Japanese-American, I read this article 5
with mixed feelings. On one level, I have much more in common with Bertha's
employer, Barbra, than I do with Bertha. Although at one time Japanese-
Americans worked in jobs similar to Bertha's and were part of the lower class,
by my generation this was not the case. I grew up in the suburbs of Chicago,
went to college and graduate school, married a pediatrician who is three-quarters
WASP and one-quarter Jewish. Although I will most likely assume a large
portion of our child care when we have children, my wife and I will probably
use some form of outside child care. Most likely, we would not employ a Black
nanny, even if we lived in New York City, but I could not help feeling a sense
of guilt and shame when I read the article. I could understand Barbra's wish
to use acts of kindness to overlook inequalities of class and race; her desire to
equate winning the affections of a Black servant with the absolution of historical
and collective guilt. I would not, in the end, act like Barbra, but I do recognize
her feelings.

At the same time, I also recognize and identify with the anger Bertha 6
feels toward her white employer. In part, Bertha's anger is a recognition of how
profoundly race has affected her and Barbra's lives, and also that Barbra does
not truly understand this fact. Although generalizations like this can sometimes
be misused—more about this later—American culture defines white middle-
class culture as the norm. As a result, Blacks and other colored minorities must
generally know two cultures to survive—the culture of middle-class whites and
their own minority culture. Middle-class whites need only to know one culture.
For them, knowledge of a minority culture is a seeming—and I use the word
"seeming" here purposely—luxury; they can survive without it.

On a smaller scale than Bertha I have experienced the inability of members 7
of the white majority to understand how race has affected my life, to come to
terms with the differences between us. Sometimes I can bridge this gap, but
never completely; more often, a gulf appears between me and white friends
that has previously been unacknowledged. I point out to them that the images
I grew up with in the media were all white, that the books I read in school—
from Dick and Jane onwards—were about whites and later, about European
civilization. I point out to them the way beauty is defined in our culture and
how, under such definitions, slanted eyes, flat noses, and round faces just don't

make it. And as I talk, I often sense their confusion, the limits of their understanding of the world. They become angry, defensive. "We all have experiences others can't relate to," they reply and equate the issue of race with prejudice against women or Italians or rich people. Such generalizations can sometimes be used to express sympathy with victims of prejudice, but as used by many whites, it generally attempts to shut down racial anger by denying the distinct causes of that anger, thereby rendering it meaningless. Another form of this tactic is the reply, "I think of you just as a white person," or, a bit less chauvinistically, "I think of you as an individual." While, at one time in my life, I would have taken this for a compliment, my reply now is, "I don't want to be a white person. Why can't I be who I am? Why can't you think of me as a Japanese-American *and* as an individual?"

I'd like to leave these questions a moment and, because I'm a writer, take up these themes in terms of literature. In my talks with whites about race, I very quickly find myself referring to history. As many have pointed out, America has never come to terms with two fundamental historical events: the enslavement of Blacks by whites and the taking of this continent by Europeans from the Native Americans and the accompanying policies of genocide. A third historical event that America hasn't come to terms with—and yet is closer to doing so than with the other two—is the internment of Japanese-Americans during World War II. Although some maintain that the camps were caused simply by wartime hysteria, the determining factors were racism and a desire for the property owned by the Japanese-Americans. Recently, in *War Without Mercy*, John Dower has demonstrated how the war in the Pacific, on both sides, took on racist overtones and used racist propaganda that were absent in the war in Europe. In wartime propaganda, while the Nazis were somehow kept separate from the rest of the German race, the Japanese, as a race, were characterized as lice and vermin. This racist propaganda was both caused by and intensified a phenomenon that led to the internment camps: A large number of white Americans were unable to distinguish between the Japanese as the enemy and Japanese-Americans.

Knowing the history behind the camps, knowing that during the internment the lives of many Japanese-Americans, particularly the Issei (first generation), were permanently disrupted; knowing the internment caused the loss of millions of dollars of property, I, as a Japanese-American, feel a kinship to both Blacks and Native Americans that I do not feel with white Americans. It is a kinship that comes from our histories as victims of injustice. Of course, our histories are more than simply being victims, and we must recognize that these histories are also separate and distinct, but there is a certain power and solace in this kinship.

This kinship is reinforced by our current position as minorities in a white-dominated culture. For instance, when Blacks or Native Americans or Chicanos complain about their image in the media, it is a complaint I easily understand. I myself have written a number of pieces about this subject, analyses of the stereotypes in such films as *Rambo* or *Year of the Dragon*. Recently, I read a play by a Sansei playwright, Philip Kan Gotanda, *Yankee Dawg You Die*, and I was struck by the similarities between this play about two Japanese-American actors and Robert Townsend's *Hollywood Shuffle*, a film about a Black actor trying to make it in Hollywood.

In both works, the actors must struggle with the battle between economics 11 and integrity, between finding no parts or playing in roles that stereotype their minority. In *Hollywood Shuffle*, we see the hero, clearly a middle-class Black, trying and failing to portray a pimp in his bathroom mirror. Later in the film, there is a mock Black acting school where Black actors learn to talk in jive, to move like a pimp, to play runaway slaves, to shuffle their feet. In *Yankee Dawg You Die*, a young third-generation Japanese-American actor, Bradley, is fired at one point because he will not mix up his r's and l's when playing a waiter. Throughout the play, he keeps chastizing an older Japanese-American actor for selling out, for playing stereotyped "coolie" and "dirty Jap" parts. Essentially, what Bradley is accusing Vincent of being is a Tom:

> The Business. You keep talking about the business. The industry. Hollywood. What's Hollywood? Cutting up your face to look more white? So my nose is a little flat. Fine! Flat is beautiful. So I don't have a double fold in my eye-lid. Great! No one in my entire racial family has had it in the last 10,000 years.
>
> My old girlfriend used to put scotch tape on her eyelids to get the double folds so she could look more "cau-ca-sian." My new girlfriend—she doesn't mess around, she got surgery. Where does it stop? "I never turned down a role." Where does it begin? Vincent? Where does it begin? All that self hate. You and your Charlie Chop Suey roles.

Vincent tells Bradley that he knows nothing about the difficulties he, Vincent, went through: "You want to know the truth? I'm glad I did it . . . in some small way it is a victory. Yes, a victory. At least an oriental was on the screen acting, being seen. We existed!" At this point, the scene slides into a father and son mode, where the father-figure, Vincent, tells Bradley that he should appreciate what those who went before him have done; it's easy now for Bradley to spout the rhetoric of Asian-American consciousness, but in the past, such rhetoric was unthinkable. (Earlier in the play, when Vincent says, "I do not really notice, or quite frankly care, if someone is oriental or caucasian . . ." Bradley makes a certain connection between Asian-American rights and other liberation movements. "It's Asian, not oriental," he says. "Asian, oriental. Black, negro. Woman, girl. Gay, homosexual.")

But Bradley then gets on a soapbox and makes a cogent point, though a 12 bit baldly, and I can easily imagine a young Black actor making a similar argument to an old Black actor who has done Stepin Fetchit roles:

> You seem to think that every time you do one of those demeaning roles, all that is lost is your dignity . . . Don't you realize that every time you do a portrayal like that millions of people in their homes, in movie theatres across the country

will see it. Be influenced by it. Believe it. Every time you do any old stereotypic role just to pay the bills, you kill the right of some Asian-American child to be treated as a human being. To walk through the school yard and not be called a "chinaman gook" by some taunting kids who just saw the last Rambo film.

By the end of the play, though, it's clear Bradley's been beaten down. 13
After scrambling through failed audition after audition, wanting to make it in the business, he cries when he fails to get a role as a butler because he doesn't know kung fu. He also reveals he has recently had his nose fixed, à la Michael Jackson.

What do the similarities I've been pointing out mean for an Asian-Amer- 14
ican writer? Recently, there have been a spate of books, such as Allan Bloom's *The Closing of the American Mind*, which call for a return to the classics and a notion of a core-cultural tradition; these critiques bemoan the relativism and "nihilism" of the sixties and the multicultural movements which, in the name of "tolerance," have supposedly left our culture in a shambles. Unfortunately, such critics never really question the political and historical bases of cultural response. If they did, they would understand why, contrary to Allan Bloom, other minority writers represent a valuable resource for Asian-American writers and vice versa: our themes and difficulties are similar; we learn from each other things we cannot receive from a Saul Bellow or John Updike or even Rousseau or Plato.

It is not just the work of Asian-American writers like Gotanda that sustain 15
me. I know a key point in my life was when I discovered the work of Frantz Fanon, particularly his book, *Black Skin, White Masks*. My experience with that work and others like it shows why multiculturalism, for a member of a racial minority, is not simply tolerance, but an essential key to survival.

In his work, Fanon, a Black psychologist, provides a cogent analysis of 16
how a majority can oppress a minority through culture: it makes the victim or servant identify with the ruler and, in so doing, causes the victim to direct whatever anger he/she feels at the situation towards himself/herself in the form of self-hatred.

> In the Antilles . . . in the magazines, the Wolf, the Devil, the Evil Spirit, the Bad Man, the Savage are always symbolized by Negroes or Indians; since there is always identification with the victor, the little Negro, quite as easily as the little white boy, becomes an explorer, an adventurer, a missionary "who faces the danger of being eaten by the wicked Negroes" . . . The black school boy . . . who in his lessons is forever talking about "our ancestors, the Gauls," identifies himself with the explorer, the bringer of civilization, the white man who carries truth to the savages—an all-white truth . . . the young Negro . . . invests the hero, who is white, with all his own aggression—at that age closely linked to sacrificial dedi-cation, a sacrificial dedication permeated with sadism.

This passage can be taken as another version of Bradley's speech to Vincent on the effects of stereotypes on an Asian-American child.

Fanon was incredibly aware of how the economic, social, and political   17
relations of power create and warp an individual's psychic identity. He was
quick to point out that psychic sickness does not always find its source in the
neuroses of an individual or that individual's family, but in the greater sickness
of a society. In such cases, for the individual to become healthy, he or she must
recognize that society is sick, and that the ideas he or she has received from
that society are part of that sickness.

In short, what Fanon recognized and taught me was the liberating power   18
of anger.

After reading Fanon and the Black French poet from Martinique, Aime   19
Cesaire, I wrote a number of poems in which I chose to ally myself with people
of color, anti-colonialist movements, and a non-Eurocentric consciousness. When
writing these poems, I was aware of how such poems can often become vehicles
for slogans and cheap rhetoric; still I tried to discover a language with a denseness
which would prevent such reduction, increase thought, and turn words like
"gook" and "nigger" against their original meaning, bending and realigning the
slang of racism. Here is the ending of one of those poems:

> . . . and we were all good niggers, good gooks and japs, good spics and rice eaters
> saying mem sab, sahib, bwana, boss-san, señor, father, heartthrob oh honored
> and most unceasing, oh devisor and provider of our own obsequious, ubiquitous
> ugliness, which stares at you baboon-like, banana-like, dwarf-like, tortoise-like,
> dirt-like, slant-eyed, kink-haired, ashen and pansied and brutally unredeemable,
> we are whirling about you, tartars of the air all the urinating, tarantula grasping,
> ant multiplying, succubused, hothouse hoards yes, it us, it us, we, we knockee,
> yes, sir, massa, boss-san, we tearee down your door!

I was scared at first by the anger of this poem, but I also saw it as an answer,
an antidote to the depression I had been feeling, a depression brought on by a
lack of self-worth and by my dropping out of English graduate school. As my
therapist had told me, depression is the repression of anger and grief. In my
diary I wrote about the unlocking of this repression:

> In the first stages of such a process, one can enter a position where the destruction
> of one stereotype creates merely a new stereotype, and where the need to point
> out injustice overwhelms and leaves the writing with a baldness that seems both
> naive and sentimental. Still, the task must be faced, and what I am now trying
> to do in both my writing and my life is to replace self-hatred and self-negation
> with anger and grief over my lost selves, over the ways my cultural heritage has
> been denied to me, over the ways that people in America would assume either
> that I am not American or, conversely, that I am just like them; over the ways
> my education and the values of European culture have denied that other cultures
> exist. I know more about Europe at the time when my grandfather came to America
> than I know about Meiji Japan. I know Shakespeare and Donne, Sophocles and
> Homer better than I know Zeami, Bashō or Lady Murasaki. This is not to say I
> regret what I know, but I do regret what I don't know. And the argument that
> the culture of America is derived from Europe will not wipe away this regret.

I am convinced if I had not read Fanon, if I had not reached these insights, 20
and gone on to explore beyond white European culture, I would have died as
a writer and died spiritually and psychically as a person. I would have ended
up denying who I am and my place in history. Thus, I think that to deny a
people a right to determine their own cultural tradition is a type of genocide.

Of course, arguing for multiculturalism is not the same thing as saying that, as 21
a minority writer, I don't need to read the works of European culture. It's not
a case of either/or. As Carlos Fuentes remarked, "We [Latin Americans] have
to know the cultures of the West even better than a Frenchman or an English-
man, and at the same time we have to know our own cultures. This sometimes
means going back to the Indian cultures, whereas the Europeans feel they don't
have to know our cultures at all. We have to know Quetzalcoatl and Descartes.
They think Descartes is enough." I think Fuentes would agree with Jesse Jackson
that there was something wrong with those students who greeted his appearance
at Stanford with the chant, "Hey hey, ho ho/Western culture's got to go." As
Jackson pointed out, Western culture was their culture. It is difficult to strike
an appropriate balance.

In the same issue of the *Village Voice* that the article about the Black nannies 22
appeared, Stanley Crouch wrote a perceptive, challenging critique of James
Baldwin. Crouch argues that at the beginning of Baldwin's career, Baldwin was
able to maneuver his way through subtleties of the Black writer's position. As
an example of this, Crouch cites Baldwin's distinction between sociology and
literature in evaluating the work of Richard Wright; Baldwin argues that despite
the good intentions of protest novels, they cannot succeed if they are "badly
written and wildly improbable." Still Crouch maintains that very early Baldwin's vision began to blur, and cites this passage from the essay "Stranger in
the Village," a depiction of Baldwin's visit to a Swiss town and his sense of
alienation from its people:

> These people cannot be, from the point of view of power, strangers anywhere in
> the world; they have made the modern world, in effect, even if they do not know
> it. The most illiterate among them is related, in a way that I am not, to Dante,
> Shakespeare, Michaelangelo, Aeschylus, da Vinci, Rembrandt, and Racine; the
> cathedral at Chartres says something to them that it cannot say to me, as indeed
> would New York's Empire State Building, should anyone here ever see it. Out
> of their hymns and dances come Beethoven and Bach. Go back a few centuries
> and they are in their full glory—but I am in Africa, watching the conquerors
> arrive.

Crouch charges Baldwin with slipping into a simplistic dualistic thinking, with
letting his rage create a we-they attitude which denies the complexity of the
race situation:

> Such thinking leads to the problems we still face in which too many so-called
> nonwhite people look upon "the West" as some catchall in which every European

or person of European descent is somehow part of a structure bent solely on excluding or intimidating the Baldwins of the world. Were Roland Hayes, Marian Anderson, Leontyne Price, Jessye Norman, or Kiri Te Kanawa to have taken such a position, they would have locked themselves out of a world of music that originated neither among Afro-Americans nor Maoris. Further, his ahistorical ignorance is remarkable, and perhaps willful.

23   If Baldwin's position is that Afro-Americans cannot learn, or enjoy or perform European culture, or that European culture is worthless to an Afro-American, that is nonsense. But that is not Baldwin's position. He is simply arguing that his relationship to that culture is different from a white European; he views that culture through the experience of a Black American, and if he is to be faulted, it is because he does not give a detailed enough explanation of how his experience as a Black American informs his experience of European culture. But none of this—including the success of opera stars like Jessye Norman—negates the fact that, in America and Europe, European culture has political—that is, ideological—effects and one effect is to reinforce the political power of those of European descent and to promote a view of whites as superior to coloreds. (It is not the only effect of that culture, but again, neither Baldwin nor I am arguing that it is.)

24   Crouch goes on to argue that "breaking through the mask of collective whiteness—collective guilt—that Baldwin imposes would demand recognition of the fact that, as history and national chauvinism prove, Europe is not a one-celled organism." I will say more about collective guilt a bit later, but it is interesting to note that Crouch refuses the concept of collectivity when it comes to guilt, yet at the same time charges that Baldwin refuses to entertain the possibility of "the international wonder of human heritage." Guilt can never be held collectively, but culture, specifically European culture, can be universal.

25   Yet, at the same time Crouch argues the non-exclusivity of European culture, he chastizes Baldwin for taking the themes of Third-World writers and adapting them to the context of America: "the denial by Europeans of non-Western cultural complexity—or parity; the social function of the inferiority complex colonialism threw over the native like a net; the alignment of Christianity and cruelty under colonialism, and the idea that world views were at odds, European versus the 'spirit of Bandung,' or the West in the ring with the Third World." How sharp the boundaries of culture should be is a difficult question; it may seem that both Crouch and Baldwin want things both ways: they just disagree on which cultures can attain universality, European culture or that of the Third World. To sort out the specifics of each of their cases requires us to connect attitudes towards culture with feelings about race, specifically the rage of Blacks and other colored minorities in America.

26   As I've already argued with my own reading of Frantz Fanon, I do think it is illuminating and useful to use Third-World problems in looking at the race issue in America. Still, I also agree with Crouch that there are fundamental

differences between the position of Blacks in America and that of colonials in the Third World. To forget these differences in a desire to be at one with all oppressed peoples is both false and dangerous. And I recognize that when borrowing or learning from the language of Third-World peoples and American Blacks, Japanese-Americans, like myself, must still recognize fundamental differences between our position and that of other people of color, whether here or in the Third World.

Part of the danger is that if we ignore the specifics of the situation of our own minority group, in essence we both deny who we are and our own complexity. We also run the risk of using our victimhood as a mask for sainthood, of letting whatever sins the white race has committed against us become a permanent absolution for us, an excuse to forgo moral and psychological introspection. Crouch argues somewhat convincingly that this is exactly the trap that Baldwin fell into and cites as evidence Baldwin's remark that "rage can only with difficulty, and never entirely, be brought under the domination of the intelligence and is therefore not susceptible to any arguments whatever." According to Crouch, Baldwin, as his career progressed, sold out to rage, despair, self-righteousness, and a will to scandalize: 27

> In America . . . fat-mouthing Negroes . . . chose to sneer at the heroic optimism of the Civil Rights Movement; they developed their own radical chic and spoke of Malcolm X as being beyond compromise, of his unwillingness to cooperate with the white man, and of his ideas of being too radical for assimilation. Baldwin was sucked into this world of intellectual airlessness. By *The Fire Next Time*, Baldwin is so happy to see white policemen made uncomfortable by Muslim rallies, and so willing to embrace almost anything that disturbs whites in general, that he starts competing with the apocalyptic tone of the Nation of Islam.

In focusing on Baldwin's inability to transform or let go his rage, I feel Crouch finally hits upon something. I also feel a shudder of self-recognition. Yet the condition Crouch pictures here is a bit more complex than he admits. Certainly, a convincing argument can be made that King's appeal to a higher yet common morality was and will be more effective than Malcolm X's in changing the hearts and minds of whites in America, yet in his very approach to the problem, Crouch seems to put the burden for change upon the Black minority rather than on the white majority. There is something intellectually and morally dishonest about this. For whether one judges King's philosophy or Malcolm X's as correct depends in part on a reading of the hearts and minds of white Americans. If those hearts and minds are fiercely unchanging, then Malcolm X's might seem the more logical stance. Either way, it is a judgment call and it involves a great deal of uncertainty, especially since that judgment involves actions in the future. Yet nowhere in his argument does Crouch concede this. 28

Shaw called hatred the coward's revenge for ever having been intimidated, says Crouch, and Crouch sees this hatred as the basis of Baldwin's 29 attitude towards whites and towards European culture. I find something skewed in Crouch's use of Shaw's quip here. Given the history of race in America, equating a Black man's sense of intimidation solely with cowardice seems a simplification; couldn't that intimidation in many cases be an acknowledgment of reality? Admittedly, there is in Baldwin that self-righteousness, that rage not quite under control. I know myself how easy it is to give in to it. But Crouch's approach to the dialectics of rage seems to me entirely unrealistic. In my poem, "Song For Artaud, Fanon, Cesaire, Uncle Tom, Tonto and Mr. Moto," I recognize a certain demagogic tone, a triumphant and self-righteous bitterness and rage. And yet, I also recognize that my rage needed to be released, that it had been held back in my own psyche for too many years, held back within my family, and held back within my race in America. That rage was liberating for me, just as it is for any oppressed people. As should be obvious to anyone, those who are oppressed cannot change their situation, cannot own themselves, unless they finally own their rage at their condition and those who have caused it. Crouch seems to have wanted Baldwin to overcome or stand above this rage, but there is a certain wishful thinking in this. One does not overcome or stand above this rage: one first goes through it, and then leaves it behind.

The problem is that this process is both long and complicated and neither Crouch nor Baldwin quite understands what it entails: one must learn first how liberating anger feels, then how intoxicating, then how damaging, and in each of these stages, the reason for these feelings must be admitted and accurately described. It may be argued that Baldwin accomplished the first of these tasks—the liberation that comes from rage—and that he alluded or hinted at the second—the intoxication that comes from rage—and even at times alluded or hinted at the third, but for the most, because he never accurately described how intoxicating the rage he felt was, he could never see how damaging it was.

For it is intoxicating after years of feeling inferior, after years of hating oneself, it is so comforting to use this rage not just to feel equal to the oppressor, but superior, and not just superior, but simply blameless and blessed, one of the prophetic and holy ones. It is what one imagines a god feels like, and in this state one does feel like a god of history, a fate; one knows that history is on one's side, because one is helping to break open, to recreate history. And how much better it is to feel like a god after years of worshipping the oppressor as one.

But once one can clearly describe all this, one realizes that such a stance represents a new form of hubris, an intoxicating blindness: human beings are not gods, are not superior to other human beings. Human beings are fallible, cannot foresee the future, cannot demand or receive freely the worship of others. In aligning one's rage with a sense of superiority, one fails to recognize how this rage is actually fueled by a sense of inferiority: one's own version of history and views on equality need, on some level, the approval, the assent, the defeat of the oppressor. The wish for superiority is simply the reverse side of feeling inferior, not its cure. It focuses all the victim's problems on the other, the oppressor. Yet until it is recognized how one has contributed to this victimhood, the chains are still there, inside, are part of the psyche. Conversely, liberation occurs only when one is sure enough of oneself, feels good enough, to admit fault, admit their portion of blame.

Given the difficulty of this process, it's no wonder so many stumble in   33
the process or stop midway through. And it is made much more difficult if the oppressor is especially recalcitrant, is implacable towards change. When this happens, fresh wound after fresh wound is inflicted, causing bundle after bundle of rage: bitterness then becomes too tempting; too much energy is required to heal. To his credit, Crouch shows some understanding of this fact in relationship to Baldwin: "Perhaps it is understandable that Baldwin could not resist the contemptuous pose of militance that gave focus to all of his anger for being the homely duckling, who never became a swan, the writer who would perhaps never have been read by so many Black people otherwise, and the homosexual who lived abroad most of his adult life in order to enjoy his preferences."

In the end, though, Crouch never comes to terms with the sources of   34
Baldwin's rage. One reason for this is Crouch's belief that "collective white-ness—and *collective guilt*" were merely a mask, a simplification for Baldwin.

Part of Crouch's problem is that he distorts Baldwin's position. On the one   35
hand, it is a simplification to pretend that collective whiteness and collective guilt are the *only* ways to view the race situation in America. But it is not a simplification to say that collective whiteness and collective white guilt *do exist*. The superior economic and political power of whites as compared to colored minorities in this country is a fact, and on some level, every white in this country benefits from that power. Of course, this does not mean that every white has more economic and political power than every member of the colored minorities. But it is not just this inequality of power that makes collective white guilt a fact; it is the way that power was acquired and the way its sources have been kept hidden from the consciousness of both whites and colored minorities that makes this term applicable.

Here I turn to the fundamental historical events I mentioned earlier in   36
this essay: the enslavement of Blacks, the taking of Native American land and the genocidal policies that accomplished it. One can think of other related historical events: the internment camps, the Asian-Exclusion Act, the conditions of the Asian workers building the American railroads, the conditions of migrant farm workers and illegal aliens. The list could go on and on. But that is to point out the obvious. What is not so obvious is how the laws of property in our society have served to make permanent what was stolen in the past. Those who bought my grandparents' property for a song still benefit from that property today; there has been no compensation, just as there has been no compensation to Blacks for the institution of slavery or to Native Americans for the taking of

a continent and the destruction of their peoples and culture. And as long as there is no movement toward a just compensation, the collective guilt will remain.

And yet I also recognize that a just compensation is not possible. The 37 wrongs are too great, run too far back in history, and human beings are fallible and forgetful. Justice demands too high a price.

Therefore we must settle for less, for a compromise. The concept of white 38 collective guilt reminds us of this compromise, that there has been and probably will always be a less than even settling of the debt. However whites protest that they want equality and justice, they are, in the end, not willing to pay the price. And when those they have wronged call for the price, the reaction of whites is almost always one of anger and resentment.

Now, in this situation, the whites have two choices. When they accept 39 the concept of collective guilt, they admit that they feel unjustifiable anger and resentment at any measure that threatens any part of their privileged position, much less any of the measures that approach just compensation. When whites don't admit collective guilt, they try to blame racial troubles on those who ask for a just settlement and remain baffled at the anger and resentment of the colored minorities.

Whether in the area of culture or in economic relations, these choices 40 remain. In the realm of culture in America, white European culture has held the floor for centuries; just as with any one-sided conversation, a balance can only be achieved if the speaker who has dominated speaks less and listens more. That is what conservative cultural critics are unwilling to do; for them there is no such thing as collective guilt, much less the obligation such guilt bestows. It is not just that the colored minorities in America need to create and receive their own cultural images, nor that, for these minorities, the culture of the Third World and its struggles against white-dominated cultures provides insights into race in America and cannot be found in European literature. This much ought to seem obvious. But there is more: only when whites in America begin to listen to the voices of the colored minorities and the Third World will they come to understand not just those voices but also themselves and their world. Reality is not simply knowing who we think we are, but also what others think of us. And only with this knowledge will whites ever understand what needs to be done to make things equal.

The situation in the *Voice* article on nannies is no different: without ad- 41 mitting the concept of collective guilt, the white middle-class Barbra remains unable to comprehend her nanny Bertha, unable to understand what this Black woman feels. Ultimately, Barbra does not want to admit that the only way she is going to feel comfortable with Bertha is if they meet as equals; that society must be changed so that Barbra and her children will not enjoy certain privileges they have taken as rights. In short, Barbra and other whites will have to give up power; that is what it means to make things equal. At the same time she must admit that no matter how much she works for change, how much society changes, there will never, on this earth, be a just settling of accounts. That is the burden she has to take up; she may think it will destroy her, but it will not. And, ultimately, this process would not only help Bertha to meet and know Barbra as an equal, but for Barbra to understand and accept who she is, to know herself. ◆

◆ Responding

1. In this reading, Barbra represents all whites. Explain what Mura wants Barbra to do to help redress the wrongs in our society. What practical steps do you think she can take? How will her actions further understanding between the races?

2. Discuss Mura's response to critics who call for "a return to the classics and a notion of a core-cultural tradition" and who "bemoan . . . the multicultural movements which, in the name of 'tolerance,' have supposedly left our culture in a shambles."

3. Mura says "the images I grew up with in the media were all white," and "the books I read in school—from Dick and Jane onwards—were about whites and later, about European civilization." What would his reaction to a text such as this one probably be? Would he want all students or only members of ethnic minorities to read such a text? Discuss the effects on both whites and members of other groups of learning about cultures other than European.

4. Working in a group, discuss what Mura means when he says, ". . . this is not to say I now regret what I know, but I do regret what I don't know." List things about your own background and culture that you would like to know more about. Share your list with the class.

◆

C O N N E C T I N G

Critical Thinking and Writing

1. Many of the readings in this chapter focus on the experiences of immigrants to America. Some of these people left their homelands for better economic opportunities; others were forced to leave because of political conditions. Write an essay classifying these immigrants according to their reasons for emigrating.

2. Compare the reasons that people immigrated to the United States in the 1970s and 1980s with the reasons that immigrants came in the 1870s and 1880s. You might compare a single group, such as the Chinese, or you might compare different groups, such as the Eastern Europeans in the 1800s and recent Latin American immigrants. Consider any changes in conditions that the immigrants encountered after they arrived in the United States.

3. For people such as Rosa in Ozick's story, it is impossible to escape the effects of the past. Using examples from the readings in this text, argue whether historical events do or do not shape an individual's or a group's behavior. Focus your discussion by referring to specific historical events such as the Holocaust, the enslavement of African Americans, the internment of Japanese Americans, or the relocation of Native Americans.

4. Immigrating to a new country can mean new opportunities or a traumatic change. Using examples from the readings and from your own experience, write an essay discussing the difficulties of adapting to a new country and a new culture.

5. Describe the misunderstandings that can arise between parents and children. Agree or disagree that there is both a generational and a cultural gap. Support your argument with evidence from the readings as well as your own experience and observations.

6. Mathabane discusses the "traumatic time" in Africa when the "black man's culture and values were decimated in the name of civilization, and the white man's culture and values, trumpeted as superior, became the standards of intelligence, excellence, and beauty." Using examples from the readings in this text, argue whether this attitude influenced the way various ethnic groups in the United State felt about themselves, about each other, and about newcomers.

7. Many new immigrants see the United States as "the promised land" where they can fulfill "the American Dream." What do you think "the American Dream" means to these people? How does this dream differ from that of the founders of the country? How is it similar?

8. Using examples from the readings, describe some of the limitations of our current educational curriculum. What reforms would authors such as Mura propose?

9. The struggle against evil concerns many groups in this country. Compare the variety of responses of individuals or groups to evil. For example, you might compare the different ways in which Dr. Martin Luther King, Jr., and Malcolm

X responded to racism, or the different ways in which Japanese Americans responded to the Internment.

10. Some of the writers in this chapter explore their personal heritages. In what ways do those heritages emerge in their creative works?

11. "Everyday Use" presents at least two ways of looking at family history and traditions. Discuss these and compare the role of tradition in that family with its role in another family, such as the one in "Puerto Rican Paradise."

12. Using examples from the readings or from your own or a friend's experience, discuss how race, gender, and/or social class help determine the circumstances of a person's life.

13. Working with the class, generate a series of essay questions concerning the issues dealt with in this chapter. Choose one question and answer it in an essay.

For Further Research

1. Research the history of apartheid in South Africa. What is its current status?

2. Choose one of the groups represented in this chapter and investigate the history of that group's immigration and its current situation in the United States. For example, you might consider the reasons for and difficulties of immigration, economic and social opportunities in the United States, and settlement patterns.

3. Research current United States immigration laws and policies. How does someone immigrate to this country? Who is allowed to enter? What procedures must they follow?

4. Study the curriculum in your university. What opportunities exist for studying other cultures? Design an ethnic literature or ethnic studies course.

◆

REFERENCES AND ADDITIONAL SOURCES

Anzaldúa, Gloria. *Borderlands/La Frontera: The New Mestiza*. San Francisco: Spinsters/ Aunt Lute Book Co., 1987.

Archdeacon, Thomas J. *Becoming American: An Ethnic History*. New York: Free Press, 1983.

Boelhower, William. *Immigrant Autobiography in the United States.* Verona: Essedue Edizioni, 1982.

Brodsky, Joseph. *Less Than One: Selected Essays.* New York: Farrar, Strauss & Giroux, Inc., 1987.

Bulosan, Carlos. *America is in the Heart.* Seattle: University of Washington Press, 1943, 1970.

Chin, Frank et al., eds. *Aiiieee: An Anthology of Asian American Writers.* Garden City: Doubleday, 1975.

Columbo, Gary, Robert J. Cullen and Bonnie Lisle, eds. *Rereading America,* New York: St. Martin's, 1989.

Delgado, Asuncion Horno. *Breaking Boundaries: Latin-Writing and Cultural Readings.* Amherst: University of Massachusetts, 1989.

de Vos, George and Lola Romanucci-Ross, eds. *Ethnic Identity: Cultural Continuities and Change.* Palo Alto: Mayfield, 1975.

Fanon, Frantz. *The Wretched of the Earth.* New York: Grove, 1966.

Fisher, Dexter, ed. *The Third Woman: Minority Women Writers of the United States.* Boston: Houghton Mifflin, 1980.

Gage, Nicholas. *A Place for Us: Eleni's Family in America.* Boston: Houghton Mifflin, 1989.

Gates, Henry Louis, Jr. *Race Writing and Difference.* Chicago: University of Chicago Press, 1987.

Hwang, David Henry. *Family Devotions.* In *Broken Promises: Four Chinese American Plays.* New York: Avon, 1983.

Iglesias, José. *The Goodbye Land.* New York: Pantheon, 1967.

Kim, Richard E. *Lost Names: Scenes from a Boyhood in Japanese-Occupied Korea.* New York: Universe Books, Inc., 1988.

Kincaid, Jamaica. *A Small Place.* New York: Farrar, Strauss & Giroux, Inc., 1988.

Marshall, Paule. *Brown Girl, Brownstone.* New York: Random, 1959.

Mehta, Ved. *Face to Face.* New York: Oxford University Press, 1978.

Milosz, Czeslaw. *Native Realm: A Search for Self Definition.* Berkeley: University of California Press, 1981.

Mirikitani, Janice, ed. *Time to Greez—Incantations from the Third World.* San Francisco: Glide Publishers, 1975.

Mukherjee, Bharati. *The Middleman and Other Stories.* New York: Grove, forthcoming.

Reed, Ishmael. *Yardbird Lives.* New York: Grove, 1978.

Rischin, Moses, ed. *Immigration and the American Tradition*. Indianapolis: Bobbs-Merrill, 1976.

Rose, Peter I., Stanley Rochman, and William Julius Wilson, eds. *Through Different Eyes: Black and White Perspectives on American Race Relations*. New York: Oxford University Press, 1973.

Said, Edward. *Literature and Society*. Baltimore: Johns Hopkins University Press, 1980.

Seller, Maxine. *To Seek America: A History of Ethnic Group Life in the United States*. Englewood, N.J.: Ozer, 1977.

Simonson, Rick and Scott Walker, eds. *Graywolf Annual Five: Multicultural Literacy*. St. Paul: Graywolf, 1988.

Smith, Derek. "A Refugee by any Other Name: An Examination of the Board of Immigration Appeals' Actions in Asylum Cases." *Virginia Law Review* (Vol. 75, 1989), pp. 681–721.

Sollors Werner. *Beyond Ethnicity: Consent and Descent in American Culture*. New York: Oxford University Press, 1986.

Sunoo, Brenda. *Korean American Writing: Selected Material from "Insight," a Korean American Bimonthly*. New York, 1975.

Takaki, Ronald, ed. *From Different Shores: Perspectives on Race and Ethnicity in America*. New York: Oxford University Press, 1987.

Tan, Amy. *The Joy Luck Club*. New York: Putnam Publishing Group, 1989.

Todorov, Tzvetan. *The Conquest of America*. trans. Richard Howard. New York: Harper, 1984.

(continued from p. iv)

"The Chicago Defender Sends a Man to Little Rock," "Medgar Evers," and "Malcolm X" by Gwendolyn Brooks from BLACKS (Chicago, IL: The David Company, 1987). Copyright © 1987 by Gwendolyn Brooks Blakely. Reprinted by permission of the author.

Héctor Calderón, "Reinventing the Border" is reprinted by permission of the author.

Ana Castillo, "Napa, California" and "Milagros" first published in WOMEN ARE NOT ROSES, by Ana Castillo. (Houston: Arte Publico Press—University of Houston, 1984).

"Such a Night" by Lincoln Chase used by permission. © 1954 Shelby Singleton Music, Inc.

César Chávez, "The Organizer's Tale," reprinted from RAMPARTS MAGAZINE, Vol. 5, No. 2 (July 1966). Copyright 1966. By permission of the author, César Chávez.

Sandra Cisneros, "Woman Hollering Creek." Copyright 1990 by Sandra Cisneros, to be published in Untitled Collection of Short Stories, Random House, Spring 1991. Reprinted by permission of Susan Bergholz Literary Services, 340 West 72nd Street, New York, NY 10023.

Excerpted from THE LINE OF THE SUN by Judith Ortiz Cofer. Copyright © 1989 by Judith Ortiz Cofer. Reprinted by permission of the author.

Jesús Colón, "Stowaway," "Easy Job, Good Wages," and "Kipling and I" from A PUERTO RICAN IN NEW YORK (New York: Mainstream, 1961). Reprinted by permission of International Publishers, New York.

"Hard Time Blues" by Waring Cuney and Josh White, copyright Thursday Music Corporation, 8425 West Third Street, Suite 300, Los Angeles, California 90048, used by permission. All Rights Reserved.

Tran Van Dinh, "Truce in Heaven, Peace on Earth," from BLUE DRAGON WHITE TIGER, TriAm Press. Reprinted by permission.

From INVISIBLE MAN by Ralph Ellison. Copyright © 1952 by Ralph Ellison. Reprinted by permission of Random House, Inc.

From LOVE MEDICINE by Louise Erdrich. Copyright © 1984 by Louise Erdrich. Reprinted by permission of Henry Holt and Company, Inc.

Excerpt from LAY BARE THE HEART by James Farmer. Copyright © 1985 by James Farmer. By permission of Arbor House, William Morrow & Co., Inc.

Reprinted from THERE IS CONFUSION by Jessie Redmon Fauset, by permission of Liveright Publishing Corporation. Copyright 1924 by Boni & Liveright, Inc. Copyright renewed 1952 by Jessie Redmon Fauset.

David M. Fine, "Attitudes Toward Acculturation in the English Fiction of the Jewish Immigrant, 1900–1917." Published with permission by the American Jewish Historical Society, Waltham, MA.

Reprinted by permission of the Modern Language Association from Juan Flores, "Puerto Rican Literature in the United States: Stages and Perspectives," from ADE Bulletin 91 (Winter 1988): 39–44.

"I am Joaquín" by Rodolpho Gonzales is reprinted by permission of Causa International.

"Luna Moth" from DOGEATERS by Jessica Hagedorn. Copyright © 1990 by Jessica Hagedorn. Reprinted by permission of Pantheon Books, a division of Random House, Inc.

"Visitor" from OUR HOUSE IN THE WORLD by Oscar Hijuelos is reprinted by permission of Persea Books. Copyright © 1983 Oscar Hijuelos.

Marlon Hom. SONGS OF GOLD MOUNTAIN: CANTONESE RHYMES FROM SAN FRANCISCO CHINATOWN, pages 76, 77, and 85. Copyright © 1987 The Regents of the University of California. Reprinted by permission.

"Manzanar, USA" from FAREWELL TO MANZANAR by Jeanne Wakatsuki and James D. Houston. Copyright © 1973 by James D. Houston. Reprinted by permission of Houghton Mifflin Co.

Langston Hughes, "The Negro Speaks of Rivers" and "Mother to Son." Copyright 1926 by Alfred A. Knopf, Inc. and renewed 1954 by Langston Hughes. Reprinted from SELECTED POEMS OF LANGSTON HUGHES, by permission of the publisher.

Langston Hughes, "Theme for English B" from MONTAGE OF A DREAM DE-FERRED, 1951, Henry Holt & Company. Reprinted by permission of Harold Ober Associates Incorporated. Copyright 1951 by Langston Hughes. Copyright renewed 1979 by George Houston Bass.

"Dream Variations" and "Afro-American Fragment" from SELECTED POEMS OF LANGSTON HUGHES. Copyright © 1959 by Langston Hughes. Reprinted by permission of Alfred A. Knopf, Inc.

"Sweat" by Zora Neale Hurston is reprinted by permission of Turtle Island Foundation.

"Flight into Egypt" from MIGRANT SOULS by Arturo Islas. Copyright 1990. Reprinted by permission of William Morrow & Co.

"Letter from Birmingham Jail" from WHY WE CAN'T WAIT by Martin Luther King, Jr. Copyright © 1963, 1964 by Martin Luther King, Jr. Reprinted by permission of Harper & Row, Publishers, Inc.

"I Have a Dream" by Martin Luther King, Jr. reprinted by permission of Joan Daves. Copyright © 1963 by Martin Luther King, Jr.

"The Grandfather of the Sierra Nevada Mountains," from CHINA MEN by Maxine Hong Kingston. Copyright © 1980 by Maxine Hong Kingston. Reprinted by permission of Alfred A. Knopf, Inc.

Kenneth Lincoln. NATIVE AMERICAN RENAISSANCE, pages 15–23. Copyright © 1983 The Regents of the University of California. Reprinted by permission.

"Father Cures a Presidential Fever" from FATHER AND GLORIOUS DESCEN-DANT by Pardee Lowe, Sr., (Boston: Little, Brown, 1943) is reprinted by permission of the author.

Reprinted with permission of Charles Scribner's Sons, an imprint of Macmillan Publishing Company from KAFFIR BOY IN AMERICA by Mark Mathabane. Copyright © 1989 Mark Mathabane.

"America" and "If We Must Die" and "Outcast" from CLAUDE McKAY: SELECTED POEMS OF CLAUDE McKAY. Copyright 1981 and reprinted with the permission of Twayne Publishers, a division of G. K. Hall & Co., Boston.

"Invocation" by Claude McKay. From SELECTED POEMS OF CLAUDE McKAY (Harcourt Brace Jovanovich) by kind permission of Hope McKay Virtue.

Excerpt from "Breaking Silence" by Janice Mirikitani published in SHEDDING SILENCE, POETRY AND PROSE BY JANICE MIRIKITANI, Celestial Arts Publishers, 1987, Berkeley, CA. © copyright by Janice Mirikitani. Reprinted by permission.

"We, the Dangerous," "Desert Flowers," and "For My Father" by Janice Mirikitani. Reprinted from AYUMI, A JAPANESE AMERICAN ANTHOLOGY. © Copyright by Janice Mirikitani.

Nicholasa Mohr, "A Thanksgiving Celebration" first published in RITUALS OF SURVIVAL, by Nicholasa Mohr (Houston: Arte Publico Press—University of Houston, 1985).

"The Priest of the Sun" from HOUSE MADE OF DAWN by N. Scott Momaday. Copyright © 1966, 1967, 1968 by N. Scott Momaday. Reprinted by permission of Harper & Row, Publishers, Inc.

Pat Mora, "Illegal Alien" and "Legal Alien," first published in CHANTS, by Pat Mora (Houston: Arte Publico Press—University of Houston, 1984).

"Unfinished Message." Acknowledgment is made to: THE CHAUVINIST AND OTHER STORIES by Toshio Mori, Asian American Studies Center, UCLA. © 1979 The Regents of the University of California, Los Angeles.

"Strangers in the Village" by David Mura appeared in THE GRAYWOLF ANNUAL FIVE: MULTI-CULTURAL LITERACY, edited by Rick Simonson and Scott Walker, Graywolf Press, and is reprinted by permission of the author.

From THE NO-NO BOY by John Okada. Copyright © 1979 by Dorothy Okada. Reprinted by permission of the University of Washington Press.

Reprinted from BEFORE THE FLAMES: A QUEST FOR THE HISTORY OF ARAB AMERICANS, by Gregory Orfalea. By permission of the author and the University of Texas Press.

Richard Oyama, "Untitled," from TRANSFER/38, San Francisco State University, 1979. Reprinted by permission of the author.

From THE SHAWL by Cynthia Ozick. Copyright © 1980, 1983 by Cynthia Ozick. Reprinted by permission of Alfred A. Knopf, Inc. Originally appeared in THE NEW YORKER.

Bernardo Vega: "The Customs and Traditions of the Tabaqueros and What It Was Like to Work in a Cigar Factory in New York City." Copyright © 1984 by Monthly Review Press. Reprinted by permission of Monthly Review Foundation.

Excerpt from POCHO by José Antonio Villarreal, copyright © 1959 by José Antonio Villarreal. Used by permission of Doubleday, a division of Bantam Doubleday Dell Publishing Group, Inc.

"Everyday Use" from IN LOVE & TROUBLE: STORIES OF BLACK WOMEN, copyright © 1973 by Alice Walker, reprinted by permission of Harcourt Brace Jovanovich, Inc.

"Plea to Those Who Matter" and "Riding the Earthboy 40" from RIDING THE EARTHBOY 40 by James Welch, Confluence Press, Lewiston, Idaho, 1990. Reprinted by permission of the author.

From EYES ON THE PRIZE by Juan Williams. Copyright © 1987, Blackside, Inc. Reprinted by permission of Viking Penguin, a division of Penguin Books USA, Inc.

Nellie Wong, "From a Heart of Rice Straw," from DREAMS IN HARRISON RAILROAD PARK, Kelsey St. Press, Berkeley, CA. Reprinted by permission.

From THE AUTOBIOGRAPHY OF MALCOLM X by Malcolm X, with the assistance of Alex Haley. Copyright © 1964 by Alex Haley and Malcolm X. Copyright © 1965 by Alex Haley and Betty Shabazz. Reprinted by permission of Random House, Inc.

Hisaye Yamamoto, "Las Vegas Charley," is reprinted by permission from the ARIZONA QUARTERLY, Vol. 17, No. 4, Winter 1961.

"The Fat of the Land" by Anzia Yezierska from HUNGRY HEARTS AND OTHER STORIES, 1985, Persea Books, New York. Copyright, Louise Levitas Henriksen. Reprinted by permission.